AF759837

Affective Computing

Focus on Emotion Expression, Synthesis and Recognition

Edited by
Jimmy Or

Affective Computing, Emotion Expression, Synthesis and Recognition

Edited by Jimmy Or

Republished by InTech

Janeza Trdine 9, 51000 Rijeka, Croatia

Copyright © 2008 InTech

Abstracting and non-profit use of the material is permitted with credit to the source. Statements and opinions expressed in the chapters are these of the individual contributors and not necessarily those of the editors or publisher. No responsibility is accepted for the accuracy of information contained in the published articles. Publisher assumes no responsibility liability for any damage or injury to persons or property arising out of the use of any materials, instructions, methods or ideas contained inside. After this work has been published by the Intech, authors have the right to republish it, in whole or part, in any publication of which they are an author or editor, and the make other personal use of the work.

Additional hard copies can be obtained from orders@intechopen.com

Affective Computing, Emotion Expression, Synthesis and Recognition, Edited by Jimmy Or
p. cm.
ISBN 978-3-902613-23-3

We are IntechOpen,
the world's leading publisher of
Open Access books

Built by scientists, for scientists

4,200+
Open access books available

116,000+
International authors and editors

125M+
Downloads

151
Countries delivered to

Our authors are among the
Top 1%
most cited scientists

12.2%
Contributors from top 500 universities

CLARIVATE ANALYTICS
BOOK CITATION INDEX
INDEXED

WEB OF SCIENCE™

Selection of our books indexed in the Book Citation Index
in Web of Science™ Core Collection (BKCI)

Interested in publishing with us?
Contact book.department@intechopen.com

Numbers displayed above are based on latest data collected.
For more information visit www.intechopen.com

For EU product safety concerns:
IN TECH d.o.o., Prolaz Marije Krucifikse Kozulić 3, 51000 Rijeka, Croatia,
info@intechopen.com or visit our website at intechopen.com.

Preface

Affective Computing is a branch of artificial intelligence that deals with the design of systems and devices that can recognize, interpret, and process emotions. Since the introduction of the term "affective computing" by Rosalind Pichard at MIT in 1997, the research community in this field has grown rapidly. Affective Computing is an important field because computer systems have become part of our daily lives. As we nowadays live in the Age of Information Overload, and computer systems are becoming more complex, there is need for more natural user interfaces for the overwhelmed computer users. Given that humans communicate with each other by using not only speech but also implicitly their facial expressions and body postures, machines that can understand human emotions and display affects through these multimodal channels could be beneficial. If virtual agents and robots are able to recognize and express their emotions through these channels, the result of that will be more natural human-machine communication. This will allow human users to focus more on their tasks at hand.

This volume provides an overview of state of the art research in Affective Computing. It presents new ideas, original results and practical experiences in this increasingly important research field. The book consists of 23 chapters categorized into four sections. Since one of the most important means of human communication is facial expression, the first section of this book (Chapters 1 to 7) presents a research on synthesis and recognition of facial expressions. Given that we not only use the face but also body movements to express ourselves, in the second section (Chapters 8 to 11) we present a research on perception and generation of emotional expressions by using full-body motions. The third section of the book (Chapters 12 to 16) presents computational models on emotion, as well as findings from neuroscience research. In the last section of the book (Chapters 17 to 22) we present applications related to affective computing.

A brief introduction to the book chapters is:

Chapter 1 presents a probabilistic neural network classifier for 3D analysis of facial expressions. By using 11 facial features and taking symmetry of the human face into consideration, the 3D distance vectors based recognition system can achieve a high recognition rate of over 90%. Chapter 2 provides a set of deterministic and stochastic techniques that allow efficient recognition of facial expression from a series of video imaging showing head motions. Chapter 3 reviews recent findings of human-human interaction and demonstrates that the tangential aspects of an emotional signal (such as gaze and the type of face that shows the expression) can affect the perceived meaning of the expression. Findings displayed in this chapter could contribute to the design of avatars and agents used in the human computer interface. Chapter 4 presents an approach to using genetic algorithm and neural network for the recognition of emotion from the face. In particular, it focuses on the eye and lip regions for the study of emotions. Chapter 5 proposes a system that analyzes facial expressions based on topographic shape structure (eyebrow, eye, nose and mouth) and the active texture.

Chapter 6 proposes a model of layered fuzzy facial expression generation (LFFEG) to create expressive facial expressions for an agent in the affective human computer interface. In this model, social, emotional and physiological layers contribute to the generation of facial expression. Fuzzy theory is used to produce rich facial expressions and personality for the virtual character. Based on recent findings that the dynamics of facial expressions (such as timing, duration and intensity) play an important role in the interpretation of facial expressions, Chapter 7 exams the analysis of facial expressions based on computer vision and behavioral science point of view. A technique that allows synthesis of photo-realistic expression of various intensities is described.

In recent years, humanoid robots and simulated avatars have gained popularity. Researchers try to develop both real and simulated humanoids that can behave and communicate with humans more naturally. It is believed that a real humanoid robot situated in the real world could better interact with humans. Given that we also use whole body movements to express emotions, the next generation humanoid robots should have a flexible spine and be able to express themselves by using full body movements. Chapter 8 points out some of the challenges in developing flexible spine humanoid robots for emotional expressions. Then, the chapter presents the development of emotional flexible spine humanoid robots based on findings from a research on belly dance. Results of psychological experiments on the effect of a full-body spine robot on human perceptions are presented.

Chapter 9 provides a review of the cues that we use in the perception of the affect from body movements. Based on findings from psychology and neuroscience, the authors raise the issue of whether giving a machine the ability to experience emotions might help to accomplish reliable and efficient emotion recognition. Given that human communications are multimodal, Chapter 10 reviews recent research on systems that are capable of multiple input modalities and the use of alternative channels to perceive affects. This is followed by a presentation of systems that are capable of analyzing spontaneous input data in real world environments. Chapter 11 draws on findings from art theory to the synthesis of emotional expressions for virtual humans. Lights, shadows, composition and filters are used as part of the expression of emotions. In addition, the chapter proposes the use of genetic algorithms to map affective states to multimodal expressions.

Since the modeling of emotion has become important in affective computing, Chapter 12 presents a computational model of emotion. The model is capable of in-

tegrating emotion, personality and motivation to allow the simulated characters to have the ability of self-control in the virtual environment. Chapter 13 provides another model for simulating emotions. This model, called SIMPLEX, operates in three interconnected layers, namely personality, mood-states and emotions. Experimental results show that the simulated agents whose emotions were generated by the model were able to exhibit emergent behavior. Chapter 14 proposes the use of psychological emotion models to construct a new generation of user interfaces that are capable of automatic emotional recognition by sensing and responding to the user's affective feedback. A Multidimensional Emotional Appraisal Semantic Space (MEAS) semantic model is introduced. Chapter 15 reviews findings from Neuroscience on the involvement of amygdala in emotion. This chapter explains a general framework of how this area of the brain processes information on emotion. Chapter 16 presents a study that shows that is possible for a computer to automatically recognize emotions of its users based on physiological signals such as PPG, GSR and SKT gathered through a specially designed mouse. Depending on the state of the user's emotion, the computer can adapt its actions correspondingly.
Chapter 17 presents the iFace facial expression training system. The system can be used for rehabilitation, improvement of business skills and daily communications. Chapter 18 introduces an automated real time virtual character based interface. The 3D agents are able to interact with the user through multimodal and emotional interaction. Depending on the emotional state the agents detect from the user's facial expression during conversation, the agents are able to modify their emotional states accordingly. The system allows more natural and interactive communications between computers and users. Chapter 19 proposes the design of an intelligent tutoring system based on hand movements around the face of the user. Chapter 20 presents a framework for affective-sensitive human-machine interaction. Based on physiological signals from children users with ASD, an affect-sensitive robot adapts its behavior to the affect of its users accordingly in real time. The system could be used for interactive autism intervention. Chapter 21 discusses the development of a plug-in interface for the storytelling authoring tools Inscape and Tetrix. Using the plug-in, the authors are able to easily create interactive stories that explore the emotional dimension of characters in the virtual world. The interesting point is that the actions of the virtual characters can be influenced by their own personal experience. Finally, Chapter 22 reviews computer therapy systems that have been used in recent years to treat emotional disorders such as phobias. These systems propose that by presenting anxiety, and provoking stimuli in a controlled virtual environment, different social and emotional disorders can be treated. A model that supports computer assisted regulation and voluntary control of emotion is presented.

Acknowledgements
This book would not have been possible without the support of my colleagues and friends. I own a great debt to Atsuo Takanishi of Waseda University. He gave me

freedom and support to pursuit my research on flexible spine humanoid robotics during my stay in his lab. I also would like to thank Robin Cohen, Lenhart Schubert, Shun-ichi Amari, Michael Arbib, Auke Ijspeert, David Willshaw, Xie Ming, Eugene Fink, Charles Sanders, Hyun Wook Park, Jungmin Han and many others for their support over the years. Many thanks to Lorna Gow for introducing me to the wonderful world of belly dance. Special thanks to KAIST President Nam Pyo Suh and Dean of Engineering Yong Hoon Lee for their support during my stay at KAIST. Many thanks to the authors of the book chapters for their contributions. Finally, I would like to express my thanks to Dr. Vedran Kordic and the staff at I-Tech Education and Publishing for their help in making the production of this book possible.

Jimmy Or
May 2008
Center for High-Performance Integrated Systems
Korea Advanced Institute of Science and Technology
Daejeon, Republic of Korea

Contents

Preface V

1. Facial Expression Recognition Using 3D Facial Feature Distances 001
Hamit Soyel and Hasan Demirel

2. Facial Expression Recognition in the Presence of Head Motion 013
Fadi Dornaika and Franck Davoine

3. The Devil is in the Details - the Meanings of Faces and How They Influence the Meanings of Facial Expressions 045
Ursula Hess, Reginald B. Adams, Jr. and Robert E. Kleck

4. Genetic Algorithm and Neural Network for Face Emotion Recognition 057
M. Karthigayan, M. Rizon, R. Nagarajan and Sazali Yaacob

5. Classifying Facial Expressions Based on Topo-Feature Representation 069
Xiaozhou Wei, Johnny Loi and Lijun Yin

6. Layered Fuzzy Facial Expression Generation: Social, Emotional and Physiological 083
Xia Mao, Yuli Xue, Zheng Li and Haiyan Bao

7. Modelling, Classification and Synthesis of Facial Expressions 107
Jane Reilly, John Ghent and John McDonald

8. The Development of Emotional Flexible Spine Humanoid Robots 133
Jimmy Or

9. The Perception of Bodily Expressions of Emotion and the Implications for Computing 157
Winand H. Dittrich and Anthony P. Atkinson

10. From the Lab to the Real World: Affect Recognition Using Multiple Cues and Modalities 185
Hatice Gunes, Massimo Piccardi and Maja Pantic

11. The Art of Expressing Emotions in Virtual Humans **219**
Celso de Melo and Ana Paiva

12. Computational Emotion Model for Virtual Characters **235**
Zhen Liu

13. SIMPLEX - Simulation of Personal Emotion Experience **255**
Henrik Kessler, Alexander Festini,
Harald C. Traue, Suzanne Filipic, Michael Weber and Holger Hoffmann

14. From Signals to Emotions:
Applying Emotion Models to HM Affective Interactions **271**
Rita Ciceri and Stefania Balzarotti

15. The Information Processing Role of the Amygdala in Emotion **297**
Wataru Sato

16. A Physiological Approach to Affective Computing **309**
Mincheol Whang and Joasang Lim

17. iFace: Facial Expression Training System **319**
Kyoko Ito, Hiroyuki Kurose, Ai Takami and Shogo Nishida

18. Affective Embodied Conversational Agents for Natural Interaction **329**
Eva Cerezo, Sandra Baldassarri, Isabelle Hupont and Francisco J. Seron

19. Exploring Un-Intentional Body Gestures for Affective System Design **355**
Abdul Rehman Abbasi, Nitin V. Afzulpurkar and Takeaki Uno

20. Towards Affect-sensitive Assistive
Intervention Technologies for Children with Autism **365**
Karla Conn, Changchun Liu, Nilanjan Sarkar, Wendy Stone and Zachary Warren

21. Authoring Emotion **391**
Nelson Zagalo, Rui Prada, Isabel Machado Alexandre and Ana Torres

22. Computer-Assisted Regulation of Emotional and Social Processes **405**
Toni Vanhala and Veikko Surakka

23. Generating Facial Expressions with Deep Belief Nets **421**
Joshua M. Susskind, Geoffrey E. Hinton, Javier R. Movellan and Adam K. Anderson

1

Facial Expression Recognition Using 3D Facial Feature Distances

Hamit Soyel and Hasan Demirel
Eastern Mediterranean University
Northern Cyprus

1. Introduction

Face plays an important role in human communication. Facial expressions and gestures incorporate nonverbal information which contributes to human communication. By recognizing the facial expressions from facial images, a number of applications in the field of human computer interaction can be facilitated. Last two decades, the developments, as well as the prospects in the field of multimedia signal processing have attracted the attention of many computer vision researchers to concentrate in the problems of the facial expression recognition. The pioneering studies of Ekman in late 70s have given evidence to the classification of the basic facial expressions. According to these studies, the basic facial expressions are those representing happiness, sadness, anger, fear, surprise, disgust and neutral. Facial Action Coding System (FACS) was developed by Ekman and Friesen to code facial expressions in which the movements on the face are described by action units. This work inspired many researchers to analyze facial expressions in 2D by means of image and video processing, where by tracking of facial features and measuring the amount of facial movements, they attempt to classify different facial expressions. Recent work on facial expression analysis and recognition has used these seven basic expressions as their basis for the introduced systems.

Almost all of the methods developed use 2D distribution of facial features as inputs into a classification system, and the outcome is one of the facial expression classes. They differ mainly in the facial features selected and the classifiers used to distinguish among the different facial expressions. Information extracted from 3D face models are rarely used in the analysis of the facial expression recognition. This chapter considers the techniques using the information extracted from 3D space for the analysis of facial images for the recognition of facial expressions.

The first part of the chapter introduces the methods of extracting information from 3D models for facial expression recognition. The 3D distributions of the facial feature points and the estimation of characteristic distances in order to represent the facial expressions are explained by using a rich collection of illustrations including graphs, charts and face images. The second part of the chapter introduces 3D distance-vector based facial expression recognition. The architecture of the system is explained by the block diagrams and flowcharts. Finally 3D distance-vector based facial expression recognition is compared with the conventional methods available in the literature.

2. Information extracted from 3D models for facial expression recognition

Conventional methods for analyzing expressions of facial images use limited information such as gray levels of pixels and positions of feature points in a face [Donato et al.,1999], [Fasel & Luttin, (2003)], [Pantic & Rothkrantz ,2004]. Their results depend on the information used. If the information cannot be precisely extracted from the facial images, then we may obtain unexpected results. In order to increase the reliability of the results of facial expression recognition, the selection of the relevant feature points is important.
In this section we are primarily concerned with gathering the relevant data from the facial animation sequences for expression recognition. The section is organised as follows. In section 2.1 we will present the description of the primary facial expressions while section 2.2 shows the muscle actions involved in the primary facial expressions and in section 2.3 we will present the optimization of the facial feature points.

2.1 Primary facial expressions

In the past, facial expression analysis was essentially a research topic for psychologists. However, recent progresses in image processing and pattern recognition have motivated significant research activities on automatic facial expression recognition [Braathen et al.,2002]. Basic facial expressions, shown in Figure 1, typically recognized by psychologists are neutral, anger, sadness, surprise, happiness, disgust and fear [P. Ekman & W. Friesen,1976]. The expressions are textually defined in Table 1.

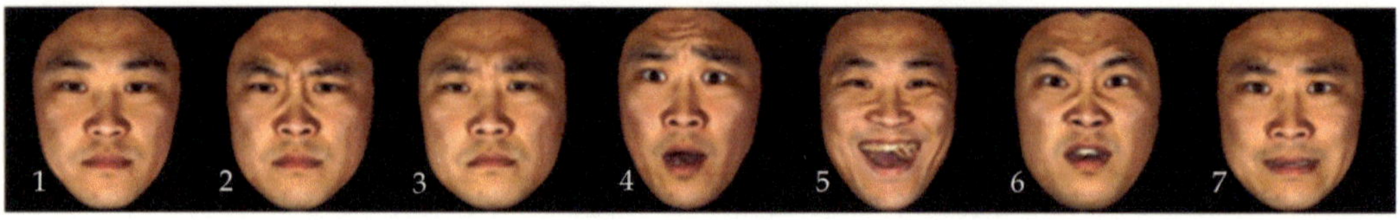

Fig.1. Emotion-specified facial expression [Yin et al., 2006]: 1-Neutral, 2-Anger, 3-Sadness, 4-Surprise, 5- Happiness, 6- Disgust, 7- Fear.

Expression	Textual Description
Neutral	All face muscles are relaxed. Eyelids are tangent to the iris. The mouth is closed and lips are in contact.
Anger	The inner eyebrows are pulled downward and together. The eyes are wide open. The lips are pressed against each other or opened to expose the teeth.
Sadness	The inner eyebrows are bent upward. The eyes are slightly closed. The mouth is relaxed.
Surprise	The eyebrows are raised. The upper eyelids are wide open, he lower relaxed. The jaw is opened.
Happiness	The eyebrows are relaxed. The mouth is open and the mouth corners pulled back toward the ears.
Disgust	The eyebrows and eyelids are relaxed. The upper lip is raised and curled, often asymmetrically.
Fear	The eyebrows are raised and pulled together. The inner eyebrows are bent upward. The eyes are tense and alert.

Table 1. Basic Facial Expressions [Pandzic & Forchheimer, 2002]

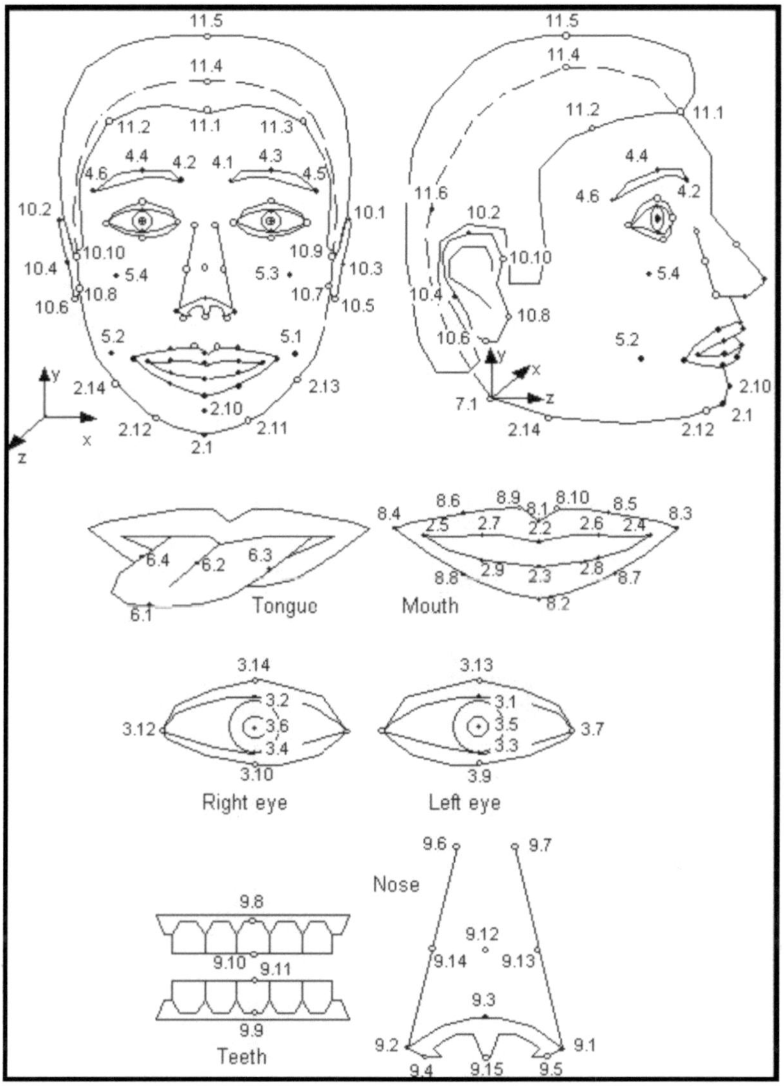

Fig. 2. The 3D orientation of the facial feature points [Pandzic & Forchheimer, 2002].

2.2 Muscle actions involved in the primary facial expressions

The Facial Definition Parameter set (FDP) and the Facial Animation Parameter set (FAP) were designed in the MPEG-4 framework to allow the definition of a facial shape and texture, as well as animation of faces reproducing expressions, emotions and speech pronunciation. The FAPs [Pandzic & Forchheimer, 2002] are based on the study of minimal facial actions and are closely related to muscle activation, in the sense that they represent a complete set of atomic facial actions; therefore they allow the representation of even the most detailed natural facial expressions, even those that cannot be categorized as particular ones. All the parameters involving translational movement are expressed in terms of the Facial Animation Parameter Units (FAPU). These units are defined with respect to specific distances in a neutral pose in order to allow interpretation of the FAPs on any facial model in a consistent way. As a result, description schemes that utilize FAPs produce reasonable results in terms of expression and speech related postures.

Expression	Muscle Actions	
Anger	squeeze_l_eyebrow (+) lower_t_midlip (-) raise_l_i_eyebrow (+) close_t_r_eyelid (-) close_b_r_eyelid (-)	squeeze_r_eyebrow (+) raise_b_midlip (+) raise_r_i_eyebrow (+) close_t_l_eyelid (-) close_b_l_eyelid (-)
Sadness	raise_l_i_eyebrow (+) close_t_l_eyelid (+) raise_l_m_eyebrow (-) raise_l_o_eyebrow (-) close_b_l_eyelid (+)	raise_r_i_eyebrow (+) close_t_r_eyelid (+) raise_r_m_eyebrow (-) raise_r_o_eyebrow (-) close_b_r_eyelid (+)
Surprise	raise_l_o_eyebrow (+) raise_l_i_eyebrow (+) raise_l_m_eyebrow (+) squeeze_l_eyebrow (-) open_jaw (+)	raise_r_o_eyebrow (+) raise_r_i_eyebrow (+) raise_r_m_eyebrow (+) squeeze_r_eyebrow (-)
Joy	close_t_l_eyelid (+) close_b_l_eyelid (+) stretch_l_cornerlip (+) raise_l_m_eyebrow (+) lift_r_cheek (+) lower_t_midlip (-) OR open_jaw (+)	close_t_r_eyelid (+) close_b_r_eyelid (+) stretch_r_cornerlip (+) raise_r_m_eyebrow (+) lift_l_cheek (+) raise_b_midlip (-)
Disgust	close_t_l_eyelid (+) close_t_r_eyelid (+) lower_t_midlip (-) squeeze_l_cornerlip (+)	close_b_l_eyelid (+) close_b_r_eyelid (+) open_jaw (+) AND / OR {squeeze_r_cornerlip (+)}
Fear	raise_l_o_eyebrow (+) raise_l_m_eyebrow(+) raise_l_i_eyebrow (+) squeeze_l_eyebrow (+) open_jaw (+) OR{ close_t_l_eyelid (-), lower_t_midlip (-)}	raise_r_o_eyebrow (+) raise_r_m_eyebrow (+) raise_r_I_eyebrow (+) squeeze_r_eyebrow (+) OR {close_t_r_eyelid (-), lower_t_midlip (+)}

Table 2. Muscle Actions involved in the six basic expressions [Karpouzis et al.,2000].

In general, facial expressions and emotions can be described as a set of measurements (FDPs and derived features) and transformations (FAPs) that can be considered atomic with respect to the MPEG-4 standard. In this way, one can describe the anatomy of a human face, as well as any animation parameters with the change in the positions of the facial feature points, thus eliminating the need to explicitly specify the topology of the underlying geometry. These facial feature points can then be mapped to automatically detected measurements and indications of motion on a video sequence and thus help analyse or reconstruct the emotion or expression recognized by the system.
MPEG-4 specifies 84 feature points on the neutral face. The main purpose of these feature points is to provide spatial references to key positions on a human face. These 84 points were chosen to best reflect the facial anatomy and movement mechanics of a human face. The location of these feature points has to be known for any MPEG-4 compliant face model. The Feature points on the model should be located according to figure points illustrated in Figure 2. After a series of analysis on faces we have concluded that mainly 15 FAP's are affected by these expressions [Soyel et al., 2005].
These facial features are moved due to the contraction and expansion of facial muscles, whenever a facial expression is changed. Table 2 illustrates the description of the basic expressions using the MPEG-4 FAPs terminology.
Although muscle actions [P. Ekman & W. Friesen,1978] are of high importance, with respect to facial animation, one is unable to track them analytically without resorting to explicit electromagnetic sensors. However, a subset of them can be deduced from their visual results, that is, the deformation of the facial tissue and the movement of some facial surface points. This reasoning resembles the way that humans visually perceive emotions, by noticing specific features in the most expressive areas of the face, the regions around the eyes and the mouth. The seven basic expressions, as well as intermediate ones, employ facial deformations strongly related with the movement of some prominent facial points that can be automatically detected. These points can be mapped to a subset of the MPEG-4 feature point set. The reader should be noted that MPEG-4 defines the neutral as all face muscles are relaxed.

2.3 Relevant facial feature points

In order to reduce the amount of time required to perform the experiments, a small set of 11 feature points were selected. Care was taken to select facial feature points from the whole set defined by the MPEG-4 standard. The MPEG-4 standard divides feature points into a number groups, which is listed in Table 3, corresponding to the particular region of the face to which they belong. A few points from nearly all the groups were taken. Nine points were selected from the left side of the face (Repetitive selection on the right side is not needed due to symmetry). The feature points selected were such that they have varying predicted extraction difficulty. The feature points selected are shown in Figure 3.

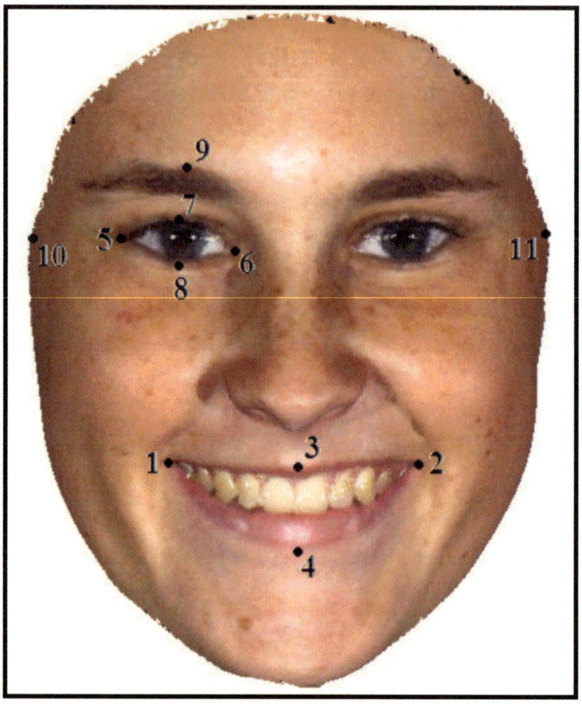

Fig. 3. 11-facial feature points: 1-Left corner of outer-lip contour, 2-Right corner of outer-lip contour, 3-Middle point of outer upper-lip contour, 4- Middle point of outer lower-lip contour, 5-Right corner of the right eye, 6-Left corner of the right eye, 7-Centre of upper inner-right eyelid, 8-Centre of lower inner-right eyelid, 9-Uppermost point of the right eyebrow, 10-Outermost point of right-face contour, 11- Outermost point of left-face contour.

Feature Point Groups	Selected Feature Points
2- Chin, innerlip	-
3- Eyes	3.10-centre of lower inner-right eyelid 3.11- left corner of the right eye 3.12-right corner of the right eye 3.14-centre of upper inner-right eyelid
4- Eye brows	4.4-uppermost point of the right eyebrow
5- Cheek	-
6- Tongue	-
7- Spine	-
8- Outer Lip	8.1-middle point of outer upper-lip contour 8.2-middle point of outer lower-lip contour 8.3-left corner of outer-lip contour 8.4 right corner of outer-lip contour
9- Nose, Nostrils	-
10- Ear	10.9-outermost point of left-face contour 10.10-outermost point of right-face contour
11-Hair Line	-

Table 3. Selected facial features points.

3. 3D distance-vector based facial expression recognition

3.1 Information extracted from 3D Space

By using the distribution of the 11 facial feature points from 3D facial model we extract six characteristic distances that serve as input to neural network classifier used for recognizing the different facial expressions shown in Table 4.

Distance No	Distance Name	Distance Description
D1	Eye Opening	Distance between the right corner of the right eye and the left corner of the right eye.
D2	Eyebrow Height	Distance between the centre of upper inner-right eyelid and the uppermost point of the right eyebrow.
D3	Mouth Opening	Distance between the left corner of outer-lip contour and right corner of outer-lip contour.
D4	Mouth Height	Distance between the middle point of outer upper-lip contour and middle point of outer lower-lip contour.
D5	Lip Stretching	Distance between the right corner of the right eye and right corner of outer-lip contour.
D6	Normalization	Distance between the outermost point of right-face contour and outermost point of left-face contour.

Table 4. Six characteristic distances.

3.2 Basic architecture of facial expression recognition system

Facial expression recognition includes both measurement of facial motion and recognition of expression. The general approach to Automatic Facial Expression Analysis (AFEA) systems, which is shown in Figure 4, can be categorised by three steps.

- Face acquisition.
- Facial feature extraction and representation.
- Facial expression recognition.

Face acquisition is the first step of the facial expression recognition system to find a face region in the input frame images. After determining the face location, various facial feature extraction approaches can be used. Mainly there are two general approaches; geometric feature-based methods and appearance-based methods. The first one utilizes the shape and the location of face components such as: mouth, nose, and eyes which are represented by a feature vector extracted from these facial components. In appearance-based methods, image filters, such as Gabor wavelets, are applied to either the whole face or specific regions in a face image to extract a feature vector.

Depending on the different facial feature extraction methods, the effects of in-plane head rotation and different scales of the faces can be eliminated, either by face normalization before the feature extraction or by feature representation before the step of expression recognition. The last stage of the facial expression analysis system is facial expression recognition using different classification approaches. Facial expression recognition usually results in classes according to either the Facial Actions Coding System (FACS) or the seven basic facial expressions.

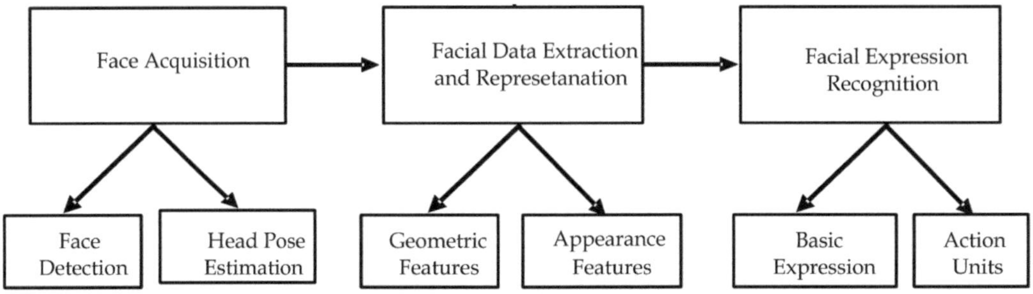

Fig. 4. Basic Architecture of Facial Expression Recognition System

3.3 Classification of the facial expressions

By using the entire information introduced in the previous section, we achieve 3D facial expression recognition in the following phases. First, we extract the characteristic distance vectors as defined in Table 3. Then, we classify a given distance vector on a previously trained neural network. The sixth distance, D6, is used to normalize the first five distances. The neural network architecture consists of a multilayered perceptron of input, hidden and output layers that is trained by using Backpropagation algorithm in the training process. The input layer receives a vector of six distances and the output layer represents 7 possible facial expressions mentioned in the preceding sections.

Backpropagation was created by generalizing the Widrow-Hoff learning rule to multiple-layer networks and nonlinear differentiable transfer functions. Input vectors and the corresponding target vectors are used to train a network until it can approximate a function to associate input vectors with specific output vectors, or classify the input vectors. Networks with biases, a sigmoid layer, and a linear output layer are capable of approximating any function with a finite number of discontinuities.

Standard backpropagation is a gradient descent algorithm, as is the Widrow-Hoff learning rule, in which the network weights are moved along the negative of the gradient of the performance function. The term backpropagation refers to the manner in which the gradient is computed for nonlinear multilayer networks. There are a number of variations on the basic algorithm that are based on other standard optimization techniques, such as conjugate gradient and Newton methods.

Properly trained backpropagation networks tend to give reasonable answers when presented with inputs that they have never seen. Typically, a new input leads to an output similar to the correct output for input vectors used in training that are similar to the new input being presented. This generalization property makes it possible to train a network on a representative set of input/target pairs and get good results without training the network on all possible input/output pairs [Rumelhart et al.,1986].

We used BU-3DFE database [Yin et al., 2006] in our experiments to train and test our model. The database we have used contains 7 facial expressions for 60 different people. We arbitrarily divided the 60 subjects into two subsets: one with 54 subjects for training and the other with 6 subjects for testing. During the recognition experiments, a distance vector is derived for every 3D model. Consecutive distance vectors are assumed to be statistically independent as well as the underlying class sequences. The vector is eventually assigned to the class with the highest likelihood score.

4. Performances analysis and discussions

4.1 Training and testing the data

Neural networks are composed of simple elements operating in parallel. These elements are inspired by biological nervous systems. As in nature, the network function is determined largely by the connections between elements. We can train a neural network to perform a particular function by adjusting the values of the connections (weights) between elements. Commonly neural networks are adjusted, or trained, so that a particular input leads to a specific target output. Such a situation is shown in Figure 5. The network is adjusted, based on a comparison of the output and the target, until the network output matches the target. Typically many such input/target pairs are used, in this supervised learning, to train a network.

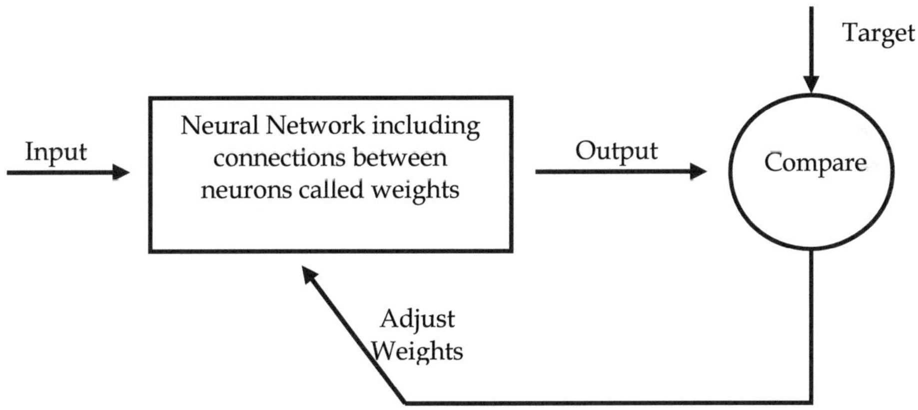

Fig.5. Basic Neural Network Structure

Batch training of a network proceeds by making weight and bias changes based on an entire set of input vectors. Incremental training changes the weights and biases of a network as needed after presentation of each individual input vector. Incremental training is sometimes referred to as "on line" or "adaptive" training.

Once the network weights and biases have been initialized, the network is ready for training. The network can be trained for function approximation, pattern association, or pattern classification. The training process requires a set of examples of proper network behaviour - network inputs and target outputs. During training the weights and biases of the network are iteratively adjusted to minimize the network the average squared error between the network outputs and the target outputs.

We have tested our neural network setup on the BU-3DFE database [Yin et al., 2006], which contains posed emotional facial expression images with seven fundamental emotional states, Anger, Disgust, Fear, Happiness, Sadness, Surprise and Neutral. In our experiment, we used the data captured from 60 subjects for each expression. The test is based on the seven fundamental expressions. The 3D distribution of the 84 feature vertices was provided for each facial model. A detail description of the database construction, post-processing, and organization can be found in [Yin et al., 2006].

4.2 System performance

Our facial expression analysis experiments are carried out in a person-independent manner, which is thought to be more challenging than a person-dependent approach. We arbitrarily divided the 60 subjects into two subsets: one with subjects for training and the other with subjects for test. The experiments assure that any subject used for testing does not appear in the training set because the random partition is based on the subjects rather than the individual expression. The tests are executed 10 times with different partitions to achieve a stable generalized recognition rate. The entire process assures that every subject is tested at least once for each classifier. For each round of the test, all the classifiers are reset and re-trained from the initial state. We show the results for all the neural network classifiers in Table 5. Note that most of the expressions are detected with high accuracy and the confusion is larger with the Neutral and Anger classes. One reason why Anger is detected with only 85% is that in general this emotion's confusion with Sadness and Neutral is much larger than with the other emotions. As we compared the proposed 3D Distance Vectors based Facial Expression Recognition method (3D-DVFER) with 2D appearance feature based Gabor-wavelet (GW) approach [Lyons et al. 1999] we found the Gabor-wavelet approach performs poorly with an average recognition rate around 80%, comparing to the performance shown in Table 5, the 3D-DVFER method is superior to the 2D appearance feature based methods when classifying the seven prototypic facial expressions.

Input/Output	Neutral	Happy	Fear	Surprise	Sadness	Disgust	Anger
Neutral	86.7%	0.0%	1.7%	0.0%	3.7%	1.7%	6.7%
Happy	0.0%	95.0%	3.3%	0.0%	0.0%	5.0%	3.3%
Fear	0.0%	3.3%	91.7%	1.7%	0.0%	1.7%	0.0%
Surprise	0.0%	0.0%	0.0%	98,3%	0.0%	0.0%	0.0%
Sadness	6.7%	0.0%	1.7%	0.0%	90.7%	0.0%	5.0%
Disgust	1.7%	1.7%	0.0%	0.0%	1.9%	91.7%	0.0%
Anger	5.0%	0.0%	1.7%	0.0%	3.7%	0.0%	85.0%

Table 5. Average confusion matrix using the NN classifier (BU-3DFE database)[H. Soyel & H. Demirel, 2007].

When we compare the results of the proposed system with the results reported in [Wang et al., 2006] which use the same 3D database through an LDA classifier, we can see that our method outperforms the recognition rates in Table 6 for all of the facial expressions except the Happy case. Both systems give the same performance for the "Happy" facial expression. Note that the classifier in [Wang et al., 2006] does not consider the Neutral case as an expression, which gives an advantage to the approach.

The average recognition rate of the proposed system is 91.3% where the average performance of the method given in [Wang et al., 2006] stays at 83.6% for the recognition of the facial expressions that uses the same 3D database.

Input/Output	Happy	Fear	Surprise	Sadness	Disgust	Anger
Happy	95.0%	3.8%	0.0%	0.4%	0.8%	0.0%
Fear	12.5%	75.0%	2.1%	7.9%	2.5%	0.0%
Surprise	0.0%	1.2%	90.8%	5.4%	0.8%	1.7%
Sadness	0.0%	2.9%	5.8%	80.4%	2.5%	8.3%
Disgust	3.8%	4.2%	0.4%	6.7%	80.4%	4.6%
Anger	0.0%	6.3%	0.8%	11.3%	1.7%	80.0%

Table 6. Average confusion matrix using of the LDA based classifier in [Wang et al., 2006]

5. Conclusion

In this chapter we have shown that probabilistic neural network classifier can be used for the 3D analysis of facial expressions without relying on all of the 84 facial features and error-prone face pose normalization stage. Face deformation as well as facial muscle contraction and expansion are important indicators for facial expression and by using only 11 facial feature points and symmetry of the human face, we are able to extract enough information from a from a face image. Our results show that 3D distance vectors based recognition outperforms facial expression recognition results compared to the results of the similar systems using 2D and 3D facial feature analysis. The average facial expression recognition rate of the proposed system reaches up to 91.3%. The quantitative results clearly suggest that the proposed approach produces encouraging results and opens a promising direction for higher rate expression analysis.

6. References

Ekman, P. & Friesen, W. (1976). Pictures of Facial Affect. *Palo Alto, CA: Consulting Psychologist*

Ekman, P. & Friesen, W. (1978). The Facial Action Coding System: A Technique for the Measurement of Facial Movement, *Consulting Psychologists Press*, San Francisco

Rumelhart, D. Hinton, G. Williams, R. (1986) Learning internal representations by error propagation, In. *Parallel Data Processing*,D. Rumelhart and J. McClelland, (Ed.), pp. 318-362,the M.I.T. Press, Cambridge, MA

Donato, G. Bartlett, M. Hager, Ekman, P. & Sejnowski, T. (1999). Classifying facial actions. *IEEE Transaction on Pattern Analysis and Machine Intelligence*, 21(10), pp. 974–989

Lyons, M. Budynek, J. & Akamatsu, S. (1999). Automatic classification of single facial images. *IEEE Trans. On PAMI*, 21, pp. 1357–1362

Karpouzis, K. Tsapatsoulis, N. & Kollias, S. (2000). Moving to Continuous Facial Expression Space using the MPEG-4 Facial Definition Parameter (FDP) Set, *In Proceedings of the Electronic Imaging*, San Jose, USA

Braathen, B. Bartlett, M. Littlewort, G. Smith, E. & Movellan, J. (2002). An approach to automatic recognition of spontaneous facial actions. *In Proceedings of International Conferance on FGR*, pp. 345-350, USA

Pandzic, I.& Forchheimer R. (Ed.) (2002). MPEG-4 Facial Animation: the Standard, Implementation and Applications, *Wiley*

Fasel, B. & Luttin, J. (2003). Automatic facial expression analysis: Survey. *Pattern Recognition,* 36(1), pp. 259–275

Pantic, M. & Rothkrantz, L. (2004). Facial action recognition for facial expression analysis from static face images. *IEEE Trans. on SMC-Part B: Cybernetics,* 34, pp. 1449–1461

Soyel, H. Yurtkan, K. Demirel, H. Ozkaramanli, H. Uyguroglu, E. Varoglu, M. (2005). Face Modeling andAnimation for MPEG Compliant Model Based Video Coding, *IASTED International Conference on Computer Graphics and Imaging.*

Yin, L. Wei, X. Sun, Y. Wang, J. & Rosato, M.(2006). A 3d facial expression database for facial behavior research. *In Proceedings of International Conferance on FGR*, pp. 211-216, UK

Wang, J. Yin, L. Wei, X. & Sun, Y.(2006). 3D Facial Expression Recognition Based on Primitive Surface Feature Distribution. *IEEE CVPR'06* - Volume 2, pp. 1399-1406

Soyel, H. Demirel, H. (2007) Facial Expression Recognition using 3D Facial Feature Distances, *Lecture Notes in Computer Science (ICIAR 07),* vol. 4633, pp. 831-838.

2

Facial Expression Recognition in the Presence of Head Motion

Fadi Dornaika[1] and Franck Davoine[2]
National Geographical Institute (IGN), 2 avenue Pasteur, 94165 Saint-Mandé [1], Heudiasyc Mixed Research Unit, CNRS/UTC, 60205 Compiègne [2], France

1. Introduction

The human face has attracted attention in a number of areas including psychology, computer vision, human-computer interaction (HCI) and computer graphics (Chandrasiri et al, 2004). As facial expressions are the direct means of communicating emotions, computer analysis of facial expressions is an indispensable part of HCI designs. It is crucial for computers to be able to interact with the users, in a way similar to human-to-human interaction. Human-machine interfaces will require an increasingly good understanding of a subject's behavior so that machines can react accordingly. Although humans detect and analyze faces and facial expressions in a scene with little or no effort, development of an automated system that accomplishes this task is rather diffcult.

One challenge is to construct robust, real-time, fully automatic systems to track the facial features and expressions. Many computer vision researchers have been working on tracking and recognition of the whole face or parts of the face. Within the past two decades, much work has been done on automatic recognition of facial expression. The initial 2D methods had limited success mainly because their dependency on the camera viewing angle. One of the main motivations behind 3D methods for face or expression recognition is to enable a broader range of camera viewing angles (Blanz & Vetter, 2003; Gokturk et al., 2002; Lu et al., 2006; Moreno et al., 2002; Wang et al., 2004; Wen & Huang, 2003; Yilmaz et al., 2002).

To classify expressions in static images many techniques have been proposed, such as those based on neural networks (Tian et al., 2001), Gabor wavelets (Bartlett et al., 2004), and Adaboost (Wang et al., 2004). Recently, more attention has been given to modeling facial deformation in dynamic scenarios, since it is argued that information based on dynamics is richer than that provided by static images. Static image classifiers use feature vectors related to a single frame to perform classification (Lyons et al., 1999). Temporal classifiers try to capture the temporal pattern in the sequence of feature vectors related to each frame. These include the Hidden Markov Model (HMM) based methods (Cohen et al., 2003) and Dynamic Bayesian Networks (DBNs) (Zhang & Ji, 2005). In (Cohen et al., 2003), the authors introduce a facial expression recognition from live video input using temporal cues. They propose a new HMM architecture for automatically segmenting and recognizing human facial expression from video sequences. The architecture performs both segmentation and recognition of the facial expressions automatically using a multi-level architecture composed of an HMM layer and a Markov model layer. In (Zhang & Ji, 2005), the authors present a new approach to spontaneous facial expression understanding in image sequences. The facial feature detection and tracking is based on active Infra Red illumination. Modeling dynamic behavior of facial expression in image sequences falls within the framework of information fusion with DBNs. In (Xiang et al., 2008), the authors propose a temporal classifier based on the use of fuzzy C means where the features are given by Fourrier transform.

Surveys of facial expression recognition methods can be found in (Fasel & Luettin, 2003; Pantic & Rothkrantz, 2000). A number of earlier systems were based on facial motion encoded as a dense flow between successive image frames. However, flow estimates are easily disturbed by illumination changes and non-rigid motion. In (Yacoob & Davis, 1996), the authors compute optical flow of regions on the face, then they use a rule-based classifier to recognize the six basic facial expressions. Extracting and tracking facial actions in a video can be done in several ways. In (Bascle & Black, 1998), the authors use active contours for tracking the performer's facial deformations. In (Ahlberg, 2002), the author retrieves facial actions using a variant of Active Appearance Models. In (Liao & Cohen, 2005), the authors used a graphical model for modeling the interdependencies of defined facial regions for characterizing facial gestures under varying pose. The dominant paradigm involves computing a time-varying description of facial actions/features from which the expression can be recognized; that is to say, the tracking process is performed prior to the recognition process (Dornaika & Davoine, 2005; Zhang & Ji, 2005).

However, the results of both processes affect each other in various ways. Since these two problems are interdependent, solving them simultaneously increases reliability and robustness of the results. Such robustness is required when perturbing factors such as partial occlusions, ultra-rapid movements and video streaming discontinuity may affect the input data. Although the idea of merging tracking and recognition is not new, our work addresses two complicated tasks, namely tracking the facial actions and recognizing expression over time in a monocular video sequence.

In the literature, simultaneous tracking and recognition has been used in simple cases. For example, (North et al., 2000) employs a particle-filter-based algorithm for tracking and recognizing the motion class of a juggled ball in 2D. Another example is given in (Zhou et al., 2003); this work proposes a framework allowing the simultaneous tracking and recognizing of human faces using a particle filtering method. The recognition consists in determining a person's identity, which is fixed for the whole probe video. The authors use a mixed state vector formed by the 2D global face motion (affine transform) and an identity variable. However, this work does not address either facial deformation or facial expression recognition.

In this chapter, we describe two frameworks for facial expression recognition given natural head motion. Both frameworks are texture- and view-independent. The first framework exploits the temporal representation of tracked facial action in order to infer the current facial expression in a deterministic way. The second framework proposes a novel paradigm in which facial action tracking and expression recognition are simultaneously performed. The second framework consists of two stages. First, the 3D head pose is estimated using a deterministic approach based on the principles of Online Appearance Models (OAMs). Second, the facial actions and expression are simultaneously estimated using a stochastic approach based on a particle filter adopting mixed states (Isard & Blake, 1998). This proposed framework is simple, efficient and robust with respect to head motion given that (1) the dynamic models directly relate the facial actions to the universal expressions, (2) the learning stage does not deal with facial images but only concerns the estimation of auto-regressive models from sequences of facial actions, which is carried out using closed- from solutions, and (3) facial actions are related to a deformable 3D model and not to entities measured in the image plane.

1.1 Outline of the chapter

This chapter provides a set of recent deterministic and stochastic (robust) techniques that perform efficient facial expression recognition from video sequences. The chapter organization is as follows. The first part of the chapter (Section 2) briefly describes a real time face tracker adopting a deformable 3D mesh and using the principles of Online Appearance Models. This tracker can provide the 3D head pose parameters and some facial actions. The second part of the chapter (Section 3) focuses on the analysis and recognition of facial expressions in continuous videos using the tracked facial actions. We propose two pose- and texture-independent approaches that exploit the tracked facial action parameters. The first approach adopts a Dynamic Time Warping technique for recognizing expressions where the training data are a set of trajectory examples associated with universal facial expressions. The second approach models trajectories associated with facial actions using Linear Discriminant Analysis. The third part of the chapter (Section 4) addresses the simultaneous tracking and recognition of facial expressions. In contrast to the mainstream approach "tracking then recognition", this framework simultaneously retrieves the facial actions and expression using a particle filter adopting multi-class dynamics that are conditioned on the expression.

2. Face and facial action tracking

2.1 A deformable 3D model

In our study, we use the *Candide* 3D face model (Ahlberg, 2002). This 3D deformable wireframe model was first developed for the purposes of model-based image coding and computer animation. The 3D shape of this wireframe model (triangular mesh) is directly recorded in coordinate form. It is given by the coordinates of the 3D vertices $\mathbf{P}_i$, $i = 1,\ldots, n$ where n is the number of vertices. Thus, the shape up to a global scale can be fully described by the $3n$ vector $\mathbf{g}$; the concatenation of the 3D coordinates of all vertices $\mathbf{P}_i$. The vector $\mathbf{g}$ is written as:

$$\mathbf{g} = \overline{\mathbf{g}} + \mathbf{S}\,\boldsymbol{\tau}_\mathbf{s} + \mathbf{A}\,\boldsymbol{\tau}_\mathbf{a} \tag{1}$$

where $\overline{g}$ is the standard shape of the model, τ_s and τ_a are shape and animation control vectors, respectively, and the columns of $\mathbf{S}$ and $\mathbf{A}$ are the Shape and Animation Units. A Shape Unit provides a means of deforming the 3D wireframe so as to be able to adapt eye width, head width, eye separation distance, etc. Thus, the term $\mathbf{S}\,\tau_s$ accounts for shape variability (inter-person variability) while the term $\mathbf{A}\,\tau_a$ accounts for the facial animation (intra-person variability). The shape and animation variabilities can be approximated well enough for practical purposes by this linear relation. Also, we assume that the two kinds of variability are independent. With this model, the ideal neutral face configuration is represented by $\tau_a = \mathbf{0}$. The shape modes were created manually to accommodate the subjectively most important changes in facial shape (face height/width ratio, horizontal and vertical positions of facial features, eye separation distance). Even though a PCA was initially performed on manually adapted models in order to compute the shape modes, we preferred to consider the *Candide* model with manually created shape modes with semantic signification that are easy to use by human operators who need to adapt the 3D mesh to facial images. The animation modes were measured from pictorial examples in the Facial Action Coding System (FACS) (Ekman & Friesen, 1977).

In this study, we use twelve modes for the facial Shape Units matrix **S** and six modes for the facial Animation Units (AUs) matrix **A**. Without loss of generality, we have chosen the six following AUs: lower lip depressor, lip stretcher, lip corner depressor, upper lip raiser, eyebrow lowerer and outer eyebrow raiser. These AUs are enough to cover most common facial animations (mouth and eyebrow movements). Moreover, they are essential for conveying emotions. The effects of the Shape Units and the six Animation Units on the 3D wireframe model are illustrated in Figure 1.

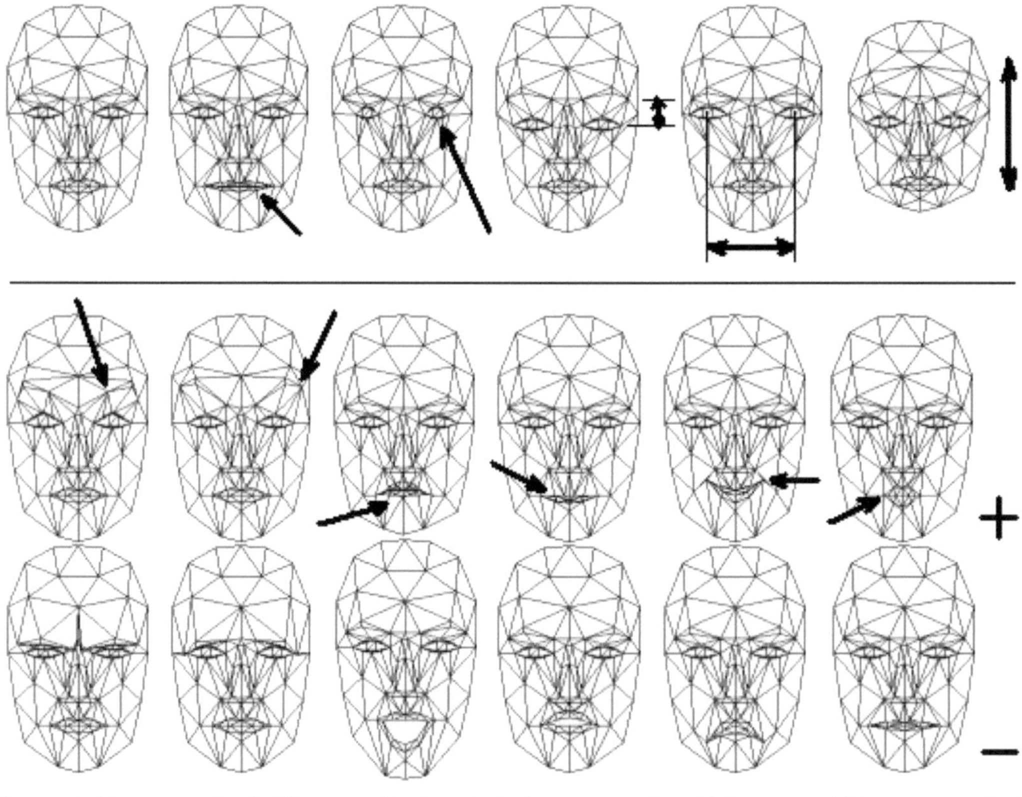

Figure 1: First row: Facial Shape units (neutral shape, mouth width, eyes width, eyes vertical position, eye separation distance, head height). Second and third rows: Positive and negative perturbations of Facial Action Units (Brow lowerer, Outer brow raiser, Jaw drop, Upper lip raiser, Lip corner depressor, Lip stretcher).

In equation (1), the 3D shape is expressed in a local coordinate system. However, one should relate the 3D coordinates to the image coordinate system. To this end, we adopt the weak perspective projection model. We neglect the perspective effects since the depth variation of the face can be considered as small compared to its absolute depth. Therefore, the mapping

between the 3D face model and the image is given by a 2×4 matrix, **M**, encapsulating both the 3D head pose and the camera parameters.
Thus, a 3D vertex $\mathbf{P}_i = (X_i, Y_i, Z_i)^T \subset \mathbf{g}$ will be projected onto the image point $\mathbf{p}_i = (u_i, v_i)^T$ given by:

$$(u_i, v_i)^T = \mathbf{M}\,(X_i, Y_i, Z_i, 1)^T \quad (2)$$

For a given subject, τ_s is constant. Estimating τ_s can be carried out using either feature-based (Lu et al., 2001) or featureless approaches (Ahlberg, 2002). In our work, we assume that the control vector τ_s is already known for every subject, and it is set manually using for instance the face in the first frame of the video sequence (the *Candide* model and target face shapes are aligned manually). Therefore, Equation (1) becomes:

$$\mathbf{g} = \mathbf{g}_s + \mathbf{A}\,\boldsymbol{\tau}_a \quad (3)$$

where $\mathbf{g}_s$ represents the static shape of the face-the neutral face configuration. Thus, the state of the 3D wireframe model is given by the 3D head pose parameters (three rotations and three translations) and the animation control vector τ_a. This is given by the 12-dimensional vector **b**:

$$\mathbf{b} \;=\; [\theta_x,\;\; \theta_y,\;\; \theta_z,\;\; t_x,\;\; t_y,\;\; t_z,\;\; \boldsymbol{\tau}_{\mathbf{a}}^T\;]^T \quad (4)$$

$$=\; [\mathbf{h}^T,\;\; \boldsymbol{\tau}_{\mathbf{a}}^T\;]^T \quad (5)$$

where the vector **h** represents the six degrees of freedom associated with the 3D head pose.

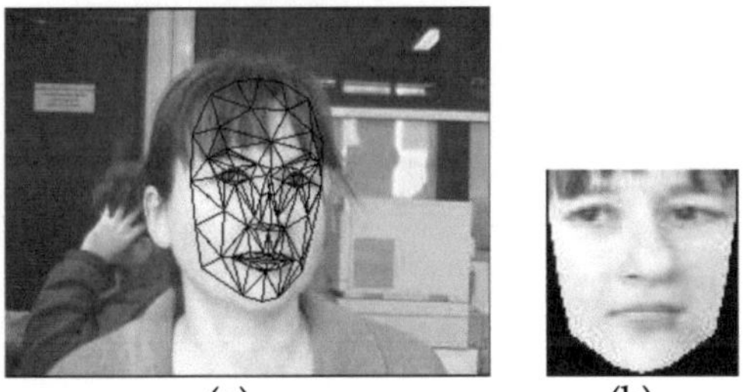

Figure 2: (a) an input image with correct adaptation of the 3D model. (b) the corresponding shape-free facial image.

2.2 Shape-free facial patches

A facial patch is represented as a shape-free image (geometrically normalized rawbrightness image). The geometry of this image is obtained by projecting the standard shape $\overline{g}$ with a centered frontal 3D pose onto an image with a given resolution. The geometrically normalized image is obtained by texture mapping from the triangular 2D mesh in the input image (see Figure 2) using a piece-wise affine transform, *W*. The warping process applied to an input image **y** is denoted by:

$$\mathbf{x}(\mathbf{b}) = \mathcal{W}(\mathbf{y}, \mathbf{b}) \quad (6)$$

where **x** denotes the shape-free patch and **b** denotes the geometrical parameters. Several resolution levels can be chosen for the shape-free patches. The reported results are obtained with a shape-free patch of 5392 pixels. Regarding photometric transformations, a zero-mean unit-variance normalization is used to partially compensate for contrast variations. The complete image transformation is implemented as follows: (i) transfer the rawbrightness facial patch **y** using the piece-wise affine transform associated with the vector **b**, and (ii) perform the gray-level normalization of the obtained patch.

2.3 Adaptive facial texture model

In this work, the facial texture model (appearance model) is built online using the tracked shape-free patches. We use the HAT symbol for the tracked parameters and patches. For a given frame t, $\hat{b}_t$ represents the computed geometric parameters and $\hat{x}_t$ the corresponding shape-free patch, that is,

$$\hat{\mathbf{x}}_t = \mathbf{x}(\hat{\mathbf{b}}_t) = \mathcal{W}(\mathbf{y}_t, \hat{\mathbf{b}}_t) \tag{7}$$

The estimation of $\hat{b}_t$ from the sequence of images will be presented in Section 2.4. $\hat{b}_0$ is set manually, according to the face in the first video frame. The facial texture model (appearance model) associated with the shape-free facial patch at time t is time-varying in that it models the appearances present in all observations $\hat{x}$ up to time t - 1. This may be required as a result, for instance, of illumination changes or out-of-plane rotated faces.

By assuming that the pixels within the shape-free patch are independent, we can model the appearance using a multivariate Gaussian with a diagonal covariance matrix Σ. In other words, this multivariate Gaussian is the distribution of the facial patches $\hat{x}_t$. Let μ be the Gaussian center and σ the vector containing the square root of the diagonal elements of the covariance matrix Σ. μ and σ are d-vectors (d is the size of x).

In summary, the observation likelihood is written as:

$$p(\mathbf{y}_t|\mathbf{b}_t) = p(\mathbf{x}_t|\mathbf{b}_t) = \prod_{i=1}^{d} \mathbf{N}(x_i; \mu_i, \sigma_i)_t \tag{8}$$

where $\mathbf{N}(x_i, \mu_i, \sigma_i)$ is the normal density:

$$\mathbf{N}(x_i; \mu_i, \sigma_i) = (2\pi\sigma_i^2)^{-1/2} \exp\left[-\frac{1}{2}\left(\frac{x_i - \mu_i}{\sigma_i}\right)^2\right] \tag{9}$$

We assume that the appearance model summarizes the past observations under an exponential envelope with a forgetting factor $\alpha = 1 - \exp\left(-\frac{\log 2}{n_h}\right)$, where n_h represents the half-life of the envelope in frames (Jepson et al., 2003).

When the patch $\hat{x}_t$ is available at time t, the appearance is updated and used to track in the next frame. It can be shown that the appearance model parameters, i.e., the μ_i's and σ_i's can be updated from time t to time (t + 1) using the following equations (see (Jepson et al., 2003) for more details on OAMs):

$$\mu_{i_{(t+1)}} = (1 - \alpha)\, \mu_{i_{(t)}} + \alpha\, \hat{x}_{i_{(t)}} \tag{10}$$

$$\sigma^2_{i_{(t+1)}} = (1-\alpha)\,\sigma^2_{i_{(t)}} + \alpha\,(\hat{x}_{i_{(t)}} - \mu_{i_{(t)}})^2 \tag{11}$$

This technique is simple, time-efficient and therefore suitable for real-time applications. The appearance parameters reflect the most recent observations within a roughly $L = 1 / \alpha$ window with exponential decay.

Note that μ is initialized with the first patch $\hat{x}_0$. However, equation (11) is not used with α being a constant until the number of frames reaches a given value (*e.g.*, the first 40 frames). For these frames, the classical variance is used, that is, equation (11) is used with α being set to $1/t$.

Here we used a single Gaussian to model the appearance of each pixel in the shape-free template. However, modeling the appearance with Gaussian mixtures can also be used at the expense of an additional computational load (e.g., see (Lee, 2005; Zhou et al., 2004)).

2.4 Face and facial action tracking

Given a video sequence depicting a moving head/face, we would like to recover, for each frame, the 3D head pose and the facial actions encoded by the state vector $\mathbf{b}_t$ (equation 5). The purpose of the tracking is to estimate the state vector $\mathbf{b}_t$ by using the current appearance model encoded by μ_t and σ_t. To this end, the current input image $\mathbf{y}_t$ is registered with the current appearance model. The state vector $\mathbf{b}_t$ is estimated by minimizing the *Mahalanobis* distance between the warped image patch and the current appearance mean - the current Gaussian center

$$\min_{\mathbf{b}} e(\mathbf{b}_t) = \min d\left[\mathbf{x}(\mathbf{b}_t), \boldsymbol{\mu}_t\right] = \min \sum_{i=1}^{d} \left(\frac{x_i - \mu_i}{\sigma_i}\right)^2_{(t)} \tag{12}$$

The above criterion can be minimized using an iterative gradient descent method where the starting solution is set to the previous solution $\hat{b}_{t-1}$. Handling outlier pixels (caused for instance by occlusions) is performed by replacing the quadratic function by the Huber's cost function (Huber, 1981). The gradient matrix is computed for each input frame. It is approximated by numerical differences. More details about this tracking method can be found in (Dornaika & Davoine, 2006).

3. Tracking then recognition

In this section, we show how the time series representation of the estimated facial actions, τ_a, can be utilized for inferring the facial expression in continuous videos. We propose two different approaches. The first one is a non-parametric approach and relies on Dynamic Time Warping. The second one is a parametric approach and is based on Linear Discriminant Analysis.

In order to learn the spatio-temporal structure of the facial actions associated with the universal expressions, we have used the following. Video sequences have been picked up from the CMU database (Kanade et al., 2000). These sequences depict five frontal view universal expressions (surprise, sadness, joy, disgust and anger). Each expression is performed by 7 different subjects, starting from the neutral one. Altogether we select 35 video sequences composed of around 15 to 20 frames each, that is, the average duration of each sequence is about half a second. The learning phase consists in estimating the facial action parameters τ_a (a 6-vector) associated with each training sequence, that is, the temporal trajectories of the action parameters.

Figure 3 shows six videos belonging to the CMU database. The first five images depict the estimated deformable model associated with the high magnitude of the five basic expressions. Figure 4 shows the computed facial action parameters associated with three training sequences: surprise, joy and anger. The training video sequences have an interesting property: all performed expressions go from the neutral expression to a high magnitude expression by going through a moderate magnitude around the middle of the sequence.

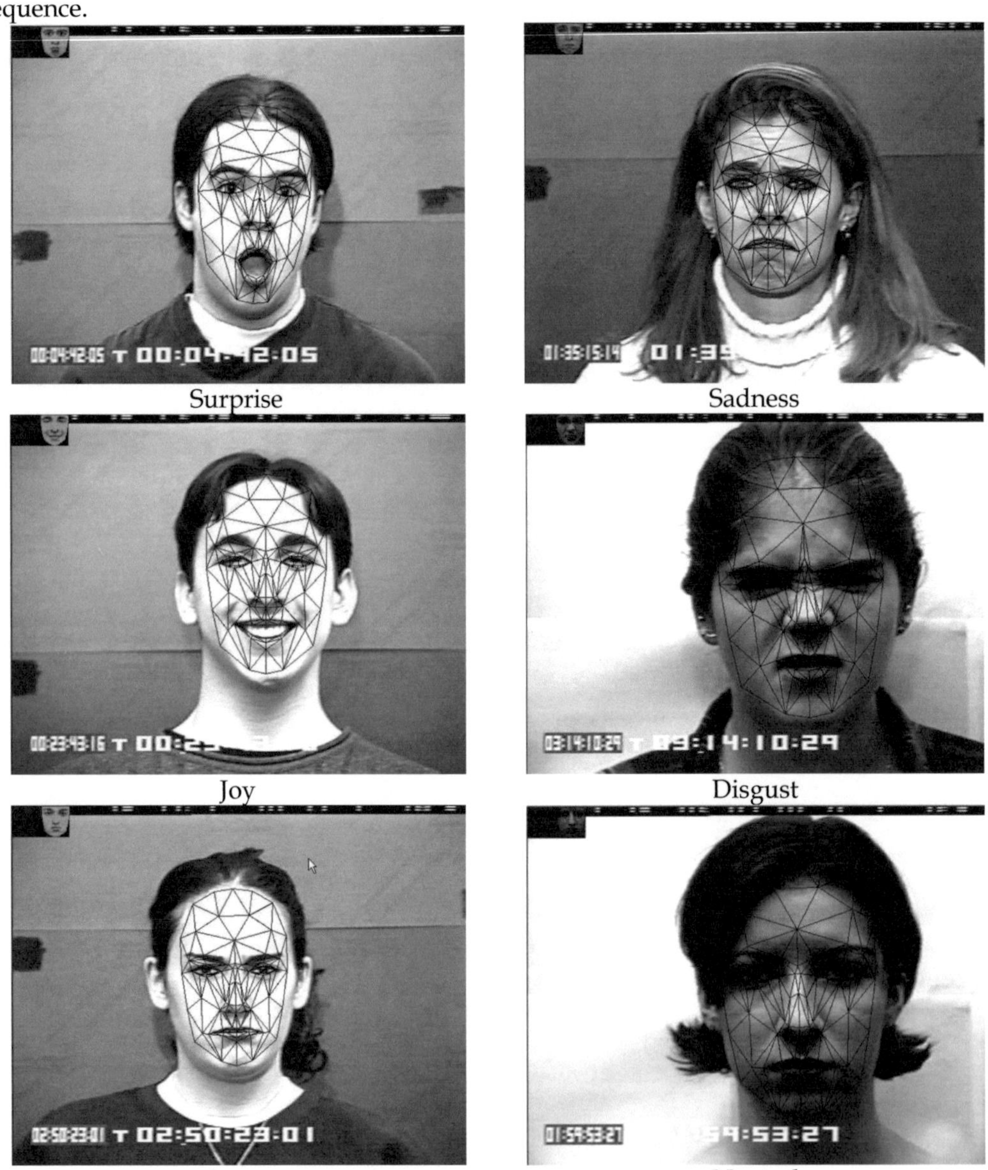

Figure 3: Six video examples associated with the CMU database. The first five images depict the high magnitude of the five basic expressions.

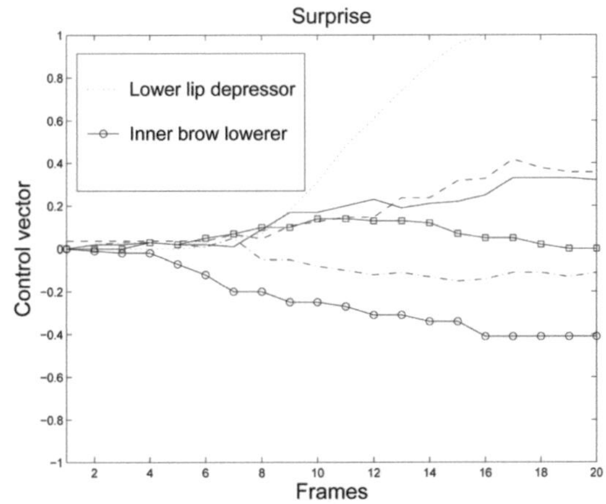

(a)

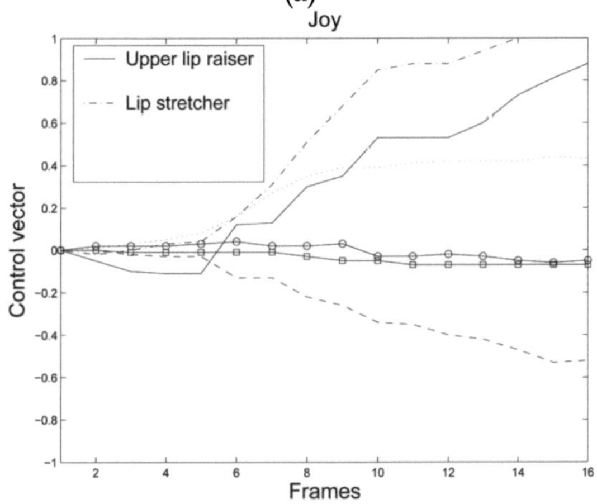

(b)

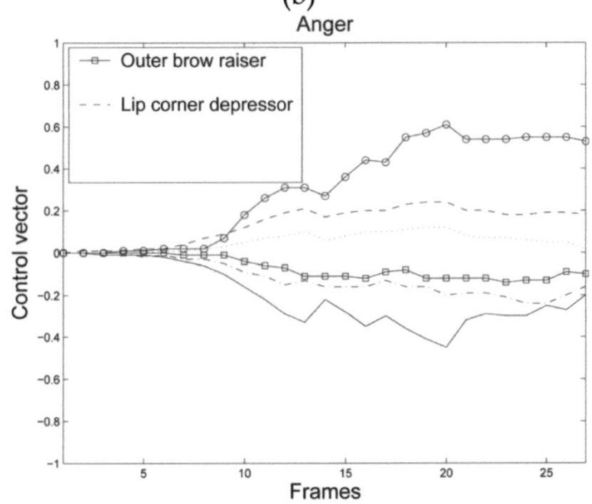

(c)

Figure 4: Three examples (sequences) of learned facial action parameters as a function of time. (a) Surprise expression. (b) Joy expression. (c) Anger expression.

3.1 Dynamic time warping

In the recognition phase, the head and facial actions are recovered from the video sequence using our developed appearance-based tracker (Dornaika & Davoine, 2006). The current facial expression is then recognized by computing a similarity measure between the tracked facial actions $\tau_{a(t)}$ associated with the test sequence and those associated with each universal expression. This recognition scheme can be carried out either online or off-line. One can notice that a direct comparison between the tracked trajectories and the stored ones is not feasible since there is no frame-to-frame correspondence between the tracked facial actions and the stored ones. To overcome this problem, we use dynamic programming which allows temporal deformation of time series as they are matched against each other.

We infer the facial expression associated with the current frame t by considering the estimated trajectory, i.e. the sequence of vectors $\tau_{a(t)}$, within a temporal window of size T centered at the current frame t. In our tests, T is set to 9 frames. This trajectory is matched against the 35 training trajectories using the Dynamic Time Warping (DTW) technique (Rabiner & Juang, 1993; Berndt & Clifford, 1994). For each training trajectory, the DTW technique returns a dissimilarity measure between the tested trajectory and the training trajectory (known universal expression). The classification rule stipulates that the smallest average dissimilarity decides the expression classifcation where the dissimilarity measures associated with a given universal expression are averaged over the 7 subjects.

The proposed scheme accounts for the variability in duration since the DTW technique allows non-linear time scaling. The segmentation of the video is obtained by repeating the whole recognition scheme for every frame in the test video.

In order to evaluate the performance, we have created test videos featuring the universal facial expressions. To this end, we have asked a volunteer student to perform each universal expression several times in a relatively long sequence. The subject was instructed to display the expression in a natural way, i.e. the displayed expressions were independent of any database. Each video sequence contains several cycles depicting a particular universal facial expression.

The performance of the developed recognition scheme is evaluated by utilizing five test videos. Table 1 shows the confusion matrix for the dynamical facial expression classifier using the DTW technique. We point out that the learned trajectories were inferred from the CMU database while the used test videos were created at our laboratory. The recognition rate of dynamical expressions was 100% for all universal expressions except for the disgust expression for which the recognition rate was 44%. The reason is that the disgust expression performed by our subject was very different from that performed by most of the CMU database subjects. Therefore, for the above experiment, the overall recognition rate is 90.4%.

	Surp.	Sad.	Joy	Disg.	Ang.
Surp.	14	0	0	0	0
Sad.	0	9	0	0	0
Joy	0	0	10	5	0
Disg.	0	0	0	4	0
Ang.	0	0	0	0	10

Table 1: Confusion matrix for the dynamical facial expression classifier using the DTW technique (the smallest average similarity). The learned trajectories were inferred from the CMU database while the used test videos were created at our laboratory. The recognition rate of dynamical expressions was 100% for all basic expressions except for the disgust expression for which the recognition rate was 44%.

3.2 Linear discriminant analysis

As can be seen from the previous section, the CPU time of the recognition scheme based on the DTW technique is proportional to the number of the subjects present in the database. Whenever this number is very large, the recognition scheme becomes computationally expensive. In this section, we propose a parametric recognition scheme by which the training trajectories can be represented in a more compact form. The computational cost of the recognition scheme does not depend on the number of examples.

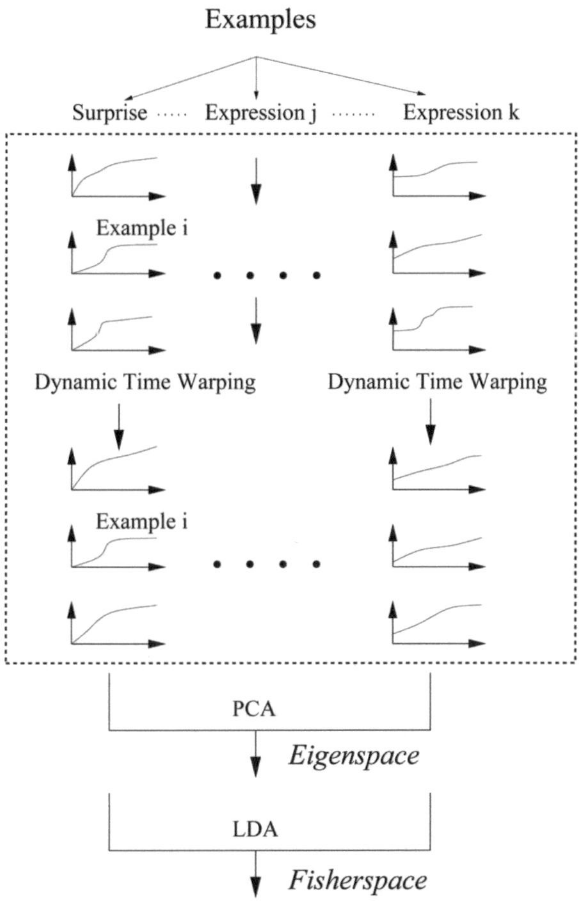

Figure 5: The parameterized modeling of facial expressions using Eigenspace and Fisherspace.

Learning. The learning phase is depicted in Figure 5. Again, we use the training videos associated with the CMU database. In order to obtain trajectories with the same number of frames (duration) the trajectories belonging to the same expression class are aligned using the DTW technique. Recall that this technique allows a frame-to-frame correspondence between two time series.

Let e_i^j be the aligned trajectory i belonging to the expression class j. The example e_i^j is represented by a column vector of dimension $1{\times}6T$ and is obtained by concatenating the facial action 6-vectors $\tau_{a(t)}$:

$$\mathbf{e}_i^j = [\boldsymbol{\tau}_{\mathbf{a}(1)}; \boldsymbol{\tau}_{\mathbf{a}(2)}; \ldots; \boldsymbol{\tau}_{\mathbf{a}(T)}]$$

Note that T represents the duration of the aligned trajectories which will be fixed for all examples. For example, a nominal duration of 18 frames for the aligned trajectories makes the dimension of all examples e_i^j (all i and j) equal to 108.

Applying a Principal Component Analysis on the set of all training trajectories yields the mean trajectory **e** as well as the principal modes of variation. Any training trajectory **e** can be approximated by the principal modes using the q largest eigenvalues:

$$\begin{aligned} \mathbf{e} &\cong \overline{\mathbf{e}} + \mathbf{U}\,\mathbf{c} \\ &= \overline{\mathbf{e}} + \sum_{l=1}^{q} c_l\,\mathbf{U}_l \end{aligned}$$

In our work, the number of principal modes is chosen such that the variability of the retained modes corresponds to 99% of the total variability. The vector **c** can be seen as a parametrization of any input trajectory, $\hat{e}$, in the space spanned by the q basis vectors $\mathbf{U}_l$. The vector **c** is given by:

$$\mathbf{c} = \mathbf{U}^T\,(\hat{\mathbf{e}} - \overline{\mathbf{e}}) \tag{13}$$

Thus, all training trajectories e_i^j can now be represented by the vectors c_i^j (using (13)) on which a Linear Discriminant Analysis can be applied. This gives a new space (the Fisherspace) in which each training video sequence is represented by a vector of dimension l -1 where l is the number of expression classes. Figure 6 illustrates the learning results associated with the CMU data. In this space, each trajectory example is represented by a 5-vector. Here, we use six facial expression classes: Surprise, Sadness, Joy, Disgust, Anger, and Neutral. (a) displays the second component versus the first one, and (b) displays the fourth component versus the third one. In this space, the neutral trajectory (a sequence of zero vectors) is represented by a star.

Recognition. The recognition scheme follows the main steps of the learning stage. We infer the facial expression by considering the estimated facial actions provided by our face tracker (Dornaika & Davoine, 2006). We consider the one-dimensional vector **e'** (the concatenation of the facial actions $\tau_{a(t)}$) within a temporal window of size T centered at the current frame t. Note that the value of T should be the same as in the learning stage. This vector is projected onto the PCA space, then the obtained vector is projected onto Fisherspace in which the classification occurs. The expression class whose mean is the closest to the current trajectory is then assigned to this trajectory (current frame).

Preformance evaluation. Table 2 shows the confusion matrix for the dynamical facial expression classifier using Eigenspace and Fisherspace. The learned trajectories were inferred from the CMU database while the used test videos were created at our laboratory. The recognition rate of dynamical expressions was 100% for all basic expressions except for the disgust expression for which the recognition rate was 55%. Therefore, for the above experiment, the overall recognition rate is 92.3%. One can notice the slight improvement in the recognition rate over the classical recognition scheme based on the DTW.

	Surp.	Sad.	Joy	Disg.	Ang.
Surp.	14	0	0	0	0
Sad.	0	9	0	0	0
Joy	0	0	10	4	0
Disg.	0	0	0	5	0
Ang.	0	0	0	0	10

Table 2: Confusion matrix for the dynamical facial expression classifier using Eigenspace and Fisherspace. The learned trajectories were inferred from the CMU database while the used test videos were created at our laboratory. The recognition rate of dynamical expressions was 100% for all basic expressions except for the disgust expression for which the recognition rate was 55%.

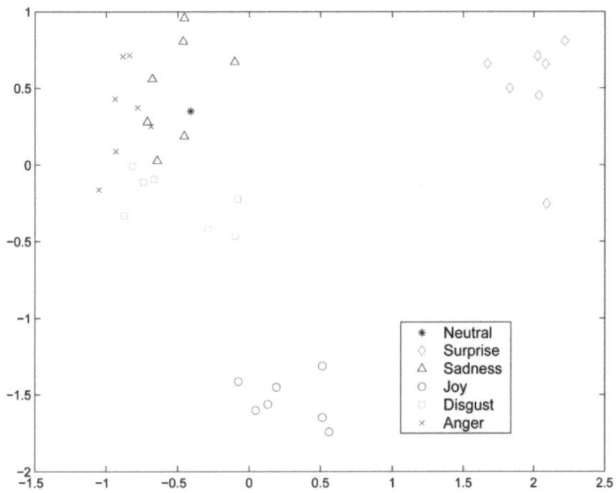

(a)

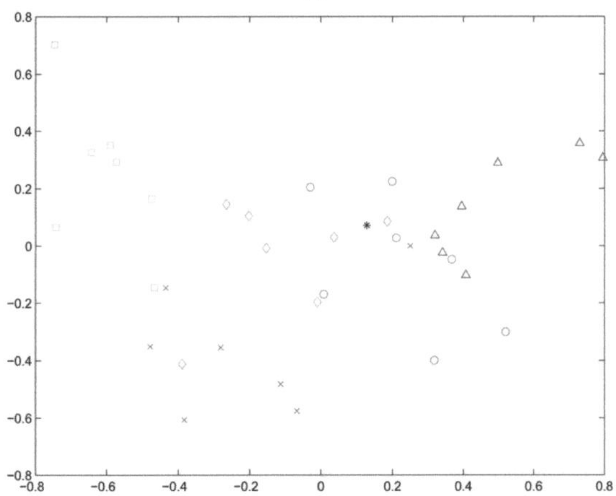

(b)

Figure 6: The 35 trajectory examples associated with five universal facial expressions depicted in Fisherspace. In this space, each trajectory example is represented by a 5-vector. Here, we use six facial expression classes: Surprise, Sadness, Joy, Disgust, Anger, and Neutral. (a) displays the second component versus the first one, and (b) displays the fourth component versus the third one. In this space, the neutral trajectory (a sequence of zero vectors) is represented by a star.

4. Tracking and recognition

In Section 3, the facial expression was inferred from the time series representation of the tracked facial actions. In this section, we propose to simultaneously estimate the facial actions and the expression from the video sequence.
Since the facial expression can be considered as a random discrete variable, we need to append to the continuous state vector $\mathbf{b}_t$ a discrete state component γ_t in order to create a mixed state:

$$\begin{pmatrix} \mathbf{b}_t \\ \gamma_t \end{pmatrix} \tag{14}$$

where $\gamma_t \in \varepsilon = \{1, 2, \ldots, N_\gamma\}$ is the discrete component of the state, drawn from a finite set of integer labels. Each integer label represents one of the six universal expressions: surprise, disgust, fear, joy, sadness and anger. In our study, we adopt these facial expressions together with the neutral expression, that is, N_γ is set to 7. There is another useful representation of the mixed state which is given by:

$$\begin{pmatrix} \mathbf{h}_t \\ \mathbf{a}_t \end{pmatrix} \tag{15}$$

where $\mathbf{h}_t$ denotes the 3D head pose parameters, and $\mathbf{a}_t$ the facial actions appended with the expression label γ_t, i.e. $\mathbf{a}_t = [\tau_{a(t)}^T, \gamma_t]^T$.
This separation is consistent with the fact that the facial expression is highly correlated with the facial actions, while the 3D head pose is independent of the facial actions and expressions. The remainder of this section is organized as follows. Section 4.1 provides some backgrounds. Section 4.2 describes the proposed approach for the simultaneous tracking and recognition. Section 4.3 describes experiments and provides evaluations of performance to show the feasibility and robustness of the proposed approach.

4.1 Backgrounds

4.1.1 Facial action dynamic models

Corresponding to each basic expression class, γ, there is a stochastic dynamic model describing the temporal evolution of the facial actions $\tau_{a(t)}$, given the expression. It is assumed to be a Markov model of order K. For each basic expression γ, we associate a Gaussian Auto-Regressive Process defined by:

$$\boldsymbol{\tau}_{\mathbf{a}(t)} = \sum_{k=1}^{K} \mathbf{A}_k^\gamma \, \boldsymbol{\tau}_{\mathbf{a}(t-k)} + \mathbf{d}^\gamma + \mathbf{B}^\gamma \, \mathbf{w}_t \tag{16}$$

in which $\mathbf{w}_t$ is a vector of 6 independent random $N(0, 1)$ variables. The parameters of the dynamic model are: (i) deterministic parameters $A_1^\gamma, A_2^\gamma, \ldots, A_K^\gamma$ and $\mathbf{d}^\gamma$, and stochastic parameters $\mathbf{B}^\gamma$ which are multipliers for the stochastic process $\mathbf{w}_t$. It is worth noting that the above model can be used in predicting the process from the previous K values. The predicted value at time t obeys a multivariate Gaussian centered at the deterministic value of (16), with $\mathbf{B}^{\gamma}\mathbf{B}^{\gamma T}$ being its covariance matrix. In our study, we are interested in second-order models, i.e. $K = 2$. The reason is twofold. First, these models are easy to estimate. Second, they are able to model complex dynamics. For example, these models have been used in (Blake & Isard, 2000) for learning the 2D motion of talking lips (profile contours), beating heart, and writing fingers.

4.1.2 Learning the second-order auto-regressive models

Given a training sequence $\tau_{a(1)},\ldots,\tau_{a(T)}$, with $T > 2$, belonging to the same expression class, it is well known that a Maximum Likelihood Estimator provides a closed-form solution for the model parameters (Blake & Isard, 2000). For a second-order model, these parameters reduce to two 6×6 matrices A_1^{γ}, A_2^{γ}, a 6-vector $\mathbf{d}^{\gamma}$, and a 6 × 6 covariance matrix $\mathbf{C}^{\gamma} = \mathbf{B}^{\gamma}\,\mathbf{B}^{\gamma\,T}$. Therefore, Eq. (16) reduces to:

$$\boldsymbol{\tau}_{\mathbf{a}(t)} = \mathbf{A}_2^{\gamma}\,\boldsymbol{\tau}_{\mathbf{a}(t-2)} + \mathbf{A}_1^{\gamma}\,\boldsymbol{\tau}_{\mathbf{a}(t-1)} + \mathbf{d}^{\gamma} + \mathbf{B}^{\gamma}\,\mathbf{w}_t \tag{17}$$

The parameters of each auto-regressive model can be computed from temporal facial action sequences. Ideally, the temporal sequence should contain several instances of the corresponding expression.

More details about auto-regressive models and their computation can be found in (Blake & Isard, 2000; Ljung, 1987; North et al., 2000). Each universal expression has its own second-order auto-regressive model given by Eq.(17). However, the dynamics of facial actions associated with the neutral expression can be simpler and are given by:

$$\tau_{a(t)} = \tau_{a(t-1)} + \mathrm{D}\mathrm{w}_t$$

where $\mathbf{D}$ is a diagonal matrix whose elements represent the variances around the ideal neutral configuration $\tau_a = \mathbf{0}$. The right-hand side of the above equation is constrained to belong to a predefined interval, since a neutral configuration and expression is characterized by both the lack of motion and the closeness to the ideal static configuration. In our study, the auto-regressive models are learned using a supervised learning scheme. First, we asked volunteer students to perform each basic expression several times in approximately 30-second sequences. Each video sequence contains several cycles depicting a particular facial expression: Surprise, Sadness, Joy, Disgust, Anger, and Fear. Second, for each training video, the 3D head pose and the facial actions $\tau_{a(t)}$ are tracked using our deterministic appearance-based tracker (Dornaika & Davoine, 2006) (outlined in Section 2). Third, the parameters of each auto-regressive model are estimated using the Maximum Likelihood Estimator.

Figure 7 illustrates the value of the facial actions, $\tau_{a(t)}$, associated with six training video sequences. For clarity purposes, only two components are shown for a given plot. For a given training video, the neutral frames are skipped from the original training sequence used in the computation of the auto- regressive models.

4.1.3 The transition matrix

In our study, the facial actions as well as the expression are simultaneously retrieved using a stochastic framework, namely the particle filtering method. This framework requires a transition matrix **T** whose entries $T_{\gamma',\gamma}$ describe the probability of transition between two expression labels γ' and γ. The transition probabilities need to be learned from training video sequences. In the literature, the transition probabilities associated with states (not necessarily facial expressions) are inferred using supervised and unsupervised learning techniques. However, since we are dealing with high level states (the universal facial expressions), we have found that a realistic *a priori* setting works very well. We adopt a 7 ×7 symmetric matrix whose diagonal elements are close to one (e.g. $T_{\gamma,\gamma} = 0.8$, that is, 80% of the transitions occur within the same expression class). The rest of the percentage is distributed equally among the expressions. In this model, transitions from one expression to another expression without going through the neutral one are allowed. Furthermore, this model adopts the most general case where all universal expressions have the same probability. However, according to the context of the application, one can adopt other transition matrices in which some expressions are more likely to happen than others.

4.2 Approach

Since at any given time, the 3D head pose parameters can be considered as independent of the facial actions and expression, our basic idea is to split the estimation of the unknown parameters into two main stages. For each input video frame $\mathbf{y}_t$, these two stages are invoked in sequence in order to recover the mixed state $[\,\boldsymbol{h}_t^T,\ \boldsymbol{a}_t^T\,]^T$. Our proposed approach is illustrated in Figure 8. In the first stage, the six degrees of freedom associated with the 3D head pose (encoded by the vector $\mathbf{h}_t$) are obtained using a deterministic registration technique similar to that proposed in (Dornaika & Davoine, 2006). In the second stage, the facial actions and the facial expression (encoded by the vector $\mathbf{a}_t = [\,\tau_{a(t)}^T,\ \gamma_t]^T$) are simultaneously estimated using a stochastic framework based on a particle filter. Such models have been used to track objects when different types of dynamics can occur (Isard & Blake, 1998). Other examples of auxiliary discrete variables beside the main hidden state of interest are given in (Perez & Vermaak, 2005). Since $\tau_{a(t)}$ and γ_t are highly correlated their simultaneous estimation will give results that are more robust and accurate than results obtained with methods estimating them in sequence. In the following, we present the parameter estimation process associated with the current frame $\mathbf{y}_t$. Recall that the head pose is computed using a deterministic approach, while the facial actions and expressions are estimated using a probabilistic framework.

4.2.1 3D head pose

The purpose of this stage is to estimate the six degrees of freedom associated with the 3D head pose at frame *t*, that is, the vector $\mathbf{h}_t$. Our basic idea is to recover the current 3D head pose parameters from the previous 12-vector $\hat{b}_{t-1} = [\,\hat{\theta}_{x(t-1)},\ \hat{\theta}_{y(t-1)},\ \hat{\theta}_{z(t-1)},\ \hat{t}_{x(t-1)},\ \hat{t}_{y(t-1)},\ \hat{t}_{z(t-1)},\ \hat{\tau}_{a(t-1)}^T]^T = [\,\hat{h}_{t-1}^T,\ \hat{\tau}_{a(t-1)}^T\,]^T$ using the same region-based registration technique outlined in Section 2.4. However, this time the unknown parameters are only given by the 3D head pose parameters:

$$\min_{\mathbf{h}} e(\mathbf{h}_t) = \min d\left[\mathbf{x}(\mathbf{b}_t), \boldsymbol{\mu}_t\right] = \min \sum_{i=1}^{d} \left(\frac{x_i - \mu_i}{\sigma_i}\right)^2_{(t)} \tag{18}$$

4.2.2 Simultaneous facial actions and expression

In this stage, our goal is to simultaneously infer the facial actions as well as the expression label associated with the current frame t given (i) the observation model (Eq.(8)), (ii) the dynamics associated with each expression (Eq.(17)), and (iii) the 3D head pose for the current frame computed by the deterministic approach (see Section 4.2.1). This will be performed using a particle filter paradigm. Thus, the statistical inference of such paradigm will provide a posterior distribution for the facial actions $\tau_{a(t)}$ as well as a Probability Mass function for the facial expression γ_t.

Since the 3D head pose $\mathbf{h}_t$ is already computed, we are left with the mixed state $\mathbf{a}_t = [\,\tau_{a(t)}^T, \gamma_t]^T$. The dimension of the vector $\mathbf{a}_t$ is 7. Here we will employ a particle filter algorithm allowing the recursive estimation of the posterior distribution $p\,(\mathbf{a}_t \mid x_{1:(t)})$ using a particle set. This is approximated by a set of J particles $\{\,(\mathbf{a}_t^{(0)}, \mathrm{w}_t^{(0)}),\ldots,(\mathbf{a}_t^{(J)}, \mathrm{w}_t^{(J)})\}$. Once this distribution is known the facial actions as well as the expression can be inferred using some loss function such as the MAP or the mean. Figure 9 illustrates the proposed two-stage approach. It shows how the current posterior $p\,(\mathbf{a}_t \mid x_{1:(t)})$ can be inferred from the previous posterior $p\,(\mathbf{a}_{t-1} \mid x_{1:(t-1)})$ using a particle filter algorithm.

On a 3.2 GHz PC, a C code of the approach computes the 3D head pose parameters in 25 ms and the facial actions/expression in 31 ms where the patch resolution is 1310 pixels and the number of particles is 100.

4.3 Experimental results

In this section, we first report results on simultaneous facial action tracking and expression recognition. Then we present performance studies, considering different perturbing factors such as robustness to rapid facial movements or to imprecise 3D head pose estimation.

4.3.1 Simultaneous tracking and recognition

Figure 10 shows the application of the proposed approach to a 748-frame test video sequence. The upper part of this figure shows 9 frames of this sequence: 50, 130, 221, 300, 371, 450, 500, 620, and 740. The two plots illustrate the probability of each expression as a function of time (frames). The lower part of this figure shows the tracking results associated with frames 130, 371, and 450. The upper left corner of these frames depicts the appearance mean and the current shape-free facial patch. Figure 11.a illustrates the weighted average of the tracked facial actions, $\hat{\tau}_{a(t)}$. For the sake of clarity, only three out of six components are shown. For this sequence, the maximum probability was correctly indicating the displayed expression. We noticed that some displayed expressions can, during a short initial phase (very few frames), be considered as a mixture of two expressions (the displayed one and another one). This is due to the fact that face postures and dynamics at some transition phases can be shared by more than one expression. This is not a problem since the frame-wise expression probabilities can be merged and averaged over a temporal patch including contiguous non-neutral frames. Figure 11.b illustrates this scheme and shows the resulting segmentation of the used test video. One remarks that this holds true for a human observer, who may fail to recognize a gesture from only one single frame.

In the above experiment, the total number of particles is set to 200. Figure 12 illustrates the same facial actions when the number of particles is set to 100. We have found that there is no significant difference in the estimated facial actions and expressions when the tracking is performed with 100 particles (see Figures 11.a and 12), which is due to the use of learned multi-class dynamics.

Figure 13 shows the tracking results associated with another 600-frame test video sequence depicting significant out-of-plane head movements. The recognition results were correct. Recall that the facial actions are related to the deformable 3D model and thus the recognition based on them is independent from the viewing angle.

A challenging example. We have dealt with a challenging test video. For this 1600-frame test video, we asked our subject to adopt arbitrarily different facial gestures and expressions for an arbitrary duration and in an arbitrary order. Figure 14 (Top) illustrates the probability mass distribution as a function of time. As can be seen, surprise, joy, anger, disgust, and fear are clearly and correctly detected. Also, we find that the facial actions associated with the subject's conversation are correctly tracked using the dynamics of the universal expressions. The tracked facial actions associated with the subject's conversation are depicted in nine frames (see the lower part of Figure 14). The whole video can be found at *http: //www.hds.utc.fr/ ~ fdavoine/MovieTrackingRecognition.wmv*.

4.3.2 Performance study

One-class dynamics versus multi-class dynamics In order to show the advantage of using multi- class dynamics and mixed states, we conducted the following experiment. We used a particle filter for tracking facial actions. However, this time the state consists only of facial actions and the dynamics are replaced with a simple noise model, i.e. motion is modelled by a random noise. Figures 15.a and 15.b show the tracking results associated with the same input frame. (a) displays the tracking results obtained with a particle filter adopting a single-class dynamics. (b) displays the tracking results with our proposed approach adopting the six auto-regressive models. As can be seen, by using mixed states with learned multi-class dynamics, the facial action tracking becomes considerably more accurate (see the adaptation of the mouth region-the lower lip).

Effect of rapid and/or discontinuous facial movements It is well known that facial expressions introduce rapid facial feature movements, and hence many developed trackers may fail to keep track of them. In order to assess the behavior of our developed tracker whenever very rapid facial movements occur, we conducted the following experiment to simulate an ultra rapid mouth motion[1]. We cut about 40 frames from a test video. These frames (video segment) overlap with a surprise transition. The altered video is then tracked using two different methods: (i) a deterministic approach based on a registration technique estimating both the head and facial action parameters (Dornaika & Davoine, 2006), and (ii) our stochastic approach. Figures 16.a and 16.b show the tracking results associated with the same input frame immediately after the cut. Note the difference in accuracy between the deterministic approach (a) and the stochastic one (b) (see the eyebrow and mouth region). Thus, despite the motion discontinuity of the mouth and the eyebrows, the particles are still

[1] This experiment also simulates a discontinuity in video streaming.

able to provide the correct state (both the discrete and the continuous components) almost instantaneously (see the correct alignment between the 3D model and the region of the lips and mouth in Figure 16.b).

Low resolution video sequences In order to assess the behavior of our developed approach when the resolution and/or the quality of the videos is low, we downloaded several low-quality videos used in (Huang et al., 2002). In each 42-frame video, one universal expression is displayed. Figure 17 shows our recognition results (the discrete probability distribution) associated with three such videos. The left images display the 25th frame of each video. Note that the neutral curve is not shown for reasons of clarity. As can be seen, the recognition obtained with our stochastic approach was very good despite the low quality of the videos used. The resolution of these videos is 320×240 pixels.

Impact of noisy estimated 3D head pose The estimated appearance-based 3D head pose may suffer from some inaccuracies associated with the out-of-plane movements, which is the case for all monocular systems. It would seem reasonable to fear that these inaccuracies might lead to a failure in facial action tracking. In order to assess the effect of 3D head pose inaccuracies on the facial action tracking, we conducted the following experiment. We acquired a 750-frame sequence and performed our approach twice. The first was a straightforward run. In the second run, the estimated out-of-plane parameters of the 3D head pose were perturbed by a uniform noise, then the perturbed 3D pose was used by the facial action tracking and facial expression recognition. Figure 18 shows the value of the tracked actions in both cases: the noise-free 3D head pose (solid curve) and the noisy 3D head pose (dotted curves). In this experiment, the two out-of-plane angles were perturbed with additive uniform noise belonging to [-7degrees, +7degrees] and the scale was perturbed by an additive noise belonging to [-2%, +2%]. As can be seen, the facial actions are almost not affected by the introduced noise. This can be explained by the fact that the 2D projection of out-of-plane errors produce very small errors in the image plane such that the 2D alignment between the model and the regions of lips and eyebrows is still good enough to capture their independent movements correctly.

Robustness to lighting conditions The appearance model used was given by one single multivariate Gaussian with parameters slowly updated over time. The robustness of this model is improved through the use of robust statistics that prevent outliers from deteriorating the global appearance model. This relatively simple model was adopted to allow real-time performance. We found that the tracking based on this model was successful even in the presence of temporary occlusions caused by a rotated face and occluding hands. Figure 19 illustrates the tracking results associated with a video sequence provided by the Polytechnic University of Madrid[2], depicting head movements and facial expressions under significant illumination changes (Buenaposada et al., 2006). As can be seen, even though with our simple appearance model the possible brief perturbations caused temporary tracking inaccuracies, there is no track lost. Moreover, whenever the perturbation disappears the tracker begins once more to provide accurate parameters.

---

[2] http://www.dia.fi.upm.es/~pcr/downloads.html

5. Conclusion

This chapter provided a set of recent deterministic and stochastic (robust) techniques that perform efficient facial expression recognition from video sequences. More precisely, we described two texture- and view-independent frameworks for facial expression recognition given natural head motion. Both frameworks use temporal classification and do not require any learned facial image patch since the facial texture model is learned online. The latter property makes them more flexible than many existing recognition approaches. The proposed frameworks can easily include other facial gestures in addition to the universal expressions.

The first framework (Tracking then Recognition) exploits the temporal representation of tracked facial actions in order to infer the current facial expression in a deterministic way. Within this framework, we proposed two different recognition methods: i) a method based on Dynamic Time Warping, and ii) a method based on Linear Discriminant Analysis. The second framework (Tracking and Recognition) proposes a novel paradigm in which facial action tracking and expression recognition are simultaneously performed. This framework consists of two stages. In the first stage, the 3D head pose is recovered using a deterministic registration technique based on Online Appearance Models. In the second stage, the facial actions as well as the facial expression are simultaneously estimated using a stochastic framework based on multi-class dynamics.

We have shown that possible inaccuracies affecting the out-of-plane parameters associated with the 3D head pose have no impact on the stochastic tracking and recognition. The developed scheme lends itself nicely to real-time systems. We expect the approach to perform well in the presence of perturbing factors, such as video discontinuities and moderate illumination changes. The developed face tracker was successfully tested with moderate rapid head movements. Should ultra-rapid head movements break tracking, it is possible to use a re-initialization process or a stochastic tracker that propagates a probability distribution over time, such as the particle-filter-based tracking method presented in our previous work (Dornaika & Davoine, 2006). The out-of-plane face motion range is limited within the interval [-45 deg, 45 deg] for the pitch and the yaw angles. Within this range, the obtained distortions associated with the facial patch are still acceptable to estimate the correct pose of the head. Note that the proposed algorithm does not require that the first frame should be a neutral face since all universal expressions have the same probability.

The current work uses an appearance model given by one single multivariate Gaussian whose parameters are slowly updated over time. The robustness of this model is improved through the use of robust statistics that prevent outliers from deteriorating the global appearance model. This relatively simple model was adopted to allow real-time performance. We found that the tracking based on this model was successful even in the presence of occlusions caused by a rotated face and occluding hands. The current appearance model can be made more sophisticated through the use of Gaussian mixtures (Zhou et al., 2004; Lee, 2005) and/or illumination templates to take into account sudden and significant local appearance changes due for instance to the presence of shadows.

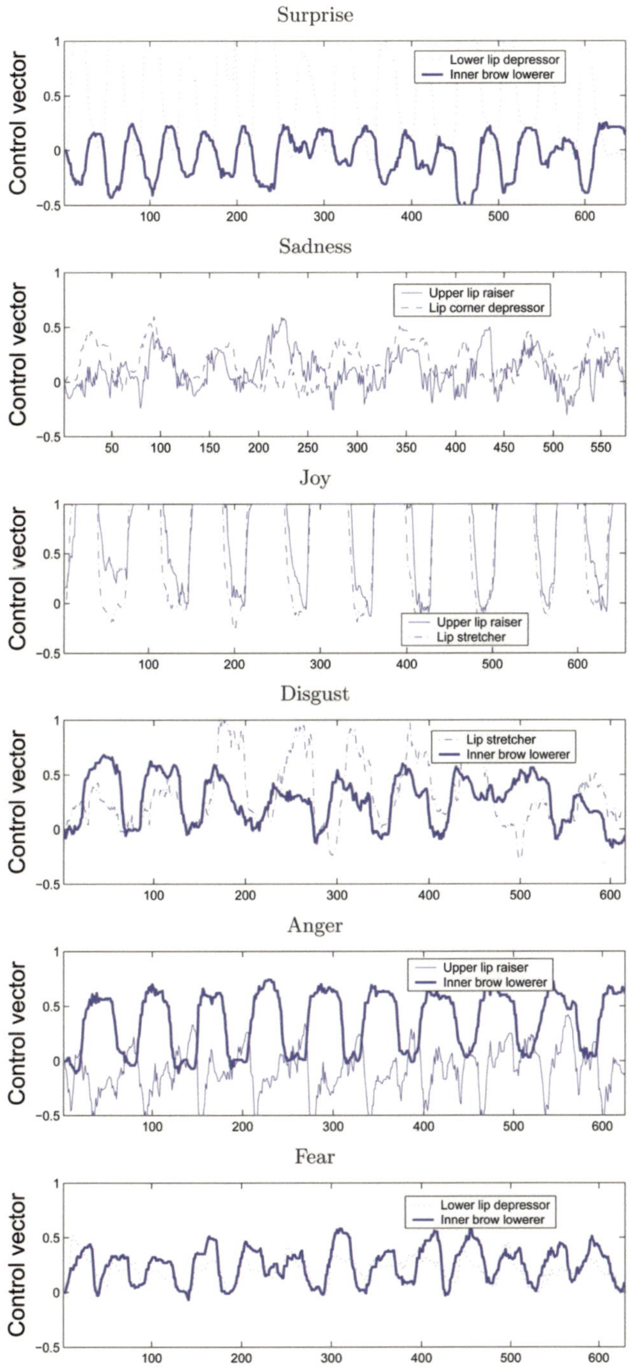

Figure 7: The automatically tracked facial actions, $\tau_{a(t)}$, using the training videos. Each video sequence corresponds to one expression. For a given plot, only two components are displayed.

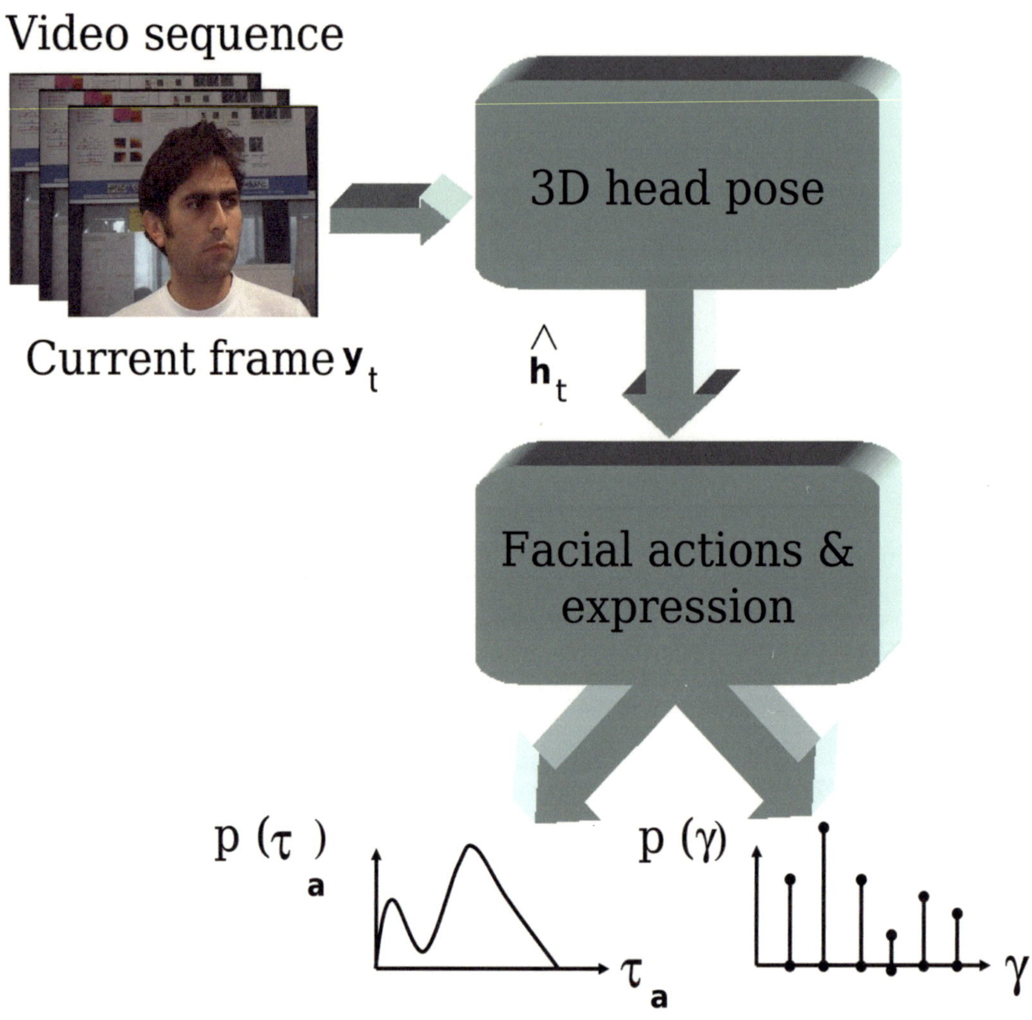

Figure 8: The proposed two-stage approach. In the first stage (Section 4.2.1), the 3D head pose is computed using a deterministic registration technique. In the second stage (Section 4.2.2), the facial actions and expression are simultaneously estimated using a stochastic technique involving multi-class dynamics.

1. **Initialization** $t = 0$:
   - Initialize the 3D head pose $\hat{\mathbf{h}}_0$
   - Generate J state samples $\mathbf{a}_0^{(1)}, \ldots, \mathbf{a}_0^{(J)}$ according to some prior density $p(\mathbf{a}_0)$ and assign them identical weights, $w_0^{(1)} = \ldots = w_0^{(J)} = 1/J$
2. **Tracking** At time step $t \leftarrow t+1$, get the input frame $\mathbf{y}_t$. Compute the corresponding 3D head pose, $\hat{\mathbf{h}}_t$, using the deterministic method outlined in Section 4.2.1. We have J weighted particles $(\mathbf{a}_{t-1}^{(j)}, w_{t-1}^{(j)})$ that approximate the posterior distribution of the state $p(\mathbf{a}_{t-1}|\mathbf{x}_{1:(t-1)})$ at the previous time step
   (a) Resample the particles proportionally to their weights, *i.e.* particles with high weights are duplicated and particles with small weights are removed. Resampled particles have the same weights
   (b) Draw J particles $\mathbf{a}_t^{(j)}$ according to the dynamic model $p(\mathbf{a}_t|\mathbf{a}_{t-1} = \mathbf{a}_{t-1}^{(j)})$. The obtained new particles approximate the predicted distribution $p(\mathbf{a}_t|\mathbf{x}_{1:(t-1)})$. For multi-class dynamics and mixed states this is done in two steps
   Discrete: Draw an expression label $\gamma_t^{(j)} = \gamma \in \mathcal{E} = \{1, 2, \ldots, N_\gamma\}$ with probability $T_{\gamma',\gamma}$, where $\gamma' = \gamma_{t-1}^{(j)}$
   Continuous: Compute $\boldsymbol{\tau}_{\mathbf{a}(t)}^{(j)}$ as

$$\boldsymbol{\tau}_{\mathbf{a}(t)}^{(j)} = \mathbf{A}_2^\gamma \, \boldsymbol{\tau}_{\mathbf{a}(t-2)}^{(j)} + \mathbf{A}_1^\gamma \, \boldsymbol{\tau}_{\mathbf{a}(t-1)}^{(j)} + \mathbf{d}^\gamma + \mathbf{B}^\gamma \, \mathbf{w}_t^{(j)}$$

   where $\gamma = \gamma_t^{(j)}$ and $\mathbf{w}_t^{(j)}$ is a 6-vector of standard normal random variables
   (c) Compute the shape-free patch $\mathbf{x}(\mathbf{b}_t^{(j)})$ according to (6) where $\mathbf{b}_t^{(j)} = [\ \hat{\mathbf{h}}_t^T,\ \ \boldsymbol{\tau}_{\mathbf{a}(t)}^{(j)T}\ ]^T$
   (d) Weight each new particle proportionally to its likelihood

$$w_t^{(j)} = \frac{p(\mathbf{x}_t|\mathbf{b}_t^{(j)})}{\sum_{m=1}^{J} p(\mathbf{x}_t|\mathbf{b}_t^{(m)})}$$

   The set of weighted particles approximates the posterior $p(\mathbf{a}_t|\mathbf{x}_{1:t})$
   (e) Set the probability of each basic expression $\gamma^\star \in \mathcal{E} = \{1, 2, \ldots, N_\gamma\}$ to

$$P(\gamma^\star) = \sum_{m=1}^{J} \begin{cases} w_t^{(m)} & \text{if } \gamma_t^{(m)} = \gamma^\star \\ 0 & \text{otherwise} \end{cases}$$

   (f) Set the facial actions to $\hat{\boldsymbol{\tau}}_{\mathbf{a}(t)} = \sum_{m=1}^{J} w_t^{(m)} \boldsymbol{\tau}_{\mathbf{a}(t)}^{(m)}$
   (g) Set the geometrical parameters as $\hat{\mathbf{b}}_t = \ [\hat{\mathbf{h}}_t^T,\ \ \hat{\boldsymbol{\tau}}_{\mathbf{a}(t)}^T\ ]^T$
   (h) Based on $\hat{\mathbf{b}}_t$, update the appearance (using Eqs. (7), (10), and (11)) as well as the 3D pose gradient matrix. Go to 2.

Figure 9: Inferring the 3D head pose, the facial actions and expression. A particle-filter-based algorithm is used for the simultaneous recovery of the facial actions and expression.

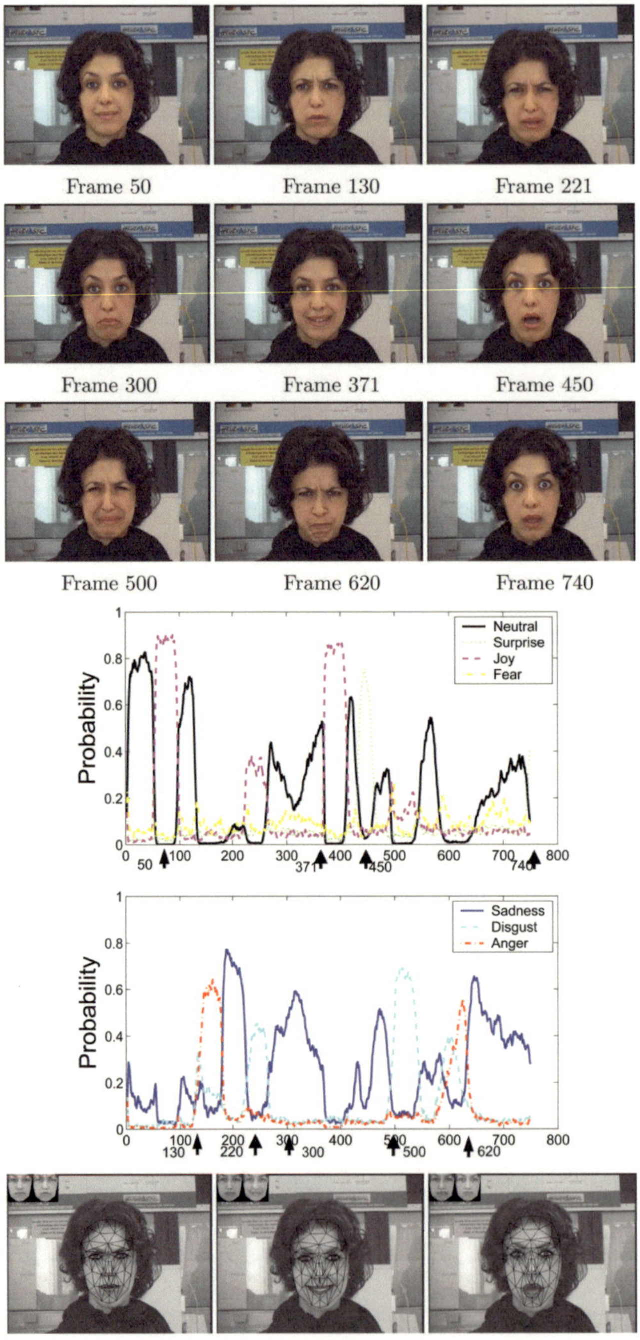

Figure 10: Simultaneous tracking and recognition associated with a 748-frame video sequence. The top illustrates some frames of the test video. The middle plots show the probability of each expression as a function of time (frames). The bottom images show the tracked facial actions where the corner shows the appearance mean and the current shape-free patch.

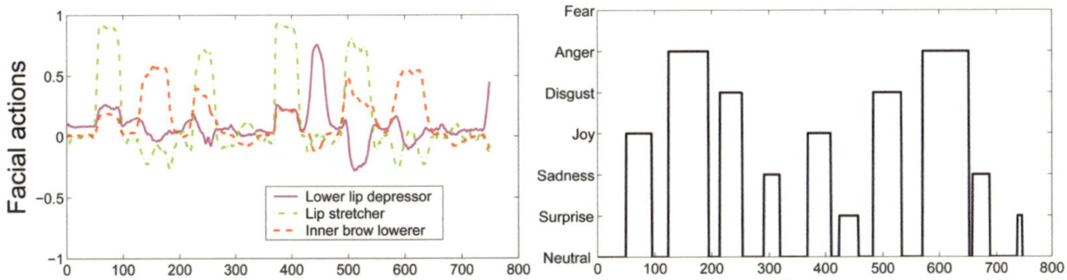

(a) (b)

Figure 11: (a) The tracked facial actions, $\hat{\tau}_{a(t)}$, computed by the recursive particle filter. (b) Segmenting the input video using the non-neutral frames.

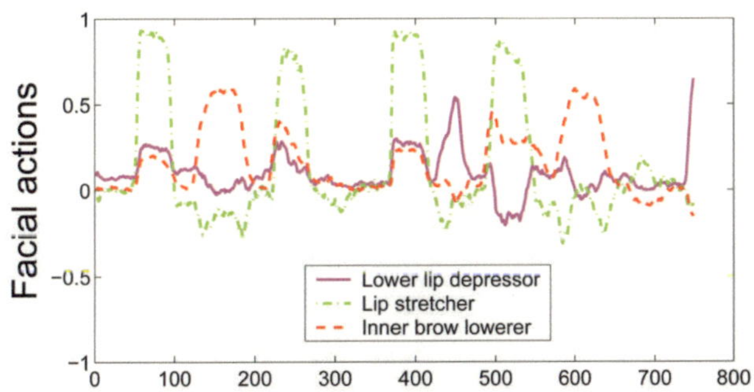

Figure 12: The tracked facial actions, $\hat{\tau}_{a(t)}$ (weighted average), computed by the recursive particle filter with only 100 particles.

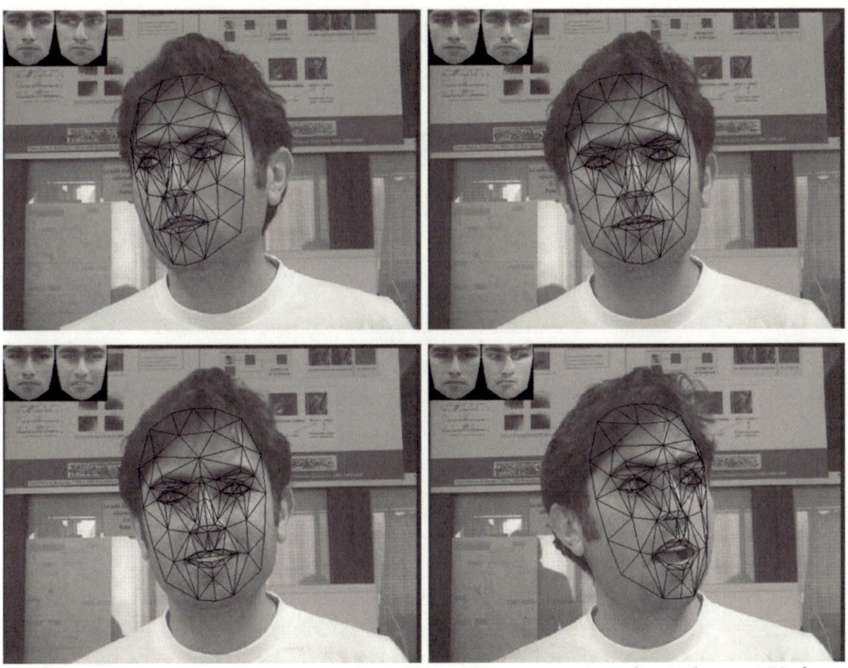

Figure 13: Simultaneous tracking and recognition associated with a 600-frame video sequence depicting non- frontal head poses.

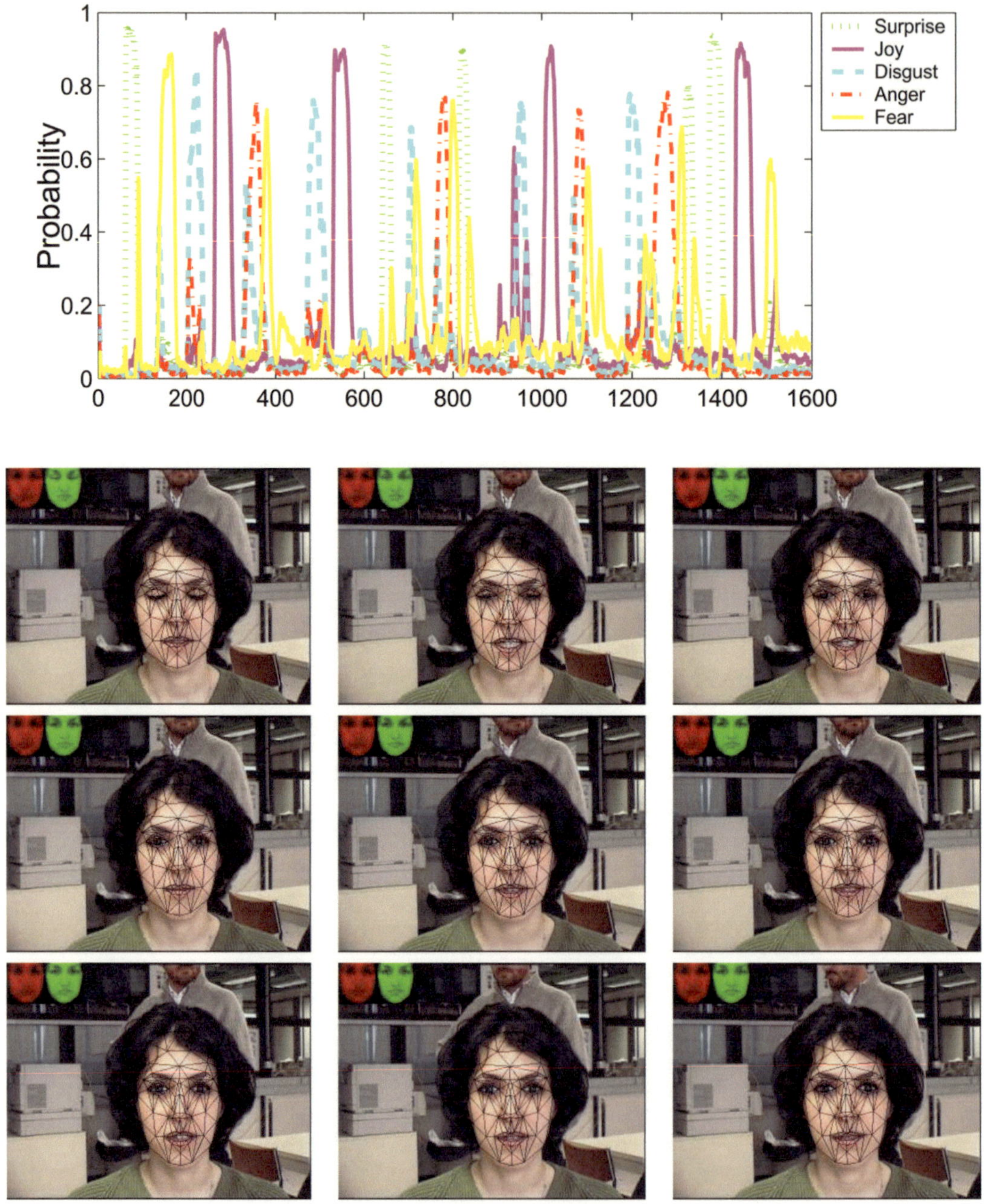

Figure 14: **Top:** The probability of each expression as a function of time associated with a 1600-frame video sequence. **Bottom:** The tracked facial actions associated with the subject's speech which starts at frame 900 and ends at frame 930. Only frames 900, 903, 905, 907, 909, 911, 913, 917, and 925 are shown.

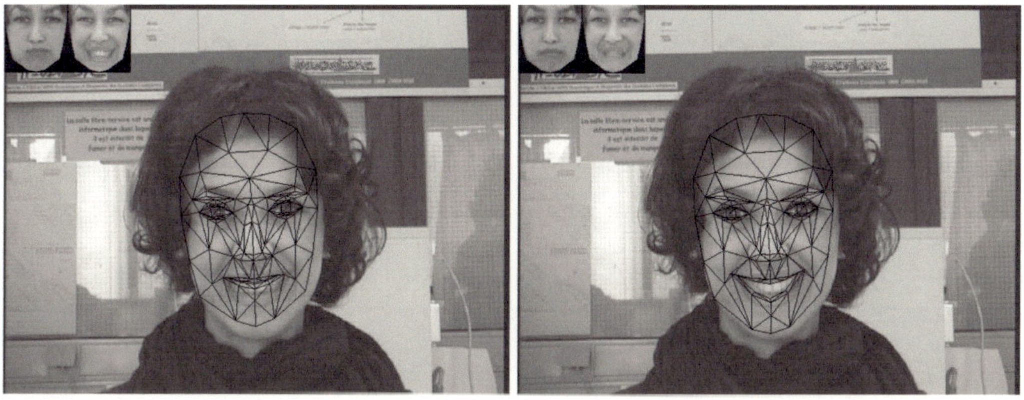

(a) (b)

Figure 15: **Method comparison:** One class dynamics **(a)** versus multi-class dynamics **(b)** (see Section 4.3.2).

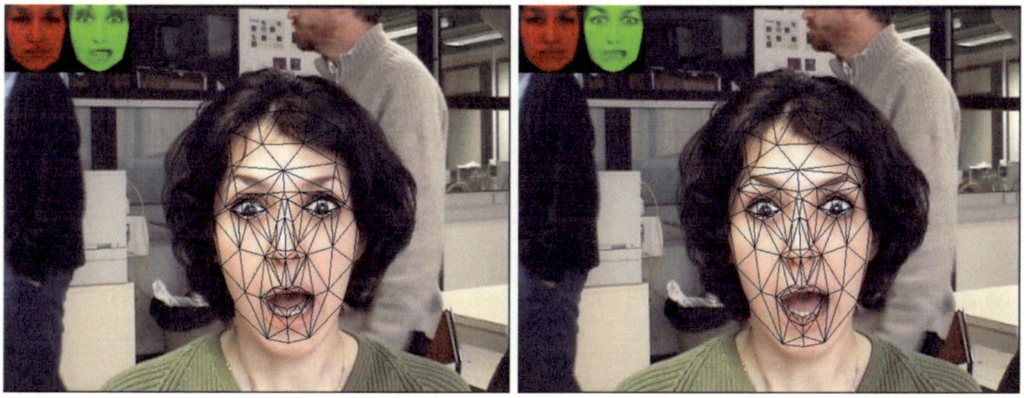

(a) (b)

Figure 16: **Method comparison:** Deterministic approach (a) versus our stochastic approach (b) immediately after a simulated mouth motion discontinuity (see Section 4.3.2).

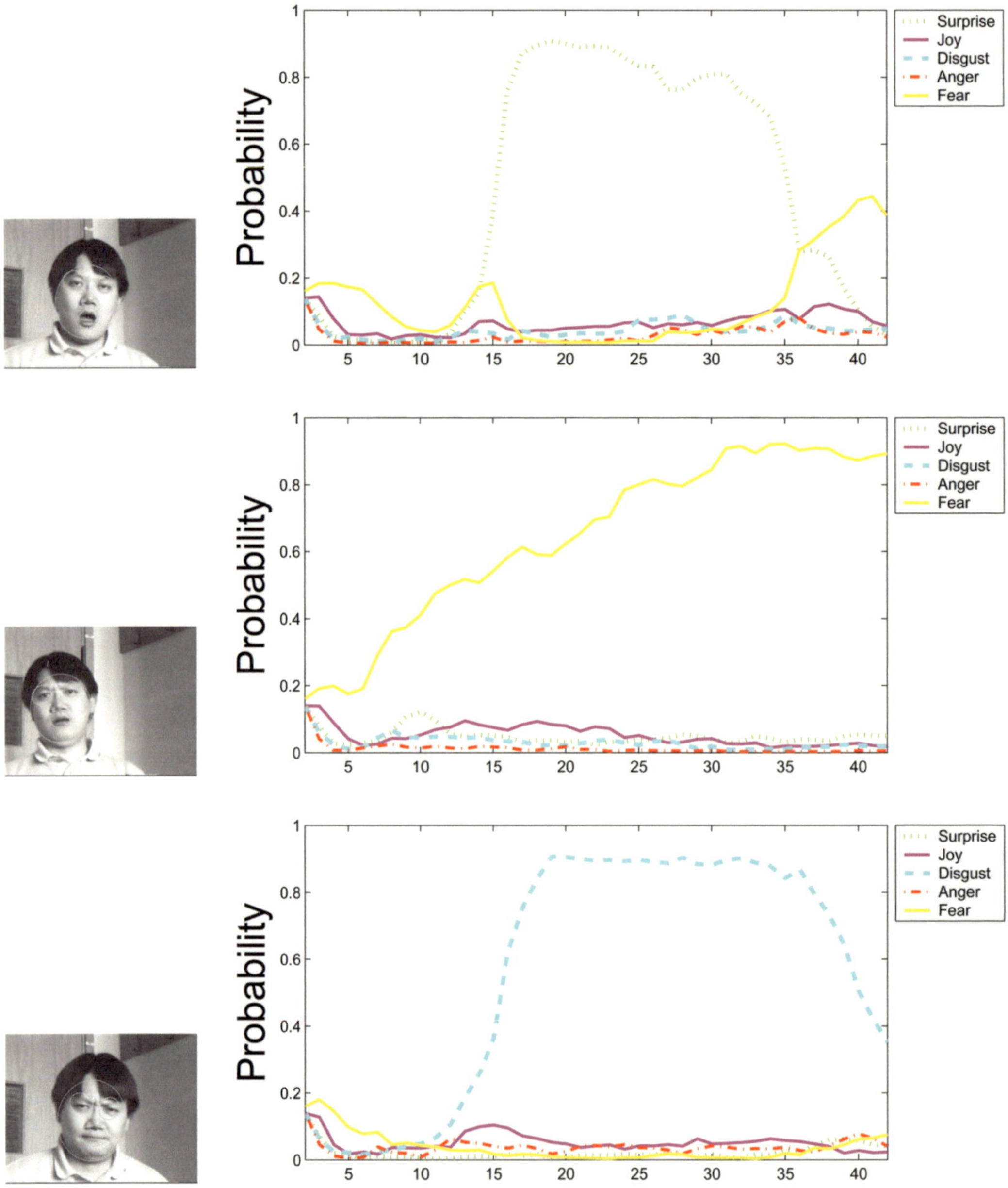

Figure 17: The probability of each expression as a function of time associated with three low resolution videos. The right images displays the 25th frame of each video.

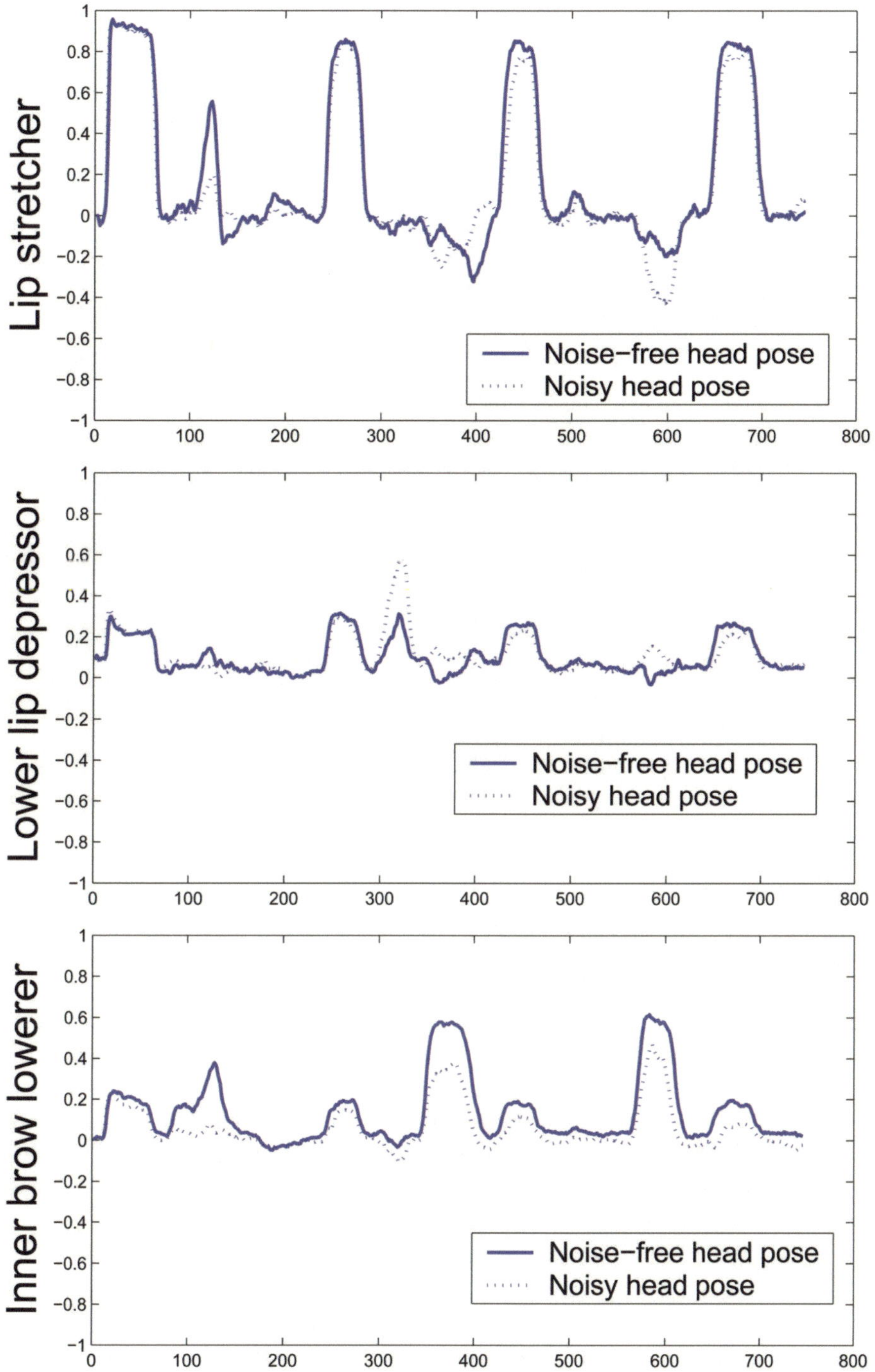

Figure 18: Impact of noisy 3D head pose on the stochastic estimation of the facial actions. In each graph, the solid curve depicts the facial actions computed by the developed framework. The dashed curve depicts the same facial actions using a perturbed 3D pose.

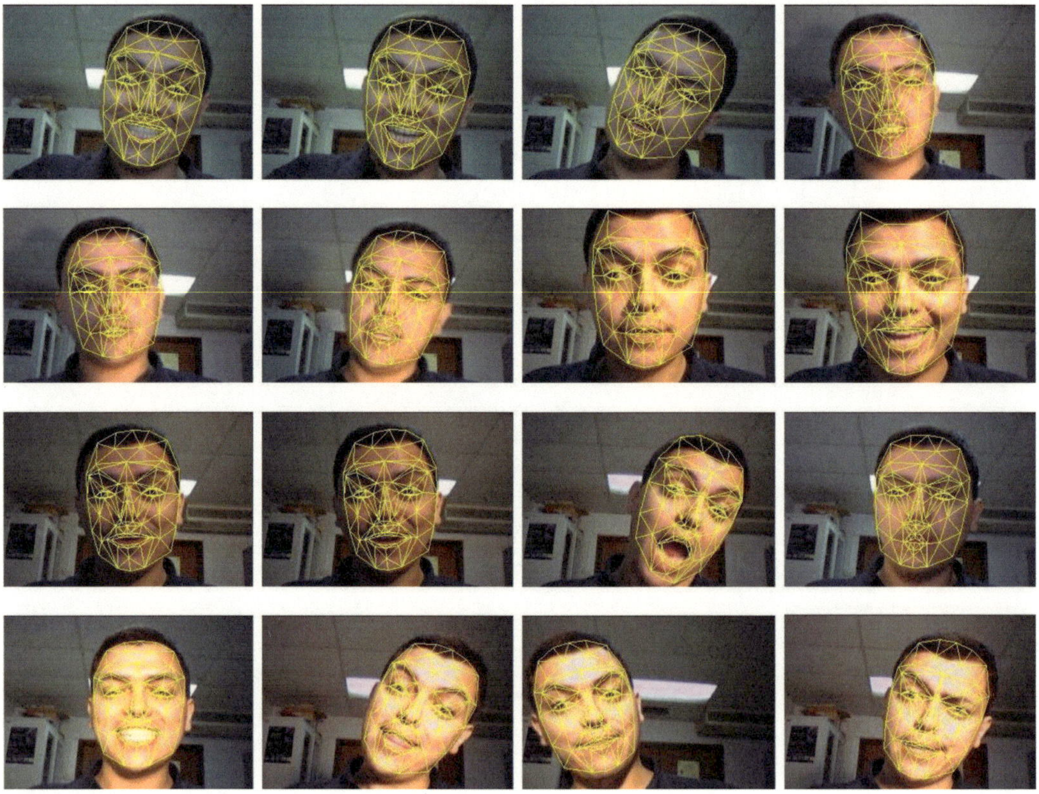

Figure 19: Tracking the head and the facial actions under significant illumination changes and head and facial feature movements.

6. References

J. Ahlberg. An active model for facial feature tracking. *EURASIP Journal on Applied Signal Processing*, 2002(6):566-571, June 2002.

M. Bartlett, G. Littlewort, C. Lainscsek, I. Fasel, and J. Movellan. Machine learning methods for fully automatic recognition of facial expressions and facial actions. In *IEEE Int. Conference on Systems, Man and Cybernetics*, 2004.

B. Bascle and A. Black. Separability of pose and expression in facial tracking and animation. In *Proc. IEEE International Conference on Computer Vision*, 1998.

D. Berndt and J. Clifford. Using dynamic time warping to find patterns in time series. In *AAAI-94 Workshop on Knowledge Discovery in Databases*, 1994.

A. Blake and M. Isard. *Active Contours*. Springer-Verlag, 2000.

V. Blanz and T. Vetter. Face recognition based on fitting a 3D morphable model. *IEEE Transactions on Pattern Analysis and Machine Intelligence*, pages 1-12, September 2003.

J.M. Buenaposada, E. Munoz, and L. Baumela. Efficiently estimating facial expression and illumination in appearance-based tracking. In *British Machine Vision Conference*, 2006.

N.P. Chandrasiri, T. Naemura, and H. Harashima. Interactive analysis and synthesis of facial expressions based on personal facial expression space. In *IEEE International Conference on Automatic Face and Gesture Recognition*, 2004.

I. Cohen, N. Sebe, A. Garg, L. Chen, and T.S. Huang. Facial expression recognition from video sequences: Temporal and static modeling. *Computer Vision and Image Understanding.*, 91(1-2):160-187, 2003.

F. Dornaika and F. Davoine. View- and texture-independent facial expression recognition in videos using dynamic programming. In *IEEE International Conference on Image Processing*, 2005.

F. Dornaika and F. Davoine. On appearance based face and facial action tracking. *IEEE Transactions on Circuits and Systems for Video Technology*, 16(9), September 2006.

P. Ekman and W.V. Friesen. *Facial Action Coding System*. Consulting Psychology Press, Palo Alto, CA, USA, 1977.

B. Fasel and J. Luettin. Automatic facial expression analysis: A survey. *Pattern Recognition*, 36(1):259-275, 2003.

S.B. Gokturk, J.Y. Bouguet, C. Tomasi, and B. Girod. Model-based face tracking for view-independent facial expression recognition. In *IEEE International Conference on Automatic Face and Gesture Recognition*, 2002.

Y. Huang, T. S. Huang, and H. Niemann. A region-based method for model-free object tracking. In *16th International Conference on Pattern Recognition*, 2002.

P.J. Huber. *Robust Statistics*. Wiley, 1981.

M. Isard and A. Blake. A mixed-state condensation tracker with automatic model switching. In *Proc. IEEE International Conference on Computer Vision*, 1998.

A.D. Jepson, D.J. Fleet, and T.F. El-Maraghi. Robust online appearance models for visual tracking. *IEEE Transactions on Pattern Analysis and Machine Intelligence*, 25(10):1296-1311, 2003.

T. Kanade, J. Cohn, and Y.L. Tian. Comprehensive database for facial expression analysis. In *International Conference on Automatic Face and Gesture Recognition*, pages 46-53, Grenoble, France, March 2000.

D. Lee. Effective Gaussian mixture learning for video background subtraction. *IEEE Transactions on Pattern Analysis and Machine Intelligence*, 27(5):827-832, 2005.

W.-K. Liao and I. Cohen. Classifying facial gestures in presence of head motion. In *IEEE Workshop on Vision for Human-Computer Interaction*, 2005.

L. Ljung. *System Identification: Theory for the User*. Prentice Hall, 1987.

L. Lu, Z. Zhang, H.Y. Shum, Z. Liu, and H. Chen. Model- and exemplar-based robust head pose tracking under occlusion and varying expression. In *Proc. IEEE Workshop on Models versus Exem- plars in Computer Vision, (CVPR'01)*, 2001.

X. Lu, A. K. Jain, and D. Colbry. Matching 2.5D face scans to 3D models. *IEEE Transactions on Pattern Analysis and Machine Intelligence*, 28(1):31-43, 2006.

M.J. Lyons, J. Budynek, and S. Akamatsu. Automatic classification of single facial images. *IEEE Transactions on Pattern Analysis and Machine Intelligence*, 21(12):1357-1362, 1999.

F. Moreno, A. Tarrida, J. Andrade-Cetto, and A. Sanfeliu. 3D real-time tracking fusing color histograms and stereovision. In *IEEE International Conference on Pattern Recognition*, 2002.

B. North, A. Blake, M. Isard, and J. Rittscher. Learning and classification of complex dynamics. *IEEE Transactions on Pattern Analysis and Machine Intelligence*, 22(9):1016-1034, 2000.

M. Pantic and L.J.M. Rothkrantz. Automatic analysis of facial expressions: The state of the art. *IEEE Transactions on Pattern Analysis and Machine Intelligence*, 22(12):1424-1445, 2000.

P. Perez and J. Vermaak. Bayesian tracking with auxiliary discrete processes. application to detection and tracking of objects with occlusions. In *IEEE ICCV Workshop on Dynamical Vision*, Beijing, China, 2005.

L. Rabiner and B. Juang. *Fundamentals of Speech Recognition*. Englewood Cliffs, N.J, Prentice Hall, 1993.

Y. Tian, T. Kanade, and J.F. Cohn. Recognizing action units for facial expression analysis. *IEEE Transactions on Pattern Analysis and Machine Intelligence*, 23:97-115, 2001.

Y. Wang, H. Ai, B. Wu, and C. Huang. Real time facial expression recognition with Adaboost. In *IEEE Int. Conference on Pattern Recognition*, 2004.

Z. Wen and T.S. Huang. Capturing subtle facial motions in 3D face tracking. In *IEEE International Conference on Computer Vision*, 2003.

T. Xiang, M.K.H. Leung, and S.Y. Cho. Expression recognition using fuzzy spatio temporal modeling. *Pattern Recognition*, 41(1):204-216, January 2008.

Y. Yacoob and L.S. Davis. Recognizing human facial expressions from long image sequences using optical flow. *IEEE Transactions on Pattern Analysis and Machine Intelligence*, 18(6):636-642, 1996.

A. Yilmaz, K.H. Shafique, and M. Shah. Estimation of rigid and non-rigid facial motion using anatomical face model. In *IEEE International Conference on Pattern Recognition*, 2002.

Y. Zhang and Q. Ji. Active and dynamic information fusion for facial expression understanding from image sequences. *IEEE Transactions on Pattern Analysis and Machine Intelligence*, 27(5):699-714, 2005.

S. Zhou, R. Chellappa, and B. Mogghaddam. Visual tracking and recognition using appearance-adaptive models in particle filters. *IEEE Transactions on Image Processing*, 13(11):1473-1490, 2004.

S. Zhou, V. Krueger, and R. Chellappa. Probabilistic recognition of human faces from video. *Com- puter Vision and Image Understanding*, 91(1-2):214-245, 2003.

3

The Devil is in the Details – the Meanings of Faces and How They Influence the Meanings of Facial Expressions

Ursula Hess[1], Reginald B. Adams, Jr.[2] and Robert E. Kleck[3]
[1]*University of Quebec at Montreal,*
[2]*The Pennsylvania State University,*
[3]*Dartmouth College,*
[1]*Canada*
[2, 3]*USA*

1. Introduction

Facial expressions have a primary role in signaling emotional states. As such they are an important source of information in social interactions and have been the focus of a large body of research in psychology and allied disciplines. This research has been drawn upon extensively in the creation of avatars and computer controlled agents in order to facilitate human-machine interactions. A great deal of effort has gone into attempting to translate the temporal and pattern features of human emotional expressions into a credible computer generated display. However, what has been ignored in this process is the fact that faces and facial movements provide other information in addition to the apparent emotional state of the individual. Specifically, facial expressions also signal behavioral intentions - such as intentions to approach or to avoid - as well as personality characteristics of the person such as dominance and affiliativeness. For example, anger signals dominance and an intention to approach, whereas fear signals submissiveness and an intention to withdraw. In this sense facial expressions not only provide information on what emotion a person is feeling, but also tell us about who a person is and what to expect from them behaviorally.

It is also important to note that a great deal of socially relevant information is transmitted via other cues directly linked to the face, in particular by physiognomy and gaze direction. Because these cues serve as the immediate context for facial expressions they can plausibly affect the interpretation we give to the facial movement. Stereotypic beliefs elicited by facial appearance, such as beliefs that men are more likely to show anger and women more likely to smile, also can impact our interpretation of expressions. It is our view that gaze, physiognomy and emotion expressions use a shared signal system in which some signals are functionally equivalent whereas others serve to reinforce each other. This means that certain combinations of expressive, gaze and physiognomic cues present a coherent message and reinforce each other, whereas others may conflict or contradict each other. Put another way, the face on which emotional expressions appear is not an empty canvas, rather, as noted above, it serves as the context within which the expression occurs and modulates the meaning of that expression.

This chapter will review and elaborate upon recent findings from research on human-human interaction. These studies demonstrate that supposedly 'tangential' aspects of an emotional signal such as eye gaze and the type of face that shows the expression can affect the perceived meaning of the expression. A central implication of this research is that the implementation of believable emotional facial expressions on avatars or other quasi-human forms will require more than just the creation of appropriate facial movement patterns. Rather, we hope to demonstrate that it is important to consider the facial appearance of the agent and the types of beliefs that people unconsciously associate with the appearance of any particular agent since these may serve to bias their perceptions of and reactions to the simulated emotional displays on the part of the agent.

2. Emotions in human computer interaction

Individuals spend more and more of their work or leisure time interacting with computers and computer controlled machines. Humans tend to treat computers in these interactions largely as they would treat humans (Reeves & Nass, 1996) and this has led to demands to make human-computer interfaces more realistically sociable. In this framework computer agents and robots have been designed that can interpret human emotions and, importantly, also signal emotions via facial expressions (e.g., Breazeal, 2003; Koda & Maes, 1996; Pelachaud & Bilvi., 2003). However, research on human-human interaction suggests that this very attempt at naturalness may mean that an agent may fail to convey the intended message because of the way it looks and the biases in perception and interpretation that this may entrain. Specifically, the human receiver is not a passive receptacle for emotion information. Rather humans actively decode this information and in this process use information other than the facial movement associated with specific expressions. One of these sources is the very face on which these expressions appear. As noted above, this implies that the relatively static appearance of the face is not an empty canvas but rather "actively" contributes to emotion communication. In what follows we will present findings from human-human interaction that demonstrate the importance of such seemingly incidental information on the decoding of emotion expressions.

3. The face and the decoding of emotions

When we see the emotional facial expressions of others we are usually able to attach some label to these, such as "he looks sad", or "she looks happy." This decoding process can be based on either or both of two important sources of information: the sender's emotion displays and the perceiver's knowledge about the sender (Kirouac & Hess, 1999). It is with regard to this second source of information that the cues present in the face in addition to movement patterns becomes critical.

Emotion displays are often quite ambiguous (Motley & Camden, 1988) and even if they seem quite clear need to be put into a context. For example, a given expression of happiness in a person we know to be very gregarious may be interpreted as suggesting less happiness than would the same expression when shown by a person known to be very socially shy.

If the sender and the receiver know each other well, the receiver usually is aware of the sender's personality, beliefs, preferences, and emotional style. This knowledge then permits the receiver to take the perspective of the sender and to deduce which emotional state the sender most likely experiences in the given situation. But what happens when we do not know the other person well?

Studies in which people are asked to judge the likely personality of complete strangers show that people can and do draw conclusions about a person's personality from no more information than is provided by the face, even though accuracy varies widely and is dependent on both encoder and decoder personality (e.g., Ambady et al., 1995). Yet more importantly, faces tell us the social categories into which our interaction partner fits. That is, faces tell us the sex, age, and race of the other person and this knowledge can be used by observers to predict the likely emotional reaction of the sender.

More recently, it has become obvious that facial expressions and knowledge or beliefs about the expresser are not the only sources of information that people use. In fact, gaze direction has to be added to the list of cues that need to be taken into account.

4. Gaze and emotion

Gaze direction has traditionally not been considered to be part of the emotional expression itself (see Fehr & Exline, 1987). Direct gaze was seen to play an important role only for the perception of the intensity of the emotion but not of it's quality (Argyle & Cook, 1976; Kleinke, 1986). And indeed, nearly all expression decoding studies have used stimuli where the encoders' gaze is directed at the perceiver. However, a set of recent studies by Adams and his colleagues and others (Adams et al., 2003; Adams & Kleck, 2003, 2005; Ganel et al., 2005; Graham & LaBar, 2007; Hess et al., 2007) serves to illustrate the important role that gaze plays in the social communication of emotions. Their specific interest was the role that gaze direction might play in the decoding of emotion expressions. They argued that the direction of a person's gaze points to the likely object of the expresser's emotion and should also be related to the intention of the expresser. And in fact, happiness and anger, which are approach emotions, tend to be expressed with direct rather than averted gaze. Conversely, emotions associated with a tendency to withdraw, such as embarrassment and sorrow, tend to be communicated more often with averted gaze (see e.g., Argyle & Cook, 1976; Fehr & Exline, 1987). References to looking behavior are also commonly used in our lexicon to describe different emotional states (e.g., downcast eyes to describe someone who is sad).

In this vein, Adams and Kleck (2003; 2005) found that direct gaze facilitates the processing of facially communicated approach-oriented emotions (e.g., anger and joy), whereas averted gaze facilitates the processing of facially communicated avoidance-oriented emotions (e.g., fear and sadness). This interaction between perceived emotion and gaze direction has also been demonstrated on the neural level (Adams et al., 2003).

Together, the studies published by Adams and his colleagues support the *shared signal hypothesis,* demonstrating that the gaze direction of the encoder can affect the efficiency with which a given display is processed as well as determine the quality of the emotion that will be perceived in a blended or ambiguous expression. They argue that when different facial cues such as the specific expression and the direction of gaze share the same signal value (e.g., approach or avoidance) the shared signal facilitates overall processing efficiency.

Similar findings were obtained for head position which was found to strongly influence reactions to anger and fear but less so in the case of sadness and happiness. For example, direct anger expressions were more accurately decoded, perceived as less affiliative, and elicited higher levels of anxiousness and repulsion, as well as less desire to approach than did head averted anger expressions (Hess, Adams et al., 2007).

However, the role of gaze seems to be a bit more complicated. Gaze direction does not only provide emotional information in the sense described above, but also has an indirect influence on emotion processing by influencing attention allocation. Specifically, direct gaze attracts attention to a larger degree than does averted gaze. In sum, the meaning of facial expressions can be clarified or obscured by gaze direction. An angry expression with gaze directed at me will lead me to think that I am the object of the anger and elicit corresponding emotions. Conversely, a fear expression directed to a point behind me will lead me to think that a dangerous object is behind me. As people – and computer agents – tend to move their heads when interacting with others, mismatches between facial and gaze signals can give rise to misunderstandings or ambiguously encoded emotional signals.

5. Beliefs about emotions

As noted above, facial expressions and gaze direction are not the only sources of emotion information transmitted by the face. Rather, since the appearance of the face tells us something about who the person is, it is reasonable to assume that this information will enter into our emotion judgments. We already know that individuals hold stereotypical beliefs about the emotions of others based on information such as their sex, their age, their culture, their status and their personality. Thus, for example, women are expected to smile more and in fact also do smile more than men. By contrast, men are expected to show more anger but do not seem to in fact do so (Brody & Hall, 2000; Fischer, 1993). These expectations are socialized early and can have dramatic consequences for the perception of emotion in male and female others. For example, even children as young as 5 years tend to consider a crying baby as "mad" when the baby is purported to be a boy but not when it is purported to be a girl (Haugh et al., 1980). Thus, the 'knowledge' that a baby is a boy or a girl, biases the perception of an otherwise ambiguous emotion display.

People also have beliefs about age and emotionality. In a recent study we showed participants photos of individuals from four different age groups (18-29; 30-49; 50-69; 70+) and asked them to indicate how likely they thought it would be that the person shown in the photo would express each of four emotions (happiness, sadness, anger, and fear) in everyday life. The responses differed with regard to both the sex and age of the stimulus persons. Thus, as they get older men were perceived to be less likely to show anger, whereas the reverse was the case for women. Men were also perceived as more likely to show sadness as they aged.

Beliefs about the emotional behavior of different ethnic groups have been most consistently studied in the context of research on decoding rule differences between collectivist Japanese and individualist US American decoders (Matsumoto, 1992; Matsumoto et al., 1999; Matsumoto & Kudoh, 1993; Yrizarry et al., 1998). Decoding rules (Buck, 1984) are the flip side of display rules. Display rules are culturally learned norms that define what emotion to show as well as when and how to show it (Ekman & Friesen, 1971). Conversely, people who are aware of such rules will adjust their interpretation of the emotional expressions of others to take account of the display rules that helped shape the expressions. For example, US Americans are usually encouraged to show emotions, especially positive emotions and tend to show emotion more intensely than is warranted by the underlying feeling state. This is not the case in Japan. Consequently, US Americans attribute less intense underlying emotions to expressions of the same intensity than do Japanese (Matsumoto et al., 1999), that is, they "correct" their estimate of a person's feeling state based on the decoding rule that people are likely to exaggerate their expressions.

Status is another characteristic that people take into account when considering the emotions of others. Thus, high status individuals are less bound by the display rules mentioned above and are presumed to be freer to express their emotions. In addition, there are also beliefs about status and emotion for rather specific situations. For example, Tiedens et al., (2000) found that participants believed that in failure situations, a high-status person would feel more angry than sad or guilty as opposed to a person with lower status who is expected to feel more sad and guilty than angry. In contrast, in response to positive outcomes, the high-status individual is expected to feel more pride and the low-status person is expected to feel more appreciation.

An individual's perceived personality is yet another source of strong beliefs that may affect our emotional attributions. Hess et al., (2005), for example, have shown that dominant individuals are believed to be more likely to show anger than are submissive ones. In fact, Hess et al. could show that some of the stereotypical beliefs about men's and women's emotions can in fact be traced to beliefs about personality - specifically to beliefs about dominance and affiliation. What makes this observation even more important in the present context is that facial expressions per se also signal these traits.

6. Facial expressions signal dominance and affiliation

Emotional facial expressions are powerful signals of dominance and affiliation. Specifically, drawing the eyebrows together in anger leads to increased attributions of dominance, whereas smiling leads to increased attributions of affiliation (Hess et al., 2000; Knutson, 1996). At the same time, anger expressions are perceived as threatening (e.g., Aronoff et al., 1988), whereas smiles are perceived as warm, friendly, and welcoming (see e.g., Hess et al., 2002). Similarly, it has been argued that fear expressions elicit affiliative reactions in conspecifics (Bauer & Gariépy, 2001; Marsh et al., 2005).

As mentioned above, people make personality judgements based on no more than a glimpse of a face. Faces that appear dominant tend to look more masculine as the features associated with dominance such as a square jaw and prominent eye-brows (Keating, 1985; Senior et al., 1999) are more typical for men than for women. At the same time men are perceived as more likely to be angry (Fischer, 1993) and angry faces appear more dominant. Thus, there is a reinforcing relationship between a dominant facial appearance and an angry expression which makes men's anger appear more intense (Hess et al., 1997) and threatening (Hess et al., 2007). Conversely, the features that make a person seem more warm and welcoming, babyfacedness (Berry & McArthur, 1985), are more common in women. Consistent with this women are perceived as more likely to express happiness and happy faces appear more affiliative, creating a reinforcing relationship between being affiliative and showing happiness, all of which serves makes women's smiles appear happier (Hess et al., 1997) and more appealing (Hess et al., 2007).

Darwin (1872/1965) was one of the first to note the equivalence between certain emotional behaviors in animals and more enduring morphological appearance characteristics. For example, he argued that piloerection and the utterance of harsh sounds by 'angry' animals are 'voluntarily' enacted to make the animal appear larger and hence a more threatening adversary (see for example, p. 95 and p.104).

This notion, in combination with the observations detailed above, led Hess et al., (2007) to propose that some aspects of facial expressive behavior and morphological cues to dominance and affiliation are equivalent in both their appearance and their effects on emotional attributions. This functional equivalence between morphology and expression also implies that there are important interactions between facial expressions and facial morphology in the decoding of expressions of emotion.

7. The functional equivalence hypothesis

We initially tested the functional equivalence hypothesis by examining differences in the attribution of emotions to men and women (Hess et al., 2004; Hess et al., 2005). As mentioned above, there is a high degree of overlap in the facial cues associated with maleness, perceived dominance and perceived anger. Likewise there are similarities in the facial cues that signal femaleness, social affiliation and happiness. In fact, this overlap in cues associated with emotional expressions, perceived dominance and affiliation, and gender is so strong that emotional displays can affect the perception of sex. Specifically, in a recent study (Hess, Adams, Grammer & Kleck, 2008) we found that an androgenous appearing avatar who shows a happy or fearful expression is perceived as more likely to represent a woman and the same avatar who looks angry is considered to be less likely to represent a woman (see Figure 1).

m = 1.86, sd = .85 | m = 2.87, sd = 1.66 | m = 2.20, sd = 1.51

Figure 1. Rated likelihood "that this person is a woman" for an avatar showing an angry, smiling, or a fearful expression.

That this perceptual overlap explains the beliefs that people have about men's and women's emotionality was shown by Hess et al. (2005). They asked separate groups of participants to rate men's and women's neutral faces either with regard to how dominant or affiliative they appeared or with regard to the likelihood that the person in the photo would show a series of emotions in everyday life. Mediational analyses showed that the tendency to perceive women as more likely to show happiness, surprise, sadness and fear was in fact mediated by their higher perceived affiliation and lower perceived dominance respectively. The tendency to perceive men as more prone to show anger, disgust, and contempt was partially mediated by both their higher level of perceived dominance and their lower level of perceived affiliation (see Figure 2). That is, if men and women were perceived to be equal on these dimensions, then we would not expect observers to rate their emotionality differently.

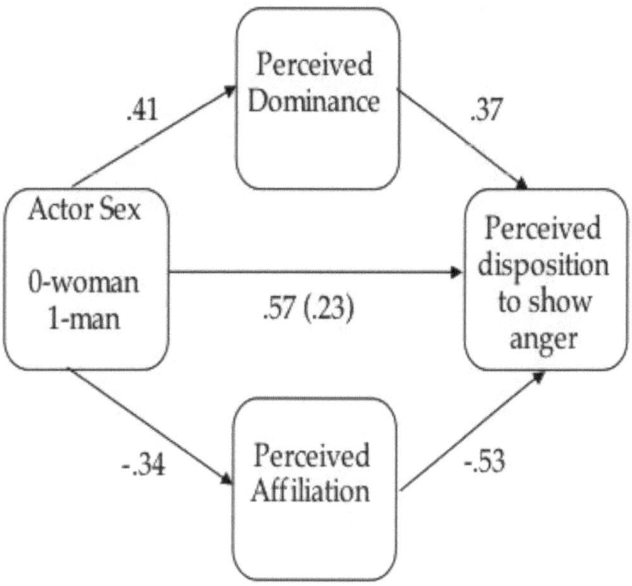

Figure 2. Mediation of expectations regarding men's and women's emotionality via perceptions of facial dominance and affiliation

More recently, we demonstrated that this is also the case for the beliefs concerning changes in emotionality over the lifespan. As reported earlier, men are perceived to be less prone to anger as they get older and women as more prone to this emotion. With happiness just the converse is the case. In our view this is mediated through the fact that as they get older men's faces appear less dominant and more affiliative, whereas women's faces appear more dominant and less affiliative.

We experimentally tested the impact of dominance and affiliation cues on perceptions of anger and fear in the context of gender manipulated facial expressions. Specifically, the interior of the face contains markers of dominance and affiliation (i.e., square versus rounded jaw, heavy versus light eyebrows), whereas hairstyle is a very potent marker of sex but not of these social motives. Thus, by combining androgynous interior faces with male and female hairstyles, apparent men and women with identical facial appearance can be created (see Figure 3).

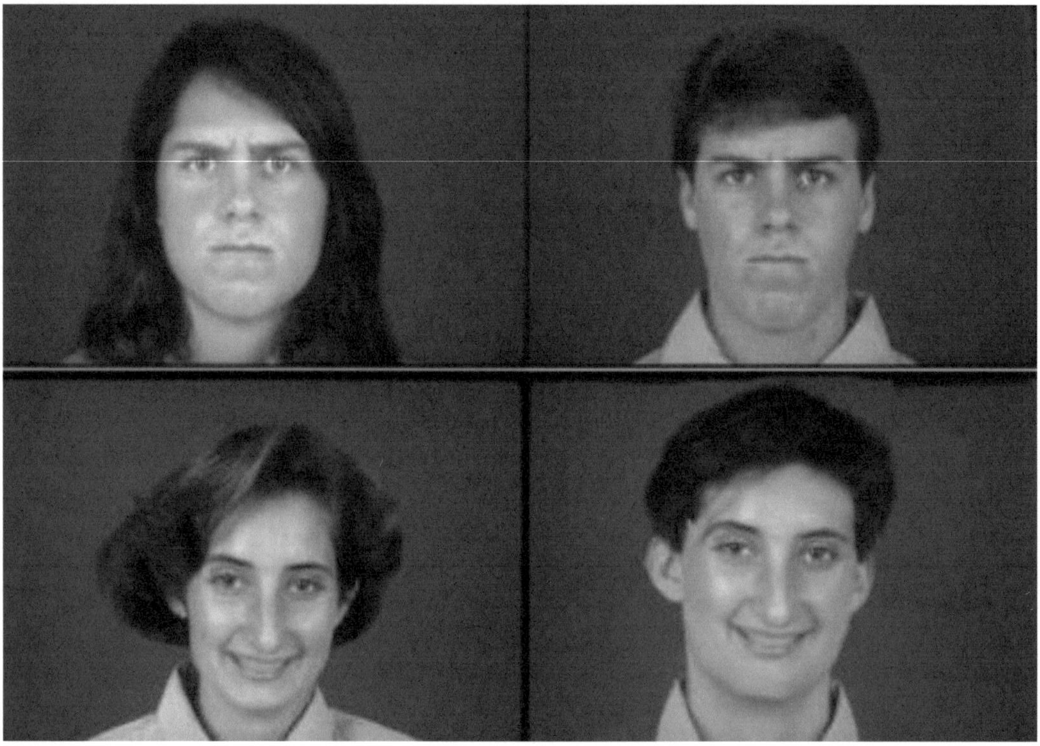

Figure 3. *Changing hairstyles to change perceived gender*

For both neutral faces and posed emotion displays (Adams et al., 2007, Study 4; Hess et al., 2004, Study 2) parallel findings obtained such that for ratings of anger and happiness, a pattern opposite to the gender stereotypical pattern was found. That is, when equated for facial appearance, apparent women were seen as more likely to show anger and less likely to show happiness than were apparent men. Similarly, expressions of anger by apparent women were rated as more intense and their expressions of happiness as less intense than when the identical expressions appeared on the faces of apparent men.

This reversal demands an explanation as it suggests that intrinsically, facial appearance being equal, women are perceived as more anger prone and less likely to be happy than are men. We propose that this reversal is due to the equivalence between morphological and expressive cues of dominance and affiliation, which leads to an interaction between these two sets of cues. That is, anger expressions emphasize some of the features that make a face appear dominant (e.g., the mouth region often appears especially square, and frowning reduces the distance between eyebrows and eyes). Conversely, smiling enhances the appearance of roundness of the face that is associated with perceived affiliation motivation and babyishness. Due to the manner in which the present stimuli were constructed, the expressive cues for anger and happiness were not 'compensated for' by gender typical appearance (the faces were chosen specifically because they were androgynous and were credible as either male or female). In some ways one could say that by depriving the interior of the face of clear gender cues we actually amplified the expressive cues to anger in women and happiness in men. These cues are normally 'obscured' or reduced by the gender typical facial appearance, which also convey domiance and affiliation information. This notion that anger on a male face presents a clearer and less ambiguous anger signal than does anger on a female face and, conversely, that happiness on a female face is a clearer signal of happiness, has recently been confirmed by Hess et al. (2007).

8. Summary

In the preceding sections we have presented research relevant to the decoding of emotional facial expressions that focuses on information other than the actual facial expression. Much is known about the specific features that make a face appear sad, angry, fearful, happy, etc. and this information has been used in recent years to implement computer controlled agents with believable facial expressions (e.g., Pelachaud & Bilvi., 2003). The research we have reviewed, however, suggests that human do not restrict themselves to facial movement information when judging the emotions of others. Rather they use *all* of the available information provided by the face. This information consists at the very least of eye gaze direction and the person information contained in faces. These sources of information interact with the facial expression information in determining which emotions a perceiver will attribute to the individual. In our view eye gaze and facial morphology are parallel message systems. Both can reinforce or obscure the emotional message transmitted by the facial expressions. Eye gaze does this because it contains information on a person's tendency to withdraw or approach and facial morphology because it informs perceivers about the person's personality - especially the dominance and affiliation domains so important for a social species - which in turn are associated with beliefs about a person's emotionality.
Overall the research presented above outlines the impact that a face has on the perception of facial expressions. These findings have obvious implications for the design of the avatars and agents used in human computer interfaces.

9. References

Adams, R. B., Jr., Gordon, H. L., Baird, A. A., Ambady, N., & Kleck, R. E. (2003). Effect of gaze on Amygdala sensitivity to anger and fear faces. *Science, 300,* 1536-1537.

Adams, R. B., Jr., & Kleck, R. E. (2003). Perceived gaze direction and the processing of facial displays of emotion. *Psychological Science, 14,* 644-647.

Adams, R. B., Jr., & Kleck, R. E. (2005). Effects of direct and averted gaze on the perception of facially communicated emotion. *Emotion, 5,* 3-11.

Ambady, N., Hallahan, M., & Rosenthal, R. (1995). On judging and being judged accurately in zero-acquaintance situations. *Journal of Personality and Social Psychology, 69,* 518-529.

Argyle, M., & Cook, M. (1976). *Gaze and mutual gaze.* Oxford, UK: Cambridge University Press.

Aronoff, J., Barclay, A. M., & Stevenson, L. A. (1988). The recognition of threatening facial stimuli. *Journal of Personality and Social Psychology, 54*, 647-665.

Bauer, D. J., & Gariépy, J. L. (2001). The functions of freezing in the social interactions of juvenile high-and low-aggressive mice. *Aggressive Behavior, 27*, 463-475.

Berry, D. S., & McArthur, L. Z. (1985). Some components and consequences of a babyface. *Journal of Personality and Social Psychology, 48*, 312-323.

Breazeal, C. (2003). Emotion and sociable humanoid robots. *International Journal of Human-Computer Studies, 59*, 119–155.

Brody, L. R., & Hall, J. A. (2000). Gender, Emotion, and Expression. In M. Lewis & J. M. Haviland (Eds.), *Handbook of emotions, 2nd Ed* (pp. 447-460). New York: Guilford Press.

Buck, R. (1984). Nonverbal receiving ability. In R. Buck (Ed.), *The communication of emotion* (pp. 209-242). New York: Guilford Press.

Darwin, C. (1872/1965). *The expression of the emotions in man and animals.* Chicago: The University of Chicago Press. (Originally published, 1872).

Ekman, P., & Friesen, W. V. (1971). Constants across cultures in the face and emotion. *Journal of Personality and Social Psychology, 17*, 124-129.

Fehr, B. J., & Exline, R. V. (1987). Nonverbal behavior and communication In A. W. Siegman & S. Feldstein (Eds.), *Social visual interaction: A conceptual and literature review* (pp. 225–325). Hillsdale, NJ: Erlbaum.

Fischer, A. H. (1993). Sex differences in emotionality: Fact or Stereotype? *Feminism & Psychology, 3*, 303-318.

Ganel, T., Goshen-Gottstein, Y., & Goodale, M. (2005). Interactions between the processin gaze direction and facial expression. *Vision Research, 49*, 1911-1200.

Graham, R., & LaBar, K. S. (2007). Garner interference reveals dependencies between emotional expression and gaze in face perception. *Emotion, 7*, 296-313.

Haugh, S. S., Hoffman, C. D., & Cowan, G. (1980). The eye of the very young beholder: Sex typing of infants by young children. *Child Development., 51*, 598-600.

Hess, U. Adams, R. B. Jr., Grammer, K., Kleck, R. E. (2008). If it frowns it must be a man: Emotion expression influences sex labeling. Manuscript submitted for publication.

Hess, U., Adams, R. B., Jr., & Kleck, R. E. (2004). Facial appearance, gender, and emotion expression. *Emotion, 4*, 378-388.

Hess, U., Adams, R. B., Jr., & Kleck, R. E. (2005). Who may frown and who should smile? Dominance, affiliation, and the display of happiness and anger. *Cognition and Emotion, 19*, 515-536.

Hess, U., Adams, R. B. J., & Kleck, R. E. (2007). Looking at you or looking elsewhere: The influence of head orientation on the signal value of emotional facial expressions. *Motivation and Emotion, 31*, 137–144

Hess, U., Beaupré, M. G., & Cheung, N. (2002). Who to whom and why – cultural differences and similarities in the function of smiles. In M. Abel & C. H. Ceia (Eds.), *An empirical reflection on the smile* (pp. 187-216). NY: The Edwin Mellen Press.

Hess, U., Blairy, S., & Kleck, R. E. (1997). The intensity of emotional facial expressions and decoding accuracy. *Journal of Nonverbal Behavior, 21,* 241-257.

Hess, U., Blairy, S., & Kleck, R. E. (2000). The influence of expression intensity, gender, and ethnicity on judgments of dominance and affiliation. *Journal of Nonverbal Behavior, 24,* 265-283.

Hess, U., Sabourin, G., & Kleck, R. E. (2007). Postauricular and eye-blink startle responses to facial expressions. *Psychophysiology, 44,* 431-435.

Keating, C. F. (1985). Human dominance signals: The primate in us. In S. L. Ellyson & J. F. Dovidio (Eds.), *Power, dominance, and nonverbal communication* (pp. 89-108). New York: Springer Verlag.

Kirouac, G., & Hess, U. (1999). Group membership and the decoding of nonverbal behavior. In P. Philippot, R. Feldman & E. Coats (Eds.), *The social context of nonverbal behavior* (pp. 182-210). Cambridge, UK: Cambridge University Press.

Kleinke, C. L. (1986). Gaze and eye contact: A research review. *Psychological Bulletin, 100,* 78-100.

Knutson, B. (1996). Facial expressions of emotion influence interpersonal trait inferences. *Journal of Nonverbal Behavior, 20,* 165-182.

Koda, T., & Maes, P. (1996). Agents with faces: the effects of personification of agents. In *Proceedings of Human-Computer Interaction '96*. August, London, UK.

Marsh, A. A., Adams, R. B., Jr., & Kleck, R. E. (2005). Why do fear and anger look the way they do? Form and social function in facial expressions. *Personality and Social Psychological Bulletin, 31,* 73-86.

Matsumoto, D. (1992). American - Japanese differences in the recognition of universal facial expressions. *Journal of Cross-Cultural Psychology, 23,* 72-84.

Matsumoto, D., Kasri, F., & Kooken, K. (1999). American-Japanese cultural differences in judgements of expression intensity and subjective experience. *Cognition & Emotion, 13,* 201-218.

Matsumoto, D., & Kudoh, T. (1993). American-Japanese cultural differences in attribution of personality based on smiles. *Journal of Nonverbal Behavior, 17,* 231-243.

Motley, M. T., & Camden, C. T. (1988). Facial expression of emotion: A comparison of posed expressions versus spontaneous expressions in an interpersonal communications setting. *Western Journal of Speech Communication, 52,* 1-22.

Pelachaud, C., & Bilvi., M. (2003). Computational model of believable conversational ahgents. In M.-P. Huget (Ed.), *Communication in Multiagent Systems: Agent Communication Languages and Conversation Policies* (pp. 300-317). Heidelberg, Germany: Springer.

Reeves, B., & Nass, C. (1996). *The Media Equation*. Stanford, CA. : CSLI Publications.

Senior, C., Phillips, M. L., Barnes, J., & David, A. S. (1999). An investigation into the perception of dominance from schematic faces: A study using the World-Wide Web. *Behavior Research Methods, Instruments and Computers, 31,* 341-346.

Tiedens, L. Z., Ellsworth, P. C., & Mesquita, B. (2000). Stereotypes about sentiments and status: Emotional expectations for high- and low-status group members. *Personality and Social Psychology Bulletin, 26,* 500-574.

Yrizarry, N., Matsumoto, D., & Wilson-Cohn, C. (1998). American-Japanese differences in multiscalar intensity ratings of universal facial expressions of emotion. *Motivation and Emotion., 22,* 315-327.

4

Genetic Algorithm and Neural Network for Face Emotion Recognition

M. Karthigayan, M. Rizon, R. Nagarajan and Sazali Yaacob,
School of Mechatronics Engineering,
Universiti Malaysia Perlis (UNIMAP),
02600 Jejawi, Perlis,
Malaysia

1. Introduction

Human being possesses an ability of communication through facial emotions in day to day interactions with others. Some study in perceiving facial emotions has fascinated the human computer interaction environments. In recent years, there has been a growing interest in improving all aspects of interaction between humans and computers especially in the area of human emotion recognition by observing facial expressions. The universally accepted categories of emotion, as applied in human computer interaction are: Sad, Anger, Joy, Fear, Disgust (or Dislike) and Surprise. Ekman and Friesen developed the most comprehensive system for synthesizing facial expression based on what they called as action units (Li, 2001). In the early 1990's the engineering community started to use these results to construct automatic methods of recognizing emotion from facial expression in still and video images (Sebe, 2002). Double structured neural network has been applied in the methods of face detection and emotion extraction. In this, two methods are proposed and carried out; they are lip detection neural network and skin distinction neural network (Takimoto et al., 2003). Facial action coding (Panti & Patras, 2006) is given to every facial points. For example, code 23 is given for lip funnel, code 4 for eye brow lower, code 10 for chin raise etc. The cods are grouped for a specific facial emotion. In order to determine the category of emotion, a set of 15 facial points in a face-profile sequence has been recommended. The work performs both automatic segmentation of an input video image of facial expressions and recognition of 27 Action Units (AUs) fitted to facial points. A recognition rate of 87% has been reported. The motion signatures (Anderson & Peter, 2006) are derived and classified using support vector machines (SVM) as either non-expressive (neutral) or as one of the six basic emotions. The completed system demonstrates in two simple but effective computing applications that respond in real-time to the facial expressions of the user. The method uses edge counting and image correlation optical flow techniques to calculate the local motion vectors of facial feature (Liyanage & Suen, 2003). Cauchy Naïve Bayes classifier is introduced in classifying the face emotion. The person-dependent and person-independent experiments have demonstrated that the Cauchy distribution assumption typically provides better results than those of the Gaussian distribution assumption (Sebe, 2002).

The current literature on emotion detection through facial images indicates the requirement of two desired directions. One on the image processing techniques highly relevant for identifying facial features under uneven lighting and the other is on interpreting the face emotion through the processed facial features. Both of these problems are under taken in this paper. Lips and eyes are used as origins of extracting facial emotion features. The methods of image processing, filtering and edge detection that are suitable for feature extraction are proposed first. Then this processed image is utilized to identify certain optimum parameters through Genetic Algorithm (GA). These parameters are employed in the interpretation of emotion characteristics. A set of new fitness functions are also suggested in extracting the lip parameters through GA. Since the emotion detection algorithm can be made as an expert system through continuous processing of available data, the suggested method of emotion interpretation is considered as suitable for a personalized face. A South East Asean (SEA) subject is considered in this work to illustrate the process (Figure 1). Figure 2 shows the outline of the process flow of estimating the emotion through facial images.

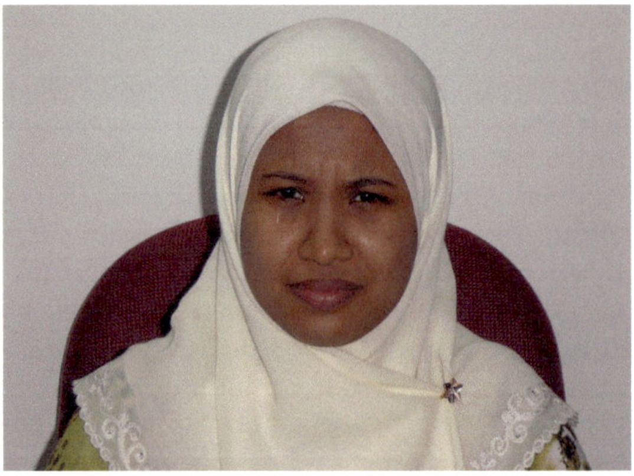

Fig.1. The Angry Emotion of South East Asian

2. Face image processing

As the first step in image processing, the region of interest (ROI) of a lip and an eye have been selected in the acquired images. The ROI image is converted into grayscale image (0-255). Before obtaining the filtered grayscale image, a histogram equalization method has been applied. Histogram equalization (Rafael et al., 2003) improves the contrast in the grayscale and its goal is to obtain an uniform histogram. The histogram equalization method also helps the image to reorganize the intensity distributions. New intensities are not introduced into the image. Existing intensity values will be mapped to new values but the actual number of intensity pixels in the resulting image will be equal or less than the original number. In the image sequence, the histogram equalized image is filtered using average and median filters in order to make the image smoother. Finally, Sobel edge detection method is applied to the filtered image with a good level of success. However, due to the intensity variations of light exposed on the face, the segmentation process is not satisfactory. In the edge detected image of the whole face, the eyes are properly segmented where as the lips segmentations are poor. Hence, the histogram equalized image is split into of lip ROI and eye ROI regions and then the regions are cropped from the full image. This has solved the problem of light intensity variations. Figure 3 and 4 show the edge detected eye and lips regions derived from their respective ROI areas.

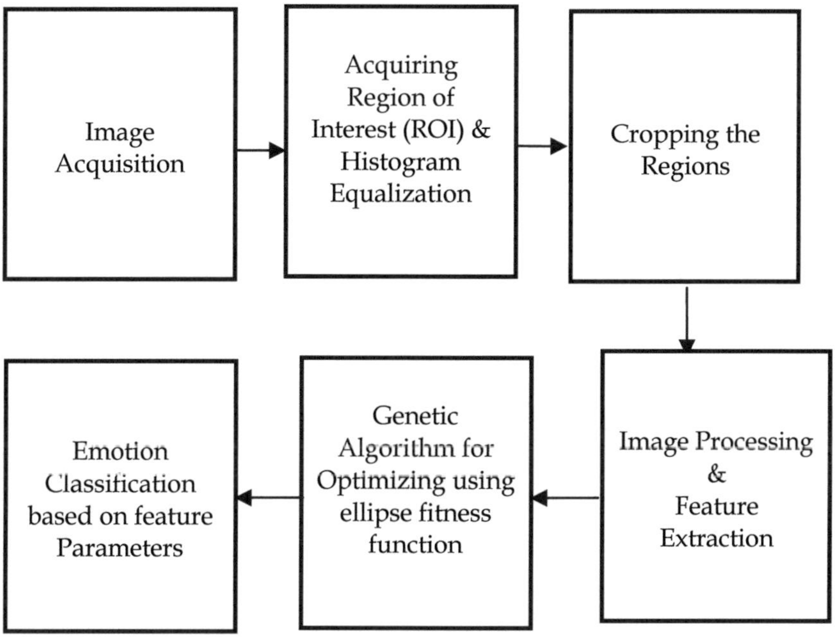

Fig. 2. Process Flow of Image Processing

Fig. 3. Sobel Edge Detected Eyes Region

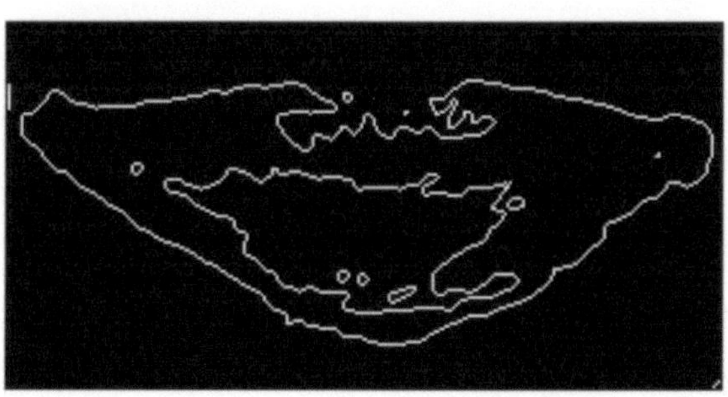

Fig. 4. Sobel Edge Detected Lip Region

3. Feature extraction

A feature extraction method can now to be applied to the edge detected images. Three feature extraction methods are considered and their capabilities are compared in order to adopt one that is suitable for the proposed face emotion recognition problem. They are projection profile, contour profile and moments (Nagarajan et al., 2006).

3.1 Projection profile

This feature extraction method is associated with the row-sum and column-sum of white pixels of edge identified image (Karthigayan et al., 2006). The pattern of row-sum (P_h) along the column and the pattern of column-sum (P_v) along the row of white pixels are defined as the feature of each region. These patterns are known as projection profiles. Let S(m,n) represent a binary image of m rows and n columns. Then, the vertical profile is defined as the sum of white pixels of each column perpendicular to the x-axis; this is represented by the vector P_v of size n as defined by

$$p_{vj} = \sum_{i=1}^{m} s(i,j) \quad , \quad j = 1, 2, 3, \ldots, n \tag{1}$$

The horizontal profile is the sum of white pixels of each row perpendicular to the y-axis; this is represented by the vector P_h of size m, where

$$p_{hi} = \sum_{j=1}^{n} s(i,j) \quad , \quad i = 1, 2, 3, \ldots, m \tag{2}$$

3.2 Moments

The moments have been widely used in pattern recognition (Karthigayan et al., 2006). Several desirable properties that can be derived from moments are also applicable to face emotion analysis. Central moments processing time is faster than Zernike moments and moments invariant. Central moments of binary image for each column of the image orders can be obtained. The image orders can be of 2 or 3. In the order 1, moment values are zeros. On the other hand, orders more than 3 produce smaller and smaller moment values that will not increase the effectiveness of feature extraction.

Let f(x,y) be an image. Then, the 2D continuous function of the moment of order (p+q), M_{pq}, is defined as

$$M_{pq} = \int_{-\infty}^{\infty}\int_{-\infty}^{\infty} x^p y^q f(x,y)\,dxdy \tag{3}$$

The central moment, μ_{pq}, of f(x,y) is defined as.

$$\mu_{pq} = \int_{-\infty}^{\infty}\int_{-\infty}^{\infty} (x-\bar{x})^p (y-\bar{y})^q f(x,y)\,dxdy \tag{4}$$

where $\bar{x} = \frac{M_{10}}{M_{00}}$ and $\bar{y} = \frac{M_{01}}{M_{00}}$.

If f(x,y) is a digital image then equation (4) becomes

$$\mu_{pq} = \sum_x \sum_y (x-\bar{x})^p (y-\bar{y})^q f(x,y) \quad (5)$$

where p and q are of nonnegative integer values. The moment values can be considered as extracted features.

3.3 Contour profile

This is one of the techniques used for object identification in the field of pattern recognition. The outer vertical and horizontal edge detected image black pixels in white background are counted. This count is named as the contour profile and can be used as the features of the lip and eye regions.

The performance of each of the above described feature extracting methods are compared with an objective of selecting one for our approach. The projection profile is found to perform well with regards to the processing time and is adopted here. The projection profile has also been found to have performed well in varied aspects in the earlier works (Karthigayan et al., 2006; Nagarajan et al., 2006; Karthigayan et al., 2007).

4. Face emotion recognition using genetic algorithm

In the early 1970s, John Holland, one of the founders of evolutionary computations, introduced the concept of genetic algorithm (GA) (Negnevitsky, 2002). The GA is a particular class of evolutionary algorithms. This is a heuristic approach used to find approximate solutions to solve problems through application of the principles from evolutionary biology. GA adopts biologically-derived techniques such as inheritance, mutation, natural selection, and recombination (or crossover). A population containing a number of trial solutions each of which is evaluated (to yield fitness) and a new generation is created from the better of them. The process is continued through a number of generations with the aim that the population evolves to contain an acceptable solution. GA is well known for optimization of nonlinear functions. It offers the best optimized value for any fitness function suitably selected for particular problems.

GA has been applied in varieties of applications which include image processing, control systems, aircraft design, robot trajectory generation, multiple fault diagnosis, traveling salesman, sequence scheduling and quality control wherein solutions to nonlinear optimization are required (Neo, 1997). Some aspects of vision system and image processing methodologies have been discussed towards approximating the face as a best ellipse using GA. In the feature extraction stage, the GA is applied to extract the facial features such as the eyes, nose and mouth, in a set of predefined sub regions. Some simulations have been carried out (Gary & Nithianandan, 2002). A method that extracts region of eyes out of facial image by genetic algorithm has also been suggested recently (Tani et al., 2001).

The human eye shape is more towards an ellipse (we call this as a regular ellipse). The edge detected eye image can be considered as an ellipse with variations. The minor axis is a feature of the eye that varies for each emotion. The major axis of the eye is more or less fixed for a particular person in varied emotions. The whitened area within the edge detected eye image for one of the emotions of SEA is shown in Figure 5. The ellipse is parameterized by its minor and major axes, respectively, as "2a" (fixed) and "2b" (to be computed). This is shown in Figure 6 and is described by the equation

$$\frac{x^2}{a^2} + \frac{y^2}{b^2} = 1 \tag{6}$$

The human lip shape is more towards a combination of two ellipses and we call this as an irregular ellipse. The word 'irregular' means that the ellipse has two different minor axes wherein the major axes remains the same. The edge detected lip image is considered as an irregular ellipse. Lengths of minor axes of the lip feature for each emotion are computed. Figure 7 shows the whitened area of edge detected lip image for a particular emotion of South East Asian. The major axis is "2a" (considered as fixed) and two minor axes are "2b1" and "2b2" (to be computed). This is shown in Figure 8 and is described by Equation (6) with b1 and b2 suitably substituted for top and bottom portions respectively.

Fig. 5 Edge detected and whitened eye image

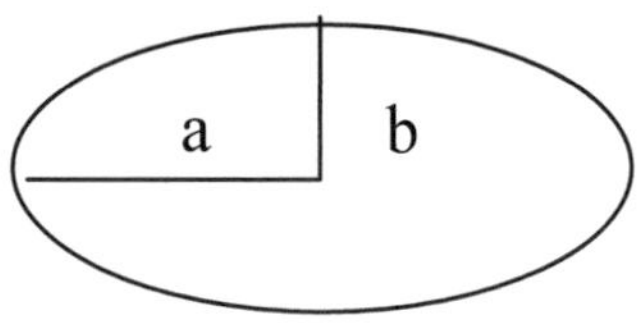

Fig. 6 The Regular Ellipse

Fig. 7. Edge detected and whitened lip image

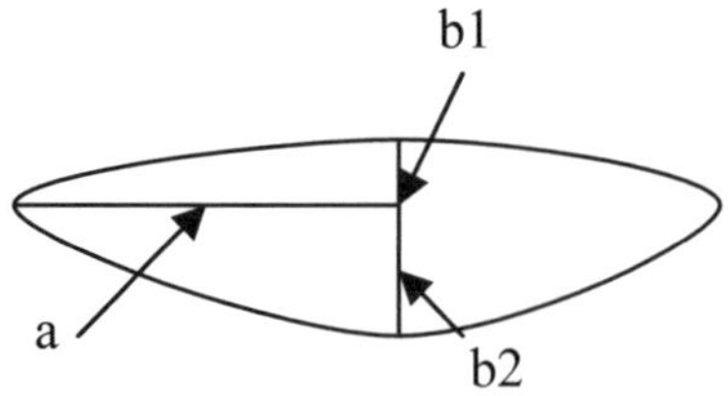

Fig 8. The Irregular Ellipse

4.1 Algorithm

GA is an iterative process (Negnevitsky, 2002). Each iteration is called generation. A chromosome of length of 6 bits and a population of 20 are chosen in our work. The selected chromosome is an approximate solution. Other selected parameters are listed in Table 1. The GA process is described in the following steps.

Step 1. Represent the problem variable domain as chromosome of a fixed length and population, with suitable cross over probability and mutation probability

Step 2. Define a fitness function to measure the performance, or fitness of an individual chromosome in the problem domain

Step 3. Randomly generate an initial population of chromosomes.

Step 4. Calculate the fitness of each individual chromosome.

Step 5. Select a pair of chromosomes for matting from the current population. Parent chromosomes are selected with a probability related to their fitness. Highly fit chromosomes have a higher probability of being selected for mating compared to less fit chromosomes.

Step 6. Create a pair of offspring chromosomes by applying the genetic operators - crossover and mutation

Step 7. Place the created offspring chromosomes in the new population

Step 8. Repeat from step 5 until the size of new chromosome population becomes equal to the size of the initial population

Stpe 9. Replace the initial chromosome population with the new population

Step 10. Go to step 4, and repeat the process until the termination criterion is satisfied.

4.2 Fitness function

A fitness function is a particular type of objective function that quantifies the optimality of a solution, a chromosome, so that the chromosome is ranked against all the other chromosomes. The fitness functions are derived from Equation(6). Equations(7) and (8) are fitness functions respectively for "b1" and "b2" to obtain optimum lip features. Equations(9) is the fitness function for "b" to obtain the optimum eye feature.

$$f(x) = \left(\sum_{i}^{m} \sum_{j}^{n} col(j) - 2\sqrt{X_1^{\,2}\left(1 - \frac{row(i)^2}{a^2}\right)}\right)^2 \qquad (7)$$

$$if X_1 \geq 0$$

$$\overline{f(x)} = \left(\sum_{i}^{m} \sum_{j}^{n} col(j) - 2\sqrt{X_2^{\,2}\left(1 - \frac{row(i)^2}{a^2}\right)}\right)^2 \qquad \textbf{(8)}$$

$$if X_2 \leq 0$$

$$f(x) = \left(\sum_{i}^{m} \sum_{j}^{n} col(j) - 2\sqrt{X^{2}\left(1 - \frac{row(i)^2}{a^2}\right)}\right)^2 \qquad (9)$$

In Equation (7) to (9), col(j) is the sum of white pixels occupied by j^{th} column and row(i) is the sum of white pixels in i^{th} row.

The lip and eye features have been given as inputs to the GA to find the optimized values of b1& b2 and b. Considering the parameters indicated in Table 1, the variance of the distribution of the Gaussian Mutation can be controlled with two parameters, the scale and the shrink. The scale parameter determines the variance at the first generation. The shrink parameter controls how variance shrinks as generations go by. These are selected as 1.0 each. Scattered crossover creates a random binary vector. It then selects the genes where the vector is a 1 from the first parent and the genes where the vector is a 0 from the second parent and combines the genes to form the child. The optimization has been carried out for 5 times for each emotion. The process of GA is found to offer a set of optimized minor axis values X1, X2 and X through fitness equations, Equations (7), (8) and (9). Table 2 indicates the manually measured values, b1, b2 and b, and the corresponding optimized values, X1, X2 and X. The emotion, based on X1, X2 and X can now be estimated. The experiment results show that values of X1, X2 and X are different for each emotion there by distinctions are possible.

Generation	250
Population size	20
Fitness scaling	Rank
Selection Function	Roulette
Mutation	Gaussian
Crossover	Scattered
Stall generation	50
Stall time	20

Table 1 Parameter Settings for GA Processing

Emotions	**Manually Computed Mean Value (in pixels)**			**Optimized Mean Value by GA (in pixels)**		
	b1	b2	b	X1	X2	X
Neutral	38	41	21	34.2644	35.2531	19.6188
Fear	25	41	16	23.0287	36.9529	14.7024
Happy	25	48	16	21.5929	43.4742	15.0393
Sad	33	34	19	30.9104	28.5235	16.9633
Angry	25	34	16	24.2781	30.8381	15.4120
Dislike	35	29	13	31.3409	21.6276	12.8353
Surprise	43	57	17	42.6892	55.5180	16.0701

Table 2 Optimized Value of the three Features

5. Emotion classification using neural network

Recently, there has been a high level of interest in applying artificial neural network for solving many problems (Negnevitsky, 2002; Pantic M. & Leon, 2000). The application of neural network gives easier solution to complex problems such as in determining the facial expression (Nagarajan, 2006). Each emotion has its own range of optimized values for lip and eye. In some cases an emotion range can overlap with other emotion range. This is experienced due to the closeness of the optimized feature values. For example, in Table 2, X_1 of Sad and Dislike are close to each other. These values are the mean values computed from a range of values. It has been found that the ranges of feature values of X_1 for Sad and dislike overlap with each other. Such overlap is also found in X for Angry and Happy. A level of intelligence has to be used to identify and classify emotions even when such overlaps occur.

A feed forward neural network is proposed to classify the emotions based on optimized ranges of 3-D data of top lip, bottom lip and eye. The optimized values of the 3-D data are given as inputs to the network as shown in Figure 9. The network is considered to be of two different models where the first model comes with a structure of 3 input neurons, 1 hidden layer of 20 neurons and 3 output neurons (denoted by (3x20x3)) and the other model with a structure of (3x20x7). The output of (3x20x3) is a 3-bit binary word indicating the seven emotional states. The output (O_i, i=1,2,.., 7) of (3x20x7) is of mutually exclusive binary bit representing an emotion. The networks with each of the above listed input sizes are trained using a back-propagation training algorithm. A set of suitably chosen learning parameters is indicated in Table 3. A typical "cumulative error versus epoch" characteristic of the training of NN models as in Figure 10 ensures the convergence of the network performances. The training is carried out for 10 trials in each case by reshuffling input data within the same network model. The time and epoch details are given in Table 3 which also indicates the maximum and minimum epoch required for converging to the test-tolerance.

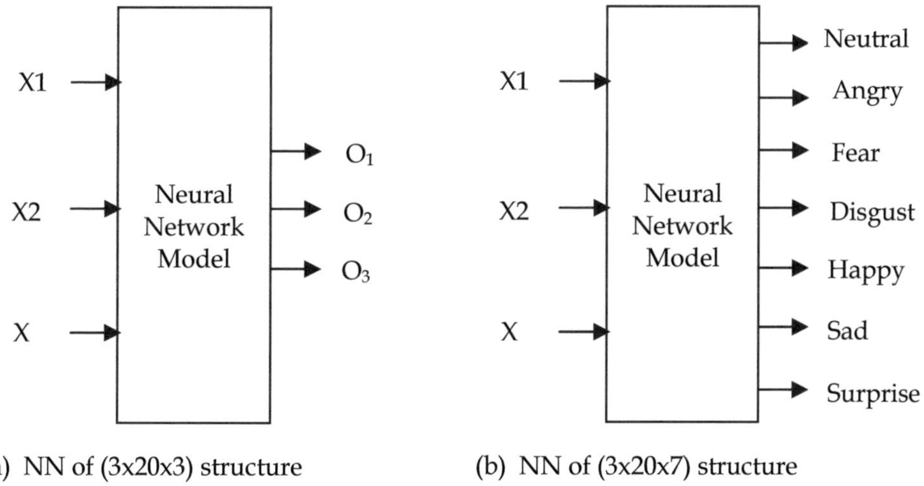

Fig. 9 Neural Network Structures

Hidden neurons: 20 Momentum factor: 0.9 Testing tolerance: 0.1			Learning rate: 0.0001 No. of samples: 70 Training tolerance: 0.0001			Activation function: (1/ $(1+e^{-x})$) Maximum no. of epoch: 1000 No. of trained samples: 50		
NN structure	**Epoch (in 10 trials)**			**Training Time (sec) (in 10 trials)**			**Classification % (in 10 trials)**	
	Min	**Max**	**Mean**	**Min**	**Max**	**Mean**	**Range**	**Mean**
3x20x3	105	323	225	2.18	7.32	5.02	75.71 – 90.00	83.57
3x20x7	71	811	294	3.43	39.25	13.76	81.42 -91.42	85.13

Table 3. Details of Neural Network Classification of Emotion

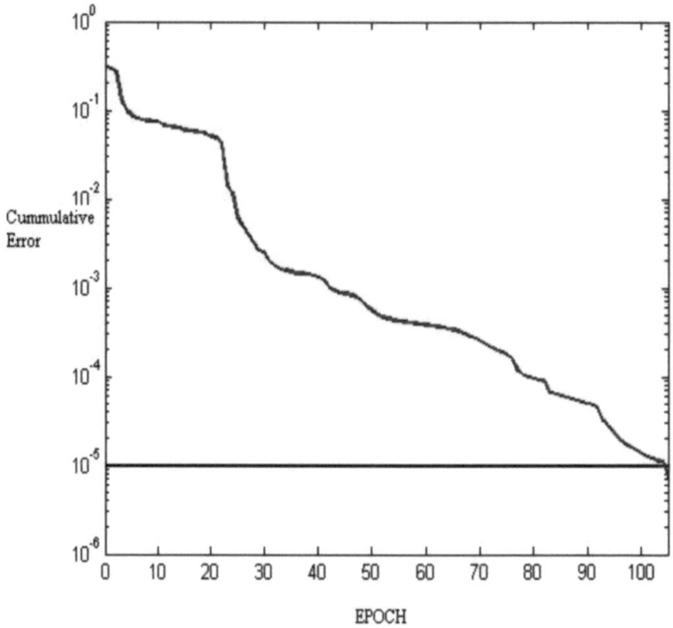

Fig. 10 Error vs Epoch Characteristic

6. Results and conclusion

In this study on a South East Asian face, the classification of six emotions and one neutral has been considered. The average and median filters are applied to smoothen the image. The Sobel edge detection is found to perform well since it offers a better segmentation even in non-structural light intensities. The eye and lip regions are used for the study on emotions. The GA is then applied to get the optimized values of the minor axes, X1 and X2, of an irregular ellipse corresponding to the lips and the minor axis, X, of a regular ellipse related to eye, by using a set of new fitness functions. The ranges of optimized values of emotion obtained from GA are found to overlap with each other resulting in an unacceptable classification. In order to overcome this problem, a NN is implemented to offer better classification. On an average of 10 trials of testing, the suggested NN processing has achieved about 85.13% and 83.57% of success rate for structure 3x20x7 and for structure 3x20x3 of NN models respectively. The successful classification even goes to the maximum of about 91.42% in the NN model of 3x20x7 structure. Even though the suggested methodology of face emotion detection and classification is general, the derived results are suitable only to a personalized South East Asian face. The software package can be developed as an expert emotion classification system for a personalized face. The applications of this emotion classification system are many such as from identifying criminals through a police enquiry to helping bedridden disabled dumb patients.

7. References

Anderson K. & Peter W. McOwan (2006, February). A Real-Time Automated System for the Recognition of Human Facial Expressions. *IEEE Transactions on Systems, Man, and Cybernetics – Part B: Cybernetics,* 36(1), 96-105.

Gary G. Yen & N. Nithianandan. (2002, May). Facial Feature Extraction Using Genetic Algorithm. *Proceedings of Congress on Evolutionary computation,* 2, 1895-1900.

Karthigayan. M, Mohammed Rizon, Sazali Yaacob & R. Nagarajan,. (2006). An Edge Detection and Feature Extraction Method Suitable for Face Emotion Detection under Uneven Lighting, *The 2nd Regional Conference on Artificial Life and Robotics (AROB'06),* July 14 - July 15, Hatyai, Thailand.

Karthigayan M, M.Rizon, S.Yaacob and R. Nagarajan. (2007). On the Application of Lip Features in Classifying the Human Emotions, *International Symposium on Artificial life and Robotics,* Japan.

Liyanage C De Silva & Suen Chun Hui. (2003). Real-time Facial Feature Extraction and Emotion Recognition, *Proceedings of Fourth Pacific RIM Conference on Multimedia,* vol. 3, pp. 1310-1314, 15-18 Dec 2003.

Li H. (2001, May 2-4). Computer Recognition of Human Emotion. *Proceedings of International Symposium on Intelligent Multimedia, Video and Speech Processing,* Hong Kong, 490-493.

Nagarajan R., S. Yaacob, P. Pandiyan, M. Karthigayan, M. Khalid & S. H. Amin. (2006). Real Time Marking Inspection Scheme for Semiconductor Industries. *International Journal of Advance Manufacturing Technology (IJAMT),* ISSN No (online): 1433-3015.

Negnevitsky M.. (2002). *Artificial Intelligence.* Addison Wesley, Pearson Education Limited, England.

Neo. (1997). http://neo.lcc.uma.es/TutorialEA/semEC/cap03/cap_3.html

Panti M. & I. Patras. (2006, April). Dynamics of Facial Expression: Recognition of Facial Actions and Their Temporal Segments from Face Profile Image Sequences. *IEEE Transactions on Systems, Man, and Cybernetics – Part B: Cybernetics,* 36(2), 433-449.

Pantic M. & Leon J. M Rothkrantz (2000, December). Automatic Analysis of Facial Expressions: The State of the Art. *IEEE Transactions on Pattern Analysis and Machine Intelligence,* 22(12), 1424-1445.

Rafael C Gonzalez, Richard E. Woods & Steven L Eddins. (2003). *Digital Image Processing using MATLAB,* Prentice Hall.

Sebe N., M. S. lew, I. Cohen, Y. Sun, T. Gevers & T. S. Huang. (2004, May 17-19) .Authentic Facial Expression Analysis. *Proc. of the sixth International Conference on Automatic Face and Gesture Recognition (FGR'04),* Seoul, Korea, 517-522.

Tani H., K. Terada, S. Oe & J. Yamaguchi. (2001). Detecting of One's Eye from facial Image by Using Genetic Algorithm. *The 27thAnnual Conference of the IEEE Industrial Electronics Society,* Colorado, USA 1937-1940.

Takimoto H., Y. Mitsukura, M. Fukumi & N. Akamatsu.(2003, July 20-24). Face Detection and Emotional Extraction System Using Double Structure Neural Network. *Proc. of the International Joint Conference on Neural Networks,* Orlando, USA, 2, 1253-1257.

5

Classifying Facial Expressions Based on Topo-Feature Representation

Xiaozhou Wei, Johnny Loi and Lijun Yin
State University of New York at Binghamton
USA

1. Introduction

Facial expression analysis and recognition could help humanize computers and design a new generation of human computer interface. A number of techniques were successfully exploited for facial expression recognition (Chang et al., 2004; Cohen et al., 2004; Cohen et al., 2003; Gu & Ji, 2004; and Littlewort et al, 2004), including feature estimation by optical flow (Mase, 1999; Yacoob & S. Davis, 2006), dynamic model (Essa & Pentland, 1997), eigen-mesh method (Matsuno et all.) and neural networks (Rosenblum et all., 1996). The excellent review of recent advances in this field can be found in (Y. Tian et al., 2001; Pantic & Rothkrantz, 2000; Zhao et al., 2000). The conventional methods on facial expression recognition concern themselves with extracting the expression data to describe the change of facial features, such as Action Units (AUs) defined in Facial Action Coding System (FACS) (Donato et al., 1999). Although the FACS is the most successful and commonly used technique for facial expression representation and recognition, the difficulty and complexity of the AUs extraction limit its application. As quoted by most previous works (Essa & Pentland, 1997; Yacoob & Davis, 1996), capturing the subtle change of facial skin movements is a dif cult task due to the difficulty to implement such an implicit representation. Currently, feature-based approaches (Reinders et al., 1995; Terzopoulos & Waters, 1993) and spatio-temporal based approaches (Essa & Pentland) are commonly used. Yacoob & Davis, 1996 integrated spatial and temporal information and studied the temporal model of each expression for the recognition purpose, a high recognition rate was achieved. Colmenarez et al. used a probabilistic framework based on the facial feature position and appearances to recognize the facial expressions, the recognition performance was improved, but only the feature regions other than the surface information were explored. Recently, Tian, Kanade and Cohn (Tian et al., 2001) noticed the importance of the transient features (i.e., furrow information) besides the permanent features (i.e, eyes, lips and brows) in facial expression recognition. They explored the furrow information for improving the accuracy of the AU parameters, an impressive result was achieved in recognizing a large variety of subtle expressions. To our knowledge, little investigation has been conducted on combining texture analysis and surface structure analysis for modeling and recognizing facial expressions. A detailed higher level face representation and tracking system is in high demand. In this paper, we explore the active texture information and facial surface features to meet the challenge - modeling the facial expression with sufficient accuracy.

Facial texture appearance plays an important role in representing a variety of facial expressions. It is possible to classify a facial expression by noting the change of facial texture. On the other hand, the facial expression change is reflected by the variation of the facial topographic deformation. It is thus of interest for us to investigate the relationship between these features and the corresponding expressions in order to model facial expressions in an intuitive way.

Facial texture consists of four major active regions: eyebrow, eye, nose and mouth. A set of active textures of a person is a class of textures with the same statistical property, which in general represents a statistical resemblance determined by the action of different facial expressions. In this paper, we propose a facial expression analysis system based on the integration of the topographic feature and the active texture. The system is composed of three major components: texture enhancement by increasing the image resolution; face surface region representation using topographic analysis; and the similarity measurement by a topographical masking method. Figure 1 outlines the system composition.

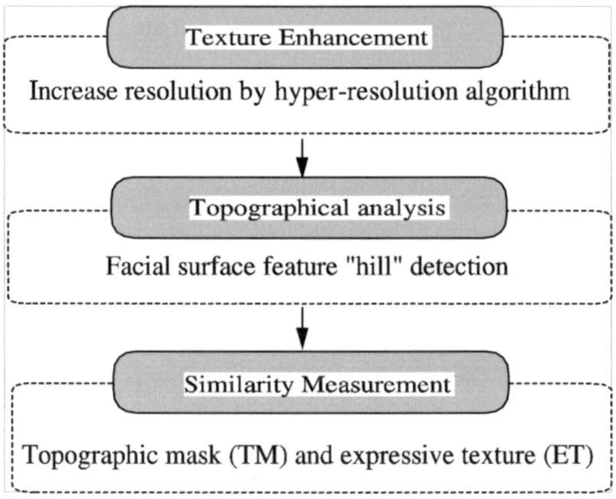

Fig. 1: Facial expression analysis system

Analysis of the facial surface features relies on the texture details. In order to detect the surface feature in a detailed level, in the first stage, we enhance the image resolution by a so called hyper-resolution algorithm. The topographical labeling process can then be carried out in the second stage. In the third stage, the texture similarity and topographic disparity between the test image and the reference image are measured for classifying different facial expressions. The method outputs a score to signify the level of similarity. In the end, a simple classification rule is defined for distinguishing six universal expressions.

In Section 2, the algorithm for texture detail recovery is described. Section 3 describes the method for facial surface representation using topographic analysis. The algorithm for similarity measurement and expression classification will be described in Section 4, followed by the experiment result presented in Section 5. Finally, the concluding remark will be given in Section 6.

2. Texture enhancement

In order to analyze and detect the face surface features from low resolution images, facial details recovery by enhancing the image resolution is necessary due to the various imaging environment where only few effective pixels could be captured in the face region. Another reason for increasing resolution is that our subsequent analysis using topographical feature relies on a surface fitting procedure, which requires accurate pixel representation within the face region. Here, we propose a super-resolution method to recover details in the facial region. Traditional methods for scaling a low resolution image to a high resolution version depend on interpolation algorithms, which suffer problems of blurred images lacking distinct edges and fine textures. Recently, *training based* super-resolution algorithms have been developed by (Baker et al., 2002; Freeman. et al., 2002; Sun et al., 2003), where an image database containing the high resolution detail of many different subjects is used. The visually plausible high resolution details for one low resolution *target image* are reconstructed based on the pattern recognition and substitution of "similar" details in a potentially large database of high resolution model images (also called *source images*.) Most existing algorithms work on either the pixel or pixel patch level. However, both humans and computers judge image sharpness and detail by the quality of an image's strong edges. This observation leads us to a novel idea: instead of matching patches in the spatial domain, we can first transform each image into a new parametric vector space structured by the image's edges. Our "patches" are then composed of only the texture details (in the form of high-pass filtered image pixels) sampled on and around image edges, with coordinates relative to these edges. Thus, we simply need to match and replace low resolution data around each target edge with the appropriate high resolution detail from a database of source edges. Central to this new method is the novel transform of image content from the orthogonal pixel space to a parametric space structured around edges.

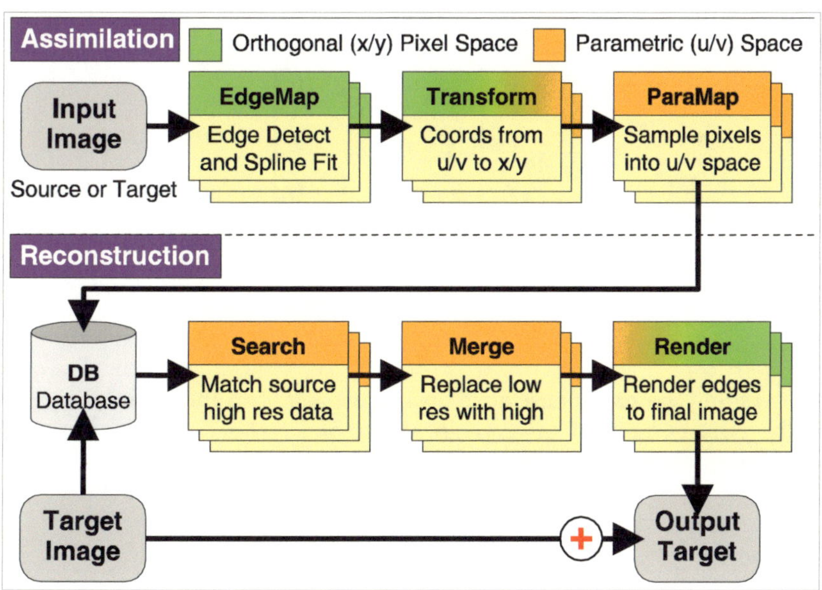

Fig. 2: HyperRes Pipeline Overview.

This so-called *hyper-resolution (HyperRes)* algorithm is illustrated in Figure 2, where the pipeline is logically split into two parts: the *Assimilation* phase, through which both source and target images are transformed and added to a database, and the *Reconstruction* phase, in which a single target image is reconstructed at a higher resolution than its original pixels provided.

2.1 Assimilation

Prior to starting the true HyperRes algorithm, the target image must be interpolated up to the desired output size (e.g., 200% or more) using the simple bi-cubic interpolation. To construct an image around its edges, we first detect those edges by using Canny edge detector, then apply the cubic splines to t the edges. This parametric curve representation allows us to establish a bidirectional mapping between two coordinate spaces: the *orthogonal space* in which the image pixels reside along *x*, *y* coordinates, and the *parametric space,* a nonlinear transformed space relative to the curvature of each edge. Each edge has its own local parametric space in the form of a warped rectangle, with the *u* coordinate running parallel to the edge and the *v* coordinate running out along the edge's normal as evaluated at *u*. The coordinate of a point **P**(u) at a parametric coordinate u in the span between any two known edge points $\mathbf{E}_n$ and $\mathbf{E}_{n+1}$ is defined as

$$P(u) = \frac{1}{2}\begin{bmatrix} 1 \\ (\frac{u-U_n}{S_n}) \\ (\frac{u-U_n}{S_n})^2 \\ (\frac{u-U_n}{S_n})^3 \end{bmatrix} \cdot M \cdot \begin{bmatrix} E_{n-1} \\ E_n \\ E_{n+1} \\ E_{n+2} \end{bmatrix} \tag{1}$$

Where

$$M = \begin{bmatrix} \frac{1}{6} & \frac{2}{3} & \frac{1}{6} & 0 \\ \frac{-1}{2} & 0 & \frac{1}{2} & 0 \\ \frac{1}{2} & -1 & \frac{1}{2} & 0 \\ \frac{-1}{6} & \frac{1}{2} & \frac{-1}{2} & \frac{1}{6} \end{bmatrix} \tag{2}$$

$$S_n = | E_{n+1} - E_n | \tag{3}$$

To completely define the parametric space, we must also find the *v* coordinate, which runs parallel to the curve's normal at a given value of *u*. The complete transform from a parametric coordinate *u, v* to an orthogonal coordinate $Q\ (u,v) \rightarrow x,\ y$ is thus:

$$Q(u,v) = P(u) + v \cdot \frac{\frac{\partial P(u)}{\partial u}}{\frac{\partial P(u)}{\partial u}} \begin{bmatrix} 0 & 1 \\ -1 & 0 \end{bmatrix} \tag{4}$$

where *Q(u, v)* is the final coordinate in the orthogonal space. $-v_\sigma \leq v \leq v_\sigma$ (v_σ is set as 8 pixels). After fitting each edge to a parametric curve representation, we warp the curve area around each edge to a standard rectangle (u, v) area, thus forming a "parametric map" (called *ParaMap*). Figure 3 shows an example of the *uv-xy* transformation and ParaMap formation.

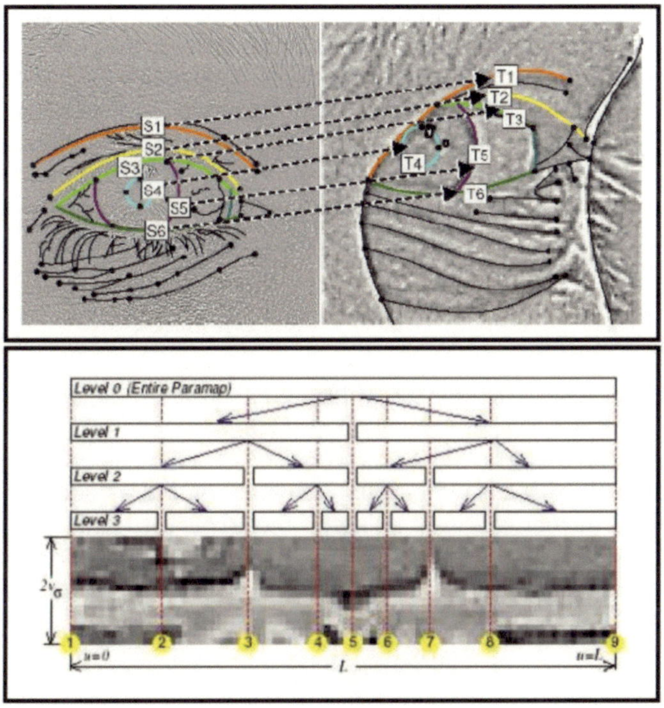

Fig. 3: Top: source-target edges match using an eye image as an example (S: source; T: target). Bottom: Paramap formation (example of S1)

2.2 Reconstruction

To reconstruct the high resolution version of a given target edge, we search for similar edge textures in the database by matching the contents of paramaps between the source and target images. To facilitate efficient operation, each edge is recursively split into two segments, such that we can always attempt to match the longest possible edge first, then subdivide as needed to optimize for accuracy.

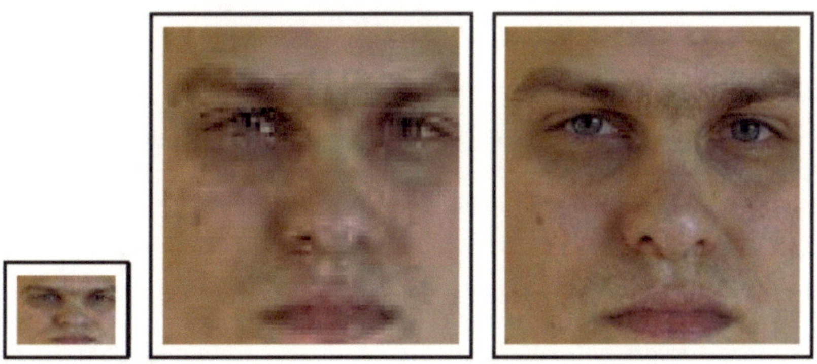

Fig. 4: left: original face region 64*64 pixels; middle: enlarged by cubic interpolation (256*256); right: enlarged by HyperRes (256*256).

The results of the Search stage are in the form of key pairs: a target key and its matching source key. In the Merge stage, we map the source key back to the corresponding subsection of the paramap owning it, and *merge* that parametric pixel data back into the correct place in the target edge's paramap. The reconstructed paramap is further rendered onto the curvature of the appropriate target edge, which is implemented by projecting the u, v coordinates back into orthogonal x, y space. As a result, the detail-reconstructed high-frequency image is created. Finally, we add this high-frequency image back into the original low resolution image to generate the new resolution-increased image. Figure 4 illustrates one example of the HyperRes results.

3. Topographic analysis

To find an explicit representation for the fundamental structure of facial surface details, the topographic primal sketch theorem is exploited (Haralick et al., 1983), where the grey level image is treated as a topographic terrain surface. Each pixel is assigned one of the topographic label peak, ridge, saddle, hill, at, ravine, or pit, as shown in Figure 5. Hill-labeled pixels can be further specified as one of the labels convex hill, concave hill, saddle hill or slope hill (Trier et al., 1997). We furthermore distinguish saddle hills as *concave saddle hill, convex saddle hill*, distinguish saddle as *ridge saddle* and *ravine saddle.*

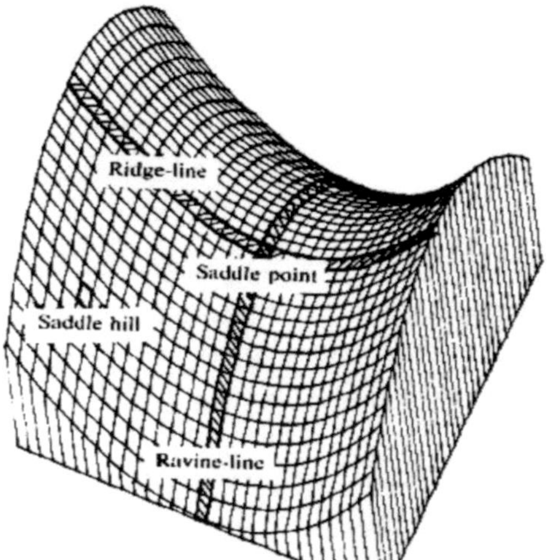

Fig. 5: Topographic labels (Haralick et al., 1983) used for facial skin details representation. The 3D topographical structure can be classified by a number of features, such as peak, pit, ridge, ravine, ridge saddle, ravine saddle, convex hill, concave hill, convex saddle hill, concave saddle hill, slope hill and at (Trier et al., 1997).

Light intensity variations on an image are caused by an object's surface orientation and its reflectance. In visual perception, exactly the same visual interpretation and understanding of a pictured scene occurs no matter how the imaging condition is. This fact suggests that topographic features can be expected to have the robustness associated with human visual perception because they are inherently capable of invariance under monotonic transformations. The topographic categories peak, pit, ridge, valley, saddle, at, and hill can reveal the three dimensional intrinsic surface of the object, and thus be possible for us to extract the facial surface features. With surface feature classification, the facial image can be segmented into a number of feature areas. The different composition of these basic primitives will give a fundamental representation of different skin surface details. The primitive label classification approach is determined by the estimation of the first-order and second-order directional derivatives. The gradient vector is

$$\nabla f = \begin{pmatrix} \frac{\partial f}{\partial x} & \frac{\partial f}{\partial y} \end{pmatrix} \tag{5}$$

The second directional derivatives can be calculated by forming the *Hessian matrix* [17].

$$H = \begin{bmatrix} \frac{\partial^2 f}{\partial x^2} & \frac{\partial^2 f}{\partial x \partial y} \\ \frac{\partial^2 f}{\partial y \partial x} & \frac{\partial^2 f}{\partial y^2} \end{bmatrix} \tag{6}$$

The eigenvalues (λ_1 and λ_2) of the Hessian are the values of the extrema of the second directional derivative, and their associated eigenvectors (ω_1 and ω_2) are the directions in which the second directional derivatives have greatest magnitude. The feature labeling is based on the values of λ_1, λ_2, ω_1, ω_2, and ∇f. For example, a pixel is labeled as a convex hill if the values in this pixel satisfied the following condition:

$$\lambda_1 < 0; \lambda_2 > 0; |\nabla f| > T_G \tag{7}$$

where T_G is a predefined threshold.
Since a temporal skin "wave" is associated with the movement of the expression, the skin surface with a certain expression at a different time will have different shape, resulting in the different label changes. The skin detail shape follows the expression's change while the expressions occur in three distinct phases: *application (from the beginning), release (from the apex)* and *relaxation (to the end)*. For example, from the concave hill to convex hill, from the ridge saddle to ravine saddle. This is known as dynamic labeling along with shape change. We can imagine that the skin surface is represented as a topographic label "map", this "map" is changed along with the skin movement. Figure 6 shows one example of facial surface features labeled by topographic analysis.

4. Facial expression representation and classification

4.1 Representation

The topographic analysis of facial surface outputs a group of topographic labels. Currently, two types of labels, convex hill and convex saddle hill, are used for feature detection. These two types of labels form a topographic mask (TM) of a specific expression, as shown in Figure 6a and Figure 6b (red and pink labels). As we can see, the areas (eye, eyebrow, nose, mouth, nasolabial, etc.) encompassed by the topographic mask are the significant regions for representing an expression. We call these textures as expressive textures (ET) or active textures (AT). Apparently TM and ET are changing along with the expression change. In terms of a specific subject, TM represents the facial expression pattern (i.e., six universal expressions have six types of TMs.) Therefore, we choose these topographic masks and expressive textures to classify different expressions. Given a specific subject A, by comparing the set of (TM, ET) of A's neutral face with the set of (TM, ET) of A's expressive face, the expression could be identified.

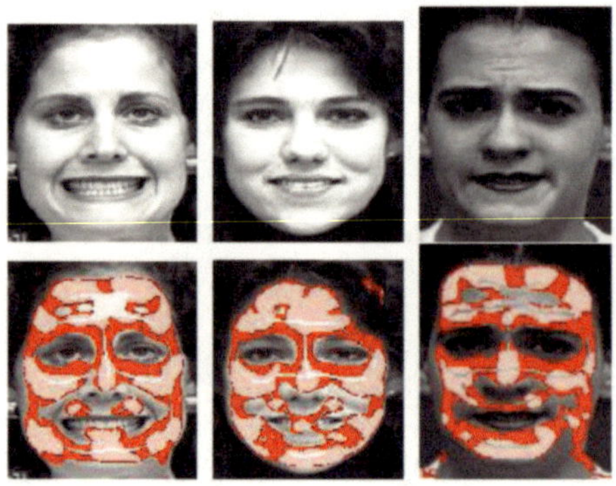

Fig. 6a: Example of topographic facial analysis on sample images of Cohn-Kanade facial expression database (Kanade et al., 2000). (top row: original faces; bottom row: labeled faces with convex hill (in red) and convex saddle hill (in pink).

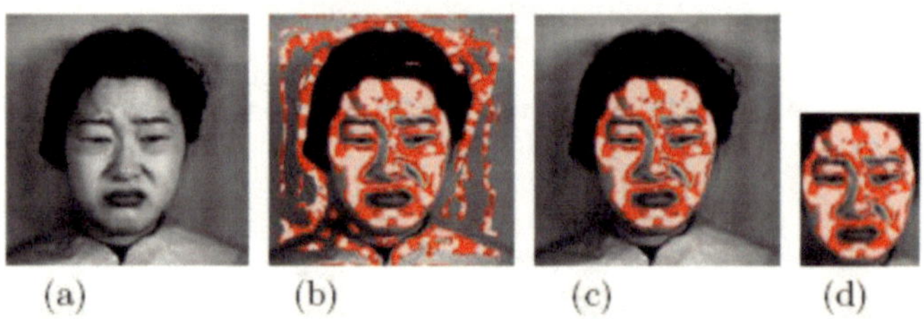

Fig. 6b: Facial expression representation by the topographic Mask from the JEFFE database (Lyons, 2005). (a) original image (KL); (b) Labeling after resolution increased from 256*256 to 512*512; (c) Background label removal; (d) Topographic Mask of "disgust" expression.

4.2 Classification

For an individual person, there is a unique topographic mask for his/her individual expression. TM is represented in a binary format, in which '1' denotes the labeled region (red and pink region) and '0' for the non-labeled region. The disparity of two masks between the neutral face and the expressive face is formulated as:

$$D_{TM} = \frac{1}{N} \sum TM_n \ xor \ \ TM_e \tag{8}$$

where N is the total number of pixels within the TM of neutral expression. TM_n is the neutral mask; TM_e is the expressive mask for one of the six universal expressions. The similarity between the neutral texture and the current expressive texture is measured by the correlation C_{ET} (Yin et al., 2003):

$$C_{ET} = \frac{E(t_n t_e) - m_{t_n} m_{t_e}}{\sigma(t_n)\sigma(t_e)} \tag{9}$$

where t_n and t_e are the neutral texture and the expressive texture, respectively. E() is a mean operation, m_{tn}, $\sigma(t_n)$ and m_{te}, $\sigma(t_e)$ are the means and variances of the two textures to be compared. In general, the similarity of two expressions is characterized by the similarity score S_{exp}, which is defined as:

$$S_{\exp} = (1 - D_{TM}) + C_{ET} \tag{10}$$

In order to differentiate the different expressions, we take a statistic method to calculate the similarity scores through a training set which contains 20 video sequences performed by 20 different subjects, each subject performed a neutral expression and six universal expressions. The average similarity score for each typical expression is obtained in Figure 7. It shows that the similarity score is within the range of [0,2] in a decreasing order from neutral to sad, fear, angry, disgust, surprise, and to happy. By the property of monotonicity of similarity curve shown in Figure 7, we classify the expressions into seven categories by the similarity scores range: [T1, 2] for neutral expression; [T2, T1) for sad; [T3, T2) for angry; [T4, T3) for fear; [T5, T4) for disgust; [T6, T5) for surprise and [0, T6) for happy. \ The thresholds T1 - T6 are obtained by the average values of two "neighbor" expressions, as shown in Figure 7 and Table 1.

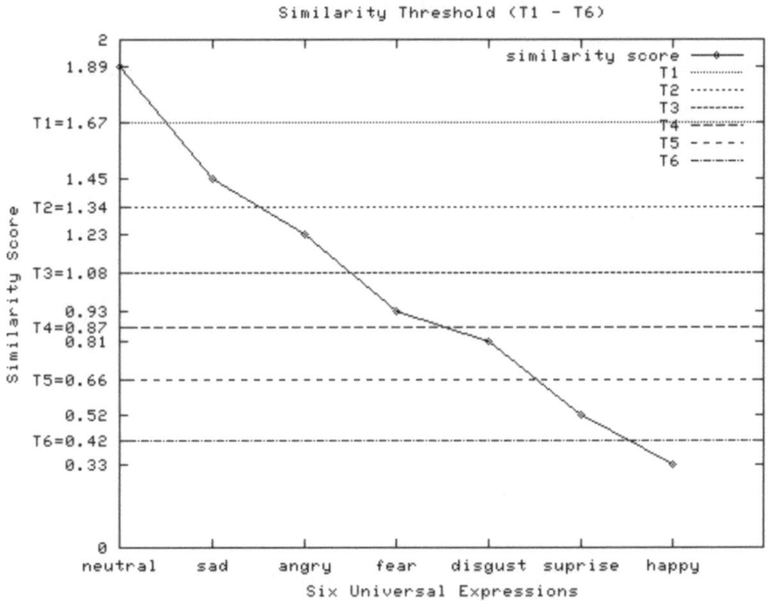

Fig. 7: Similarity scores and threshold values

T1	T2	T3	T4	T5	T6
1.67	1.34	1.08	0.87	0.66	0.42

Table 1: Thresholds for distinguishing six expressions plus a neutral expression. As shown in Figure 7, T1 is the threshold between neutral and sad; T2 between sad and angry; T3: angry and fear; T4: fear and disgust; T5: disgust and surprise; T6: surprise and happy.

5. Experiments

5.1 The JAFFE facial expression database (Lyons, 2005) is used in our experiment. The database contains 212 frontal facial images including ten female subjects performing seven types of expressions (six universal expressions plus one neutral expression). After increasing the resolution to the double size, the face images are labeled by convex hill and convex saddle hill features. Figure 8 shows two sets of topographic masks obtained from two female subjects (KL and TM). The results show that topographic labeling method can accurately capture the facial surface regions.

For each subject, we take one of the neutral expressions as a reference expression to which all other expressions of her own can be compared. In order to remove the background hill regions, we detect the connected components of the hill regions, and take the largest region as the face region to form the topographic mask. Based on the obtained TM, we use the similarity score to classify the expressions. Note that before the similarity calculation, the TM and EM are normalized (by the width, height and orientation) to the size of the neutral TM and ET. The similarity score is calculated to classify the input facial expression using thresholds and categories defined in Table 1 and figure 7.

The classification results show that the average correct recognition rate is at 85.8%. Table 2 enumerates the recognition results on seven expressions of JEFFE database.

The experimental result shows that recognition rates are encouraging in view of such a condition that no action units are extracted. The possible extension of this work is to use the similarity score of other topographic labels for classifying richer range of fine expressions.

	(1)	(2)	(3)	(4)	(5)	(6)	(7)
(1)angry	25	1	1	0	1	1	1
(2)disgust	1	26	1	1	0	1	1
(3)fear	1	1	24	0	1	2	2
(4)happy	0	0	1	28	0	0	0
(5)neutral	1	0	1	0	27	1	0
(6)sad	1	2	1	1	1	26	0
(7)suprise	1	0	2	0	0	0	26
RR(%)	83.3	86.7	77.4	93.3	90.0	83.9	86.7

Table 2: Correct expression recognition rate (RR). 212 frontal face images captured from 10 female subjects, including 30 images for each of following expressions: (1) angry, (2) disgust, (4) happy, (5) neutral, (7) surprise; and 31 images for each of following expressions: (2) fear and (6) sad. (Average RR: 85.8%).

5.2 The Cohn-Kanade (CK) facial expression database is used for our second test. We randomly choose 180 sequences performed by 30 subjects, in which each prototypic expression has 30 sequences. Since the first frame of each sequence shows the neutral expression and the last frame shows the peak of a prototypic expression, we select the first frame as a reference frame and the last frame as a probe frame to form an image pair, with a total of 180 pairs in our experiment. In addition, we also generate 30 image pairs from 30 sequences by selecting the first frame and the third frame as the neutral expression pairs. The classification results show that the average correct recognition rate is at 80.9%. Table 3 enumerates the classification results by the confusion matrix. Note that from the experiments, we find that the labeling algorithm works best when the face region has over

256*256 pixels. Although the above two databases contain images with the size larger than 256*256, the valid face region may not have sufficient resolution. Therefore, to keep the operation consistent and efficient, we always increase the image resolution from its original size to the double size using AugRes algorithm before the topographic labeling. The experiment demonstrates the efficiency and the feasibility of this scheme. The possible extension of this work is to use the similarity score of other topographic labels for classifying wide range of fine expressions.

	(1)	(2)	(3)	(4)	(5)	(6)	(7)
(1)angry	23	1	1	1	2	1	2
(2)disgust	1	24	1	1	0	2	0
(3)fear	1	2	22	1	0	2	2
(4)happy	1	1	1	25	0	0	1
(5)neutral	1	0	1	0	27	1	0
(6)sad	2	2	2	0	1	24	0
(7)suprise	1	0	2	2	0	0	25
RR(%)	76.7	80.0	73.3	83.3	90.0	80.0	83.3

Table 3: Confusion matrix and correct expression recognition rate (RR) on CK database. (Average RR: 80.9%).

5.3 Analysis: Identifying facial expression is a challenging problem. However, there is no baseline algorithm or standard database for measuring the merits of new methods. The unavailability of an accredited common database and evaluation methodology make it difficult to compare any new algorithm quantitatively with the existing algorithms. Although the CK database is widely used, some recent work (Cohen et al., 2004; Cohen et al., 2003) utilized a portion of the database because not all the subjects in CK database have six prototypic expressions. This makes the algorithm comparison not feasible without knowing the exact test set in the existing approaches. Here we use the JAFFE database as a common test data to compare the result reported by (Lyons et al., 1999). Lyons et al (1999) developed a elastic graph matching and a linear discriminant analysis approach to classify expressions of JAFFE database. The very impressive results were achieved in classifying facial images in terms of gender, race and expression. In particular, the correct recognition rate for the prototypic expressions is at 92% for a person-dependent test, and at 75% for the person-independent test. Here, we report our average recognition rate for JAFFE database is at 85.8%. Note that this rate is obtained under the person-independent circumstance, which means that the person to be tested has never appeared in the training set. Our system therefore improves the expression classification performance to a certain degree.

Our system has certain pros and cons:

(1) Although our system can work based on the static images, the expression recognition is dependent on the first frame, which means we need a reference face image with neutral expression for each instance. It is frame-dependent. Because the dynamic expression is obtainable by the video capture, it is feasible to select a neutral expression frame in the video.

(2) Our system works on the facial expressions in frontal view. The selection of image pairs with a neutral expression and a test expression is conducted manually. We selected the "peak" (exaggerated) expression as the test data. More spontaneous expressions will be used in the future work.

(3) Our system is person-independent. It appears that topographic structure significantly differs from person to person, in other words, TM is person specific. However, the normalized similarity between a neutral TM and an expressive TM falls in a certain range with respect to the certain expression regardless of subjects to be tested. Therefore, the classification of facial expression is person independent. Moreover, it does not require complete sampling of the expression space for each person. A large training set and a large sampling space for each expression could help improve the accuracy and robustness of the classification.

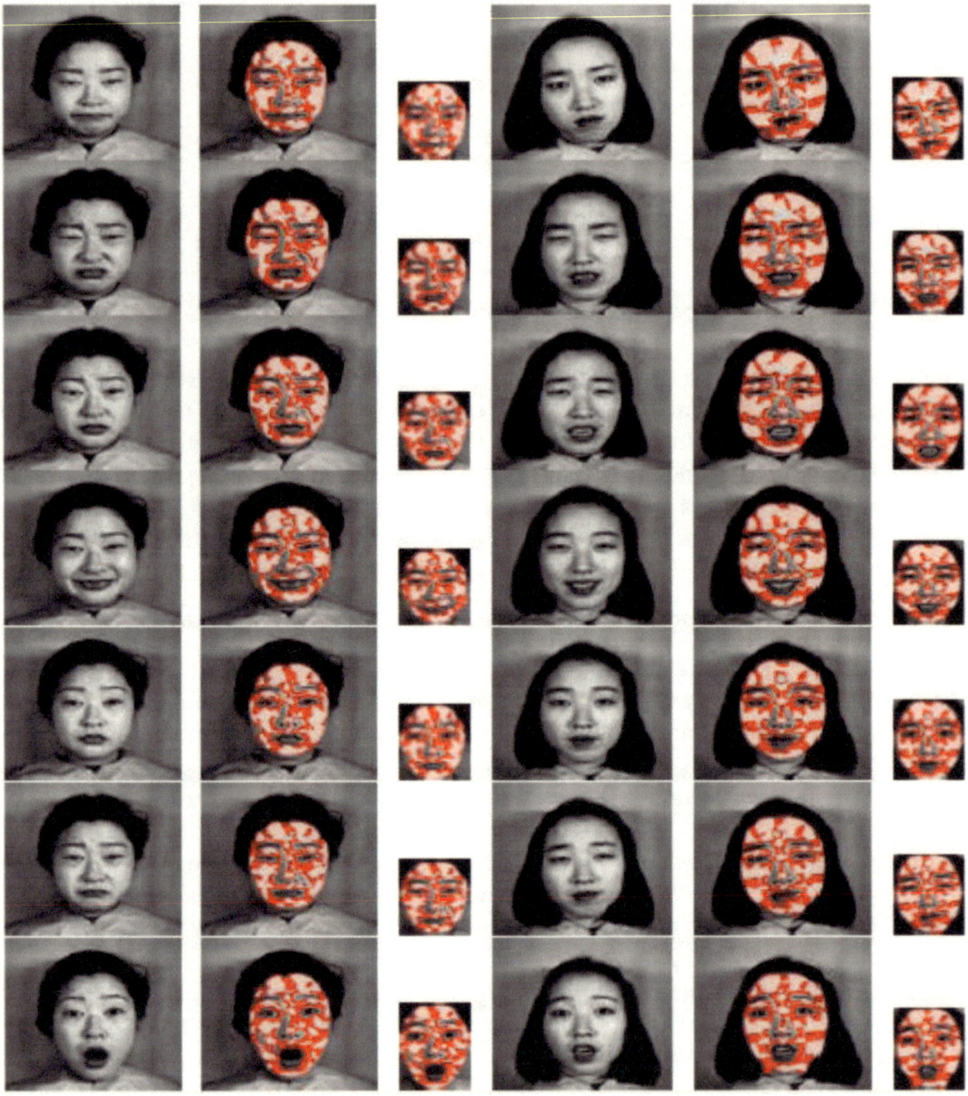

Fig. 8: Example of labeling on JAFFE facial expressions (Lyons et al., 2005) (names: KL for left three columns and YA for right three columns). From top to bottom: angry, disgust, fear, happy, neutral, sad, and surprise. Each row shows the expression, labeled face region, and the Topographic Mask, respectively.

6. Conclusion

We presented a new scheme to model and recognize facial expressions based on the topographic shape structure and the enhanced textures. The encouraging results demonstrate the efficiency and the feasibility of the proposed scheme. This work can be the first step for the coarse classification of the expressions. A fine classification approach will be investigated as the second step by taking the probability of appearance of topographic mask and other labels into account (e.g., ridge and ravine). In the future, the similarity score can be used as an input in order to design the classifier to classify subtle facial expressions recognition, for example, using the Bayesian recognition framework (Colmenarz et al; Gu & Ji, 2004). In addition, the intensive test on a larger amount of facial expression data will be conducted in the future.

7. Acknowledgment

This material is based upon the work supported in part by the National Science Foundation under grant No. IIS-0414029, IIS-0541044, NYSTAR, and AFRL.

8. References

G. Donato, P. Ekman, and et al. Classifying facial actions. *IEEE Trans. PAMI*, 21(10):974-989, 1999.

I. Essa and A. Pentland. Facial expression recognition using a dynamic model and motion energy. In *ICCV95*, pages 360–367.

I. Essa and A. Pentland. Coding, analysis, interpretation, and recognition of facial expressions. *IEEE Trans. PAMI*, 19(7), 1997.

A. Colmenarz *et al.* A probalilistic framework for embedded face and facial expression recognition. In *CVPR99*.

S. Baker *et al.* Limits on super-resolution and how to break them. *IEEE PAMI*, 24(9), 2002.

W. Freeman. *et al.* Example-based super-resolution. *IEEE Comp. Graphics and App.*, 22(2):56–65, 2002.

Y. Tian *et al.* Recognizing action units for facial expression analysis. *PAMI*, 23(2), 2001.

R. Haralick and et al. The topographic primal sketch. *The Int. J of Robotics Research*, 2(2):50–72, 1983.

T. Kanade, J.F. Cohn, and Y. L. Tian. Comprehensive database for facial expression analysis. In *IEEE 4th International conference on Automatic Face and Gesture Recognition*, France, 2000. http://vasc.ri.cmu.edu/idb/html/face/facial expression/.

K. Mase. Recognition of facial expression from optical flow. *IEICE Transactions*, E74(10):3474–3483, October 1991.

K. Matsuno, C. Lee, S. Kimura, and S. Tsuji. Automatic recognition of human facial expressions. In *ICCV95*, pages 352–359.

M. Pantic and L. Rothkrantz. Automatic analysis of facial expressions: the state of the art. *IEEE Trans. PAMI*, 22(12), 2000.

M. Reinders, P. Beek, B. Sankur, and J. Lubbe. Facial feature localization and adaptation of a generic face model for model-based coding. *Signal Processing: Image Communication*, 7:57–74, July 1995.

M. Rosenblum, Y. Yacoob, and L. Davis. Human expression recognition from motion using a radial basis function network architecture. *IEEE Trans. on Neural Network*, 7(5):1121-1138, 1996.

J. Sun, N. Zheng, H. Tao, and H. Shum. Image hallucination with primal sketch priors. In *CVPR*, 2003.

D. Terzopoulos and K. Waters. Analysis and synthesis of facial image sequences using physical and anatomical models. *IEEE Trans. PAMI*, 15(6):569, 1993.

O. Trier, T. Taxt, and A.K. Jain. Recognition of digits in hydrographic maps: binary versus topographic analysis. *IEEE Trans. PAMI*, 19(4), April 1997

Y. Yacoob and L. S. Davis. Recognizing human facial expressions from long image sequences using optical flow. *IEEE Trans. PAMI*, 18(6):636-642, June 1996.

L. Yin, S. Royt, et al. Recognizing facial expressions using active textures with wrinkles. In *IEEE Inter. Conf. on Multimedia and Expo 2003*, pages 177-180, Baltimore, MD, July 2003.

W. Zhao, R. Chellappa, A. Rosenfeld, and P. Phillips. Face recognition: A literature survey. *Technique report: CAR-TR-948, CS-TR-4167, University of Maryland, College Park*, October 2000.

Y. Chang, C. Hu, and M. Turk. Probabilistic expression analysis on manifolds. In IEEE Inter. Conf. on CVPR, Washington DC, June 2004.

I. Cohen, F. Cozman, N. Sebe, M. Cirelo, and T. Huang. Semi-supervised learning of classifiers: Theory, algorithms for bayesian network classifiers and application to human-computer interaction. IEEE Trans. PAMI, 26(12), 2004.

I. Cohen, N. Sebe, A. Garg, L. Chen, and T. Huang. Facial expression recognition from video sequences: temporal and static modeling. Computer Vision and Image Understanding, 91(1), 2003.

H. Gu and Q. Ji. Facial event classification with task oriented dynamic bayesian network. In CVPR, 2004.

G. Littlewort, M. Bartlett, I. Fasel, J. Susskind, and J. Movellan. Dynamics of facial expression extracted automatically from video. In CVPR Workshop on FPIV'04, 2004.

M. Lyons. http://www.mis.atr.co.jp/ mlyons/jaffe.html. 2005.

M. Lyons, J. Budynek, and S. Akamatsu. Automatic classi_cation of single facial images. IEEE Trans. PAMI, 21(12):1357{1362, December 1999.

6

Layered Fuzzy Facial Expression Generation: Social, Emotional and Physiological

Xia Mao, Yuli Xue, Zheng Li and Haiyan Bao
School of Electronic and Information Engineering, Beihang University
China

1. Introduction

Facial expression plays an important role in human's daily life, as indicated by (Mehrabian, 1968), in face-to-face human communication, only 7% of the communicative message is due to linguistic language, 38% is due to paralanguage, while 55% of it is transferred by facial expressions. Currently, facial expression has been widely researched in psychology, sociology, cognitive science, biology, pathology, neuroscience, computer science, and so on, thus different views of facial expressions have been formed.

Facial expression has been researched in the "Emotion View" for a long time. In the 19th century, kinds of facial expressions of emotions were studied by (Darwin, 1872), who argued that there is a link between emotions and expressive behaviour. Later, facial expressions of 6 basic emotions or fundamental emotions were pointed to be universally recognized in the cross culture studies by (Ekman & Friesen, 1971). However, the assumption of universality of human facial expressions of emotion was suggested to be premature by (Russell, 1994). As there are some shortcomings in the emotion view (Fridlund, 1997), the "Behavioral Ecology View" treats facial displays as social signals of intent. Facial display may depend upon the intent of the displayer, the topographic features of the niche, the behaviour of the recipient, and the context of the interaction (Fridlund, 1994). Recently, facial expressions have been considered as emotional activators and regulators (Lisetti & Schiano, 2000). It has been found that voluntary facial action can generate subjective experience of emotion and emotion specific autonomic nervous system activity.

Along with the rapid development of the research fields of computer science, human-computer interaction, affective computing, etc., the generation of facial expressions in computer has been actively researched. The Improvisational Animation system (Perlin, 1997) generated facial expressions such as angry, daydreaming, disgusted, distrustful, fiendish, haughty etc. by relating lower level layer facial movements to higher level moods and attitudes. (Yang et al., 1999) proposed a facial expression synthesis system, in which 34 facial expressions were generated by converting emotion into combination of upper, middle and lower expressions. The CharToon system (Hendrix & Ruttkay, 2000) generated kinds of facial expressions by interpolation between the 7 known expressions (neutral, sadness, happiness, anger, fear, disgust, and surprise) positioned on the emotion disc. (Bui et al., 2001) realized a fuzzy rule-based system, in which the animated agent's representations of 7 single expressions and blending expressions of 6 basic emotions were mapped onto muscle contraction values. Recently, (Ochs et al., 2005) introduced emotional intelligence into an animated character to express felt emotions and expressed emotions. These works have developed kinds of methods for emotional facial expression generation. However there are some limits in the above researches.

1. The first limit is that most works of facial expression generation are constrained in the 6 basic emotions. In another word, they are in the "Basic Emotion View". Although some works try to generate mixed facial expressions simply through blending basic expressions, these expressions do not often appear in our daily life and cannot be well related to distinct emotional categories. It is necessary for computer to display lifelike facial expressions of abundant emotions like human does.
2. The second limit is that most works of facial expression generation are merely related to emotions. Generally speaking, they are in the "Emotion View". However, emotion is not the only source of facial expressions, and some facial expression can signal much. For example, one may wink just because he is too tired or is to give a hint to someone. Lifelike facial expression generation should be more complicated to accommodate the complex environment in human computer interaction.
3. The third limit is that facial expression generation is mostly monotone, or in the "Invariable View". They usually correlate one model of facial expression to one emotion, and generate facial animation based on that. However, human tend to act more complicatedly to express one emotion. For example, human display kinds of facial expressions to express happiness, such as smile with mouth open or closed, symmetrically or asymmetrically, even with head wobbled.

Meeting the above limits, (Heylen, 2003) has deduced some guiding principles for building embodied conversational agents, such as the inclusion of more than 6 basic emotions, the voluntary control of emotional expressions, and the variation in expression. Although some works have also been done in the non-emotional expressions, such as gaze and eye-movements (Cassell et al., 1999; Colburn et al., 2000), there are few works to overcome all the limits in one work.

This chapter aims at generating humanoid and expressive facial expressions of agent to achieve harmonious and affective human computer interface. Based on the cues of sources and characteristics of facial expression, we propose a novel model of layered fuzzy facial expression generation, in which the social, emotional and physiological layers contribute to the facial expression generation and fuzzy theory helps to generate mutative and rich facial expressions.

This chapter is organized as follows. In section 2, the model of layered fuzzy facial expression generation (LFFEG) is proposed. In section 3, the layered fuzzy facial expression generation system (LFFEGS) is founded, and the modules for social, emotional and physiological expression generation are described in detail. In section 4, evaluation of the generated facial expressions is carried out to prove the validity of the LFFEG model. Subsequently, potential applications of the LFFEG are illustrated. In section 5, the conclusion and future research are given.

2. Model of layered fuzzy facial expression generation

This section proposes a novel model of layered fuzzy facial expression generation for humanoid and lifelike facial expression generation of agent. Firstly, theoretic reasons of the model are given, and then detailed explanation of the model is introduced.

2.1 Fuzzy facial expression

Fuzziness is the ubiquitous character of human mind and common objects. Human displays facial expressions fuzzily in daily life. As human face is extremely expressive (Christine & Diane, 2000; Terzopoulos & Waters, 1993), it is impossible to relate an expression to an exact emotion or intention, thus facial expressions are usually classified into different families, such as happiness, sadness, etc. For example, more than 60 kinds of facial expressions about anger have been found (Ekman, 1992), and each of the anger expressions shares certain configurational features to differ from the family of other expressions. However, some facial expressions can be recognized as in different families. (Russell, 1997) argued that facial expressions are ambiguous, and its meaning can depend on the context. For example, the "expression of fear" can be chosen as "anger" if a story about the expresser's context is told to the observer. Also, the observer's context such as the relativity of judgement and response format can influence the judgement of facial expression. So, human facial expression has the character of fuzziness. Some examples of facial expressions from Beihang University Facial Expression Database (Xue, Mao, et al., 2006) are illustrated in figure 1.

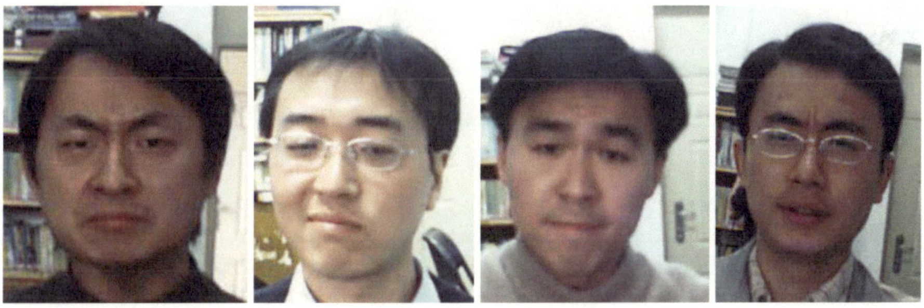

Figure 1. Examples of fuzzy facial expressions

The fuzzy theory arises from the incessant human request for better understanding of mental processes and cognition. (Zadeh, 1965) proposed the idea of "fuzzy set" from the observation that classes of objects usually have no well-defined boundary. Currently, fuzzy systems have been successfully employed in modeling of many real-life phenomena involving uncertainty. Facial expression generation can be well managed by fuzzy theory.

2.2 What influence facial expression

(Fasel & Luettin, 2003) have concluded that the sources of facial expressions include mental states (e.g. felt emotions, conviction and cogitation), verbal communication (e.g. illustrators, listener responses and regulators), non-verbal communication (e.g. unfelt emotions, emblems and social winks), and physiological activities (e.g. manipulators, pain and tiredness). Herein, we conclude the factors that influence facial expressions into social, emotional and physiological factors, together with expression personality, as seen in figure 2.

The terms of illustrators, regulators, emblems and manipulators are what (Ekman & Friesen, 1969) suggested facial paralanguage, as seen in table 1, where illustrators, regulators and emblems are social communication related, while manipulators are physiological activities related.

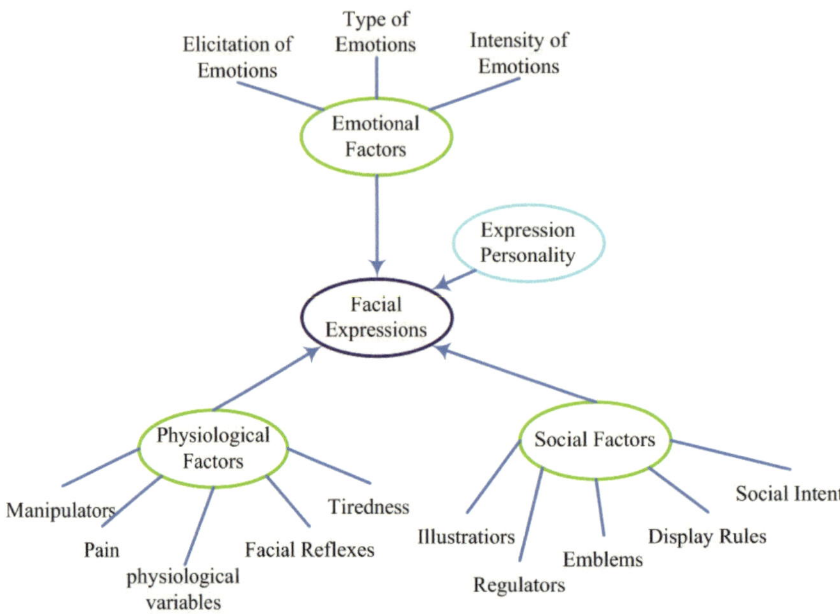

Figure 2. Factors that influence facial expressions

Facial Paralanguage	Short Description	Examples
illustrators	give vividness and energy to our spoken words	we raise our brows when we say beseechingly, "What do you want?" (Fridlund, 1994)
regulators	conversation requires regulation	with brow raises if we like what others are saying, with frowns and head shakes if we don't like it, with yawns if we find it tiresome (Rosenfeld, 1987)
emblems	symbolic gestures we enact with our faces	"facial shrug" which announces "I don't know" or "You've stumped me" (Ekman, 1985)
manipulators	self-manipulative facial actions	biting our lips, wiping our lips, running our tongues in the crevices between our teeth and cheeks, clamping and then widening our eyelids, working our jaws, and brushing our teeth (Ekman & Friesen, 1969)

Table 1. Explanation of facial paralanguage

Emotional factors are the most important factors for facial expression. In our daily life, we smile when we are happy, and cry when sad, so we call the facial expression that reflecting emotion the "emotional facial expression" or "facial expression of emotion". There are many factors that influence mapping emotional state to facial expression, such as the type and intensity of emotion, and how emotional state elicited (Picard, 1997).

Social factors include illustrators, regulators, emblems, social intent, and the "display rules" which designates attempts to manage involuntary expressions of emotion that include attenuating, amplifying, inhibiting or covering the involuntary expression with the sign of another emotion (Ekman & Friesen, 1969). Display rules specify not only what type of management is required, but when, in what social situation.

Physiological factors include manipulators, pain, tiredness, physiological variables, and "facial reflexes". Facial reflexes are considered innate and immutable, and characterized by few synapses in the human facial physiology (Fridlund, 1994). Sneezing to nasal membrane irritation, pupillary dilation to pain, jaw closure to tap, yawning and laughing are examples of facial reflexes (Fridlund, 1994; Provine & Hamernik, 1986).

Expression Personality describes the character of individual's facial expressions. For example, the speed, amount and duration of facial expression are different from individuals (Christine & Diane, 2000).

In summary, facial expressions are influenced by social, emotional, and physiological factors, and can vary with different expression personalities, thus these factors should be considered in the modeling of facial expression generation.

2.3 Facial expression generation via multiple mechanisms

In the book "Affective Computing" (Picard, 1997), emotion generation via multiple mechanisms was introduced, where human's emotion is generated not only by cognitive illation but also by low-level non-cognitive factors. An example is the three layered structure that includes reactive layer, deliberative layer and self-monitoring layer. In the structure, reactive layer is used to generate fast and first emotion; deliberative layer is related to second emotion generated by cognition; and the self-monitoring layer is the layer where self concept worked weightily.

Facial expression and emotion are alike in some aspects, such as the characteristics of innateness and sociality. (Darwin, 1872; Lorenz, 1965; Eibl-Eibesfeldt, 1972) argued that facial expressions are innate, evolved behaviour. (Klineberg, 1940; LaBarre, 1947; Birdwhistell, 1970) argued that facial expressions are socially learned, culturally controlled, and variable in meaning from one setting to another.

In the Emotion View, the well-known "two-factor" model emphasizes the influence of emotion and social conventions (Fridlund, 1991), where innate, prototype facial expressions namely "felt faces" are generated from emotional state, while learned, instrumental facial expressions namely "false faces" are modified by social conventions.

However, the Emotion View may fail to account for the poor relationship between emotions and facial displays (Fridlund, 1994). For example, the "cry" face is generally thought to be sadness. Nonetheless, we also cry when we are happy, angry, frightened, or relieved. The Behavioral Ecology View suggests the function of the cry-face display is to signal readiness to receive attention or succour, regardless of one's emotional status.

The Emotion View and Behavioral Ecology View can be regarded as the two mechanisms for facial expression generation. With both mechanisms, facial expression generation can be better explained than with any single mechanism. Nevertheless, the physiological aspect in facial expression generation can not be ignored.

As human's facial expression is innate and social, influenced by physiological, emotional and social factors, a layered structure for facial expression generation via mechanisms of low level of physiological factors, middle level of emotional factors, and high level of social factors is proposed. A comparison of the two-factor model and the layered model for facial expression generation is seen in figure 3.

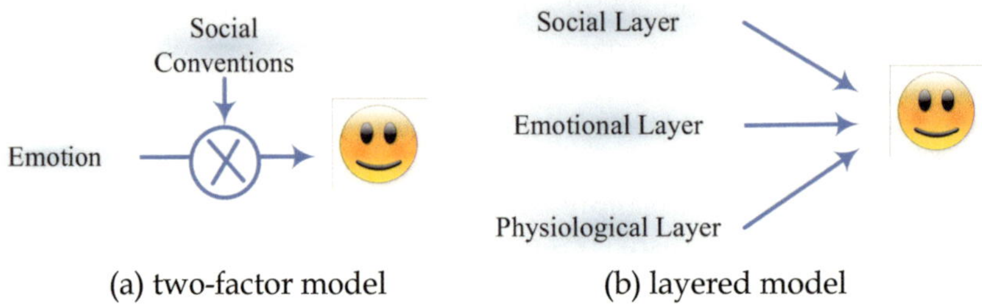

Figure 3. Two-factor model and layered model for facial expression generation

2.4 Layered fuzzy facial expression generation

Based on the fuzzy character of facial expression, kinds of factors that influence facial expression and the elicitation of generation via multiple mechanisms, the model of layered fuzzy facial expression generation is proposed (Xue, Mao, et al., 2007). As seen in figure 4, the physiological layer at low level, emotional layer at middle level and social layer at high level determine the fuzzy facial expression generation.

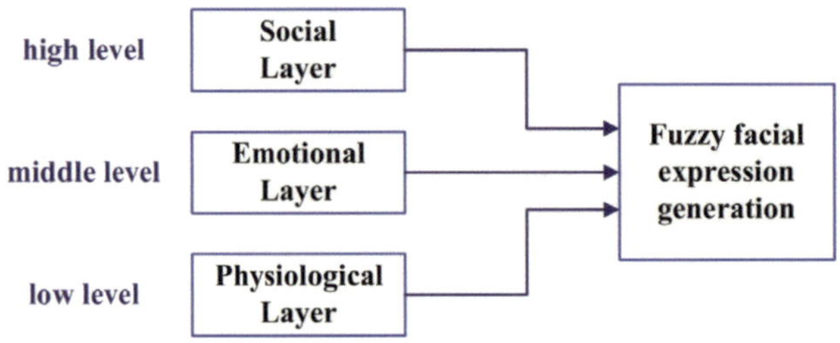

Figure 4. Model of layered fuzzy facial expression generation

The physiological layer includes physiological variables which influence human's emotion and expression. (Picard, 1997) recognized that hunger or pain can influence the activation of emotional states. For example, hunger can increase irritability, and pain can spur anger. Also, changes in brain blood temperature along with other physiological changes may lead to the feeling of excitation or depressed (Christine & Diane, 2000). In the LFFEG model, the physiological variables influence the emotional expressions or lead to physiological expressions such as grimace of pain; the physiological expressions such as facial reflexes can also be directly specified.

The emotional layer includes multiple emotions based on the OCC model (Ortony et al., 1988). As the 22 emotion types in OCC model are well accepted in the research of affective computing, it is reasonable to research the facial expressions to display the emotions. In the LFFEG model, multiple facial expressions can be fuzzily generated according to the emotions. For example, kinds of smile facial expressions can be elicited by the emotions such as joy, appreciation, gloating, satisfaction and happy-for, fuzzily controlled by the factors such as the intensity of the emotion, the type of the emotion and the expression personality.

The social layer includes social intent and display rules. When, where and how to express facial expressions is restricted by the social rules. A felt emotion may be masked by a fake emotion due to some display rules. In the LFFEG model, the social expressions generated by social rules can override the affect of the emotional layer. For example, whatever a waiter felt, he should show a smile of politeness to the customer.

The module of **fuzzy facial expression generation** maps one emotion type to different modes of facial expressions and realizes fuzzy intensity control through fuzzy theory, making facial expressions smart and expressive.

In the LFFEG model, **social expression, emotional expression** and **physiological expression** are generated from the social layer, emotional layer and physiological layer respectively, their relation is shown in figure 5. Social expressions are the facial expressions such as smile of politeness, social wink and social plea regardless of the emotion behind. Emotional expressions are the facial expressions elicited by kinds of emotions such as happiness, sadness and so on. Physiological expressions are the facial expressions elicited by physiological activities, alike facial reflexes, including quick expressions such as startle, horror and other expressions such as frown, blink and gape.

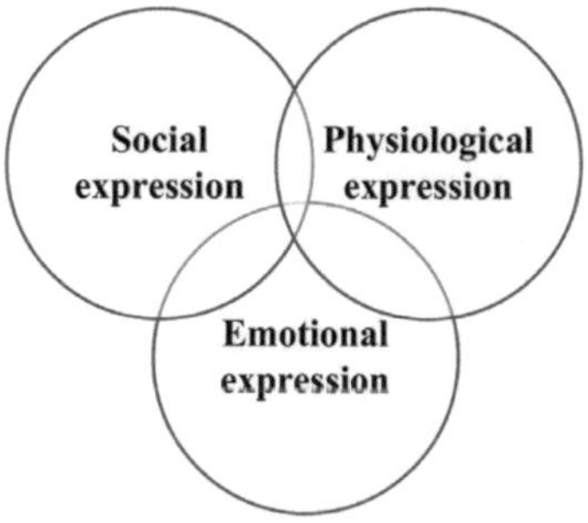

Figure 5. The relation of social, emotional and physiological expression

3. The layered fuzzy facial expression generation system

Based on the model of layered fuzzy facial expression generation, this section sets up a layered fuzzy facial expression generation system. Firstly, we give an overview of the system, and then the realization of each part is explained in detail.

3.1 System overview

The overview of the layered fuzzy facial expression generation system (LFFEGS) is shown in figure 6. The social layer, emotional layer and physiological layer have respective priority, denoting the weight of the layer at a time. The module of fuzzy facial expression generation processes the output of the three layers, giving the final facial expression. Social expression is determined by the parse module from the social layer. Emotional expression is determined by the fuzzy control function block from the emotional layer. Physiological expression is determined by the parse module from the physiological layer. According to the priorities of the three layers, final expression is determined from the social expression, emotional expression and physiological expression through the module of MUX.

The inputs of the facial expression generation are defined as followed:

1. Time: t;

2. Social layer parameters: $S(t)=\{S_P(t),S_E(t),S_R(t)\}$ is the interface of the social layer, where S_P: Priority, S_E: Social expressions, S_R:Social rules;

3. Emotional layer parameters: $E(t)=\{E_P(t),E_S(t),E_M(t),E_P(t)\}$ is the interface of the emotional layer, where E_P: Priority, E_S: Specific emotions, E_M: Mood, E_P: Expression personality;

4. Physiological layer parameters: $P(t)=\{P_P(t),P_E(t),P_V(t)\}$ is the interface of the physiological layer, where P_P: Priority, P_E: Physiological expressions, P_V: Physiological variables.

Consequently, the layered fuzzy facial expression generation function is:

$$F(t)=F(S(t),E(t),P(t)),\ \text{where } F(t) \text{ is the fuzzy function.}$$

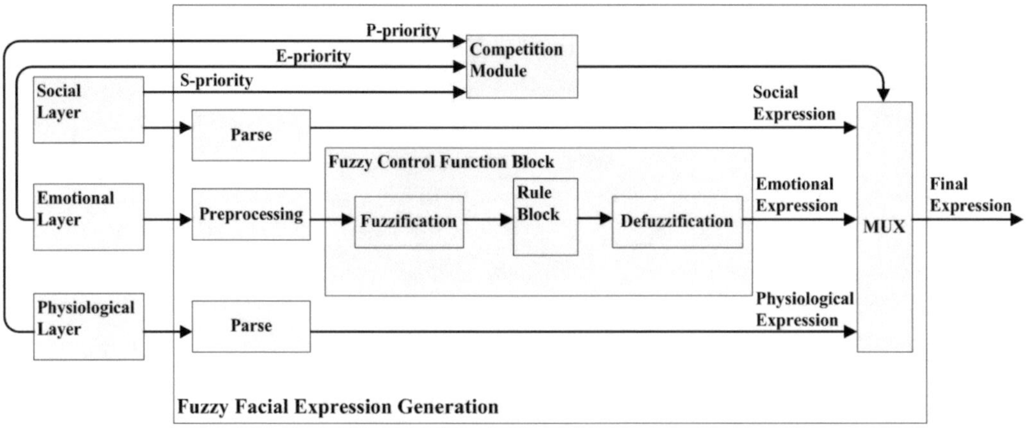

Figure 6. Overview of the Layered Fuzzy Facial Expression Generation System

3.2 The lingual realization of the LFFEGS

The LFFEGS is realized based on extensible markup language (XML), which provides an easy way to control the agent's behavior. Previous efforts in the XML-based languages are Human Markup Language (HML), Multimodal Presentation Markup Language (MPML) (Prendinger et al., 2004a), Synchronized Multichannel Integration Language (SMIL) (Not et al., 2005), etc. In this chapter, the Layered Fuzzy Facial Expression Generation Language (LFFEGL) is developed to realize the LFFEG model.

In the LFFEGL script, the tags of "social", "emotional" and "physiological" relate to the social layer, emotional layer and physiological layer respectively, as seen in figure 7. The attribute "priority" gives the weight of the layers.

```
<seq>
  <Social priority="0.7" positive_threshold="0.4" negative_threshold="0.3">
        <Smile intensity="0.5"/>
  </Social>
  <Emotional priority="0.5" mood="positive" positive_weight="1">
        <Joy intensity="0.5"/>
  </Emotional>
  <Physiological priority="0.9">
        <Pain intensity="1"/>
  </Physiological>
</seq>
```

Figure 7. Sample of LFFEGL Script

Possible parameters of the LFFEGL are shown in figure 8, where 6 social expressions are provided in the social layer, 26 emotions are provided in the emotional layer and 14 physiological variables are provided in the physiological layer. Note that the parameters can be easily extended according to the requirement.

```
<!-- specification of possible social expressions -->

<!ENTITY %Social
"(normal | smile | plea | agreement | disagreement | wink) ">

<!-- specification of possible emotions -->

<!ENTITY %Emotional
"(happyfor | pity | resentment | gloating | joy |distress | hope | fear | satisfaction |
  fearsconfirmed | relief | disappointed | pride | selfreproach | appreciation |
  reproach | gratitude | anger | gratification | remorse | liking | disliking | surprise |
  disgust | sadness | sorryfor) ">

<!-- specification of possible physiological variables -->

<!ENTITY %Physiological
"(adrenaline | bloodpressure | bloodsugar | dopamine | endorphine | energy | heartrate |
  respirationrate | temperature | vascularvolume | pain | tiredness | sneeze | yawning) ">
```

Figure 8. Specification of the Parameters in LFFEGL

(Ortony, Clore & Collins, 1988) suggested that the research for and postulation of basic emotions is not a profitable approach, as there are significant individual and cultural differences in the experience of emotions. Hence, according to the description of tokens of emotion types in (Ortony, Clore & Collins, 1988), numerous emotion words related to each of the 26 emotion types are accepted in the LFFEGL, as seen in table 2.

3.3 Facial expressions related to emotional layer

Based on the modules of fuzzy emotion-expression mapping, the novel arousal-valence-expressiveness emotion space, expression personality, and facial expression generation model, the fuzzy emotional facial expression generation subsystem is developed to generate lifelike emotional facial expressions, as seen in figure 9.

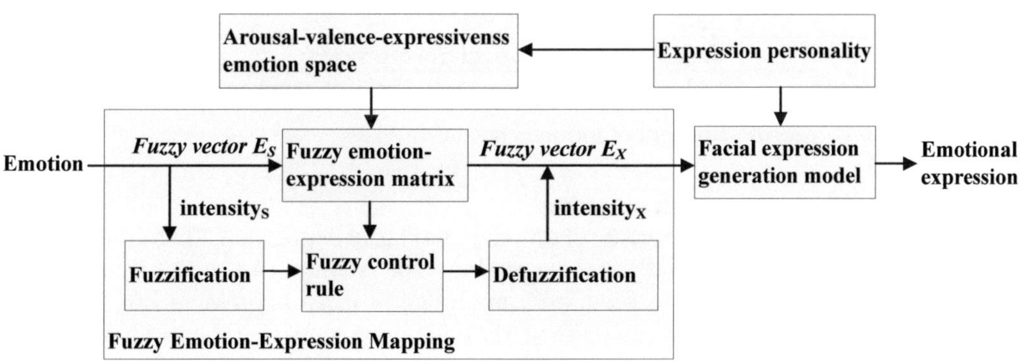

Figure 9. Overview of the fuzzy emotional facial expression generation system

Emotion type	Emotion words
Joy	contented, cheerful, delighted, ecstatic, elated, glad, happy, joyful, jubilant, pleased
Distress	depressed, distressed, displeased, dissatisfied, distraught, grief, miserable, sad, shock, uneasy, unhappy, upset
Happy-for	delighted-for, happy-for, pleased-for
Sorry-for	compassion, pity, sorry-for, sympathy
Resentment	envy, jealousy, resentment
Gloating	gloating, schadenfreude
Hope	anticipation, anticipatory excitement, expectancy, hope, hopeful, looking forward to
Fear	apprehensive, anxious, cowering, fear, fright, nervous, petrified, scared, terrified, timid, worried
Satisfaction	gratification, hopes-realized, satisfaction
Fears-confirmed	fears-confirmed
Relief	relief
Disappointment	despair, disappointment, frustration, heartbroken
Pride	pride
Self-reproach	embarrassment, guilty, mortified, self-blame, self-reproach, shame, uncomfortable, uneasy
Appreciation	admiration, appreciation, awe, esteem, respect
Reproach	appalled, contempt, despise, disdain, indignation, reproach
Gratitude	appreciation, gratitude, thankful
Anger	anger, annoyance, exasperation, fury, incensed, indignation, irritation, livid, offended, outrage, rage
Gratification	gratification, satisfaction, smug
Remorse	penitent, remorse
Liking	adore, affection, like, love
Disliking	aversion, detest, disgust, dislike, hate, loathe
Pity	pity, compassion, commiseration, sympathy, condolence, empathy
Surprise	surprise, astonish, amaze, astound, dumbfound, flabbergast
Disgust	disgust, nauseate, repel, revolt, sicken
Sadness	sad, melancholy, sorrowful, doleful, woebegone, desolate

Table 2. Emotion words of different emotion types

3.3.1 Fuzzy emotion-expression mapping

Fuzziness is one common characteristic of emotion and facial expression. There is also fuzzy relationship between emotion and facial expression. One emotion can be fuzzily expressed by multiple modes of facial expression, and one mode of facial expression can be fuzzily recognized as multiple emotions. (Baldwin at al., 1998) have suggested the mechanisms of a mapping of many expressions to a few emotions, a given expression mapped to more than one emotional state, and a mapping from one expression to different emotional states. Here, we give the model of fuzzy emotion-expression mapping.

The mapping of emotion to expression is many-to-many. Firstly, one emotion can be mapped to many facial expressions. For example, the fuzzy emotional facial expression of happy-for can be expressed as formula (1). Secondly, a predefined facial expression can express many emotions. For example, the emotions of joy and happy-for can be expressed as the facial expression of "SmileOpen" with different intensities.

$$E_{\text{happyfor}} = \begin{cases} a, SmileClosed \\ b, SmileOpen \\ \cdots \end{cases} \quad a, b, \cdots \in (0,1] \tag{1}$$

Where a, b are respectively the probabilities that happy-for is mapped to the facial expression of "SmileClosed" or "SmileOpen".

Fuzzy Emotion-Expression Matrix

Based on the correlation of multiple facial expressions of emotions, fuzzy emotion-expression mapping is proposed, in which emotion and facial expression are supposed to be fuzzy vectors, and a fuzzy relation matrix consisting of degrees of membership maps the fuzzy emotion vector to the fuzzy facial expression vector.

Define the emotion space as $X = \{x_1, x_2, \cdots, x_m\}$, where x_i is any emotion, such as surprise, disgust. Define the facial expression space as $Y = \{y_1, y_2, \cdots, y_n\}$, where y_i indicates any mode of facial expression.

The fuzzy relation $\widetilde{R}$ from the emotion space X to the facial expression space Y is shown in formula (2):

$$R = (r_{ij})_{m \times n} \tag{2}$$

where $r_{ij} = \widetilde{R}(x_i, y_j) \in [0,1]$ indicates the correlation degree of (x_i, y_i) to $\widetilde{R}$.

Some key frames of facial expressions with their memberships are shown in table 3. The memberships compose a sparse matrix R.

Emotion	Facial expression membership					
	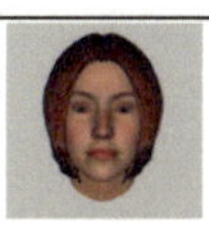 y_1	 y_2	 y_3	 y_4	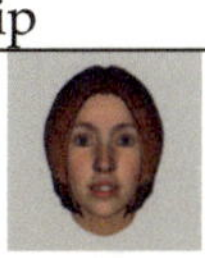 y_5	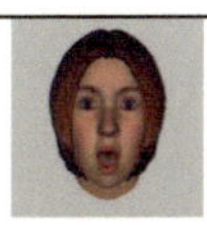 y_6
Disliking (x_1)	0.6	0.8	1.0	1.0	0	0
Disgust (x_2)	0.3	0.5	1.0	1.0	0	0
Sadness (x_3)	0.4	0.7	0	0	0	0
Surprise (x_4)	0	0	0	0	0.9	1.0

Table 3. Membership of some facial expressions

Given the input emotional fuzzy vector E_S, the fuzzy facial vector E_X can be obtained via fuzzy mapping, as seen in formula (3).

$$E_X = E_s \circ R = (ex_1, ex_2, \cdots, ex_n) \quad (3)$$

where ex_i is the membership of the mode of facial expression y_i to the fuzzy facial expression $\widetilde{E}_X$, $\circ$ means the compositional operation of the fuzzy relations.

Once the fuzzy facial expression $\widetilde{E}_X$ is determined, its intensity will also be computed. The intensity of selected emotion x_i is fuzzified to the linguistic value, which is then mapped to the linguistic value of related facial expressions according to fuzzy control rule. The intensity of facial expression y_i is obtained by defuzzifying its linguistic value.

Emotion-Expression Intensity Mapping

Intensity control of predefined facial expression has been realized in (Not et al., 2005), however, the intensity of facial expression is not mapped directly to the intensity of the emotion. As seen in figure 10(a), the largest intensity of facial expression of "SmileClosed" may be not enough to express the largest intensity of happy-for. As seen in figure 10(b), moderate intensity of facial expression of "Disgust" may be enough to express the largest intensity of disliking.

If the emotion comes on slowly, or is less expressive, or is rather weak, the impulse might not be enough to trigger the expression, so sometimes there will be emotion without expression. Figure 10(c) shows that low intensity of love may not trigger expression, unless it achieves a certain level, the expression of SmileClosed plus Gaze appears. Similar in figure 10(d) that certain degree of hate may reveal low level of Disliking expression.

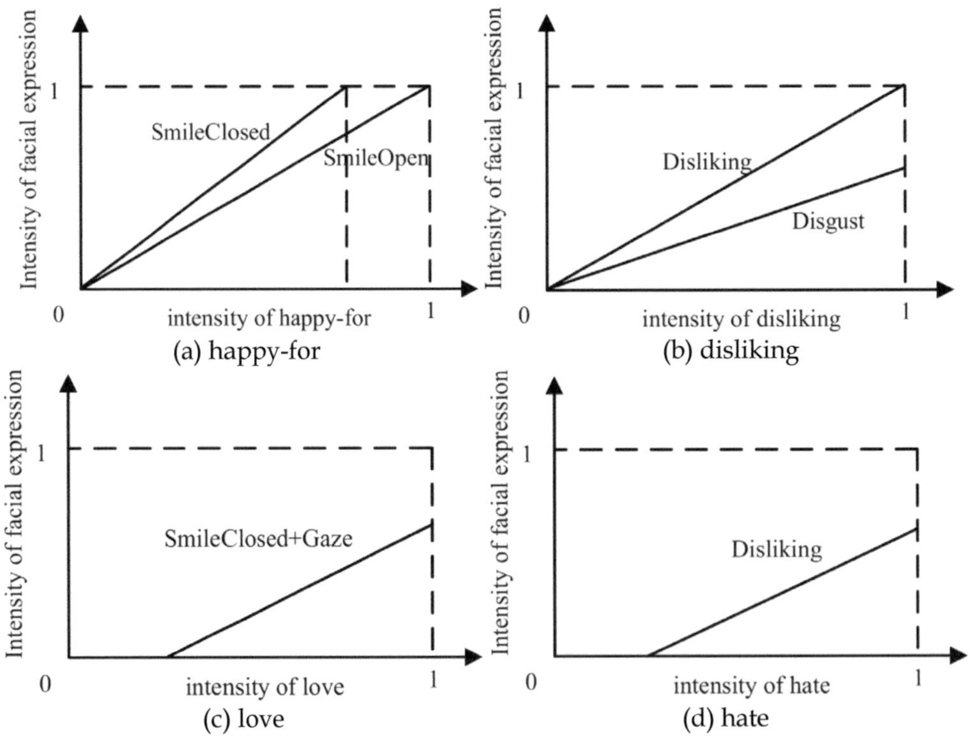

Figure 10. Mapping of intensity of emotions to intensity of facial expressions

Fuzzification of Emotion and Facial Expression

The emotion intensity and facial expression intensity also have fuzzy characteristics. The fuzzy linguistic values of emotion and facial expression are listed as very low, low, middle, high and very high, as seen in figure 11.

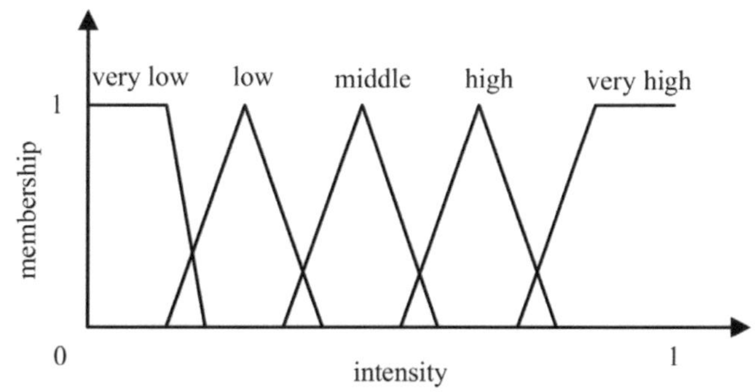

Figure 11. Memberships of linguistic values of emotion and facial expression

Fuzzy Control Rule

According to the emotion-expression intensity mapping, the mapping from linguistic value of emotion intensity to linguistic value of facial expression intensity was realized through fuzzy control. An example of fuzzy control rule is shown in table 4. Where emotion x_4 (surprise) can be fuzzily expressed by facial expression y_5 or y_6. The very low intensity of x_4 can be expressed by small intensity of y_5 or very small intensity of y_6.

Emotion x_4 (surprise)	Facial expression y_5	Facial expression y_6
Very low	small	Very small
low	middle	small
middle	large	middle
high	Very large	large
Very high	– –	Very large

Table 4. Fuzzy control rule for emotion-expression intensity mapping

3.3.2 The novel emotion space of arousal-valence-expressiveness

Given the emotion space X and the facial expression space Y, the fuzzy emotion-expression matrix R can be determined based on the novel arousal-valence-expressiveness emotion space. The expression personality has the function as scaling factor to the arousal-valence-expressiveness emotion space.

Expressive Difference of Emotions

Psychologists have acknowledged the sex differences in emotional expressiveness (Tucker & Friedman, 1993). For example, most studies find that women better convey emotions than men, though not in most cases and situations (Buck et al., 1974; Hall, 1984).

Besides the sex difference of emotional expressions, there are also expressive differences between different emotions. To look into the relation between emotion and facial expression, a questionnaire about how hard or easy to express an emotion through facial expression and recognize an emotion from facial expression was put to subjects. 51 subjects gave their answers in ratings of very hard (1), hard (2), middle (3), easy (4), and very easy (5) on 23 emotions.

The result of the investigation is shown in figure 12. The line of how hard or easy to express emotion through facial expression is approximate to the line of how hard or easy to recognize emotion from facial expression. It demonstrates that some emotions such as happy-for, joy and anger are easy to express and be recognized, while some emotions such as jealousness, resentment and love are hard to express and be recognized. It is obvious that expressive differences of emotions exist on human face.

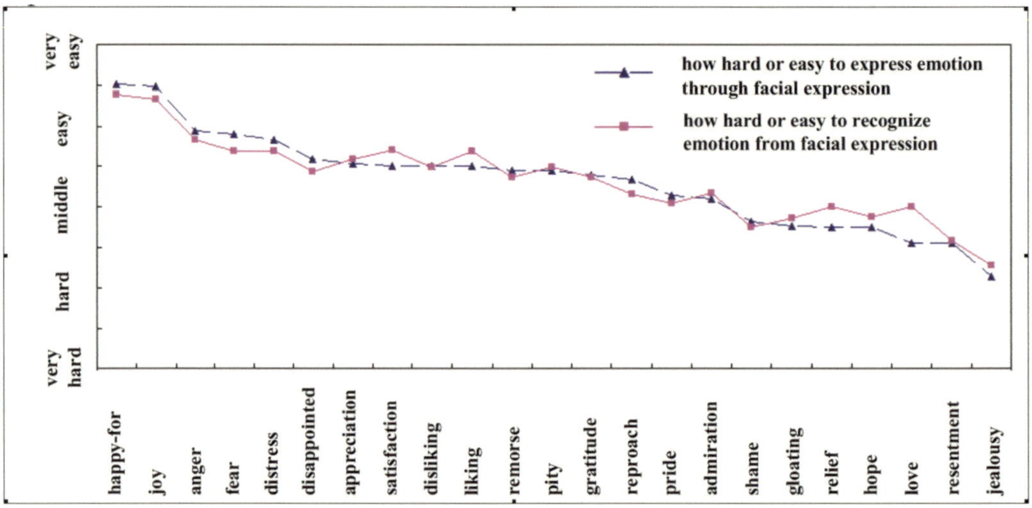

Figure 12. Mean value of how hard or easy to express or recognize emotion through facial expression

As to the expressive differences of emotions, it is further inferred that the emotions quickly aroused are easy to be expressed and recognized, or more expressive, while the emotions in a long term are hard to be expressed and recognized, or less expressive. For those categories of human emotional phenomena: specific emotions, moods and emotional dispositions (Sarmento, 2004), their expressiveness come down gradually.

Expressive differences exist not only in different emotions, but also in different persons. For example, one person may open his eyes and mouth widely and furrows deeply when he is in great anger, while another person just furrows with the same degree of anger. If you are not familiar with one's expression personality, you can not recognize his emotion from his facial expression exactly.

The Novel Arousal-Valence-Expressiveness Emotion Space

Kinds of emotion models have been proposed for affective reasoning, such as the arousal-valence emotional plane (Lang, 1995) and the PAD model (Mehrabian, 1996). In the arousal-valence emotional plane, valence denotes if the emotion is positive or negative, and arousal denotes the intensity of the emotion. In the PAD Emotional State Model, three nearly independent dimensions are used to describe and measure emotional states: pleasure vs. displeasure, arousal vs. nonarousal, and dominance vs. submissiveness. Pleasure-displeasure distinguishes the positive-negative affective quality of emotional states, arousal-nonarousal refers to a combination of physical activity and mental alertness, and dominance-submissiveness is defined in terms of control versus lack of control.

According to the different expressiveness of various emotions, a dimension of expressiveness is added to the arousal-valence emotion plane to compose a novel three-dimensional emotion space, which can be useful to found the relation between emotion and facial expression.

The dimensions of arousal and valence are necessary to the emotion-expression mapping, and the dimension of expressiveness is useful to map emotion intensity to facial expression intensity. For example, emotion with low expressiveness is mapped to the facial expression with low intensity, such as sadness, hate and love; emotion with high expressiveness is mapped to the facial expression with high intensity, such as fury and surprise. Thus, the new emotion space is called arousal-valence-expressiveness emotion space, as seen in figure 13. Expression personality can be reflected by the expressiveness distribution of emotions.

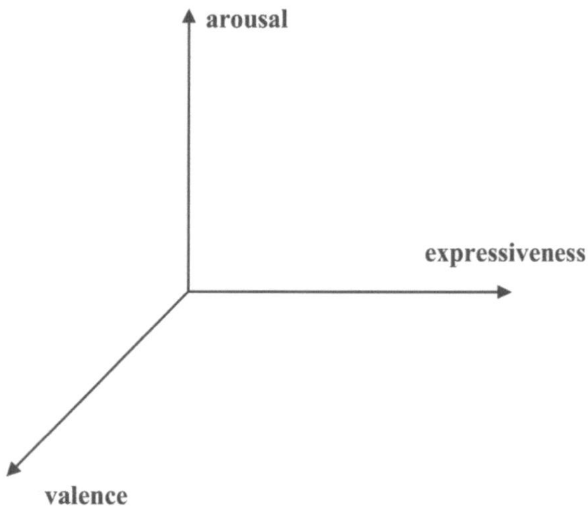

Figure 13. Arousal-valence-expressiveness emotion space

3.3.3 Expression personality

Facial expressiveness, like other forms of sentic modulation, is influenced by a person's innate physiology, which is related to temperament. Affected by the personality, different person with the same intensity of emotion may express facial expressions with different intensities. For example, inhibited ones have lower overall facial expressiveness than uninhibited ones.

To realize the personality in facial expression, (Miwa et al., 2001) introduced the module of Expression Personality in the signal processing structure of the robot, which is defined as a matrix of expression personality, weighting 7 emotions. Here, as there are more emotion types in this system, the intensity of the emotional expression is gained by weighting the positive emotion or negative emotion with the attribute of "positive_weight" or "negative_weight"; furthermore, even the weight of specific emotion such as "happyfor_weight" can be given. Thus the expression personality is realized.

Also, the fuzzy emotion-expression matrix can be variable according to different expression personalities or different expressiveness distribution of emotions, thus the output emotional expression can be different with the same input emotion.

3.3.4 Facial expression generation model

The facial expression generation model is the module that accepts input of the fuzzy facial expression $\widetilde{E}_X$ with its intensity and output the agent's facial expression animation. The facial expression generation model can also be regulated by expression personality. For example, different agents with the same emotion may exhibit very different facial actions, expression intensities and durations. Even the same agent's facial expressions can be modified by the user.

3.4 Facial expressions related to social layer

Until the late 1970s, there were few studies on facial displays in social settings (Chovil, 1997). Facial displays appear to be sensitive to the sociality of the situation. For example, smiles may occur more frequently when individuals are in social contact with others than when they are not facing or interacting with others. (Buck, 1991) argued that social factors can facilitate or inhibit facial expression depending upon the nature of emotion being expressed and the expresser's personal relationship with the other. (Fridlund, 1994) contended that facial expressions are inherently social. For example, even when someone is alone he is holding an internal dialogue with another person, or imaging himself in a social situation. The social communicative approach has provided an alternative to the emotional expression approach for understanding and studying facial displays.

(Matsumoto, 1990) has measured display rules by requesting subjects to judge the appropriateness of displaying emotions in different situations. When viewing the photo of each emotion, subjects were asked to rate how appropriate it was for them to express that emotion in eight social situations: alone, in public, with close friends, with family members, with casual acquaintances, with people of higher status, with people of lower status, and with children.

```
<Social priority="0.7" positive_threshold="0.4" negative_threshold="0.3">
</Social>
```

(a) social rules for both positive and negative emotions specified

```
<Social priority="0.7" >
        <Smile intensity="0.5"/>
</Social>
```

(b) social expression "Smile" specified

```
<Social priority="0.7" situation="alone">
</Social>
```

(c) predefined situation specified

Figure 14. Examples of LFFEGL scripts with tag "social"

In the LFFEGS, if the layer of social rules has higher priority than layer of emotional model, the attributes "positive_threshold" and "negative_threshold" will restrict the largest intensities of the positive facial expressions and negative facial expressions respectively, acting as inhibiting facial expression, as seen in figure 14(a). The element such as "smile" or "agreement" specifies social expression to take the place of emotional expression, sometimes operates as facilitating facial expression, as seen in figure 14(b). Social rules can be predefined in a specific situation to adjust the expression of the agent. For example, figure 14(c) gives the situation of "alone" to specify the social rules related to that situation instead of the ways of "positive_threshold" or specified social expression "smile".

3.5 Facial expressions related to physiological layer

Kinds of facial expressions may occur when physiological state changes. For example, characteristics of facial expressions that occur most frequently in the headache state include furrowed eyebrows, closed eyes, slow eye blinks, lip pursuing, facial grimacing, and flat facial affect (Anthony et al., 1991).

(Ekman, 1984) studied how a reflex differs from an emotion. For example, startle is considered a reflex, as it is very easy to elicit and cognition does not play a causal role in eliciting it. Although startle resembles surprise in some respect, it has much briefer latency than surprise.

The bodily reactions associated with emotions have been researched in psychophysiology and psychobiology. Many bodily or physiological responses may co-occur with an emotion or rapidly follows it. For example, essential hypertension is thought to be primarily due to chronic states of tension, stress, and anxiety (Grings & Dawson, 1978). Physiological responses such as sweaty palms and rapid heart beat inform our brain that we are aroused, and then the brain must appraise the situation we are in before it can label the state with an emotion such as fear or love (Schachter, 1964). So, it is inferred that facial expression of emotion with different physiological states may be different, thus physiological states may influence the facial expressions of emotions.

In the layer of physiological layer, the physiological variables are chosen based on (Grings & Dawson, 1978; Fridlund, 1994; Canamero, 1997). The physiological variables are adrenaline, blood pressure, blood sugar, dopamine, endorphine, energy, heart rate, respiration rate, temperature, vascular volume, pain, tiredness, sneeze and yawning, which may influence the emotional expressions or lead to physiological expressions. For example, high levels of endorphines can increase the expressiveness of positive emotions or decrease the expressiveness of negative emotions, or trigger a state of happiness. Some examples of LFFEGL scripts with tag "physiological" are shown in figure 15.

```
<Physiological priority="0.9">
        <Tiredness intensity="1"/>
</Physiological>
```

(a) physiological expression specified

```
<Physiological priority="0.9">
        <Endorphines intensity="high"/>
</Physiological>
```

(b) linguistic value for intensity description available

```
<Physiological priority="0.9">
        <Temperature intensity="0.3"/>
</Physiological>
```

(c) real value for intensity description available

Figure 15. Examples of LFFEGL scripts with tag "physiological"

3.6 Facial expression generation strategy

In the LFFEGS, facial expression is generated according to the priorities of different layers. The flow chart of the facial expression generation strategy is shown in figure 16. As seen in the figure, after the priority comparison in the competition module, the layers are arranged as layer 1, layer 2, and layer 3 with degressive priorities. If expression is generated in one layer, it will be modified considering the influence of the layer with higher priority, otherwise the next layer will be examined.

For example, in the LFFEGL script in figure 7, the physiological layer is first checked, as pain is specified, the expression "pain" will be generated with its intensity "very high". If the physiological priority changes to "0.3", the social layer will be first checked, and expression "smile" will be generated with its intensity "middle".

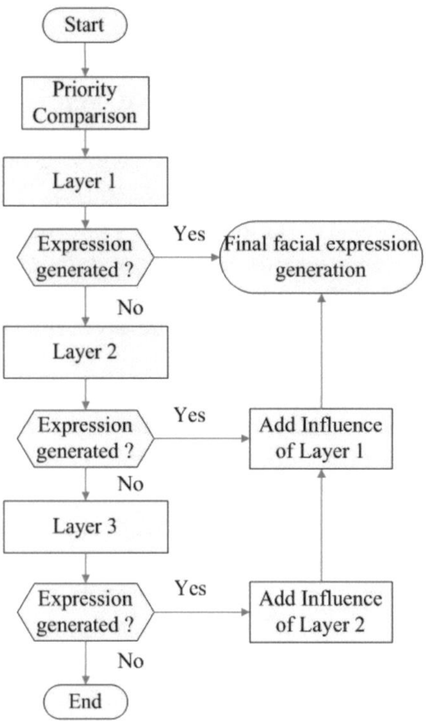

Figure 16. Facial expression generation strategy

4. Evaluation of the LFFEGS

To evaluate the LFFEGS, lively facial expression animations of the character should be presented to the subjects. Xface toolkit (Not et al., 2005) was utilized to generate keyframes of facial expressions to display kinds of emotions. The interface of the LFFEGS is shown in figure 17. The list of key frames of facial expressions can be seen in the top left of the interface, and the work space of the LFFEGL is positioned in the bottom left. Fuzzy facial expression animation can be generated through LFFEGL script, as seen in the right region of the interface. Some keyframes of facial expressions such as disgust, surprise, disliking, pain and tiredness are shown in figure 18.

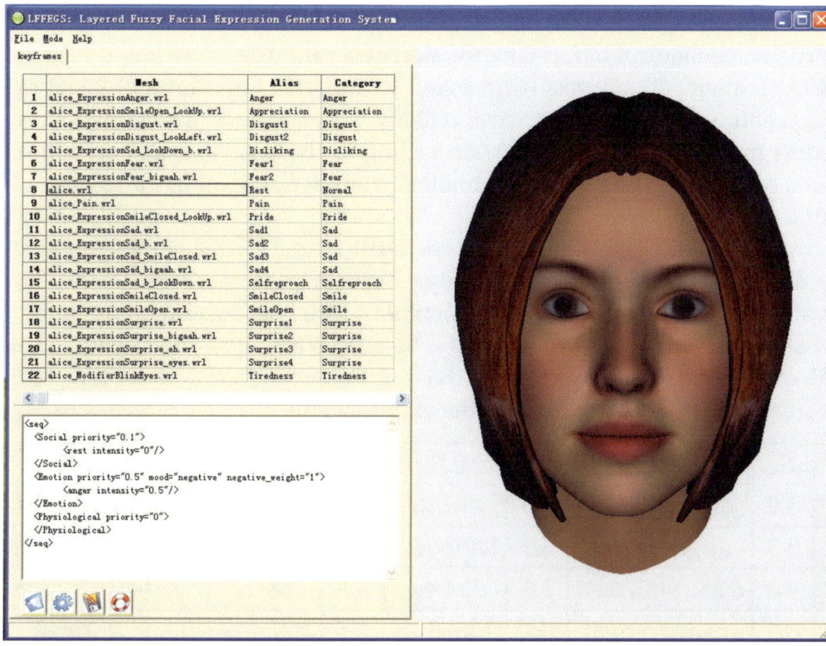

Figure 17. Interface of the LFFEGS

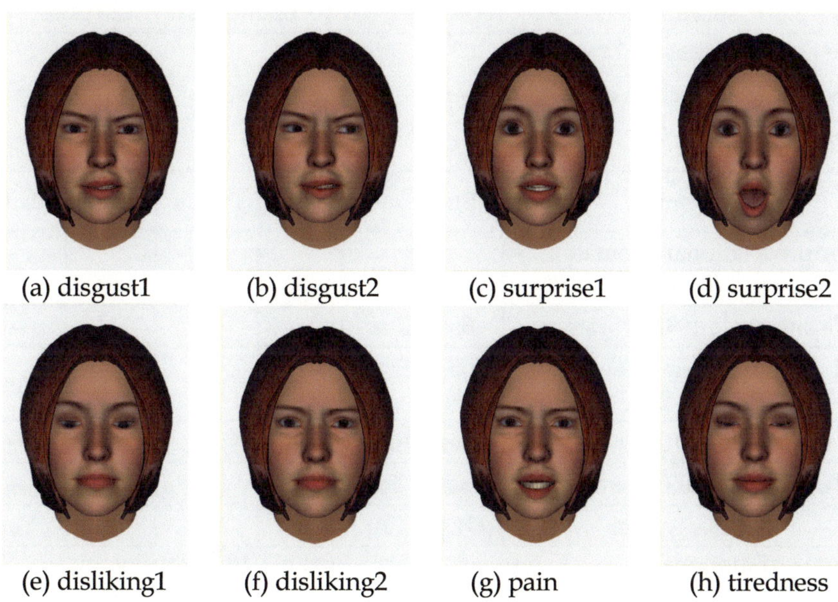

Figure 18. Some keyframes of facial expressions

Experiment 1

Although there are thousands of facial expressions, it is unnecessary for agent to present so many facial expressions as even human cannot distinguish them clearly. The important thing is to let user understand the agent's emotions and intentions. Dozens of prototype

facial expressions are competent to cover facial expression types defined in the system with the help of fuzzy mechanism of facial expression generation.
In the first experiment, 10 subjects were asked to judge 21 keyframes of facial expressions, giving what emotions each facial expression likely to present and the corresponding score of expressiveness from 1 (low) to 5 (high). According to the results, each emotion was related to some facial expressions and fuzzy parameters were determined in the LFFEGS.

Experiment 2

In the following experiment, 30 scripts were written in LFFEGL to generate fuzzy facial expression animations with middle intensity. 20 subjects were asked to run each script 5 times to evaluate the effect of the fuzzily generated facial expression animations, giving the score of satisfaction from 1 (low) to 5 (high). The results are showed in table 5, denoting that most facial expressions acted well. For those facial expressions with low scores, better keyframes should be taken to strengthen the expressiveness.

F.E.	S.	F.E.	S.	F.E.	S.	F.E.	S.	F.E.	S.
anger	3.9	disappointed	2.8	gratitude	2.9	sadness	3	agreement	4.8
fear	3.5	appreciation	3.3	happyfor	4.0	sorryfor	2.8	resentment	4.1
joy	4.0	fearsconfirmed	3.4	distress	3.3	relief	3	satisfaction	3.7
pity	3.2	disagreement	3.7	gloating	3.5	remorse	3.1	disgust	4.8
pride	4.2	gratification	3.7	disliking	3.2	liking	3.5	tiredness	4.0
hope	2.8	selfreproach	2.5	reproach	3.4	pain	4.6	surprise	4.3

Note: F.E.=facial expression, S.=score

Table 5. Score of satisfaction of fuzzily generated facial expressions

Comparison

Systems	Em. View	F.Ex	Ph.Ex.	S.Ex.	Ex.P.
Improvisational Animation system (Perlin, 1997)	others	–	Yes	–	–
(Yang et al., 1999)'s system	Basic Em.	–	–	–	–
CharToon system (Hendrix & Ruttkay, 2000)	Basic Em. +others	–	–	–	Yes
(Bui et al., 2001)'s system	Basic Em.	Yes	–	–	–
(Ochs et al., 2005)'s system	OCC's Em.	Yes	–	Yes	–
LFFEG system	OCC's Em.	Yes	Yes	Yes	Yes

Note: Em. =Emotional, Ex.=Expression, F.= Fuzzy, Ph.=Physiological, S.=Social, P.=Personality

Table 6. Comparison of facial expression generation systems

A comparison of facial expression generation systems was given in the items of Emotion View, Fuzzy Expression, Physiological Expression, Social Expression and Expression Personality, as seen in table 6. In the LFFEG system, facial expressions fuzzily generated by the social, emotional and physiological layers in different levels are richer and more reasonable, tally well with the character of human.

Potential Applications

The LFFEG can help improving the intelligence of facial expression generation and will be useful in kinds of applications such as lifelike characters and robots.

Lifelike characters are one of the most exciting technologies for human computer interface applications (Prendinger & ishizuka, 2004b). Animating the visual appearance of life-like characters and integrating them into an application environment involves a large number of complex and highly inter-related tasks. The expression of personality and affective state by means of body movement, facial displays, and speech can easily be realized by emotional layer. The coordination of the bodily behaviour of multiple characters should be instructed by social rules. The characters also need to show their bodily state such as sleepy to coordinate the communication.

The humanoid shape has evolved over eons of interaction with the world to cope efficiently and effectively with it. So, (Norman, 2003) suggested that where the demands upon a robot are similar to those upon people, having a similar shape might be sensible. Thus, robot should display facial expression like human does to achieve similar intelligence. Recent research demonstrates that robot need emotion. Accompany with emotion, social intent and rules are necessary to instruct the robot to display appropriate expressions. As robot has its own body, if it is damaged somewhere, it can show facial expression such as pain to inform people that there is something wrong with it.

5. Conclusion

In this chapter, we proposed a novel model of layered fuzzy facial expression generation and developed the corresponding facial expression generation system. In the LFFEG model, the affects of the social, emotional and physiological factors are considered in different layers, and facial expressions are fuzzily generated. In the LFFEG system, the LFFEG language provides an easy way for facial expression generation, and the fuzzy emotion-expression mapping and the novel arousal-valence-expressiveness emotion space help realize the fuzzy facial expression with personality.

There are three primary novelties in our work: layered, fuzzy, and expression personality. Firstly, the factors that affect facial expression generation are considered in different layers, not only emotion but also social and physiological factors. Secondly, fuzzy facial expressions are realized to display multiple emotions, making the expression of the agent smart and rich. Thirdly, expression personality is realized via the expressiveness difference of emotions in the facial expression generation. So the facial expression generation of the agent is more like human, making the agent intelligent in displaying facial expressions in human computer interaction.

To achieve affective and harmonious human computer interaction, the LFFEG model can be further studied in the following directions:

- Further study the mechanisms of facial expression generation.
- Develop an effective way to generate various facial expressions of agent.
- Embed the LFFEG model in a multi-modal human computer interaction system.

6. Acknowledgments

This work is supported by the National Nature Science Foundation of China (No.60572044), High Technology Research and Development Program of China (863 Program,

No.2006AA01Z135), the National Research Foundation for the Doctoral Program of Higher Education of China (No.20070006057) and the Innovation Foundation for Doctoral Student of Beihang University, China. We also appreciate ITC-irst to provide the open source Xface toolkit for 3D facial animation.

7. References

Anthony, I. (1991). Facial expressions of pain in muscle-contraction headache patients. *Journal of Psychopathology and Behavioral Assessment*, vol.13, No.3, 269-283, ISSN: 0882-2689.

Baldwin, J.F. et al. (1998). Machine interpretation of facial expressions. *BT Technol J.* Vol.16, No.3, 156-164, ISSN: 1358-3948.

Birdwhistell, R.L. (1970). *Kinesics and context*. Philadephia: University of Pennsylvania Press. ISBN: 0-8122-1012-3.

Buck, R. et al. (1974). Sex, personality and physiological variables in the communication of emotion via facial expression. *Journal of Personality and Social Psychology*, Vol.30, No. 4, 587-596.

Buck, R. (1991). Social factors in facial display and communication: a reply to Chovil and others. *J. Nonverb. Behav*, Vol.15, No.3, 155-161, ISSN: 0191-5886.

Bui, TD., et al. (2001). Generation of facial expressions from emotion using a fuzzy rule based system. *14th Australian Joint Conf. on Artificial Intelligence*, pp.83-94. ISBN: 3-540-42960-3, Australia, December, 2001, Springer-Verlag, London, UK.

Canamero, D. (1997). Modeling motivations and emotions as a basis for intelligent behavior. *Proceedings of the 1st Int. Conf. on Autonomous agents*, pp.148-155. ISBN: 0-89791-877-0, California, United States, February, 1997, ACM New York, NY, USA

Cassell, J. et al. (1999). Turn taking vs. discourse structure : how best to model multimodal conversation, In: *Machine Conversations*. Wilks Y. (ed.), 143-154, Springer, ISBN: 0-7923-8544-8.

Chovil, N. (1997). Facing others: a social communicative perspective on facial displays. In: *The Psychology of Facial Expression*. Russell, J. A. & Fernandez-Dols, J. (Eds.), 321-333, Cambridge University Press, ISBN: 0-521-49667-5, Cambridge.

Colburn, R.A. et al. (2000). The role of eye gaze in avatar mediated conversational interfaces. *Microsoft Technical Report*, MSR-TR-2000-81, July 2000.

Darwin, C. (1872). *The Expression of the Emotions in Man and Animals*. London, John Murray

Matsumoto, D. (1990). Cultural similarities and differences in display rules. *Motivation and Emotion*, Vol. 14, No. 3, 195-214, ISSN: 0146-7239

Ekman, P. & Friesen, W.V. (1969). The repertoire of nonverbal behaviour: categories, origins, usage, and coding, *Semitotica*, Vol.1, 49-98.

Ekman, P. & Friesen, W.V. (1971). Constants across cultures in the face and emotion. *J. Personality and Social Psychology*, Vol.17, No.2, 124-129.

Ekman, P. (1984). Expression and the nature of emotion. In: *Approaches to emotion*. Scherer, K. & Ekman, P. (Eds.), 319-343, Lawrence Erlbaum, ISBN: 0898594065.

Ekman, P. (1985). *Telling lies*. New York: Norton. ISBN: 0393019314.

Ekman, P. (1992). An argument for basic emotions. *Congnition and Emotion*, 6(3/4): 169-200.

Ekman, P. (1997). Should we call it expression or communication? *Innovations in Social Science Research*, Vol.10, 333-344.

Eibl-Eibesfeldt, I. (1972). Similarities and differences between cultures in expressive movements. In: *Nonverbal Communication*. Hinde, R. (Ed.), Cambridge: Cambridge University Press.

Fasel, B. & Luettin, J. (2003). Automatic facial expression analysis: a survey. *Pattern Recognition,* Vol.36, 259-275.

Fridlund, A. J. (1991). Evolution and facial action in reflex, social motive, and paralanguage. *Biological Psychology*, 32, 3-100. ISSN: 0301-0511.

Fridlund, A. J. (1994). *Human Facial Expression: An Evolutionary View*. San Diego, CA: Academic Press. ISBN: 0-12-267630-0.

Fridlund, A. J. (1997). The new ethology of human facial expressions. In: *The Psychology of Facial Expression*. Russell, J. A. & Fernandez-Dols, J. (Eds.), 103-129, Cambridge University Press, ISBN: 0-521-49667-5, Cambridge.

Grings, W.W. & Dawson, M.E. (1978). *Emotions and Bodily Responses: A Psychophysiological Approach*. Academic Press, New York, San Francisco London. ISBN: 0-12-303750-6.

Hall, J.A. (1984). *Nonverbal sex difference: Communication accuracy and expressive style*. Baltimore, MD: The John Hopkins University Press, ISBN: 080184018X.

Hendrix, J. et al. (2000). A facial repertoire for avatars. *Proceedings of the Workshop "Interacting Agents"*, Enschede, The Netherlands, 27-46.

Heylen, D. (2003). Facial expressions for conversational agents. *CHI Workshop on Subtle Expressivity*.

Klineberg, O. (1940). *Social Psychology*. New York: Henry Holt & Co.

LaBarre, W. (1947). The culture basis of emotions and gestures. *Journal of Personality*, Vol.16, 49-68.

Lang, P.J. (1995). The emotion probe. *American Psychologist*, Vol.50, No.5, 372-385.

Lisetti, C.L. & Schiano, D.J. (2000). Automatic facial expression interpretation: where human-computer interaction, artificial intelligence and cognitive science intersect. *Pragmatics and Cognition*, Vol. 8, No.1, 185-235. ISSN: 0929-0907

Lorenz, K. (1965). *Evolution and modification of behaviour*. Chicago: University of Chicago Press.

Mehrabian, A. (1968). Communication without words, *Psychology Today*, Vol.2, No.4, 53-56.

Mehrabian, A. (1996). Pleasure-arousal-dominance: a general framework for describing and measuring individual differences in temperament. *Current Psychology: Developmental, Learning, Personality, Social*, Vol.14, 261-292.

Miwa, H. et al. (2001). Experimental study on robot personality for humanoid head robot. *IEEE/RSJ Int. Conf. on Intelligent Robots and Systems*, Vol.2, 1183-1188.

Norman, D.A. (2003). Emotional machines. Chapter 6 in *Emotional Design*, Basic Books, ISBN: 0465051359, New York, NY.

Not, E. et al. (2005). Synthetic characters as multichannel interfaces. *7th Int. Conf. on Multimodal Interfaces*, pp.200-207, ISBN: 1-59593-028-0, Torento, Italy, Oct. 2005, Association for Computing Machinery, New York, NY, USA.

Ochs, M., et al. (2005). Intelligent expressions of emotions. *1st Int. Conf. on Affective Computing and Intelligent Interaction*, pp.707-714, ISBN: 3-540-29621-8, Beijing, China, Nov. 2005, Springer Berlin / Heidelberg.

Ortony, A. et al. (1988). *The Cognitive Structure of Emotions*. Cambridge, UK: Cambridge University Press, ISBN: 0521386640.

Picard, R. W. (1997). *Affective Computing*. Cambridge, MA: MIT Press, ISBN: 0262161702.

Perlin, K. (1997). Layered compositing of facial expression. *SIGGRAPH'97 Technical Sketch*, New York University Media Research Lab

Predinger, H. et al. (2004a). MPML: a markup language for controlling the behaviour of life-like characters. *Journal of Visual Languages and Computing*, 15, 183-203, ISSN: 1045-926X.

Prendinger, H. & Ishizuka, M. (2004b). Introducing the cast for social computing. In: *Life-like Characters--Tools, Affective Functions, and Applications*, Prendinger, H. & Ishizuka, M. (Eds.), 3-16, Springer-Verlag, ISBN: 3-540-00867-5.

Provine, R.R. & Hamernik, H.B. (1986). Yawning: Effects of stimulus interest. *Bulletin of the Psychonomic Society*, Vol.24, No.6, 437-438.

Rosenfeld, H.M. (1987). The experimental analysis of interpersonal influence process. *Journal of Communication*, Vol.22, 424-442.

Russell, J.A. (1994). Is there universal recognition of emotion from facial expression? *Psychological Bulletin*, Vol.115, No.1, 102-141.

Russell, J. (1997). Reading emotions from and into faces: Resurrecting a dimensional-contextual perspective. In: *The Psychology of Facial Expression*. Russell, J. A. & Fernandez-Dols, J. (Eds.), 295-320, Cambridge University Press, ISBN: 0-521-49667-5, Cambridge.

Sarmento, L.M. (2004). An emotion-based agent architecture. Master Thesis in Artificial Intelligence and Computing, Universidade do Porto.

Schachter, S. (1964). The interaction of congnitive and physiological determinants of emotional state. *Adavances in Experimental Social Psychology*. Vol.1, 49-80, ISSN: 0065-2601.

Tterzopoulos, D. & Waters, K. (1993). Analysis and synthesis of facial image sequences using physical and anatomical models. *IEEE Transactions on Pattern Analysis and Machine Intelligence*, Vol.15, No.6, 569-579, ISSN: 0162-8828.

Tucker, J.S. & Friedman, H.S. (1993). Sex differences in nonverbal expressiveness: emotional expression, personality, and impressions. *Journal of Nonverbal Behavior*, Vol.17, No.2, 103-117. ISSN: 0191-5886.

Xue, YL., Mao, X. et al. (2006). Beihang University facial expression database and multiple facial expression recognition. *Proceedings of the Fifth Int. Conf. on Machine Learning and Cybernetics*, pp.3282-3287, ISBN: 1-4244-0061-9, Dalian, China, Aug. 2006.

Xue, YL., Mao, X. et al. (2007). Modeling of layered fuzzy facial expression generation. *HCI International 2007*, pp.22-27, ISBN: 3-540-73318-8, Beijing, China, July 2007.

Yang, D. et al. (1999). A study of real-time image processing method for treating human emotion by facial expression. *Proceedings of the IEEE Int. Conf. on Systems, Man and Cybernetics*, Vol.2, pp.360-364, ISBN: 0-7803-5731-0, Tokyo, Japan, Dec. 1999.

Zadeh, L.A. (1965). Fuzzy sets. *Information and Control*, Vol.8, 338-353.

7

Modelling, Classification and Synthesis of Facial Expressions

Jane Reilly, John Ghent and John McDonald
Computer Vision and Imaging Laboratory
Department of Computer Science
National University of Ireland Maynooth,
Ireland

1. Introduction

The field of computer vision endeavours to develop automatic approaches to the interpretation of images from the real world. Over the past number of decades researchers within this field have created systems specifically for the automatic analysis of facial expression. The most successful of these approaches draw on the tools from behavioural science. In this chapter we examine facial expression analysis from both a behavioural science and a computer vision perspective. First we will provide details of the principal approach used in behavioural science to analyze facial expressions. This will include an overview of the evolution of facial expression analysis, where we introduce the field of facial expression analysis with Darwin's initial findings (Darwin, 1872). We then go on to show how his findings were confirmed nearly 100 years later by Ekman *et al.* (Ekman et al., 1969). Following on from this we provide details of recent works investigating the appearance and dynamics of facial expressions.

Given these foundations from behavioural science, we appraise facial expression analysis from a computer vision perspective. Here researchers attempt to create automated computational models for facial expression classification and synthesis. This chapter is divided into three sections, each of which deals with a different, but related problem within the field of facial expression analysis:

I. Classification of facial expressions:

Facial expressions play a major role in human communication. A system capable of interpreting and reacting to facial expressions would represent a major advancement in the field of human computer interaction. Although initial investigations into facial expressions focussed on classifying the six primary expressions (joy, sadness, fear, surprise, anger and disgust), in more recent years the focus has changed, due to a need for a consistent representation of facial expressions. Researchers began to concentrate on classifying expressions in terms of the individual movements that make up facial expressions. In this section, we appraise the current state of the art in facial expression classification, and provide details of our research to date in this area.

II. Modelling the dynamics of facial expressions:

Recent research has shown that it is not just the particular facial expression, but also the associated dynamics that are important when attempting to decipher its meaning. The dynamics of facial expressions, such as the timing, duration and intensity of facial activity plays a critical role in their interpretation. Once we have classified which expression has been portrayed, we subsequently extract information regarding the dynamics of the expression.

III. Synthesis of facial expressions:

In the final section of this chapter we describe a technique which we have developed that allows for photo-realistic images of a person depicting a desired expression to be synthesised in real-time once a neutral image of the subject is present (Ghent, 2005a; Ghent, 2005b). This is achieved by applying machine learning techniques to the modelling of *universal facial expression mapping functions* (i.e. functions that map facial expressions independent of identity). We also demonstrate how the representation of expression used allows the intensity of the output expression to be varied. This ability to vary intensity means that the technique can also be used to generate image sequences of expression formation.

2. Behavioural and computational approaches for facial expression analysis

In this section we first review the state-of-the-art in expression analysis from a behavioural science perspective. Subsequent to this we detail computer vision based approaches for the classification and synthesis of facial expressions.

2.1 Facial expressions from a behavioural science perspective

Darwin first recognised the importance of facial expressions and the role which they play in human communication in 1872 (Darwin, 1872). During the subsequent years as behavioural scientists sought a means to objectively measure facial expressions, many different techniques and methodologies for describing facial expressions were developed (see (Fasel & Luettin, 2003) for a comprehensive review). Recent research has shown that it is not just the expression itself, but also its dynamics that are important when attempting to interpret its underlying meaning. In this section we provide details of the principal approach used in behavioural science to analyze, interpret and encode facial expressions.

2.1.1 Facial expression analysis

Within the field of facial expression analysis there has been a significant amount of research carried out investigating the six prototypical expressions (anger, fear, sadness, joy, surprise, and disgust). This focus is partially due to observations made by Darwin in 1872, when he observed that although people from different countries spoke different languages, from looking at their faces he could interpret their feelings and emotions. This idea coincided with his theory of evolution and the continuity of the species (Darwin, 1872).

In the subsequent years, the field of facial expression analysis remained an active research area within behavioural science. However, from a computer vision perspective, the research carried out by Ekman *et al.* has come to represent the seminal works on facial expression analysis. Approximately 100 years after Darwin's initial findings, Ekman *et al.* established that there are six universal facial expressions. They did so by performing a number of experiments to discover if American and Japanese students responded in a similar manner to a series of emotion evoking films. The reactions of the students to the films were captured and labelled as being one of the six primary expressions. While, they found that the students had similar responses to the films, Ekman *et al.* were unable prove conclusively that the student's responses were not as a result of exposure to the American culture (Ekman & Friesen, 1969).

In the 1970's Ekman *et al.* came across footage of a remote tribe from New Guinea called the South Fore, which had little or no exposure to modern culture. Upon analysing the video footage they recognised the expressions portrayed by tribesmen as being variations of the six primary expressions. Ekman *et al.* subsequently travelled to New Guinea where they performed a number of studies. For example, they showed the tribesmen photographs of caucasians depicting the primary facial expressions. As anticipated, the South Fore tribe were able to recognise these expressions. Ekman *et al.* then asked the tribesmen to show what their face would be like if, for example, *'friends had come to visit'*, or *'their son was injured'*. Using the results of these experiments, they were able to prove that the South Fore people responded to and performed the facial expressions as anticipated (Ekman et al., 1971).

What distinguished these experiments from previous work was that as the South Fore people had not been exposed to modern culture, Ekman *et al.* were able to conclusively prove that these six primary facial expressions were not culturally determined. These results support Darwin's hypothesis that these primary facial expressions are biological in origin, and are expressed and perceived in a similar way across all cultures.

In everyday life, while these primary expressions do occur frequently, when analysing human interaction and conversation, researchers have found that displays of emotion are more often communicated by small subtle changes in the face's appearance (Ambadar et al., 2005). As a consequence, the focus of research into facial expressions has shifted from concentrating on identifying the six basic expressions to identifying the individual movements that make up an expression. The *Facial Action Coding System* (FACS) provides a means for coding expression in terms of these elementary facial actions. In Section 2.2.3 we look at the FACS in detail.

2.1.2 Facial expressions dynamics

Recent research has shown that it is not only the expression itself, but also its dynamics that are important when attempting to decipher its meaning (Cohn et al., 2005). The dynamics of facial expression can be defined as the intensity of the AUs coupled with the timing of their formation. Ekman *et al.* suggest that the dynamics of facial expression provides unique information about emotion that is not available in static images (Ekman & Friesen, 2002).

However, according to Ambadar *et al.*, only a few investigators have examined the impact of dynamics in deciphering faces. These studies were largely unsuccessful due to their reliance on extreme facial expressions. Ambadar *et al.* also highlighted the fact that facial expressions are frequently subtle. They found that subtle expressions that were not identifiable in individual images suddenly became apparent when viewed in a video sequence (Ambadar et al., 2005).

There is now a growing body of psychological research that argues that these dynamics are a critical factor for the interpretation of the observed behaviour. Zheng *et al.*, state that in many cases, an expression sequence can contain multiple expressions of different intensities sequentially, due to the evolution of the subject's emotion over time (Zheng, 2000). Despite the fact that facial expressions can be either subtle or pronounced in their appearance, and fleeting or sustained in their duration, most of the studies to date have focused on investigating static displays of extreme posed expressions rather than the more natural spontaneous expressions. The following definitions explain the differences between *posed* and *spontaneous* facial expressions:

- **Posed facial expressions** are generally captured by asking subjects to perform specific facial actions or expressions. They are usually captured under artificial conditions, i.e. the subject is facing the camera under good lighting conditions, there is a limited degree of head movement, and the expressions are usually exaggerated.
- **Spontaneous facial expressions** are more representative of what happens in the real world, typically occurring under less controlled circumstances. With spontaneous expression data, subjects may not necessarily be facing the camera, the image size may be smaller, there will undoubtedly be a greater degree of head movement, and the facial expressions portrayed are in general less exaggerated.

The dynamics of posed expressions can not be taken as representative of what would happen during natural displays of emotions, similar to how individual words spoken on command would differ from the natural flow of conversation. Consequently, when analysing the dynamics of facial expressions, one must realise that while the final image in a posed sequence will be the requested facial expression, the entire sequence as a whole will not allow for the accurate modelling of the interplay between the different movements that make up the facial expression during its natural formation. This is because subjects often use different facial muscles when asked to pose an emotion such as fear as opposed to when they are actually experiencing fear.

2.1.3 Encoding facial expressions

While the importance of facial expressions was established in 1872, it wasn't until the 1970's that researchers began to analyse the individual movements that make up facial expressions. Many different techniques were developed which claimed to provide means for objectively measuring facial expressions. Although, the *Facial Action Coding System* (FACS) introduced by Ekman and Friesen in 1978 is arguably the most widely used of these techniques, as a result we have chosen to use it as a basis for describing expressions in our research.

The Facial Action Coding System (FACS)

The FACS was first introduced by Ekman & Friesen in 1978 (Ekman & Friesen, 1978). It is the most comprehensive standard for describing facial expressions and is widely used in research. It provides an unambiguous quantitative means of describing all movements of the face in terms of 47 *Action Units* (AUs). Unlike previous systems that use emotion to describe facial expressions, the advantage that FACS has over its competitors is the way in which the FACS explicitly distinguishes between AUs, and inferences about what they mean. However should one wish to make emotion based inferences from the FACS codes, resources such as the FACS interpretive database developed by Ekman, Rosenberg and Hager in 1998 are available (Ekman et al., 1998). For a complete list of AUs and descriptions of these AUs see (Ekman & Friesen, 1978).

As the field of facial expression analysis has evolved, so too has the FACS, with its latest amendment occurring in 2002 where intensity codes were included for all AUs (Ekman et al., 2002). There are five intensity ranges defined in total, ranging from ***A*** to ***E***, with ***A*** representing a subtle change in appearance, and ***E*** representing a maximum change in appearance. It should be noted that although there are five intensity levels, these intensities do not occur equally, for example intensity **C** occurs for a longer duration than intensity ***A*** during the formation of a given AU. An example of the affect that increasing intensity has on the appearance a facial expression is shown in Fig. 1.

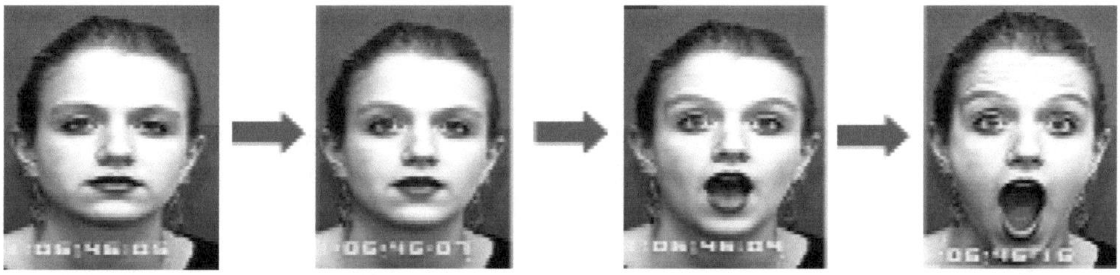

Fig. 1: Expression intensity ranges, intensities displayed, from left to right, are: neutral, and intensities A, C, E

While the 2002 version of the FACS is a significant improvement on the previous version of the FACS, in that it included descriptions on how to grade the different intensities for all AUs, these FACS guidelines for intensity coding are somewhat subjective. Hence special effort is required to establish and maintain acceptable levels of reliability, especially in the mid-range. Sayette *et al.*, suggest that the reliability of intensity coding may be problematic and state that further work is needed (Sayette et al., 2001).

2.2. Computational approaches for facial expression analysis

Using the foundations laid down by behavioural science researchers, in this section we appraise computer vision solutions for the problems of classifying and synthesising facial expressions. Here researchers attempt to create automated computational models for facial expression classification and synthesis.

Although the FACS provides a good basis for AU coding of facial images by human observers, the way in which the AU codes have been defined does not easily translate into a computational test. The reason for this is that the FACS is an appearance based technique with the AUs being defined as a series of descriptions. As a consequence of this description based method, a certain element of subjectivity occurs with human coders.

Due to this subjectivity, the development of a system to automatically FACS code facial images is a difficult task. Although the development of such as system would be an important step in the advancement of studies on human emotion and non-verbal communication, potentially enhancing numerous applications in fields as diverse as security, medicine and education. However, this is as yet an unsolved problem. According to Cohn *et al.*, further development is required within the area of automatic facial AU recognition before the need for manual FACS coding of facial images is eliminated (Cohn et al., 2002).

The automated analysis of facial expressions is a challenging task because everyone's face is unique and interpersonal differences exist in how people perform facial expressions. Numerous methodologies have been proposed to solve this problem such as Expert Systems (Pantic & Patras, 2006), Hidden Markov Models (Cohen et al., 2003); Gabor filters (Bartlett et al., 2006a; Bartlett et al., 2006b; Bartlett et al., 2004; Bartlett et al., 2001,) and Optical Flow analysis (Goneid & Kalioby, 2002). For an overview of these techniques see (Tian et al., 2004).

While the computational analysis of facial expressions and their dynamics have received a lot of interest from various different research groups, in the past decade the techniques developed by Bartlett *et al.* have come to represent the state of the art in facial expression analysis. Bartlett *et al.* proposed a technique which combines *Gabor wavelets* and *Support Vector Machines (SVMs)* to classify the six primary facial expressions and neutral in a seven-way forced decision, achieving an accuracy rate of 93.3% (Bartlett et al., 2001). In (Bartlett et al., 2004), Bartlett *et al.* extended on this technique to classify 18 AUs[1] with an agreement rate of 94.5% with human FACS coders.

Although this agreement rate is impressive, the most important contribution of this work lies in the design and training of the context independent classifiers. These classifiers are capable of identifying the presence of an AU whether it occurs singly or in combination with other AUs. The benefit of this approach is clear as there are an estimated 7000 possible AU combinations, if context independent classifiers were used, then potentially all possible AU combinations could be classified using only 47 classifiers.

In (Bartlett et al., 2006a), Bartlett *et al.* present a system that accurately performs automatic recognition of 20 AUs[2] from near frontal image sequences in real time, once again using Gabor wavelets and SVMs with a 91% agreement with human FACS coders. Following recent trends in using standardised approaches for characterising the performance of classification systems, Bartlett *et al.* have begun to use *Receiver Operating Characteristic* (ROC) curve analysis, whereby they report the success/failure of their classifiers in terms of the *area under the ROC curve* (AUC). In (Bartlett et al., 2006b), Bartlett *et al.*, present the results of their experiments using ROC analysis, reporting an AUC of 0.926. For details on ROC analysis see Section 4.1.2.

Within the field of facial expression synthesis, a number of approaches have been reported in the literature over the past 10 years (Raouzaiou et al., 2002; Zhang et al., 2006; Wang & Ahuja, 2003; Choe & Ko, 2001; Gralewski, 2004; Ghent, 2005a; Ghent 2005b). The approach presented in this chapter combines the FACS, statistical shape and texture models, and machine learning techniques to provide a novel solution to this problem.

In the past *Radial Basis Function Networks* (RBFN) have been applied to facial expression synthesis (King & Hou, 1996; Arad et al., 1994). However, in these approaches redundancy reduction techniques were not applied prior to calculating the mapping functions. This kept the dimensionality of the mapping functions high and meant that irrelevant information was used in calculating the mapping functions. In King's (King & Hou, 1996) approach, mapping functions were used to modify the locations of *Facial Characteristic Points* (FCP) which in turn were used to warp an image to depict an alternative expression. A weakness with this approach was, that in order to adequately model the appearance change due to expression, one must take account of the variation of both shape and texture. For example, to synthesise a smile the texture of the image must be modified to produce wrinkles. The technique described in this chapter overcomes this problem by manipulating both shape and texture of the input image.

More recently, Abboud (Abboud et al., 2004) applied PCA to the shape and texture of unseen images to lower the dimensionality of the problem in order to produce synthetic facial expressions. However, their approach used linear regression to perform facial expression synthesis. Our technique improves on this approach by using a RBFN to describe the non-linear nature of facial expressions. The results of the technique described in this chapter considerably outperform the results found in (Abboud et al., 2004).

---

[1] AUs {1, 2, 4, 5, 6, 7, 9, 10, 12, 15, 17, 20, 23, 24, 25, 26, 27, 44}

[2] AUs {1, 2, 4, 5, 6, 7, 9, 10, 11, 12, 14, 15, 16, 17, 20, 23, 24, 25, 26, 27}

3. Building facial expression models

A common problem within the areas of machine learning and computer vision is the extraction of relevant features from high-dimensional datasets such as video sequences. Feature extraction refers to the process of transforming the input data set to a lower dimension where the resulting dimensions exhibit high information packing properties (i.e. they accurately represent the original data). In general dimensionality reduction techniques are possible due to the fact that datasets have a lower implicit dimensionality in that their input representation is redundant. For this reason dimensionality reduction techniques are often referred to as redundancy reduction techniques.

Images of faces exhibit these properties in that the dimensionality of the space of faces is far lower than that of the images themselves (Meytlis & Sirovich, 2007). Given this fact, prior to both classification and synthesis, we apply redundancy reduction techniques to reduce the dimensionality of the input images. This has the advantages of reducing the complexity of the machine learning task and as a consequence increasing their accuracy.

Dimensionality reduction techniques can be either linear, such as *Principal Component Analysis (PCA),* or non-linear, such as *Locally Linear Embedding (LLE).* Linear dimensionality reduction techniques can in general be represented by $y=Ax$, where the A represents a linear transformation which when applied to the input data x maps it to the lower dimensional output vector y. Nonlinear dimensionality reduction techniques can be represented by $y=fx$ where f is typically a particular family of nonlinear mappings and again, x and y are the high-dimensional input and low-dimensional output vectors, respectively.

In our research we have investigated the application of both PCA and LLE for facial expression analysis. Details of each of these techniques are provided in the Sections 3.2 and 3.3. For completeness, prior to explaining these techniques, we give details of the dataset used in our experiments.

3.1 Facial expression dataset

In order to fully utilize the FACS AU and intensity coding we use a database containing videos of individuals performing a series of facial expressions which are fully FACS coded. In our research to date we use the Cohn-Kanade AU-Coded Facial Expression Database (Cohn & Kanade, 1999). This database contains approximately 2000 images sequences from over 200 subjects. The subjects come from a cross-cultural background and are aged between 18 - 30. This database contains full AU coding and partial intensity coding of facial images and is the most comprehensive database currently available.

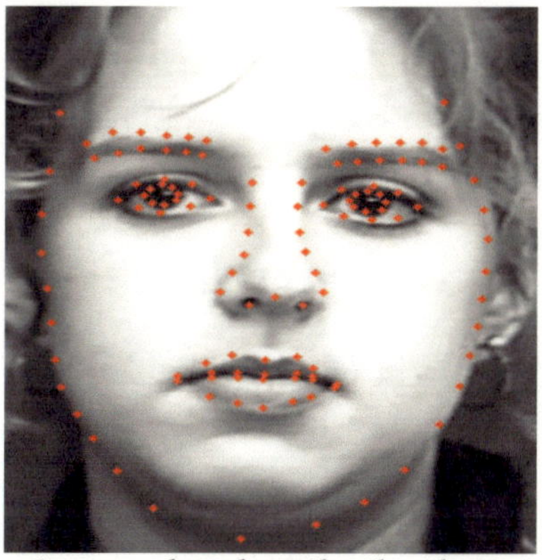

Fig. 2: Example of landmark points used to describe the shape of a particular face

Prior to experimentation, we extract the expression features from our dataset by manually identifying a set of 122 landmark points on the face as shown in Fig. 2. To ensure that the variance in the data set is due to change in expression rather than subject we perform a global alignment step known as *Generalised Procrustes Alignment* (GPA) (Ghent, 2005a). Applying GPA minimises the sum of the squared distances between corresponding landmark points and in effect normalises the shapes with respect to scale, translation, and rotation. Given the set of globally aligned shapes there will be a high degree of correlation in the variation of landmark positions due to expression.

3.2 Principal Component Analysis – PCA

PCA is used to map high dimensional data to a low dimensional subspace. This method takes a set of data points and constructs a lower dimensional linear subspace that maximises the variance in the training set. PCA essentially performs an orthonormal transformation on the input data such that the variance of the input data is accurately captured using only a few of the resulting principal components.

These principal components are calculated in such a way that the squared reconstruction error between the input and output data are minimized. This is achieved by performing eigenvector decomposition on the covariance matrix of the input data. The resulting eigenvectors and eigenvalues represent the degrees of variability where the first eigenvalue is the most significant mode of variation. This process of maximising the variability of the input data and minimizing the reconstruction error can be achieved by rotating the axes. This axis rotation is the core idea behind PCA.

The higher the correlation between the input data the fewer the number of principal components needed to represent the majority of variance in the training set. However, if the input data points are co-linear then the data can be represented without any information loss using only one dimensional data along the principal axis. In correlated input data there also exists redundant information in the input space. PCA removes this by de-correlating the input data. The uncorrelated low dimensional features can be used to represent the correlated high dimensional input data making PCA a powerful data compression technique.

Given the set of globally aligned shapes there will be a high degree of correlation in the variation of landmark positions due to expression. In order to reduce this redundancy we perform PCA on the data set. To do this each shape is represented as a one-dimensional vector of the form:

$$\mathbf{P}_i = \left[\mathbf{p}_i^1 \;\; \mathbf{p}_i^2 \;\; \dots \;\; \mathbf{p}_i^n\right]^{\mathrm{T}} = \left[x_i^1 \;\; y_i^1 \;\; x_i^2 \;\; y_i^2 \;\; \dots \;\; x_i^n \;\; y_i^n\right]^{\mathrm{T}} \tag{1}$$

For each $\mathbf{P}_i$, we define the difference vector as:

$$\boldsymbol{\delta}\mathbf{P}_i = \overline{\mathbf{P}} - \mathbf{P}_i \tag{2}$$

Where, $\overline{\mathbf{P}} = \frac{1}{n}\sum_{i=1}^{n} \mathbf{P}_i$ is the *mean shape*, using Equation (2) we may now define the covariance matrix of the dataset as:

$$\mathbf{S} = \frac{1}{n-1}\sum_{i=1}^{n} (\boldsymbol{\delta}\mathbf{P}_i)(\boldsymbol{\delta}\mathbf{P}_i)^{\mathrm{T}} \tag{3}$$

The m eigenvectors corresponding to the m largest eigenvalues of **S** are known as the *principal components* and are orientated in the directions of the m highest modes of variation of the original dataset. These eigenvectors form the basis of a low-dimensional subspace capable of representing the input shapes far more efficiently whilst capturing the majority of the variance in dataset. We refer to this space as the *Facial Expression Shape Model* (FESM). For example in our experiments the input space is 244-dimensional whilst the maximum number of dimensions that we use in an FESM is 20, which captures over 98% of the variance of the variance in the input dataset. Given an input point, $\mathbf{P}_i$, we can compute the corresponding FESM vector using:

$$\mathbf{b} = \mathbf{B}^{\mathrm{T}}\left(\overline{\mathbf{P}} - \mathbf{P}_i\right) \tag{4}$$

Where, **B** is an $n \times m$ matrix where the columns are the m eigenvectors described above. Conversely given an FESM vector we can project it into the input space by inverting Equation (4).

3.2 Locally Linear Embedding - LLE

According to Kayo *et al.*, as real world data is often inherently nonlinear, linear dimensionality reduction techniques such as PCA, do not accurately capture the structure of the underlying manifold, i.e. relationships which exist in the high dimensional space are not always accurately preserved in the low dimensional space (Kayo et al., 2006). This means that in order to capture the underlying manifold of real world data, a nonlinear dimensionality reduction technique is required. On one such nonlinear dimensionality reduction technique is LLE.

LLE was introduced as an unsupervised learning algorithm that computes low dimensional, neighbourhood preserving embeddings of high dimensional data (Saul & Roweis, 2003). The LLE algorithm is based on simple geometric intuitions, where it essentially computes a low dimensional representation of the input data in such a way that nearby points in the high dimensional space remain nearby and similarly co-located with respect to one another in the low dimensional space.

The LLE algorithm takes a dataset of N real valued vectors $\boldsymbol{X}_i$, each of dimensionality $\boldsymbol{D}$, sampled from some smooth underlying manifold as its input. Provided that the manifold is sufficiently sampled by the dataset, we can expect each point and its neighbours to lie on or close to a locally linear patch of the manifold. The LLE algorithm involves three main steps. Firstly, the manifold is sampled and the $\boldsymbol{K}$ nearest neighbours per data point are identified. Secondly each point $\boldsymbol{X}_i$ is approximated as a linear combination of its neighbours $\boldsymbol{X}_j$.

These linear combinations are then used to construct the sparse weight matrix $\boldsymbol{W}_{ij}$. Reconstructions errors are then measured by the cost function given in Equation 5, which sums the squared distances between each point and its reconstruction.

$$\varepsilon W = \sum_i \left| \overrightarrow{X_i} - \sum_j W_{ij} \overrightarrow{X_j} \right|^2 \tag{5}$$

In the final step of the LLE algorithm, each point $\boldsymbol{X}_i$ in the high dimensional space is mapped to a point $\boldsymbol{Y}_i$ in the low dimensional space which best preserves the structure and geometry of $\boldsymbol{X}_i$'s neighbourhood. The geometry and structure is represented by the weight matrix W_{ij}. The mapping from X_i to Y_i is achieved by fixing the weights W_{ij}, and selecting the bottom d non zero coordinates of each output Y_i to minimise Equation 6. For more details on the LLE algorithm see (Saul & Roweis, 2003).

$$\Phi Y = \sum_i \left| \overrightarrow{Y_i} - \sum_j W_{ij} \overrightarrow{Y_j} \right|^2 \tag{6}$$

4. Classifying facial expressions

In this section we provide details of our approach towards the automatic classification of facial expressions, and the extraction and modelling of their dynamics. In our experiments we use *Support Vector Machine* (SVM) classifiers, and characterise the performance of our technique by performing *Receiver Operating Characteristic* (ROC) analysis on the results of our experiments. Details of both of these techniques are given in section 4.1. Following on from this we detail a number of experiments which demonstrate our approaches towards the automatic classification of facial expressions.

4.1 Facial expression classification and validation

4.1.1 Support Vector Machines - SVMs

SVMs are a type of learning algorithm based upon advances in statistical learning theory, and are based on a combination of techniques. One of the principal ideas behind SVMs is the kernel trick, where data is transformed into a high dimensional space making linear discriminant functions practical. SVMs also use the idea of large margin classifiers. Suppose we have a dataset $(x_1, y_1), \ldots, (x_m, y_m) \in X \times \{\pm 1\}$ where X is some space from which the x_i have been sampled. We can construct a dual Lagrangian of the form:

$$W(\alpha) = \sum_{i=1}^{m} \alpha_i - \frac{1}{2} \sum_{i,j=1}^{m} \alpha_i \alpha_j y_i y_j (x_i \cdot x_j) \tag{7}$$

The solution to Equation 7, subject to the constraints $\alpha_i \geq 0 \forall i$ and $\sum_{i=1}^{m} \alpha_i y_i = 0$, is a set of α values which define a hyperplane that is positioned in an optimal location between the classes.

A number of methods have been proposed for multi-class classification using SVMs, the *one-against-all* and the *Directed Acyclic Graph* (DAG) algorithms are the two main approaches (Ghent, 2005a). In our experiments we use the *one-against-all* approach.

4.1.2 Receiver Operating Characteristic (ROC) curve analysis

ROC analysis is a technique for visualizing, organising, and selecting classifiers based on their performance (Fawcett, 2003). Within the field of computer science, ROC analysis is becoming increasingly important in the area of cost sensitive classification, classification in the presence of unbalanced classes, robust comparison of classifier performance under imprecise class distribution and misclassification costs.

Given a classifier and an instance, there are four possible outcomes:

- True Positive (TP) - test correctly returns a positive result
- True Negative (TN) –test correctly returns a negative result

- False Positive (FP) -test incorrectly returns a positive result
- False Negative (FN) -test incorrectly returns a negative result

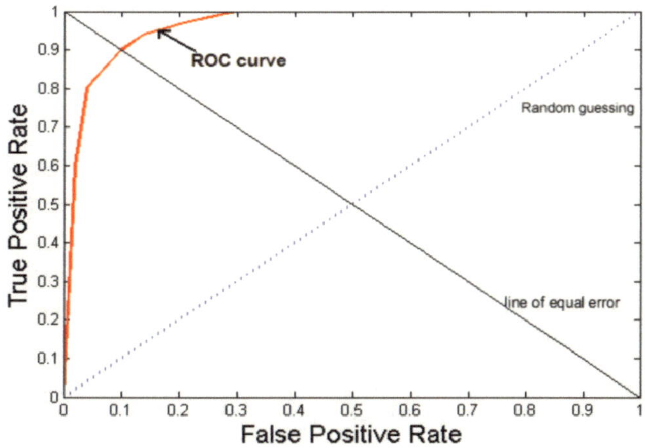

Fig. 3: Example ROC curve, with line of equal error & random guess line

These values are used to compile various ratios such as the *True Positive Rate* (TPR), which is *the number of true positives divided by the total number of positives*, and the *False Positive Rate* (FPR) is 1 - *the number of false positives divided by the total number of negatives*. ROC graphs are two dimensional graphs with the TPR plotted on the Y-axis, and the FPR plotted on the X-axis. A ROC graph depicts the relative trade offs between the benefits and costs of a particular classifier. An example of a ROC curve is shown in Fig. 3. The most frequently used performance metric in ROC analysis is the *area under the ROC Curve* (AUC). The AUC of a classifier is equivalent to the probability that the classifier will rank a randomly chosen positive instance higher than a randomly chosen negative instance. The AUC ranges from 0-1, and a random classifier has an AUC of 0.5.

4.2 Facial expression classification

The area of facial expression classification was originally concerned with classifying the six primary facial expressions (joy, sadness, fear, surprise, anger, and disgust). However, as the need for a consistent representation of facial expressions became apparent, this focus has changed, with researchers concentrating on classifying expressions in terms of the individual movements or AUs that make up the facial expressions. In this section we provide details of our work within these two distinct areas, concluding with details of our technique which models the dynamics of facial expression in terms of intensity and timing.

4.2.1 Classification of the six primary expressions

To date the research group at the *Computer Vision and Imaging Laboratory* (CVIL) at the National University of Ireland, Maynooth, have proposed a computational model for the classification of facial expressions (Ghent, 2005a). This model which is based on PCA and SVMs, can accurately classify the primary facial expressions at extreme levels of intensity. This model was created by firstly reducing the dimensionality of our data using PCA. This lower dimensional data was then used to train one-against-all SVMs, in this example we have three expressions to classify (happiness, sadness and surprise), so we used three one-against-all SVMs (For more details on SVMs see Section 4.1.1.).

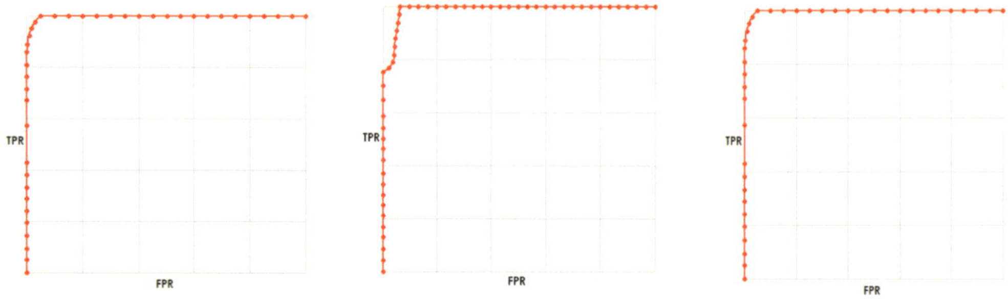

Fig. 4: ROC Curves for the three of the primary facial expressions, from left to right, Happiness, Sadness & Surprise

Following on from this, test data was projected into the training space, and presented as input to the SVMs. As a means of validating our results we performed ROC analysis. The resulting ROC curves are shown in Fig. 4, and the confusion matrices shown in Table 1. Our PCA-SVM technique has achieved a mean AUC of 0.91. Once we demonstrated the success of our technique at classifying a number of the primary facial expressions, such as happiness, sadness and surprise, we then extended on this work to analyse the individual movements that make up facial expressions.

4.2.2 Classification of individual action units (AUs)

Although FACS provides a good basis for the AU coding of facial images by trained individuals, the automatic recognition of AUs by computers remains a difficult challenge. As mentioned earlier, one issue with automating FACS coding is that 47 AUs have been defined and these can occur in a large number of combinations (estimated at over 7000 (Pantic & Rothkrantz, 2003)). One approach to overcome this problem is to subdivide the face into regions and classify expressions within these regions independently.

Emotion	AUC	#Neg	#Pos	FP	TP	FN	TN
Happiness	0.94	98	40	2	12	28	96
Sadness	0.804	121	17	0	2	15	121
Surprise	0.996	118	20	0	3	17	118

Table 1: ROC Results, AUC = Area under the ROC Curve, **#Neg** = number of negative samples, **#Pos** = number of positive samples, **FP** = False Positives, **TP** = True Positives, **FN** = False Negatives, **TN** = True Negatives

As the FACS separates facial expressions into upper and lower facial AUs, in this section we demonstrate our technique at classifying AUs in both of these regions of the face. In Experiment 1 we report our results for the classification of lower facial expressions involving the mouth, while in Experiment 2 we provide details of our experiments for the classification of upper facial expressions involving the eyebrow.

In these experiments we used LLE to reduce the dimensionality of our datasets. An LLE shape space is established by pre-processing training face shapes and using these as inputs to into an LLE algorithm. SVMs are then trained on this data. In our experiments we use one-against-all SVM classifiers, so if for example there were four expressions in our training set, we would use 4 one-against-all SVMs. Once these classifiers have been trained, individual unseen shapes are pre-processed and projected into the LLE expression shape space. The results of this projection are then used as inputs to a previously trained SVM classifiers which output a FACS coding for this unseen shape. We perform ROC analysis on the results of the experiments.

Experiment 1 - Classification of lower face AUs

In our first experiment we classify four lower facial expressions; AU20+25, AU25+27, AU10+20+25 and AU12, the affect that these AUs have on the face is shown in Fig. 5. Our training data consisted of 73 images of an individual performing these four AU combinations, from neutral to extreme expression intensity. It should be noted that expression I & III are very similar and therefore we hypothesise that a technique that can accurately differentiate between these two expressions can accurately classify subtle changes in appearance. Our test set consisted of 522 images of multiple subjects from multi-cultural backgrounds performing the four lower facial expressions as shown in Fig. 5. In our test dataset we sampled the sequences at each intensity rating, including neutral (6 in total). In our training set we used the entire sequence and labelled each frame with an intensity score.

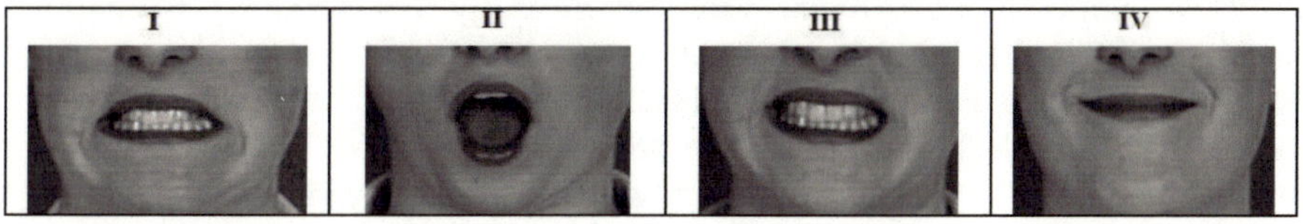

Fig. 5: This Figure illustrates the effect of portraying four different AU combinations on the mouth. From left to right the expressions portrayed are: I = AU20+25, II = AU25+27, III = AU10+20+25, IV = AU12

Results:

Using the outputs of our SVM classifiers we preformed ROC analysis, the optimal ROC curve for each of the four expressions are shown in Fig. 6. While from first glance it appears that our technique did not perform as well at the task of classifying the two similar expressions I - AU20+25 and III - AU10+20+25, it is important to note that the classifiers were tested across the entire intensity range. Possible reasons for the lower AUC's for these two expressions could be that as these two expressions are quite similar, in the more subtle intensities they may have been miss-classified.

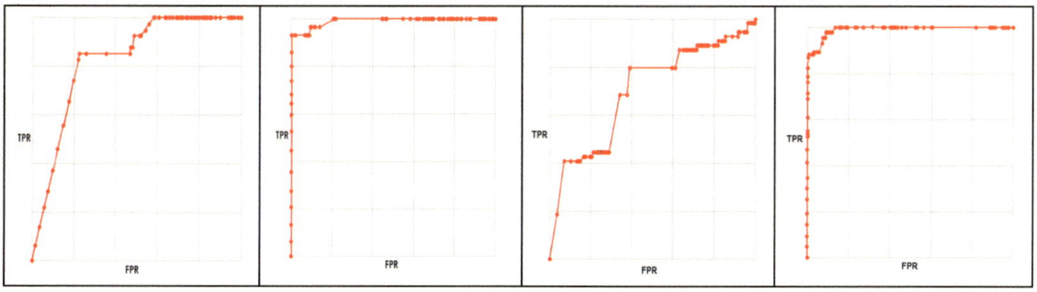

Fig. 6: ROC results from the application of LLE to lower facial expressions. From left to right: I=AU20+25, II=AU25+27, III=AU10+20+25, IV=AU12

Expression	AUC	#Neg	#Pos	FP	TP	FN	TN
AU20+25	0.803	422	20	93	15	93	329
AU25+27	0.951	382	28	1	22	6	381
AU10+20+25	0.687	432	18	31	8	10	401
AU12	0.989	417	105	0	62	43	417

Table 2: ROC Results, AUC=Area under the ROC Curve, **#Neg**=number of negative samples, **#Pos**=number of positive samples, **FP**=False Positives, **TP**=True Positives, **FN**=False Negatives, **TN**=True Negatives

From looking at the confusion matrices for these two classifiers, (see Table 2), for expressions I & III, we can see that there is a higher level of false positives than with the other expressions. However, this is still a positive result as the classification and differentiation between two such similar facial expressions across the entire intensity range is a non-trivial task. (For an in-depth analysis of these results across the entire intensity range see (Reilly, 2007)).

Experiment 2 - Classification of upper face AUs

The structure of our second experiment is similar to that of our previous experiment except that instead of attempting to classify each AU or AU group separately, we wanted to classify AU1 and AU4 independent of context. What we mean by this is that we wanted to classify AU1 regardless of whether it occurs on its own or in combination with other AUs within the eyebrow region such as AU2 and AU4. The motivation for the development of context independent classifiers is that the 47 AUs defined by the FACS can occur in over 7000 possible combinations. Due to this large number of possible combinations, it is not practical to design an independent classifier for each of these cases. Hence, in order to simplify this classification problem, if we design classifiers that will classify the presence of an AU regardless of whether it occurs in isolation or in combination with other AUs, we could potentially classify all of these possible AU combinations using 47 classifiers. This is a challenging problem as there is a significant overlap in how these AUs can alter the appearance of the face. This overlap is demonstrated in Fig. 7, where all the possible combinations of AU1 and AU4, within the eyebrow region, which are available within the Cohn-Kanade database are displayed.

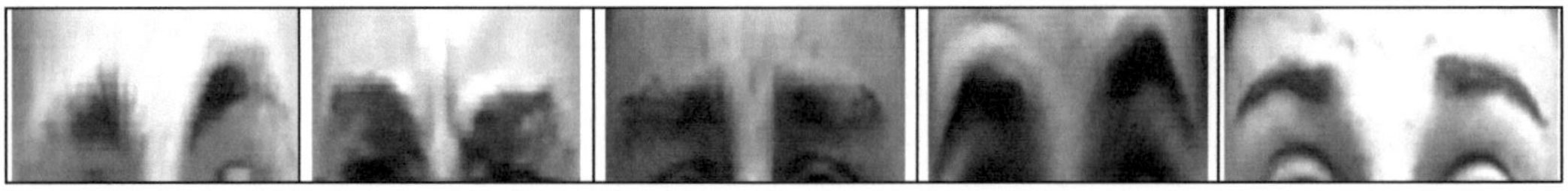

Fig. 7: Example of AU combinations that can occur in the eyebrow region, from left to right they are, AU1, AU4, AU1+4, AU1+2, AU1+2+4

Our training data consisted of 42 images of an individual performing the five eyebrow movements as illustrated in Fig. 7, across the entire intensity range from neutral to extreme AU intensity. Our test set consisted of 84 images from multiple subjects from multi-cultural backgrounds performing the AUs as shown above. In our test dataset we sampled our data at each level of intensity from neutral to extreme, where 6 samples per sequence were taken. While there are three AUs associated with the eyebrow, there were not sufficient samples of AU2 within the Cohn-Kanade database to include this AU in this particular experiment. However, we hypothesise that a technique that can accurately classify the remaining AUs:

AU1 & AU4, regardless of whether they occur together or in isolation has the potential to perform similar classification in more complex regions of the face such as the mouth.

Results:

Using the outputs of our SVM classifiers we preformed ROC curve analysis, the optimal ROC curves for the context independent classification of AU1 and AU4 are shown in Fig. 8. From analysing the ROC curves we can see that our technique was successful at classifying AUI, where it achieved an AUC of 0.789. Our technique was less successful at classifying AU4, achieving an AUC of 0.62. This could possibly be because we had more samples containing AU1 in our training set. Although it could also be attributed to the fact that one of the indicators of the presence of AU4 is the appearance of wrinkles and bulges between the brows, and as our technique is shape based, this information is not captured.

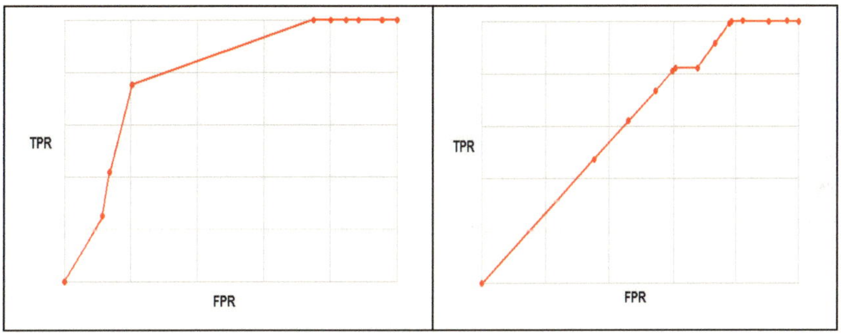

Fig. 8: ROC curves for the context independent classification of AU1 (Left), and AU4 (Right)

An example of the affect that AU4 has on the face is shown in detail in Fig. 9, where it can be seen that the presence of AU4 causes bulges to appear between the brows. Nonetheless, the development of context independent classifiers is a difficult problem. We envisage that our results will improve when we extend on our current models to also include texture information.

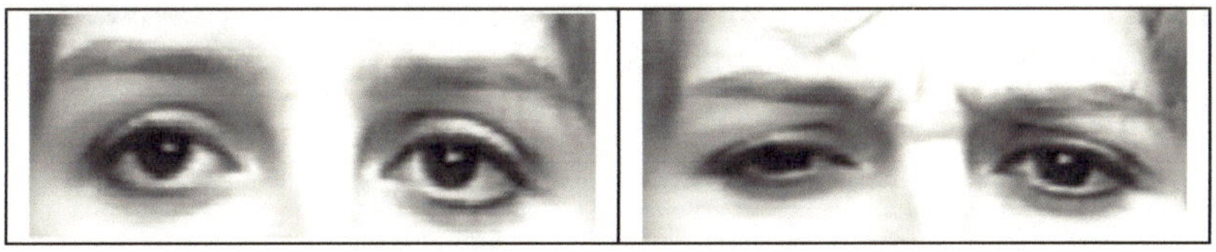

Fig. 9: Effect of AU4 on the eyebrow region, the neutral expression is shown on the left, and the extreme is shown in the right

Experiment 3 - capturing the dynamics of facial expression.

When investigating the dynamics of facial expression, we are interested in capturing the appearance changes that occur during facial expression formation in terms of the intensity and timing of those changes. When referring to facial expressions, intensity refers to the magnitude of the appearance change resulting from any facial activity, and the timing refers to the speed and duration of that activity. The dynamics of facial expression, such as the timing, duration and intensity of facial activity plays a critical role for the interpretation of the observed behaviour.

In the following experiment we extract information regarding the intensity and timing of a previously classified AU. The extraction of this information provides a means for analyzing

the dynamics of facial expression. In this experiment we estimate the intensity of AU25 – *which parts the lips*. The input to this experiment consisted of 24 subjects performing AU25, sampled at each intensity rating (i.e. per subject we sampled at intensity Neutral, A, B, C, D and E).
As we wish to capture the dynamics of AU formation, we perform an extra pre-processing step called *Shape Differencing*, whereby the neutral mouth shapes of each subject are subtracted from the sample set for that subject. The reason being is that we are only interested in the difference between the two shapes and not the actual shapes themselves. This is a valid step as in order to analyse the dynamics of facial expression it is necessary to have a sequence containing a neutral image.

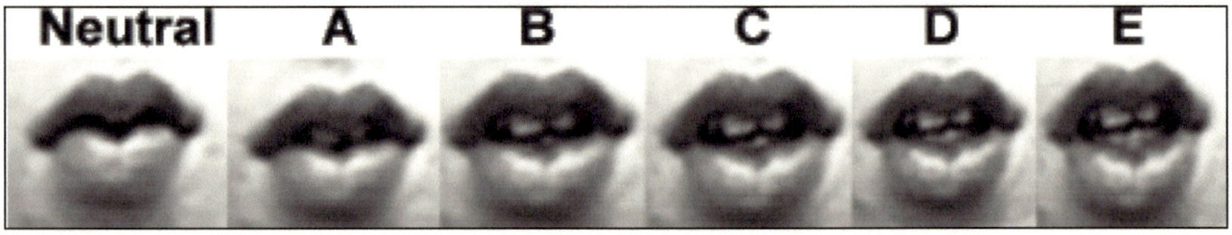

Fig. 10: Examples of sequences of AU25 from the Cohn-Kanade database

As mentioned earlier in Section 2.2.3, the 2002 version of the FACS contains intensity ranges for each AU. The FACS intensity range goes from A to E, with A representing a minor change in appearance and E representing the maximum change in appearance. As the data for this experiment was taken from the Cohn-Kanade database, full intensity coding of the image sequences was not available. Therefore we manually selected the frames from the expression sequences which correspond to the FACS intensity coding descriptions, examples of our selections can be seen in Fig. 10.
In our initial experiments we developed the dynamical model as shown in Fig. 11. However, there is a significant overlap between intensities in the mid ranges, for example intensity D covers a large portion of the axis. We hypothesise that this is due to the fact that the FACS intensity codes are quite subjective and as a result the distinction between the different intensities across our dataset is a difficult task.

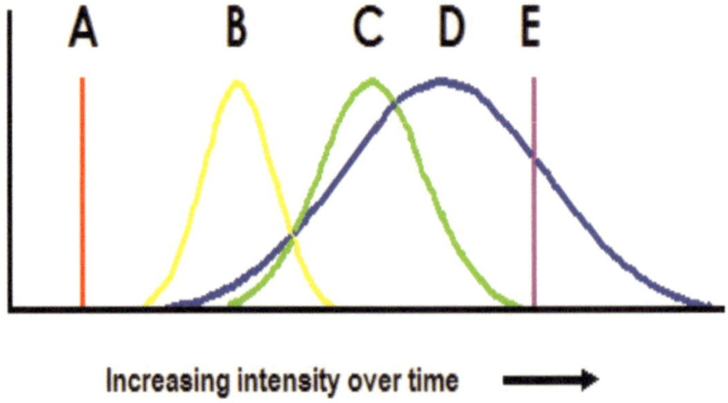

Fig. 11: Distributions for our FACS based dynamical model

To deal with this problem we relabelled our dataset based on three categories corresponding to low, medium, and high intensity displays of the AUs. As a result of this relabelling the outputs of the estimation process became more repeatable and representative of the underlying dynamics of expression formation. The results of the clustering of the dataset under the three-category labelling can be seen in Fig. 12. This is an extension of our previous works on modelling the dynamics of facial expression (Reilly, 2006).

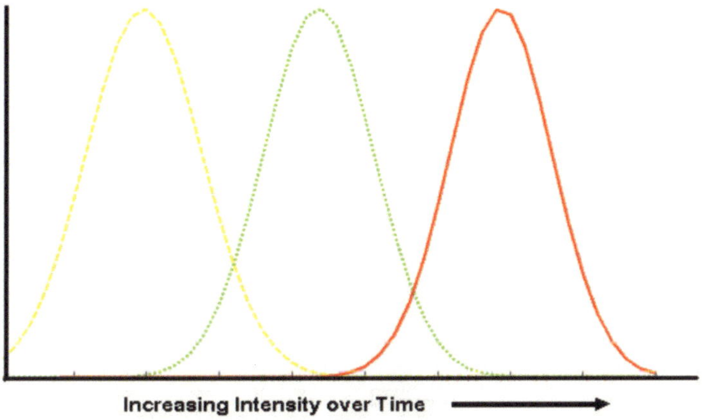

Fig. 12: Distributions for our new 3 stage simplified intensity model

Facial Expression Synthesis

In this section we describe a technique which we have developed that allows for photo-realistic images of a person depicting a desired expression to be synthesised in real-time once a neutral image of the subject is present (Ghent, 2005a; Ghent, 2005b). We also demonstrate how through simple linear interpolation in the expression space the intensity of the output expression can be varied and hence can be used to generate image sequences of expression formation. The approach combines facial appearance models, machine learning techniques, and the FACS to compute a *universal facial expression mapping function* (i.e. a function which maps facial expressions independent of identity).

5.1 Modelling the appearance of facial expressions

In our approach we use active appearance models to first derive low-dimensional spaces, known as *expression spaces*, which are capable of representing the variation in appearance of facial expressions. Active appearance models (Cootes et al., 2001) model the variation of appearance of a class of objects in terms of the variation of both the shape and texture of images of instances of the class. The shape of an object is characterised by the locations of a set of fiducial points on the object, known as landmarks, whereas the texture is defined as the set of pixel intensity values contained within the convex hull of the set of landmarks. By considering the complete collection of landmark sets, independent of the underlying texture data, we can derive a model of the variation in the image due to shape alone. By applying this technique to our dataset we derive separate shape and texture models which we call the *Facial Expression Shape Model* (*FESM*) and the *Facial Expression Texture Model* (FETM). Computation of the FESM is described in Section 3.2.

To compute the FETM we must first warp each input image to the mean shape. This provides us with a *shape independent* representation of the facial texture. Representing the resulting image as a one-dimensional vector (i.e. by concatenating each row of pixels).

$$\mathbf{P}_i = \begin{bmatrix} g_i^1 & g_i^2 & \dots & g_i^n \end{bmatrix}^T \tag{8}$$

A similar procedure can be applied to the texture data as was applied to the shape data in deriving the FESM. That is, the covariance of the texture data and corresponding principal components may be computed. For example in our experiments each shape independent image contains approximately 90,000 dimensions (i.e. pixels) whilst the maximum number of dimensions that we use in an FETM is 20 in which case captured 92% of the variance in the input dataset.

These spaces allow us to constrain the expression synthesis mapping functions such that we can ensure that both the input and output of the functions represent facial images. This is achieved by using the projection of the input image in the expression space, as opposed to the input image itself, as input to the function. Furthermore since the output of the function is also a point in the expression space we ensure that the function only outputs facial images.

5.2 Learning universal expression mapping functions

As mentioned above, an expression mapping function maps a point corresponding to one expression type (e.g. neutral) for a particular individual to the point corresponding to a different expression (e.g. surprise) for that individual. The term "universal expression mapping function" is used to emphasize the fact that the function should perform this mapping for all individuals independent of identity.

To model this function we use *artificial neural networks* (ANN's) in conjunction with the FESM and FETM. Since we represent the shape and texture separately, it follows that for a given expression mapping we must construct the universal mapping as two separate functions. To do this we use a Linear Network (LN) and a Radial Basis Function Network (RBFN) to model the universal mapping function in the FESM and FETM, respectively (Ghent, 2005b). The reason for the different choice of network architecture is due to the fact that we have found the mapping in the FETM to be highly non-linear and hence cannot be modelled accurately using a LN.

Both networks are trained in a supervised manner using a subset of the database described in Section 3.1. For each image, the landmark set and the shape normalised texture are projected into the FESM and FETM, respectively, producing two vectors, $\mathbf{b}_s$ and $\mathbf{b}_t$. Training of the LN involves presenting the network with pairs of $\mathbf{b}_s$ vectors corresponding to the FESM representation of the neutral and expression shape for each individual. Training of the RBFN is performed in the same manner using the $\mathbf{b}_t$ vectors.

Once both networks are trained, synthesis is performed on an input image by identifying the landmark positions and computing the shape normalised texture. Again these are both projected into the FESM and FETM producing vectors $\mathbf{b}_s$ and $\mathbf{b}_t$. These vectors are then used as input to the respective ANN's resulting in two new vectors $\tilde{\mathbf{b}}_s$ and $\tilde{\mathbf{b}}_t$ corresponding to the predicted vectors for the individual portraying the output expression used in the training set. Reconstruction of the image is achieved by inverting Equation 2 for both the shape and texture.

5.3. Experiments

Many interactive media applications involving faces require the ability to animate a face in real-time. Such applications include personalised media creation (i.e. inserting an individual into a pre-captured sequence or movie), personalised online avatars, or giving a character in a computer game the identity of the user. In these situations the user typically presents themselves to the system in a cooperative manner and hence the system can request that the user portray a neutral expression.

To evaluate the performance of our approach in the context of this type of application we have applied it to the synthesis of non-neutral expressions where the input is a neutral expression. Universal mapping functions were developed for synthesising joy (AU6 + AU12 + AU25), surprise (AU1 + AU2 + AU5 + AU26), and sadness (AU15 + AU17).

To create a FESM and a FETM we use images from the Cohn–Kanade AU coded Facial Expression Database described in Section 3.1. Again, each face was manually labelled with 122 landmark points as shown in Fig. 2. Given both the images and the landmark sets the procedure described above was applied to produce the facial expression appearance model (i.e. the FESM and FETM). Since for each expression mapping function we assume that the input and output are specific expressions, only those two expressions are used in building the appearance model. Hence for each new expression mapping function we create an expression space tailored to that mapping. The neural networks are then trained on sample input-output pairs of the expression vectors under consideration in that space.

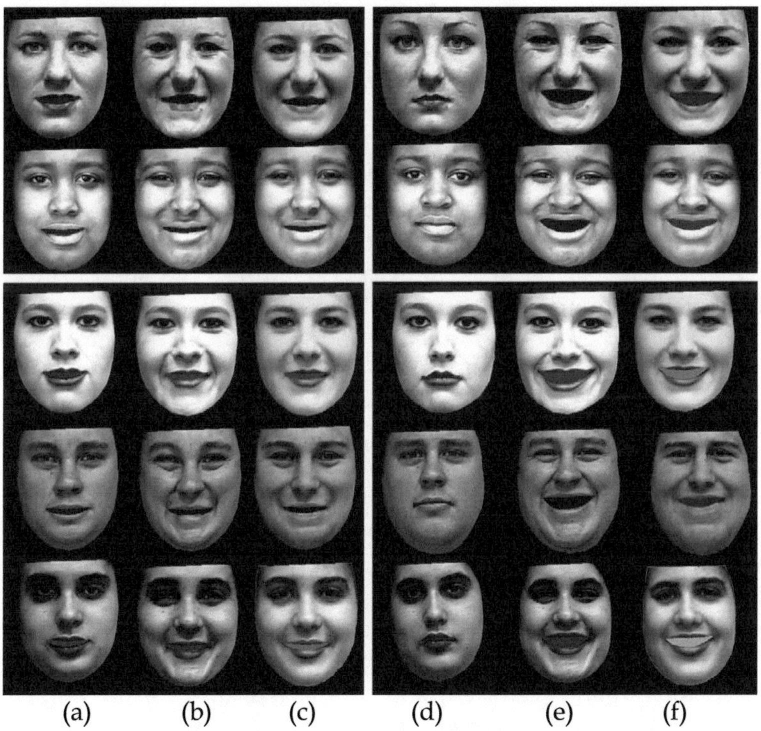

Fig. 13: Columns (a)-(c) show the shape-free neutral, non-neutral, and synthesised images, respectively. Columns (d)-(f) show the same texture as columns (a)-(c) but here the correct shape is used (i.e. the original shape in (d) and (e), and the synthesised shape in (f))

(a) (b) (c)

Fig. 14: Examples of the (a) input, (b) desired output, and (c) actual output of the mapping functions for surprise, joy and sadness

Fig. 13 shows examples of the outputs of one of these mappings for five different subjects. The first two rows consist of images of subjects that were used during the training of the networks while the next three individuals (rows 3–6) were not used during the training of the networks. Column one consists of shape free original images of individuals depicting neutral expressions. Column two consists of shape free original images of individuals depicting AU6C+AU12C+AU25 as described by the FACS. Column three consists of synthetic images of individuals portraying these AU's as calculated by the RBFN with the neutral texture vector as input. Columns 4–6 are the same as the first three columns, respectively, except with shape taken into consideration. The shapes in column 6 are calculated using a LN in conjunction with the FESM.

Fig. 14 shows examples of original neutral and non-neutral images of unseen individuals in conjunction with images where the synthesised expression has been overlaid on the original neutral. As can be seen from the figure the rows 1-3 show the outputs for the surprise, joy, and sadness mapping functions, respectively. In order to quantitatively evaluate the performance of the technique we compute the correlation coefficient between the synthesised data and the real data.

Table 3 and Table 4 show the correlation coefficients between the estimated and real principal components for the FESM using a LN and FETM using an RBFN, respectively. Here, N_I is the number of individuals (i.e. image pairs) used in the experiments, *Pram* is the number of principal components used as input and output to and from the neural networks and, *Perc* is the percentage of variance that *Pram* can describe. N_S is the total number of individuals used for training (i.e. seen) and testing (i.e. unseen) the mapping functions, while *Avg*, *Max* and *Min* are the average, maximum and minimum correlation coefficients between the estimated shape parameters and the real shape parameters, respectively.

From the average of correlation coefficient of the unseen shape and texture taken from Tables 3 and 4 we can compute that the overall average for unseen data is 0.757. Using a similar technique Yangzhou and Xueyin (Yangzhou & Xueyin, 2003) showed how a universal mapping function achieves results of *Avg*=0.51. Given that the input and output to LN and RBFN are vectors representing the neutral and extreme expression, respectively, a natural next step is to try to develop mapping functions for outputting expressions at intermediate intensities. By treating the neutral and extreme vectors as the end points of the trajectory traced out by the expression vector during the expression formation process, generating intermediate intensity expressions can be treated as equivalent to identifying intermediate points on this trajectory. We have found that by approximating this trajectory as linear and hence using linear interpolation to identify intermediate point yields excellent results.

AU	N_I	*Parm*	*Perc*		N_S	*Avg*	*Min*	*Max*
6,12,25	40	15	94.04	Seen	35	0.959	0.753	0.998
				Unseen	5	0.875	0.589	0.997
1,2,5,26	20	20	98.61	Seen	15	0.976	0.899	0.999
				Unseen	5	0.777	0.522	0.971
15,17	17	20	99.35	Seen	15	0.969	0.776	0.999
				Unseen	2	0.699	0.554	0.845
Total	**77**	**N/A**	**N/A**	**Seen**	**65**	**0.968**	**0.754**	**0.999**
				Unseen	**12**	**0.784**	**0.522**	**0.997**

Table 3: Correlation coefficients between real and synthesised shape vectors using a LN

AU	N_I	*Parm*	*Perc*		N_S	*Avg*	*Min*	*Max*
6,12,25	40	15	95.59	Seen	35	0.997	0.936	1.00
				Unseen	5	0.780	0.628	1.00
1,2,5,26	20	20	89.18	Seen	15	0.991	0.875	1.00
				Unseen	5	0.776	0.317	0.875
15,17	17	20	92.03	Seen	14	0.977	0.737	1.00
				Unseen	3	0.635	0.501	0.737
Total	**77**	**N/A**	**N/A**	**Seen**	**64**	**0.988**	**0.737**	**1.00**
				Unseen	**13**	**0.730**	**0.317**	**1.00**

Table 4: Correlation coefficients between real and synthesised texture vectors using a RBFN

Fig. 15 shows an example of applying this interpolation process to the FESM only. Here we have taken the input neutral shape and used the universal mapping function to estimate the shape of the extreme expression. We then linearly interpolate 3 equally spaced points between the two corresponding vectors in the FESM. Using the 4 new shapes as warp targets we warp the input (neutral) texture producing the images shown. Note here that due to the fact that we are just using the LN and FESM that we do not need to convert the original image to greyscale and hence we can use this approach to generate colour image sequences. Also even though the image is not taken from the Cohn-Kanade database the results are still accurate. We have applied the technique to a number of images which are not part of this database and achieved similar results and so are confident that the technique generalises well.

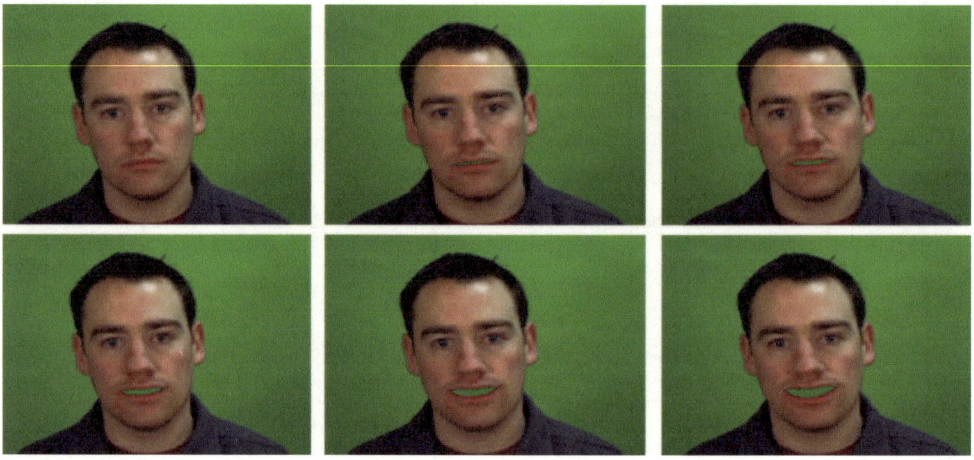

Fig. 15: Examples of our synthesis results, by varying the interpolation in the FESM

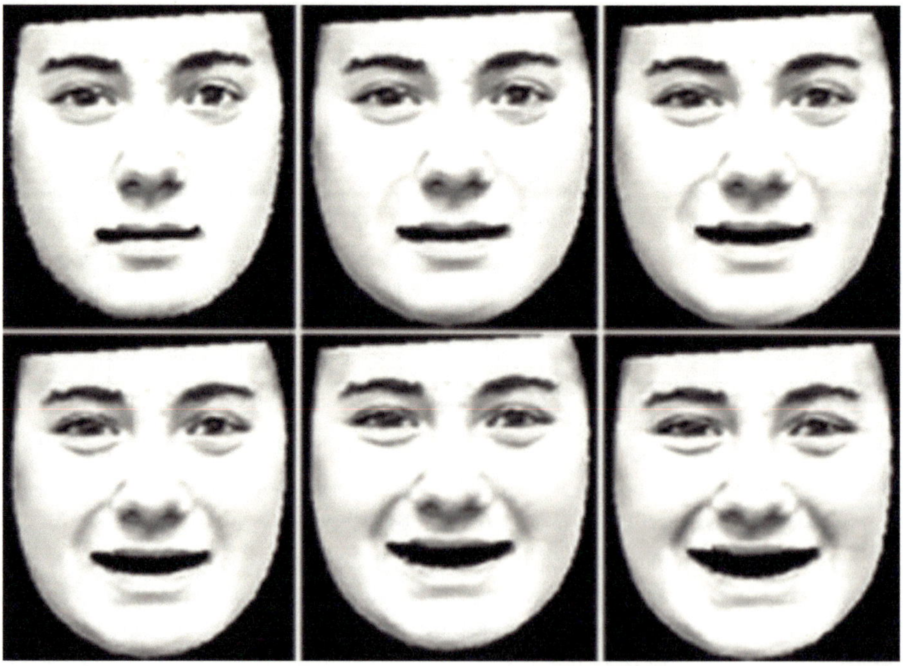

Fig. 16: Examples of our synthesis results, by varying intensity by interpolation in the FESM and FETM

Fig. 16 shows the result of applying the same procedure to both the shape and texture vectors of a given neutral image (i.e. interpolating both simultaneously). Since the FETM is computed using greyscale images the input and output of the process are also greyscale images. The advantage of interpolation in both spaces simultaneously can be seen in that here the texture is both warped and altered appropriately. This can best be seen by inspecting the cheek region (known as the *intraorbital triangle*) across the sequence. Specifically, in the neutral image there no creasing in this region, however in each subsequent image the creasing increases as would be expected in the expression associated with joy (due to the action of AU12). This alteration of the texture could not be achieved by simple warping alone and so requires a complete shape and texture model.

7. Conclusion

In this chapter we have discussed the field of facial expression analysis from both a Behavioural Science and a Computer Vision perspective. We introduced the field of facial expression analysis with Darwin's initial findings and then went on to provide details of the research conduced by Ekman *et al.* on facial expression analysis highlighting the importance of facial expression dynamics.

We then provided details of the current state-of-the-art in automated facial expression analysis, and presented our contribution to this field. In our facial expression classification section we demonstrated the success of our PCA based technique at classifying the primary facial expressions achieving and average AUC of 0.91. We developed separate LLE based shape models for the classification of upper and lower face AUs. Context independent classifiers were used to discriminate between two of the three AUs that occur within the eyebrow area.

Given our approaches to classification of static expressions, we then extended on this work to create dynamical models which estimate the AU intensity. The performance of this approach was evaluated using both the full FACS intensity system and a simpler system of low, medium, and high intensities. Distributions of the resulting intensity estimations for a sample of the Cohn-Kanade database were presented.

In the final section of this chapter we described a technique which allows for photo-realistic expression synthesis (Ghent, 2005a; Ghent, 2005b). This was achieved by applying machine learning techniques to the modelling of *universal facial expression mapping functions.* Three mapping functions were developed for mapping from neutral to joy, surprise, and sadness. We also demonstrated how the representation of expression used allowed the intensity of the output expression to be varied. This ability to vary the intensity of output enabled us to generate image sequences of expression formation.

8. References

Abboud, B., Davoine, F. & Dang, M. (2004) , Facial expression recognition and synthesis based on an appearance model, *Signal Processing: Image Communication*, 19, 8, (September 2004), pp. 723-740.

Ambadar, Z., Schooler, J., Cohn, J. (2005) Deciphering the enigmatic face: The importance of facial dynamics to interpreting subtle facial expressions. *Psychological Science* (2005)

Arad, N., Dyn, N., Reisfeld, D. & Yeshurun, Y. (1994) Image warping by Radial Basis Functions:Application to Facial Expressions, *CVGIP: Graphical Models & Image Processing*,56,2, (March 1994), pp.161–172.

Bartlett, M.S. B. Braathen, G.L.T.J.S., Movellan, J.: Automatic analysis (2001)of spontaneous facial behavior(2001) MPLABTR-2001-06, Institute for Neural Computation, University of California, San Diego.

Bartlett, M.S., Littlewort, G., Lainscsek, C., Fasel, I., Movellan, J.: Machine learning methods for fully automatic recognition of facial expressions and facial actions. *IEEE International conference on systems, man and cybernetics (2004) 592–597*

Bartlet, M., Littlewort, G., Lainscsek, C., Fasel, I., Frank, M., Movellan, J. (2006a): Fully automatic facial action recognition in spontaneous behavior, *conference on Face and Gesture Recognition* (2006)

Bartlet, M., Littlewort, I., Frank,G., Lainscsek, C., Fasel, M., Movellan, J.: (2006b) Automatic Recognition of Facial Actions in Spontaneous Expresions, *Journal of Multimedia*, Vol 1. No. 6 September 2006

Choe B. & Ko H.S., (2001) Analysis & synthesis of facial expression with hand generated muscle actuation basis, *Proc 14th Conference on Computer Animation*, pp.12-19, Seoul, South Korea, November 2001

Cohen, I., Sebe, N., Huang, T.S. (2003) Facial expression recognition from video sequences: Temporal and static modeling. *Computer Vision and Image Understanding*, 91(1-2) (2003)

Cohn, J., Kanade: (1999) Cohn-Kanade au-coded facial expression database. *Technical report*, Pittsburgh University 1999

Cohn, J.F., Schmidt, K., Gross, R., Ekman, P. (2002) Individual differences in facial expression: Stability over time, relation to self-reported emotion, and ability to inform person identification. *Proceedings of Intel. Conf. On Multimedia and Expo*, 2002

Cohn, J.(2005) Automated analysis of the configuration and timing of facial expression. (2005) Afterword of What the face reveals (2nd edition): Basic and applied studies of spontaneous expression using the FacialAction Coding System (FACS) by P. Ekman and E. Rosenberg, ed., 2005.

Cootes, T.F.; Edwards, G.J.; Taylor, C.J. (2001) Active appearance models, *IEEE Transactions on Pattern Analysis and Machine Intelligence*, 23, 6, (June 2001), pp. 681 - 685

Darwin, C (1872), *The expression of the emotions in man and animal*, University of Chicago Press, ISBN-13: 978-0195112719, Chicago, USA

Ekman, P., Sorenson, E. R., & Friesen, W. V. (1969) Pan-cultural elements in facial displays of emotions. *Science*, 1969, 164(3875), pp. 86-88

Ekman, P., Friesen, W., Hager, J. (1978) Facial Action Coding System , consulting psychologists press, Palo Alto,CA 1978

Ekman, P. Friesen, W. (1979) Constants across cultures in the face and emotion, Journal of personality and social psychology 1971

Ekman, P. Friesen, W. (1999a) Facial expression handbook of cognition and emotion, new york, john Wiley and sons ltd. Chapter 16. 2002

Ekman, P, Rosenberg, E., Hager, J., (1999b) Facial action coding system aect interpretive database FACSAID http://nirc.com/expression/facsaid/facsaid.htm 1999

Ekman, P., Friesen, W., Hager, J. (2002) Facial Action Coding System Manual. (2002)

Fasel, B., Luettin, J. (2003) Automatic facial expression analysis: A survey, *Pattern Recognition,* Vol., 36(1) (2003), pp. 259-275.

Fawcett, T. (2003) Roc graphs: Notes and practical considerations for data mining researchers. (2003)

Ghent, J. (2005a). *A Computational Model of Facial Expression*, PhD thesis,National University of Ireland, Maynooth, Co. Kildare, Ireland, July 2005.

Ghent, J. & McDonald, J. (2005b) Photo-realistic facial expression synthesis.*Image and Vision Computing*, 23, 12, (November 2005), pp. 305-328

Goneid, A., el Kaliouby, R.: Facial feature analysis of spontaneous facial expression. In Proceedings of the 10th International AI Applications Conference (2002)

Gralewski, L, Campbell, N., Thomas, B., Dalton, C. & Gibson, D., (2004) Statistical synthesis of facial expressions for the protraying of emotion, *2nd international conf. on Computer graphics and interactive techniques in Australasia and South East Asia*, pp. 190–198, Singapore, June 2004

Kayo, nee Kouropteva, O., (2006). Locally Linear Embedding Algorithm. Extensions and Applications. PhD thesis, University of Oulu, Oulu, Finland,2006.

King, I. & Hou, H.T. (1996) Radial Basis Network for Facial Expression Synthesis, *Proceedings of the International Conference on Neural Information Processing*, pp. 1127-1130, Hong Kong, 1996,

Meytlis, M. & Sirovich, L.; On the Dimensionality of Face Space, *IEEE Transactions on Pattern Analysis and Machine Intelligence*, 29, 7, (July 2007), pp. 1262 - 1267

Pantic, M., Rothkrantz, L.J.M. (2000) Automatic analysis of facial expressions:the state of the art. *IEEE transactions on pattern analysis and machine learning* 22 (2000)

Pantic, M., Patras, I.: Dynamics of facial expression: Recognition of facial actions and their temporal segments from face profile image sequences. *SMC-B* 36 (2006) 433–449

Raouzaiou, A., Tsapatsoulis, N. & Karpouzis, K. (2002). ParameterizedFacial Expression Synthesis Based on MPEG-4, *EURASIP Journal on Applied Signal Proccessing*, vol. 10, (October 2002), pp. 1021–1038

Reilly, J., Ghent, J., McDonald, J., 2006 Investigating the Dynamics of facialexpressions, *International symposium on visual computing* 2006

Reilly, J., Ghent, J., McDonald, J., 2007 Nonlinear Approaches towards the classification of facial expressions *International Machine Vision and Image Processing conference*, 2007

Saul, L. K., and Roweis, S. T., (2003). Think globally, fit locally: unsupervised learning of low dimensional manifolds. *Journal of Machine Learning Research*, 4(119), 2003.

Sayette M., Cohn, J F, Parrott, D.J (2001) Psychometric Evaluation of the Facial Action Coding System for Assessing Spontaneous Expression. (Springer Netherlands) 2001

Wang, H. & Ahuja, N. (2003) Facial Expression Decomposition, *Proceedings of International Conference on Computer Vision*, pp. 958-965, Nice, France, October 2003

Yangzhou, D. & Xueyin, L. (2003) Emotional facial expression model building, *Pattern Recognition Letters*, 24, 16, (December 2003), pp. 2923-2934.

Zhang, Q., Liu, Z., Guo, B., Terzopoulos, D. & Shum, H. (2006). Geometry-Driven Photorealistic Facial Expression Synthesis, *IEEE Trans on Visualization and Computer Graphics*, vol.12, no.1, (Jan/Feb 2006), pp. 48-60

Zheng, A. (2000) Deconstructing motion. Technical report, EECS department, U. C. Berkley (2000)

8

The Development of Emotional Flexible Spine Humanoid Robots

Jimmy Or
Korea Advanced Institute of Science and Technology (KAIST)
Republic of Korea

1. Introduction

Over the past 15 years, there has been an increasing interest in humanoid robots. Researchers worldwide are trying to develop robots that look and move more like humans because they believe that anthropometric biped robots have several advantages over wheeled robots. For instance, humanoid robots can communicate with us and express their emotions by facial expressions, speech and body language. They can also work in our living environment without the need of special infrastructure. Moreover, they can serve as companions and take care of the elderly in our aging society. Due to the usefulness of humanoid robots, some research labs and companies, especially in Japan and Korea, have spent an enormous amount of financial and human resources in this research area.

With advances in computer and robot technologies (RT), several impressive biped walking humanoid robots have been developed. For instance, the Honda's ASIMO, Sony's QRIO and the Kawada's HRP-3P. Although these robots are able to walk stably, their movements are not as natural looking as a human's. One of the reasons is that they do not have a flexible spine as we do. Instead, they have a box-like torso. Since it is very difficult to design and control a biped walking spine robot, researchers have been treating their robots as a rigid mass carried by the legs. They neglect the contributions of the spine in daily activities. We believe that in order for the next generation of humanoid robots to better express themselves through body language and to achieve tasks that cannot be accomplished by conventional humanoid robots, they should have a flexible spine as we do.

This chapter is organized as follows. In Section 2 we give an overview of related research on flexible spine humanoid robotics and point out some of the problems faced by researchers in this research area. Then, in Section 3, we describe our approach for solving these problems. In Section 4, we present psychological experiments on the effect of a flexible spine humanoid robot on human perceptions. Finally, in Section 5, we conclude this chapter.

2. Related research

Compared with wheeled robots, it is more costly and difficult to develop biped walking humanoid robots. One of the main reasons is that full-body biped humanoid robots have more joints. Depending on the type of actuators being used, the total development cost could go up significantly. Another reason is that unlike wheeled robots, biped robots need to be able to maintain stability. The task of coordinating different actuators to produce stable walking in a real-world environment is a challenging one.

Based on the concept of Zero Moment Point (ZMP) proposed by Miomir Vukobratovic (Vukobratovic et al., 1970; Vukobratovic & Borovac, 2004), Atsuo Takanishi at Waseda University applied the ZMP criterion to realize stable walking for biped robots (Takanishi et al., 1988; Takanishi, 1993). His approach contributes greatly to the development of walking humanoid robots. In addition to his ZMP-based compensation approach, other methods such as inverted pendulum, central pattern generator (CPG) and passive walking have also been used to control biped humanoid robots (Sugihara et al., 2002; Nagashima, 2003; Kajita et al., 2003; Collins et al., 2005).

Realizing that the spine is very important in daily activities, several research groups have started to build flexible spine humanoid robots. At the University of Tokyo, Mizuuchi attempted to build a full-body humanoid robot which had a spine controlled by eight tendons. However, it looked like the robot could not stand up without external support (Mizuuchi et al., 2001; Mizuuchi et al., 2003a). Mizuuchi then developed a more sophisticated human-size robot called "Kenta" (Mizuuchi et al., 2002; Mizuuchi et al., 2003b). Although the torso of the robot has a spine-like structure, it does not seem to be as flexible as the neck is because it holds heavy electronics and mechanical components. Also, there has been no data to show that the torso is able to move dynamically and by itself while the robot is sitting on a desk. Later, Mizuuchi developed another robot named "Kotaro". The robot is able to bend to the left and right automatically while sitting in a chair.[1] Although Mizuuchi claimed that the robot is able to stand still by itself, there has been no experimental data to support the claim or to show that the robot can move while standing without external support from above (Mizuuchi et al., 2006a; Mizuuchi et al., 2006b). Recently, Mizuuchi has been working on a new robot named "Kojiro" (Mizuuchi et al., 2007; Nakanishi et al., 2007). The robot has only a lower-spine and two legs. Thus far, there is no experimental data to show that the lower-body robot is able to exhibit dynamic motions while standing by itself without external support. Using the same tendon-based approach, Holland and his group at the University of Essex developed the CRONOS series of anthropomimetic robots (Holland & Knight, 2006). However, their robots are also unable to stand up. This shows that building and controlling full-body spine robots using tendons might not be the ideal approach.

At EPFL in Switzerland, Billard and her group developed a new Robota doll for research on human-robot interactions. In order for the robot to communicate with humans more naturally, her group added a 3-DOF spine to the robot (Guenter et al., 2005; Roos et al., 2006). Unlike the robots developed by Mizuuchi, the spine of this robotics doll is driven by hydraulic power. Due to its actuating system, the robot has no mobility. It is fixed on a platform. At the German Space Agency (DLR), Hirzinger and his group developed an upper-torso robot named "Justin". The robot has light weight arms and dexterous hands. Moreover, it has a 3-DOF movable torso. Unlike the tendon-based approach used by Mizuuchi and Holland, each controllable spinal joint of Justin is directly actuated by a DLR ILM DC Motor via Harmonic Drive Gear. Although the robot is fixed on a platform, the added degrees of freedom in the torso allow the robot to manipulate objects both on the floor and on an evaluated shelf (Ott et al., 2006).

In November, 2007, researchers from Sugano Lab of Waseda University announced a new humanoid robot called "Twendy-One". The robot was developed to carry out household

[1] Such movement has been achieved by a few non-flexible spine humanoid robots using only one motor.

work in today's aging society. It has a 4-DOF spine each joint of which is directly controlled by a Maxon DC Motor via Harmonic Drive Gear. Because of the flexibility in the torso, the robot is able to lift a handicapped person from bed. Also, it can handle objects without flattening them due to the 241 pressure sensors embedded in each hand. However, in order to avoid having it fall, the designers fixed the robot on a wheeled mobile platform.

3. Our approach

In the previous section, we mentioned that a few groups worldwide have started to develop flexible spine humanoid robots. However, they have not yet made a full-body walking prototype. Some of their robots cannot even stand up. The main reason for this is that it is very costly and difficult to build a walking spine robot that has a high degree of freedom. Moreover, it is difficult to coordinate all the motors to generate stable walking motions for the robot.

Since our goal is to develop sociable flexible spine humanoid robots that can express emotions through full-body motions, the robots need to be able to stand and maintain balance by themselves without external support. In order to achieve this goal, we need to simplify the mechanical structure of the robots to reduce the weight of the upper body. We need to take an approach different from that used by other groups. Rather than trying to develop robots that have an equal number of spine segments as humans, we have developed robots that have just enough joints to perform all human torso movements. Instead of using tendons or expensive DC motors with Harmonic Drive Gear to control the robots, we use low-cost off- the-shelf RC servo motors.

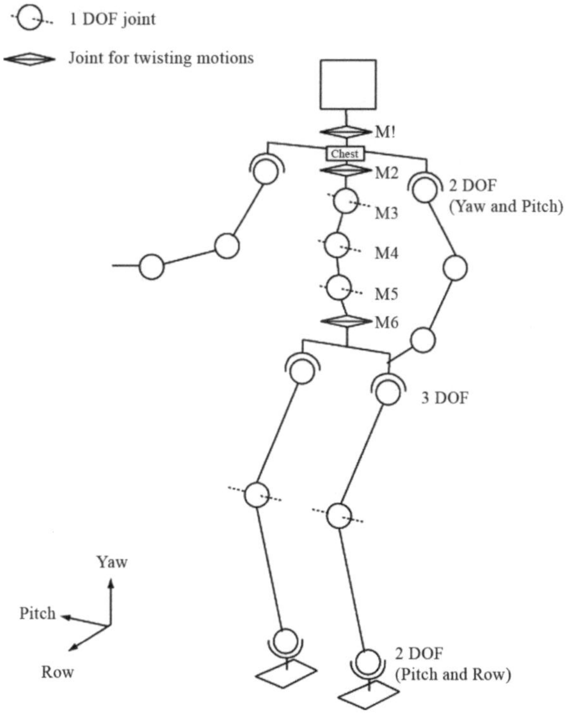

Fig. 1. A schematic diagram of the WBD-1. The robot has 26 DOF joints. Each joint is actuated by a low-cost RC servo motor (from Or & Takanishi, 2005).

Inspired by the dexterity and flexibility of belly dancers, we conducted research on belly dance. After analyzing the motions of professional dancers, we confirmed that a lot of seemingly complex belly dance movements are composed of simple wave-like, circular, sliding motions (Or, 2006). We further noticed that some of the spine motions exhibited by belly dancers are similar to those exhibited by the lamprey, a prototype vertebrate. We then extended our work from belly dance and the motor control of the lamprey to the design and control of flexible spine humanoid robots (Or & Takanishi, 2005). At first, we designed a 6-DOF mechanism that is capable of exhibiting all human-like spine motions with significantly less joints. Then, we added limbs to the mechanical spine to create a full-body humanoid robot called the "Waseda Belly Dancer No. 1" (WBD-1). The spine mechanism of our robot works as follows (see Fig. 1): to generate forward-backward bending on the sagittal plane, we turn motors M3 to M5. To create lateral flexion on the frontal plane, we rotate motors M2 and M6 in opposite directions by 90 degrees. This changes the orientation of the spine so that when we turn motors M3 to M5, the robot's upper torso bends towards the left or right. In order for the robot to twist its body on a transverse plane, we turn motors M2 or M6.

In terms of coordinating different motors in the mechanical spine to generate human-like spine motions, we used a model of the lamprey central pattern generator as the controller. Using the CPG, we are able to control the mechanical spine with only three control parameters (Or & Takanishi, 2005; Or, 2006). Unlike the robots developed by other groups, the WBD-1 is able to exhibit dynamic spine motions even when it is standing without external support. This is accomplished by widening the supporting polygon formed by the feet of the robot.

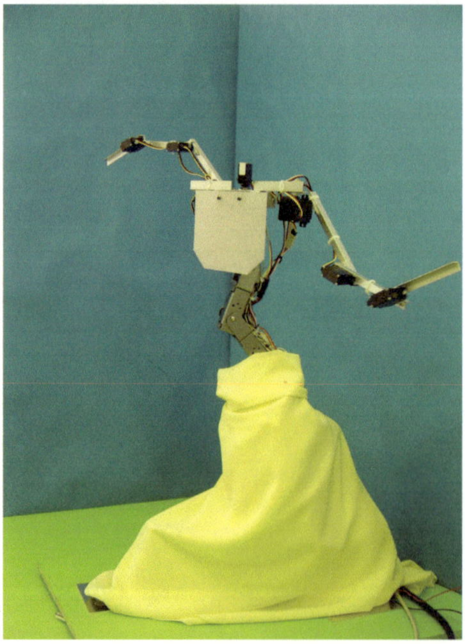

Fig. 2. The WBD-1 performing belly dance (*Nature*, 2004). The robot is able to exhibit dynamic upper body motions without being hung from above.

For emotional expressions using full-body motions, the robots need to be able to maintain balance without external support. To investigate real-time balancing for flexible spine humanoid robots, we developed a hybrid CPG-ZMP based control system for a simple four-segment spine robot (Or & Takanishi, 2004). The robot is made of serially connected RC servo motors. Each motor serves as a spinal joint and the four actuators are stacked on top of each other (Figs. 3 and 4). The motor at the bottom of the mechanical spinal column is connected to a plastic foot-sole. The entire robot is free to move on the desk. In our controller, the biologically-inspired CPG module generates rhythmic belly dancing motions for the mechanical spine. Meanwhile, the ZMP Monitor measures the torque at the base joint. If the torque is larger than an experimentally pre-determined threshold, the robot is on the verge of falling.[2] Whenever this happens, the ZMP Monitor sends negative feedback signals to the CPG module to modulate its neural activities. Depending on the state of the robot and timing, different emergent spine motions can be generated. Using our approach, the robot is able to perform belly dance-like motions while dancing freely on the desk (Fig. 4). The robot's behavior can be interpreted as emotional expressions. For instance, slow wave-like motions correspond to *calm* while fast motions correspond to *happiness* or *excitement*.

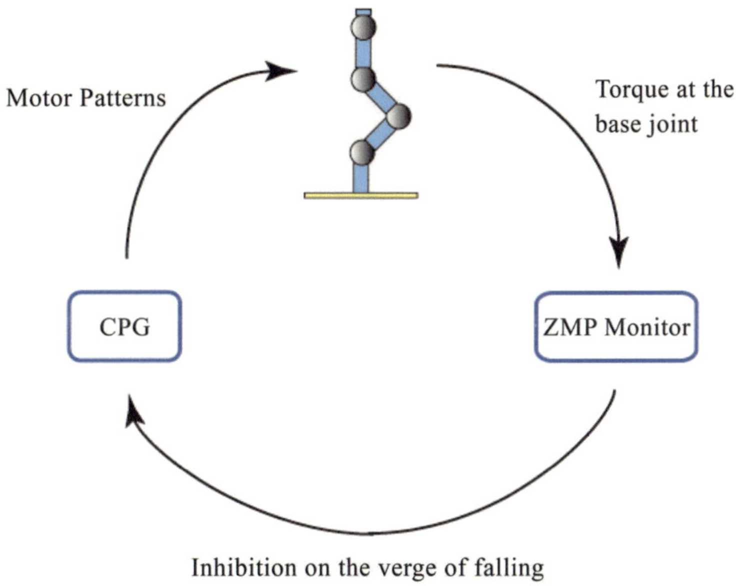

Fig. 3. Schematic diagram of the hybrid CPG-ZMP control system (from Or & Takanishi, 2004).

---

[2] In our studies, we measured the current consumption of the robot's base joint motor using a current sensor. Since current is proportional to torque and a large torque is generated at the base joint motor when the robot is going to fall, we are able to predict when the robot is on the verge of falling by comparing the measured current with an experimentally pre-determined threshold.

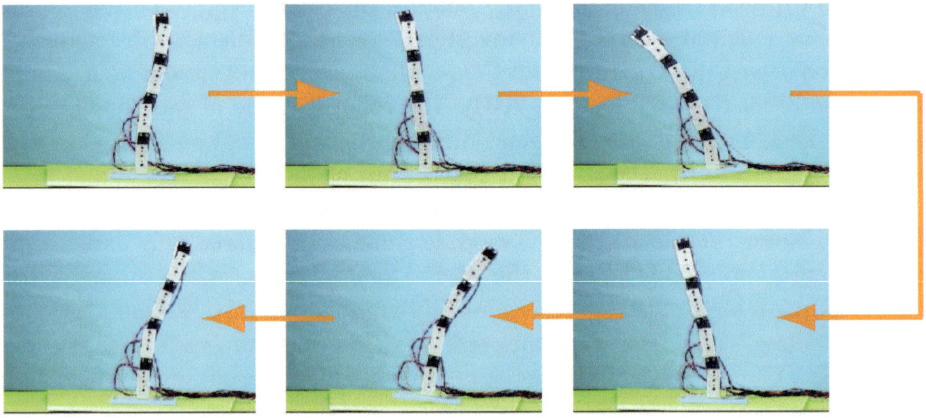

Fig. 4. Snapshot of a four-segment belly dancing mechanical spine controlled by the hybrid CPG-ZMP controller.

Based on the WBD-1, we developed another prototype called the WBD-2 in 2004 (Fig. 5). The robot is capable of expressing emotions using full-body dynamic motions due to an improved lower-body design (Fig. 6). However, because the leg joints are made of low-cost, off-the-shelf RC servo motors, the robot has limited walking capabilities. Later, we developed a new robot called the WBD-3. This robot is able to walk stably at different speeds with dynamic spine motions. In Section 4 of this chapter, we present results of psychological experiments on the effect of an emotional belly dancing robot on human perceptions.

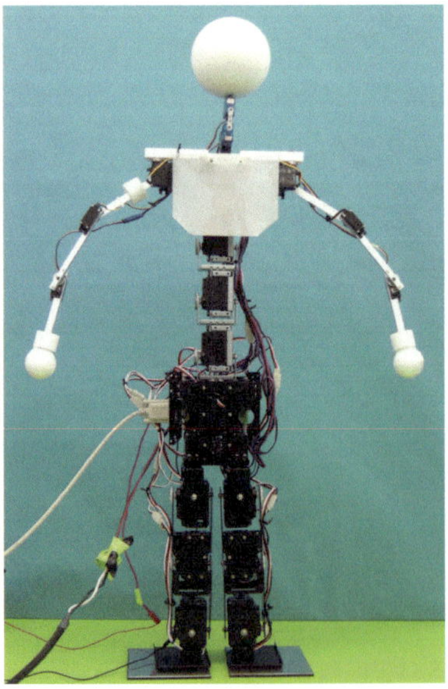

Fig. 5. The Waseda Belly Dancer No.2 (WBD-2) humanoid robot. The world's first full-body, flexible spine humanoid robot capable of full-body motions without external support (as of March 7, 2008).

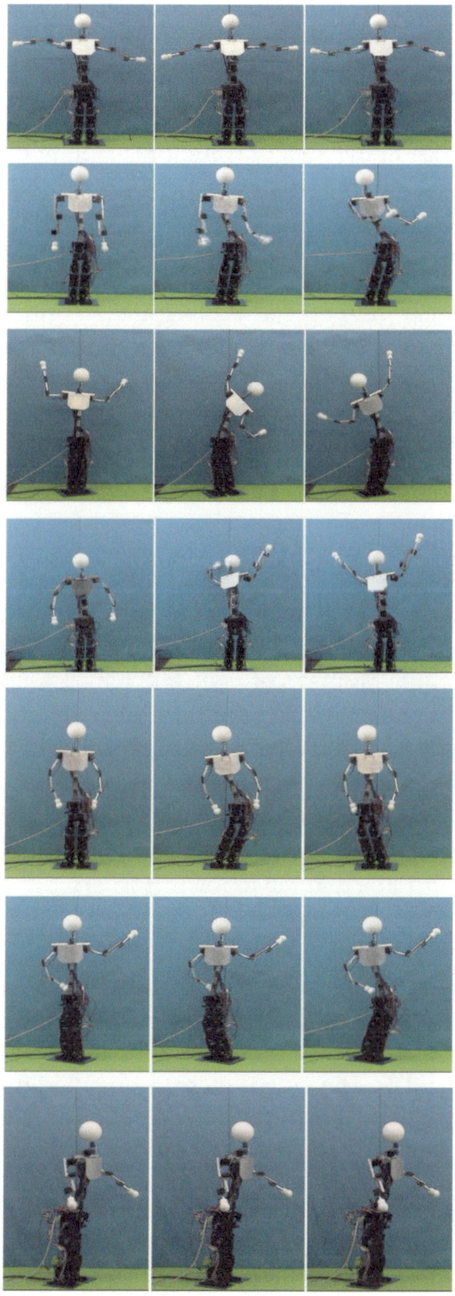

Fig. 6. Emotional expressions of the WBD-2 humanoid robot. Note that the robot is able to exhibit full-body dynamic motions without external support from the top. Behavior for *confident, disgust, happy, relieved, patient, angry* and *sexy* (from top to bottom). For details on behavioral generation, refer to Or & Takanishi, 2007.

4. Experiments on the effect of a flexible spine emotional belly dancing robot on human perceptions

Since much of human communication is non-verbal and we often use body language to express emotions, it is important for humanoid robots to have a similar capability. So far, there have been several studies in the area of communication of emotion from both human and robot body movements (Walk & Homan, 1984; Sogon & Masutani, 1989; Ayama et al., 1996; Dittrich et al., 1996; Brownlow et al., 1997; Shibata & Inooka, 1998; Pollick et al., 2001). Moreover, several impressive robots that can express emotions have been developed (Lim et al., 1999; Kobayashi et al., 2001; Breazeal, 2002; Breazeal, 2003; Itoh et al., 2004; Ishiguro, 2005; Oh et al., 2006). However, besides the WBD-2, there is no humanoid robot that can express emotions using spine motions. We conducted a series of psychological experiments using both the WBD-2 and human actors to investigate whether it is possible for human subjects to categorize effects of the movements of a flexible spine humanoid robot through body motions alone, and how effectively it does so.[3]

4.1 General procedure

Forty subjects were randomly selected to participate in the experiments. The male subjects came from two different labs in the Department of Mechanical Engineering at Waseda University in Japan. Due to the limited number of females in this group, 11 female subjects were also selected from two different dance classes. The age of our subjects ranged from 20 to 34 years old. There were equal numbers of male and female subjects. At the beginning of the experiments, the subjects were provided with three pages of questionnaires (one for each experiment), and they were asked to match a series of video clips to the list of emotions given in each questionnaire, based on their first impressions. They were then shown the video clips on a laptop computer (Thinkpad X40 with a 12.1" LCD screen). Forced-choice paradigm was used. During the experiments, the subjects were not allowed to talk with each other. The experiments were arranged in the following order:

1. Categorization of affective movements from a robot actor
2. Categorization of affective movements from a human actor (with face covered)
3. Categorization of affective movements from a human actor (with facial expressions)

The goals of the experiments were to test whether human subjects could categorize affective movements performed by the different actors. In each experiment, subjects saw a series of seven video clips (Figs. 6, 7 and 8). The videos were arranged in the same order and each of them corresponded to a particular emotion the actor was trying to express. Given that seven choices were provided, the base level at which observers could have been guessing is one out of seven.

In order to statistically test our hypotheses and investigate the patterns of categorizations with respect to the video clips, we used one-way repeated-measures analysis of variance (ANOVA) to analyze the data in each experiment. To carry out the analysis, we used the statistical software program SPSS (version 13.0; SPSS, Inc.). In the analyses described below we follow the convention that a difference is considered to be significant when the p-value of the associated ANOVA test is less than 0.05.

---

[3] The remainder of this section are orginated from Or & Takanishi, 2007. Copied and modified with permission.

Fig. 7. Snapshot of video images shown in Experiment 2. Movements for *confident, disgust, happy, relieved, patient, angry* and *sexy* (from top to bottom).

Fig. 8. Snapshot of video images shown in Experiment 3. Movements for *confident, disgust, happy, relieved, patient, angry* and *sexy* (from top to bottom).

4.2 Results of experiment 1: categorization of affective movements from the robot actor

The results of our subjects' responses (on an interval scale) are shown in Table 1.[4] We used Mauchly's test of sphericity to ascertain that the assumption of sphericity was met. We then conducted a test of within-subjects effects on how well the movements of the robot actor were correctly categorised. The result shows that there was a significant difference among some of the responses toward the seven affective movements exhibited by the robot. $F(6, 39) = 7.695, p < 0.01$.

Affective Movement	Mean	Standard Deviation	Standard Error of the Mean
confident	(0.150, 0.100, 0.150)	(0.362, 0.304, 0.362)	(0.057, 0.048, 0.057)
disgust	(0.450, 0.375, 0.725)	(0.504, 0.490, 0.452)	(0.080, 0.077, 0.071)
happy	(0.500, 0.725, 0.950)	(0.506, 0.452, 0.221)	(0.080, 0.067, 0.035)
relieved	(0.150, 0.725, 0.625)	(0.362, 0.452, 0.490)	(0.057, 0.067, 0.077)
patient	(0.600, 0.425, 0.625)	(0.496, 0.501, 0.490)	(0.078, 0.079, 0.077)
angry	(0.125, 0.350, 0.475)	(0.335, 0.483, 0.506)	(0.053, 0.076, 0.080)
sexy	(0.375, 0.400, 0.550)	(0.490, 0.496, 0.504)	(0.077, 0.078, 0.080)

Table 1. Descriptive statistics for the responses to each of the emotions expressed by the three actors. Under the columns "Mean," "Standard Deviation" and "Standard Error of the Mean," the elements in parentheses (*from left to right*) represent the responses toward the robot, faceless human and human actor, respectively. Higher mean values correspond to more correct responses.

In order to compare the means of responses to each movement, we examined the pairwise comparisons. Table 2 shows that the movement which corresponds to *happy* elicited significantly more correct responses than the ones corresponding to *confident, relieved* and *angry*. Similarily, the movement which corresponds to *patient* elicited significantly more correct responses than the ones for *confident, relieved* and *angry*. Finally, significantly more subjects correctly categorized the movement for *disgust* than the one for *angry*. These results confirmed the hypothesis that a flexible spine humanoid robot can be used to convey recognisable emotions through body movements.

Note that if we take the confidence intervals of the means into consideration, our subjects' responses could roughly be classified into two groups (see Fig. 9). The first group includes *patient, happy, disgust* and *sexy* while the second group includes *confident, relieved* and *angry*.

[4] The raw data can be found later in Fig. 12.

Comparison Pair		Mean Difference	Std. Error	Sig	95% CI
confident	disgust	-0.300	0.103	0.120	[-0.633, 0.033]
	happy	-0.350*	0.098	0.021	[-0.670, -0.030]
	relieved	0.000	0.088	1.000	[-0.285, 0.285]
	patient	-0.450*	0.094	0.001	[-0.757, -0.143]
	angry	0.025	0.084	1.000	[-0.248, 0.298]
	sexy	-0.225	0.104	0.782	[-0.564, 0.114]
disgust	happy	-0.050	0.101	1.000	[-0.378, 0.278]
	relieved	0.300	0.096	0.071	[-0.012, 0.612]
	patient	-0.150	0.098	1.000	[-0.470, 0.170]
	angry	0.325*	0.090	0.019	[0.031, 0.619]
	sexy	0.075	0.121	1.000	[-0.318, 0.468]
happy	relieved	0.350*	0.098	0.021	[0.030, 0.670]
	patient	-0.100	0.112	1.000	[-0.464, 0.264]
	angry	0.375*	0.099	0.011	[0.052, 0.698]
	sexy	0.125	0.125	1.000	[-0.281, 0.531]
relieved	patient	-0.450*	0.094	0.001	[-0.757, -0.143]
	angry	0.025	0.067	1.000	[-0.192, 0.242]
	sexy	-0.225	0.091	0.380	[-0.521, 0.071]
patient	angry	0.475*	0.095	0.000	[0.167, 0.783]
	sexy	0.225	0.091	0.380	[-0.071, 0.521]
angry	sexy	-0.250	0.106	0.490	[-0.594, 0.094]

Table 2. Pairwise comparisons for the performance of the robot actor. *The mean difference is significant at the 0.05 level. Adjustment for multiple comparisons: Bonferroni.

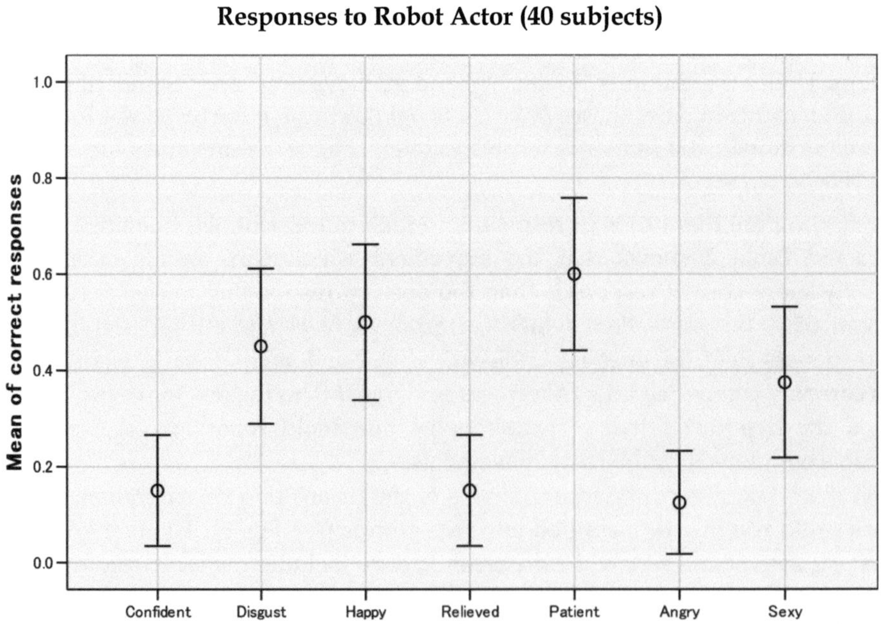

Fig. 9. Responses to affective movements exhibited by the robot. The vertical bars in the graph denote the 95% confidence intervals.

4.3 Results of experiment 2: categorization of affective movements from a human actor (with face covered)

To investigate whether our subjects could categorize emotions from human movements alone, we showed them videos of a human actor performing the same type of movements as the robot. However, in order to prevent the subjects from making their decisions based on facial expressions, we digitally covered the face of the actor.

Table 1 shows the results of our subjects' responses. Mauchly's test showed that the assumption of sphericity was violated (χ^2 (20) = 31.780, $p < 0.05$), so the Greenhouse-Geisser correction was used ($\varepsilon = 0.824$). We then performed the test of within-subjects effects and found that there were significant differences among some of the responses toward the seven affective movements displayed by a faceless human actor. F (4.94, 192.83) = 10.557, $p < 0.01$.

The results of the pairwise comparisons are shown in Table 3. The table shows that the movements which correspond to *happy* elicited significantly more correct responses than the movements for *confident, disgust* and *angry.* Also, the movement which corresponds to *relieved* was significantly more recognizable than the ones for *confident, disgust, sexy* and *angry.* As for the movement for *patient,* it significantly outperformed the one for *confident.* Finally, the movement for *sexy* elicited significantly more correct responses than the one for *confident.* Hence, our analysis confirmed the hypothesis that the subjects could categorize affects based on human body movements alone.

Comparison Pair		Mean Difference	Std. Error	Sig	95% CI
confident	disgust	-0.275	0.088	0.068	[-0.560, 0.010]
	happy	-0.625*	0.078	0.000	[-0.877, -0.373]
	relieved	-0.625*	0.085	0.000	[-0.903, -0.347]
	patient	-0.325*	0.075	0.002	[-0.569, -0.081]
	angry	-0.250	0.086	0.124	[-0.529, 0.029]
	sexy	-0.300*	0.073	0.004	[-0.538, -0.062]
disgust	happy	-0.350*	0.105	0.039	[-0.690, -0.010]
	relieved	-0.350*	0.098	0.021	[-0.670, -0.030]
	patient	-0.050	0.094	1.000	[-0.357, 0.257]
	angry	0.025	0.076	1.000	[-0.222, 0.272]
	sexy	-0.025	0.104	1.000	[-0.364, 0.314]
happy	relieved	0.000	0.113	1.000	[-0.368, 0.368]
	patient	0.300	0.114	0.260	[-0.072, 0.672]
	angry	0.375*	0.106	0.021	[0.032, 0.718]
	sexy	0.325	0.110	0.109	[-0.032, 0.682]
relieved	patient	0.350	0.096	0.071	[-0.012, 0.612]
	angry	0.375*	0.099	0.011	[0.052, 0.698]
	sexy	0.325*	0.097	0.039	[0.009, 0.641]
patient	angry	0.075	0.097	1.000	[-0.241, 0.391]
	sexy	0.025	0.098	1.000	[-0.293, 0.343]
angry	sexy	-0.050	0.107	1.000	[-0.398, 0.298]

Table 3. Pairwise Comparisons for the performance of faceless human actor. *The mean difference is significant at the 0.05 level. Adjustment for multiple comparisons: Bonferroni.

Just like the first experiment, our subjects had difficulty in characterizing the affective movement for *confident*. However, unlike the responses to the robot actor, the responses of our subjects in this experiment can clearly be divided into three distinct groups (see Fig. 10): 1. high performance (*happy* and *relieved*); 2. moderate performance (*disgust, patient, angry* and *sexy*); and 3. low performance (*confident*).

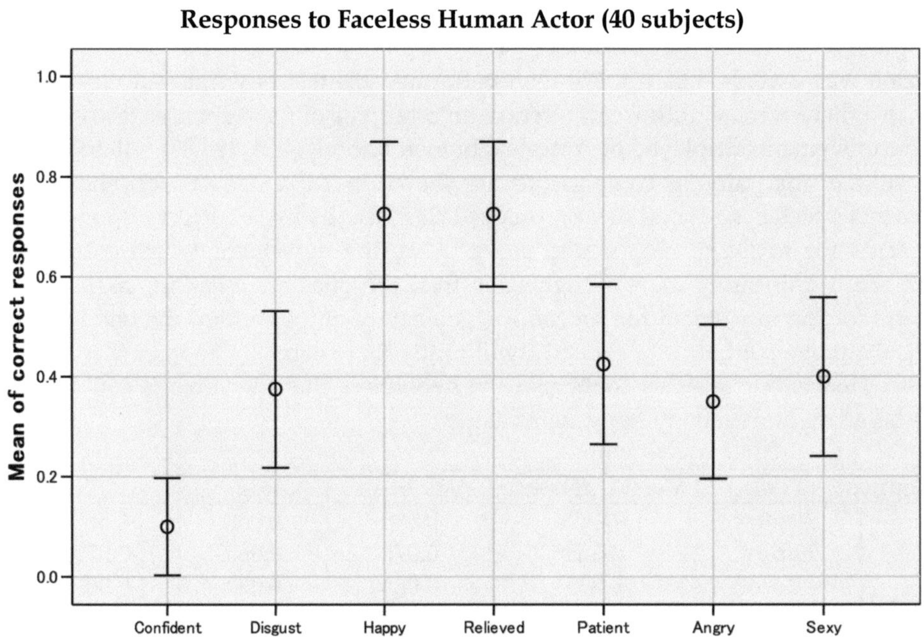

Fig. 10. Responses to affective movements exhibited by a human actor with face covered. The vertical bars in the graph denote the 95% confidence intervals.

4.4 Results of experiment 3: categorization of affective movements from a human actor (with facial expressions visible)

In this experiment, we investigated whether our subjects could categorize emotions from a human actor when they could see the actor's facial expressions. The same video clips used in Experiment 2 were used here, except that in this experiment the face of the human actor was not obscured. We should therefore be able to attribute any change in the pattern of our subjects' responses to the visibility of the actor's facial expressions or due to experience from previous clarification tasks.

Table 1 shows the means and standard deviations of our subjects' responses. Again, Mauchly's test of sphericity indicates that the assumption of sphericity has been violated (χ^2 (20) = 32.967, $p < 0.05$), and again we used the Greenhouse-Geisser estimates of sphericity ($\varepsilon = 0.826$). The result shows that there was a significant difference among some of the responses toward the seven emotive movements exhibited by the human actor. $F(4.957, 193.311) = 13.807$, $p < 0.01$.

Results from the pairwise comparisons are shown in Table 4. The table shows that the movement for *confident* elicited significantly fewer correct responses than those for the other affective movements. Compared with the results from the previous two experiments, this indicates that the poor performance of this movement in all experiments was not caused by the form of the stimulus. Rather, it was caused by a poor choice of movement to express this emotion. The movement for *happy*, on the other hand, was significantly more recognizable than the movements for *relieved, patient, angry* and *sexy*. Its confidence interval is also much shorter than that of other emotive moves. Our analysis confirmed that human subjects were able to categorize emotions from a human dancer with facial expressions shown.

Comparison Pair		Mean Difference	Std. Error	Sig	95% CI
confident	disgust	-0.575*	0.087	0.000	[-0.857, -0.293]
	happy	-0.800*	0.064	0.000	[-1.008, -0.592]
	relieved	-0.475*	0.107	0.002	[-0.824, -0.126]
	patient	-0.475*	0.080	0.000	[-0.735, -0.215]
	angry	-0.325*	0.097	0.039	[-0.641, -0.009]
	sexy	-0.400*	0.093	0.002	[-0.703, -0.097]
disgust	happy	-0.225	0.076	0.108	[-0.472, 0.022]
	relieved	0.100	0.106	1.000	[-0.245, 0.445]
	patient	0.100	0.106	1.000	[-0.245, 0.445]
	angry	0.250	0.093	0.221	[-0.052, 0.552]
	sexy	0.175	0.087	1.000	[-0.107, 0.457]
happy	relieved	0.325*	0.075	0.002	[0.081, 0.569]
	patient	0.325*	0.083	0.008	[0.055, 0.595]
	angry	0.475*	0.088	0.000	[0.190, 0.760]
	sexy	0.400*	0.086	0.001	[0.120, 0.680]
relieved	patient	0.000	0.107	1.000	[-0.349, 0.349]
	angry	0.150	0.098	1.000	[-0.170, 0.470]
	sexy	0.075	0.097	1.000	[-0.241, 0.391]
patient	angry	0.150	0.105	1.000	[-0.190, 0.490]
	sexy	0.075	0.104	1.000	[-0.262, 0.412]
angry	sexy	-0.075	0.097	1.000	[-0.391, 0.241]

Table 4. Pairwise comparisons for the performance of the human actor with facial expressions visible. *The mean difference is significant at the 0.05 level. Adjustment for multiple comparisons: Bonferroni.

As in Experiment 2, the responses of our subjects can clearly be divided into three distinct groups (see Fig. 11): 1. excellent performance (*happy*); 2. good performance (*disgust, relieved, patient, angry* and *sexy)*; and 3. low performance *(confident)*.

Just like the previous two experiments, the movement corresponding to *confident* does not lead to a high recognition rate. This might be due to the fact that the movement which we used to represent this emotion is ambigious and uncommon in daily lives. Note that generally speaking, the means of correct responses obtained in this experiment are higher than those obtained in the previous two experiments. In this study, a mean of 0.15 is slightly above chance level.

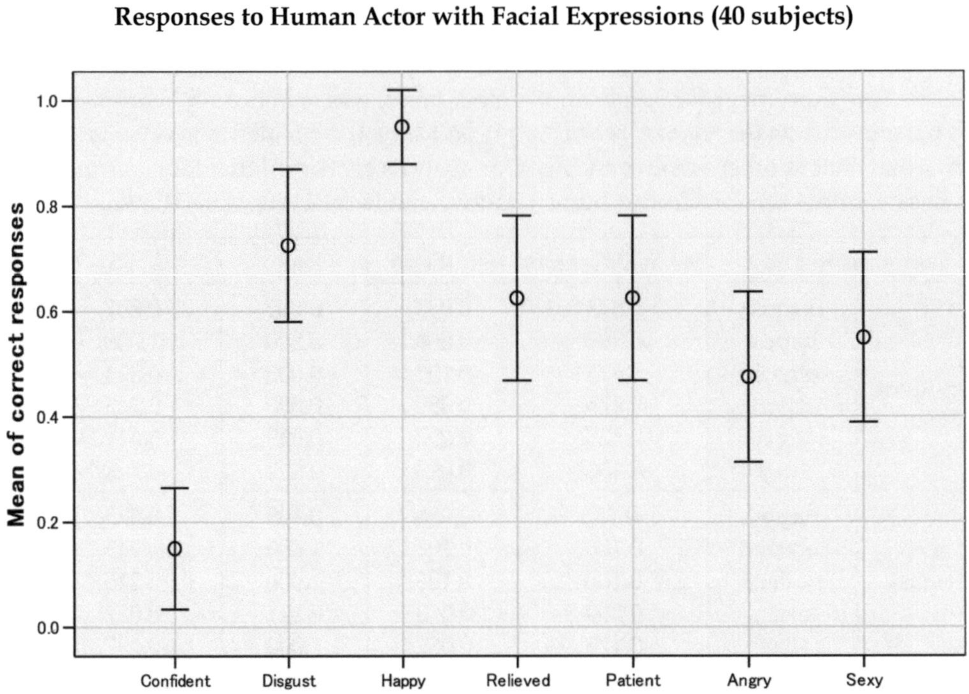

Fig. 11. Responses to affective movements exhibited by a human actor with facial expressions. The vertical bars in the graph denote the 95% confidence intervals.

4.5 Exploration of the effect of type of actor on human perceptions of affective movements

In this section, we are interested in testing the following hypotheses:

1. Does the type of actor influence the overall subjects' responses?
2. Do both human-form actors elicit more correct responses than the robot actor?
3. Does the faceless human actor elicit more correct responses than the robot actor?
4. Does the human with visible facial expressions elicit more correct responses than the faceless human actor?
5. Does the human with facial expressions elicit more correct responses than the robot actor?

To get an overview of how the type of actor affected the overall responses, for each emotion under investigation, we plotted our subjects' responses to each actor as shown in Fig. 12.
In order to analyze the effects of the type of actor on our subjects' responses, we could have done a 7x3 repeated-measures ANOVA. However, this would have resulted in so many interactions that it would have been very difficult to interpret. For this reason we analyzed the data corresponding to each affective movement separately. For each analysis, we conducted Mauchly's test of sphericity and confirmed that the assumption of sphericity was met. The overall results of the effect of different actors on the subject's responses are summarized in Table 5. Our results confirmed the hypothesis that for some movements (*disgust, relieved, happy* and *angry*), the type of actor could influence our subjects' responses.

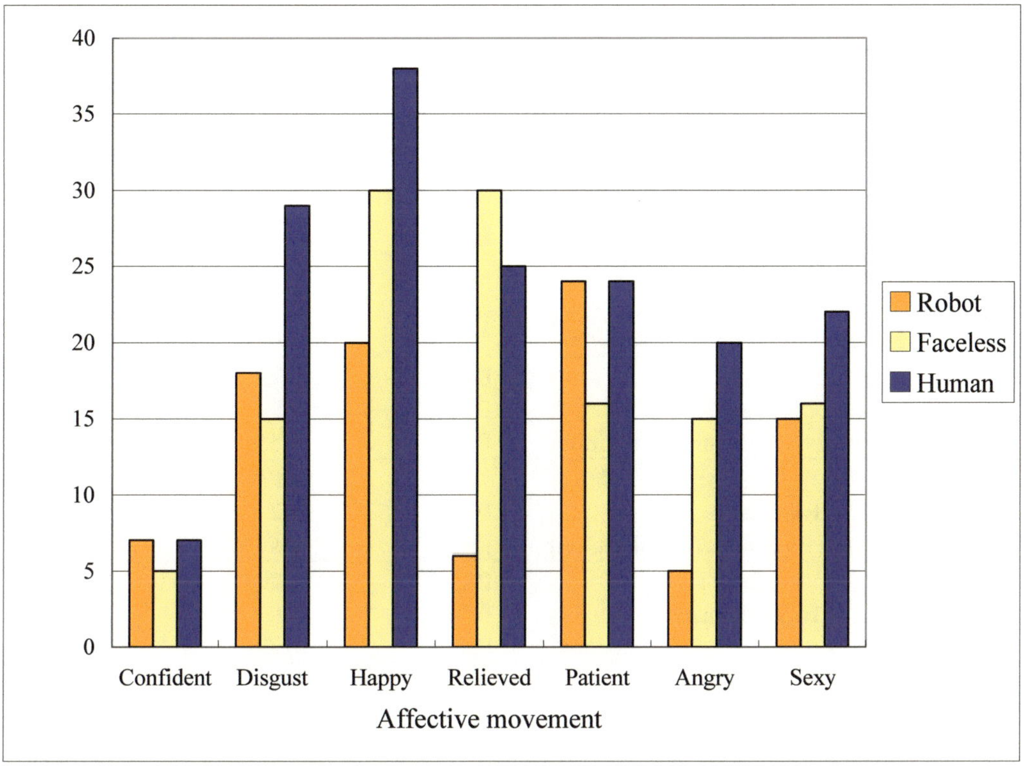

Fig. 12. Responses to movements exhibited by different actors. *Robot* means robot actor. *Faceless* means human actor with face covered. *Human* means human actor with facial expressions visible.

In order to test Hypotheses 2 to 5, we tested subjects' responses to each actor for each affective movement presented. The results of the ANOVA for the within-subjects variable (*actor*) with respect to different emotive movements are summarized in Table 6. The table shows that for *confident*, there was no significant difference in overall responses toward the different actors ($F(2, 78) = 0.358$, $p > 0.05$). However, for *disgust*, there was a significant difference in overall responses based on the type of actor ($F(2, 78) = 5.903$, $p < 0.05$): comparing the means shown in Table 5 shows that for the movements corresponding to *disgust*, having facial expressions visible elicited significantly more correct responses.

Similarly, Table 6 indicates that there was a significant difference in responses toward the three actors' expression of *relieved* ($F(2, 78) = 22.449$, $p < 0.01$). In particular, Table 8 indicates that there were significant differences in performance between the robot vs. faceless human and the robot vs. human with facial expressions. In both cases, the human-form actors performed significantly better. It might be the case that our subjects were more familiar with this movement through their daily interactions with other humans. Interestingly, although the human actors performed this movement more recognizably than the robot actor, there was no significant difference in performance between the two human actors. In other words, showing facial expressions did not significantly improve the recognition rate for this affective movement.

Emotion	Actor	Mean	Standard Deviation	Significant
confident	Robot Faceless human Human with facial expressions	0.150 0.100 0.150	0.362 0.304 0.362	No
disgust	Robot Faceless human Human with facial expressions	0.450 0.375 0.725	0.504 0.490 0.452	Yes ($p < 0.01$)
relieved	Robot Faceless human Human with facial expressions	0.150 0.725 0.625	0.362 0.452 0.490	Yes ($p < 0.01$)
happy	Robot Faceless human Human with facial expressions	0.500 0.725 0.950	0.506 0.452 0.221	Yes ($p < 0.01$)
patient	Robot Faceless human Human with facial expressions	0.6 0.425 0.625	0.496 0.501 0.49	No
angry	Robot Faceless human Human with facial expressions	0.125 0.350 0.475	0.335 0.483 0.506	Yes ($p < 0.01$)
sexy	Robot Faceless human Human with facial expressions	0.375 0.400 0.550	0.490 0.496 0.504	No

Table 5. Summary of the effect of different actors on subject's responses.

Emotion	Source	SS	df	MS	F	Significant
confident	actor error (actor)	0.067 7.267	2 78	0.033 0.093	0.358	0.700
disgust	actor error (actor)	2.717 17.950	2 78	1.358 0.230	5.903	0.004
relieved	actor error (actor)	7.550 13.117	2 78	3.775 0.168	22.449	0.000
happy	actor error (actor)	4.050 12.617	2 78	2.025 0.162	12.519	0.000
patient	actor error (actor)	0.950 13.717	2 78	0.475 0.176	2.701	0.073
angry	actor error (actor)	2.517 12.150	2 78	1.258 0.156	8.078	0.001
sexy	actor error (actor)	0.717 11.950	2 78	0.358 0.153	2.339	0.103

Table 6. Summary of tests of within-subjects effects on the type of actor presented. SS and MS stand for Sum of Squares and Mean of Squares, respectively. Note that *actor* is the repeated-measures variable.

Table 6 indicates that there was also a significant difference in our subjects' responses toward the actors when they were expressing the emotion *happy* ($F(2, 78) = 12.519, p < 0.01$). In particular, the human with visible facial expressions elicited significantly more correct responses than the other two actors (Table 9). In contrast, Table 6 shows that there was no significant difference in our subjects' responses toward the three actors when they were expressing *patient* ($F(2, 78) = 2.701, p > 0.05$) or *sexy* ($F(2, 78) = 2.339, p > 0.05$).
Finally, Table 6 shows that for the movement which corresponds to *angry*, there was a significant difference in responses towards the three actors ($F(2, 78) = 8.078, p < 0.01$). Table 10 shows that the human with visible facial expressions elicited significantly more correct responses than the robot actor. However, compared with the faceless human, showing facial expressions did not significantly improve the recognition rate.
Based on the above analyses, a summary of our findings is provided in Table 11. The results indicate that for the affective moves (*disgust, happy, relieved* and *angry*), the type of actor can significantly influence the subjects' responses. Contrary to the common belief that human-form (face and faceless) actors are always able to elicit more correct responses than a robot actor, only the movement for *relieved* agreed with this hypothesis. As for the hypothesis that a faceless human actor is able to elicit more correct responses than the robot actor, this was only confirmed for the movements corresponding to *relieved.* Interestingly, the same human actor, showing facial expressions did not always elicit more correct responses than when the face was covered. In fact, only two (*disgust* and *happy)* out of seven emotive moves showed that this was the case. This calls into question the talents of the human actor and the quality of the human displays. Finally, experimental results show the surprising finding that the human actor with visible facial expressions did not always elicit more correct responses than the robot actor. Of the seven movements under investigation, only those for *happy, relieved* and *angry* did show a higher recognition for the actor with facial expressions over the robot actor. (For discussions on our experiments, refer to Or & Takanishi, 2007.)

Comparison Pair	Mean Difference	Std. Error	Sig	95% CI
Robot, Faceless human	0.075	0.115	1.000	[−0.214, 0.364]
Robot, Human with face	-0.275	0.113	0.059	[−0.558, 0.008]
Faceless human, Human with face	-0.350*	0.092	0.001	[−0.579, −0.121]

Table 7. Pairwise comparisons for the movements for *disgust* performed by the different actors. *The mean difference is significant at the 0.05 level.

Comparison Pair	Mean Difference	Std. Error	Sig	95% CI
Robot, Faceless human	-0.575*	0.087	0.000	[-0.792, -0.358]
Robot, Human with face	-0.475*	0.095	0.000	[-0.712, 0.238]
Faceless human, Human with face	0.000	0.093	0.872	[-0.134, 0.334]

Table 8. Pairwise comparisons for the performance of *relieved* by the different actors. *The mean difference is significant at the 0.05 level.

Comparison Pair	Mean Difference	Std. Error	Sig	95% CI
Robot, Faceless human	-0.225	0.098	0.081	[-0.470, 0.020]
Robot, Human with face	-0.450*	0.087	0.000	[−0.668,−0.232]
Faceless human, Human with face	-0.225*	0.084	0.032	[−0.435,−0.015]

Table 9. Pairwise comparisons for the performance of *happy* by the different actors. *The mean difference is significant at the 0.05 level.

Comparison Pair	Mean Difference	Std. Error	Sig	95% CI
Robot, Faceless human	−0.225	0.091	0.054	[−0.453, 0.003]
Robot, Human with face	−0.350*	0.092	0.001	[−0.579,−0.121]
Faceless human, Human with face	−0.125	0.082	0.400	[−0.329, 0.079]

Table 10. Pairwise comparisons for the performance of *angry* by the different actors. *The mean difference is significant at the 0.05 level.

Hypothesis	1	2	3	4	5
Emotion:					
confident					
disgust	**o**			**o**	
happy	**o**			**o**	**o**
relieved	**o**	**o**	**o**		**o**
patient					
angry	**o**				**o**
sexy					

Table 11. Summary of the analysis of the effect of type of actor on human perception of affective movements. Hypothesis 1: Does the type of actor influence the overall subjects' responses? Hypothesis 2: Do both human-form actors elicit more correct responses than the robot actor? Hypothesis 3: Does the faceless human actor elicit more correct responses than the robot actor? Hypothesis 4: Does the human with visible facial expressions elicit more correct responses than the faceless human actor? Hypothesis 5: Does the human with facial expressions elicit more correct responses than the robot actor? The symbol "**o**" shows that the hypothesis is confirmed for that specific affective movement.

5. Conclusion

Based on the work presented above, we believe that with current technologies, it is unrealistic to build a flexible spine humanoid robot that has as many vertebrae as a human. Also, controlling the robots using the tendons or hydraulic power approach might not be ideal. Our research has shown that by carefully designing the spine mechanism, it is possible to build a flexible spine humanoid robot that can use full-body motions to express emotions. Compared with the robots developed by other groups, the development costs of our robots are relative low. Results from the psychological experiments show that it is possible for humans to recognize the emotions which the robot's movements are intended to express. Statistical analyses indicated that the movements of the robot dancer (WBD-2) are often as recognizable as the movements of the human dancer, both when subjects based their responses on only the movements of the human actor (his face was obscured) and when the human's face was visible along with his movements. Although having the human actor's facial expressions visible does improve the recognition rate for some movements, the availability of the facial expressions does not always elicit more correct responses than the faceless robot actor.

6. Acknowledgment

This research was funded by JSPS under the Japanese grant-in-aid for Scientific Research. The experiments were conducted in Takanishi Lab of Waseda University. The author would like to thank Jungmin Han for creating the tables shown in this chapter.

7. References

Ayama, K.; Bruderlin, A. & Calvert, T. (1996). Emotion from motion. in *Proc. Graphics Interface'96* (Canadian Information Processing Society, 1996), pp. 222-229.

Breazeal, C. (2002). *Designing Sociable Robots* (MIT Press, Cambridge, 2002).

Breazeal, C. (2003). Emotion and sociable humanoid robots, *Int. J. Human-Comput. Studies*, **59** (2003), pp. 119-155.

Brownlow, S.; Dixon, A. R.; Egbert, C. A. & Radcliffe, R. D. (1997). Perception of movement and dancer characteristics from point-light displays of dance, *Psychol. Rec.* **47** (3) (1997), pp. 411-421.

Collins, S.; Ruina, A.; Tedrake, R. & Wisse, M. (2005). Efficient bipedal robots based on passive-dynamic walkers. *Science* **307** (February 18, 2005), pp. 1082-1085.

Guenter, F.; Roos, L.; Guignard, A. & Billard, A. G. (2005). Design of a Biomimetic Upper Body for the Humanoid Robot, in *Proc. 2005 IEEE-RAS Int. Conf. on Humanoid Robots*, Tsukuba, Japan (2005), pp. 56-61.

Holland, O. & Knight, R. (2006). The Anthropomimetic Principle, in Burn, Jeremy and Wilson, Myra (eds.), *Proc. AISB06 Symposium on Biologically Inspired Robotics*, 2006.

Ishiguro, H. (2005). Android Science - Toward a new cross-interdisciplinary framework -, Toward Social Mechanisms of Android Science, *Cogsci 2005 Workshop*, Stresa, Italy, Cognitive Science Society, pp.1-6.

Itoh, K.; Miwa, H.; Nukariya, K.; Imanishi, K.; Takeda, D. & Saito, M. (2004). Development of face robot to express the facial features, in *Proc. 2002 IEEE Int. Workshop on Robot and Human Interactive Communication*, Okayama, Japan (2004), pp. 347-352.

Kajita, S.; Kanehiro, F.; Fujiwara, K.; Harada, K.; Yokoi, K. & Hirukawa, H. (2003). Biped walking pattern generation by using preview control of zero-moment point., in *Proc. 2003 IEEE Int. Conf. on Robotics and Automation*, Taipei, Taiwan (2003), pp. 1620-1626.

Kobayashi, H.; Ichikawa, Y.; Tsuji, T. & Kikuchi, K. (2001). Development on face robot for real facial expressions, in *Proc. 2001 IEEE/RSJ Int. Conf. on Intelligent Robots and Systems*, Maui, USA (2001), pp. 2215-2220.

Lim, H. Ishii, A. & Takanishi, A. (1999). Basic emotional walking using a biped humanoid robot, in *Proc. 1999 IEEE Int. Conf. on Systems, Man, and Cybernetics*, Tokyo, Japan (1999), **4**, pp. 954-959.

Mizuuchi, I.; Inaba, M. & Inoue, H. (2001). A flexible spine human-form robot - Development and control of the posture of the spine, in *Proc. 2001 IEEE/RSJ Int. Conf. on Intelligent Robots and Systems*, Maui, Hawaii **3** (2001), pp. 2099-2104.

Mizuuchi, I.; Tajima, R.; Yoshiaki, T.; Sato, D.; Nagashima, K.; Inaba, M.; Kuniyoshi, Y. & Inoue, H. (2002). The design and control of a flexible spine of a fully tendon-driven humanoid "Kenta", in *Proc. 2002 IEEE/RSJ Int. Conf. on Intelligent Robots and Systems*, Lausanne, Switzerland **3** (2002), pp. 2527-2532.

Mizuuchi, I.; Yoshida, S.; Inaba, M. & Inoue, H. (2003a). The development and control of the flexible-spine of a human-form robot, *Adv. Robot.* **17** (2), (2003), pp.179-196.

Mizuuchi, I.; Yoshikai, D.; Sato, S.; Yoshida, M.; Inaba, M. & Inoue, H. (2003b). Behavior developing environment for the large-dof muscle driven humanoid equipped with numerous sensors, in *Proc. 2003 IEEE Int. Conf. on Robotics and Automation*, Taipei, Taiwan (2003), pp.1940-1945.

Mizuuchi, I.; Yoshiaki, T.; Sodeyama, Y.; Nakanishi, Y.; Miyadera, A.; Yamamoto, T.; Nimela, T.; Hayashi, M.; Urata, J.; Namiki, Y.; Nishino, T. & Inaba, M. (2006a). Development of musculoskeletal humanoid kotaro, in *Proc. 2006 IEEE Int. Conf. on Intelligent Robots and Systems*, (2006), pp. 82-87.

Mizuuchi, I.; Nakanishi, Y.; Nammiki, Y.; Yoshikai, T.; Sodeyama, Y.; Nishino, T.; Urata, J. & Inaba, M. (2006b). Realization of Standing of the Musculoskeletal Humanoid Kotaro by Reinforcing Muscles, in *Proc. 2006 IEEE-RAS Int. Conf. on Humanoid Robots*, Genoa, Italy (2006), pp. 176-181.

Mizuuchi, I.; Nakanishi, Y.; Sodeyama, Y.; Namiki, Y.; Nishino, T.; Muramatsu, N.; Urata, J.; Hongo, K.; Yoshikai, T. & Inaba, M. (2007). An Advanced Musculoskeletal Humanoid Kojiro, in *Proc. 2007 IEEE-RAS Int. Conf. on Humanoid Robots*, Pennsylvania, USA (2007), pp. 101-106.

Nagashima, F. (2003). A motion learning method using CPG/NP. In *CD Proc. 2nd Int. Symp. Adaptive Motion of Animals and Machines*. Presentation number: ThP-II-3.

Nakanishi, Y.; Namiki, Y.; Hongo, K.; Urata, J.; Mizuuchi, I. & Inaba, M. (2007). Design of the Musculoskeletal Trunk and Realization of Powerful Motions Using Spines, in *Proc.*

2007 IEEE-RAS Int. Conf. on Humanoid Robots, Pennsylvania, USA (2007) http://planning.cs.cmu.edu/humanoids07/p/85.pdf

Oh, J.; Hanson, D.; Kim, W.; Han, I.; Kim, J. & Park, I. (2006). Design of Android type Humanoid Robot Albert HUBO, in *Proc. 2006 IEEE/RSJ Int. Conf. on Intelligent Robots and Systems*, Beijing, China (2006), pp. 1428-1433.

Or, J. & Takanishi, A. (2004). A biologically inspired CPG-ZMP control system for the real-time balance of a single-legged belly dancing robot, in *Proc. 2004 IEEE/RSJ Int. Conf. on Intelligent Robots and Systems*, Sendai, Japan (2004), pp. 931-936.

Or, J. & Takanishi, A. (2005). From lamprey to humanoid: the design and control of a flexible spine belly dancing humanoid robot with inspiration from biology. *Int. J. Humanoid Robot.* **2** (1) (2005), pp. 81-104.

Or, J. (2006). A Control System for a Flexible Spine Belly-Dancing Humanoid. *Artificial Life*, **12** (1) (2006), pp. 63-87.

Or, J. & Takanishi, A. (2007). Effect of a Flexible Spine Emotional Belly Dancing Robot on Human Perceptions. *Int. J. Humanoid Robot.* **4** (1), (2007), pp. 21-47.

Ott, C.; Eiberger, O.; Friedl, W.; Bauml, B.; Hillenbrand, U.; Borst, C.; Albu-Schaffer, A.; Brunner, B.; Hischmuller, H.; Kielhofer, S.; Konietschke, R.; Suppa, M.; Wimbock, T.; Zacharias, F. & Hirzinger, G. (2006). A Humanoid Two-Arm System for Dexterous Manipulation, in *Proc. 2006 IEEE-RAS Int. Conf. on Humanoid Robots*, Genova, Italy (2006), pp. 276-283.

Pollick, F.; Petersn, H.; Bruderlin, A. & Sanford, A. (2001). Perceiving affect from arm movement, *Cognition* **82**, B51-B61.

Roos, L.; Guenter, F.; Guignard, A. & Billard, A. G. (2006). Design of a Biomimetic Spine for the Humanoid Robot Robota, in *Proc. IEEE/RAS-EMBS Int. Conf. on Biomedical Robotics and Biomechatronics*, Piza, Italy (2006), pp. 329-334.

Shibata, S. & Inooka, H. (1998). Psychological evaluations of robot motions - An experimentally confirmed mathematical model, *Int. J. Ind. Ergonom.* **21** (6) (1998), pp.483-494.

Sogon, S. & Masutani, M. (1989). Identification of emotion from body movements: A cross-cultural study of Americans and Japanese, *Psychol. Rep.* **65** (1998), pp.35-46.

Sugihara, T.; Nakamura, Y. & Inoue, H. (2002). Realtime humanoid motion generation through zmp manipulation based on inverted pendulum control, in *Proc. 2002 IEEE Int. Conf. on Robotics and Automation*, Washington, DC, USA (2002), pp. 1404-1409.

Takanishi, A.; Egusa, Y.; Tochizawa, M.; Takeya, T. & Kato, I. (1988). Realization of dynamic biped walking stabilized with trunk motion, in *Proc. ROMANSY 7*, Udine, Italy (1988), pp. 68-79.

Takanishi, A. (1993). Biped walking robot compensation moment by trunk motion. *Journal of Robotics and Mechatronics*, **5**, pp. 505-510.

Vukobratovic, M.; Frank, A. & Juricic, D. (1970). On the stability of biped locomotion. *IEEE Transactions on Biomedical Engineering* **17** (1), pp. 25-36.

Vukobratovic, M. & Borovac, C. (2004). Zero-moment point - thirty five years of its life. *Int. J. Humanoid Robot.* **1** (1) (2004), pp. 157-173.

Walk, R. & Homan, C. (1984). Emotion and dance in dynamic light displays, *Bull. Psychon. Soc.* **22** (5) (1984), pp. 437-440.

9

The Perception of Bodily Expressions of Emotion and the Implications for Computing

Winand H. Dittrich¶ and Anthony P. Atkinson‡
¶University of Hertfordshire;
‡Durham University
UK

1. Introduction

Increasingly rapid technological developments in robotics, human-computer interaction (HCI), and the computer and video games industry have led to the development of quite sophisticated, intelligent robots and realistic, computer-generated characters. These robots and characters vary in their human-like qualities, from visual and behavioural replicas of humans, to androids, aliens or other beings that have some human characteristics, to creatures that have little in common with humans. The most common human-like qualities evidenced by these robots and characters are intelligence, looks, movements and language. Yet until very recently they were often not endowed with much in the way of emotions, and when they were they typically appeared emotionally underdeveloped, stilted, or false. For example, in James Cameron's film *Terminator 2*, Arnold Schwarzenegger plays an emotionless but intelligent humanoid robot. The film character explains that it is equipped with a microchip based on connectionist neural-net architecture. He comes to understand the patterning of human emotional behaviour but, of course, he does not have feelings or emotions. This was also true of other animated or computer-generated characters in films. Even if the characters gave rise to highly emotional video game or film scenes, the users or audience were in agreement that the characters were emotionally impoverished or did not have emotions at all. In large part this was and still is a technological issue: advances made in endowing machines and computer-generated characters with realistic emotions have not kept pace with the rapid advances in endowing such machines and characters with realistic intelligence, looks, movements and language. Nonetheless, given that these robots and characters are designed to interact with humans, and that emotions are so central to successful social interactions, effective implementation of emotions in these robots and characters is vital.

The latest developments in HCI include an area that is concerned with implementing emotions with mostly human-like characteristics into HCI technology. About 10 years ago, even a completely new field of computer science emerged that is based on such an attempt, namely "affective computing" (Picard, 1997). Since then, various attempts have been made either to implement emotions into machines or have machines that express emotional reactions. A close examination of these examples reveals two ways of implementing emotions and emotional reactions in HCI technology. First, emotions are seen as constituting a state variable affecting the range or diversity of responses available to the machine or interface (Suzuki et al., 1998; Arkin et al., 2003) without changing the responses themselves. Second, emotions are linked to overt responses shaping directly the response characteristics of the machine or interface (e.g., Breazeal, 2003; Fujita, 2001), i.e. changing the response characteristics noticeably. This variation in how to implement emotions in machines seems to mirror the ambiguities in the understanding of human emotions.

Before the scientific study of emotions had disappeared almost completely in the wake of behaviourism, emotions were often introduced as the undesired side effect of behaviour. "I was so enraged" one says, "that I couldn't think straight". Emotions and cognitions were considered strange bedfellows and strictly separated for decades (for reviews and discussion, see e.g., Prinz, 2004; Oatley, 2004; Mandler, 2007). This concept of emotion as distinct from and irrelevant to cognition, in other words rather a disturbing factor in information processing, seems no longer tenable. Emotions play an important part in cognition and in the adaptive significance of ongoing behavioural decisions (e.g., Schachter & Singer, 1962; Damasio, 1994). We argue that the psychology of emotions, especially that which characterizes the relation between specific emotional states and the related facial, bodily, and vocal patterns, may provide a useful theoretical framework for model-driven applications in affective computing.

For this purpose a functional approach to emotion research seems to be the most promising (e.g., Frijda, 1986; Izard, 1991; Lazarus, 1991; Plutchik, 1980; Scherer, 1984). Schneider and Dittrich (1989) proposed a functional system-analytic approach to studying emotions. Following this approach, emotion can be described as a phylogenetically evolved mechanism for behavioural adaptation. Adaptation can take place both with respect to preparation for appropriate responses to environmental challenges and to providing chances for evaluation and communication of intentions in order to optimize response characteristics (see Schneider & Dittrich, 1989). In line with this approach, we shall highlight two essential functions of emotions with respect to computing and summarize research on the perception of emotional expressions. The two functional processes that are essential for emotional processing consist of (a) the intra-individual regulation of cognition and actions and (b) the inter-individual regulation in communication.

In human psychology, emotion research has concentrated on the study of, on the one hand, basic and unique human emotions as shown in facial, vocal and body expressions and their role in communication, and on the other hand, on affective states and internal bodily reactions and their role in cognition or behavioural organization. With respect to the latter research programme, Arbib and Fellous (2004) point out that the neural and chemical basis of animal function differs greatly from the mechanics and electronics of current machines, such that implementing emotions in such machines will require functional theories of emotion that abstract away from the details of the biological substrates. Our concern in this chapter is primarily with the former research programme and its implications for affective computing. Nonetheless, it is important to note that in animals these two aspects of emotions (expression/communication and behavioural organization) co-evolved and remain intimately linked, and as we shall point out below, implementing one might be aided by implementing the other.

The recognition of emotions in communicative social situations relies strongly on visual cues. Following Darwin, Paul Ekman and colleagues (e.g., Ekman et al., 1972; Ekman, 1992) proposed that there are only a limited number of basic and unique facial expressions. They characterized six emotional facial expressions on the basis of a unique subset of facial muscle movements: disgust, surprise, fear, joy, anger, and sadness. These emotions were found in infants and blind people, who had no opportunity to imitate them. Also, the appearance, range and interpretation of these emotions are supposed to be similar in Papua New Guinea or Hatfield, England. These facial expressions of basic emotions have been systematically characterized in terms of individual facial muscle movements using the Facial Action Coding System, or FACS (Ekman & Friesen, 1978).

As exemplified by the above work, the study of emotion perception has relied primarily on visually presented static facial expressions. While faces are a vitally important - arguably the most important - source of cues in non-verbal communication in humans, they are not the only source of such cues. In the visual modality, postures and movement of the body and its parts also make a substantial contribution to non-verbal communication, including the communication of emotions; yet relatively little work has been devoted to the study of the perception of emotional body expressions. A central aim of this chapter is to review the current state of knowledge about what cues the human visual system uses in the perception of body postures and movements, with particular focus on emotion perception, and about the functional organization of the underlying neural systems.

An important reason why robots and animated characters can appear emotionally impoverished is that they rarely express emotions in realistic ways. The attribution of emotions by an observer or interactant depends a lot on the character's emotional expressions - not just what she does but how she expresses her (real, simulated, or intended) inner feelings. Only if someone shows emotional reactions are we likely to attribute emotional states to this person. Indeed, humans even tend to interpret very simple cues as indications of emotional reactions. For example, in animated scenarios a simple change of colour might give rise to emotional interpretations in the viewer or user (e.g. Miwa et al., 2001). Furthermore, when viewing a moving abstract stimulus, people tend to attribute social meaning and purpose to the movement (e.g., Heider & Simmel, 1944; Dittrich & Lea, 1994) (reviews: Dittrich, 1999; Scholl & Tremoulet, 2000).

Research on visual recognition has been dominated by studies about the recognition of objects. In these studies, the roles of form and motion cues have been investigated and various models of object recognition rely on the dissociation of the processing of form and motion cues. In sections 2 and 3 we will outline major lines of research in human psychology and neuropsychology that have applied this approach to the study of form and motion cues in the perception of social objects, and specifically bodies, and in the perception of emotional expressions from postures and movements of the body. Then in section 4 we shall place this work in the wider context of affective computing.

2. The perception of bodily form and motion

2.1 The visual cues that humans use to perceive bodies and their motion

The *form* of the human body could be represented in several different ways, demarcating points on a configural-processing continuum, from part-based to holistic processing. Thus bodies could be represented in terms of individual body parts or features, the relative positions of those parts (i.e., first-order spatial relations), the structural hierarchy of body parts (i.e., first-order configuration plus information about the relative position of features with respect to the whole body), or in terms of whole body posture templates (Reed et al., 2006). Unlike faces, the relative positions of body parts change as people move, which suggests the need for a relatively fine-grained structural description of the spatial relationships among body parts.

A series of experiments by Reed and colleagues (2006) suggests that the recognition of body postures depends on the processing of the structural hierarchy of body parts. This study drew on the well-known inversion effect in face recognition, that turning faces upside down impairs the ability to recognize their identity more than inverting nonface objects impairs the recognition of their identity. It is generally considered that face inversion disrupts configural processing, specifically the coding of second-order relational information, that is, the metric distances amongst features (e.g., Diamond & Carey, 1986; Rhodes et al., 1993; Maurer et al., 2002). In Reed et al.'s (2006) study, participants had to judge whether two sequentially presented images were the same or different. Each pair of images was presented either upright or inverted. Performance was significantly impaired for inverted compared to upright whole-body postures but not houses, replicating their earlier finding (Reed et al., 2003). The matching of isolated body parts (arms, legs, heads) was unaffected by inversion, indicating that, as with isolated facial features, individual body parts do not evoke configural processing. Disrupting first-order spatial relations, by rearranging the body parts around the trunk (by e.g., putting the arms in the leg and head positions), abolished the inversion effect, indicating that such first-order configural cues do not contribute to body posture recognition. Presenting half-body postures that were divided along the vertical midline (i.e., left or right halves), which preserves the structural hierarchy of body parts but disrupts holistic template matching, did not abolish the body inversion effect. In contrast, presenting half-body postures that were divided along the horizontal midline (the waist), which preserves salient parts (e.g., both arms) but disrupts structural hierarchy information, did not produce an inversion effect. Thus the particular form of configural processing critical to body posture recognition, as indexed by the presence of an inversion effect, appears to be the structural hierarchy of body parts, that is, the positions of body parts relative to themselves and to the whole body.

There are three main classes of information pertaining to the *movements* of human bodies: the changes of structural or form information over time (including motion-mediated structural information), kinematics (e.g., velocity, acceleration, displacement) and dynamics (motion specified in terms of mass and force). Considerable attention has been given to the role of kinematics in specifying cues for action and person perception (e.g., Westhoff & Troje, 2007). Typically, these studies employ *point-light* or patch-light displays of human or other biological motion, in which static form information is minimal or absent but motion information (kinematics and dynamics) and motion-mediated structural information are preserved (Johansson, 1973). Point-light displays of body movements provide a sufficient basis for observers to discriminate biological motion from other types of motion, and to make accurate judgements about the people making the movements, including sex from gait (e.g., Barclay et al., 1978), identity from gait (Richardson & Johnston, 2005) or actions (Loula et al., 2005), the weight of boxes from the lifting movement (Runeson & Frykholm, 1981), and complex individual or social actions from whole-body movements (Dittrich, 1993). Some of this evidence shows equivalent or near equivalent performance with point-light compared to full-light (or solid-body) displays, in which the whole body is visible (e.g., Runeson & Frykholm, 1981), which suggests that static form cues are rather less important than motion cues and may often be unnecessary for successful judgements about people and their actions based on their visible behaviour. Evidence for the relative importance of kinematic cues comes from studies that measure the effects on recognition of changes in certain kinematic or structural dimensions of point-light stimuli. For example, accuracy in judging the sex of point-light walkers was influenced more by "body sway" than by the ratio of shoulder to hip width, in Mather and Murdoch's (1994) study, and was greater when point-light walkers were normalized with respect to their size (thus providing only motion information) than when they were normalized with respect to their motion information (thus providing only size cues), in Troje's (2002) study.

It has been argued that the ability to discriminate at least simple biological movements in point-light displays may be based on relatively low-level or mid-level visual processing that does not involve the reconstruction of the form of body parts or of the whole body, either from static form or motion-mediated structural cues (e.g., Casile & Giese, 2005; Mather et al., 1992). Nevertheless, neuropsychological and neurophysiological evidence demonstrates that form information can indeed subserve biological motion perception from point-light displays (e.g., Hirai & Hiraki, 2006; McLeod et al., 1996; Peelen et al., 2006; Vaina et al., 2002). The processing of changes in the form of the body over time may be particularly important (e.g., Beintema & Lappe, 2002), especially in the context of more sophisticated tasks, such as recognizing emotional states or complex actions (Casile & Giese, 2005; Giese & Poggio, 2003). This conclusion gains some support from inversion effects in biological motion perception. The spontaneous identification of point-light motion displays as biological motion is impaired when they are shown upside down (Bertenthal & Pinto, 1994; Pavlova & Sokolov, 2000; Shipley, 2003; Troje, 2003), even given prior knowledge about display orientation (Pavlova & Sokolov, 2003). Moreover, neural activation characteristic of upright biological motion displays is attenuated or absent when such displays are inverted (Grossman & Blake, 2001; Pavlova et al., 2004). Inversion of point-light displays also disrupts the ability to distinguish the identity of the actors from their actions (Loula et al., 2005), and sex judgements based on gait tend to be reversed (Barclay et al., 1978). While it is likely that inversion of biological motion disrupts the processing of dynamic cues related to movement within the earth's gravitational field (Barclay et al., 1978; Bertenthal et al., 1987; Pavlova & Sokolov, 2000; Shipley, 2003), there is also some evidence to suggest that inversion of whole-body movements impairs the processing of configural information (Lu et al., 2005; Pinto & Shiffrar, 1999).

2.2 The human brain contains regions specialized for processing bodily form and motion

The form of the human (or primate) body is a category of visual object for which there appears to be both selectivity and functional specialization in higher-level visual cortices. By *selectivity* we mean the extent to which a mechanism is activated by or operates over a particular stimulus class, such as faces or bodies, as compared to other stimulus classes. By *functional specialization* (or function for short) we mean a mechanism's specificity for performing a particular process. Evidence for body-selective visual mechanisms comes from studies of both humans and non-human primates (reviewed by Peelen & Downing, 2007). In humans, the evidence points to two distinct regions, dubbed the extrastriate body area (EBA), located in lateral occipitotemporal cortex (Downing et al., 2001), and the fusiform body area (FBA), located in fusiform gyrus (Peelen & Downing, 2005; Schwarzlose et al., 2005). The EBA and FBA respond selectively to human bodies and body parts compared with objects, faces, and other control stimuli, despite considerable anatomical overlap between the FBA and the face-selective fusiform face area (FFA) (Peelen & Downing, 2005; Schwarzlose et al., 2005; Peelen et al., 2006) and between the EBA, motion processing area V5/MT, and object-form-selective lateral occipital complex (Peelen et al., 2006; Downing et al., 2007).

With respect to functional specialization, the EBA represents the static structure of viewed bodies (Downing et al., 2006; Peelen et al., 2006; Michels et al., 2005), although these representations appear to be at the level of individual body parts rather than at the level of whole-body configuration (Taylor et al., 2007; Urgesi et al., 2007a). As discussed above, configural cues in body perception include the relative positions of body parts and the positions of those parts with respect to the whole body (Reed et al., 2006), and there is evidence indicating that the processing of one or other or both of these configural cues is more a function of the FBA than of the EBA (Taylor et al., 2007).

Another region implicated as having a critical role in processing configural body cues is left ventral premotor cortex (Urgesi et al., 2007a). This region of inferior frontal cortex is known for its role in both the planning of motor actions (Johnson & Grafton, 2003) and in the visual discrimination of such actions (Grafton et al., 1996; Pobric & Hamilton, 2006; Urgesi et al., 2007b), which has led to the suggestion that it forms part of a system for simulating the observed action to allow it to be understood (Gallese et al., 2004; Rizzolatti & Craighero, 2004).

The EBA appears to constitute a critical early stage in the perception of other people (Chan et al., 2004), rather than a later processing stage via, for example, top-down effects related to imaginary gestures and movement (de Gelder, 2006). Evidence in support of this claim comes from recent studies using either intracranial recordings or transcranial magnetic stimulation (TMS). Pourtois et al. (2007) recorded highly body-selective visual evoked potentials over the EBA of a patient that started approximately 190ms and peaked 260ms after stimulus onset. Consistent with this finding are reports of selectively impaired perception of body form following application of TMS over EBA at 150–250 ms (Urgesi et al., 2004; Urgesi et al., 2007a) and at 150-350ms (Urgesi et al., 2007b) post-stimulus onset. Despite this evidence, however, it is entirely possible that, in addition to its role in the early visual processing of body form, the EBA also plays a role in later processing stages of person perception. Little is yet known about the timing of the FBA and ventral premotor cortex involvement in body and person perception, although given that they preferentially represent configural over body-part cues it is likely that their initial involvement occurs subsequent to that of the EBA. Nonetheless, as Taylor et al. (2007) comment, a strictly serial model is probably too simplistic, given the widespread bi-directional connectivity in visual cortex.

Our brains contain systems specialized for processing the *movements* of bodies and their parts (including faces), in addition to those systems specialized for processing bodily facial form. (Although as we shall soon see, the computations performed by these biological motion-processing systems may well draw on form information.) Important early evidence came from neuropsychological lesion studies, which demonstrated spared ability to discriminate biological motion stimuli despite severe impairments in discriminating other types of motion (Vaina et al., 1990; McLeod et al., 1996). However, not all aspects of biological motion perception are normal in such 'motion blind' patients. For example, McLeod et al. (1996) report a case of a subject who was able to describe accurately a variety of actions from whole-body movements represented in point-light displays, but was unable to report in which direction the figure was facing, or whether it was approaching or retreating from her. Furthermore, this same patient was severely impaired at identifying natural speech from point-light or fully illuminated facial movements, despite being unimpaired in recognizing speech-patterns from face photographs (Campbell et al., 1997).

In patients with relatively spared biological motion perception despite deficits in perceiving other sorts of motion, the lesions are restricted to ventral and middle occipito-temporal cortices, sparing superior temporal and parietal areas. Electrophyshiological and neuroimaging studies confirm a particularly important role for superior temporal cortex in the perception of body and facial movement (Puce & Perrett, 2003; Allison et al., 2000). Single-cell recording studies in monkeys revealed neurons in superior temporal sulcus (STS) and superior temporal gyrus (STG), especially in the anterior portion of superior temporal polysensory area (STPa), selective for various types of face, limb and whole body motion (e.g., Jellema et al., 2000; Oram & Perrett, 1994; Perrett et al., 1985). Functional imaging studies in humans show that whole-body movements as represented in point-light displays elicit activation in pSTS compared to a variety of non-biological movements (e.g., Bonda et al., 1996; Grossman et al., 2000; Grossman & Blake, 2002; Pelphrey et al., 2003; Peuskens et al., 2005; Vaina et al., 2001). Regions of posterior and middle STS and surrounding superior and middle temporal gyri are also selectively activated by movements of the face or other body parts, as represented in fully-illuminated displays, compared to static images of the same body parts (Wheaton et al., 2004) and to non-biological motion (Puce et al., 1998). Disruption of the activity of right pSTS using TMS has confirmed a critical role for this region in perceiving body movement (Grossman et al., 2005). More recently, a lesion-overlap study with 60 brain-damaged subjects showed that impairments in the ability to discriminate whole-body from non-biological motion in point-light displays were most reliably associated with lesions in posterior temporal and ventral premotor cortices, which corresponded with the regions whose activity in neurologically intact subjects was selective for the same point-light whole-body movements (Saygin, 2007). The critical involvement of ventral premotor cortex in this study confirms earlier studies showing selectivity in this region for point-light whole-body movements (Saygin et al., 2004; Pelphrey et al., 2003).

There are also reports of selectivity to biological motion, in the form of whole-body movements, in the posterior inferior temporal sulcus/middle temporal gyrus (Grossman & Blake, 2002; Michels et al., 2005; Peuskens et al., 2005; Saygin et al., 2004), which might reflect activation of body-selective neurons in the EBA or motion-selective neurons in the overlapping V5/MT. There is even a report of selectivity to whole-body movements in the face-selective FFA (Grossman & Blake, 2002), which might reflect activation of body-selective or face-selective neurons, or of both body- and face-selective neurons. These last two issues have been resolved by a recent study: biological (whole-body) motion selectivity in occipitotemporal cortex was correlated on a voxel-by-voxel basis to body selectivity (i.e., EBA and FBA activation) but not to face selectivity (i.e., FFA activation) or to non-biological motion selectivity (i.e., V5/MT activation) (Peelen et al., 2006).

Neuroimaging studies in humans have also revealed distinct regions of STS selective for the movements of different body parts. While face, hand, mouth, and leg movements activate substantially overlapping regions of right pSTS (Thompson et al., 2007; Wheaton et al., 2004; Pelphrey et al., 2005), movements of the face (Thompson et al., 2007; Wheaton et al., 2004) and mouth (Pelphrey et al., 2005) are also associated with activity along the mid-posterior STS, as are leg movements (Wheaton et al., 2004). Moreover, whereas both facial speech (principally mouth) and visually similar but linguistically meaningless facial movements activate right pSTS, speech and non-speech facial movements also elicit dissociable patterns of temporal cortex activation, with speech movements activating traditional language processing areas in both hemispheres, including auditory cortex (Campbell et al., 2001; Calvert et al., 1997). In addition to activating pSTS, hand motion is associated with activity in inferior right pSTS and inferior parietal lobule (Thompson et al., 2007), extending into middle occipital and lingual gyri (Pelphrey et al., 2005), whereas eye movements are associated with activity in more superior and posterior portions of the right pSTS (Pelphrey et al., 2005) and elicit stronger responses in these pSTS regions for mutual than for averted gaze (Pelphrey et al., 2004). Other areas, including ventral premotor and intraparietal cortex, also show differential selectivity to the motion of different body parts, in a somatotopic manner (Wheaton et al., 2004; Buccino et al., 2001).

Selectivity to whole-body movements relative to non-biological motion is evident as early as 80-100ms post-stimulus onset over the left parieto-occipital region (Pavlova et al., 2006; Pavlova et al., 2004), regardless of whether the participant is attending to the stimuli (Pavlova et al., 2006). Subsequent selectivity for whole-body motion is evident at several different stages, each associated with different brain regions, including fusiform and superior temporal cortices, but typically only when the stimuli are attended (2006; Pavlova et al., 2004; 2007; Hirai et al., 2005; Jokisch et al., 2005; Hirai & Hiraki, 2006).

The distribution of responses in STS and surrounding cortex to the motion of different body parts suggests a functional organization in which distinct but overlapping patches of cortex extract body-part specific representations of biological motion, with a posterior region of STS, especially in the right hemisphere, encoding a higher-level representation of biological motion that is not dependent on the particular body part generating that motion. Consistent with the first part of this hypothesis is the considerable evidence for an important role for areas of STS in the integration of motion and form information, especially that related to social perception (e.g., Beauchamp, 2005; Oram & Perrett, 1996; Puce et al., 2003; Vaina et al., 2001). With respect to the second part of this hypothesis, there is some debate over whether pSTS analyzes local image motion and higher-level optic flow or some more global motion of the whole figure (Lange & Lappe, 2006; Giese & Poggio, 2003; Thompson et al., 2005; Beintema & Lappe, 2002). While this issue has yet to be fully resolved, recent evidence is building up in favour of the latter proposal. Two computational models of biological motion perception (Giese & Poggio, 2003; Lange & Lappe, 2006) propose that a ventral form pathway derives 'snapshots' that represent the various static postures comprising a movement sequence. Neuroimaging evidence indicates these snapshots are derived by the EBA and FBA (Peelen et al., 2006). In one model (Giese & Poggio, 2003), these snapshots are summated and temporally smoothed in ventral visual areas on the basis of local image motion information derived in separate areas, including pSTS. The other model (Lange & Lappe, 2006) proposes that more superior cortical areas, especially pSTS, temporally integrate sequences of intact body configurations, a suggestion also supported by neuroimaging evidence (Thompson et al., 2005; Peuskens et al., 2005). Nonetheless, it is possible that pSTS both analyzes local image motion, at an early stage, and, at later stage, the more global motion information related to changes in body and body part configurations over time, subsequent to the analysis of individual configurations of body form in the EBA and FBA and facial form in the face-selective areas of occipital and fusiform cortex and perhaps also STS.

2.3 Putting it all together: How we perceive and understand bodily actions

We have been emphasizing the use of structural form and motion information in the perception and identification of bodies (as distinct from other visual objects), body postures and movements. The evidence reviewed above points to the following account. The human visual system contains mechanisms specialized for processing the form of the human body, with distinct mechanisms encoding the form of body parts and configural relations between those parts. The ability to recognize (at least non-emotional) body postures relies on configural cues towards the template end of a continuum that extends from part-based to holistic processing, specifically, on cues specifying the structural hierarchy of body parts. The human visual system also contains mechanisms specialized for processing the motion of human bodies and body parts, as distinct from other forms of motion. Some mechanisms encode local image motion and higher-level optic flow, and a full model of how these various routines and processes are integrated and work together is captured in the Interactive Encoding Model of e-motion perception (Dittrich, 1999). He argues that it seems unlikely that one or both types of these mechanisms will be found to be specific to the processing of biological motion. Other mechanisms, which have been suggested to be specific to biological motion (see reviews below), encode the translations of body form over time, integrating form information captured in snapshots of the moving body with the local motion and optic flow information. Again, Dittrich (1999) argues that neither of these general mechanisms (snapshot capturing or optic flow) seem specific to or even necessary for perceiving biological motion. Instead, as proposed in the Interactive Encoding Model, the processing of biological motion depends on a particular way of neuronal coding in the brain by motion integrators (instead of motion detectors) and three cognitive routines depending on the motion information available. The first routine is strictly associated with the analysis of the structural components of human motion to reconstruct 3D body-related emotion information out of the 2D motion trajectory. The second routine is part of the working memory system and allows the application of cognitive constraints relating to human emotions and their motion trajectories for the 3D reconstruction. The third routine relies on visual semantics related to emotion categories as stored in long-term memory.

Our review here has been necessarily brief. For readers interested in finding out more about the intricacies of human body and biological motion perception, in addition to Dittrich's (1999) Interactive Encoding model, we suggest the following reviews: de Gelder (2006), Giese and Poggio (2003), Puce and Perrett (2003), Blake and Shiffrar (2007), and Peelen and Downing (2007).

Is such an image-processing account, or an extension of it, sufficient for explaining our ability to perceive and understand bodily *actions*? The majority of human postures and movements are not aimless but are directed towards some purpose or goal and thus reflect that person's intentions and may also or instead reflect their emotional and other internal states. Moreover, humans are not passive observers but like the people whose postures and movements they are observing, have intentions and emotions and act in a purposive, goal-directed manner. Research and theory over the past decade or so suggests that one (and perhaps the main or even the only) route to understanding others' actions depends on the observer's own action capabilities (Rizzolatti & Craighero, 2004; Gallese et al., 2004). One productive source of evidence for this view is the body of findings showing neural mechanisms with dual functions in action perception and action production. For example, so-called mirror neurons in the premotor cortex of monkeys were found to respond not only when the monkey prepares to perform an action itself, but also when the monkey observes the same visually presented action performed by someone else (e.g., Rizzolatti et al., 1996). Various supportive findings suggesting the existence of a mirror neuron system, if not actual mirror neurons, have also been obtained in humans. Observing another's actions results in desynchronization in motor cortex as measured with magnetoencephalography (Hari et al., 1998), and lowers the threshold for producing motor responses when transcranial magnetic stimulation is used to activate motor cortex (Strafella & Paus, 2000). Imitating another's actions via observation activates premotor cortex in functional imaging studies (Iacoboni et al., 1999); moreover, such activation is somatotopic with respect to the body part that is observed to perform the action, even in the absence of any overt action on the part of the subject (Buccino et al., 2001).

These and numerous other findings indicating the existence of a human mirror neuron system suggest a simulation account of action understanding, according to which observing another perform an action triggers in the observer an offline simulation of the viewed action. Work on motor control indicates ways in which such simulations may be computationally instantiated, in the form of forward models, inverse models, or both (Miall, 2003; Grush, 2004; Wolpert et al., 2003). Forward models use copies of the motor commands to map the current sensory states and motor commands to the future sensory and motor states that will result once the current motor commands have been executed. Inverse models perform the opposite transformations, by mapping sensory representations associated with the intended action to the motor commands to execute the action. One suggestion, for example, is that proposed by Wolpert et al. (2003) and also comprehensively envisaged in the Interactive Encoding Model (Dittrich, 1999): When observing another's action, the observer's brain generates a set of motor commands that would be produced given the observed movements and the current state of the observed person. Rather than driving the observer's own motor behaviour, these motor commands are used to predict the sensory and motor consequences of the observed action, which are then compared with the observed new state of the actor.

3. Bodily form and motion cues in emotion perception

There is compelling evidence that the kinematics of body and body-part movements are at least sufficient, and may often be important, in furnishing cues for the perception of emotional expressions. For example, using point-light knocking and drinking arm movements as stimuli, Pollick et al. (2001) found that judgements of anger and happiness were more likely when the movements were fast and jerky, and that judgements of sadness were more closely associated with slow and smooth movements. And Sawada et al. (2003) reported that arm movements made with the intention of expressing joy, sadness, or anger varied in their velocity, acceleration, and displacement, and that differences in these factors predicted the ability of observers to distinguish between the three types of emotional expression. Nonetheless, there is also evidence that form-related cues in moving bodies and faces, in addition to kinematics, contribute to emotion perception. Bassili (1978) reported greater emotion classification accuracy for full-light compared to point-light facial movements, except for happy expressions. Dittrich (1991) found equivalent emotion recognition performance for point-light face stimuli in which the dots demarcated key facial structures (e.g., eyes, mouth) and those in which the dots were positioned randomly on the face. This result contrasts with Hill et al.'s (2003) finding that sex judgements from facial movements were more accurate with spatially normalized than pseudo-random dot placement, and thus highlights the relationship between form and motion information in specifying cues for emotion perception. In our own work, we have reported a reduction in emotion recognition performance with point-light (Dittrich et al., 1996) and patch-light (Atkinson et al., 2004) compared to full-light displays of body movements.

Building on this earlier work, we have demonstrated robust effects of stimulus inversion and motion reversal on the classification of basic emotions from patch-light and full-light movie clips of bodily expressions (Atkinson et al., 2007). Inverting the 3-second long movies significantly impaired emotion recognition accuracy, but did so more in the patch-light than in the full-light displays, indicating that inversion disrupts the processing of form cues more than it does the processing of kinematic and dynamic cues. Playing the movies backwards also significantly impaired emotion recognition accuracy, but this effect was only marginally greater for the patch-light than for the full-light displays, providing qualified support for the importance of the sequencing of changes in form to judgements of emotions from body gestures. While we cannot be certain that our stimulus manipulations completely eliminated all cues other than kinematics, even when in combination, the substantial reduction in emotion classification performance, especially for the inverted, reversed patch-light displays, attests to the importance of form cues in emotion perception; conversely, the fact that emotion classification performance was still substantially above chance, even in the inverted, reversed patch-light displays, attests to the importance of kinematics in providing cues for emotion perception. While it is likely that inversion of biological motion disrupts the processing of dynamic cues related to movement within the earth's gravitational field, if that were *all* that inversion impaired, then we should not have seen a greater effect of orientation for the patch-light compared to full-light stimuli.

The results of this study provide partial support for Dittrich et al.'s (1996) modified version of Walk and Homan's (1984) "alarm hypothesis", insofar as the identification of fearful and disgusted body movements was disproportionately impaired by inversion, suggesting a more important role for static form cues in the recognition of these emotions compared to the other emotions. On this reasoning, however, one would also expect a similar effect for anger, the identification of which was not disproportionately impaired by inversion. Consistent with the idea that an important diagnostic feature of fearful body movements is that they often involve cowering or retreating, which when reversed would appear as advancements, fear recognition was also disproportionately impaired by motion reversal.

What specific form-related cues are utilized in emotion perception from body expressions? One suggestion is that the overall shape of particular body postures, such as their angularity or roundedness, informs emotion judgements (Aronoff et al., 1992). The inversion effects that we found (Atkinson et al., 2007) highlight the importance of relational or configural cues, adding weight to previous claims that configural information plays an important role in subserving emotion perception from body expressions (Dittrich et al., 1996; Stekelenburg & de Gelder, 2004). In contrast, the effects of motion reversal tentatively suggest a possible role for spatiotemporal cues (changes in form over time) in emotion recognition. Given the conventional and sometimes symbolic (Buck, 1984) nature of our actors' movements (see Atkinson et al., 2004 for details), we speculate that configurations of static form and their changes over time are more closely associated with representations of *what* people do with their bodies than with how they move them, the latter being specified mostly by kinematics (see also Giese & Poggio, 2003).

In emphasizing the roles of configural form cues and kinematics in the recognition of emotions from body movements, we do not wish to deny the possible importance of simulation accounts of emotion recognition. As with action understanding in general (discussed in Section 2.3), purely image-processing accounts may not be sufficient for emotional expression understanding, or at any rate may not detail the only means by which we can understand others' emotional expressions. One way in which we might be able to recognize the emotional state of another is via our perception of an emotional response within ourselves (Adolphs, 2002; Atkinson & Adolphs, 2005; Gallese et al., 2004; Atkinson, 2007; Heberlein & Adolphs, 2007; Goldman & Sripada, 2005). One version of this idea is that a visual representation of another's expression leads us to experience what that person is feeling (i.e., emotional contagion), which allows us then to infer that person's emotional state. That is, the grounds for inferring the viewed person's emotional state is knowledge from the 'inside'; experiencing the emotion for oneself (even in an attenuated or unconscious form) is an important, perhaps necessary, step to accurate judgements about the other's emotion. A different but conceivably compatible idea is that coming to know what another is feeling involves simulating the viewed emotional state via the generation of a somatosensory image of the associated body state (Adolphs, 2002), or simulating the motor programs for producing the viewed expression (Carr et al., 2003; Gallese et al., 2004; Leslie et al., 2004).

4. Implications for computer vision and AI

The implementation of an emotion model into computer vision and AI has widespread consequences for future technologies and research approaches. For example, virtual reality scenarios recently have tried to include emotions in various ways. We will briefly mention the implications of the psychology of emotion expression and recognition for affective computing in such fields as AI, HCI, robotics and telecommunications. The use of emotions for future technologies will be discussed and some strengths and weaknesses of the application of emotional behaviours will be addressed.

In the previous sections we reviewed evidence for and argued that the ability to identify bodily expressions of emotion relies on specific types of both visual form and motion cues, and that the relative reliance on these different types of cue can vary across emotions. Several suggestions for affective computing can be drawn from this work, especially when viewed in the light of the Interactive Encoding Model proposed by Dittrich (1999). He argues for the integration of low-level processing of structural motion routines with more conceptually-driven semantic processing. These integrative processes are strictly resource-dependent but amenable to learning through continuous updating in working memory (see Figure 1).

A prediction of the Interactive Encoding model is that there is a strategic transition from input-driven to conceptually-driven processing as the performer develops more elaborate cognitive processes. The level of stimulus encoding therefore seems to be variable, depending on the amount and type of information available to the observer. Such an information flow characterized by multiple interactions and continuous updating is linked together through what are termed 'motion integrators'. The idea is that 'motion integrators' operating at a perceptual and cognitive level of visual processing and requiring attention are integral to skilled pattern recognition in a domain such as emotion recognition and can be directly translated to affective computing (see Dittrich, 1999). This model is, on the one hand, brain-inspired, as recent models of artificial computing are, but on the other hand, guided by the functional process model of emotion processing. Emotions are seen as grounded in the overall interactive nature of input-output characteristics of the artificial device (where between input and output one has to infer some intervening variables, such as homeostatic variables of the system state, or emotional variables), and as playing a regulatory role, both internally and externally.

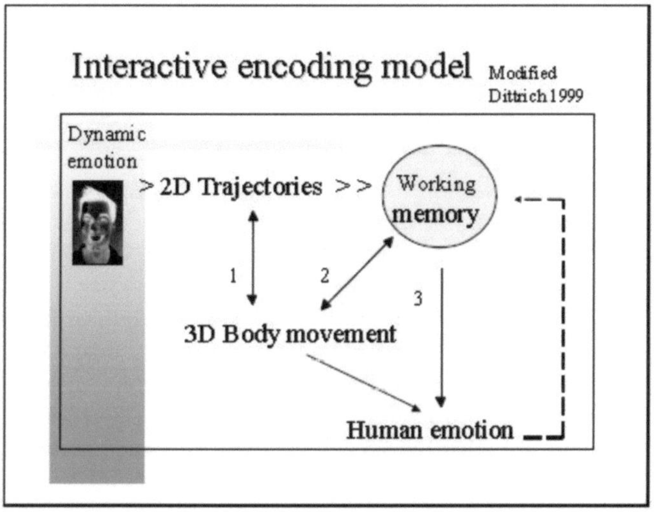

Fig. 1. Sketch of the Interactive Encoding Model for E-Motion Perception. (Note: 'Dynamic emotions' include body as well as facial expressions, and are usually dynamic events.)

In this sense, a developmental or ethological approach to implementing emotions in artifacts ("understanding by building"), favoured by many robot designers at present (e.g., Breazeal, 2002; Pfeifer, 2002; Brooks & Stein, 1994), might, however, not necessarily be regarded as the only or most efficient way to equip artifacts with emotional capabilities. As Brooks (1991; 2002) quite rightly pointed out, the notion of embodiment seems one possible avenue of how to achieve the necessary grounding of emotions. However, for implementing and linking biological input–output characteristics, several avenues and theoretical models from the behavioural and brains sciences become available. For example, we argue that the role of emotions is not restricted to expressive display characteristics; rather, emotions have a much wider impact on behavioural regulation in multi-layered and multi-agent artifacts. They form part of more general structures or are instrumental for a wide range of adaptive functions in an organism (Schneider & Dittrich, 1989). Analogously, the roles of emotions in artifacts may reach from a simple indication of its state (e.g., energy needs, spatial arrangements) to the highest levels of mental regulation (e.g., consciousness, imagination or turn-taking, and intentionality). Following this line of argument, we consider the role of emotions as ideally suited to fit perfectly Brooks's (1991) demand for structures that form part of the control systems in a way that fits exactly into existing structures, and are both totally distributed and also local in their operations. In this sense, we argue that the role of emotions and emotion recognition is not only crucial but the key for any artificial device or robot to pass the 'Total Turing Test' as specified by Harnad (2000). Therefore, an Emotional Turing Test has to form part of any Total Turing Test. The Emotional Turing Test will satisfy

Harnad's (2000) useful criterion of some kind of embodiment for a Turing test in which there is no screen between the candidate and the interrogator. Why and how could it be?
In a useful overview article "Multiagent systems: milestones and new horizons", which summarizes the immense progress made by a second generation of multiagent architectures, Sen (1997) quite rightly sees the field at a critical juncture. Nevertheless, it is revealing that in the whole article the term 'emotion' is not mentioned once. Similarly, when Schaal (1999) asked the question "Is imitation learning the route to humanoid robots?" not once is emotion addressed. This situation has dramatically changed over the last 10 years, not the least through Picard's (1997) influential book "Affective Computing". One of the early researchers to implement social features and emotional signals in robots is Cynthia Breazeal (for overviews, see Breazeal, 2002; 2003) with KISMET. But see also the pioneering work of Takeuchi and Nagao (1992), who developed a computer interface with synthetic facial displays. In these approaches the importance of emotional displays is strongly recognized and seen as crucial for the successful development of robots. For example, KISMET's skills include the ability to direct the robot's focus to establish shared reference ('joint viewing'), the ability to display readable expressions to the human, the ability to recognize expressive movements such as praise and rejection, the ability to take turns during social learning and the ability to regulate interaction to provide sensible learning situations ('emotion-driven learning'). Often, as in the case of KISMET, the implementation of expressive movements and emotion recognition is based on (a) facial expressions, (b) gestures or body movement in the visual modality, and (c) affective speech or affective sound variations in the auditory modality.
Generally, in affective computing, emotions can mirror the two regulatory roles emotions have, namely intra-individual and inter-individual. Emotions can be used, on the one hand, in the form of emotional visual expressions for social interactions and communication and, on the other hand, in order to organise and prioritise behaviours. The first aspect is more concerned with the relationship between people whereas the second aspect refers to the internal regulation of behaviours through selection, coordination or shifting of output priorities. The latter roles seem closely linked to some of the most evolved mental activities in humans such as consciousness or intentionality and would constitute the core of any "autonomous agent" (e.g., Dean, 1998; Kozma & Fukuda, 2006). Nevertheless, one needs to acknowledge that sometimes emotions are of no direct use, as Arbib (2005) quite rightly pointed out. Queuing for the bus seems a useful activity but showing anger about the length of the queue might be of no use when it is the last bus to make the journey into town. In other words, to display emotions or not seems closely linked to the debate on "autonomous agents".
Occasionally, in addition to changes in the form of the body and in its movements, changes in body colour are associated with emotional responses in humans; for example, a reddening of the face in anger or increased pallor in fear (Drummond & Quah, 2001; Drummond, 1997). Similarly, colours could be used to generate some kind of emotional display in virtual reality scenarios and computing. However, as the association between colours and emotional interpretations is quite vague and often subjective, if not spurious, such attempts seem less fruitful in the long run. Colours might be used as a common frame of reference as with traffic lights, but emotional significance should not be assumed as self-evident; rather, it needs to be defined for each instance as, for example, a red light should be taken unambiguously as a stop signal. It does not seem fruitful to rely on peoples' feelings

or interpretations of colour as emotional signals. Various attempts to use colour as emotional signals in sports environments testify to the difficulties of relying on emotional colour information. A controversial study by Frank and Gilovich (1988), for example, reported that the wearing of black uniforms in professional sports leads to increased aggression and more penalties. Movement from a non-black to a black uniform team results in an increase in penalties. When watching sport events on a colour monitor where teams wear black and non-black uniforms, increases in perceived rule violations for the referees and the actions of the players themselves are reported by observers. A more recent study by Hill and Barton (2005), which seems not to be as methodologically problematic as the one by Frank and Gilovich (1988), found, across a range of competitive sports, a tendency for individuals or teams who wore red to have a higher probability of winning. While the underlying principles for such an advantage remain unclear, their uncovering will have the potential for greatly stimulating affective computing as well as psychology. Yet, whereas colour is without doubt a very strong stimulus, its significance for emotion processing is not as clear-cut as necessary to suggest in a straightforward way its use in affective computing.

One implication from findings on how we perceive visual facial expressions can be seen in the development of automatic systems to detect and categorize facial expressions. In order to do this the coding of facial behaviours has to be automated. A prime candidate for such attempts, Ekman and Friesen's (1978) Facial Action Coding System (FACS), has been used because of the precise description of facial movements and the standardized catalogue of corresponding emotion labels. The development of such automated systems is not without its difficulties, however, primarily because of the wide range of physiognomic differences between individuals, which affects the variability of visual display characteristics such as eyebrow or mouth movements. Kaiser and Wehrle (1992) tried to solve such problems by adopting a combined approach using FACS as an expert system teaching a connectionist network fuzzy rules to measure facial movements automatically. The combination of fuzzy rules together with an artificial neural network has proven more successful in overcoming the variability problem than traditional methods such as expert systems or connectionist systems on their own.

The use of visual signals as emotional indicators is particularly relevant for telecommunications, and highlights two opposing principles. On the one side, despite the ever-increasing storage capacities of computer chips one tenet in telecommunication is nevertheless the reduction of the information flow between sender and receiver to save processing costs and minimise errors. On the other side, emotional signals are more often than not characterized by subtle changes in form or motion. Now the dilemma for the telecommunication architect seems obvious. First, there is the question of how much information is necessary to portray the emotional state in addition to the identity. Second, there is the question of how to build a system that is able to pick up reciprocal behaviour. Such new systems would have to go far beyond the FACS model or the concept of a small set of basic emotions (see Ortony & Turner, 1990). But which psychological emotion theory should be embraced instead?

One option is the appraisal model of emotions. Quite interestingly, the majority of the computer models of emotions, if they refer expressly to psychological theories, are based on the so-called appraisal theories. The fascination with these theories most likely stems from the fact that they can be converted into programme code in a more or less direct way. Consider, for example, Ortony, Clore and Collins's view (1988), which assumes that emotions develop as a consequence of certain cognitions and interpretations. This view concentrates exclusively on the cognitive elicitors of emotions: events, agents and objects. Their central assumption is that emotions represent value-based reactions to our perceptions of the world. One can be pleased about the consequences of an event or not; one can endorse or reject the actions of an agent or one can like or not like aspects of an object. Furthermore, events can have consequences for others or for oneself, and an acting agent can be another or oneself. The consequences of an event for another can be desirable or undesirable; the consequences for oneself can lead to relevant or irrelevant expectations. Relevant expectations for oneself finally can be differentiated again according to whether they actually occur or not. The authors further define a set of global and local intensity variables, which operate over all three emotion categories. Although no formalization of their model is explicitly provided, every emotion can be described using a formal notation, which makes their model so attractive to the computing community. A problem with the model is that not all stimuli can be directly evaluated because, quite often, there are strong pre-wired stimulus-response relationships for which explicit appraisal procedures would not apply or stimuli that are processed subliminally in emotion processing without further appraisal. Thus whereas the phenomenon of implicit emotion processing is common in humans, it seems a major unsolved challenge for full implementation in affective computing.

Another elaborate appraisal model has been suggested by Scherer (1984; Ellsworth & Scherer, 2003), in which five functionally defined subsystems at various levels of consciousness are involved with emotional processes. An information-processing subsystem evaluates the stimulus through perception, memory, forecast and evaluation of available information. A supporting subsystem adjusts the internal condition through control of neuroendocrine, somatic and autonomous states. A leading subsystem plans, prepares actions and selects between competitive motives. An acting subsystem controls motor expression and visible behaviour. Finally, a monitor subsystem controls the attention that is assigned to the present states and passes the resulting feedback on to the other subsystems. Emotion-related appraisals are implemented by the information-processing subsystem, which in Scherer's model are called stimulus evaluation checks, and which lead to changes in the other subsystems. Each emotion can be clearly characterized by a mix of the stimulus evaluation checks and subchecks.

A very interesting appraisal model has been suggested in the form of the "communicative theory of emotions" (Oatley & Johnson-Laird, 1996). This model proposes a hierarchy of simultaneously operative processing modules, which work asynchronously on different tasks. These instances are coordinated by a central control or operating system. This control system contains a model of the entire system. The functioning of the whole system depends on communication between modules. According to Oatley and Johnson-Laird (1996) there are two kinds of communication between modules: propositional or symbolic, through which actual information about the environment is conveyed, and non-propositional, whose primary role is related to the emotions. The task of the non-propositional form of communication is less to convey information and more to shift the entire system of modules into a state of increased attention, the so-called emotion mode. This function seems not unlike the global interrupt programs on computers.

The appraisal models of emotion outlined above are just three of the most prominent of a wide range of cognitive approaches (see also e.g., Frijda, 1986, 1993; Roseman et al., 1996; Lerner & Keltner, 2000; Levine et al., 2001). This variety of models, all linked to one or another kind of appraisal process, clearly demonstrates a dilemma for the computing community. Which of the many models should be adopted as the most promising in affective computing? Again, it seems as if the hope for general answers to such a question is futile. Instead, computer scientists concentrate more on the criteria of applicability for their solutions. In this sense, questions of implementation and availability of programming tools have had priority in the past. In the future, there are challenges ahead to look beyond valence models of emotion in psychology and equip artifacts with a range of different emotional processes that work together in the end. To highlight the challenges ahead and hint at possible solutions for the most complicated area of emotional processing linked to consciousness and intentionality, we focus on a concrete example below.

At the other end of the spectrum when considering the regulatory contributions of emotional features in multi-agent systems, the concepts of meaning and intentionality have to be taken more seriously (see Dittrich, 1999). It is argued that progress is made only if designers move away from the gestalt or beyond a valence view when combining multi-feature input characteristics and fully embrace a more holistic view based on the overall input-output and intervening variable states, including emotional states. For a holistic design approach the question of emotional regulation between multiple agents and, finally, intentionality seems of utmost importance. However, implementing intentional features in artifacts is one of the greatest challenges affective computing faces, as it requires the combination of emotional and cognitive states. Intentionality seems to have two aspects to it, namely target-directed and goal-directed. Both functions fall together sometimes, for example, when a pack of wolves target and hunt a sheep herd to catch a prey. Such a rather narrative scenario has been simplified, simulated and studied by Dittrich and Lea (1994), in order to investigate directly the perception of intentional motion. A visual display was developed in which multiple objects moved randomly except one (see Figure 2). This one object always moved towards one of the other randomly moving objects. This is typical for predator/prey scenarios. Three separate factors were identified, all of which contributed to the perception of intentional motion in an object by an observer: (1) the object moved in a direct fashion; (2) the object moved faster than other objects; and (3) the goal towards which the object was moving was visible. The fact that identification of intentional motion depended on three separate factors suggests that the perception of intentionality is a rather complex concept depending on the integration of different dynamic features of multiple objects. Therefore, one of the challenges for the architecture of artificial devices is how such 'motion integrators' can be designed in multi-layered systems. The successful implementation of such e-motion features in artifacts would not only be seen as a major step in realizing the tenets of embodiment but as central to understand the workings of the animal and human brains at a psychological level. The notion of intelligence would be demystified in a major way. Only then would interaction with robots be able to constitute significant relationships in people's lives. Real-life scenarios could be entered into or re-enacted and virtual reality become a reality in life.

Fig. 2. The wolf-sheep scenario: The thin lines denote the movement trace of random moving objects. The thick line is the movement trace of the objects imbued with intention (for more detailed explanation, see text).

5. Conclusion

We suggest two recommendations for affective computing. First, affective computing researchers should heed the findings of psychology and neuroscience. We grant that machines that recognize emotional expressions or that behave emotionally need not achieve these feats in exactly the way humans and their brains do. Nonetheless, a better understanding of human perception and human emotions can aid affective computing by narrowing down the search space of possible solutions and by providing a rich set of clues for alternative solutions within that space. We have tried to give a flavour of how emotion perception, as well as emotions more generally, are implemented in humans. In summary: Emotions have roles in both communication and behavioural organization. The communication of emotions is multimodal. With respect to the perception of bodily expressed emotions, humans rely on a mixture of visual form and motion cues, particularly configural form and motion as well as kinematic cues. The relative reliance on these different types of cue can vary across emotions. Evidence reviewed here suggests the functional architecture of human emotion perception is both modular and interactive. In particular, visual emotion perception involves, *inter alia*, subsystems specialized for processing the form and motion of others' bodies, and other, modality-general subsystems that evaluate and signal the value of stimuli and events to the observer's own welfare and interests. At least in some cases, these latter processes subsequently modulate the activity of the visual mechanisms. Evidence also suggests that existence of other subsystems that simulate observed expressions or actions and/or that simulate the changes in internal body state associated with the viewed expression or action. Attempts to emulate human emotion recognition in machines will require detailed knowledge not only of how all these different subsystems operate but also of how they interact, so it is heartening to note that this is now a focus of research in cognitive neuroscience. With respect to the role of emotions in behavioural organization, research on human emotions indicates the importance of basic level regulatory functions as well as high-order mental activities related to consciousness and intentionality, which also in turn influence perception and communication.

Our second recommendation is that, on the basis of the findings from psychology and neuroscience, affective computing researchers might want to give serious consideration to the question of whether giving a machine the capacity to experience emotions might be one way in which it could achieve reliable and efficient emotion recognition. Indeed, it might also or instead be beneficial to consider the flipside of this question, that is, whether installing an ability to recognize emotions in others might be an important or even necessary step in building a machine that experiences genuine emotions.

Affective computing could be a powerful tool to produce a new generation of artificial devices. However, we suggest that a new approach to affective computing based on the above recommendations may support the design of emotional agents as well as the implementation of emotional reactions into different types of machinery. It is possible that the features of human emotions that we have outlined above are not directly applicable to AI or computer science models of emotions. Even so, we suggest that the role of emotions in regulating the internal functioning and external behaviour of multi-layered and multi-agent systems needs to form the core of affective computing attempts to simulate the overall distribution and at the same time local display of emotional characteristics.

6. References

Adolphs, R. (2002). Recognizing emotion from facial expressions: Psychological and neurological mechanisms. *Behavioral and Cognitive Neuroscience Reviews, 1*(1), 21-62.

Allison, T., Puce, A., & McCarthy, G. (2000). Social perception from visual cues: role of the STS region. *Trends in Cognitive Sciences, 4*(7), 267-278.

Arbib, M. A. (2005). Beware the passionate robot. In J.-M. Fellous & M. A. Arbib (Eds.), *Who needs emotions? The brain meets the robot*,Oxford University Press, New York.

Arbib, M. A., & Fellous, J. M. (2004). Emotions: from brain to robot. *Trends in Cognitive Sciences, 8*(12), 554-561.

Arkin, R. C., Fujita, M., Takagi, T., & Hasegawa, R. (2003). An ethological and emotional basis for human-robot interaction. *Robotics and Autonomous Systems, 42*(3-4), 191-201.

Aronoff, J., Woike, B. A., & Hyman, L. M. (1992). Which are the stimuli in facial displays of anger and happiness? Configurational bases of emotion recognition. *Journal of Personality and Social Psychology, 62*(6), 1050-1066.

Atkinson, A. P. (2007). Face processing and empathy. In T. F. D. Farrow & P. W. R. Woodruff (Eds.), *Empathy in mental illness* (pp. 360-385), Cambridge University Press, Cambridge.

Atkinson, A. P., & Adolphs, A. (2005). Visual emotion perception: Mechanisms and processes. In L. F. Barrett, P. M. Niedenthal & P. Winkielman (Eds.), *Emotion and consciousness* (pp. 150-182), Guilford Press, New York.

Atkinson, A. P., Dittrich, W. H., Gemmell, A. J., & Young, A. W. (2004). Emotion perception from dynamic and static body expressions in point-light and full-light displays. *Perception, 33*(5), 717-746.

Atkinson, A. P., Tunstall, M. L., & Dittrich, W. H. (2007). Evidence for distinct contributions of form and motion information to the recognition of emotions from body gestures. *Cognition, 104*(1), 59-72.

Barclay, C. D., Cutting, J. E., & Kozlowski, L. T. (1978). Temporal and spatial factors in gait perception that influence gender recognition. *Perception and Psychophysics, 23*(2), 145-152.

Bassili, J. N. (1978). Facial motion in the perception of faces and of emotional expression. *Journal of Experimental Psychology: Human Perception and Performance, 4*, 373-379.

Beauchamp, M. S. (2005). See me, hear me, touch me: multisensory integration in lateral occipital-temporal cortex. *Current Opinion in Neurobiology, 15*(2), 145-153.

Beintema, J. A., & Lappe, M. (2002). Perception of biological motion without local image motion. *Proceedings of the National Academy of Sciences, 99*(8), 5661-5663.

Bertenthal, B. I., & Pinto, J. (1994). Global processing of biological motions. *Psychological Science, 5*(4), 221-225.

Bertenthal, B. I., Proffitt, D. R., & Kramer, S. J. (1987). Perception of biomechanical motions by infants: implementation of various processing constraints. *Journal of Experimental Psychology: Human Perception & Performance, 13*(4), 577-585.

Blake, R., & Shiffrar, M. (2007). Perception of human motion. *Annual Review of Psychology, 58*, 47-73.

Bonda, E., Petrides, M., Ostry, D., & Evans, A. (1996). Specific involvement of human parietal systems and the amygdala in the perception of biological motion. *Journal of Neuroscience, 16*(11), 3737-3744.

Breazeal, C. (2003). Emotion and sociable humanoid robots. *International Journal of Human-Computer Studies, 59*(1-2), 119-155.

Breazeal, C. L. (2002). *Designing sociable robots*, MIT Press, Cambridge, MA.

Brooks, R. (2002). *Robot: The future of flesh and machines*, Allen Lane/Penguin, London.

Brooks, R. A. (1991). *Intelligence without reason.* Paper presented at the 12th International Joint Conference on Artificial Intelligence, Sydney, Australia.

Brooks, R. A., & Stein, L. A. (1994). Building brains for bodies. *Autonomous Robots, 1*(1), 7-25.

Buccino, G., Binkofski, F., Fink, G. R., Fadiga, L., Fogassi, L., Gallese, V., et al. (2001). Action observation activates premotor and parietal areas in a somatotopic manner: an fMRI study. *European Journal of Neuroscience, 13*, 400-404.

Buck, R. (1984). *The communication of emotion*, Guilford Press, New York.

Calvert, G. A., Bullmore, E. T., Brammer, M. J., Campbell, R., Williams, S. C. R., McGuire, P. K., et al. (1997). Activation of auditory cortex during silent lipreading. *Science, 276*(5312), 593-596.

Campbell, R., MacSweeney, M., Surguladze, S., Calvert, G., McGuire, P., Suckling, J., et al. (2001). Cortical substrates for the perception of face actions: an fMRI study of the specificity of activation for seen speech and for meaningless lower-face acts (gurning). *Cognitive Brain Research, 12*(2), 233-243.

Campbell, R., Zihl, J., Massaro, D., Munhall, K., & Cohen, M. M. (1997). Speechreading in the akinetopsic patient, L.M. *Brain, 120*, 1793-1803.

Carr, L., Iacoboni, M., Dubeau, M. C., Mazziotta, J. C., & Lenzi, G. L. (2003). Neural mechanisms of empathy in humans: a relay from neural systems for imitation to limbic areas. *Proceedings of the National Academy of Sciences, 100*(9), 5497-5502.

Casile, A., & Giese, M. A. (2005). Critical features for the recognition of biological motion. *Journal of Vision, 5*(4), 348-360.

Chan, A. W., Peelen, M. V., & Downing, P. E. (2004). The effect of viewpoint on body representation in the extrastriate body area. *Neuroreport, 15*(15), 2407-2410.

Damasio, A. R. (1994). *Descartes' error: Emotion, reason and the human brain*, Picador, London.

de Gelder, B. (2006). Towards the neurobiology of emotional body language. *Nature Reviews Neuroscience, 7*(3), 242-249.

Dean, J. (1998). Animats and what they can tell us. *Trends in Cognitive Sciences, 2*(2), 60-67.

Diamond, R., & Carey, S. (1986). Why faces are and are not special: An effect of expertise. *Journal of Experimental Psychology: General, 115*, 107-117.

Dittrich, W. (1991). Das Erkennen von Emotionen aus Ausdrucksbewegungen des Gesichts. *Psychologische Beitrage, 33*, 366-377.

Dittrich, W. H. (1993). Action categories and the perception of biological motion. *Perception, 22*(1), 15-22.

Dittrich, W. H. (1999). Seeing biological motion – Is there a role for cognitive strategies? In A. Braffort, R. Gherbi, S. Gibet, J. Richardson & D. Teil (Eds.), *Gesture-based communication in human-computer interaction* (pp. 3-22),Springer, Berlin.

Dittrich, W. H., & Lea, S. E. (1994). Visual perception of intentional motion. *Perception, 23*(3), 253-268.

Dittrich, W. H., Troscianko, T., Lea, S., & Morgan, D. (1996). Perception of emotion from dynamic point-light displays represented in dance. *Perception, 25*(6), 727-738.

Downing, P. E., Jiang, Y., Shuman, M., & Kanwisher, N. (2001). A cortical area selective for visual processing of the human body. *Science, 293*(5539), 2470-2473.

Downing, P. E., Peelen, M. V., Wiggett, A. J., & Tew, B. D. (2006). The role of the extrastriate body area in action perception. *Social Neuroscience, 1*(1), 52-62.

Downing, P. E., Wiggett, A. J., & Peelen, M. V. (2007). Functional magnetic resonance imaging investigation of overlapping lateral occipitotemporal activations using multi-voxel pattern analysis. *Journal of Neuroscience, 27*(1), 226-233.

Drummond, P. D. (1997). Correlates of facial flushing and pallor in anger-provoking situations. *Personality and Individual Differences, 23*(4), 575-582.

Drummond, P. D., & Quah, S. H. (2001). The effect of expressing anger on cardiovascular reactivity and facial blood flow in Chinese and Caucasians. *Psychophysiology, 38*(2), 190-196.

Ekman, P. (1992). An argument for basic emotions. *Cognition & Emotion, 6*(3-4), 169-200.

Ekman, P., & Friesen, W. V. (1978). *The facial action coding system*, Consulting Psychologist's Press, Palo Alto, CA.

Ekman, P., Friesen, W. V., & Ellsworth, P. (1972). *Emotion in the human face*, Pergamon Press, New York.

Ellsworth, P. C., & Scherer, K. R. (2003). Appraisal processes in emotion. In R. J. Davidson, K. R. Scherer & H. H. Goldsmith (Eds.), *Handbook of affective sciences* (pp. 572-595), Oxford University Press, New York.

Frank, M. G., & Gilovich, T. (1988). The dark side of self-perception and social perception: Black uniforms and aggression in professional sports. *Journal of Personality and Social Psychology, 54*(1), 74-85.

Frijda, N. H. (1986). *The emotions*, Cambridge University Press, Cambridge.

Frijda, N. H. (1993). The place of appraisal in emotion. *Cognition & Emotion, 7*(3-4), 357-387.

Fujita, M. (2001). AIBO: Toward the era of digital creatures. *The International Journal of Robotics Research, 20*(10), 781-794.

Gallese, V., Keysers, C., & Rizzolatti, G. (2004). A unifying view of the basis of social cognition. *Trends in Cognitive Sciences, 8*(9), 396-403.

Giese, M. A., & Poggio, T. (2003). Neural mechanisms for the recognition of biological movements. *Nature Reviews Neuroscience, 4*(3), 179-192.

Goldman, A. I., & Sripada, C. S. (2005). Simulationist models of face-based emotion recognition. *Cognition, 94*(3), 193-213.

Grafton, S. T., Arbib, M. A., Fadiga, L., & Rizzolatti, G. (1996). Localization of grasp representations in humans by positron emission tomography. 2. Observation compared with imagination. *Experimental Brain Research, 112*(1), 103-111.

Grossman, E., Donnelly, M., Price, R., Pickens, D., Morgan, V., Neighbor, G., et al. (2000). Brain areas involved in perception of biological motion. *Journal of Cognitive Neuroscience, 12*(5), 711-720.

Grossman, E. D., Battelli, L., & Pascual-Leone, A. (2005). Repetitive TMS over posterior STS disrupts perception of biological motion. *Vision Research, 45*(22), 2847-2853.

Grossman, E. D., & Blake, R. (2001). Brain activity evoked by inverted and imagined biological motion. *Vision Research, 41*(10-11), 1475-1482.

Grossman, E. D., & Blake, R. (2002). Brain areas active during visual perception of biological motion. *Neuron, 35*(6), 1167-1175.

Grush, R. (2004). The emulation theory of representation: motor control, imagery, and perception. *Behavioral and Brain Sciences, 27*(3), 377-396; discussion 396-442.

Hari, R., Forss, N., Avikainen, S., Kirveskari, E., Salenius, S., & Rizzolatti, G. (1998). Activation of human primary motor cortex during action observation: a neuromagnetic study. *Proceedings of the National Academy of Sciences, 95*(25), 15061-15065.

Harnad, S. (2000). Minds, machines and Turing: The indistinguishability of indistinguishables. *Journal of Logic, Language, and Information, 9*(4), 425-445.

Heberlein, A. S., & Adolphs, R. (2007). Neurobiology of emotion recognition: Current evidence for shared substrates. In E. Harmon-Jones & P. Winkielman (Eds.), *Social neuroscience: Integrating biological and psychological explanations of social behavior*, Guilford Press, New York.

Heider, F., & Simmel, M. (1944). An experimental study of apparent behavior. *American Journal of Psychology, 57*, 243-259.

Hill, H., Jinno, Y., & Johnston, A. (2003). Comparing solid-body with point-light animations. *Perception, 32*(5), 561-566.

Hill, R. A., & Barton, R. A. (2005). Red enhances human performance in contests. *Nature, 435*(7040), 293-293.

Hirai, M., & Hiraki, K. (2006). The relative importance of spatial versus temporal structure in the perception of biological motion: An event-related potential study. *Cognition, 99*(1), B15-B29.

Hirai, M., Senju, A., Fukushima, H., & Hiraki, K. (2005). Active processing of biological motion perception: an ERP study. *Cognitive Brain Research, 23*(2-3), 387-396.

Iacoboni, M., Woods, R. P., Brass, M., Bekkering, H., Mazziotta, J. C., & Rizzolatti, G. (1999). Cortical mechanisms of human imitation. *Science, 286*, 2526-2528.

Izard, C. E. (1991). *The psychology of emotions*, Kluwer Academic Amsterdam.

Jellema, T., Baker, C. I., Wicker, B., & Perrett, D. I. (2000). Neural representation for the perception of the intentionality of actions. *Brain and Cognition, 44*(2), 280-302.

Johansson, G. (1973). Visual perception of biological motion and a model for its analysis. *Perception and Psychophysics, 14*(2), 201-211.

Johnson, S. H., & Grafton, S. T. (2003). From 'acting on' to 'acting with': the functional anatomy of object-oriented action schemata. *Progress in Brain Research, 142*, 127-139.

Jokisch, D., Daum, I., Suchan, B., & Troje, N. F. (2005). Structural encoding and recognition of biological motion: evidence from event-related potentials and source analysis. *Behavioural Brain Research, 157*(2), 195-204.

Kaiser, S., & Wehrle, T. (1992). Automated coding of facial behavior in human-computer interactions with FACS. *Journal of Nonverbal Behavior, 16*(2), 67-84.

Kozma, R., & Fukuda, T. (2006). Intentional dynamic systems: Fundamental concepts and applications. *International Journal of Intelligent Systems, 21*(9), 875-879.

Lange, J., & Lappe, M. (2006). A model of biological motion perception from configural form cues. *Journal of Neuroscience, 26*(11), 2894-2906.

Lazarus, R. S. (1991). *Emotion and adaptation*, Oxford University Press, New York.

Lerner, J. S., & Keltner, D. (2000). Beyond valence: Toward a model of emotion-specific influences on judgement and choice. *Cognition & Emotion, 14*(4), 473-493.

Leslie, K. R., Johnson-Frey, S. H., & Grafton, S. T. (2004). Functional imaging of face and hand imitation: towards a motor theory of empathy. *Neuroimage, 21*(2), 601-607.

Levine, L. J., Prohaska, V., Burgess, S. L., Rice, J. A., & Laulhere, T. M. (2001). Remembering past emotions: The role of current appraisals. *Cognition & Emotion, 15*(4), 393-417.

Loula, F., Prasad, S., Harber, K., & Shiffrar, M. (2005). Recognizing people from their movement. *Journal of Experimental Psychology: Human Perception and Performance, 31*(1), 210-220.

Lu, H., Yuille, A., & Liu, Z. (2005). Configural processing in biological motion detection: Human versus ideal observers. *Journal of Vision, 5*(8), 23-23.

Mandler, G. (2007). *A history of modern experimental psychology: From James and Wundt to cognitive science*, MIT Press/ Bradford Books, Cambridge, MA.

Mather, G., & Murdoch, L. (1994). Gender dscrimination in biological motion displays based on dynamic cues. *Proceedings of the Royal Society of London, Series B: Biological Sciences, 258*(1353), 273-279.

Mather, G., Radford, K., & West, S. (1992). Low-level visual processing of biological motion. *Proceedings of the Royal Society of London Series B: Biological Sciences, 249*(1325), 149-155.

Maurer, D., Le Grand, R., & Mondloch, C. J. (2002). The many faces of configural processing. *Trends in Cognitive Sciences, 6*(6), 255-260.

McLeod, P., Dittrich, W., Driver, J., Perrett, D., & Zihl, J. (1996). Preserved and impaired detection of structure from motion by a "motion-blind" patient. *Visual Cognition, 3*(4), 363-391.

Miall, R. C. (2003). Connecting mirror neurons and forward models. *Neuroreport, 14*(17), 2135-2137.

Michels, L., Lappe, M., & Vaina, L. M. (2005). Visual areas involved in the perception of human movement from dynamic form analysis. *Neuroreport, 16*(10), 1037-1041.

Oatley, K. (2004). *Emotions: A brief history*, Blackwell, Oxford.

Oatley, K., & Johnson-Laird, P. N. (1996). The communicative theory of emotions: Empirical tests, mental models, and implications for social interaction. In L. L. Martin & A. Tesser (Eds.), *Striving and feeling: Interactions among goals, affect, and self-regulation* (pp. 363-393),Erlbaum, Hillsdale, NJ.

Oram, M. W., & Perrett, D. I. (1994). Responses of anterior superior temporal polysensory (STPa) neurons to "biological motion" stimuli. *Journal of Cognitive Neuroscience, 6*(2), 99-116.

Oram, M. W., & Perrett, D. I. (1996). Integration of form and motion in the anterior superior temporal polysensory area (STPa) of the macaque monkey. *Journal of Neurophysiology, 76*(1), 109-129.

Ortony, A., Clore, G. L., & Collins, A. (1988). *The cognitive structure of emotions*, Cambridge University Press, Cambridge.

Ortony, A., & Turner, T. J. (1990). What's basic about basic emotions? *Psychological Review, 97*(3), 315-331.

Pavlova, M., Birbaumer, N., & Sokolov, A. (2006). Attentional modulation of cortical neuromagnetic gamma response to biological movement. *Cerebral Cortex, 16*(3), 321-327.

Pavlova, M., Lutzenberger, W., Sokolov, A., & Birbaumer, N. (2004). Dissociable cortical processing of recognizable and non-recognizable biological movement: Analysing gamma MEG activity. *Cerebral Cortex, 14*(2), 181-188.

Pavlova, M., Lutzenberger, W., Sokolov, A. N., Birbaumer, N., & Krageloh-Mann, I. (2007). Oscillatory MEG response to human locomotion is modulated by periventricular lesions. *Neuroimage, 35*(3), 1256-1263.

Pavlova, M., & Sokolov, A. (2000). Orientation specificity in biological motion perception. *Perception and Psychophysics, 62*(5), 889-899.

Pavlova, M., & Sokolov, A. (2003). Prior knowledge about display inversion in biological motion perception. *Perception, 32*(8), 937-946.

Peelen, M. V., & Downing, P. E. (2005). Selectivity for the human body in the fusiform gyrus. *Journal of Neurophysiology, 93*(1), 603-608.

Peelen, M. V., & Downing, P. E. (2007). The neural basis of visual body perception. *Nature Reviews Neuroscience, 8*(8), 636-648.

Peelen, M. V., Wiggett, A. J., & Downing, P. E. (2006). Patterns of fMRI activity dissociate overlapping functional brain areas that respond to biological motion. *Neuron, 49*(6), 815-822.

Pelphrey, K. A., Mitchell, T. V., McKeown, M. J., Goldstein, J., Allison, T., & McCarthy, G. (2003). Brain activity evoked by the perception of human walking: Controlling for meaningful coherent motion. *Journal of Neuroscience, 23*(17), 6819-6825.

Pelphrey, K. A., Morris, J. P., Michelich, C. R., Allison, T., & McCarthy, G. (2005). Functional anatomy of biological motion perception in posterior temporal cortex: An fMRI study of eye, mouth and hand movements. *Cerebral Cortex, 15*(12), 1866-1876.

Pelphrey, K. A., Viola, R. J., & McCarthy, G. (2004). When strangers pass: Processing of mutual and averted social gaze in the superior temporal sulcus. *Psychological Science, 15*(9), 598-603.

Perrett, D. I., Smith, P. A., Mistlin, A. J., Chitty, A. J., Head, A. S., Potter, D. D., et al. (1985). Visual analysis of body movements by neurones in the temporal cortex of the macaque monkey: a preliminary report. *Behavioural Brain Research, 16*(2-3), 153-170.

Peuskens, H., Vanrie, J., Verfaillie, K., & Orban, G. A. (2005). Specificity of regions processing biological motion. *European Journal of Neuroscience, 21*(10), 2864-2875.

Pfeifer, R. (2002). Robots as cognitive tools. *International Journal of Cognition and Technology, 1*, 125-143.

Picard, R. W. (1997). *Affective computing*, MIT Press, Cambridge, MA.

Pinto, J., & Shiffrar, M. (1999). Subconfigurations of the human form in the perception of biological motion displays. *Acta Psychologica, 102*(2-3), 293-318.

Plutchik, R. (1980). *Emotion: A psychoevolutionary synthesis*, Harper and Row, New York.

Pobric, G., & Hamilton, A. F. (2006). Action understanding requires the left inferior frontal cortex. *Current Biology, 16*(5), 524-529.

Pollick, F. E., Paterson, H. M., Bruderlin, A., & Sanford, A. J. (2001). Perceiving affect from arm movement. *Cognition, 82*(2), B51-61.

Pourtois, G., Peelen, M. V., Spinelli, L., Seeck, M., & Vuilleumier, P. (2007). Direct intracranial recording of body-selective responses in human extrastriate visual cortex. *Neuropsychologia, 45*(11), 2621-2625.

Prinz, J. J. (2004). *Gut reactions: A perceptual theory of emotion*, Oxford University Press, New York.

Puce, A., Allison, T., Bentin, S., Gore, J. C., & McCarthy, G. (1998). Temporal cortex activation in humans viewing eye and mouth movements. *Journal of Neuroscience, 18*(6), 2188-2199.

Puce, A., & Perrett, D. (2003). Electrophysiology and brain imaging of biological motion. *Philosophical Transactions of the Royal Society of London, Series B: Biological Sciences, 358*(1431), 435-445.

Puce, A., Syngeniotis, A., Thompson, J. C., Abbott, D. F., Wheaton, K. J., & Castiello, U. (2003). The human temporal lobe integrates facial form and motion: evidence from fMRI and ERP studies. *Neuroimage, 19*(3), 861-869.

Reed, C. L., Stone, V. E., Bozova, S., & Tanaka, J. (2003). The body-inversion effect. *Psychological Science, 14*(4), 302-308.

Reed, C. L., Stone, V. E., Grubb, J. D., & McGoldrick, J. E. (2006). Turning configural processing upside down: Part and whole body postures. *Journal of Experimental Psychology: Human Perception and Performance, 32*(1), 73-87.

Rhodes, G., Brake, S., & Atkinson, A. P. (1993). What's lost in inverted faces? *Cognition, 47*(1), 25-57.

Richardson, M. J., & Johnston, L. (2005). Person recognition from dynamic events: The kinematic specification of individual identity in walking style. *Journal of Nonverbal Behavior, 29*(1), 25-44.

Rizzolatti, G., & Craighero, L. (2004). The mirror-neuron system. *Annual Review of Neuroscience, 27*, 169-192.

Rizzolatti, G., Fadiga, L., Gallese, V., & Fogassi, L. (1996). Premotor cortex and the recognition of motor actions. *Cognitive Brain Research, 3*, 131-141.

Roseman, I. J., Antoniou, A. A., & Jose, P. E. (1996). Appraisal determinants of emotions: Constructing a more accurate and comprehensive theory. *Cognition & Emotion, 10*(3), 241-277.

Runeson, S., & Frykholm, G. (1981). Visual perception of lifted weight. *Journal of Experimental Psychology: Human Perception and Performance, 7*(4), 733-740.

Sawada, M., Suda, K., & Ishii, M. (2003). Expression of emotions in dance: relation between arm movement characteristics and emotion. *Perceptual and Motor Skills, 97*(3 Pt 1), 697-708.

Saygin, A. P. (2007). Superior temporal and premotor brain areas necessary for biological motion perception. *Brain, 130*(9), 2452-2461.

Saygin, A. P., Wilson, S. M., Hagler, D. J., Bates, E., & Sereno, M. I. (2004). Point-light biological motion perception activates human premotor cortex. *Journal of Neuroscience, 24*(27), 6181-6188.

Schaal, S. (1999). Is imitation learning the route to humanoid robots? *Trends in Cognitive Sciences, 3*(6), 233-242.

Schachter, S., & Singer, J. E. (1962). Cognitive, social, and physiological determinants of emotional state. *Psychological Review, 69*(5), 379-399.

Scherer, K. R. (1984). On the nature and function of emotion: A component process approach. In K. R. Scherer & P. Ekman (Eds.), *Approaches to emotion*, Lawrence Erlbaum, Hillsdale, NJ.

Schneider, K., & Dittrich, W. (1989). Functions and evolution of emotions (Germ.). In K. Scherer (Ed.) *Enzyklopaedie der Psychologie, Bd. C/IV/3* (pp.41-115). Goettingen: Hogrefe.

Scholl, B. J., & Tremoulet, P. D. (2000). Perceptual causality and animacy. *Trends in Cognitive Sciences, 4*(8), 299-309.

Schwarzlose, R. F., Baker, C. I., & Kanwisher, N. (2005). Separate face and body selectivity on the fusiform gyrus. *Journal of Neuroscience, 25*(47), 11055-11059.

Sen, S. (1997). Multiagent systems: milestones and new horizons. *Trends in Cognitive Sciences, 1*(9), 334-340.

Shipley, T. F. (2003). The effect of object and event orientation on perception of biological motion. *Psychological Science, 14*(4), 377-380.

Stekelenburg, J. J., & de Gelder, B. (2004). The neural correlates of perceiving human bodies: an ERP study on the body-inversion effect. *Neuroreport, 15*(5), 777-780.

Strafella, A. P., & Paus, T. (2000). Modulation of cortical excitability during action observation: a transcranial magnetic stimulation study. *Neuroreport, 11*(10), 2289-2292.

Suzuki, K., Camurri, A., Ferrentino, P., & Hashimoto, S. (1998). *Intelligent agent system for human-robot interaction through artificial emotion.* Paper presented at the IEEE International Conference on Systems, Man, and Cybernetics, San Diego, CA, USA.

Takeuchi, A., & Nagao, K. (1992). *Communicative facial displays as a new conversational modality.* Tokyo: Sony Computer Science Laboratory.

Taylor, J. C., Wiggett, A. J., & Downing, P. E. (2007). fMRI analysis of body and body part representations in the extrastriate and fusiform body areas. *Journal of Neurophysiology, 98* (3), 1626-1633.

Thompson, J. C., Clarke, M., Stewart, T., & Puce, A. (2005). Configural processing of biological motion in human superior temporal sulcus. *Journal of Neuroscience, 25*(39), 9059-9066.

Thompson, J. C., Hardee, J. E., Panayiotou, A., Crewther, D., & Puce, A. (2007). Common and distinct brain activation to viewing dynamic sequences of face and hand movements. *Neuroimage, 37*(3), 966-973.

Troje, N. F. (2002). Decomposing biological motion: a framework for analysis and synthesis of human gait patterns. *Journal of Vision, 2*(5), 371-387.

Troje, N. F. (2003). Reference frames for orientation anisotropies in face recognition and biological-motion perception. *Perception, 32*(2), 201-210.

Urgesi, C., Berlucchi, G., & Aglioti, S. M. (2004). Magnetic stimulation of extrastriate body area impairs visual processing of nonfacial body parts. *Current Biology, 14*(23), 2130-2134.

Urgesi, C., Calvo-Merino, B., Haggard, P., & Aglioti, S. M. (2007a). Transcranial magnetic stimulation reveals two cortical pathways for visual body processing. *Journal of Neuroscience, 27*(30), 8023-8030.

Urgesi, C., Candidi, M., Ionta, S., & Aglioti, S. M. (2007b). Representation of body identity and body actions in extrastriate body area and ventral premotor cortex. *Nature Neuroscience, 10*(1), 30-31.

Vaina, L. M., Cowey, A., LeMay, M., Bienfang, D. C., & Kikinis, R. (2002). Visual deficits in a patient with 'kaleidoscopic disintegration of the visual world'. *European Journal of Neurology, 9*(5), 463-477.

Vaina, L. M., Lemay, M., Bienfang, D. C., Choi, A. Y., & Nakayama, K. (1990). Intact "biological motion" and "structure from motion" perception in a patient with impaired motion mechanisms: A case study. *Visual Neuroscience, 5*(4), 353-369.

Vaina, L. M., Solomon, J., Chowdhury, S., Sinha, P., & Belliveau, J. W. (2001). Functional neuroanatomy of biological motion perception in humans. *Proceedings of the National Academy of Sciences, 98*(20), 11656-11661.

Walk, R. D., & Homan, C. P. (1984). Emotion and dance in dynamic light displays. *Bulletin of the Psychonomic Society, 22*, 437-440.

Westhoff, C., & Troje, N. F. (2007). Kinematic cues for person identification from biological motion. *Perception & Psychophysics, 69*, 241-253.

Wheaton, K. J., Thompson, J. C., Syngeniotis, A., Abbott, D. F., & Puce, A. (2004). Viewing the motion of human body parts activates different regions of premotor, temporal, and parietal cortex. *Neuroimage, 22*(1), 277-288.

Wolpert, D. M., Doya, K., & Kawato, M. (2003). A unifying computational framework for motor control and social interaction. *Philosophical Transactions of the Royal Society of London, B: Biological Sciences, 358*(1431), 593-602.

10

From the Lab to the Real World: Affect Recognition Using Multiple Cues and Modalities

Hatice Gunes[1], Massimo Piccardi[1] and Maja Pantic[2,3]
[1]*University of Technology, Sydney (UTS)*
[2]*Imperial College, London, United Kingdom*
[3]*University of Twente, the Netherlands*
[1]*Australia*
[2]*United Kingdom*
[3] *The Netherlands*

1. Introduction

Human affect sensing can be obtained from a broad range of behavioral cues and signals that are available via visual, acoustic, and tactual expressions or presentations of emotions. Affective states can thus be recognized from visible/external signals such as gestures (e.g., facial expressions, body gestures, head movements, etc.), and speech (e.g., parameters such as pitch, energy, frequency and duration), or invisible/internal signals such as physiological signals (e.g., heart rate, skin conductivity, salivation, etc.), brain and scalp signals, and thermal infrared imagery.

Despite the available range of cues and modalities in human-human interaction (HHI), the mainstream emotion research has mostly focused on facial expressions (Hadjikhani & De Gelder, 2003). In line with this, most of the past research on affect sensing and recognition has also focused on facial expressions and on data that has been posed on demand or acquired in laboratory settings. Additionally, each sense such as vision, hearing, and touch has been considered in isolation. However, natural human-human interaction is multimodal and not occurring in predetermined, restricted and controlled settings. In the day-to-day world people do not present themselves to others as voice- or body-less faces or face- or body-less voices (Walker-Andrews, 1997). Moreover, the available emotional signals such as facial expression, head movement, hand gestures, and voice are unified in space and time (see Figure 1). They inherently share the same spatial location, and their occurrences are temporally synchronized. Cognitive neuroscience research thus claims that information coming from various modalities is combined in our brains to yield multimodally determined percepts (Driver & Spence, 2000). In real life situations, our different senses receive correlated information about the same external event. When assessing each others' emotional or affective state, we are capable of handling significantly variable conditions in terms of viewpoint (i.e. frontal, profile, even back view), tilt angle, distance (i.e., face to face as well as at a distance) , illumination (i.e., both day and night conditions), occlusions (e.g., even when some body parts are occluded), motion (e.g., both when stationary and moving, walking and talking) and noise (e.g., while many people are chatting and interacting simultaneously).

The fact that humans perceive the world using rather complex multimodal systems does not necessarily imply that the machines should also posses all of the aforementioned functionalities. Humans need to operate in all possible situations and develop an adaptive behavior; machines instead can be highly profiled for a specific purpose, scenario, user, etc. For example, the computer inside an automatic teller machine probably does not need to recognize the affective states of a human. However, in other applications (e.g., computer agents, effective tutoring systems, clinical settings, monitoring user's stress level) where computers take on a social role such as an *instructor* or *helper,* recognizing users' affective states may enhance the computers' functionality (Picard, 1997).

A number of survey papers exist within the affect sensing and recognition literature (e.g., Gunes & Piccardi, 2008; Zeng & et al., 2008). For instance, the shift from monomodal to multimodal affect recognition, together with systems using vision as one of the input modalities and analyzing affective face and body movement either as a pure monomodal system or as part of a multimodal affective framework, is discussed in (Gunes & Piccardi, 2008). An exhaustive survey of past efforts in audiovisual affect sensing and recognition, together with various visual, audio and audio-visual databases, is presented in (Zeng & et al., 2008). However, no effort so far has attempted to compile and discuss visual (i.e., facial and bodily expression), audio, tactile (i.e., heart rate, skin conductivity, thermal signals etc.) and thought (i.e., brain and scalp signals) modalities together. Accordingly, this chapter sets out to explore recent advances in affect sensing and recognition by explicitly focusing on systems that are based on multiple input modalities and alternative channels, and is organized as follows. The first part is concerned with the challenges faced when moving from affect recognition systems that were designed in and for laboratory settings (i.e., analyzing posed data) to systems that are able to analyze spontaneous data in a multimodal framework. It discusses the problem domain of multimodal affect sensing, when moving from posed to spontaneous settings. The chapter initially focuses on background research, reviewing the theories of emotion, monomodal expression and perception of emotions, temporal information, posed vs. spontaneous expressions, and multimodal expression and perception of emotions. The chapter then explores further issues in data acquisition, data annotation, feature extraction, and multimodal affective state recognition. As affect recognition systems using multiple cues and modalities have only recently emerged, the next part of the chapter presents representative systems introduced during the period 2004 - 2007, based on multiple visual cues (i.e., affective head, face and/or body movement), haptic cues (physiological sensing) or combination of modalities (i.e., visual and physiological channels, etc.) capable of handling data acquired either in the laboratory or real world settings. There exist some studies analyzing spontaneous facial expression data in the context of cognitive-science or medical applications (e.g., Ashraf & et al., 2007). However, the focus of this chapter is on multimodal or multicue affective data, accordingly, systems analyzing spontaneous data are presented in the context of human-computer interaction (HCI) and human-robot interaction (HRI). The last part of this chapter discusses issues to be explored in order to advance the state-of-the-art in multimodal and multicue affect sensing and recognition.

2. From posed to spontaneous: changes and challenges

Affect sensing and recognition is a relatively new research field. However, it should be realized that affect recognition from multiple modalities has an even shorter historical background and is still in its infancy. It was not till 1998 that computer scientists attempted to use multiple modalities for recognition of emotions/affective states (Riseberg & et al., 1998). The initial interest was on fusing visual and audio data. The results were promising; using multiple modalities improved the overall recognition accuracy helping the systems function in a more efficient and reliable way. Starting from the well-known work of Picard (Picard & et al., 2001), interest in detecting emotions from physiological signals emerged. Although a fundamental study by Ambady and Rosenthal suggested that the most significant channels for judging behavioral cues of humans appear to be the visual channels of face and body (Ambady & Rosenthal, 1992), the existing literature on automatic emotion recognition did not focus on the expressive information that body gestures carry till 2003 (e.g., Camurri & et al., 2003). Following the new findings in psychology, a number of researchers have attempted to combine facial expressions and body gestures for affect recognition (e.g., Gunes & Piccardi, 2007; Karpouzis & et al., 2007; Martin & et al., 2006). A number of approaches have also been proposed for other sensorial sources such as thermal and brain signals (e.g., Nakasone & et al., 2005; Takahashi, 2004; Pun & et al., 2006; Puri & et al., 2005; Savran & et al., 2006; Takahashi, 2004; Tsiamyrtzis & et al., 2007). With all these new areas of research in affect sensing, a number of challenges have arisen (e.g., synchronization, fusion, etc.). The stage that affective computing has reached today is combining multiple channels for affect recognition and moving from laboratory settings towards real world settings.

Figure 1: Examples of socially visible multimodal expression (facial expression, body gesture and speech) of emotions in real-life situations.

We start with the description of what is meant by *laboratory* vs. *real world settings.* The so-called laboratory/posed/controlled settings refer to:

- an experimental setup or environment (e.g., a laboratory), with controlled and uniform background/illumination/placement conditions (e.g., a static background without any clutter, no audiovisual noise, with predetermined level of illumination and number of lights etc.),
- human subject restricted in terms of free movement of head/body and in terms of location/seating and expressivity s(he) is allowed/able to display,
- a setup where people are instructed by an experimenter on how to show the desired actions/expressions (e.g., by moving the left eyebrow up or producing a smile), where occurrences of occlusion/noise/missing data are not allowed,
- a setup without considering any of the issues related to user, task or context.

The so-called real world/spontaneous/natural settings instead refer to:

- a realistic environment, for instance, home/office/hospital, without attempting to control the varying conditions,

- where people might show all possible affective states, expressed synchronously (e.g., speech and facial expression) or asynchronously (e.g., facial expression and body gesticulation), expressed with intention (e.g., irony) or without intention (e.g., fatigue),
- with large head or body movements as well as moving subjects in various environments (e.g., office or house, not just restricted to one chair or room),
- where people are not aware of the recording (or are, depending on the context),
- where people will not restrain themselves unlike the case when they are part of an experiment, and will express emotions due to real-life event or trigger of events (e.g., stressed at work),
- with possible occurrences of occlusions (e.g., hands occluding each other or hand occluding the face), noise (e.g., in audio recordings) and missing data,
- where the recordings are acquired with multiple sensing devices (e.g., multiple cameras & microphones & haptic/olfactory/taste/brain sensors etc.), under non-uniform and noisy (lighting/voice recording) conditions and in long sessions (e.g., one whole day and possibly a couple of weeks or longer),
- capturing all variations of expressive behavior in every possible order/combination/scale,
- being able to adapt to user, task and context.

As the real world settings pose many challenges to the automatic sensing and recognition of human affect, there have been a relatively higher number of research studies on affect recognition that have dealt with laboratory settings rather than real world settings. The shift from the laboratory to the real world is driven by various advances and demands, and funded by various research projects (e.g., European Union FP 6, HUMAINE and European Union FP 7, SEMAINE). However, similar to that of many other research fields, the shift is gradual and the progress is slow. The multimodal systems introduced so far can only partially handle challenges mentioned as part of the more naturalistic or real world settings. Although multimodal systems or machines aimed at assisting human users in their tasks might not need to function exactly as humans do, it is still necessary to investigate which modalities are the most suitable ones for which application context. To date, many research questions remain unexplored while advancing toward that goal.

3. Background research

Emotions are researched in various scientific disciplines such as neuroscience, psychology, and cognitive sciences. Development of affective multimodal systems depends significantly on the progress in the aforementioned sciences. Accordingly, we start our analysis by exploring the background in emotion theory, perception and recognition.

3.1 Theories of emotion

One of the most discussed issues in the emotion literature is the definition, categorization and elicitation of emotions. As far as definition of emotion is concerned emotions are defined as affectively valenced states (Ortony & Turner, 1990). In general, emotions are short-term (seconds/minutes), whereas moods are long-term (several days), and temperaments or personalities are very long-term (months, years or a lifetime) (Jenkis & et al., 1998).

As far as the categorization is concerned, a significant number of researchers in psychology advocate the idea that there exists a small number of emotions that are basic as they are hard-wired to our brain and are recognized universally (e.g., (Ekman & et al., 2003). Ekman and his colleagues conducted various experiments on human judgment on still photographs of posed facial behavior and concluded that the six basic emotions can be recognized universally, namely, happiness, sadness, surprise, fear, anger and disgust (Ekman, 1982). To date, Ekman's theory on universality is the most widely used theory in affect sensing by machines.

Some other researchers argue about how many emotions are basic, which emotions are basic, and why they are basic (Ortony & Turner, 1990). Some researchers claim that the list of basic emotions (i.e., happiness, surprise, desire, fear, love, rage, sadness etc.) includes words that do not refer to emotions. For instance, a few researchers claim that surprise is an affectively neutral state; therefore is not an emotion (Ortony & Turner, 1990).

Among the various classification schemes, Baron-Cohen and his colleagues, for instance, have investigated cognitive mental states (e.g., agreement, concentrating, disagreement, thinking, unsure and interested) and their use (see Figure 2a) in daily life via analysis of multiple asynchronous information sources such as facial actions, purposeful head gestures and eye-gaze direction. They showed that cognitive mental states occur more often in day to day interactions than the so-called basic emotions (Baron-Cohen & Tead, 2003). These states were also found relevant in representing problem-solving and decision-making processes in HCI context and have been used by a number of researchers (e.g., El Kaliouby & Robinson, 2005).

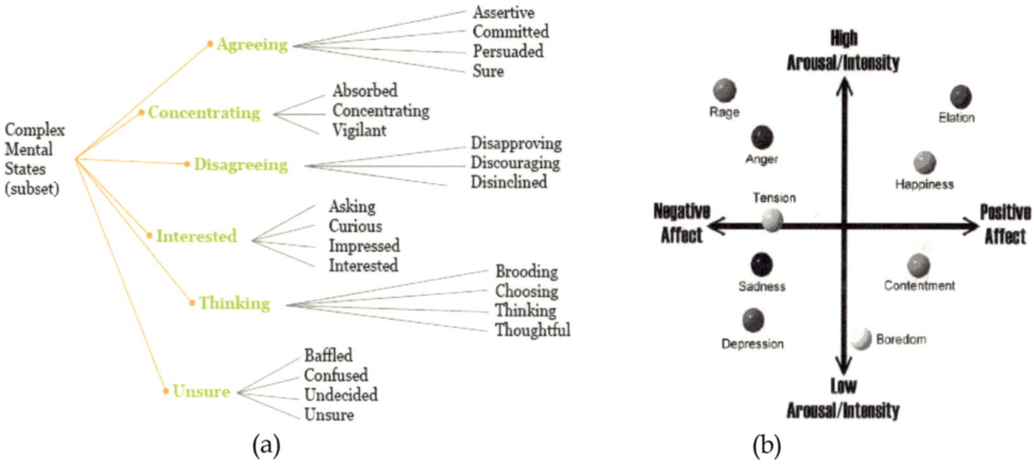

Figure 2. Illustration of a) Baron-Cohen's cognitive mental states (from Autism and Affective-Social Computing Tutorial at ACII 2007), and b) Russell's circumflex model (Russell, 1980).

A number of emotion researchers take the dimensional approach and they view affective states not independent of one another; rather, related to one another in a systematic manner (e.g., Russell, 1980). Russell (Russell, 1980) among others argues that emotion is best characterized in terms of a small number of latent dimensions, rather than in terms of a small number of discrete emotion categories. Russell proposes that each of the basic emotions is a bipolar entity as part of the same emotional continuum. The proposed polars are arousal (relaxed vs. aroused) and valence (pleasant vs. unpleasant). Arousal is a feeling state that ranges from sleepiness or boredom to frantic excitement. Valence ranges from

unpleasant feelings to pleasant feelings of happiness. The model is illustrated in Figure 2b.
Another issue in the emotion research is that of certain emotions' co-occurrence. Russell and Carroll (Russell & Carroll, 1999), in accordance with Russell's circumflex model, propose that happiness and sadness are polar opposites and, thus, mutually exclusive. In other words, "when you are happy, you are not sad and when you are sad, you are not happy". In contrast, Cacioppo and Berntson (Cacioppo & Berntson, 1994) propose that positive and negative affect are separable, and mixed feelings of happiness and sadness can co-occur.
As far as the labeling is concerned, different labels are used by different researchers when referring to the same emotion (e.g., anger - rage, happiness - joy - elation). The problem of what different emotion words are used to refer to the same emotion is by itself a topic of research for linguists, emotion theorists, psychologists and potentially ethnologists (Ortony & Turner, 1990).
After all, even with over a century of research, all of the aforementioned issues still remain under discussion and psychologists do not seem to have reached consensus yet. In relevance to this chapter, in the following sections, background in nonverbal communication of emotions is provided. In particular, studies that explore the characteristic nonverbal expressions of emotions in HHI from various channels are reviewed under two categories: i) monomodal expression and perception of emotions and ii) multimodal expression and perception of emotions.

3.2 Monomodal expression and perception of emotions

Emotional information is conveyed by a broad range of modalities, including speech and language, gesture and head movement, body movement and posture, as well as facial expression. One limitation of prior work on human emotion perception is the focus on separate channels for expression of affect, without adequate consideration for the multimodal emotional signals that people encounter in their environment (Ekman, 1982; Pantic & Rothkrantz, 2003; Van den Stock & et al., 2007). Most research on the development of emotion perception has focused on human recognition of facial expressions and posed emotional data. The investigation of various ways in which people learn to perceive and attend to emotions multimodally is likely to provide a more complete picture of the complex HHI.
Herewith, we provide a summary of the findings from emotion research in emotion communication from facial and bodily expression, audio or acoustic signals, and bio-potential signals (physiological signals, brain signals and thermal infrared signals). Figure 3 presents examples of sensors used for acquiring affective data from these channels.

3.2.1 Facial expression

Ekman and his colleagues conducted various experiments on human judgment on still photographs of posed face behavior and concluded that six basic emotions can be recognized universally: happiness, sadness, surprise, fear, anger and disgust. Several other emotions and many combinations of emotions have been studied but it remains unconfirmed whether they are universally distinguishable. Although prototypic expressions, like happiness, surprise and fear, are natural, they occur infrequently in daily life and provide an incomplete description of facial expression. To capture the subtlety of human emotion and paralinguistic communication, Ekman and Friesen developed the Facial Action Coding System (FACS) for coding of fine-grained changes on the face (Ekman &

Friesen, 1978). FACS is based on the enumeration of all *face action units* causing face movements. In addition to this, Friesen and Ekman (Friesen & Ekman ,1984) developed Emotion FACS (EMFACS) as a method for using FACS to score only the facial actions that might be relevant to detecting emotion.

To date, Ekman's theory of emotion universality (Ekman & Friesen, 2003) and the Facial Action Coding System (FACS) (Ekman &Friesen, 1978) are the most commonly used schemes in vision-based systems attempting to recognize facial expressions and action units.

3.2.2 Bodily expression

Researchers in social psychology and human development have long emphasized the fact that emotional states are expressed through body movement (Hadjikhani & De Gelder, 2003). However, compared to research in facial expression, the expressive information body gestures carry has not been adequately exploited yet.

Darwin (Darwin, 1872) was the first to describe in detail the bodily expressions associated with emotions in animals and humans and proposed several principles underlying the organization of these expressions. It is also well known from animal research that information from bodily expressions can play a role in reducing the ambiguity of facial expression (Van Hoof, 1962). It has been shown that observers' judgments of infant emotional states depend on viewing whole-body behaviors more than facial expression (Camras & et al., 2002). Following Darwin's early work, there have been a number of studies on human body postures communicating emotions (e.g., Argyle, 1975). Coulson presented experimental results on attribution of six emotions (anger, disgust, fear, happiness, sadness and surprise) to static body postures by using computer-generated figures (Coulson, 2004). He found out that in general, human recognition of emotion from posture is comparable to recognition from the voice, and some postures are recognized as effectively as facial expressions. Van den Stock & et al. (Van den Stock & et al., 2007) also presented a study investigating emotional body postures (happiness, sadness, surprise, fear, disgust and anger) and how they are perceived. Results indicate good recognition of all emotions, with angry and fearful bodily expressions less accurately recognized compared to sad bodily expressions. (Gross & et al., 2007) presented a study where bodily expression of felt and recognized emotions was associated with emotion specific changes in gait parameters and kinematics (content, joy, angry, sad and neutral). After recalling an emotion, participants walked across the laboratory while video and whole-body motion capture data were acquired. Walkers felt and observers recognized the same emotion in 67% of the available data. On average, sadness was most recognized and anger was least recognized. Gait velocity was greatest in high-activation emotion trials (anger and joy), and least in sad trials. Velocity was not different among neutral and low-activation emotion trials (content and sad). Both posture and limb motions changed with emotion expressed.

In general, the body and hand gestures are much more varied than face gestures. There is an unlimited vocabulary of body postures and gestures with combinations of movements of various body parts. Despite the effort of Laban in analyzing and annotating body movement (Laban & Ullmann, 1988) unlike the face action units, body action units that carry expressive information have not been defined or coded with a Body Action Coding System. Communication of emotions by bodily movement and expressions is still a relatively unexplored and unresolved area in psychology, and further research is needed in order to obtain a better insight on how they contribute to the perception and recognition of the various affective states.

3.2.3 Audio

Speech is another important communicative modality in human-human interaction. It is between 200 thousand and 2 million years old, and it has become the indispensable means for sharing ideas, observations, and feelings. Speech conveys affective information through explicit (linguistic) messages, and implicit (paralinguistic) messages that reflect the way the words are spoken. If we consider the verbal part (linguistic message) only, without regarding the manner in which it was spoken (paralinguistic message), we might miss important aspects of the pertinent utterance and even misunderstand the spoken message by not attending to the non-verbal aspect of the speech. However, findings in basic research indicate that spoken messages are rather unreliable means to analyze and predict human (affective) behavior (Ambady & Rosenthal, 1992). Anticipating a person's word choice and the associated intent is very difficult: even in highly constrained situations, different people choose different words to express exactly the same thing. Yet, some information about the speaker's affective state can be inferred directly from the surface features of words, which were summarized in some affective word dictionaries and lexical affinity (e.g., Whissell, 1989). The rest of affective information lies below the text surface and can only be detected when the semantic context (e.g., discourse information) is taken into account. The association between linguistic content and emotion is language-dependent and generalizing from one language to another is very difficult to achieve.

When it comes to implicit, paralinguistic messages that convey affective information, the research in psychology and psycholinguistics provides an immense body of results on acoustic and prosodic features which can be used to encode affective states of a speaker. For a comprehensive overview of the past research in the field, readers are referred to Juslin & Scherer (2005). The speech measures which seem to be reliable indicators of the basic emotions are the continuous acoustic measures, particularly pitch-related measures (range, mean, median, and variability), intensity and duration. For a comprehensive summary of acoustic cues related to vocal expressions of basic emotions, readers are referred to Cowie & et al. (2001). However, basic researchers have not identified an optimal set of voice cues that reliably discriminate among emotions. Nonetheless, listeners seem to be accurate in decoding some basic emotions from prosody (Juslin & Scherer, 2005) as well as some nonbasic affective states such as distress, anxiety, boredom, and sexual interest from nonlinguistic vocalizations like laughs, cries, sighs, and yawns (Russell & Fernandez-Dols, 1997).

3.2.4 Bio-potential signals

Brain signals measured via functional Near Infrared Spectroscopy (fNIRS), scalp signals measured via electroencephalogram (EEG), and peripheral signals, namely, cardiovascular activity, including interbeat interval, relative pulse volume, pulse transit time, heart sound, and pre-ejection period; electrodermal activity (tonic and phasic response from skin conductance) or galvanic skin response (GSR), electromyogram (EMG) activity (from corrugator supercilii, zygomaticus, and upper trapezius muscles), are commonly referred to as physiological or bio-signals (Changchun & et al., 2005; Savran & et al., 2006; Takashi, 2004). While visual modalities such as facial expressions and body gestures provide a visible/external understanding of the emotions, bio-signals such as EEG and fNIRS provide an invisible/internal understanding of the emotion phenomenon (see (Savran & et al., 2006) and Figure 3).

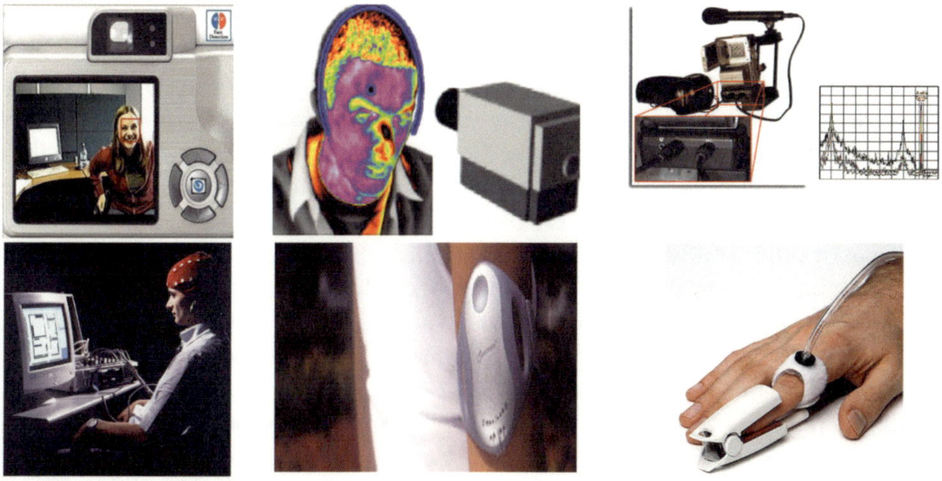

Figure 3: Examples of sensors used in multimodal affective data acquisition: (a) camera for visible imagery, (b) microphone(s) for audio recording, (c) infrared camera for thermal infrared (IR) imagery, (d) body media sense wear for physiological signal recording, (e) pulse wave signal recorder clipped on the finger, and (f) electroencephalogram (EEG) for brain/scalp signals recording and measurement.

Researchers claim that all emotions can be characterized in terms of judged valence (pleasant or unpleasant) and arousal (calm or aroused) (Lang, 1995). Emotions can thus be represented as coordinates in the arousal-valence space. The relation between physiological signals and arousal/valence is established in psychophysiology that argues that the activation of the autonomic nervous system changes while emotions are elicited (Levenson, 1988). Galvanic skin response (GSR) is an indicator of skin conductance (SC), and increases linearly with a person's level of overall arousal and Electromyography (EMG) measures muscle activity and has been shown to correlate with negatively valenced emotions (Nakasone & et al., 2005). The transition from one emotional state to another, for instance, from state of boredom to state of anxiety is accompanied by dynamic shifts in indicators of autonomic nervous system activity (Changchun & et al., 2005). Moreover, there is evidence suggesting that measurements recorded over various parts of the brain including the amygdala enable observation of the emotions felt (Pun & et al., 2006). For instance, approach or withdrawal response to a stimulus is known to be linked to the activation of the left or right frontal cortex, respectively. Therefore, such responses can be used as correspondence to positive/negative emotions (Pun & et al., 2006). BCIs can assess the emotions by assuming that negative/positive valence corresponds to negative/ positive emotions and arousal corresponds to the degree of excitation, from none to high (e.g., (Pun & et al., 2006)). However, in general, researchers have not identified an optimal set of bio-potential cues that can assist in reliably discriminating among various affective states.

3.2.5 Thermal infrared signals

A number of studies in the fields of neuropsychology, physiology and behavior analysis suggest that there exists a correlation between mammals' core body temperature and their affective states. Nakayama & et al. conducted experiments by monitoring the facial temperature change of monkeys under stressful or threatening conditions. Their study revealed that decrease in nasal skin temperature is relevant to a change from neutral to negative affective state (Nakayama & et al., 2005). Vianna & Carrive conducted another independent experiment by monitoring the temperature changes in rats when they were experiencing fearful situations (Vianna & Carrive, 2005). The observation was that the temperature increased in certain body parts (i.e., eyes, head and back), while in other body parts (i.e., tail and paws) the temperature dropped simultaneously.

There also exist other studies indicating that contraction or expansion of the facial/bodily muscles of humans causes fluctuations in the rate of blood flow (e.g., Khan & et al., 2006a, 2006b; Tsiamyrtzis & et al., 2007). This thermo-muscular activity results in a change in the volume of blood flow under the surface of the human facial and/or bodily skin. Thus, skin temperature is heavily modulated by superficial blood flow and environmental temperature. However, influence of environmental temperature blends in the background once the person is in that environment and can be modeled or ignored. This in turn implies that it is possible to obtain objective measurements of skin temperature change.

Unlike other bio-physiological signal measurement, sensing using infrared thermal imagery does not rely on contact with the human body. Thus, the noninvasive detection of any changes in facial and/or bodily thermal features may help in detecting, extracting, and interpreting human affective states. For instance, (Pavlidis & et al., 2001) and (Tsiamyrtzis & et al., 2007) have shown that there is a correlation between increased blood perfusion in the orbital muscles, and anxiety and stress levels of humans, respectively. Similarly, Puri & et al. reported that users' stress level was correlated with increased blood flow in the frontal vessels of forehead causing dissipation of convective heat (Puri & et al., 2005).

A generic model for estimating the relationship between fluctuations in blood flow and facial/bodily muscle activity is not yet available. Such a model could enhance our understanding of the relationship between affective states and the facial/bodily thermal and physiological characteristics.

3.3 Temporal information

Studies show that the temporal dynamics play an important role for interpreting emotional displays (Ambady & Rosenthal, 1993; Schmidt & Cohn, 2001). The temporal aspect of a facial movement is described by four segments: neutral, onset, apex and offset (Ekman, 1979). The neutral phase is a plateau where there are no signs of muscular activation, the face is relaxed. The onset of the action/movement is when the muscular contraction begins and increases in intensity and the appearance of the face changes. The apex is a plateau usually where the intensity reaches a stable level and there are no more changes in facial appearance. The offset is the relaxation of the muscular action. A natural facial movement evolves over time in the following order: neutral- onset- apex-offsetneutral. Other combinations such as multiple-apex facial actions are also possible.

Similarly, the temporal structure of a body gesture consists of (up to) five phases: preparation (pre-stroke)- hold- stroke- (post-stroke) hold-retraction. The preparation moves to the stroke's starting position and the stroke is the most energetic part of the gesture. Holds are optional still phases which can occur before and/or after the stroke. The retraction returns to a rest pose (e.g., arms hanging down, resting in lap, or arms folded) (Wilson & et al., 1997).

As stated previously, research on bodily expression of emotions is relatively new. Moreover, most of the present studies on bodily expression of emotion have used static images, in line with the large majority of studies on facial expressions. Due to such reasons issues such as the importance of motion, timing, and spontaneity have not been considered as extensively as in the facial expression literature.

The importance of temporal information has also not been widely explored for bio-potential signals. Overall, similar body of research to the facial expressions needs to be conducted in order to identify the importance of such factors for bodily or bio-potential signal-based expressions of emotions and correlation between these cues and modalities. After all, detection of the temporal phases and/or dynamics can effectively support automated recognition of affective states (e.g., Gunes, 2007).

3.4 Posed vs. spontaneous expressions

Most of the studies supporting the universality of emotional expressions are based on experiments related to deliberate/posed expressions. Studies reveal that both deliberate/posed and natural/spontaneous emotional expressions are recognized equally accurately; however, deliberate expressions are significantly different from natural ones. Deliberate facial behavior is mediated by separate motor pathways and differences between natural and deliberate facial actions may be significant. Schmidt and Cohn (Schmidt & Cohn, 2001) found that an important visual cue signaling a smile as deliberate or spontaneous is the timing of the phases. A major body of research has been conducted by Cohn and his colleagues in order to identify such differences for other facial expressions of emotions (Affect analysis group, 2008).

In natural situations, a particular bodily expression is most likely to be accompanied by a congruent facial expression being governed by a single emotional state. Darwin argued that because our bodily actions are easier to control on command than our facial actions, the information contained in the signal of body movements should be less significant than the face, at least when it comes to discerning spontaneous from posed behavior. Ekman however, argued that people do not bother to censor their body movements in daily life and therefore, the body would be the *leakier* source (Ekman, 2003). Furthermore, research in nonverbal behavior and communication theory stated that truthful and deceptive behavior differ from each other in lack of head movement (Buller & et al., 1994) and lack of illustrating gestures which accompany speech (DePaulo, 2003).

Compared to visible channels of face and body, the advantage of using bio-signals for recognizing affective states is the fact that physiological recordings cannot be easily faked or suppressed, and can provide direct information as to the user's state of mind.

Overall, perceiving dynamics for spontaneous emotional face and body language and recognition of dynamic whole bodily expressions has not been studied extensively. In day-today life people express and communicate emotions multimodally. Research that study posed vs. spontaneous expressions in a multicue and/or multimodal context therefore is needed in order to obtain a better understanding of the natural communication of emotions in HHI to be later used in HCI.

3.5 Multimodal expression and perception of emotions

In noisy situations, humans depend on access to more than one modality, and this is when the nonverbal modalities come into play (Cassell, 1998). It has been shown that when speech is ambiguous or in a speech situation with some noise, listeners do rely on gestural cues (McNeill, 1985).

Cross-modal integration is known to occur during multi-sensory perception. Judgments for one modality are influenced by a second modality, even when the latter modality can provide no information about the judged property itself or increase ambiguity (Driver & Spence, 2000). A number of studies reported that facial expressions and emotional tone of voice or emotional prosody influence each other (De Gelder & et al.,1999; Massaro & Cohen, 2000).. In a study with static facial expressions and emotional spoken sentences, de Gelder and Vroomen observed a cross-modal influence of the affective information. Recognition of morphed vocal expressions was biased toward the simultaneously presented facial expression, even when the participants were instructed to ignore the visual stimuli. A follow up study suggested that this cross-modal integration of affective information takes place automatically, independent of attentional factors (Vroomen & et al., 2001). Van den Stock & et al. (Van den Stock & et al., 2007) investigated the influence of wholebody expressions of emotions on the recognition of facial and vocal expressions of emotion. The recognition of facial expression was strongly influenced by the bodily expression. This effect was a function of the ambiguity of the facial expression. In another experiment they found that the recognition of emotional tone of voice was similarly influenced by task irrelevant emotional body expressions. Taken together, the findings illustrate the importance of emotional whole-body expressions in communication when viewed in combination with facial expressions and emotional voices.

When input from multiple expressive sources or channels is available the affective message conveyed by different modalities might be congruent (i.e., agreeing) or incongruent (i.e., disagreeing). Observers judging a facial expression were found to be strongly influenced by emotional body language (Meeren & et al., 2005). (Meeren & et al., 2005) investigated the combined perception of human facial and bodily expressions. Participants were presented compound images of faces on bodies and their emotional content was either congruent or incongruent. The results showed that responses were more accurate and faster when face and body expressed the same emotion. When face and body convey conflicting emotional information, judgment of facial expression is hampered and becomes biased toward the emotion expressed by the body. The results show that the whole-body expression has the most influence when the face ambiguity is highest and decreases with reduced facial ambiguity.

Emotion research has not reported such cross-modal interaction for other pairs of modalities such as tactile and visual, or tactile and audio etc. These issues need to be addressed in follow-up studies to obtain a better understanding of the interaction between various expressive cues, sources and modalities in HHI. The multimodal affect systems should potentially be able to detect incongruent messages and label them as *incongruent* for further/detailed understanding of the information being conveyed (Paleari & Lisetti, 2006) .

Different to the cross-mode compensation but still part of the multicue or multimodal perception, there exist findings reporting that when distance is involved humans tend to process the overall global information rather than considering configurations of local regions. Researchers found that if a face is present at close range, especially the eyes are important, but when the distance increases, the configural properties of the whole face play an important role (Van den Stock & et al., 2007). Whole-body expressions seem to be preferentially processed when the perceiver is further away from the stimulus. When the facial expression of the producer is not visible, emotional body language becomes particularly important. Such issues are yet to be explored in multimodal affect recognition.

If humans are presented with temporally aligned but conflicting audio and visual stimuli, the perceived sound may differ from that present in either channel. This is known as McGurk effect in the audio-visual speech perception literature. (Ali & et al., 2003) examined the effect of temporal misalignment of audio and visual channels when users interact with multimodal interfaces (e.g., talking heads). Their study showed that when the audio is not in synchrony with the visual channel, the McGurk effect is observed and participants need to apply extra mental effort for recognition. Such an analysis has not yet been applied in the field of affect sensing and recognition.
Overall, further research is needed in multicue and multimodal affect sensing and recognition in order to explore the issues that have been discussed in this section.

4. Data acquisition

A recent discussion in the automatic affect sensing field is the creation and use of posed vs. spontaneous databases. Affective data may belong to one of the following categories: posed (i.e., produced by the subject upon request), induced (i.e., occurring in a controlled setting and designed to create an affective activation or response such as watching movies) or spontaneous (i.e., occurring in real-life settings such as interviews or interactions between humans or between humans and machines) (Bänziger and Scherer, 2007).
When acquiring posed affective multimodal data, the experiments are usually carried out in a laboratory setting where the illumination, sounds, and room temperature are controlled to maintain uniformity. The stimulated emotions usually include the so-called six basic emotions (e.g., Takashi, 2004). Posed databases are recorded by asking "actors" to act specific affective-cognitive states. The easiest way to create a posed multimodal affect database is by having an experimenter direct and control the expression/display and the recordings. The creation of such database usually depends on the restrictions imposed on the actors: e.g., where the subject should sit or stand, where the subject should look, how a smile should be displayed, whether or not head motion, body motion or speech are allowed etc. Moreover, transitions between affective states are not allowed. Depending on which modalities are recorded, the experimenters typically use a number of sensors: two cameras where face and upper body are recorded simultaneously (e.g., the FABO database (Gunes & Piccardi, 2006)), a camera and a microphone when recording facial expressions and audio signals (e.g., the University of Texas Database (O'Toole & et al., 2005)) etc. A typical affective state recorded thus consists of neutral-onset-apex-offset-neutral temporal segments. When acquiring spontaneous affective multimodal data, the subjects are recorded without their knowledge while they are stimulated with some emotionally-rich stimulus (e.g., Zuckerman & et al., 1979). In the facial expression recognition literature the so-called spontaneous data is facial behavior in less constrained conditions such as an interview setting where subjects are still aware of placement of cameras and their locations (e.g., Littlewort & et al., 2007; Pantic & Bartlett (2007).
Recording of the physiological or bio-potential signals is a bit more complicated compared to the aforementioned recordings. In the brain-computer interface (BCI) or bio-potential signal research context, the subject being recorded usually wears headphones, a headband on which electrodes are mounted, a clip sensor, and/or touch type electrodes. The subject is then stimulated with emotionally-evocative images/videos/sounds. EEG recordings capture neural electrical activity on a millisecond scale from the entire cortical surface while fNIRS records hemodynamic reactions to neural signals on a seconds scale from the frontal

lobe. The skin conductance meter is usually composed of a number of electrodes and an amplifier. The electrodes are mounted on a surface, for example a mouse in order to contact the fingers of the subject. The variation of the skin conductance at the region of interest is then measured (Takahashi, 2004). In summary, the bio-potential affect data acquisition is *induced,* however, due to its invasive nature, the experimental settings provided do not encourage spontaneity.

Recently, there have been a number of attempts to create publicly available affect databases using multiple sensors or input modalities. Some examples can be listed as follows: the SmartKom Corpora, the FABO Database, the Database collected at the University of Amsterdam and the Database collected at the University of Texas. These databases have been reviewed in (Gunes & Piccardi, 2006b) in detail. Such affect databases fall in either the posed or induced category. A number of databases (e.g.,: Drivawork Database, SAL Database and Mixed/spaghetti Data) have also been created as part of HUMAINE EU FP6 and have been presented in (Douglas-Cowie & et al., 2007). Among these, the Belfast database is a naturalistic audio-visual database consisting of clips taken from television and realistic interviews with a research team, and the SAL database contains induced data where subjects interacted with artificial listener with different personalities were recorded audio-visually.

Creation and annotation of affect databases from face and body display has been reviewed in (Gunes & Piccardi, 2006b). Various visual, audio and audio-visual databases have been reviewed in (Zeng & et al., 2008).

Overall, very few of the existing multimodal affect databases contain spontaneous data. Although there is a recent attempt to collect spontaneous facial expression data in real-life settings (in the context of autism disorder) (El Kaliouby & Teeters, 2007), such an attempt is lacking for multimodal affect database creation. Overall, acquiring data in fully unconstrained environments with multiple sensors involves ethical and privacy concerns together with technical difficulties (placement of sensors, controlling the environmental conditions such as noise, illumination, occlusions, etc., consistency, repeatability etc.).

5. Data annotation

The relative weight given to facial expression, speech, and body cues depend both on the judgment task (i.e. what is rated and labeled) and the conditions in which the behavior occurred (i.e. how the subjects were simulated to produce the expression) (Ekman, 1982). People do not judge the available communicative channels separately and the information conveyed by these channels cannot be assumed simply additive (i.e., cross-mode compensation). However, in general, annotation of the data in multimodal affect databases, both for posed and spontaneous data, has been done separately for each channel assuming independency between the channels.

The experimental setup for labeling or annotating emotional behaviors expressed via the visual channels usually consist of static photographs (e.g., Van den Stock & et al., 2007) or videos containing semi-professional actors expressing six basic (or more) emotions with face (e.g., Bänziger & Scherer, 2007), face and upper body (e.g., Gunes & Piccardi, 2006a), whole-body with faces blurred (e.g., Van den Stock & et al., 2007), or stick figures (e.g., Coulson, 2004). Visual data are presented on a computer screen, and participants are asked to view and choose an emotion label from a predetermined list of labels that best describes the expressed emotion. Such studies usually aim to determine rates of observer recognition in visual stimuli, and to use motion analysis to quantify how emotions change patterns in characteristic ways.

In general, when annotating or labeling affect data from face display, Ekman's theory of emotion universality and the Facial Action Coding System (FACS) are used. When it comes to annotating body gestures, unlike the AUs, there is not one common annotation scheme that can be adopted by all the research groups. Laban and Ullman defined and analyzed body movement by using the following information and descriptions: body part (e.g., left hand), direction (e.g., up/down), speed (e.g., fast/slow), shape (hands made into fists), space (flexible/direct), weight (light/strong), time (sustained/quick), and flow (fluent/controlled) (Laban & Ullmann, 1988). Overall, the most time-costly aspect of current facial/body movement manual annotation is to obtain the onset-apex-offset time markers. This information is crucial for coordinating facial/body activity with simultaneous changes in physiology, voice, or speech.

Hereby we describe some attempts or the so-called *coding schemes* for annotating multimodal affect data. In (Allwood & et al., 2004) authors designed a coding scheme for the annotation of 3 videos of TV interviews. Facial displays, gestures, and speech were coded using the following parameters: form of the expression and of its semantic-pragmatic function (e.g. turn managing) and the relation between modalities: repetition, addition, substitution, contradiction. (Martin & et al., 2005) designed a coding scheme for annotating multimodal behaviors during real life mixed emotions (i.e., TV interviews). They focused on the annotation of emotion specific behaviors in speech, head and torso movements, facial expressions, gaze, and hand gestures. They grounded their coding scheme on the following parameters: the expressivity of movements, the number of annotations in each modality, their temporal features (duration, alternation, repetition, and structural descriptions of gestures), the directions of movements and the functional description of relevant gestures. (Martin & et al., 2007) designed a multilevel coding scheme for the representation of emotion at several levels of temporality and abstraction. At the global level there is the annotation of emotion (categorical and dimensional including global activation). Similar annotations are available at the level of emotional segments of the video. At the level of multimodal behaviors there are tracks for each visible behavioral cue: torso, head, shoulders, facial expressions, gaze, and hand gestures. The head, torso and hand tracks contain a description of the pose and the movement of these cues. For the annotation of emotional movements, they use a model which describes expressivity by a set of six dimensions: spatial extent, temporal extent, power, fluidity, repetition, overall activity. The annotation also includes the structural descriptions (phases) of gestures.

When annotating or labeling affect data from audio participants are asked to identify an emotion (e.g., happy or sad) given an auditory spoken sentence. Thus, again Ekman's theory of emotion universality or Russell's theory of arousal and valence is the most common way to annotate audio signals.

For bio-potential signal annotation, ground truth usually consists of the participant's self-assessment (e.g., Pun & et al., 2006). In general, Ekman's theory of emotion universality or Russell's theory of arousal and valence is used. However, obtaining a correlation between emotions and the neural, thermal and other signals is not a straightforward process and is inherently different compared to visual or audio channels. The data labeling for bio-signals is directly dependant on the individuals' evaluation of his own emotional situation during the experimental setup (i.e., emotion elicitation) or recordings. This implies that, the ground truth coding or labeling is very subjective and cannot be evaluated by independent observers or emotion research experts.

Another major challenge in affect data annotation is the fact that there is no coding scheme that is agreed upon by all the researchers to accommodate all possible communicative modalities like facial expressions, body gestures, voice, bio-potential signals etc. Addressing the aforementioned issues will potentially extend the state-of-the-art in multimodal affect sensing and recognition.

6. Feature extraction

After multimodal affect data has been acquired and annotated, representative and relevant features need to be extracted prior to the automatic affect recognition procedure. The feature extraction is only broadly covered here under each communicative source or channel: facial expression, body gestures, audio, bio-potential signals and thermal infrared imagery.

6.1 Facial expression

There exists an extensive literature for human face detection, feature extraction and expression recognition. Possible strategies for face detection vary significantly depending on the type of input images. Face detection can become a simplified problem with the assumption that an input image contains only one face. The so-called appearance-based methods have proved very robust and fast in recent years. They usually are based on training a classifier using positive and negative examples of faces. Various classifiers can be used for this purpose: Naive Bayes classifier, Hidden Markov model (HMM), Sparse network of windows (SNoW), Support Vector Machines (SVM), Adaboost etc. For face detection, the current state-of-the-art is based on the robust and well-known method proposed by Viola and Jones (Viola & Jones, 2001) and extended by Lienhart and Maydt based on a set of rotated Haar-like features (Lienhart & Maydt, 2002), and improved by (Fasel & et al., 2005) using GentleBoost.

Facial feature extraction aims to detect the presence and location of features such as eyes, nose, nostrils, eyebrow, mouth, lips, ears, etc. Similar to face detection, for facial feature extraction usually it is assumed that there is only one face in the image. There exists an extensive literature for face feature extraction for the detection of facial region and facial features using texture, depth, shape, color information or statistical models. Such approaches can be categorized under two categories: feature-based approaches and appearance-based approaches. In the feature-based approach, specific facial features such as the pupils, inner/outer corners of the eyes/ mouth are detected and tracked, distances between these are measured or used and prior knowledge about the facial anatomy is utilized. In the appearance-based approach, certain regions are treated as a whole and motion, change in texture are measured. A similar approach to face detection can also be used for training a separate classifier on each facial feature (eyes, lips etc.). Such an approach can handle inplane rotation and tolerate variations in lighting. Methods based on Haar features or wavelets, also known as appearance-based methods, in general have demonstrated good empirical results. They are fast and fairly robust and can be easily extended to detect objects in different pose and orientation.

(Tian & et al., 2002) have shown that appearance-based methods alone perform poorly for the facial expression recognition. They found that when image sequences include nonhomogeneous subjects with small head motions, appearance-based methods have a relatively poor recognition rate compared to using an approach based on the geometric features and locations. Combining the two approaches (appearance based methods and geometric features) resulted in the best performance (Tian & et al., 2002). On the other hand, Bartlett and her colleagues have shown that appearance-based methods perform better than feature-based methods (Pantic & Bartlett, 2007). For further details on facial feature extraction and tracking for facial expression or action unit recognition the reader is advised to see (Pantic & Bartlett, 2007).

6.2 Body gesture

There exists an extensive literature for body feature extraction, tracking and gesture recognition from video sequences. In the context of affect sensing, we only briefly summarize the existing trends in body gesture recognition.

The existing approaches for hand or body gesture recognition and analysis of human motion in general can be classified into three major categories: model-based (i.e., modeling the body parts or recovering three-dimensional configuration of articulated body parts), appearance-based (i.e., based on two dimensional information such as color/gray scale images or body silhouettes and edges), and motion-based (i.e., using directly the motion information without any structural information about the physical body) (Elgammal, 2003). In the aforementioned approaches, Dynamic Time Warping (DTW) or Hidden Markov Models (HMM) are typically used to handle the temporal properties of the gesture(s).

An overview of the various tasks involved in motion analysis of the human body such as motion analysis involving human body parts, tracking of human motion using single or multiple cameras from image sequences is presented in (Yilmaz & et al., 2006). The literature on visual interpretation of hand gestures mainly focuses on HCI rather than affect sensing. (Mitra & Acharya, 2007) provide a recent survey on gesture recognition, with particular emphasis on hand gestures and facial expressions. Applications involving hidden Markov models, particle filtering and condensation, finite-state machines, optical flow, skin color, and connectionist models are discussed in detail. (Poppe, 2007) also provides a recent survey on vision-based human motion analysis and discusses the characteristics of human motion analysis via modeling and estimation phases.

Vision based gesture recognition is a challenging task due to various complexities including segmentation ambiguity and the spatio-temporal variability involved. Gesture tracking needs to handle variations in the tracked object (i.e., shapes and sizes of hands/arms) illumination, background, noise and occlusions. Recognition requires spotting of the gesture (i.e., determining the start and end points of a meaningful gesture pattern from a continuous stream) and segmenting the relevant gesture. Hand gestures may occlude each other as they switch from one gesture to another. Moreover, there occur intermediate and transition motions that may or may not be part of the gesture, and the same gesture may dynamically vary in shape and duration even for the same gesturer. Color as a distinct feature has been widely used for representation and tracking of multiple objects in a scene. Several tracking methods have been used in the literature; amongst them, the Kalman filter, Condensation tracking, Mean-shift tracking, and Cam-shift tracking. (Dreuw & et al. , 2006), for instance, present a dynamic programming framework with the possibility to integrate multiple scoring functions e.g. eigenfaces, or arbitrary objects, and the possibility of tracking multiple objects at the same time. Various techniques for extracting and tracking specific features such as shoulders have also been proposed in the literature. (Ning & et al., 2006) introduce a system that can detect shoulder shrug by firstly using a face detector based on AdaBoost and then detecting shoulder positions by fitting a parabola to the nearby horizontal edges using weighted Hough Transform to recognize shrugs. There are also more recent works using different (or a combination of) tracking schemes depending on what they aim to track and recognize. An example system is that of Valstar & et al. (Valstar & et al.,2007) that uses a cylindrical head tracker to track the head motion, an auxiliary particle filtering to track the shoulders motion, and a particle filtering with factorized likelihood tracking scheme to track movements of facial salient points in an input video. Overall, most of the existing hand/body gesture recognizers work well in relatively constrained environments (e.g., assuming that the person is seated on a chair) with relatively small changes in terms of illumination, background, and occlusions (Pantic & et al., 2007).

Compared to automatic gesture analysis and recognition, affective body gesture recognition per se has not been widely explored. For recognition of emotions from body movement and gesture dynamics, some researchers propose to extract the whole-body silhouette and the hands of the subjects from the background (e.g., Villalba & et al., 2007). Different motion cues are then calculated: amount of motion computed with silhouette motion images, the degree of contraction and expansion of the body computed using the bounding region, velocity and acceleration computed based on the trajectory of the hands etc. However, despite the challenges pertaining in the field, advance tracking techniques need to be created and used to be able to track body parts such as torso, head, shoulders, and hands in real world settings.

6.3 Audio features

Most of the existing approaches to vocal affect recognition use acoustic features, particularly pitch-related measures (range, mean, median, and variability), intensity, and duration, based on the acoustic correlations for emotion expressions as summarized by Cowie & et al. (2001). In addition, and mostly because they proved very suitable for speaker identification task, spectral features (e.g., MFCC, cepstral features) have been used in many of the current studies on automatic vocal affect recognition. Various studies have shown that pitch and energy among these features contribute most to affect recognition (Zeng & et al, 2008). A few efforts have been also reported that use some alternative features such as voice-quality features (Campbell & Mokhtari, 2003) and speech disfluencies (e.g., filler and silence pauses; Devillers & et al., 2004).

However, with the research shift towards analysis of spontaneous human behavior, it became clear that analysis of acoustic information only will not suffice for identifying subtle changes in vocal expression (Batliner & et al., 2003). In turn, several recent studies investigated the combination of acoustic features and linguistic features (language and discourse) to improve recognition of emotions from speech signal (e.g., Fragopanagos & Taylor, 2005). Examples include using spoken words and acoustic features, using prosodic features, spoken words, and information of repetition, and using prosodic features, Part-of-speech (POS), dialogue act (DA), repetitions, corrections, and syntactic-prosodic boundary to infer the emotion. For more details on such studies, readers are referred to the comprehensive survey of the past efforts in the field by Zeng & et al (2008). It must be noted, however, that although the above-mentioned studies reported an improved performance by using information of language, these systems typically depend on both accurate recognition of verbal content of emotional speech, which still cannot be reliably achieved by existing automatic speech recognition systems, and on accurate extraction of semantic discourse information, which is attained manually in the present systems.

6.4 Bio-potential features

Prior to extracting features, affect recognition systems that use bio-potential signals or modalities as input usually pre-process signals to remove noise (e.g., Savran & et al., 2006). Peripheral signals (e.g., GSR, respiration and blood volume pressure) are first filtered by a mean filter to remove noise (i.e., the resistance of the skin) or depending on the signal used, the environmental noise is removed by applying a bandpass filter. Various signal processing techniques such as Fourier transform, wavelet transform, thresholding, and peak detection, are commonly used to derive the relevant features from the physiological signals (Changchun & et al., 2005).

Following the preprocessing stage, there are various alternatives for feature extraction. For physiological signals, usually the following features are calculated: means, the standard deviations, the means of the absolute values of the first differences, the means of the absolute values of the first differences of the normalized signals, the means of the absolute values of the second differences, the means of the absolute values of the second differences of the normalized signals etc. (e.g., Picard & et al., 2001; Takahashi, 2004).

For brain signals, one alternative is to collect EEG energies at various frequency bands, time intervals and locations in the brain. The gathered signals are separated using frequency domain analysis algorithms and are then analyzed in terms of frequency bands (i.e., low, middle and high frequency band), and center frequency etc. (Takahashi, 2004). (Aftanas & et al., 2003, 2004) used the correlation between arousal variation and power in selected frequency bands and electrodes. Another possibility is to compute the STFT (Short Term Fourier Transform) on a pre-determined time segment of each electrode, assuming that the signal remains stationary within the chosen time widow (Savran & et al., 2006).

After these procedures, various pattern recognition techniques such as evaluation of subsets or feature selection, transformations of features, or combinations of these methods are applied. The extracted and calculated feature values then make up the overall feature vector used for classification.

Researchers reported that muscle activities (e.g., opening the mouth, clenching the jaw etc.) due to expression generation contaminate EEG signals with strong artifacts. Use of multiple sensors can thus cause cross-sensor noise (e.g., Savran & et al., 2006). Design of an appropriate filter or use of other techniques such as Independent component analysis (ICA) should be explored to remove this type of noise. Estimating a Laplacian reference signal by subtracting for each electrode the mean signal of its neighbors might potentially provide a better representation for the brain activity.

6.5 Thermal infrared imagery

Systems analyzing affective states from thermal infrared imagery perform feature extraction and selection, exploit temporal information (i.e., infrared video) and rely on statistical techniques (e.g., Support Vector Machines, Hidden Markov Models, Linear Discriminant Analysis, Principal Component Analysis etc.) just like their counterparts in visible spectrum imagery.

Current research in the thermal infrared imagery has utilized several different types of representations, from shape contours to blobs (Tsiamyrtzis & et al., 2007). Some studies estimate differential images between the averaged neutral face/body and the expressive face/body (e.g., Yoshitomi, 2000) and perform a transformation (e.g., discrete cosine transformation (DCT)). Other researchers divide each thermal image into grids of squares, and the highest temperature in each square is recorded for comparison (Khan & et al., 2006b). Patterns of thermal variations for each individual affective state are also used (Khan et al., 2006a). Similar tracking techniques to those in the visible spectrum are utilized (e.g., Condensation algorithm, Kalman/Particle Filtering etc.) and therefore, similar challenges pertain to tracking in the thermal infrared imagery domain (Tsiamyrtzis & et al., 2007).

7. Affective state recognition

The main problem overarching affect sensing is the recognition of affective states in their nature of complex spatio-temporal patterns. Should emotion recognition be regarded as an easier or a harder problem than an equivalent recognition problem in a *generic* domain? In the following, we identify its main characteristics as challenges or facilitators, alongside the main pattern recognition techniques that have been or can be used to deal with them.

7.1 Challenges

The main challenges we identify from the pattern recognition perspective can be listed as feature extraction, high inter-subject variation during recognition, dimensionality reduction, and optimal fusion of cues/modalities.

The value range of certain features is very limited compared to typical noise levels. Let us consider, for instance, the raising of an eyebrow that has to be recognized as an expression of surprise. When sensed by a camera, such a movement may translate into just a few pixels extent. Facial feature extraction from videos is typically affected by comparable errors, thus undermining recognition accuracy. Higher-resolution cameras (and lenses - in the order of several equivalent megapixels per frame) are required for effective feature extraction in such cases.

The space in which emotions have to be recognized is typically a feature space with very high dimensionality: for instance, (Gunes, 2007) uses a feature set with 152 face features and 170 upper-body features; (Bhatti2004) uses a feature set with 17 speech features; (Kim & et al, 2004) uses a feature set with 29 features from a combination of ECG, EMG, skin conductivity and respiration measurements. This aspect of emotion recognition is certainly a challenge and imposes the use of dimensionality reduction techniques. Linear combination techniques such as PCA and LDA and non-linear techniques such as KPCA have been used for that purpose, and so have been feature selection techniques such as Sequential Forward Selection (Bhatti & et al.,2004) and Genetic Algorithms (Noda & et al., 2006). However, feature-space dimensionality reduction for sequential data (not to be confused with reduction along the time dimension)is still an open problem.

High inter-subject variation is reported in many works. This challenges generalization over unseen subjects that are, most often, the actual targets of the emotion recognition process. The search for features with adequate discriminative power-invariance trade-off is an attempt at solving this problem (Varma & Ray, 2007).

Eventually, as modalities are heterogeneous and possibly asynchronous, their optimal fusion adds to the list of challenges. The asynchrony between modalities may be two fold: (a) asynchrony in subject's signal production (e.g., face movement might start earlier than the body movement), and (b) asynchrony during recording (e.g., a video recorded at 25 Hz frame rate while the audio recorded at 48 kHz) and processing of the signals coming from various sensing devices. For instance when fusing effective information coming from the EEG, the video or fNIRS, it should be noted that these have orders of magnitude difference in their relative time scales (Savran & et al., 2006).

The most straightforward approach to tackle modality fusion is at the decision or score level since feature- and time-dependence are abstracted. In decision level fusion each classifier processes its own data stream, and the two sets of outputs are combined at a later stage to produce the final hypothesis. There has been some work on combining classifiers and providing theoretical justification for using simple operators such as majority vote, sum, product, maximum/minimum/median and adaptation of weights (Kittler & et al., 1998). Decision-level fusion can also be obtained at the soft-level (a measure of confidence is associated with the decision); or at the hard-level (the combining mechanism operates on single hypothesis decisions).

Recent works have attempted at providing synchronization between multiple cues to also support feature-level fusion, reporting greater overall accuracy when compared to decisionlevel fusion (e.g., Gunes, 2007 and Shan & et al., 2007). Feature-level fusion becomes more challenging as the number of features increases and they are of very different natures (e.g. distances and times). Synchronization then becomes of utmost importance.

Outside the affect sensing and recognition field, various techniques have been exploited for implicit synchronization purposes. For instance, dynamic time warping (DTW) has been used to find the optimal alignment between two time series if one time series may be warped non-linearly by stretching or shrinking it along its time axis. This warping between two time series can then be used to find corresponding regions between the two time series or to determine the similarity between them. Variations of HMM have also been proposed for this task. The pair HMM model was proposed to align two non-synchronous training sequences and an asynchronous version of the Input/Output HMM was proposed for audio-visual speech recognition (Bengio, 2004). Coupled HMM and fused HMM have been used for integrating tightly coupled time series, such as audio and visual features of speech (Pan & et al., 2004). Bengio (Bengio, 2004), for instance, presents the Asynchronous HMM that could learn the joint probability of pairs of sequences of audiovisual speech data representing the same sequence of events (e.g., where sometimes lips start to move before any sound is heard for instance). There are also a number of efforts within the affect sensing and recognition field to exploit the correlation between the modalities and relax the requirement of synchronization by adopting the so-called model-based fusion approach using Bayesian Networks, Multi-stream Fused HMM, tripled HMM, Neural Networks etc. (see Zheng & et al., 2008 for details on these).

A number of approaches have also been reported for explicit synchronization purposes. (Gunes, 2007) identifies the neutral-onset-apex-offset-neutral phases of face and body inputs and synchronizes the sequences at the phase level (i.e., apex phase). (Savran & et al., 2006) have obtained feature/decision level fusion of the fNIRS and EEG feature vectors and/or decision scores on a block-by-block basis. In their experiments a block is 12.5 seconds long and represents all emotional stimuli occurring within that time frame. Video features and fNIRS features can be fused at the feature or decision level on a block-by-block basis. (Paleari & Lisetti, 2006) introduce a generic framework with 'resynchronization buffers'. They aim to compare the different estimations, and realign the different evaluations so that they correspond to the same phenomenon even if one estimation is delayed compared to the other one.(e.g., in the case of delay).

For affective multimodal recognition, synchronization between the modalities is a very interesting and challenging problem and needs to be investigated further. In particular, synchronization other than feature-level, for example at higher levels of abstraction such as temporal phase or segment-level or even task-level synchronization, has not been be explored.

7.2 Facilitators

Affective data can be thought of as uninterrupted streams originating from a variety of sensors (cameras, microphones etc): prior to recognition, or simultaneously with it, it is also required to identify the data sequences corresponding to atomic emotions - a typical time segmentation problem in time series. In some applications, it is possible that a special neutral state can be recognized per se as the marker of the end of an emotion/start of the next, thus easing the time segmentation problem. This is the case, for instance, of a sequence of affective body gestures where each gesture concludes to an identifiable rest state.

Affective data are generated by humans under anatomical and biological constraints. This offers an unrivalled opportunity to simplify the recognition approach by exploiting such prior information. For instance, the generation of facial and bodily expressions undergo muscular constraints: a plateau is reached and maintained for a few seconds in which the features are at their maximum extent. (Gunes, 2007) uses this fact to decouple the temporal and spatial aspects of the recognition process: the plateau is identified first, prior to and independently of the specific emotion thanks to the constrained dynamics; emotion recognition is performed then by assuming that the feature values at the plateau are i.i.d. in the presence of noise. Similarly, (Elgammal & et al., 2003) posits a layer of "exemplars" that separate the spatial and temporal sides in a gesture recognition application. Use of such constraints should be incorporated in approaches to mitigate the high-dimensionality issue.

Affect is naturally expressed via multiple cues and channels. An adaptive framework based on fusion of the available cues and modalities thus offers an opportunity to improve the analysis and recognition of affective states. However, to date, most of the existing fusion algorithms have not been made adaptive to the input quality and therefore do not consider eventual changes on the reliability of the different information channels. (Paleari & Lisetti, 2006) proposed a generic fusion framework that is able to accept different single and multimodal recognition systems and to automatically adapt the fusion algorithm to find optimal solutions, and be adaptive to channel (and system) reliability. They describe a bufferized approach where two different fusion chains would be active in parallel. The first chain, treats close to real time signals and interpretations returning fast interpretations of the recognized emotion. The second chain works on the same bufferized and re-aligned data in order to have the possibility to resynchronize data just before fusion. The objective of this double chain is to have both a fast but less reliable and a longer but more accurate evaluations of the user's affective states.

Further research is needed to test the feasibility of the framework proposed by (Paleari & Lisetti, 2006) and/or create a more generic and common framework that can be easily adopted by the research community.

8. Affect sensing and recognition from multiple cues and modalities: representative systems

In this section we briefly review a number of automated systems that attempt to recognize affect from multicue or multimodal expressive behavior. This review is intended to be illustrative rather than exhaustive. For an exhaustive survey of past efforts in audiovisual affect sensing and recognition, the readers are referred to Zeng & et al. (Zeng & et al. , 2008).Here, we present representative projects/systems introduced in the multimodal affect recognition literature during the period 2004-2007 by grouping these systems under three categories: i) the lab, ii) from the lab to the real world and iii) the real world.

The lab systems analyze posed affect from multicue or multimodal expressive behavior. An example system is that of (Gunes, 2007) that recognizes 12 affective states (anger, anxiety, boredom, disgust, fear, happiness, negative surprise, positive surprise, neutral surprise, uncertainty, puzzlement and sadness) and their temporal segments (neutral-onset-apex-offset-neutral) from either face/upper-body/combined face-and-body display, acquired by two cameras simultaneously. The temporal segmentation of face and body display is achieved explicitly, a phase-synchronization scheme is introduced to deal with simultaneous yet asynchronous face and upper-body data and affective state recognition is performed both on a frame-basis and a video-basis. Experiments were conducted on the FABO database (Gunes & Piccardi, 2006a) from 10 subjects and 539 videos. The approach explores the usefulness of the temporal segment/phase detection to the overall task of affect recognition with various experiments. It also proposes fusion of information coming from multiple visual cues by phase synchronization and selective fusion, and proves the greater performance of this approach by comparative experiments. Using 50% of the data for training and remaining 50% for testing, the FABO system obtains an average recognition rate of 35% for facial expressions alone, 77% for bodily expression alone, %82.6 (frame-basis) and %85 (video-basis) by fusing face and upper-body data. From the experiments the authors concluded that explicit detection of the temporal phases can improve the accuracy of affective state recognition, recognition from fused face and body cues performs better than from facial or bodily expression alone, and synchronized feature-level fusion achieves better performance than decision-level fusion. (Shan & et al., 2007) also report affective state recognition results using the FABO database. They exploit the spatial-temporal features based on space-time interest point detection for representing body gestures in videos. They fuse facial expressions and body gestures at the feature-level by using the Canonical Correlation Analysis (CCA), a statistical tool that is suited for relating two sets of signals. For their experiments they selected 262 videos of seven affective states (anger, anxiety, boredom, disgust, happiness, puzzle, and surprise) from 23 subjects in the FABO database and obtained 88.5% recognition accuracy.

Systems that analyze (more) spontaneous or real world affect data from multiple cues or modalities are described as *from the lab to the real world systems*. An example system is that of (Valstar & et al., 2007). It automatically distinguishes between posed and spontaneous smiles by fusing information from multiple visual cues including the head, face, and shoulder actions. It uses a cylindrical head tracker to track the head motion; particle filtering with factorized likelihoods to track fiducial points on the face and auxiliary particle filtering to track the shoulders motion (see Figure 4a). Based on tracking data, the presence of AU6 (raised cheeks), AU12 (lip corners pulled up), AU13 (lip corners pulled up sharply), head movement (moved off the frontal view), and shoulder movement (moved off the relaxed state), are detected first. For each of these visual cues, the temporal segments (neutral, onset, apex, and offset) are also determined. Classification is then performed by combining

GentleBoost ensemble learning and Support Vector Machines (SVM). A separate SVM is trained for each temporal segment of each of the five behavioral cues (i.e., in total 15 GentleSVMs). The authors combined the results using a probabilistic decision function and investigated two aspects of multicue fusion: the level of abstraction (i.e., early, mid-level, and late fusion) and the fusion rule used (i.e., sum, product and weight criteria). Experimental results from 100 videos displaying posed smiles and 102 videos displaying spontaneous smiles were presented. Best results were obtained with late fusion of all cues when 94.0% of the videos were classified correctly (with 0.964 recall, and 0.933 precision). The results seem to indicate that using video data from face, head and shoulders increases the accuracy, and the head is the most reliable source, followed closely by the face.

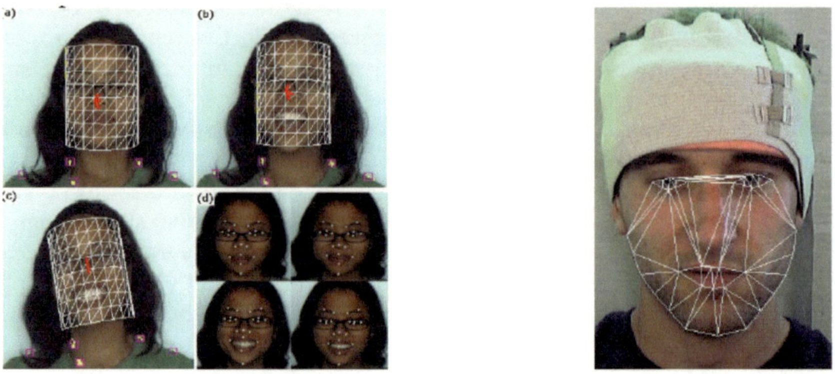

(a) (b)

Figure 4. System of (a) (Valstar & et al., 2007) and (b) (Savran & et al., 2006).

(Savran & et al., 2006) present a project as part of the eNTERFACE Workshop on multimodal emotion detection from three modalities: brain signals via fNIRS, face video and the scalp EEG signals (see Figure 4b). fNIRS sensors were used to record frontal brain activity and EEG sensor was used to capture activity in the rest of the brain. In addition to these, a respiration belt, a GSR (Galvanic Skin Response) and a plethysmograph (blood volume pressure) were also used to record aperipheral body processes. All these devices were synchronized using a trigger mechanism. Three emotions (i.e., calm, exciting positive and exciting negative corresponding to neutral, happiness and disgust) were elicited in five subjects using emotionally evocative images evaluated on valence and arousal dimensions. Participants were then asked to self-assess their emotions by giving a score between 1 and 5 for valence and arousal components. For facial feature extraction an active contour-based technique and active appearance models (AAM) were used. For classification, Transferable Belief Model (TBM) was utilized. The authors considered fusion of fNIRS with video and of EEG with fNIRS. Fusion of all three modalities was not considered due to the extensive noise on the EEG signals caused by facial muscle movements. Both feature and decision level fusion was considered by adopting a block for each emotional stimuli (12.5 seconds long in their experiment) and a block-by-block fusion was applied. Assessment of emotion detection performance of individual modalities and their fusion has not been explored.
Takahashi proposed an emotion recognition system from multimodal bio-potential signals collected using an EEG sensor, a pulseoxymeter, and a skin conductance meter (Takahashi, 2004). Recordings of 12 subjects were obtained in a laboratory where the illumination, noise, and room temperature were controlled to maintain uniformity. To stimulate emotions (joy, anger, sadness, fear, and relax), several commercial films broadcasted on TV were used.

Recognition was carried out with NN and SVM using leave-one-out cross-validation method. The averaged recognition rate of 63.9% for NN and 66.7% for SVM was achieved. Pun & et al. describe the work they conducted in the domain of multimodal interaction via the use of EEG and other physiological signals for assessing a user's emotional status (Pun & et al., 2006). The experimental setup consisted of three participants viewing strongly positive or negative images. Ground truth consisted of the participant's self-assessment. The following physiological signals were recorded: EEGs, blood pressure, GSR, breathing rate, and skin temperature. Each participant was asked to provide valence and arousal values for each image they viewed. These values were then divided into either two classes (calm versus exciting for arousal, positive versus negative for valence), or three classes (same two classes plus an intermediate one). Features extracted such as signal power in particular frequency bands, means, standard deviations, and extreme values were saved as vectors. A Naïve Bayes classifier and a Fisher discriminant analysis were applied in a leave-one-out manner for classification. Depending on the classifier used, the participant, the use of either EEGs, or of peripheral signals only, or of both EEGs and peripheral signals, accuracies ranged between about chance level to 72% for the two classes problem, and between chance levels to 58% for the three classes problem.

Systems that analyze (more) realistic multimodal affect data are described as *the real world systems*. An example system is that of (Kapoor & et al., 2007) that assesses whether a learner is about to click on a button saying *I'm frustrated.* To this aim they use multiple nonverbal channels of information: a chair and a mouse both equipped with pressure sensors, a wireless skin conductance sensor placed on the wristband of the user, two cameras (one video camera for offline coding and the Blue-Eyes camera to record elements of facial expressions). See Figure 5a for details on the sensors used. The data obtained by the aforementioned sensors are classified into *pre-frustration* or *not pre-frustration* behavior using Gaussian process classification and Bayesian inference. The system deals with data synchronization in a similar manner to (Paleari & Lisetti, 2006). In other words, it gathers data for a predetermined time window (i.e., window size of 150 s), normalizes and then averages them. The proposed method was tested on data gathered from 24 participants using an automated learning companion. The experimental setup is described as follows. The users were asked to sit in front of a wide screen plasma display where an agent appears in a 3D environment. The user can interact with the agent and can attend to and manipulate objects and tasks in the environment. In the aforementioned experimental setup, the system was able to predict the indication of frustration from the collected data with 79% accuracy.

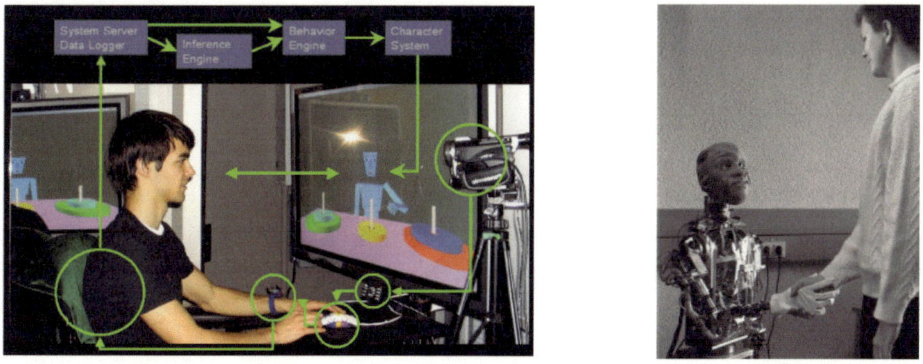

(a) (b)

Figure 5. (a) The system of (Kapoor & et al., 2007) and (b) a humanoid interacting in a humanlike manner (Spexard & et al., 2007).

(Spexard & et al., 2007)present an anthropomorphic robot framework (BARTHOC) bringing together different interaction concepts and perception capabilities with the goal of creating an interdisciplinary research platform for multimodal human-robot interaction (HRI). The framework uses two cameras and two microphones only, has components for face detection, a tracking module based on anchoring, and extended interaction capabilities based on both verbal and nonverbal communication (see Figure 5b). Sounds are validated as voices by using the results of a face detector. The robot is equipped with an attention system for tracking and interacting with multiple persons simultaneously in real time. As sensors cover a limited area only, people are tracked by utilizing a short-time person memory that extends the existing anchoring of people. A long-time memory stores person specific data into file enabling robust tracking in real time. A modular integration approach utilizing XML-based data exchange is used for implementing different interaction capabilities like deictic gestures, natural adaptive dialogs, and emotion awareness on the robot. The robot can recognize affect by classifying the prosody of an utterance to seven emotional states (happiness, anger, fear, sadness, surprise, disgust, and boredom) independently from the content in emotional states of the speaker. The robot is thus able to realize when a communication partner is getting angry and can react showing a calming facial expression on its face. The appropriate facial expression can be invoked from different modules of the overall system, e.g., BARTHOC starts smiling when it is greeted by a human and "stares" onto an object presented to it. The framework also contains a 3-D body tracker based on 2-D video data and a 3-D body model to compensate the missing depth information from the video data. Deictic gestures and the position a person is referring to are estimated using the direction and speed of the body extremity trajectories. The robot is then able to perform pointing gestures to presented objects itself. Robot's emotion recognition and facial expression generation capabilities were evaluated by creating a setup in which multiple persons were invited to read out a shortened version of the fairy tale to the robot. For this experiment, an office-like surrounding with common lighting conditions was used. The robot mirrored the classified prosody of the utterances during the reading in emotion mimicry at the end of any sentence, grouped into happiness, fear, and neutrality. As the neutral expression was also the base expression, a short head movement toward the reader was generated as a feedback for non-emotional classified utterances. Overall, the use of emotion recognition and mimicry of the robot was found to be encouraging for further research in a robotic platform for multimodal human-robot interaction.

9. Conclusion and discussion

This chapter focused on the challenges faced when moving from affect recognition systems that were designed and experimented in laboratory settings (i.e., analyzing posed data) to the real world systems (i.e., analyzing spontaneous data) in a multicue and/or multimodal framework. It discussed the problem domain of affect sensing and recognition by explicitly focusing on multiple input modalities (audio, vision, tactile, and thought) and cues (facial expressions, head and body gestures, etc.) together with alternative channels (brain and thermal infrared signals), and explored a number of representative systems introduced during the period 2004-2007, either capable of handling laboratory, more realistic or real world settings.

The analysis provided in this chapter indicates that the automatic multimodal affect recognition systems have slowly but steadily started shifting their focus from the lab to the real world settings. There already exist a number of efforts for automatic multimodal affect recognition in real world settings. Existing systems deal with the so-called spontaneous data obtained in less-controlled or restricted environment (i.e., subjects are taking part in the interaction, subjects are not always stationary, etc.), and can handle a limited number of emotion categories (e.g., 2-6). These real world systems have been mostly trained to have expertise in a specific interaction context. As stated by (Kapoor & et al., 2007), generalization thus might be affected by various factors such as: the experimental setup (i.e., the tasks and situations the users are presented), age of the users, availability/robustness of the sensors (e.g. the skin conductance sensor is effected by sweat) etc.

One of the main disadvantages of the bio-potential based affect recognition systems is the fact that they are cumbersome and invasive and require placing sensors physically on the human body (e.g., a sensor clip that is mounted on subject's earlobe, a BCI mounted on the subject's head etc. (Takahashi, 2004). Moreover, EEG has been found to be very sensitive to electrical signals emanating from facial muscles while emotions are being expressed via face. Therefore, in a multimodal affect recognition system the simultaneous use of these modalities needs to be reconsidered. Additionally, during recording the fNIRS device is known to cover the eyebrows. This in turn poses another challenge (i.e., occluding facial features) for multimodal affective data recordings if the simultaneous use of these modalities is intended. However, new forms of non-contact psychological sensing might help spreading the use of psychological signals as input to multimodal affect recognition systems.

The most notable issue is the fact that there exists a gap between different communities researching emotions or affective states. For instance, affect recognition communities seem to use different databases compared to psychology or cognitive science communities. Moreover, for annotation of the data, a more uniform and multi-purpose scheme that can accommodate all possible modalities should be explored. Another issue to consider is fusion of multimodal affect data. Researchers claim that the choice of fusion strategy depends on the targeted application (Wu & et al., 1999, Busso & et al., 2004). Accordingly, all available multimodal recognizers have designed and/or used ad hoc solutions for fusing information coming from multiple modalities but cannot accept new modalities. In summary, there is not a general consensus when fusing multiple modalities.

An important point to note is that experimentation with all possible human behavioral cues (linguistic terms/words, audio cues such as pitch, facial expression/AUs, body postures and gestures, physiological signals, brain and thermal infrared signals etc.) has been impossible to date due to lack of a generic and shared platform for automatic affect recognition. We would like to stress that it is highly likely that machines aimed at assisting human users in their tasks will need neither the human-like flexibility to adapt to any environment and any situation nor will they need to function exactly as humans do. Machines can be highly profiled for a specific purpose, scenario, user, etc. Nonetheless, it is necessary to investigate which modalities are the most suitable for which application context. The representative systems covered in this chapter are thus encouraging towards such a goal.

However, further research is still needed in order to identify the importance/feasibility of the following questions/factors for creating multimodal affect recognizers that can handle the so-called more natural or real world settings:

- Among the available *external* and *internal* modalities, which ones should be used for automatic affect recognition? In which context? Will the affect recognition accuracy increase as the number of modalities a system can analyze/integrate increases?
- In automated multimodal affect systems, can global processing replace local processing (i.e., whole-body expression analysis instead of facial expression analysis) by still providing means for fast and accurate analysis (e.g., when distance between the subject and the cameras/sensors poses a challenge)?
- What cross-modal interactions between pairs of various modalities (e.g., tactile and visual, tactile and audio etc.) can be exploited for multimodal affect analysis? Can we follow the example of HHI where judgments for one modality are influenced by a second modality even at the cost of increased ambiguity? How can such analysis be integrated for fusion of modalities?
- How can automated systems detect and label an affective message conveyed by different modalities as either *congruent* (i.e., agreeing) or *incongruent* (i.e., disagreeing)? After labeling, how can such knowledge be incorporated into the multimodal systems for detailed understanding of the information being conveyed? Should the goal be towards detecting and decreasing ambiguity, and increasing the reliability and accuracy of the automatic recognition process? Should/can we use the so-called *internal signals* (e.g., thermal infrared or physiological signals) for resolving ambiguity, instead of relying purely on the *external ones*?
- For the fusion purposes, how can an automated system include and integrate a new modality (when it becomes available) automatically? How can the system dynamically adapt to the channel conditions (e.g., when noise increases) in order to find an optimal solution?
- For the recognition purposes, how can a system estimate different affective phenomena (emotions, moods, affects and/or personalities)? How should the system include the knowledge about the environment and the user to the overall multimodal recognizer?
- How should the requirements of an automated system be decided? Is real-time processing and outputting labels as quickly as possible the priority? Or is the priority having a better, more accurate understanding of the user's affective state, regardless of the computational time it will take (Paleari & Lisetti, 2006)?

Overall, the research field of multimodal affect sensing and recognition is relatively new, and future efforts have to follow to address the aforementioned questions.

10. Acknowledgement

The authors would like to thank Arman Savran, Bulent Sankur, Guillaume Chanel, Rana el Kaliouby, Rosalind Picard and Thorsten Spexard for granting permission to use figures from their works/papers. The research of Maja Pantic leading to these results has been funded in part by the European IST Programme Project FP6-0027787 (AMIDA) and the European Community's 7th Framework Programme [FP7/2007-2013] under grant agreement no 211486 (SEMAINE).

11. References

Affect analysis group (2008): http://www.pitt.edu/%7Eemotion/publications.html.

Aftanas, L. I.; Pavlov, S. V.; Reva, N. V. & Varlamov, A. A. (2003) Trait anxiety impact on the EEG theta band power changes during appraisal of threatening and pleasant visual stimuli, *International Journal of Psychophysiology*, Vol. 50, No. 3, 205-212.

Aftanas, L.I.; Reva, A.A.; Varlamov; Pavlov, S.V. & Makhnev, V.P. (2004). Analysis of Evoked EEG Synchronization and Desynchronization in Conditions of Emotional Activation in Humans: Temporal and Topographic Characteristics. *Neuroscience and Behavioral Physiology*, (859-867).

Ali, A. N. & Marsden, P. H. (2003). Affective multi-modal interfaces: the case of McGurk effect, *Proc. of the 8th Int. Conf. on Intelligent User Interfaces*, pp. 224 - 226.

Allwood, J. & et al. (2004), The MUMIN multimodal coding scheme, *Proc. Workshop on Multimodal Corpora and Annotation*.

Ambady, N. & Rosenthal, R. (1993). Half a minute: Predicting teacher evaluations from thin slices of nonverbal behavior and physical attractiveness. *Journal of Personality and Social Psychology*, Vol. 64, 431-441.

Ambady, N. & Rosenthal, R. (1992). Thin slices of expressive behavior as predictors of interpersonal consequences: A meta-analysis. *Psychological Bulletin*, Vol. 11, No. 2, 256–274.

Argyle, M. (1975) , *Bodily communication*, Methuen, London.

Ashraf, A.B.; Lucey, S.; Cohn, J.F.; Chen, T.; Ambadar, Z.; Prkachin, K.; Solomon, P.; & Theobald, B. J. (2007). The painful face: Pain expression recognition using active appearance models. *Proc. of the ACM Int. Conf. on Multimodal Interfaces*, pp. 9-14.

Banziger, T. & Scherer, K. R. (2007) Using actor portrayals to systematically study multimodal emotion expression: The gemep corpus, *Proc. of the Second Int. Conf. on Affective Computing and Intelligent Interaction*, pp. 476–487.

Baron-Cohen, S. & Tead, T. H. E. (2003) *Mind reading: The interactive guide to emotion*, Jessica Kingsley Publishers Ltd.

Batliner, A.; Fischer K.; Hubera, R.; Spilkera, J. & Noth, E. (2003). How to find trouble in communication. *Speech Communication*, Vol. 40, 117-143.

Bengio, S. (2004). Multimodal speech processing using asynchronous hidden markov models, *Information Fusion*, Vol. 5, 81–89.

Bhatti, M.W.; Yongjin Wang & Ling Guan (2004). A neural network approach for human emotion recognition in speech, *Proc. International Symposium on Circuits and Systems*, Vol. 2, pp. 181-184.

Buller, D.; Burgoon, J.; White, C. & Ebesu, A. (1994). Interpersonal deception: Vii. behavioral profiles of falsification, equivocation and concealment. *Journal of Language and Social Psychology*, Vol. 13, No. 5, 366–395.

Busso, C.; Deng, Z.; Yildirim, S.; Bulut, M.; Lee, C.; Kazemzadeh, A.; Lee, S.; Neumann, U. & Narayanan, S. (2004). Analysis of emotion recognition using facial expressions, speech and multimodal information, *Proc. Int. Conf. on Multimodal Interfaces*, pp. 205–211.

Cacioppo, J. T. & Berntson, G. G. (1994). Relationship between attitudes and evaluative space: A critical review, with emphasis on the separability of positive and negative substrates, *Psychological Bulletin*,Vol. 115, 401-423.

Campbell, N. & Mokhtari, P. (2003). Voice quality: the 4th prosodic dimension, *Proc. Int'l Congress of Phonetic Sciences*, pp. 2417-2420.

Camras, L.A.; Meng, Z. ; Ujiie, T. ; Dharamsi, K.; Miyake, S.; Oster, H.; Wang, L.; Cruz, A.; Murdoch, J. & Campos, J. (2002). Observing emotion in infants: facial expression, body behavior, and rater judgments of responses to an expectancy-violating event, *Emotion*, Vol. 2, 179-193.

Camurri, A.; Mazzarino, B. & Volpe, G. (2003) Analysis of Expressive Gesture: The EyesWeb Expressive Gesture Processing Library. *Proc. of Gesture Workshop*, pp. 460-467.

Cassell, J. (1998). A framework for gesture generation and interpretation, In: *Computer Vision in Human-Machine Interaction*, A. Pentland & R. Cipolla (Ed.), Cambridge University Press.

Changchun Liu; Rani, P. & Sarkar, N. (2005). An empirical study of machine learning techniques for affect recognition in human-robot interaction, *Proc. of IEEE/RSJ International Conference on Intelligent Robots and Systems*, pp. 2662- 2667.

Coulson, M. (2004). Attributing emotion to static body postures: Recognition accuracy, confusions, and viewpoint dependence, *Nonverbal Behavior*, Vol. 28, No. 2, 117–139.

Cowie, R.; Douglas-Cowie, E.; Tsapatsoulis, N.; Votsis, G.; Kollias, S.; Fellenz, W. & Taylor, J.G. (2001). Emotion Recognition in Human-Computer Interaction, *IEEE Signal Processing Magazine*, Vol. 18, No. 1, 32-80.

Darwin, C. (1872). *The expression of the emotions in man and animals*, John Murray, London.

De Gelder, B.; Bocker, K. B.; Tuomainen, J.; Hensen, M. & Vroomen, J. (1999). The combined perception of emotion from voice and face: Early interaction revealed by human electric brain responses, *Neuroscience Letters*, Vol. 260, 133–136.

DePaulo, B. Cues to deception (2003). *Psychological Bulletin*, Vol. 129, No. 1, 74–118.

Devillers, L.; Vasilescu, I. & Vidrascu, L. (2004). Anger versus fear detection in recorded conversations, *Proc. Speech Prosody*, pp. 205-208.

Douglas-Cowie, E.; Cowie, R., Sneddon; Cox, C.; Lowry, McRorie, Martin, J.-C.; Devillers, L. & Batliner, A. (2007). The HUMAINE Database: addressing the needs of the affective computing community, *Proc. of the Second International Conference on Affective Computing and Intelligent Interaction*, pp. 488-500.

Dreuw, P.; Deselaers, T.; Rybach, D.; Keysers, D. & Ney, H. Tracking using dynamic programming for appearance-based sign language recognition (2006). *Proc. of the IEEE Int. Conf. on Automatic Face and Gesture Recognition*, pp. 293–298.

Driver, J. & Spence, C. (2000). Multisensory perception: Beyond modularity and convergence, *Current Biology*, Vol. 10, No. 20, 731-735.

Ekman, P. (2003). Darwin, deception, and facial expression. *Annals of New York Ac. of sciences*, Vol. 1000, 105–221.

Ekman, P.(1982) *Emotion in the human face*. Cambridge University Press.

Ekman, P.(1979) About brows: Emotional and conversational signals, In: *Human Ethology: Claims and Limits of a New Discipline: Contributions to the Colloquium*, M.V. Cranach, K. Foppa, W. Lepenies, and D. Ploog (Ed.), 169–248, Cambridge University Press, New York.

Ekman, P. & Friesen, W.V. (2003) *Unmasking the face: a guide to recognizing emotions from facial clues*. Cambridge, MA.

Ekman, P. & Friesen, W. V. (1978). *Facial action coding system: A technique for the measurement of facial movement*, Palo Alto, Calif.: Consulting Psychologists Press.

Elgammal, A.; Shet, V.; Yacoob, Y. & Davis, L.S. (2003). Learning dynamics for exemplar-based gesture recognition, *Proc. of the IEEE Conf. on Computer Vision and Pattern Recognition*, pp. 571–578.

El Kaliouby, R. & Teeters, A. (2007) Eliciting, capturing and tagging spontaneous facial affect in autism spectrum disorder, *Proc. of the 9th Int. Conf. on Multimodal Interfaces*, pp. 46-53.
El Kaliouby, R. & Robinson, P. (2005). Real-time Inference of Complex Mental States from Facial Expressions and Head Gestures, *In: Real-Time Vision for HCI*, pp. 181–200, Spring-Verlag.
Fasel, I. R.; Fortenberry, B. & Movellan, J. R. (2005). A generative framework for real-time object detection, and classification, *Computer Vision and Image Understanding*, Vol. 98.
Fragopanagos, F. & Taylor, J.G., Emotion recognition in human-computer interaction, *Neural Networks*, Vol. 18, 389-405.
Friesen, W. V., & Ekman, P. (1984). EMFACS-7: *Emotional Facial Action Coding System*, Unpublished manuscript, University of California at San Francisco.
Gross, M. M.; Gerstner, G. E.; Koditschek, D. E.; Fredrickson, B. L. & Crane, E. A. (2006) Emotion Recognition from Body Movement Kinematics:http://sitemaker.umich.edu/mgrosslab/files/abstract.pdf.
Gunes, H. (2007) Vision-based multimodal analysis of affective face and upper-body behaviour, Ph.D. dissertation, University of Technology, Sydney (UTS), Sydney, Australia.
Gunes, H. & Piccardi, M. (2008). From Mono-modal to Multi-modal: Affect Recognition Using Visual Modalities, In: *Ambient Intelligence Techniques and Applications*, D. Monekosso, P. Remagnino, and Y. Kuno (Eds.), Springer-Verlag (in press).
Gunes, H. & Piccardi, M. (2007). Bi-modal emotion recognition from expressive face and body gestures. *J. Network and Computer Applications*, Vol. 30, No. 4, 1334-1345.
Gunes, H. & Piccardi, M. (2006a).A bimodal face and body gesture database for automatic analysis of human nonverbal affective behavior, *Proc. of the Int. Conf. on Pattern Recognition*, Vol. 1, pp. 1148–1153.
Gunes, H. & Piccardi, M. (2006b), Creating and annotating affect databases from face and body display: A contemporary survey, *Proc. of the IEEE Int. Conf. on Systems, Man and Cybernetics*, pp. 2426–2433.
Hadjikhani, N. & De Gelder, B. (2003). Seeing fearful body expressions activates the fusiform cortex and amygdala, *Current Biology*, Vol. 13, 2201-2205.
Jenkins, J.M.; Oatley, K. & Stein, N.L. (1998). *Human emotions: A reader*, Blackwell Publishers, Malden, MA.
Juslin, P.N. & Scherer, K.R. (2005), Vocal expression of affect, In: *The New Handbook of Methods in Nonverbal Behavior Research*, Harrigan, J., Rosenthal, R. & Scherer, K. (Ed.), Oxford University Press, Oxford, UK.
Kapoor, A.; Burleson, W. & Picard, R. W. (2007). Automatic Prediction of Frustration, *Int. Journal of Human Computer Studies*, Vol. 65, No. 8, 724-736.
Karpouzis, K.; Caridakis, G.; Kessous, L.; Amir, N.; Raouzaiou, A. ; Malatesta, L. & Kollias, S. (2007). Modeling naturalistic affective states via facial, vocal and bodily expressions recognition, In: *Lecture Notes in Artificial Intelligence*, vol. 4451, pp. 92–116.
Khan, M. M.; Ingleby, M. & Ward, R. D. (2006a). Automated facial expression classification and affect interpretation using infrared measurement of facial skin temperature variations, *ACM Transactions on Autonomous and Adaptive Systems*, Vol. 1, No. 1, 91 - 113.

Khan, M. M.; Ward, R. D. & Ingleby, M. (2006b). Infrared Thermal Sensing of Positive and Negative Affective States, Proc. of the IEEE Conf. on Robotics, Automation and Mechatronics, pp. 1-6.

Kim, K.H.; Bang, S. W. & Kim, S. R. (2004). Emotion recognition system using short-term monitoring of physiological signals., *Medical & Biological Engineering & Computing*, Vol. 42, 419–427.

Kittler, J.; M.; Hatef, Duin, R.P.W. & Matas, J. (1998). On combining classifiers, *IEEE Tran. on Pattern Analysis and Machine Intelligence*, Vol. 20, No. 3, 226–239.

Laban, R. & Ullmann, L. (1988). *The mastery of movement*, 4th revision ed., Princeton Book Company Publishers.

Lang, P. J. (1995). The emotion probe: Studies of motivation and attention, *American Psychologist*, Vol. 50, No. 5, 372–385.

Lienhart, R. & Maydt, J. (2002). An extended set of haar-like features for rapid object detection, *Proc. of the IEEE Int. Conf. on Image Processing*, Vol. 1, pp. 900–903.

Littlewort, G. C.; Bartlett, M. S. & Lee, K. (2007). Faces of pain: automated measurement of spontaneous facial expressions of genuine and posed pain, *Proc. of the 9th Int. Conf. on Multimodal interfaces*, pp. 15-21.

Martin, J. -C.; Caridakis, G.; Devillers, L.; Karpouzis, K. & Abrilian, S. (2007). Manual annotation and automatic image processing of multimodal emotional behaviors: validating the annotation of TV interviews, *Personal and Ubiquitous Computing*.

Martin, J. -C.; Abrilian, S. & Devillers, L. (2005). Annotating Multimodal Behaviours Occurring During Non Basic Emotions, *Proc. of the First Int. Conf. on Affective Computing and Intelligent Interaction*, pp. 550–557.

Massaro, D. W. & Cohen, M. M. (2000), Fuzzy logical model of bimodal emotion perception: Comment on "The perception of emotions by ear and by eye" by de Gelder and Vroomen, *Cognition and Emotion*, Vol. 14, No. 3, pp. 313-320.

McNeill, D. (1985). So you think gestures are nonverbal?, *Psychological Review*, Vol. 92, 350-371.

Meeren, H. K.; Van Heijnsbergen, C. C. & De Gelder, B. (2005). Rapid perceptual integration of facial expression and emotional body language, *Proc. of the National Academy of Sciences of the USA*, Vol. 102, 16518–16523.

Mitra, S. & Acharya, T. (2007). Gesture Recognition: A Survey, *IEEE Tran. on Systems, Man, and Cybernetics, Part C*, Vol. 37, No. 3, 311-324.

Nakasone, A.; Prendinger, H. & Ishizuka, M. (2005). Emotion Recognition from Electromyography and Skin Conductance, *Proc. of the 5th International Workshop on Biosignal Interpretation*, Tokyo, Japan, pp. 219-222.

Nakayama, K. ; Goto, S.; Kuraoka, K. & Nakamura, K. (2005). Decrease in nasal temperature of rhesus monkeys (Macaca mulatta) in negative emotional state, *Journal of Physiology and Behavior*, Vol. 84, 783-790.

Ning, H.; Han, T.X.; Hu, Y.; Zhang, Z.; Fu, Y. & Huang, T.S. (2006). A real-time shrug detector, *Proc. of the IEEE Int. Conf. on Automatic Face and Gesture Recognition*, pp. 505–510.

Noda, T.; Yano, Y.; Doki, S. & Okuma, S. (2006). Adaptive Emotion Recognition in Speech by Feature Selection Based on KL-divergence, *Proc. IEEE International Conference on Systems, Man and Cybernetics*, Vol. 3, pp. 1921 - 1926.

Ortony, A. & Turner, T. J. (1990). What's basic about basic emotions?, *Psychological Review*, Vol. 97, pp. 315–331.

O'Toole, A. J. & et al. (2005). A video database of moving faces and people, *IEEE Tran. on Pattern Analysis and Machine Intelligence*, vol. 27, No. 5, 812-816.

Paleari, M. & Lisetti, C. L. (2006). Toward multimodal fusion of affective cues, *Proc. of the 1st ACM Int. Workshop on Human-Centered Multimedia*, pp. 99–108.

Pan, H.; Levinson, S.E. ; Huang, T.S. & Liang, Z.-P. (2004). A fused hidden markov model with application to bimodal speech processing, *IEEE Transactions on Signal Processing*, Vol. 52, No. 3, 573–581.

Pantic, M. & Bartlett, M.S. (2007). Machine Analysis of Facial Expressions, In: *Face Recognition*, Delac, K. & Grgic, M. (Ed.), Vienna, Austria: I-Tech Education and Publishing, 377-416.

Pantic, M.; Pentland, A.; Nijholt, A. & Huang, T. (2007). Machine understanding of human behavior, In: *Lecture Note in Artificial Intelligence*, Vol. 4451, pp. 47-71.

Pantic, M. & Rothkrantz, L.J.M. (2003). Towards an Affect-Sensitive Multimodal Human-Computer Interaction, *Proceedings of the IEEE*, Vol. 91, No. 9, 1370-1390.

Pavlidis, I. T.; Levine, J.; Baukol, P. (2001). Thermal image analysis for anxiety detection, *Proc. of the International Conference on Image Processing*, Vol. 2, pp. 315 - 318.

Picard, R.W. (1997). *Affective computing*, The MIT Press, MA, USA.

Picard, R.W.; Vyzas, E. & Healey, J. (2001). Toward machine emotional intelligence: analysis of affective physiological state, *IEEE Transactions on Pattern Analysis and Machine Intelligence*, Vol. 23, No. 10, 1175-1191.

Poppe, R. (2007). Vision-based human motion analysis: An overview, *Computer Vision and Image Understanding*, Vol. 108, No. 1-2, 4-18.

Pun, T.; Alecu, T. I.; Chanel, G.; Kronegg, J. & Voloshynovskiy, S. (2006). Brain-Computer Interaction Research at the Computer Vision and Multimedia Laboratory, University of Geneva, *IEEE Tran. on Neural Systems and Rehabilitation Engineering*, Vol. 14, No. 2.

Puri, C.; Olson, L.; Pavlidis, I.; Levine, J. & Starren, J. (2005). StressCam: Non-contact measurement of users' emotional states through thermal imaging, Proc. of the CHI, pp. 1725-1728.

Riseberg, J.; Klein, J.; Fernandez, R. & Picard, R.W. (1998). Frustrating the User on Purpose: Using Biosignals in a Pilot Study to Detect the User's Emotional State, *Proc. of CHI*.

Russell, J. A. (1980). A circumplex model of affect, *Journal of Personality and Social Psychology*, Vol. 39, 1161-1178.

Russell, J.A. & Carroll, J. M. (1999). On the bipolarity of negative and positive affect, Psychological Bulletin 125 (1999), 3-30.

Russell, J.A. & Fernández-Dols, J.M., (1997). The Psychology of Facial Expression. New York: Cambridge Univ.

Savran, A.; Ciftci, K.; Chanel, G.; Mota, J. C.; Viet, L. H.; Sankur, B.; Akarun, L.; Caplier, A. & Rombaut, M. (2006). Emotion Detection in the Loop from Brain Signals and Facial Images, *Proc. of the eNTERFACE 2006*, July 17th - August 11th, Dubrovnik, Croatia, Final Project Report (www.enterface.net).

Schmidt, K.L. & Cohn, J.F. (2001). Human facial expressions as adaptations: Evolutionary questions in facial expression research, *Yearbook of Physical Anthropology*, Vol. 44, 3–24.

Shan, C.; Gong, S. & McOwan, P. W. (2007). Beyond facial expressions: Learning human emotion from body gestures, *Proc. of the British Machine Vision Conference*.

Spexard, T. P.; Hanheide, M. & Sagerer, G. (2007). Human-Oriented Interaction With an Anthropomorphic Robot, *IEEE Tran. on Robotics*, Vol. 23, No. 5.

Takahashi, K. (2004). Remarks on Emotion Recognition From Multi-Modal Bio-Potential Signals, *Proc. IEEE International Conference on Industrial Technology*, pp. 1138-1143.

Tian, Y. L.; Kanade, T. & Cohn, J. F. (2002), Evaluation of gabor-wavelet-based facial action unit recognition in image sequences of increasing complexity, *Proc. of the IEEE Int. Conf. on Automaitc Face and Gesture Recognition*, pp. 218-223.

Tsiamyrtzis, P.; Dowdall, J.; Shastri, D.; Pavlidis, I.; Frank, M. G. & Ekman, P. (2007). Imaging Facial Physiology for the Detection of Deceit. *International Journal of Computer Vision*, Vol. 71, No. 2, 197-214.

Valstar, M. F.; Gunes, H. & Pantic, M. (2007). How to distinguish posed from spontaneous smiles using geometric features, *Proc. of the 9th Int. Conf. on Multimodal Interfaces*, pp. 38–45.

Van den Stock J.; Righart R. & De Gelder B. (2007). Body expressions influence recognition of emotions in the face and voice, *Emotion*, Vol. 7, No. 3, 487-494.

Van Hoof, J.A. (1962). Facial expressions in higher primates, *Proceedings of the Symposium of the Zoological Society of London*, Vol. 8, pp. 97-125.

Varma, M. & Ray, D. (2007). Learning The Discriminative Power-Invariance Trade-Off, *Proc. IEEE 11th International Conference on Computer Vision*, pp. 1-8.

Vianna, D.M. & Carrive, P. (2005). Changes in cutaneous and body temperature during and after conditioned fear to context in the rat, *European Journal of Neuroscince*, Vol. 21, No. 9, 2505-25012.

Villalba, S. D. ; Castellano, G. & Camurri, A. (2007). Recognising human emotions from body movement and gesture dynamics, *Proc. of the Second Int. Conf. on Affective Computing and Intelligent Interaction*, pp. 71–82.

Viola, P. & Jones, M. (2001). Rapid object detection using a boosted cascade of simple features, *Proc. of the IEEE Conf. on Computer Vision and Pattern Recognition*, vol. 1, pp. 511–518.

Vroomen, J.; Driver, J. & De Gelder, B. (2001). Is cross-modal integration of emotional expressions independent of attentional resources? *Cognitive, Affective & Behavioral Neuroscience*, Vol. 1, 382–387.

Walker-Andrews, A. S. (1997). Infants' perception of expressive behaviors: differentiation of multimodal information, *Psychol Bull*, Vol. 121, No. 3, 437-456.

Whissell, C. M. (1989). The dictionary of affect in language, In: *Emotion: Theory, research and experience. The measurement of emotions*, Plutchik R. & Kellerman H. Ed., Vol.4. 113-131. New York: Academic Press.

Wilson, A. D.; Bobick, A. F. & Cassell, J. (1997). Temporal classification of natural gesture and application to video coding, *Proc. of the IEEE Conf. on Computer Vision and Pattern Recognition*, pp. 948–954.

Wu, L.; Oviatt, S.L. & Cohen, P.R. (1999). Multimodal integration–a statistical view, *IEEE Tran. on Multimedia*, Vol. 1, No. 4, 334–341.

Yilmaz, A.; Javed, O. & Shah, M. (2006). Object Tracking: A Survey, *ACM Journal of Computing Surveys*, Vol. 38, No. 4.

Yoshitomi, Y.; Kim, S.-I.; Kawano, T. & Kilazoe, T. (2000) Effect of sensor fusion for recognition of emotional states using voice, face image and thermal image of face, *Proc. of the IEEE International Workshop on Robot and Human Interactive Communication*, pp. 178 – 18.

Zeng, Z.; Pantic, M.; Roisman, G.I. & Huang, T.S. (2008). A Survey of Affect Recognition Methods: Audio, Visual, and Spontaneous Expressions, *IEEE Tran. on Pattern Analysis and Machine Intelligence*, 2008 (in press).

Zuckerman, M.; Larrance, D. T.; Hall, J. A.; DeFrank, R. S. & Rosenthal, R. (1979). Posed and spontaneous communication of emotion via facial and vocal cues, *Journal of Personality*, Vol. 47, No. 4, 712–733.

11

The Art of Expressing Emotions in Virtual Humans

Celso de Melo and Ana Paiva
University of Southern California and IST-Technical University of Lisbon
United States of America and Portugal

1. Introduction

Artists express emotions through art. To accomplish this, they rely on lines, shapes, textures, color, light, sounds, music, words and the body (Sayre, 2007). It is the flexibility of artistic media which affords the expression of complex affective states (Bell, 1913; Oatley, 2003). In fact, many artists use art as a means to come to terms and understand the subtlety and peculiarity of their feelings (Collingwood, 1938). Furthermore, it is not uncommon for artists to claim they need these media, which are not limited to the body or language, for the expression of their feelings (Gardner, 1982). But art is not simply an outlet for the artist's emotions. From the perspective of the receiver, through its empathetic emotional response to a work of art, it is also seen as a means to learn about the human condition (Elliot, 1966; Oatley, 2003). Emotions are, therefore, intrinsically related to the value of art.
Affective computing has been neglecting the kind of expression we see in the arts. Instead, researchers have focused on expression signals, spanning face, voice and body, which accompany affective processes (Davidson, Scherer & Goldsmith, 2003). Four reasons could help explain why this has been so. First, it is natural to focus on overt expression signals as these are directly observable and, thus, can be measured objectively. In contrast, it is rather difficult to measure objectively what is being expressed in a work of art. In fact, whereas some argue for the importance of understanding the artist's production process and culture when interpreting an art artefact (Davies, 1987; Wollheim, 1980; Goodman, 1968), others argue that the interpretation and aesthetics of an artefact is independent of its creation process (Beardsley, 1958; Baxandall, 1987; Sontag, 1966). Second, art is certainly not limited to the expression of affective states and sometimes it is difficult to discern what constitutes such expression. In fact, there are several conceptions about what expression in the arts is: (a) it relates to beauty as the creative expression of beauty in nature (Batteux, 1969); (b) it relates to culture as the expression of the values of a given society (Geertz, 1976); (c) it relates to individuality as the expression of the artist's liberties and creativity (Kant, 1951); (d) finally, it relates to the expression of affective states. Third, the romantic perspective of art as the creative expression of affective states in all its complexity is problematic (Averill, Nunley & Tassinary, 1995; Oatley, 2003). In general, the subject of art is not the habitual emotions we experience in our daily lives but, subtle and peculiar affective states. Therefore, it is only natural that researchers choose to begin by addressing the simpler affective states. Finally, the affective sciences field is itself relatively recent and we are only now beginning

to move beyond all-encompassing grand theories of emotions to more specialized conceptions of affective phenomena (Davidson, Scherer & Goldsmith, 2003). It is, perhaps, time to start taking more seriously the kind of expression we see in the arts.

In this context, this work proposes to draw on accumulated knowledge from art theory to synthesize expression of emotions in virtual humans. Virtual humans are embodied characters which inhabit virtual worlds and look, think and act like humans (Gratch et al, 2002). The state-of-the-art in virtual human research is symptomatic of the narrow view of the affective computing field we described above. Indeed, researchers have, thus far, tended to focus on gesture (Cassell, 2000), face (Noh & Neumann, 1998) and voice (Schroder, 2004) for the expression of emotions. But, of course, in the digital medium we need not be limited to the body. In this sense, this work goes beyond embodiment and explores the expression of emotions in virtual humans using lights, shadows, composition and filters. Our approach, thus, focuses on two expression channels: lights and screen. In the first case, we inspire on the principles of lighting, regularly explored in theatre or film production (Millerson, 1999; Birn, 2006), to convey the virtual human's affective state through the environment's light sources. In the second case, we acknowledge that, at the meta level, virtual humans are no more than pixels in the screen which can be manipulated, in a way akin to the visual arts (Birn, 2006; Gross, 2007; Zettl, 2008), to convey affective states. Finally, because artistic expression is essentially a creative endeavor (Sayre, 2007), more than trying to find the right set of rules, we explore an evolutionary approach which relies on genetic algorithms to learn mappings from affective states to lighting and screen expression.

The remainder of the chapter is organized as follows. Section 2 provides background on virtual humans and describes the digital medium's potential for expression of emotions, focusing on lighting and screen expression. Section 3 describes our virtual human model, detailing the lighting and screen expression channels, and introduces our evolutionary model. Section 4 describes some of our results. Finally, section 5 draws some conclusions and discusses future work.

2. Background

2.1 Expression of emotions in the digital medium

Digital technology is a flexible medium for the expression of emotions. In virtual worlds, inhabited by virtual humans, besides embodiment, at least four expression channels can be identified: camera, lights, sound, and screen. The camera defines the view into the virtual world. Expressive control, which inspires on cinema and photography, is achieved through selection of shot, shot transitions, shot framing and manipulation of lens properties (Arijon, 1976; Block, 2001). Lights define which areas of the scene are illuminated and which are in shadow. Furthermore, lights define the color in the scene. Expressive control, which inspires in the visual arts, is achieved through manipulation of (Millerson, 1999; Birn, 2006): light type, placement and angle; shadow softness and falloff; color properties such as hue, brightness and saturation. Sound refers to literal sounds (e.g., dialogues), non-literal sounds (e.g., effects) and music. Expressive control, which inspires in drama and music, is achieved through selection of appropriate content for each kind of sound (Juslin & Sloboda, 2001; Zettl, 2008). Finally, the screen is a meta channel referring to the pixel-based screen itself. Expression control, which inspires on cinema and photography, is achieved through manipulation of pixel properties such as depth and color (Birn, 2006; Zettl, 2008). This work shall focus on the lighting and screen expression channels.

2.2 Expression of emotions in virtual humans

Virtual humans are embodied characters which inhabit virtual worlds (Gratch et al, 2002). First, virtual humans look like humans. Thus, research draws on computer graphics for models to control the body and face. Second, virtual humans think and act like humans. Thus, research draws on the social sciences for models to produce synchronized verbal and nonverbal communication as well as convey emotions and personality. Emotion synthesis usually resorts to cognitive appraisal theories of emotion, being the Ortony, Clore and Collins (OCC) theory (Ortony et al, 1988) one of the most commonly used. Emotion expression tends to focus on conveying emotions through synchronized and integrated gesture (Cassell, 2000), facial (Noh & Neumann, 1998) and vocal (Schroder, 2004) expression. In contrast, this work goes beyond the body using lights, shadows, composition and filters to express emotions.

A different line of research explores *motion modifiers* which add emotive qualities to neutral expression. Amaya (Amaya et al, 1996) uses signal processing techniques to capture the difference between neutral and emotional movement which would, then, be used to confer emotive properties to other motion data. Chi and colleagues (Chi et al., 2000) propose a system which adds expressiveness to existent motion data based on the effort and shape parameters of a dance movement observation technique called Laban Movement Analysis. Hartmann (Hartmann et al, 2005) draws from psychology six parameters for gesture modification: overall activation, spatial extent, temporal extent, fluidity, power and repetition. Finally, closer to this work, de Melo (de Melo & Paiva, 2005) proposes a model for expression of emotions using the camera, light and sound expression channels. However, this model did not focus on virtual humans, used a less sophisticated light channel than the one proposed here, did not explore screen expression and used simple rules instead of an evolutionary approach.

2.3 Expression of emotions using lights

This work explores *lighting* to express virtual humans' emotions. Lighting is the deliberate control of light to achieve expressive goals. Lighting can be used for the purpose of expression of emotions and aesthetics (Millerson, 1999; Birn, 2006). To achieve these goals, artists usually manipulate the following elements: (a) type, which defines whether the light is a point, directional or spotlight; (b) direction, which defines the angle; (c) color, which defines color properties. In Western culture, color is regularly manipulated to convey emotions (Fraser, 2004); (d) intensity, which defines exposure level; (e) softness, which defines how hard or soft the light is; (f) decay, which defines how light decays with distance; (g) throw pattern, which defines the shape of the light. Shadows occur in the absence of light. Though strictly related to lights, they tend to be independently controlled by artists. Shadows can also be used to express emotions and aesthetics (Millerson, 1999; Birn, 2006). In this case, this is achieved by manipulation of shadow softness and size. Lighting transitions change the elements of light and shadow in time. Transitions can be used to change the mood or atmosphere of the scene (Millerson 1999; Birn 2006).

2.4 Expression of emotions using pixels

At a meta level, virtual humans and virtual worlds can be seen as pixels in a screen. Thus, as in painting, photography or cinema, it is possible to manipulate the image itself for expressive reasons. In this view, this work explores composition and filtering for the expression of emotions. Composition refers to the process of arranging different aspects of the objects in the scene into layers which are then manipulated and combined to form the final image (Birn, 2006). Here, aspects refer to the ambient, diffuse, specular, shadow, alpha or depth object components. Composition has two main advantages: increases efficiency as different aspects can be held fixed for several frames; and, increases expressiveness as each aspect can be controlled independently. Composition is a standard technique in film production. Filtering is a technique where the scene is rendered into a temporary texture which is then manipulated using *shaders* before being presented to the user (Zettl, 2008). Shaders replace parts of the traditional pipeline with programmable units (Moller & Haines, 2002). Vertex shaders modify vertex data such as position, color, normal and texture coordinates. Pixel shaders modify pixel data such as color and depth. Filtering has many advantages: it has constant performance independently of the scene complexity; it can be very expressive due to the variety of available filters (St-Laurent, 2004); and, it is scalable as several filters can be concatenated.

3. The model

3.1 Overview

The virtual human model is summarized in Fig.1. The virtual human itself is structured according to a three-layer architecture (Blumberg & Galyean, 1995; Perlin & Goldberg, 1996). The *geometry layer* defines a 54-bone human-based skeleton which is used to animate the skin. The skin is divided into body groups - head, torso, arms, hands and legs. The *animation layer* defines keyframe and procedural animation mechanisms. The *behaviour layer* defines speech and gesticulation expression. Finally, several expression modalities are built on top of this layered architecture. Bodily expression manipulates face, postures and gestures. Further details on bodily expression, which will not be addressed here, can be found in (de Melo & Paiva, 2006a; de Melo & Paiva, 2006b). Lighting expression explores the surrounding environment and manipulates lights and shadows. Screen expression manipulates the virtual human pixels themselves.

3.2 Lighting expression

Lighting expression relies on a local pixel-based lighting model. The model supports multiple sources, three light types and shadows using the shadow map technique (Moller & Haines, 2002). The detailed equations for the lighting model can be found in (de Melo & Paiva, 2007). Manipulation of light and shadow elements (subsection 2.3) is based on the following parameters: (a) *type*, which defines whether to use a directional, point or spotlight; (b) *direction* and *position*, which, according to type, control the light angle; (c) *ambient, diffuse* and *specular colors*, which define the color of each of the light's components in either RGB (red, green, blue) or HSB (hue, saturation and brightness) space; (d) *ambient, diffuse* and *specular intensity*, which define the intensity of each of the components' color. Setting intensity to 0 disables the component; (e) *attenuation, attnPower, attnMin, attnMax*, which simulate light falloff. Falloff is defined as $attenuation^{attnPower}$ and is 0 if the distance is less than *attnMin* and 1 beyond a distance of *attnMax*; (f) *throw pattern*, which constraints the light to a texture using component-wise multiplication; (g) *shadow color*, which defines the shadow color. If set to grays, shadows become transparent; if set to white, shadows are disabled; (h) *shadow softness*, which defines the falloff between light and shadow areas.

Finally, sophisticated lighting transitions, such as accelerations and decelerations, are based on parametric cubic curve interpolation (Moller & Haines, 2002) of parameters.

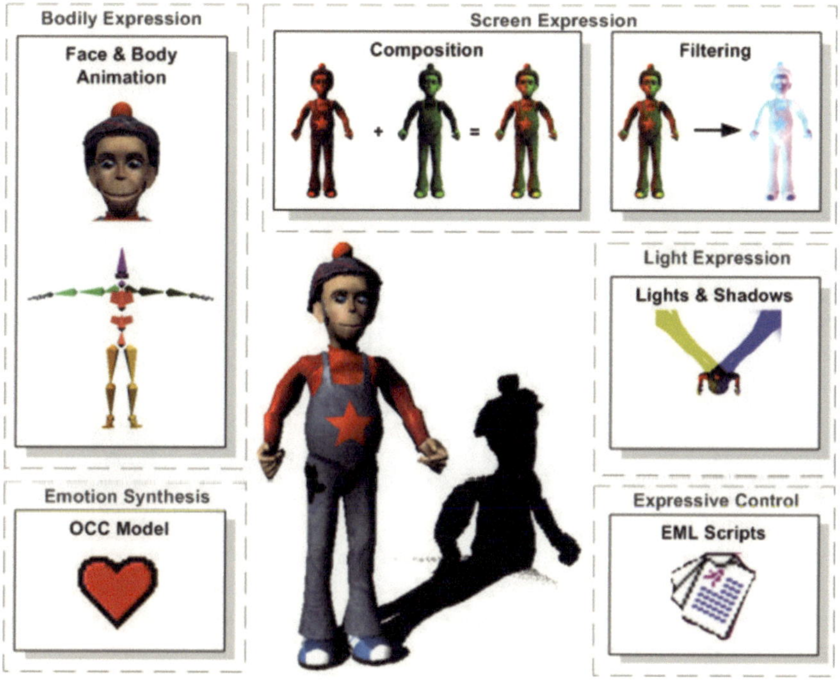

Fig. 1. The virtual human model

3.3 Screen expression

Screen expression explores composition and filtering. Filtering consists of rendering the scene to a temporary texture, modifying it using shaders and, then, presenting it to the user. Several filters have been explored in the literature (St-Laurent, 2004) and this work explores some of them: (a) the *contrast* filter, Fig.2-(b), which controls virtual human contrast and can be used to simulate exposure effects; (b) the *motion blur* filter, Fig.2-(c), which simulates motion blur and is usually used in film to convey nervousness; (c) the *HSB* filter, Fig.2-(c), which controls the virtual human hue, saturation and brightness; (d) the *style* filter, Fig.2-(d), which manipulates the virtual human's color properties to convey a stylized look. Filters can be concatenated to create compound effects and its parameters interpolated using parametric cubic curve interpolation (Moller & Haines, 2002).
Composition refers to the process of (Birn, 2006): arranging different aspects of the objects in the scene into layers; independently manipulating the layers for expressive reasons; combining the layers to form the final image. A layer is characterized as follows: (a) is associated with a subset of the objects which are rendered when the layer is rendered. These subsets need not be mutually exclusive; (b) can be rendered to a texture or the backbuffer. If rendered to a texture, filtering can be applied; (c) has an ordered list of filters which are

successively applied to the objects. Only applies if the layer is being rendered to a texture; (d) is associated with a subset of the lights in the scene. Objects in the layer are only affected by these lights; (e) defines a lighting mask, which defines which components of the associated lights apply to the objects; (f) can render only a subset of the virtual human's skin body groups. Finally, layer combination is defined by order and blending operation. The former defines the order in which layers are rendered into the backbuffer. The latter defines how are the pixels to be combined.

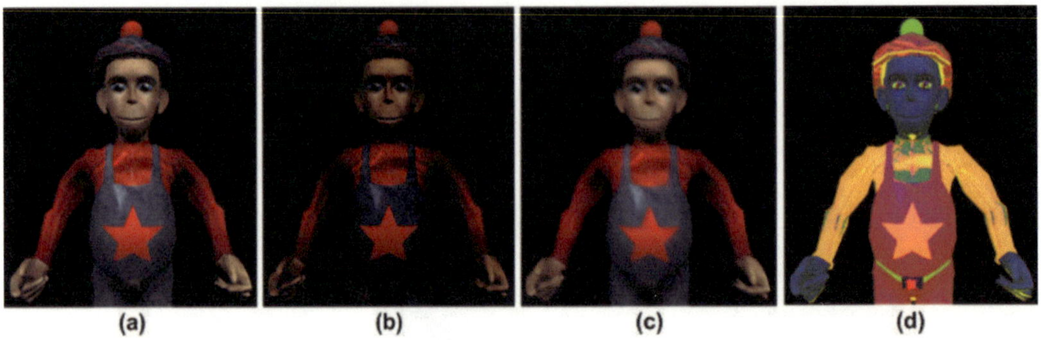

Fig. 2. Filtering manipulates the virtual human pixels. In (a) no filter is applied. In (b) the contrast filter is used to reduce contrast and create a more mysterious and harsh look. In (c) the motion blur is used to convey nervousness. In (d) the style filter, which is less concerned with photorealism, conveys an energetic look.

3.4 Synthesis of emotions

Emotion synthesis is based on the Ortony, Clore and Collins (OCC) model (Ortony, Clore & Collins, 1988). All 22 emotion types, local and global variables are implemented. Furthermore, emotion decay, reinforcement, arousal and mood are also considered. Emotion decay is, as suggested by Picard (1997), represented by an inverse exponential function. Emotion reinforcement is, so as to simulate the saturation effect (Picard, 1997), represented by a logarithmic function. Arousal, which relates to the physiological manifestation of emotions, is characterized as follows: is positive; decays linearly in time; reinforces with emotion eliciting; and, increases the elicited emotions' potential. Mood, which refers to the longer-term effects of emotions, is characterized as follows: can be negative or positive; converges to zero linearly in time; reinforces with emotion eliciting; if positive, increases the elicited emotions' potential, if negative, decreases it. Further details about this model can be found in (de Melo & Paiva, 2005).

3.5 Expression of emotions

Expression in the arts is a creative endeavor (Kant, 1951; Mill, 1965; Gombrich, 1960; Batteux, 1969; Sayre, 2007). Art is not a craft were artists can simply follow a set of rules to reach a result (Collingwood, 1938) and, according to the Romantic view, art is the creative expression of latent affective states (Oatley, 2003). Art can also be seen as the manifestation of the artist's individuality and liberties (Kant, 1951). In fact, Gombrich (1960) argues that this idiosyncrasy is inescapable as the artist's visual perceptions are necessarily confronted with its mental schemas, including ideas and preconceptions. Thus, the simple rule-based approach is unlikely to capture the way artistic expression works. A better approach should, therefore, rely on machine learning, which would support adaptation to dynamic artistic values and automatic learning of new rules and sophisticated mappings between emotional states and bodily, environment and screen expression.

In this work, we propose an evolutionary approach for learning such mappings which is based on genetic algorithms. Genetic algorithms seem appropriate for several reasons. First, there are no available datasets exemplifying what correct expression of emotions using lights or screen is. Thus, standard supervised machine learning algorithms, which rely on a teacher, seem unsuitable. Furthermore, art varies according to time, individual, culture and what has been done before (Sayre 2007). Therefore, the artistic space should be explored in search of creative - i.e., new and aesthetic - expression. Genetic algorithms, defining a guided search, are, thus, appropriate. Second, the virtual humans field is new and novel forms of expression are available. Here, the genetic algorithm's clear separation between generation and evaluation of alternatives is appropriate. Alternatives, in this new artistic space, can be generated using biologically inspired operators - selection, mutation, crossover, etc. Evaluation, in turn, could rely on fitness functions drawn from art theory.

3.6 Evolutionary expression of emotions

The evolutionary model we propose revolves around two key entities: the *virtual human* and the *critic ensemble*. The virtual human tries to evolve the best way to express some affective state. For every possible state, it begins by generating a random set of *hypotheses*, which constitute a *population*. The population evolves resorting to a genetic algorithm under the influence of feedback from the critic ensemble. The ensemble is composed of human and artificial critics. The set of evolving populations (one per affective state) are kept on the *working memory*. The genetic algorithm only operates on populations in working memory. These can be saved persistently in the *long-term memory*. Furthermore, high fitness hypotheses (not necessarily from the same population) are saved in the long-term memory's *gallery*. Hypotheses from the gallery can, then, provide elements to the initial population thus, promoting high fitness hypotheses evolution. This model is summarized in Fig. 3.

At the core of the model lies a standard implementation of the genetic algorithm (Mitchell, 1999). The algorithm's inputs are: (a) the *critic ensemble* for ranking candidate hypotheses; (b) *stopping criteria* to end the algorithm; (c) the *size of the population*, p, to be maintained; (d) the *selection method*, *SM*, to select among the hypotheses in a population. In general, the higher the fitness, the higher the probability of being selected; (e) r, the *crossover rate*, defining the population percentage which is subjected to crossover; (f) m, the *mutation rate*, defining the population percentage subjected to mutation; (g) e, the *elitism rate*, defining the population percentage which propagates unchanged to the next generation.

The hypothesis space encodes the different expression modalities. Section 4 shows some possibilities for this encoding. Hypotheses are subjected to two genetic operators: crossover and mutation. Crossover takes two parent hypotheses from the current generation and creates two offspring by recombining portions of the parents. Mutation exists to provide a continuous source of variation in the population. This operator essentially randomizes the values of a random number of the hypothesis' parameters. Selection among hypotheses is probabilistic and proportional to the fitness. Fitness is assigned by the critic ensemble.

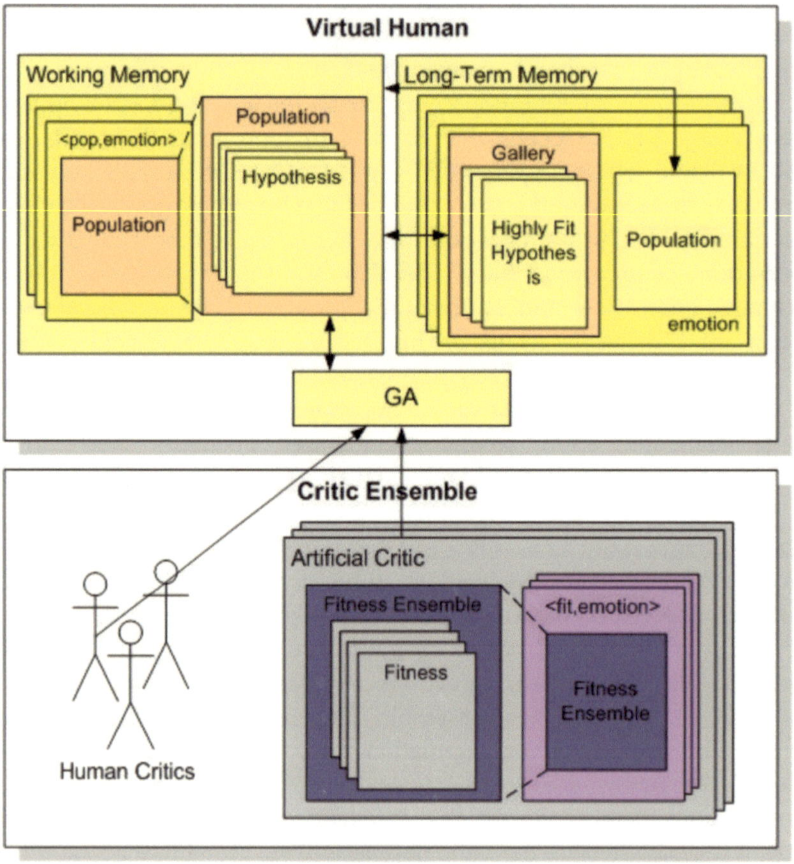

Fig. 3. The evolutionary model for expression of emotions in virtual humans

The critic ensemble defines several *critics* per affective state. Critics can be artificial, in which case fitness is inspired on art theory, or human, in which case fitness reflects the subjective opinion of the critic. An artificial critic consists of a set of *population fitness functions* and a set of *hypothesis fitness functions*. A population fitness function calculates a hypothesis' fitness with respect to the other hypotheses in the population. A hypothesis fitness function assigns an absolute fitness to each hypothesis, independently of the others. Both kinds of function are normalized to lie in the range [0.0;1.0] and the final fitness is calculated as the weighted average among all fitness functions. Regarding human critics, there are several advantages to bringing humans to the selection loop (Sayre, 2007): (a) art literature is far from being able to fully explain what is valued in the arts; (b) art is dynamic and values different things at different times. Furthermore, bringing humans into the evaluation process accommodates individual, social and cultural differences in expression of emotions (Keltner et al., 2003; Mesquita, 2003). Moreover, as discussed in future work, if the fitness functions are unknown, then the model might be made to learn from human experts. Two disadvantages are that humans may reduce variety in the population, causing convergence to a specific style, and that the evolution process becomes much slower. For these reasons, the human fitness function (as well as any other) may be selectively deactivated.

Finally, notice the virtual human needs to keep track of several populations, one per affective state, even though only a single one is evolving at any instant of time. The working memory keeps the current state of evolving populations. In real life, creating an artistic product may take a long time (Sayre, 2007). Therefore, to accommodate this characteristic, the whole set of evolving populations can be saved, at any time, in long-term memory. Implementation-wise this corresponds to saving all information about the population in XML format. The interaction between working and long-term memory provides the foundations for life-long learning, where the virtual human can adapt to changing critics.

4. Results

The models we propose for lighting and screen expression are very expressive. For screen expression, consider the space which is defined by the application of one filter to each of the virtual human's body groups. Implementation-wise this is accomplished by having one composition layer per body group, where only that body group is active. Each layer is assigned its own filter. Rendering all layers will compose the whole virtual human. Examples of points in this exploration space are shown on the first eight images of Fig. 4. For lighting expression, let us restrict ourselves to configurations of the *three-point lighting technique* (Millerson, 1999; Birn, 2006). It is a configuration composed of the following light "roles": (a) *key light*, which is the main source of light focusing the character; (b) *fill light*, which is a low-intensity light that fills an area that is otherwise too dark; (c) *back light*, which is used to separate the character from the background. Moreover, we'll use only the key and fill lights, as these define the main illumination in the scene (Millerson 1999) and the back light can be computationally expensive (Birn 2006). Both lights are modeled as directional lights and, according to standard lighting practice (Birn 2006), only the key light is set to cast shadows. Examples of points in the lighting expression space are shown in the last seven images in Fig. 4.

Having shown that we are dealing with a very large expression space, what remains to be defined is how to define the mappings between affective states and lighting and screen expression. Here we'll exemplify our evolutionary model for the case of learning how to express 'anger' with lighting expression. The lighting hypothesis encoding is as described in the previous paragraph. Furthermore, we'll ignore all human critics and use a single artificial critic with the following fitness functions:

- The *red color* function, with weight 4.0, assigns higher fitness the smaller the Euclidean distance between the light's diffuse color to pure red. This function is applied both to the key and fill lights. Red is chosen because, in Western culture, red tends to be associated with excitation or nervousness (Fraser & Banks, 2004);
- The *low-angle illumination* function, with weight 1.5, assigns higher fitness the closer the Euclidean distance between the key light's angle about the x axis to 20°. The rationale is that illumination from below is unnatural, bizarre and frightening (Millerson, 1999);
- The *opaque shadow* function, with weight 1.0, assigns higher fitness the closer the key light's shadow opacity parameter is to 0. The rationale is that hard, crisp shadows convey a mysterious and harsh character (Millerson, 1999; Birn, 2006);

- The *low complexity* function, with weight 0.5, assigns higher fitness to less complex hypotheses. The rationale is that humans naturally value artefacts which can express many things in a simple manner (Machado, 2006). A lowest complexity hypothesis was defined to be one which has: diffuse color equal to a grayscale value (i.e. with equal R,G,B components); K_d equal to 2.0; and K_s equal to 0.0;
- The *key high-angle* function, with weight 0.5, assigns higher fitness the closer the Euclidean distance between the key light's angle about the x axis to ±30°. This is a standard guideline for good illumination (Millerson, 1999). Notice this function contradicts the low-angle illumination function. This is acceptable, as guidelines in art can be contradictory (Sayre, 2007);
- The *key-fill symmetry* function, with weight 0.5, which assigns higher fitness if the fill light angles are symmetrical to the key light's. This is also a standard guideline for good illumination (Millerson, 1999);
- The *novelty* function, with weight 0.5, which assigns higher fitness the more novel the hypothesis is w.r.t. the rest of the population. This is a population fitness function. The idea is that novelty is usually appreciated in the arts (Sayre, 2007).

Having defined the artificial critic, the genetic algorithm was run for 50 iterations with the following parameters: p = 50, r = 0.70, m = 0.00, e = 0.10 and SM = *tournamentSelection*. The 44th generation was evaluated as having the best value of 2.3324, with its best hypothesis having a fitness of 0.9005. Five of the initial populations' hypotheses as well as five of the 44th generation are shown in Fig. 5. Finally, a graph showing population value and highest fitness evolution is shown in Fig. 6.

5. Conclusions and future work

This chapter argues for the importance of the kind of expression we find in the arts to the affective computing field. Emotions are intrinsically related to the value of art. For the artist, it is a means to come to terms with what he is experiencing affectively. For the audience, through empathy, it is a means to learn about the human condition. Furthermore, the kind of affective states which are reflected in works of art go beyond the kind of emotions we experience in our regular daily lives. The artist seeks to express an affective state in all its subtlety and peculiarity. This is why artists require flexible media and use lines, shapes, words, sounds and the body to express themselves. The affective computing field has been neglecting the kind of expression we find in the arts. Virtual humans are a case in point. Thus far, research has focused on the expression of emotions using body, face and voice. But why limit ourselves to the body?

Drawing on accumulated knowledge from the arts, we propose a virtual human model for the expression of emotions which goes beyond the body and uses lights, shadows, composition and filters. Regarding light expression, a pixel-based lighting model is defined which provides several control parameters. Parameter interpolation based on parametric cubic curves supports sophisticated lighting transitions. Regarding screen expression, filtering and composition are explored. Filtering consists of rendering the scene to a temporary texture, manipulating it using shaders and, then, presenting it to the user. Filters can be concatenated to generate a combined effect. In composition, aspects of the scene objects are separated into layers, which are subjected to independent lighting constraints and filters, before being combined to generate the final image. Regarding emotion synthesis, the OCC emotion model is integrated. To learn mappings from affective states to multimodal expression, we propose an evolutionary approach based on genetic algorithms.

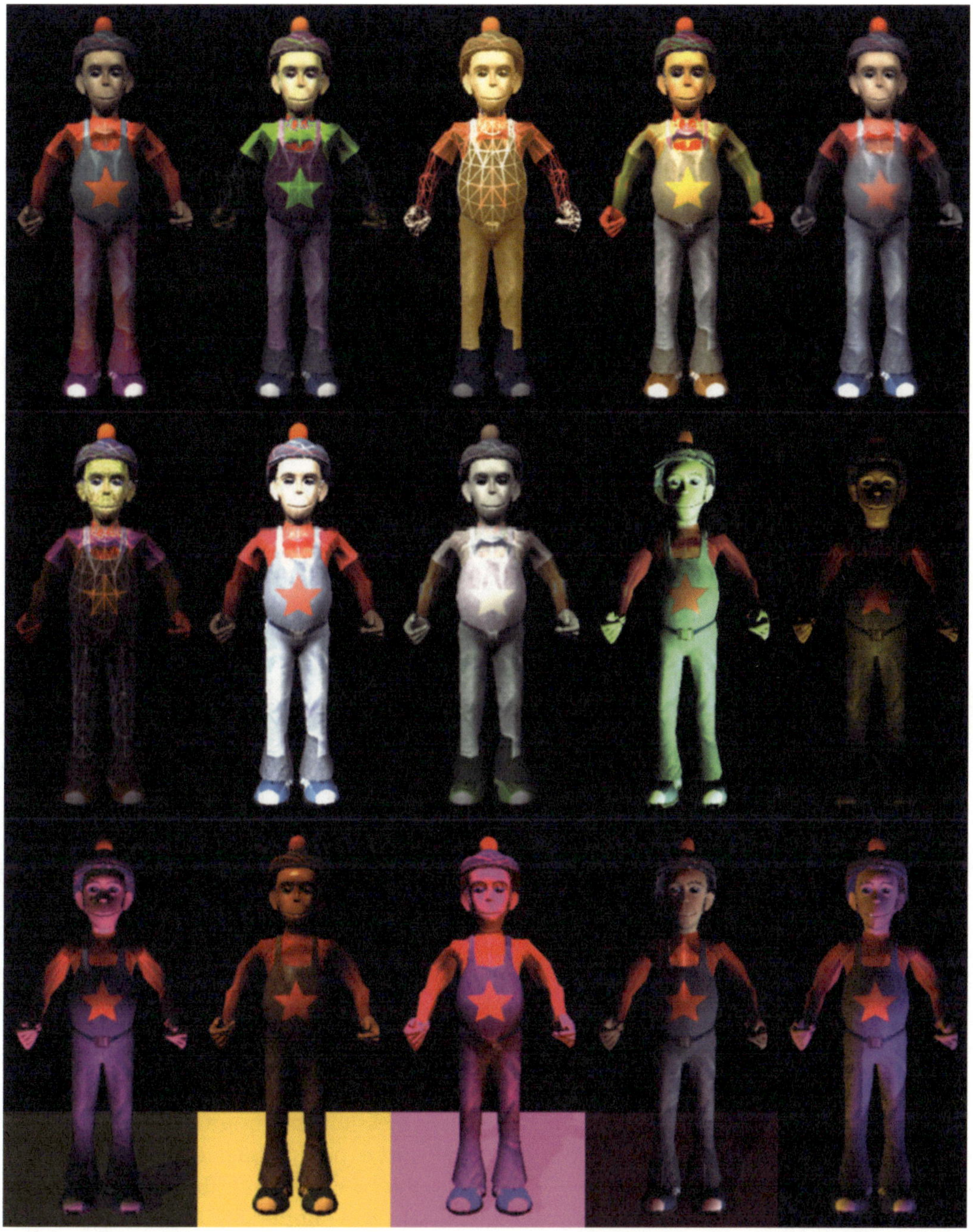

Fig. 4. The lighting and screen expression space. The first eight pictures correspond to assigning different filters to the virtual human's body groups, without manipulating lights. The last seven pictures correspond to variations of the three-point lighting configuration, without manipulation of filters. Bodily expression is kept constant in all images.

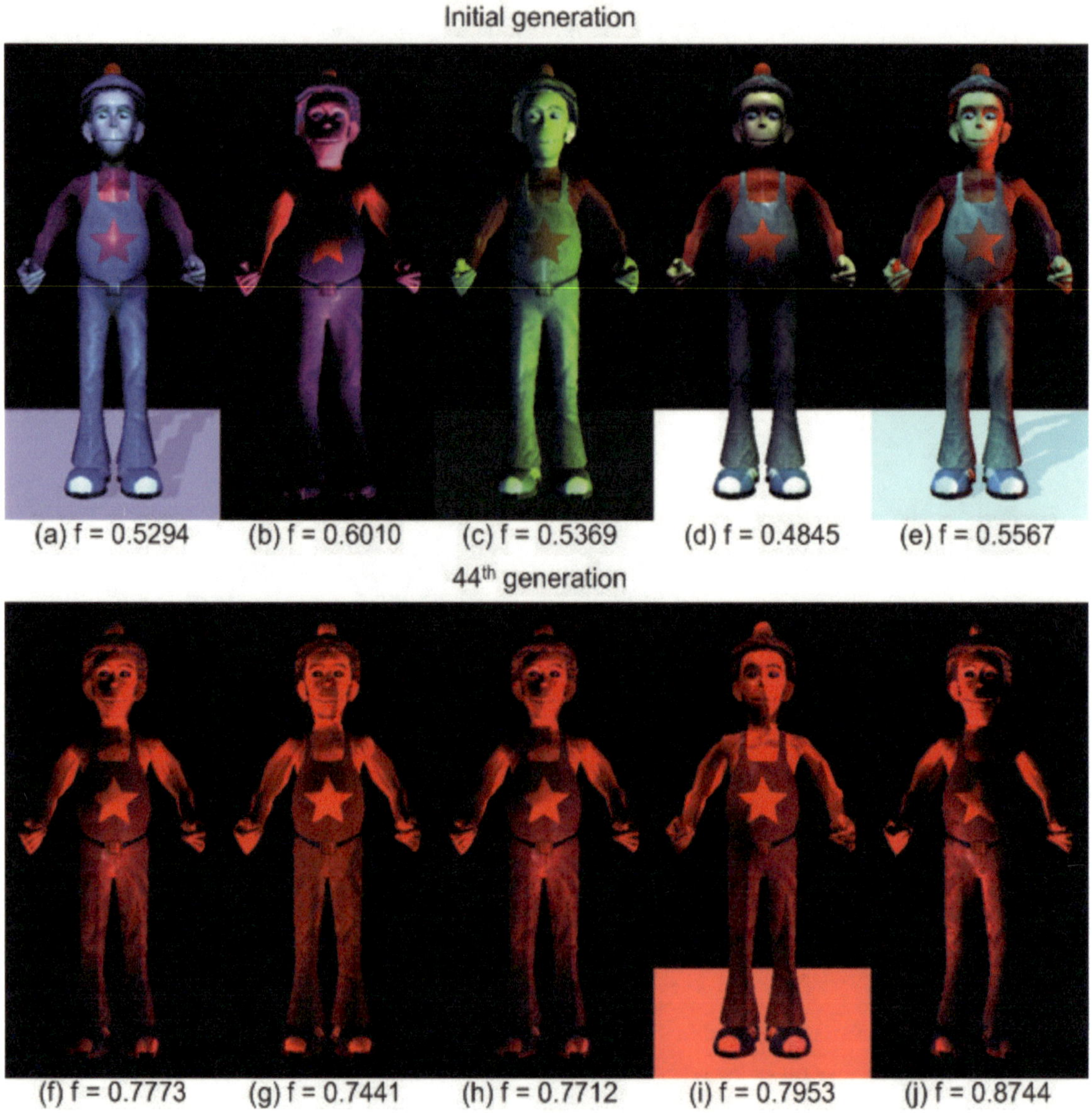

Fig. 5. The initial and 44th generation of a 50-iteration run of the evolutionary model

We've shown how broad our lighting and screen expression spaces are and demonstrated our evolutionary approach for the case of learning to express anger using lights. In the future, we'll explore fitness functions. This will require us to survey the literature on art theory and contact artists themselves. Artificial and human critics, respectively, accommodate, in our model, both of these forms of feedback. An interesting line of research would be to learn, through human critics, new fitness functions. In fact, this seems unavoidable, since it is clear for us that the literature is insufficient to fully comprehend the kind of expression we find in the arts. Furthermore, not only should the fitness functions be learned but, also their weights. The gallery could also be used to feed supervised learning algorithms to generate models which explain highly fit hypotheses. These models could, then, feed a self-critic which would, in tandem with the usual artificial and human critics, influence the selection process. Finally, two obvious extensions to this work include exploring the camera and sound expression channels of which much knowledge already exists in the arts (Sayre, 2007).

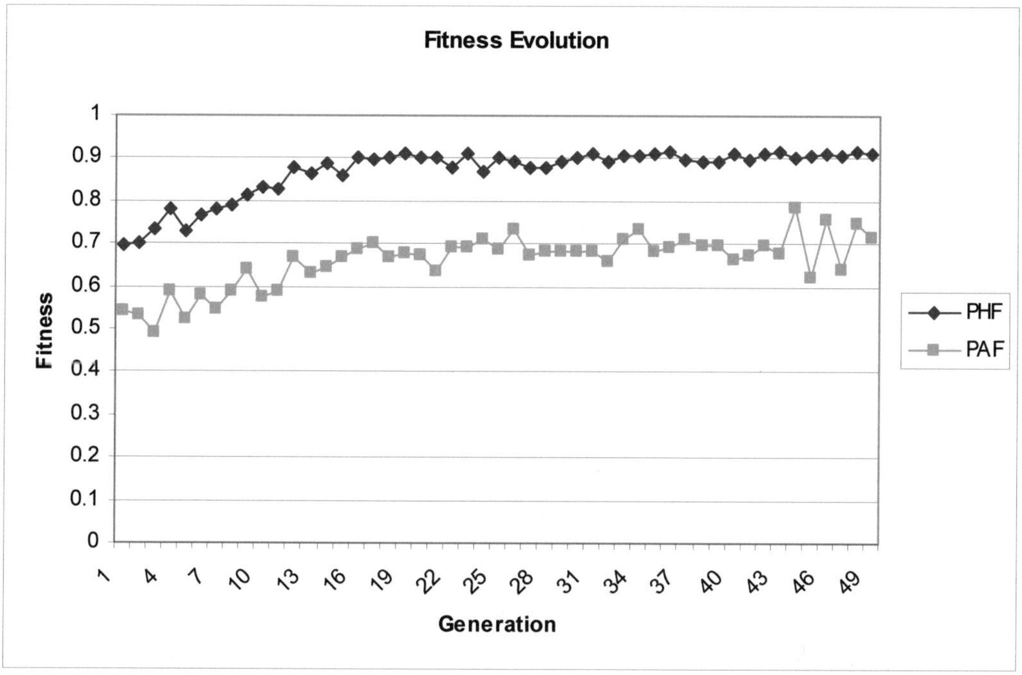

Fig. 6. Fitness evolution of a 50-iteration run of the evolutionary model

6. References

Amaya, K., Bruderlin, A. & Calvert, T. (1996). Emotion from motion, *Proceedings of Graphics Interface'96*, pp.222-229

Arijon, D. (1976). *Grammar of Film Language*, Hastings House, 0-80-382675-3, New York, USA

Averill, J., Nunley, E. & Tassinary L. (1995). Voyages of the Heart: Living an Emotionally Creative Life, *Contemporary Psychology*, Vol. 40, No.6, pp.530, 0010-7549

Batteux, C. (1969). *Les Beaux Arts Réduits à un meme Principe*, Slatkine Reprints, Genève, Switzerland

Baxandall, M. (1987). *Patterns of Intention*, Yale University Press, 0-30-003763-5, New Haven, UK

Bell, C. (1913). *Art*, Frederick A. Stokes, New York, USA

Beardsley, M. (1958). *Aesthetics: Problem in the Philosophy of Criticism*, Harcourt, New York, USA

Birn, J. (2006). *[digital] Lighting and Rendering – 2nd edn*, New Riders, 0-32-131631-2, London, UK

Block, B. (2001). *The Visual Story: Seeing the Structure of Film, TV, and New Media*, Focal Press, 0-24-080467-8, Boston, USA

Blumberg, B. & Galyean, T. (1995). Multi-Level Direction of Autonomous Creatures for Real-Time Virtual Environments, *Proceedings of SIGGRAPH'95*, Vol.30, No. 3, pp.173-182

Cassell, J. (2000). Nudge, nudge, wink, wink: Elements of face-to-face conversation for embodied conversational agents, In: *Embodied Conversational Agents*, S. P. J. Cassell, J. Sullivan and E. Churchill, (Eds.), pp. 1-27, The MIT Press, 0-26-203278-3, Massachusetts, USA

Chi, D., Costa, M., Zhao, L. & Badler, N. (2000). The EMOTE model for effort and shape, *Proceedings of SIGGRAPH 2000*, pp.173-182

Collingwood, R. (1938). *The Principles of Art*, Clarendon Press, Oxford, UK

Davidson, R., Scherer K. & Goldsmith J. (2003). *Handbook of Affective Sciences*, Oxford University Press, 0-19-512601-7, New York, USA

Davies, S. (1987). Authenticity in Musical Performance, *The British Journal of Aesthetics*, Vol. 27, No.1, pp.39-50, doi:10.1093/bjaesthetics/27.1.39

de Melo, C. & Paiva, A. (2005). Environment Expression: Expressing Emotions through Cameras, Lights and Music, *Proceedings of Affective Computing Intelligent Interaction (ACII'05)*, pp.715-722, Springer

de Melo, C. & Paiva, A. (2006a). Multimodal Expression in Virtual Humans, *Computer Animation and Virtual Worlds Journal*, Vol.17, No.3, pp.215-220

de Melo, C. & Paiva, A. (2006b). A Story about Gesticulation Expression, *Proceedings of Intelligent Virtual Agents (IVA'06)*, pp.270-281

de Melo, C. & Paiva, A. (2007). The Expression of Emotions in Virtual Humans using Lights, Shadows, Composition and Filters, *Proceedings of Affective Computing Intelligent Interaction (ACII'07)*, pp.546-557

Elliot, R. (1966). Aesthetic Theory and the Experience of Art paper, *Proceedings of the Aristotelian Society*, NS 67, III-26

Fraser, T. & Banks, A. (2004). *Designer's Color Manual: the Complete Guide to Color Theory and Application*, Chronicle Books, San Francisco, USA

Gardner, H. (1982). *Art, mind and brain: A cognitive approach to creativity*, Basic Books, 0-46-500445-8, New York, USA

Geertz, C. (1976). Art as a Cultural System, *Modern Language Notes*, Vol. 91, No.6, pp.1473-1499

Gombrich, E. (1960). *Art and Illusion; a Study in the Psychology of Pictorial Representation*, Pantheon Books, New York, USA

Goodman, N. (1968). *Languages of Art; an Approach to a Theory of Symbols*, Bobbs-Merrill, Indianapolis, USA

Gratch, J., Rickel, J., Andre, E., Badler, N., Cassell, J., Petajan, E. (2002). Creating Interactive Virtual Humans: Some Assembly Required, *IEEE Intelligent Systems*, Vol.17, No.4, pp.54–63

Gross, L. & Ward, L. (2007). *Digital Moviemaking - 6th edn*, Thomson/Wadsworth, 0-49-505034-2, Belmont, USA

Hartmann, B., Mancini, A. & Pelachaud, C. (2005). Implementing Expressive Gesture Synthesis for Embodied Conversational Agents, *Proceedings of Gesture Workshop*, pp.173-182, LNAI, Springer

Juslin, P. & Sloboda, J. (2001). *Music and Emotion: Theory and Research*, Oxford University Press, 0-19-263188-8, New York, USA

Kant, I. & Bernard, J. (1951). *Critique of judgment*, Hafner Pub. Co., New York, USA

Keltner, D., Ekman, P., Gonzaga G. & Beer, J. (2003). Facial Expression of Emotion, In: *Handbook of Affective Sciences*, R. J. Davidson, K. R. Scherer and J. H. Goldsmith, (Eds.), 415-433, Oxford University Press, 0-19-512601-7, New York, USA

Machado, F. (2006). *Inteligencia Artificial e Arte*, PhD thesis, Universidade de Coimbra

Mesquita, B. (2003). Emotions as Dynamic Cultural Phenomena, In: *Handbook of Affective Sciences*, R. J. Davidson, K. R. Scherer and J. H. Goldsmith, (Eds.), 871-890, Oxford University Press, 0-19-512601-7, New York, USA

Mill, J. (1965). What is Poetry?, In: *Mill's Essays on Literature and Society*, J. B. Schneewind, (Eds.), 103-117, Collier Books, New York, USA

Millerson, G. (1999). *Lighting for Television and Film - 3rd edn*, Focal Press, 0-24-051582-X, Oxford, USA

Mitchell, M. (1998). *An Introduction to Genetic Algorithms*, MIT Press, 0-26-263185-7, Massachusetts, USA

Moller, T. & Haines, E. (2002). *Real-Time Rendering - 2nd edn*, AK Peters, 1-56-881182-9, Massachusetts, USA

Noh, J. & Neumann, U. (1998). *A survey of facial modelling and animation techniques*, Technical report, USC Technical Report 99-705

Oatley, K. (2003). Creative Expression and Communication of Emotions in the Visual and Narrative Arts, In: *Handbook of Affective Sciences*, R. J. Davidson, K. R. Scherer and J. H. Goldsmith, (Eds.), 481-502, Oxford University Press, 0-19-512601-7, New York, USA

Ortony, A., Clore, G. & Collins, A. (1988). *The Cognitive Structure of Emotions*, Cambridge University Press, Cambridge, USA

Perlin, K. & Goldberg, A. (1996). Improv: A System for Scripting Interactive Actors, *Virtual Worlds in Proceedings of SIGGRAPH'96*, pp.205-216

Picard, R. (1997). *Affective Computing*, MIT Press, 0-58-500319-X, Massachusetts, USA

Sayre, H. (2007). *A World of Art - 5th edn*, Prentice Hall, 978-0-132221-86-3, New Jersey, USA

Schroder, M. (2004). *Speech and emotion research: an overview of research frameworks and a dimensional approach to emotional speech synthesis*, PhD thesis, Institute of Phonetics, Saarland University

Sontag, S. (1966). *Against Interpretation and Other Essays*, Farrar, Straus & Giroux, New York, USA

St-Laurent, S. (2004). *Shaders for Game Programmers and Artists*, Thomson/Course Technology, Massachusetts, USA

Wollheim, R. (1980). *Art and its Objects – 2nd edn*, Cambridge University Press, 0-52-129706-0, Cambridge, UK

Zettl, H. (2008). *Sight, Sound, Motion: Applied Media Aesthetics – 5th edn*, Thomson/Wadsworth, 0-49-509572-9, Belmont, USA

12

Computational Emotion Model for Virtual Characters

Zhen Liu
Faculty of Information Science and Technology, Ningbo University
China

1. Introduction

Computer game is becoming a new computer application field, its one of key technology is to set up intelligent virtual characters. Emotion is of the highest importance in modern computer games. The essence of computer game lies in waking a user's emotion experience; modeling virtual character's emotion is the key goal in computer game. David Freeman pointed out in his best-seller book "Creating Emotion in Games"(Freeman, 2003) : the revolution in the future of computer game is not the technology, but to create emotion experience. Truthfully, many directors of computer game products have already realized that the contents must be full of emotion experience.

Computer game industry needs more clever virtual characters with an intelligent model. Intelligent virtual character is a new research field that integrates artificial life and computer animation together. Artificial life is the research field that tries to describe and simulate life by set-ting up virtual artificial systems with the properties of life. We can get more understanding from the developing history of computer animation. Early computer animation only includes shape and movement of a geometry model, it is very difficult to draw complex natural landscape, and artificial life can help to solve these problems. In a general, an artificial life model is based on bottom-up strategy. Emergence is the key concept of artificial life. It means a complex system is from the simple location interactions of individuals. Another key concept of artificial life is adaptation, which means evolution. In 80 years of the 20th century, many models of computer animation were presented, such as particle models, L-system, kinematics and dynamics, facial animation, etc. In 90 years of the 20th century, artificial life influenced the development of the computer animation greatly (Tu, 1994); Funge presented the cognitive model for computer animation (Funge, 1999), On the basis of the Funge's a cognitive model for computer animation, we can illustrate a virtual character's hierarchy of computer animation in Fig 1. In order to create believable characters, people hope to set up computational emotion models for virtual characters.

There are a lot of relative researches on virtual character and emotion model; we only introduce part of them. Badler et al. use finite state machine to control a virtual character's behavior, personality characteristic was expressed by locomotion parameters (Badler, 1997), they also built a system called Emote to add personality and emotion for virtual characters (Chi, 2000), Ball et al. proposed a Bayesian network-based model of personality for speaking

(Ball, 2000), they only used two traits (dominance and friendliness). Goldberg realized a script-based animation system for virtual characters (Goldberg, 1997), users could add some personality parameters in script file. Rousseau et al. used a value for a personality on social psychology (Rousseau, 1998). The OZ project at CMU made a lot of researches on emotion and personality for believable agents (Bates, 1994; Loyall, 1997; Reilly, 1996). Blumberg in MIT presented a mental model of an autonomous virtual dog with a cognitive architecture (Blumberg, 1997). A virtual dog had a motivation system to express its behavior and personality. Blumberg also presented a learning method of the virtual dog, and his technique was based on Reinforcement Learning (RL)(Blumberg, 2002). Moffat presented a personality frame by emotion theory in psychology (Moffat, 1997), he used Frijda's theory of emotion to illustrate the relation between emotion and personality, but his model is abstract and lacks in mathematical details. N.M.Thalmann suggested that virtual character should not only look visual, they must have behavior, perception, memory and some reasoning intelligence (Thalmann, 1994), D.Thalman presented the concept of virtual character society (Thalmann, 2004; Noser, 1995), which is built according to agent architecture, Musse et al. depicted a crowd model for virtual characters (Musse, 2001). Egges et al. built a multi-layer personality model by the Big Five theory (Egges, 2004), their goal was to create believable virtual avatar that could interact with natural language, emotions and gestures, this personality model set up the relation between personality and emotion by a matrix. Gratch et al. presented a domain-independent framework for modeling emotion, they supposed that people had beliefs about past events, emotions about those events and could alter those emotions by altering the beliefs (Gratch, 2004). Cassell et.al realized a behavior animation toolkit (Cassell, 2001), and Pelachaud et.al presented a method to create facial expression for avatars (Pelachaud, 2002). Human emotion is related to stimulus and cognitive appraisal (Ekman, 1979; Ortony, 1988; Picard, 1997), most of emotion models in psychology are qualitative, there are little researching on formalization of emotion, personality and motivation. On the basis of previous research (Liu, 2002;Liu, 2005), a computational emotion model is presented in this chapter; the goal is to construct virtual characters with the ability of emotion self-control in environment. The emotion model gives a quantitative description for an emotion process; it can integrate emotion, personality and motivation together.

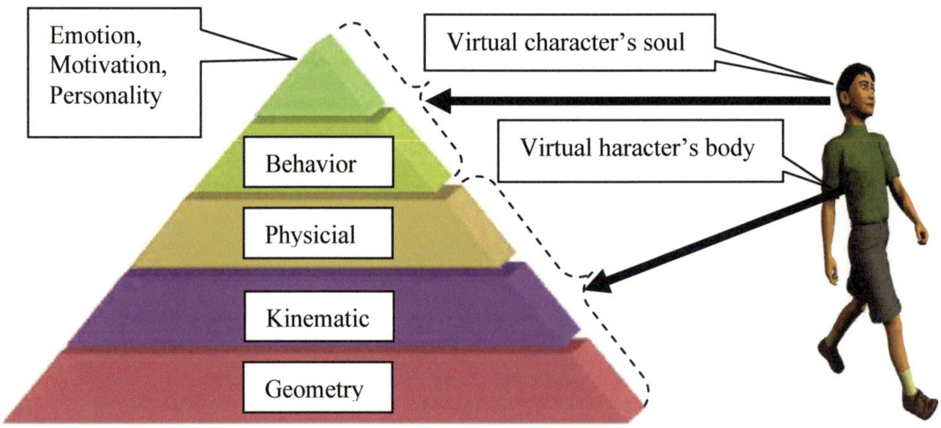

Fig. 1. Intelligent virtual character 's modelling hierarchy

The remainder of this chapter is organized as follows: In the section 2, mental architecture of virtual character is presented by cognitive model. In the section 3, a formalization model of emotion is set up. In the section 4, animation expression of 3D virtual characters is proposed. In the section 5, an example of the model is introduced, and conclusion is in Section 6.

2. Mental architecture of a virtual character

A virtual character is regarded as an agent with a built-in structure. It should be provided with the mechanism of physical or mental variables that include emotion, personality, motivation and social norm. Based on Freud theory (Bernstein,1997; Satrongman, 2003), ID is the inborn, unconscious portion of the personality where instincts reside, and it operates on the pleasure principle. Libiduo is a source of psychic energy. Ego is responsible for organizing ways in the real world, and it operates on the reality principle. Superego is the rulers that control what a virtual character should do or not. The research is mainly based on behavior animation, and the goal is setting up a mental state-based animation model for 3D virtual character. The cognitive structure of a virtual character is shown in Fig 4:

(1) Sensors module collects environment's information from memory module. In this chapter, we only consider visual sensors, which can read from memory module to get current information of a 3D environment.

(2) Perception module is different from sensor module, and a virtual character can perceive the meaning of objects in environment through perception module. The perception module reads and filtrates information from sensor module and collect information of outer stimuli, a simplified attention mechanism can be integrated in perception module. In a dynamic environment, a virtual character needs not focus on all objects in environment. In this chapter, an attention object list can be set up beforehand for different virtual character. If an object is in the scope of perception, and is not in attention object list, character will not perceive the object. Moreover, the perception module reads the memory module to get mental variables, knowledge, and social norm. Meanwhile, perception module can communicate with mental variables by memory module.

In this chapter, we only discuss the visual perception. Synthetic vision is an important method for visual perception, which can accurately simulate the vision from view of a virtual character, the method synthesis vision on PC. When a virtual character needs to observe the virtual environment, the demo system can render the scene in invisible windows with no texture, and get a synthesis vision image. The virtual character can decide what he (she) could see from the values in color buffer and depth buffer. The purpose of using color buffer is to distinguish objects with different color code. The purpose of using depth buffer is to get the space position of a pixel in the window. In order to simulate perception for space, we can use static partition of scene octree that is a hierarchical variant of spatial-occupancy enumeration (Noser, 1995). We partition the static part of the scene in advance and record octree in data base module. We can use octree to solve path searching problem, as scene octree and the edges among them compose a graph, and so the path searching problem can be transformed to the problem of searching for a shortest path from one empty node to another in the graph (See Fig.2). In a complex virtual environment in which there are a lot of virtual characters, synthetic vision will be costly. Furthermore, this method cannot get the detail semantic information of objects. Therefore, we present another efficient method for simulation of visual perception. The visual perception of virtual character is limited to a sphere, with a radius of R and angle scope of θ_{max}. The vision sensor is at point O_{eyes} (the midpoint between the two eyes), and sets up local left-handed coordinate system. O_{eyes} is the origin and X_{axis} is along front orientation (See Fig.3). To determine whether the object P_{ob} is visible, the first step is to judge whether P_{ob} is in the vision scope. If the distance from P_{ob} to O_{eyes} is less than R and the angle between the ray and X_{axis} is less than $\theta_{max/2}$, the object P_{ob} is in the vision scope. The second step is to detect whether other obstacle occlude P_{ob}. We can shoot a ray OP from the O_{eyes} to P_{ob}, cylinders can serve as the bounding boxes of obstacles. In order to check the intersection of OP with an obstacle's bounding box, we can check whether OP intersects with a circle that is a projection of the obstacle's bounding box, and further to check whether OP intersects with the obstacle's bounding box. In a 3D virtual environment, there are a lot of dynamic objects, on which we set up feature points (such as geometric center). If one feature point is visible, the object is regarded as visible. In our demo system, all obstacles are building.

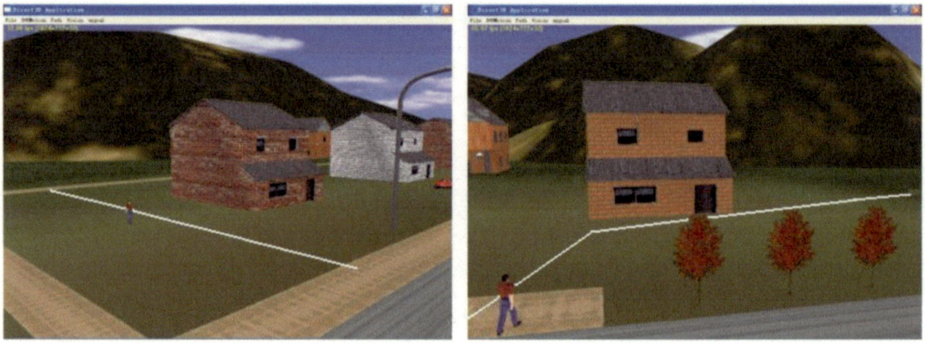

Fig. 2. A* path searching (the left is no obstacle and the right is near a house)

Based on the Gibson's theory of affordances (Gibson, 1986), affordances are relations among space, time and action. A character can perceive these affordances directly. An affordance is invariance for environment. In this chapter, we use the Gibson's theory to guide navigation, affordances of objects hints navigation information. We set up some navigation information in database for special area or objects in the 3D virtual environment. For example, when a character wants to walk across a road, we set navigation information of the zebra crossing is accessible, so that the character will select zebra crossing. We use scene octree to simulate the character's perception for static object in 3D virtual environment. The locations of all dynamic objects are recorded in memory module in animation time step. If an object is visible, we suppose that a virtual character moves on a 2D plane, let D_{ovc} is detection radius, d_{min} is avoiding distance for the character, if $D_{ovc}<d_{min}$, the virtual character will read navigation information of the object from memory. With doing so, when a virtual character wants to move from one place to another. We can set up some navigating points in a 3D environment, and a virtual character can seek the navigating point that is nearest to him and move to it. Usually, a virtual character moves from one navigating point to another. A default plan is a script file that records default-navigating points. If there is no external stimulus, a virtual character walks by a walking plan. When a virtual character perceives an object or events, he may stop walking and make some actions, then he continues walking to the nearest navigating point.

A virtual character has the sensor of detection barrier or stimulus, if a barrier or stimulus is in the fan-shaped region, the character will sense the barrier or stimulus, and read the semantic information for navigation. The navigation arithmetic of a virtual character is as follows(see Fig.3):

Step1: Read first location and goal location, stimulus location, octree of virtual environment, and motion step. Go to **Step2**.

Step2: If the distance from current location to goal location is less than motion step, the navigation is over; or else, go to **Step3**.

Step3: If the virtual character is in a navigation area (the distance from current location to navigation point is less than motion step), he will read the semantic navigation information navigation area from database, the navigation information will guide the virtual character to select a possible motion path; or else, go to **Step4**.

Step4: the virtual character will move along on the road, he will detect any barrier or stimulus by his sensors, if he senses a barrier, he will read the semantic navigation information on the barrier from memory, he will change motion direction and move by navigation information, go to **Step5**. If he senses a stimulus, he will read the semantic interaction information on the stimulus from memory module and knowledge module, in the emergent condition, the virtual character will leave road, he will move in free area and detect buildings by octree. When the emergent behavior is over, he will return to road, go to **Step 5**.

Step 5: the virtual character will move to the next navigation area, go to **Step2**.

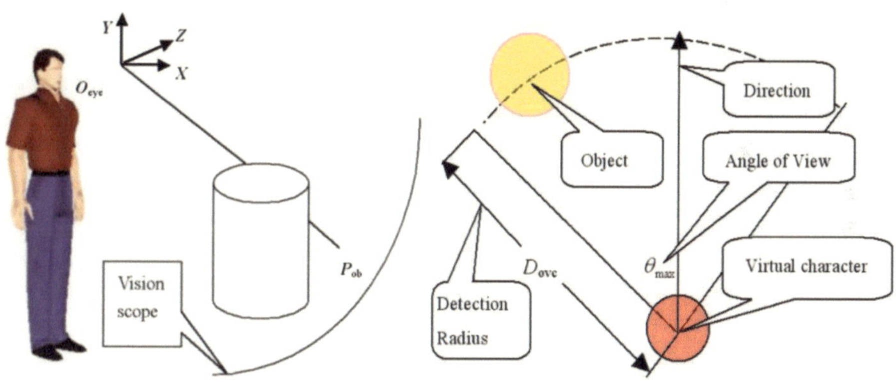

Fig. 3. Visible detection and detection of object's affordance

(3)Plan module executes navigation behavior code by perception model, it also executes a (expressive) behavior code by stimuli, emotion, personality, motivation, norm and knowledge, the detail is in section 3.

(4) Behavior module reads plan module and creates action codes for actuator module. There are several behaviors in the same time, for example, a virtual character can have smile behavior , calling to other's behavior and walking to a place behavior. Inhibitory gain and fatigue are time sequence characteristic of behavior. The higher Inhibitory gain, the longer the duration of the behavior is and new behavior is excited only under new stimuli. Fatigue means that behavior with low degree of priority can obtain the chance to carry out, once a certain behavior is carried out, the behavior will stop at some time (Tu, 1994). We can introduce the inhibitory gain coefficient (a real number greater than one) and fatigue

coefficient (a real number smaller than one) to measure inhibitory gain and fatigue correspondingly.
(5) Actuator module executes the behavior in behavior code, it includes inverse kinematics arithmetic to drive locomotion, and read motion capture data from memory module (memory module will read motion capture data in database). When actuator module successful executes a behavior code, it will write to memory module with an action sign that indicate whether the character moves to or executes a behavior code.
(6) Database module includes 3D geometry of virtual environment, original information, such as, the original location and parameters of virtual character, motion capture data, 3D model and location of objects, default motion plan scripts that record some goal location.
(7) Memory module serves as a center of information share among all other modules.
(8) Id module includes gender and need variables, gender variable is related to behaviors. Need variables include physical needs (hungry, etc) and psychic needs(safety). Let *GD* is a gender variable for a virtual character, $-1 \leq GD \leq 1$. If $GD<0$, the virtual character is a female, If GD>0, the virtual character is a male if $GD=0$, the virtual character is neutral. |GD| is the measure of gender, if |GD|=1, the virtual character is a pure female or male. A virtual character can have many needs, Let ***NED*** is need vector, $\boldsymbol{NED}=\{ned_1, \ldots, ned_{\mathrm{ne}}\}$, ned_i is a need variable, $i \in [1, ne]$, *ne* is the number of needs, for example, let ned_1 is food energy, $0 \leq ned_1 \leq 1$, if $ned_1=0$, the virtual character is not hungry, if $ned_1=1$, the virtual character is very hungry.
(9) Ego module includes emotion, personality and motivation. This module read external stimuli from memory (the perception module write stimuli information to memory module). Activation of an emotion is relative to external stimuli and inner mental variables. If an emotion is active, this module will create emotion expression, emotion expression code will be sent to behaviour module. Emotion is the core of the module, personality is some stable psychological traits of a virtual character, and motivation variables include some physiology parameters of a virtual character.
(10) Superego module includes norm and knowledge. Norm module includes status, interaction information and interaction rules, it controls the process of a nonverbal social interaction, and knowledge provides the social knowledge for virtual character.

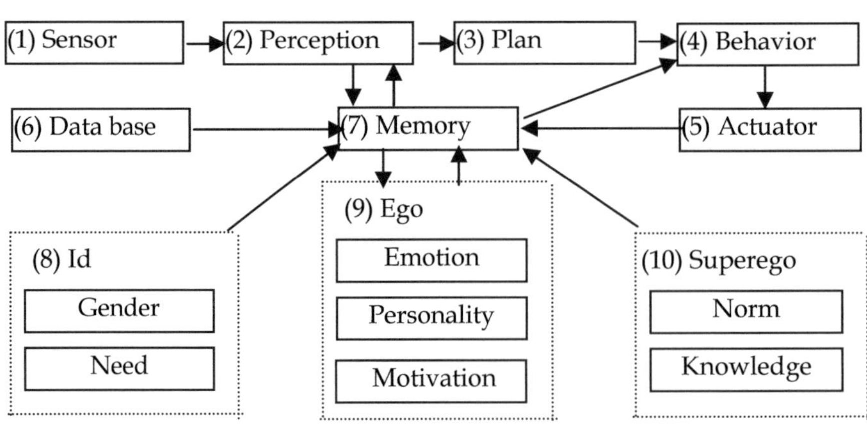

Fig. 4. Virtual character 's cognitive structure

3. Emotion model of virtual character

3.1 Formalization of some relative concepts about emotion

There are some classical research works in emotion model. The theories of emotion in psychology demonstrate that emotion is a cognitive interpretation of those responses to emotional experiences. Emotion associates the environment stimulus with the character personality on the basis of James-Lange theory of emotion and Schachter-Singer theory of emotion, and occurs with motivation simultaneously. In some sense, motivation can intensify emotion, but emotion can also create motivation. Emotion is usually transitory, with a relatively clear beginning and ending, and a short duration. Ortony et al set up an emotion cognitive model that is called OCC model (Ortony, 1988)(see Fig.5 and Fig.6). In the model, emotions are generated in reaction to objects, actions of agents and events. They outlined specifications for 22 emotion types.

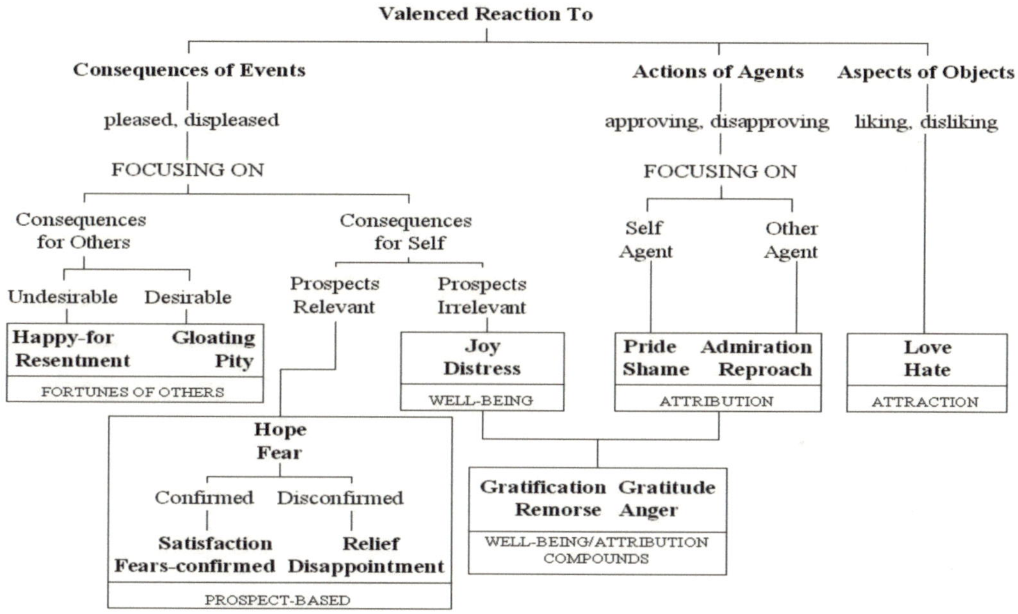

Fig. 5. Emotion types of OCC model

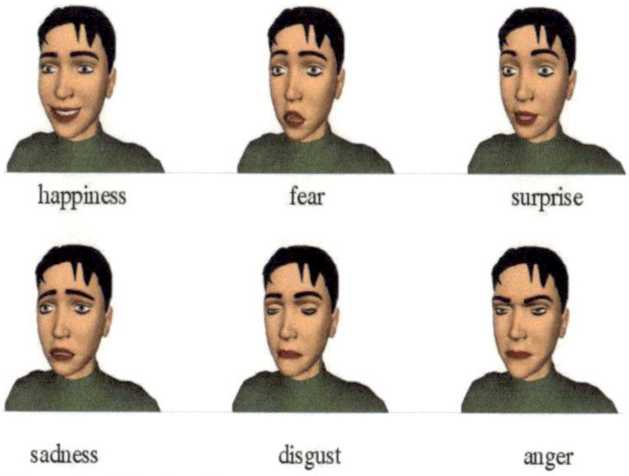

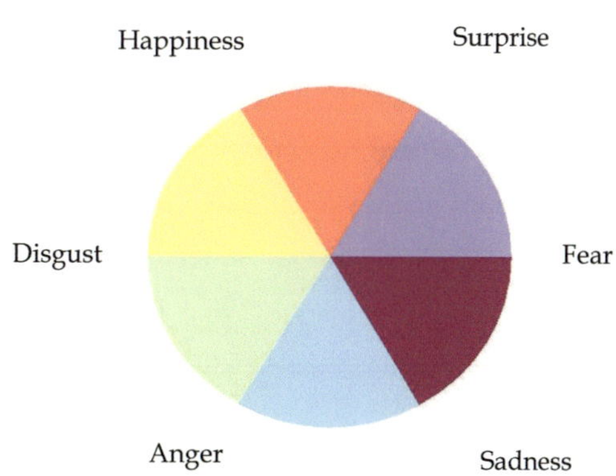

Fig. 6. Six basic emotions expression

Picard gave the concept of affective computing for interface between character and computer (Picard, 1997). In the opinion of Plutchik's emotion classification (Satrongman, 2003), emotion intensity distributes on a "circle" with eight basic categories of emotion that motivate various kinds of adaptive behavior of character. In the center of "circle", emotion intensity is zero, while in the edge of "circle" emotion intensity is one. In this chapter, the simplified Plutchik's emotion classification on face expression is as follows: happiness, surprise, sadness, fear, disgust, and anger. We can integrate OCC emotion model and Plutchik's emotion classification together; a virtual character can have 22 types emotion in OCC model, and six basic face expressions. We can set a function from OCC emotion types to six face expressions in table 1.

Plutchik's types	Emotion types in OCC model
Happiness	Happy-for, Gloating, Joy, Pride, Admiration, Love, Hope, Satisfaction, Relief, Gratification, Gratitude
Disgust	Hate
Anger	Anger, Reproach, Hate
Sadness	Resentment, Pity, Distress, Shame, Disappointment, Remorse
Fear	Fear, Fear-confirmed
Surprise	By context

Table 1. Relation between Plutchik's simplified emotion types and OCC emotion types

In this section, we give some new definitions for describing emotion process of virtual characters.

For a certain virtual character, ***BE*** is a basic emotion set, ***BE***={be_1, …… ,be_N}, $i \in [1, N]$, be_i is a basic emotion (such as happiness). N is the number of basic emotion class. $EI_i(t)$ is the intensity of be_i, $EI_i(t) \in [0, 1]$, t is time variable. $\boldsymbol{be}_i$ is the unit vector of be_i. For example, be_1={1,…,0}, be_N={0,…,1}. Let ES is emotion state, ***E*** is represented emotion vector of ES, the projection length of ***E*** on $\boldsymbol{be}_i$ is $EI_i(t)$. ***E*** can be represented as formula (1):

$$\boldsymbol{E} = \sum_{i=1}^{N} EI_i(t)\, \boldsymbol{be}_i \,. \tag{1}$$

Let $\boldsymbol{E}_1$ and $\boldsymbol{E}_2$ are two emotion vectors, the synthesis of $\boldsymbol{E}_1$ and $\boldsymbol{E}_2$ is represented as $\boldsymbol{E}_1 + \boldsymbol{E}_2$ in formula (2).

$$\boldsymbol{E}_1 + \boldsymbol{E}_2 = \sum_{i=1}^{N} [\, EI_{i1}(t)\, \boldsymbol{be}_{i1} + EI_{i2}(t)\, \boldsymbol{be}_{i2} \,]. \tag{2}$$

Let ***EP*** is the set of all emotion vectors, if any element of ***EP*** satisfies to formula (1)(2), ***EP*** is called emotion vector space, $\boldsymbol{be}_i$ is called the basic emotion vector.

Let ***PS*** is a personality set, $PS_k(t)$ is the personality variable, ***PS***={ $PS_k(t)$}, Θ [$PS_k(t)$] is the intensity of $PS_k(t)$, *nps* is the number of personality(k=1,…, *nps*), and $0 \leq \Theta[PS_k(t)] \leq 1$.
MV is a motivation variable set, $MV_m(t)$ is the motivation variable, ***MV*** ={ $MV_m(t)$}, *w* is the number of motivation variable(m=1,…,*w*). Θ [$MV_m(t)$] is the intensity of $MV_m(t)$, $0 \leq \Theta[MV_m(t)] \leq 1$.

3.2 How an emotion is active

Let $O_j(t)$ is an external stimuli, *no* is the number of stimuli(j=1,…, *no*). Θ [$O_{ji}(t)$] is the stimuli intensity function of $O_j(t)$ for emotion be_i , and $0 \leq \Theta[O_{ji}(t)] \leq 1$.
In a virtual environment, there are a lot of stimuli, a virtual character can express emotion under stimuli or not, any virtual character has the ability of resisting external stimuli, let $C_i(t)$ is the average resistive intensity for emotion be_i. If stimuli intensity is bigger than $C_i(t)$, emotion expression for emotion be_i is active. The weaker $C_i(t)$ of a virtual character is, the more emotion expressive the virtual character becomes to be with emotion be_i, and $0 \leq C_i(t) \leq 1$.
In a general, a $C_i(t)$ is different for two virtual characters, personality and motivation will influence $C_i(t)$. We can give a simple method to update a $C_i(t)$.
For a certain $C_i(t)$, personality has impact on emotion state, α_{ki} is an impact coefficient from personality $PS_k(t)$ to $C_i(t)$. $NC_i(t)$ is the updating $C_i(t)$ with considering impact from personality $PS_k(t)$, $NC_i(t)=\min[\alpha_{ki} C_i(t),1]$, $\alpha_{ki}>=0$. If $\alpha_{ki}=1$, $NC_i(t)= C_i(t)$, personality has no impact on resistive intensity of emotion. $NC_i(t)$ is the updating Ci(t) with considering impact from all personality variable,

$$NC_i(t) = \sum_{k=1}^{nps} \Theta[PS_k(t)]\, NC_{ki}(t) \Big/ \sum_{k=1}^{nps} \Theta[PS_k(t)]. \qquad (3)$$

For a certain C_i(t), motivation has impact on emotion state, β_{mi} is an impact coefficient from motivation variable MV_m(t) to C_i(t). MC_{mi}(t) is the updating C_i(t) with considering impact from motivation variable MV_m(t) , $MC_{mi}(t)=\min[\beta_{mi} Ci(t),1]$, $\beta_{mi}>=0$. If $\beta_{mi}=1$, $MC_{mi}(t)= C_i(t)$, motivation variable has no impact on emotion. MC_i(t) is the updating C_i(t) with considering impact from all motivation variable, and so:

$$MC_i(t) = \sum_{m=1}^{w} \Theta[MV_m(t)]\, R_m\, MC_{mi}(t) \Big/ \sum_{m=1}^{w} \Theta[MV_m(t)]\, R_m. \qquad (4)$$

For a certain $C_i(t)$, motivation and personality has impact on emotion state in the same time, $TC_i(t)$ is the updating $C_i(t)$ with considering impact both from personality and motivation. $TC_i(t)=\min(NC_i(t), MC_i(t))$.
When an emotion be_i is active, emotion expression include three phases as follows:
(1) **Growth phase**: the intensity of an emotion class grows from its minimum value $[EI_{ji}(t)]_{min}$ to its maximum value $[EI_{ji}(t)]_{max}$. $[DT_{ji}]_{growth}$ is the duration time.

(2) **Delay phase**: the intensity of an emotion class is equal to its maximum value $[EI_{ji}(t)]_{max}$. $[DT_{ji}]_{delay}$ is the duration time.
(3) **Decay phase**: the intensity of an emotion class decrease to its minimum value $[EI_{ji}(t)]_{min}$. $[DT_{ji}]_{decay}$ is duration time.
In order to simplify the three phases, for a given be_i, we can give a default duration time for a certain external stimuli $O_{ji}(t)$ with $\Theta\,[O_{ji}(t)]_{max}=1$.The corresponding default duration time of the three phases are indicated by $DT[O_{ji}(t)]_{s\text{-}growth}$, $DT[O_{ji}(t)]_{s\text{-}delay}$ and $DT[O_{ji}(t)]_{s\text{-}decay}$. We suppose the intensity of an emotion changes with linear rule in growth phase or decay phase. The three phases are described as formula (5)-(9):

$$[EI_{ji}(t)]_{min} = [\,\Theta\,[O_{ji}(t)\text{- TCi(t)}]/(1\text{- TCi(t)}). \tag{5}$$

$$[EI_{ji}(t)]_{max} = \Theta\,[\,O_{ji}(t)]. \tag{6}$$

$$[DT_{ji}]_{growth} = [EI_{ji}(t)]_{max}\;.\;DT[O_{ji}(t)]_{s\text{-}growth} \tag{7}$$

$$[DT_{ji}]_{delay} = [EI_{ji}(t)]_{max}\;.\;DT[O_{ji}(t)]_{s\text{-}delay} \tag{8}$$

$$[DT_{ji}]_{decay} = [EI_{ji}(t)]_{max}\;.\;DT[O_{ji}(t)]_{s\text{-}decay} \tag{9}$$

4. Animation expression of 3D virtual characters

4.1 Creating expressive pose animation

In our method, a kinematic chain is used to simulate the pose animation of virtual character (Tolani, 2001), while an analytical method is used to solve inverse kinematics. In general, the kinematic chain can be expressed as: $\Delta\theta = J^{+}\,\Delta X + (I - J^{+}J)\,\Delta Z$, $\Delta\theta$ is the joint variation vector, I is the identity matrix, J is the Jacobian matrix of the set of cartesian constraints, J^{+} is the pseudo-inverse of J, ΔX is the variations of the set of cartesian constrints, ΔZ is used to minimise the distance to the attraction posture. Numerical algorithms for solving inverse kinematics are too slow to meet the demands of real-time applications. Deepak Tolani presented an analytical method for solving inverse kinematics and more accurate (Tolani, 2001). In his opinion, human limb kinematic chain can be expressed as Fig 7. Let T_1 denote the rotation matrix from the proximal to the distal site of S_1 as function of θ_1, θ_2, θ_3. T_2 similarly represents the rotation matrix from proximal to the distal site of S_2 as function of θ_5, θ_6, θ_7, and T_y is the rotation matrix produced by revolute joint F as a function of θ_4, let A is transformation matrix from proximal of F to distal S_1, B is transformation matrix from proximal S_2 to distal of F, G is the goal matrix of end effector. The kinematic chain can be denoted as: $G=T_1\,A\,T_y\,B\,T_2$, and so θ_1, θ_2, θ_3, θ_4, θ_5, θ_6, θ_7 can be solved.
Motions of whole virtual character body can be realized in the motion capture data process software, and can accumulate a motion library M. Let $M=\{m_i\}$, $i=1,....,L$, L is the number of motion in M, m_i is a motion capture data including the three dimension rotation of a joint of body, m_i is stored as BVH format file. We can blend motion capture data to create an emotional walking pose.

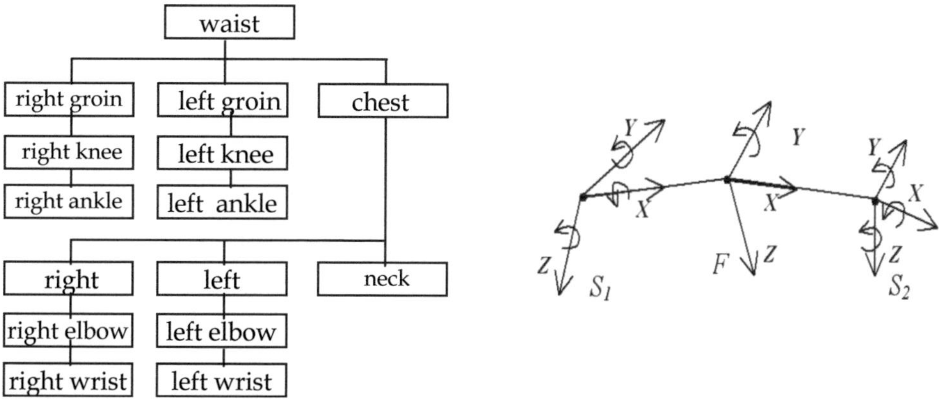

Fig. 7. Skeleton of virtual character and kinematic chain with seven degree

We can blend motion capture clips to create an emotional walking pose (see Fig. 8 and Fig. 9). The target of motion blending is to support motion concurrency. Motion concurrency means the avatar performs multiple motions at the same time. It is quite natural in our life. For example, we can greet to others while walking and we can lift a bag by one hand while making a phone call by the other hand. Motion concurrency results in different limbs performing different actions. Take greeting while walking: legs perform walking motion and arms perform greeting motion. Motion blending is to embed one motion into another and to simulate the effect of motion concurrency. We use signal interpolation to solve the problem of transition between two motions (Kovar, 2002; Lee, 2002). To calculate the phasing of each motion, generic time is needed. A motion signal can be represented as:

$$A_i = \{ \theta_{ij}(T), K_m, P_s, P_e \mid j=0,\ldots,numDof-1, m=0,\ldots,num\text{Keytime}-1\}$$

Where A_i represents the ith motion signal, θ_{ij} represents the jth freedom of A_i, Kim represents the m th key time of A_i, Ps is the starting phasing and Pe is the end phasing. Rose defines the mapping from real time T to uniform t as follows (Rose , 1998):

$$t(T)=\left(m+ \frac{T-K_m}{K_{m+1}-K_m} \right) \frac{1}{N_k-1} \tag{10}$$

Where m=max ($i \mid K_i<T$) and N_k is the number of key times.

As walking is the most frequent motion, so we do phasing calculation based on one walking cycle. For each motion signal, we find the most similar time point in the walking signal and use the generic time of this time point as the phasing value. This can be done by hand. But to be more accurate and efficient, we can use some frame mapping algorithms (Kovar, 2002; Lee, 2002). Signal interpolation is actually signal fade-in and fade-out mechanism. We define a function:

$$f=(1-\cos(\alpha\pi))/2 \tag{11}$$

In the transition time, we use (1-f) and f as the coefficients to do interpolation between the two motion signals and generate the transition motion.

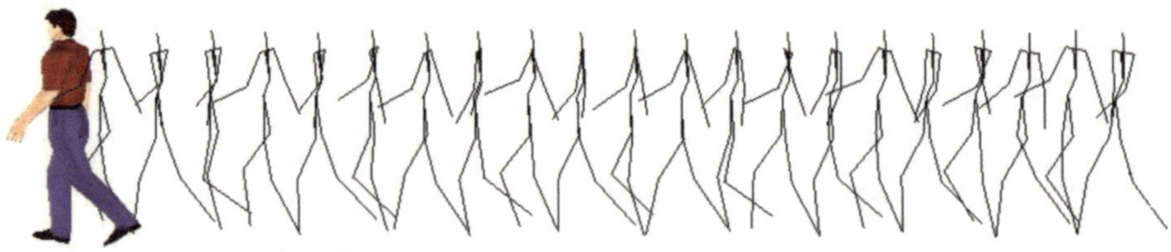

Fig. 8. Skeleton of natural walking

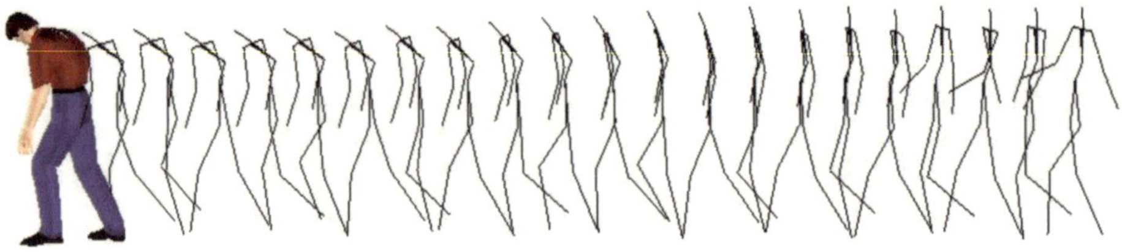

Fig. 9. Skeleton of sad walking (blend sad motion capture data to natural walking)

4.2 Facial animation

A face's geometry model is described by polygons, the location of any vertex can be represented as vector v_k , $k \in [0, L]$, L is the number of all vertex. Let $\boldsymbol{V}$ is a vector for all vertex, $\boldsymbol{V}$ is called expression vector. $\boldsymbol{V}$ is represented as formula (12).

$$\boldsymbol{V} = (v_1 ,\ldots\ldots, v_L) . \tag{12}$$

There are two rulers on $\boldsymbol{V}$:

1) For two expression vector $\boldsymbol{V}_1$ and $\boldsymbol{V}_2$, $\boldsymbol{V}_1=(v_{11} ,\ldots\ldots, v_{L1})$, $\boldsymbol{V}_2=(v_{12} ,\ldots\ldots, v_{L2})$, the synthesis of $\boldsymbol{V}_1$ and $\boldsymbol{V}_2$ is represented as formula(13):

$$\boldsymbol{V}_1 + \boldsymbol{V}_2 =(v_{11} + v_{12} ,\ldots\ldots, v_{L1}+ v_{L2}). \tag{13}$$

2) For any real number C, the multiplication of expression vector by C is represented in formula (14):

$$\mathrm{C}\boldsymbol{V} =(\mathrm{C}v_1 ,\ldots\ldots, \mathrm{C}v_L). \tag{14}$$

Let $\boldsymbol{E}_1$ and $\boldsymbol{E}_2$ are two emotion vectors, if an emotion vector changes from $\boldsymbol{E}_1$ to $\boldsymbol{E}_2$, the corresponding expression vector changes from $\boldsymbol{V}_1$ to $\boldsymbol{V}_2$. In order to describe the process of facial expression, let λ is interpolation function, $\lambda \in [0, 1]$, $\boldsymbol{FV}$ is a expression vector generated by interpolation of $\boldsymbol{V}_1$ and $\boldsymbol{V}_2$, $\boldsymbol{FV} =(fv_1 ,\ldots\ldots, fv_L)$, fv_k is the corresponding vertex vector, $k \in [0, L]$, fv_k is calculated by formula(15):

$$fv_k = \lambda\, v_{k1} +(1- \lambda)v_{k2}. \tag{15}$$

The formula (15) can be transformed to formula (16):

$$\boldsymbol{FV} = \lambda\ \boldsymbol{V}_1 +(1- \lambda)\ \boldsymbol{V}_2 . \tag{16}$$

There are some expression vector, pn is the number of expression vector, $\boldsymbol{V}_i$ is an expression vector, $i \in [0, pn]$, λ_i is the corresponding interpolation function of $\boldsymbol{V}_i$, $\boldsymbol{FV}$ is an expression vector generated by interpolation among different $\boldsymbol{V}_i$, $\boldsymbol{FV}$ is calculated by formula (17):

$$FV = \sum_{i=1}^{N} \lambda_i V_i. \quad (17)$$

All **FV** is in formula (17) is called expression vector linear space, *pn* is called the dimension number of **FV**, $\boldsymbol{V_i}$ is called a base expression vector.In general, there are some expression vector, *pn* is the number of expression vector, $\boldsymbol{V_i}$ is an expression vector, $i \in [0, pn]$, SY is an synthesis function among all $\boldsymbol{V_i}$, **FV** is calculated by formula (18):

$$FV = SY\ (V_1, \ldots\ldots, V_{pn}). \quad (18)$$

All **FV** is in formula (18) is called expression vector space.In general, **EP** is emotion vector space, **FV** is called expression vector space, *T* is a function from **EP** to **FV**, for any $\boldsymbol{E} \in \boldsymbol{EP}$, $T(\boldsymbol{E}) \in \boldsymbol{FV}$.In general, $\boldsymbol{be_i}$ is a unit vector, $i \in [1, N]$, $\boldsymbol{T}(\boldsymbol{be_i})$ is called base expression vector. If $pn=N$, **FV** is calculated by formula (19):

$$FV = SY\ (T(\boldsymbol{be_1}), \ldots, T(\boldsymbol{be_N})). \quad (19)$$

In order to simplify the formula (19), let SY is linear function, $\lambda_i = EI_i$, **FV** is calculated by formula (20):

$$FV = \sum_{i=1}^{N} (EI_i)\ T(\boldsymbol{be_i}). \quad (20)$$

A demo of synthesis on expression by formula (20) is realized on PC, the programming tools are Visual c++ language and Direct3D API. In the demo, six basic facial expressions are selected in Fig.6, some of synthesis results are shown in Fig.10. For example, in Fig.10(1), "1/2 happiness+1/2 sadness" is represented the synthesis of happiness and sadness, each basic emotion intensify is equal to 1/2.

4.3 Norm and social knowledge of virtual characters

Virtual characters live in a virtual society; a believable virtual character should have the ability of social interaction to other virtual characters with verbal and nonverbal manner. In this section, we give a method to construct norm and social knowledge.

For a certain virtual character, a status is a social degree or position. In general, a virtual character may own many status, let $ST(CA)$ is a status set for virtual character CA, $ST(CA)=\{st_1, \ldots, st_{NS}\}$, $i \in [1, NS]$, st_i is a status (such as mother or son).NS is the number of $ST(CA)$.

Status plays an important role in a social interaction. For example, in a virtual office, there are two kinds of social status altogether, namely the manager and staff member. The manager's status is higher than the status of the staff member. In general, a person will control emotion expression by one's status.

For two certain virtual characters CA_1 and CA_2, let $FD(CA_1/CA_2)$ is friendliness value from CA_1 to CA_2. If $FD(CA_1/CA_2)=1$, CA_2 is a friend of CA_1; If $FD(CA_1/CA_2)=-1$, CA_2 is an enemy of CA_1; If $FD(CA_1/CA_2)=0$, CA_2 is a stranger of CA_1; If $FD(CA_1/CA_2)=2$, CA_2 is a lover of CA_1; If $FD(CA_1/CA_2)=3$, CA_2 is a mother or father of CA_1; If $FD(CA_1/CA_2)=4$, CA_1 is a mother or father of CA_2.

A virtual character judges others with friendliness value. In general, a virtual character will not interact with a stranger unless in some exceptive conditions (calling help in danger etc.).

For two certain virtual characters CA_1 and CA_2, let ET_1 (CA_1/CA_2) is default-ending time of interaction from CA_1 to CA_2, let ET_2 (CA_2/CA_1) is default-ending time of interaction from CA_2 to CA_1, and ET is the time from beginning to ending in interaction.

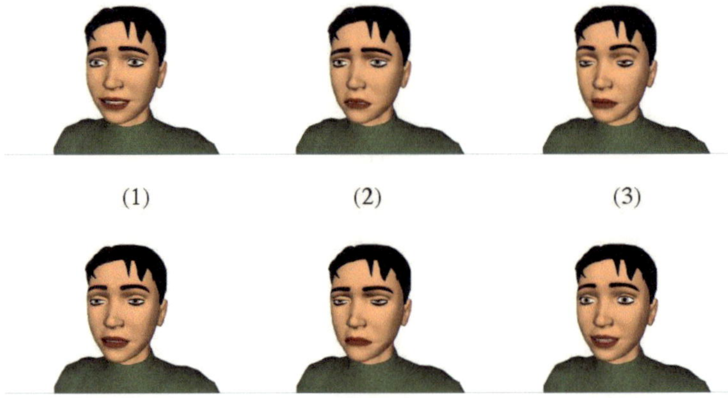

(1) (2) (3)

(4) (5) (6)

Fig.10. Some synthesis of expressions :(1) "1/2happiness+1/2sadness"; (2) "1/2sadness+1/2anger";(3)"1/2surprise+1/2disgust";(4)"1/3happiness+1/3fear+1/3disgust";(5)"1/3sadness+1/3disust+1/3anger";(6)"1/3happiness+1/3sadness +1/3 anger ".

In general, if ET $\geq$min (ET_1 (CA_1/CA_2), ET_2 (CA_2/CA_1), the interaction will end. For two certain virtual characters CA_1 and CA_2, let IR (CA_1/CA_2) is interaction radius of CA_1 to CA_2, let DS (CA_1/CA_2) is distance from CA_1 to CA_2. In general, if DS (CA_1/CA_2)> IR (CA_1/CA_2), CA_1 will not make interaction to CA_2; if $(CA_1/CA_2) \leq IR$ (CA_1/CA_2), CA_1 may make interaction to CA_2.

In default condition, when two agents encounter together, interaction radius is critical distance of interaction triggering.

For two certain virtual characters CA_1 and CA_{12}, let PN (CA_1, CA_2) is priority value of social interaction between CA_1 and CA_2. If PN (CA_1, CA_2)=0, CA_1 first interact with CA_2, CA_1 is initiator; If PN (CA_1, CA_2)=1, CA_2 first interact with CA_1, CA_2 is initiator; If PN (CA_1, CA_2)=2, CA_1 and CA_2 interact each other at the same time.

In general, a virtual character acts different status with interaction to others. For instance, there are three virtual characters CA_1, CA_2 and CA_3, CA_2 is mother of CA_1, CA_3 is a student of CA_1, when CA_1 meet CA_2 or CA_3, CA_1 usually first interact with CA_2, CA_3 usually first interact with CA_1, and PN (CA_1, CA_2)=0, PN (CA_1, CA_3)=1.

For two certain virtual characters CA_1 and CA_2, let INS $(CA_1 \leftarrow CA_2)$ is an interaction signal set from CA_2 to CA_1, INS $(CA_1 \leftarrow CA_2)=\{ins_1, \ldots ,ins_N \}$, ins_i is a nonverbal interaction signal (such as "calling help pose"), $j \in [1, NI]$, NI is the number of INS $(CA_1 \leftarrow CA_2)$.

In a virtual environment, when two virtual characters begin to interact each other, Each of them is supposed to be able to know interaction signal. In a practical demo system, interaction signals are sent to memory module by social norm module.

For a certain virtual characters CA, let IR (CA) is an interaction rule for virtual character CA, IR control the manner of interaction, IR include some production rulers.

A high-level algorithm can illustrate how to construct IR, which is related to context. There are two virtual characters CA_1 and CA_2 in a virtual environment. The algorithm procedure of emotion social interaction is as follows step:

Step 1: The procedure gets current emotion state and social norms (status, all friendliness degree, default-ending time of interaction, all interaction radius, and all priority degree of social interaction).

Step 2: The procedure judge whether a character can interact with others according to the current emotion state and social norm. If a character can interact with others, go **Step 3**; else go **Step 4**.

Step 3: Interaction signals are transferred between CA_1 and CA_2. If one of interaction signal is "ending interaction", then go to **Step 4**.

Step 4: Ending interaction.

5. An example of the model

A virtual town is set up on PC, we can use this example to illustrate the above method, all the 3D geometry models of objects in the town are drawn by 3D software and stored in Microsoft DirectX format files. There are dynamic objects (vehicles) and virtual characters; Tom, John and Mary are three virtual characters in the demo system. They can move from one place to another, and can express their emotions. We can suppose John is a friend of Tom, when Tom meets to John, Tom will smile to John, and we can construct the social norm for Tom in a script file as follows:

```
Status (Tom):={a worker};
GD=1; //Gender of Tom is male.
Social relationships:=(John is friend, no enemy)
Friendliness value (to John)=1;
Friendliness value (to others)=0;
Default-ending time of interaction (to John)=1 minutes;
Default-ending time of interaction (to others)=0.1 minutes;
Interaction radius (to John)= 3 meter;
Interaction radius (to others)= 5 meter;
Priority value of social interaction( to John)=0;
Priority value of social interaction( to others)=1;
Interaction signal set=(angry, calling help, happy,…….., );
Emotion Interaction rules of sending information to others
{If Friendliness value=-1 then Emotion to other = angry
        Else
          If other  GD=-1;//other person's gender is female.
          Emotion to other =happy;
          End
        Emotion to other =Null; //no any emotion to others
        End
}
Emotion Interaction rules of receiving information from others
{If Emotion from friend= sad then Emotion to friend=sad
        Else
        Emotion to friend=happy
        End
End }
```

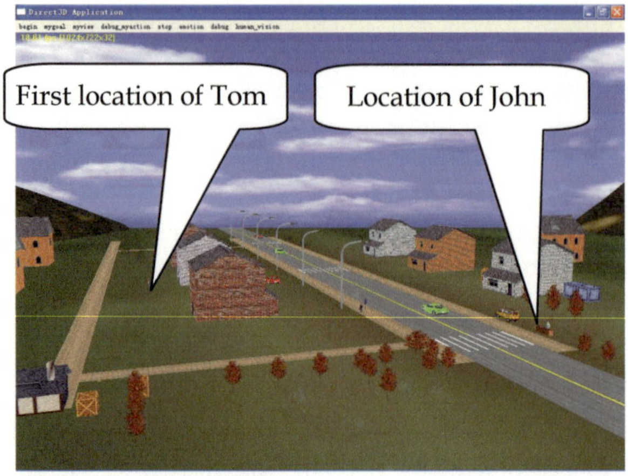

Fig. 11. A bird view of virtual environment

Fig. 12. Tom can move from one place to another

Fig. 13. Tom communicates with John with hand moving and facial expression

Let Mary is a female virtual character, she is watching TV in a room, a TV program is a stimulus, if a TV program is interesting, Mary will be happy on face. We can suppose some parameters for Mary:

1) Mary has six basic emotions (Happiness, Disgust, Anger, Sadness, Fear, Surprise).
2) Let a virtual character may have five personalities: agreeableness, openness, conscientiousness, extraversion, and neuroticism. If Mary's personality is agreeableness, PS_1 is agreeableness, and Θ $[PS_1(t)]$ =1(all other intensity of $PS_k(t)$ is equal to 0). If Mary's personality is conscientiousness, PS_3 is conscientiousness, and Θ $[PS_3(t)]$ =1(all other intensity of $PS_k(t)$ is equal to 0).
3) On the basis of Maslow's theory, human can have five motivations (Physiological, Safety, Affiliation, Achievement, Self-Actualization). In a certain environment, we suppose a virtual character only has one motivation. In the example, Mary only has Affiliation motivation, all R_m are equal, Θ $[MV_3]$ =1,
4) Let O_j ={TV program}, in a certain time, the number of stimulus is one, Θ $[O_{11}]$=0.8, other Θ $[O_{ji}]$ =0.
5) Let $C_i(t)$=0.7 (i=1,...,6), we can define a rule for $NC_i(t)$ and $MC_i(t)$. If a character's personality is agreeableness, $NC_1(t)=C_1(t)$, $MC_1(t)= \min[1.2\times C_1(t), 1]$; if a character's personality is conscientiousness, $NC_1(t)=\min[1.2 \times C_1(t),1]$, $MC_1(t)=\min[1.2\times C_1(t), 1]$.

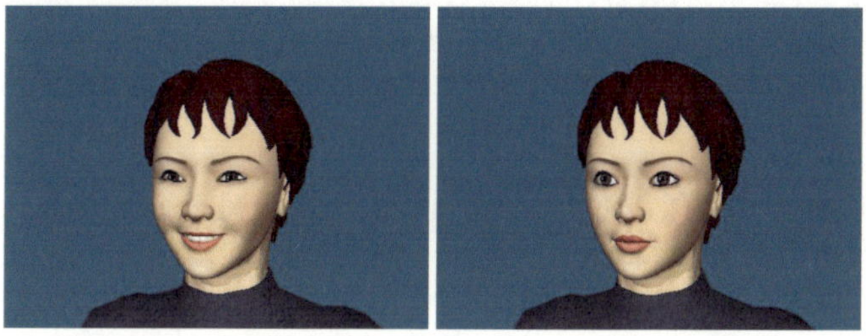

Fig. 14. Mary's personality (1) agreeableness (2) conscientiousness

6) If Mary's personality is agreeableness, $TC_1(t)$=0.7, Θ $[O_{11}]>TC_1(t)$, the emotion "Happiness" is active. If Mary's personality is conscientiousness, $TC_1(t)$=0.84, the emotion "Happiness" is not active. Mary's expressions are in Fig.14.

6. Conclusion

Emotion is related to stimulus and cognitive appraisal. Emotion is very important for modern computer game. Emotion model of virtual characters is a challenging branch of computer science. A believable character should be provided with emotion and perception. In general, a virtual character is regarded as an autonomous agent with sense, perception, emotion behavior and action. A computational emotion model of virtual characters is presented in this chapter. The method is to construct virtual characters that have internal sensor and perception for external stimuli. First, architecture of a virtual character is set up by cognitive model; Second, emotion model is proposed by a formalization method, some new concepts are presented with a general mathematical model, the model integrates emotion, stimuli, motivation, personality, and social knowledge together. As a result, an emotional animation demo system of virtual character is implemented on PC.

7. Acknowledgements

The work described in this chapter was co-supported by the National Grand Fundamental Forepart Professional Research (grant no: 2005cca04400) and the Natural Science Foundation of NingBo City(grant no:2007A610038) .

8. References

Freeman, D. (2003).*Creating Emotion in Games: The Craft and Art of Emotioneering*, New Riders Games publisher, ISBN: 1592730078.

Tu, X.; Terzopoulos, D. (1994). Artificial fishes: Physics, locomotion, perception, behavior, *Proceedings of SIGGRAPH'1994*, pp.43-50, ISBN 0-89791-667-0, Orlando, FL USA, July.1994, ACM Press/Addison-Wesley Publishing Co. New York, NY, USA.

Funge, J.; Tu, X.; Terzopoulos D.(1999).Cognitive Modeling: Knowledge, Reasoning and Planning for Intelligent Characters, *Proceedings of SIGGRAPH'1999*, pp.29-38, ISBN:0-201-48560-5 , Los Angeles, CA, August, 1999, ACM Press/Addison-Wesley Publishing Co. New York, NY, USA.

Badler, N.I. ; Reich B.D. ; Weber, B.L.(1997) Towards person-alities for animated agents with reactive and planning behaviors, In :*Creating Per-sonalities for Synthetic Actors: Towards Autonomous Personality Agents*, Trappl, R& Petta, P. (Ed.), pp. 43-57, Springer-Verlag, Berlin.

Chi, D. ; Costa, M. ; Zhao,L. ; Badler, N.(2000). The Emote Model for Effect and Shape, *Proceedings of SIGGRAPH'2000*, pp.173-182, New Orleans, Louisiana USA, July,2000, ACM Press/Addison-Wesley Publishing Co. New York, NY, USA.

Ball, G. ; Breese, J.(2000). Emotion and Personality in a con-versational agent, In : *Embodied conversational agents*, Cassell,J ; Sullivan,J. ; Prevost,S. ; Churchill,E.(Ed.), pp.189-219, MIT Press, Cambridge, MA.

Goldberg, A.(1997).IMPROV: A system for real-time anima-tion of behavior-based interactive synthetic actors, In :*Creating Per-sonalities for Synthetic Actors: Towards Autonomous Personality Agents*, Trappl, R& Petta, P. (Ed.), pp.58-73, Springer-Verlag,Berlin.

Rousseau,D. ;Hayes-Roth,B.(1998)A Social-Psychological Model for Synthetic Actors, *Proceedings of the Second International Conference on Autonomous Agents*, Minneapolis, MN, May, 1998.

Bates, J.(1994).The role of emotion in believable characters, *Communications of the ACM*, Vol.37,No.7, pp.122-125.

Loyall, A.B.(1997) Some requirements and approaches for natural language in a believable agent, In :*Creating Per-sonalities for Synthetic Actors: Towards Autonomous Personality Agents*, Trappl, R& Petta, P. (Ed.), pp.113-119, Springer-Verlag, ,Berlin.

Reilly, W.S.N.(1996). *Believable Social and Emotional Agents*, Ph.D. Dissertation, Carnegie-Mellon University.

Blumberg, B.(1997). Multi-level Control for Animated Autonomous Agents:Do the right Thing.Oh,Not That, In :*Creating Per-sonalities for Synthetic Actors: Towards*

Autonomous Personality Agents, Trappl, R& Petta, P. (Ed.), pp.74-82, Springer-Verlag, Berlin.

Blumberg, B. ; Downie, M. ; Ivanov, Y. ; Berlin, M. ; Johnson,M. ; Tomlinson, B.(2002). Integrated learning for interactive synthetic characters, *Proceedings of SIGGRAPH'02*, pp.417-426, San Antonio, Texas, USA, July 23 - 26, 2002, ACM Press/Addison-Wesley Publishing Co. New York, NY, USA.

Moffat, D.(1997). Personality parameters and programs, In :*Creating Per-sonalities for Synthetic Actors: Towards Autonomous Personality Agents*, Trappl, R& Petta, P. (Ed.), pp.120-165, Springer-Verlag, Berlin.

Thalmann, N.M. ; Thalman, D.(eds).(1994).*Artifical Life and Virtual Reality*, John Wiley&sons chichester,England.

Thalmann, N.M. ; Thalmann, D. (eds). (2004). *Handbook of Virtual Humans*, John Wiley & Sons, chichester,England.

Noser, H. ; Renault, O. ; Thalmann, D. ; Thalmann, N.M.(1995). Navigation for Digital Actors Based on Synthetic Vision, Memory, and Learning, *Computer& Graphics*, Vol. 19, No.1, pp 7-19.

Musse, S.R. ; Thalmann, D.(2001). Hierachical Model For Real Time Simulation of Virtual Character Crowds, *IEEE Transactions on Visualization and Computer Graphics*, vol.7, no.2, pp.152-163.

Egges, A. ; Kshirsagar, S. ; Thalmann, N.M.(2004). Generic personality and emotion simulation for conversational agents, *Computer Animation and Virtual Worlds*, Vol.15, 2004, pp:1-13.

Gratch, J. ; Marsella, S. (2004).A Domain-independent framework for modeling emotion, *Journal of Cognitive Systems Research*, Vol.5, No.4, pp.269-306.

Cassell, J. ; Vilhjalmsson, H.H. ; Bickmore T.(2001). BEAT: the behavior expression animation toolkit, *Proceedings of SIGGRAPH'2001*, pp. 477–486, Los Angeles, California, USA, ACM Press/Addison-Wesley Publishing Co. New York, NY, USA.

Pelachaud, C. ; Poggi, I.(2002). Subtleties of facial expressions in embodied agents, *Journal of Visualization and Computer Animation*, Vol.13 ,pp: 287–300.

Ekman, P. ; Oster, H. (1979).*Facial Expression of Emotion*. Annual Review of Psychology, 1979, 20: 527-554.

Ortony, A. ; Clore, G.L.; Collins, A.(1988). *The cognitive structure of emotions*, Cambridge University Press, ISBN 0-521-35364-5,New York.

Picard, R. W.(1997). *Affective Computing*, The MIT Press, Massachusetts.

Liu, Z. ; Pan, Zhi-Geng. ; Xu, Weiwei.(2002). A method of Emotional Behavior Animation of Virtual Human, *Proceedings of Virtual Environment on PC Cluste* , pp.277-283,, Protvino-St.Petersburg, 2002.

Liu, Z. ; Pan, Zhi-Geng.(2005). An Emotion Model of 3D Virtual Characters In Intelligent Virtual Environment. In: *Affective computing and intelligent interaction*, Tao, JH ; Tan,TN ;Picard, R,W., (Ed.), pp.629-636, Springer-Verlag, ISBN 3-540-29621-2,Berlin.

Bernstein, D.A. ; Stewart, A.C. ; Roy, E.J. ; Wickens, C.D. (1997). *Psychology*, Houghton Miffin Company, New York.

Satrongman, K.T.(2003). *The Psychology of Emotion*, John Wiley&sons, ISBN 0471485683, chichester,England.

Gibson, J.J.(1986).*The ecological approach to visual perception*, NJ:Lawrence Erlbaum Associates,Inc,Hillsdale.

Tolani,D. ; Goswami,A. ; Badler,N.(2001).Real-Time Inverse Kinematics Techniques for Anthropomorphic Limbs, *Graphical Models and Image Processing*, Vol.62, No.5, pp.353-388.

Kovar, L. ; Gleicher, M. (2002). Motion Graph, *Proceedings of SIGGRAPH'2002*, pp.473-482, San Antonio, Texas, USA,July23-26, 2002, ACM Press/Addison-Wesley Publishing Co. New York, NY, USA.

Lee, J. ; Chai, J. ; Reitsma, Paul S. A. (2002), Interactive Control of Avatars Animated with Human Motion Data, *Proceedings of SIGGRAPH2002*, pp. 491-500, San Antonio, Texas,USA, July 23 - 26, 2002, ACM Press/Addison-Wesley Publishing Co. New York, NY, USA.

Rose, C.F. ; Cohen,M. ; Bodenheimer, B.(1998). Verbs and Adverbs: Multidimensional Motion Interpolation, *IEEE Computer Graphics & Application*, Vol. 18, No.5, pp.32-40.

13

SIMPLEX – Simulation of Personal Emotion Experience

Henrik Kessler, Alexander Festini, Harald C. Traue,
Suzanne Filipic, Michael Weber and Holger Hoffmann
University of Ulm, Medical Psychology, Institute for Media Computing
Germany

1. Introduction

Emotion modelling is becoming increasingly important for emotion computing, computer games, interactive storytelling or life-like wizards and assistants because it is necessary to make human-computer interaction more natural. Reeves & Nass (1996) showed that humans like to communicate with computers as they do with people. Software applications which include models of emotional processes are needed to model the social and emotional aspects of human-machine interaction. Extending classic AI and logic by adding simulated emotions can be useful to improve the user's experience in many ways. This chapter will provide a brief overview of existing solutions and models used for artificial emotions (AE) and present a novel model of emotion simulation (SIMPLEX). Empirical data will be reported on its performance, especially the occurrence of emotions, in a game environment. This chapter concludes with a comment on the usefulness of separating AI and AE considering recent advances in cognitive neuroscience.

2. Models for artificial emotions

2.1 Historical roots

The 70s saw what might have been the first debate about emotions and artificial intelligence. The main and - as we know now - most important point was that purely cognitive systems lacked emotions, which strongly influence human thought processes. Two of the models that emerged at that time will be described here.

Simon's interrupt system

Herbert Simon was the first to propose that emotions should be part of a model of cognitive processes (Simon, 1967). His intention was to provide a theoretical foundation for a system incorporating emotions and multiple goals. Within this system, important processes could be interrupted so that more attention went into satisfying important needs (e.g. hunger, safety). Herbert Simon imagined two parallel systems, one designed to achieve goals (cognition, planning) and one observing the environment for events that require immediate attention (emotions). Indeed, the possibility of interrupting current cognitive processes is vital for survival, as it makes it possible to react to threats, but also to pay more attention to one's surroundings when a threat is expected.

Toda's Fungus Eater

Another step towards a theory for the computer modelling of emotions was made by the psychologist Masanoa Toda (Toda, 1982) between 1961 and 1980, with a model called the Fungus Eater. This model resulted in the design of an autonomous robot system and partial implementations.

At first, Toda only wanted to create a scenario for a cognitive system that would require concentrating on multiple issues at the same time. In this scenario, the task was collecting as much ore as possible with the help of a mining robot. Operating this robot required energy that could only be gained by collecting a special fungus. Additionally, different Fungus Eaters were competing for the same resources, thus making the scenario more complicated. Toda came to the conclusion that in order to survive on their own, these Fungus Eaters would need to have emotions and to be partially controlled by them. However, Toda named them "urges" instead of emotions and on closer examination, it is apparent that some of these are actual emotions like joy or anger, while others are needs, goals or motives (e.g. hunger).

2.2 Theoretical approach and recent models

There are roughly three areas where emotion models are applied. Artificial emotions (AE) can be used to improve problem-solving in complex environments, as in the early approaches mentioned above. Emotion models can also be used to test psychological emotion theories in experiments using controlled scenarios. Finally, emotions are essential to make computer characters more believable. Emotion models which synthesize and express emotions are necessary to make AI characters more human-like. These models will be the focus of the next sections as they have inspired our own emotional model. The most influential theoretical approach, OCC, will be presented in detail, as it is the basis of many computational models of emotion. Then, three interesting recent models are briefly described.

OCC - a theoretical approach to simulate emotions

The OCC model by Ortony, Clore and Collins is an emotion theory based on appraisal which was explicitly developed to offer a foundation for artificial emotion systems (Ortony, Clore, & Collins, 1988). Its authors succeeded as it inspired many modern models and approaches to artificial emotions.

The basis of the model is that emotions are reactions to the attributes of objects, to events or to actions. Note that internal events (like bodily sensations or memories) which are a part of most modern emotion theories are neglected in the OCC approach. Objects, events and actions are evaluated in an appraisal process based on specific criteria, and result in multiple emotions of different intensities. Figure 1 gives an overview of the OCC approach.

Appraising the *aspects of objects* requires the agent to have *attitudes* (tastes or preferences) in order to decide whether the object is *appealing* or not. This appraisal process results in either love or hate.

Events, or rather *consequences of events*, are appraised by analyzing their impact on the agent's *goals*. This determines the *desirability* of events. The degree of desirability depends on how much closer to or further away from achieving the goal the agent will be after the event. The emotions of joy and distress are direct results of desirable and undesirable events, considering the consequences they have for the agent himself. Some emotions, like for example pity, are triggered when processing events that have consequences for other agents. An open issue is whether this appraisal should be based upon the agent's own goals or rather the other agent's goals. How much should an agent be empathic if another one looses something that is not important to the first agent? In an attempt to solve this issue, abstract goals were introduced (such as for example, not losing property). It eventually became clear that it is very important to keep the goals general and abstract, to avoid having to define too many specific goals. The emotions triggered by reacting to other agents' good or bad fortune depend on how well-liked they are. Another agent's bad fortune can trigger pity or gloating, while happy events can result in either feeling of happiness or of resentment, depending on the relationship between the agents.

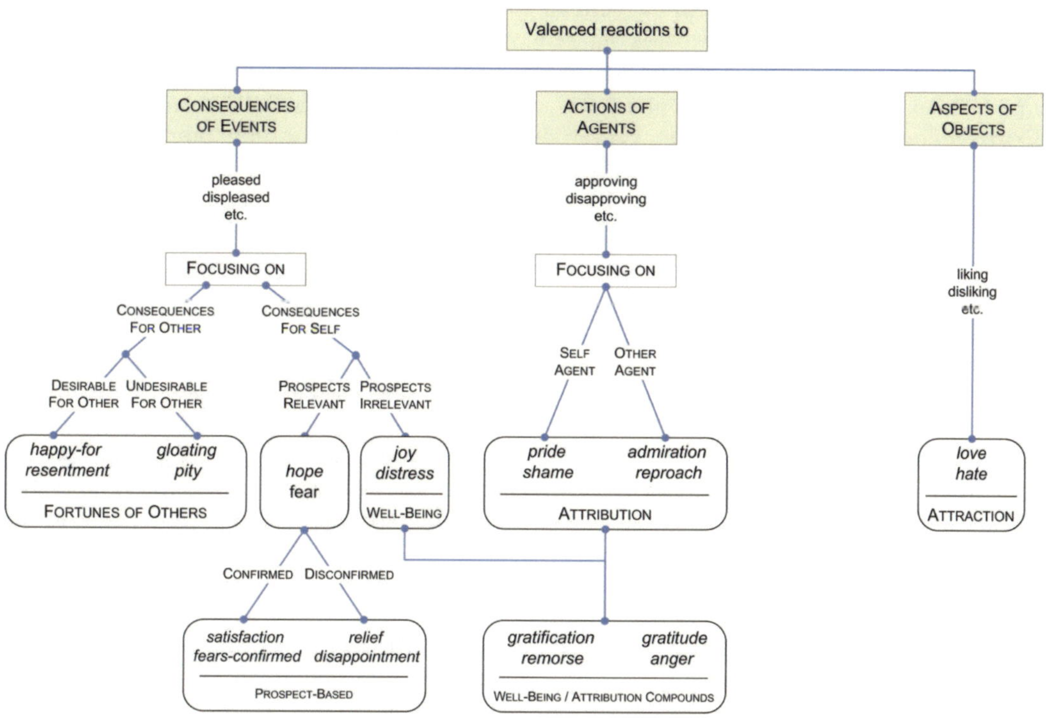

Fig. 1. The OCC model

Appraising an event also means evaluating its *prospects* - hoping or fearing that something will or will not occur. Prospect-based emotions include disappointment and relief. The intensity of these emotions is usually based on the intensity of the preceding hope or fear.

The criterion used to appraise the *actions of agents* is their *praiseworthiness*, which is based on the agent's *standards*. Generally, praiseworthy actions cause pride and blameworthy actions cause shame, if the agent himself is the one acting. When the actions of other agents are appraised, the emotions triggered are admiration or reproach. Standards can be as complex as attitudes (aspects of objects) and goals (consequences of events), and are almost as subjective and individual. Again, the problem of listing them was solved by describing actions in an abstract way. An interesting phenomenon is the ability of feeling proud or ashamed of someone else's actions. Simply put, the closer an agent feels related to the acting agent(s), the more he will identify with him in appraising his actions. Examples of this phenomenon (called the strength of the cognitive unit) can range from parents being proud of their child to soccer fans being ashamed of their team's performance.

One of the many practical implementations of OCC is the model by Staller & Petta (1999). They constructed a virtual agent which emotion architecture links discrete emotions categories to 14 action response categories, comprising a large range of individual actions.
The OCC emotion model is also partly congruent with Nico Frijda's reknowed theory of emotions (Frijda, 1986). For more details on emotion theory, see Traue & Kessler (2003).
Artificial Emotion Engine
The aim of the Emotion Engine (EE) is to control the behavior of an artificial agent in complex scenarios. It is made of three layers- emotions, mood and personality (Wilson, 2000). If an emotion is triggered, the actions will be based on this emotion. When emotions are not triggered, the engine bases its actions on the current mood; when no mood is activated, then personality serves as a basis for behavior. The emotion engine is based on the EFA model, which is a three-dimensional space, describing personality traits in terms of Extroversion, Fear and Aggression. Within this space, an area around the point representing an artificial agent's personality is determined and all traits located inside this area are considered to be available to the specific character. For Wilson, the EFA is congruent with the three central systems of the human brain which according to Gray (Gray & McNaughton, 1996) determine behavior: the Approach system, the Behavior Inhibition system and the Fight/Flight system. These three basic dimensions are intuitive, which makes programming easy.
Different personalities trigger some moods more frequently than others: extroversion is linked to good moods, and fear to negative moods. Aggression affects the speed of mood changes. Reward and punishment signals work as the main inputs, and this is comparable with the desirability of events in OCC. Inputs are adjusted based on personality, but also on how often this input occurred before. An agent can get used to a certain input, and this lowers the impact it will eventually have (habituation). On the contrary, a rare or unprecedented input will have more effect (novelty).
Needs are organized hierarchically. Physiological needs, such as hunger, thirst, and the need for warmth and energy are the most important. Each of these needs can become a priority, as when for example a very hungry agent will consider eating as his most important goal. Safety, affiliation and esteem needs are the remaining layers. While physiological needs are the most important, the order of the other layers can vary, depending on what is more important to the agent. Memory is very limited; an agent only remembers how much he likes the other agents. In the same way, in OCC, sympathy is used to cause different emotions for liked and disliked entities.
Only the six basic emotions of fear, anger, joy, sadness, disgust and surprise can be triggered. This might appear like a limited selection compared to the 24 emotions of OCC, but given the reactive nature of emotions in this model (working without inner events and triggers) and since some emotion theorists consider the broad spectrum of emotions as mixtures of these basic emotions, this is quite a sensible choice. Personality is used to adjust the intensity or the frequency of the occurrence of emotions, so that a character with personality that is "low in Fear" will simply not experience as much fear as others.
FLAME
The Fuzzy Logic Adaptive Model of Emotion (FLAME) is partially based on OCC, but what differentiates FLAME from other models is the use of fuzzy logic. This results in a relatively simple appraisal process.
FLAME can integrate multiple emotions at the same time (in a process called emotional filtering), as emotions at times inhibit one another. For example, imagine an agent feeling

joy and pride because he just obtained a new position, but who at the same time feels anger, because a relative of the boss of the company was given a higher position than himself. At this point, his anger may prevent him from feeling joy any longer. When opposite emotions occur, FLAME lets the stronger emotion inhibit the weaker one(s), giving a slightly stronger weight to negative emotions. Another way to handle conflicting emotions is through mood, which is determined by comparing the intensities of positive and negative emotions over the last few steps. If the summed up intensities of positive emotions are higher than that of the negative emotions, then the mood will be positive. If a positive and a negative emotion of comparable intensities occur at the same time, the mood determines which of these emotions will inhibit the other one.

As there is little research about the decay of emotions, FLAME uses a simple constant decay, though positive emotions decay faster than negative emotions. FLAME does not make it possible to implement an agent's personality; instead, differences in behavior are created through learning. For example, an agent may learn that reacting in an angry way will enable him to reach his goals, thus enticing him to be more choleric. FLAME implements multiple types of learning, such as classical conditioning (associating expectations with objects) which occurs in many situations, triggering fear or hope. Another type of learning is learning about consequences of actions or events. This is simple whenever an action directly causes a result. For example, learning that eating will result in feeling less hungry is rather trivial. In the case of more complex causal relations over time, FLAME is using Q-learning, a form of reinforcement learning.

Another form of learning, quite similar to model learning, is the ability to recognize patterns in the behavior of a user by observing sequences of actions. For this type of learning, FLAME simply counts the occurrences of sequences. The last type of learning in FLAME, but one of the most important, is learning about the value of actions. Remember that OCC relies on the praiseworthiness of actions, which is based on the agent's standards. In FLAME, these standards are not predefined knowledge, but they are learned from the interaction between users. Using learning instead of predefined knowledge seems like a very sensible way to avoid most of the troubling issues that come with using OCC. Additionally, learning allows agents to adjust, which makes them all the more believable.

ALMA

The intention in designing A Layered Model of Affect (ALMA) was to control agents in conversational scenarios. In interactive game or learning environments, the artificial characters display facial expressions of emotions and moods through their postures to appear more believable. Emotions, moods and personalities are implemented and interact with each other. Events and actions are described in terms of abstract tags which are then evaluated during the appraisal process and describe things like for example the expressed emotion or gesture accompanying an action or simply if something is a good or bad event. As ALMA is aimed at conversations, an action is often a statement. Hence, there are tags to describe the kind of statement, for example if it was an insult or a compliment. In addition, ALMA requires defining personality profiles for each agent. Essentially, these profiles already contain the desirability and praiseworthiness the agent assigns to certain tags.

Since our own emotion model shares some features with ALMA (see below) a key difference should be pointed out. In SIMPLEX we considered it impractical to explicitly specify this information, as this would have limited the model to a small number of agents. So instead of using tags, our model requires to specify goals and their priorities for an agent, where generic goals can be used for all agents. Events still need to be described in a special way, but this is reduced to a relatively objective list of which agents goals are affected and in which way. All other information like praiseworthiness is automatically derived from this and the agent's personality. Although this approach is providing less control over an agent's appraisal process, it is better suited for a generic system meant to be used with minimal extra effort.

3. SIMPLEX – Simulation of Personal Emotion Experience

3.1 Overview

SIMPLEX is a context-independent module to create emotions as a result of primary application (environment) events. Goals, emotions, mood-states, personality, memory and relationships between agents have been modelled so they could interact as in real life. Figure 2 shows an overview of the model.

SIMPLEX is based on the OCC model by Ortony, Clore and Collins (1988) in that it creates discrete emotions by appraising events based on the desirability of their consequences and the praiseworthiness of the actions of agents. The appraisal process was modified by including the personality of virtual agents. The personality component is based on the Five Factor Model (FFM) introduced by psychologists McCrae & Costa (1987), which includes extroversion, conscientiousness, agreeableness, neuroticism and openness. The personality module influences the emotion module on multiple levels during appraisal processes and in the development of mood-states.

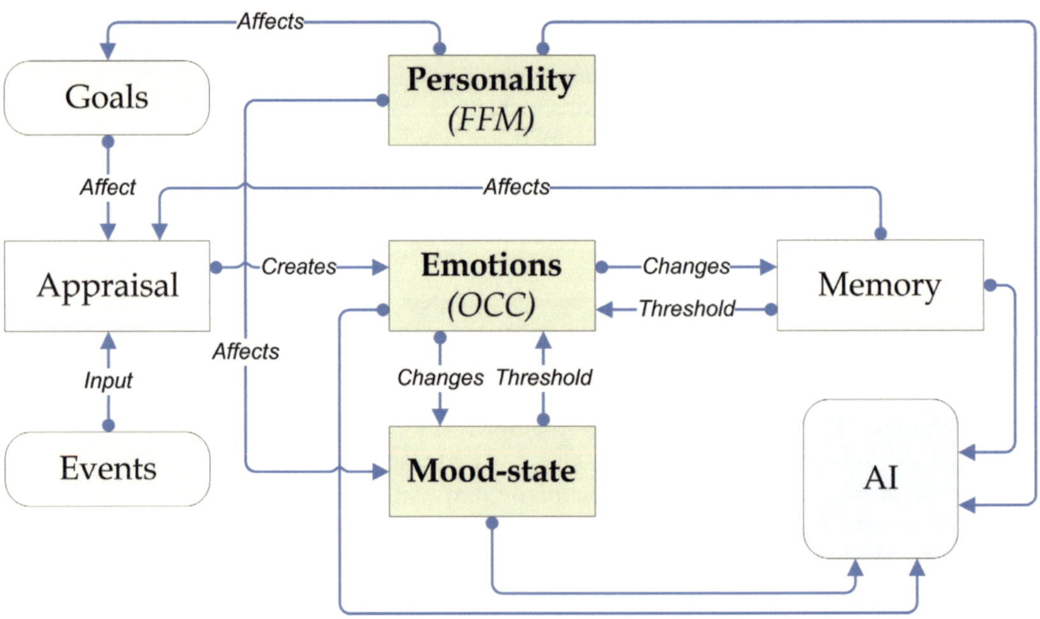

Fig. 2. The emotion module SIMPLEX

Other important aspects of the model are mood-states and relationships. Mood-states are represented in a three-dimensional space which dimensions are pleasure, arousal and dominance (Bradley & Lang, 1994), and they are based on active or recently experienced emotions (implemented by pull-functions). In the absence of emotions, a mood state will slowly gravitate back to a default mood-state based on the agent's personality. A mood-state also functions as a threshold to determine whether an emotion is strong enough to become active at a given time.

Relationships are handled as if they were mood-states towards other agents (for instance a player in a game scenario): they are based on emotions caused by other agents and they can be considered as a simplified way to store memories of experiences with these agents. They are used as thresholds as well; for example, an agent will be more likely to become angry at another agent when their relationship is in the range of negative valence.

Personality (long-term), mood-state (mid-term) and emotions (short-term) thus represent three levels of the emotion module that interact with each other in order to create believable agents. Events from the scenario serve as the model's inputs. They are appraised according to the OCC algorithm (see figure 1). This appraisal is influenced by the agent's goals, his personality and his relationships with other agents. At the end of an appraisal one or several discrete emotions are generated. These emotions and the current mood-state are represented in the same three-dimensional PAD space: on the one hand, the emotion(s) serve(s) as an attractor for the recent mood-state position (pull function). On the other hand, the closer an emotion is located to the current mood-state, the more probable it will be that the emotion will be activated. The speed at which the mood-state changes, is influenced by the agent's neuroticism (a personality variable). Additionally, emotions that are caused by other agents will influence another mood-state representation (stored on another PAD space) representing the relationship with that agent. Thus, every agent has specific relationships with other agents, which influences his behavior towards others. Emotions, mood-states and relationships with other agents are the outputs of the model and can be used by the AI application.

Originally, the PAD space was designed to represent emotions in a dimensional rather than a discrete way (Russell, 1978). In our model, PAD is used as a common space where three different constructs (discrete OCC emotions, continuous mood-states and personality), are represented in order to be handled together by the SIMPLEX algorithm. An agent's current mood-state is thus the result of a mathematical function which takes into account the default mood (defined by personality), the pulling behaviour of OCC emotion(s) triggered by appraisals, and weighed factors influencing movement speed (see equation 1).

$$\text{Mood-state} = f(PAD_{FFM}, PAD_{Emotions}, Filter_{FFM}) \tag{1}$$

3.2 Basic components

Mood-state represented in the PAD-Space (Pleasure-Arousal-Dominance)

Beyond discrete emotions, which are typically short-term, mood-states are a powerful way to model emotional shifts and explain affective influences over longer periods of time. To implement mood-states in our model, we chose to use Russell's three-dimensional space to describe emotions (Russell, 1978) and Mehrabian's concept of how emotions are linked to personality traits (Mehrabian, 1996).

The dimension of Pleasure encompasses valence ranging from very positive to very negative. Arousal is an indicator of how intensely something is perceived, or of how much it affects the organism. Dominance is a measure of experienced control over the situation. For example, a different degree of dominance can make the difference between fear and anger. Both of these emotions are states of negative valence and high arousal, but not feeling in control is what differentiates fear from anger. When an agent is angry, it is because he believes he can have a potential influence.

Although emotions are triggered by OCC appraisals and are therefore discrete, they are handled in a continuous three-dimensional space by SIMPLEX. The advantage of treating emotions in this way and not just as a fixed set of possible emotions is that it makes it possible to represent emotions that do not even have a name. It also creates the possibility to combine emotions, mood-state and personality in one space. First, a coordinate in PAD space can obviously represent an agent's mood-state. But emotions and personalities can also be described in terms of Pleasure, Arousal and Dominance values. For example, the value of arousal can be not only the degree of arousal associated with a specific emotion, but also the arousability of a person.

Mehrabian (1996) gives specific names to the resulting different octants in PAD-space and describes the diagonally opposite octants as Exuberant/Bored, Dependent/Disdainful, Relaxed/Anxious, Docile/Hostile. Thus mood-states are not points but octants of the PAD-space. However, positioning a personality (based on FFM) within a PAD-space could have been a rather difficult task, since there is no mathematically-correct way to make the conversion. Luckily, this transformation can be based upon empirical data. Mehrabian provided such a conversion table from FFM to PAD after correlational analyses of questionnaires measuring both constructs in healthy subjects (Mehrabian, 1996).

Five Factor Model of Personality (FFM)

The implementation of personality is a key factor when creating believable agents that differ from each other. OCC already offers a few possibilities: different goals, standards and attitudes automatically result in differences during the appraisal process. However, since personality goes beyond preferences, it was necessary to find a model of personality that made it possible to adjust the appraisal process, to shift the agent's perception and to influence mood-states.

The model chosen for SIMPLEX was the Five Factor Model (McCrae & Costa, 1987). After years of research, an agreement emerged that five groups of traits are sufficient to describe a personality. Using self-report questionnaires with multiple items, a personality profile can be provided for each individual scoring high or low in each of the five factors (this approach is called "dimensional"). In the case of our model, the value for each factor can be typed in when defining the artificial agent.

Agreeableness refers to a tendency to cooperate and to compromise, in order to interact with others in an agreeable way. High agreeableness often means having a positive outlook on human nature, assuming people to be good rather than bad. Low agreeableness is essentially selfishness, putting your own needs above the needs of others and not caring about the consequences your actions might have for others.

Conscientiousness is usually high in people who plan a lot, who think everything through, and who are very tidy or achievers. Extreme cases can appear to be compulsive or pedantic. The opposite personality trait includes sloppiness or ignoring one's duties.

Extroversion can be a measure of how much people experience positive emotions. An enthusiastic and active person that enjoys company and attention is extraverted, while a quiet individual who needs to spend more time alone is introverted.

Neuroticism is partly an opposite of Extroversion in being a tendency to experience negative emotions. However, being neurotic also means being more sensitive in general, and reacting emotionally to unimportant events that wouldn't usually trigger a response. Neurotics can

be prone to mood swings and tend to be more negative in their interpretation of situations. Low neuroticism means high emotional stability and describes calm people who are not easily upset.
Finally, those scoring high on *Openness to Experience* are creative and curious individuals, interested in art and more in touch with their own emotions than others. Those scoring low on that dimension are conservative persons with few interests, they prefer straight and simple things rather than fancy ones, and they do not care about art or science. It is suspected that Openness can be influenced by education.

3.3 Technical implementation

The appraisal process and the generation of emotions

There are three categories of inputs to the appraisal process of the emotion model: consequences of events, actions of agents and objects (see the OCC model in figure 1). The following section will describe the respective mechanisms applied when mapping each type of input to emotions.
Each event handled by a character is first adjusted according to the agent's personality.
First, the consequences are adjusted based on the agent's *neuroticism*. As neurotic people tend to see things more negatively, consequences are rated worse than what they actually are. The factor by which neuroticism can reduce the desirability of events is adjustable. Note that all personality traits are in the range of [-1; 1], so that negative neuroticism actually makes consequences more positive. In real life, positive people could think "it could have been worse".
The desirability of events is determined by (predefined) goals during the event appraisal. A goal consists of two aspects: relevance [0; 1] and state of realization [0; 1], which means to which percentage the goal is already achieved.
Afterwards, the *praiseworthiness* of actions is determined. Basically, the more positive consequences an action has, the more praiseworthy it is considered to be. Sympathy plays a role in this process, as it is added to positive values and subtracted from negative ones. Consequences for self are considered to be more important than consequences for others, which are currently factored in at 50% of their value.
After the adjusted values for all consequences have been summed up, *conscientiousness* is used to obtain the final result, by being scaled and subtracted. Thus the more conscientious an agent is, the harder it will be to commit an action positive enough to be deemed praiseworthy. This applies to both actions of other agents and actions of the agent himself.
Agreeableness works the opposite way, but only for the actions of others. This is based on the psychological notion that agreeable people tend to be more forgiving in order to get along with others. Apart from having a different weight, factoring in agreeableness has the same results as negative conscientiousness.
The remaining factors serving as parameters for the action (*responsibility,unexpectedness, publicness*) are averaged and used to scale the result of the above calculations. Finally, as cost is attempted to be derived from consequences for self, it is subtracted, before the calculated praiseworthiness is averaged over the number of consequences or rather the number of affected agents. The resulting value of praiseworthiness is used as the intensity for admiration or reproach, depending on whether it is positive or negative. If the agent is appraising his own actions, the emotions are pride or shame instead of admiration and reproach.

Once the praiseworthiness has been calculated, a search is conducted through the list of prospects for all the ones that are active and that match the name of the event. For each, the *prospect appraisal* function is called, which determines the net desirability by multiplying it with the affected goal's relevance. This value will be compared to the expected desirability for this event. The simplest situation is when a positive consequence was expected but a negative one occurs. This would obviously cause disappointment. However, this is also the case if a very high desirability was hoped for and the actual consequences are less positive, but still not negative. Having a hope fulfilled results in satisfaction. If an event has exactly the expected consequences, it results in the full intensity for the emotion.

The intensity of emotions is the product of the determined *quality* of the event and of the intensity of the prospects. For example, if there was very little hope, there cannot be strong satisfaction. Which emotion is created depends on the kind of prospect and on the sign of the quality value. Hope and positive quality result in satisfaction, hope and negative quality in disappointment, fear and positive quality in fears-confirmed and fear and negative quality in relief. After the prospect appraisal is done, short term or one-shot prospects (only valid for one round) are removed.

Appraisal concerning joy and distress is done for each consequence affecting the agent himself, while appraisal for pity/gloating and happy-for/resentment is done for the remaining consequences. The former is straightforward, weighs the desirability with the goal's relevance and directly uses the absolute value as intensity. The intensity of joy and distress is obtained by multiplying the relevance of a goal with its desirability. To determine the intensity of emotions that are reactions to consequences for others, this value is additionally multiplied with the sympathy to this entity (see below). When the agent is indifferent to the entity, the emotions will have very low intensities. High desirability and sympathy for another agent leads to the emotion "happy for", high desirability and negative sympathy to resentment, low desirability and sympathy to pity, and low desirability and negative sympathy to gloating.

The remaining emotions are referred to as *compound emotions*, as they are the result of combining the consequences for the self and the praiseworthiness. If the agent himself was the cause, the emotion is determined based on the desirability of the event. Positive consequences cause gratification, negative ones result in remorse. Appraisal for compound emotions regarding other entities' actions are handled in a similar way and cause either gratitude or anger. An overview of emotions and their criteria is given in Table 1.

The interplay of emotions, mood-state and personality

Emotions (short-term), mood-states (mid-term) and personality (long-term) interact in multiple ways, which will be described in this section. First of all, the personality of an agent is stored under the form of user-defined values for the five personality dimensions (Five Factor Model, FFM): the values for extroversion, conscientiousness, agreeableness, neuroticism and openness are defined at the beginning and remain the same throughout the scenario. Empirical research has shown that with healthy subjects, FFM dimensions correlate with trait dimensions of pleasure, arousability and dominance (Mehrabian, 1996). Mehrabian also provided equations (2) to convert FFM into PAD. This is used in our emotion model to set the default mood-state according to an agent's personality.

$$P = 0.21 \cdot \text{Extroversion} + 0.59 \cdot \text{Agreeableness} + 0.19 \cdot \text{Neuroticism}$$

$$A = 0.15 \cdot \text{Openness} + 0.30 \cdot \text{Agreeableness} - 0.57 \cdot \text{Neuroticism}$$

$$D = 0.25 \cdot \text{Openness} + 0.17 \cdot \text{Conscientiousness} + 0.60 \cdot \text{Extroversion} - 0.32 \cdot \text{Agreeableness} \quad (2)$$

	Emotion	Cause
Positive Emotions	Admiration	Praiseworthy deed by other
	Gloating	Bad consequence for disliked other
	Gratification	Good consequence through own deed
	Gratitude	Good consequence through others deed
	Happy for	Good consequence for liked other
	Hope	Potential good consequence expected
	Joy	Good consequence
	Love	Attractive entity
	Pride	Praiseworthy deed
	Relief	Expected bad consequence not confirmed
	Satisfaction	Expected good consequence confirmed
Negative Emotions	Anger	Bad consequence through others deed
	Disappointment	Expected good consequence not confirmed
	Distress	Bad consequence
	Fear	Potential bad consequence expected
	Fears confirmed	Expected bad consequence confirmed
	Hate	Repelling entity
	Pity	Bad consequence for liked other
	Remorse	Bad consequence through own deed
	Reproach	Blameworthy deed by other
	Resentment	Good consequence for disliked other
	Shame	Blameworthy deed

Table 1. OCC emotions and their respective causes

When no other emotions are active, the current mood-state is slowly changing back to the default mood-state corresponding with the agent's personality traits. Each of the five traits has a range of [-1; 1]. The current range is based on 0 typically being used as the average, and values above or below are in relation to an average persons rating in this factor. Neuroticism additionally influences mood-states as it is positively correlated with the speed of mood change (see below).

Each appraisal results in one or multiple emotions. On the one hand, these emotions are projected into PAD space and attract the current mood-state (pull function). On the other hand, an emotion is active or inactive depending on its proximity to the current mood-state. All of these changes are implemented in an *update* function with the time that has passed since the last emotional trigger. This update function will make the agent update its internal state, which results for example in the intensity of emotions being reduced depending on their decay values and the current mood-state. Active emotions dropping below their threshold will become inactive, emotions dropping to zero or less are removed from the update function. Changes to the mood-state may also cause inactive emotions to become active. All remaining active emotions are used to calculate the emotion centre, which then attracts the current mood-state. This is done with a pull function: if the mood-state is located between the origin and the emotion centre, the mood-state is moved closer to the emotion centre. The emotions should not all have the same influence for the emotion centre, so instead, the intensities of all emotions are added up and the ratio is used as a weight. The average intensity of all emotions is used to determine how much the mood-state is attracted to the (calculated) emotion centre. Another factor is the agent's neuroticism. Higher neuroticism means a tendency to be moody and experience mood swings, which is simulated by simply allowing the mood-state to change faster than for other non-neurotic agents.

To decay an emotion, the distance of the emotion to the mood-state is used. The decay time is given as the time needed for the emotion to fully decay from 100% to 0.

Relations between agents are stored as simple PAD values linked to the name of every other agent that has caused emotions in the agent so far. Essentially, the relations are just an emotion average and can, for example, be considered as an associated mood-state towards the entity.

4. Empirical data in a game scenario

To test our emotion module a simplified game scenario was created, where players have to take over squares in a battlefield. The goal was to create an environment where the virtual agents can develop emotions and mood-states while the game would be kept simple enough, so the observed effects could be understood. Virtual players were made to react to game events by experiencing emotions and mood-state shifts, and these factors were also made to have an influence back on their their decision making. The results of pure AI and AE players were compared. Apart from the fact that many different and realistic emotions appeared, AE agents have shown somewhat of an emergent behavior, resembling cooperation.

The simplest possible scenario that could still trigger all possible emotions was created. This scenario was reduced to one abstract resource and one possible action. The resource was squares on a board; the action was stealing a square adjacent to one of your own. An addition had to be made to allow for explicit cooperation: before an attempt to take over a square is made, the other players can be asked for help to improve chances of success. However, if the other players disagree, the chances to succeed are reduced, so the other player that is chosen to help should be chosen carefully.

Before describing the behavior of the emotional agents, a short introduction will be given on the way pure AI worked in this scenario. The AI module was set to always pick the player with the least number of squares to eliminate him from the game as quickly as possible in an attempt to reduce the potential attackers. Players with more than 80% of all squares are to be considered close to winning and be attacked as well. The decision to ask other players for help is purely based on their previous responses. If they agreed in 50% of all cases, then they are asked again. Before they have been asked at least five times, this statistic is ignored and they are always asked. The response of the agent(s) asked for help depends on the number of squares of the affected players. Typically, an AI agent would always agree, as long as the attacker had less squares than the agent himself.

Since this scenario was only used to test whether the emotion model was adequate to produce emotions as reactions to events, the emotion module did not affect AI decisions. Because of the simple nature of this scenario, the emotion module alone could play the game, which allows a direct comparison between AI and AE. Events were still evaluated by the module, but all decisions were based on sympathy. The least-liked player would be attacked and only players which 'inspired' positive sympathy would be asked for help or supported.

In order to test the emerging emotions, data was collected from thousands of test runs with virtual agents playing against each other. The first batch consisted of one thousand games with four agents using the emotion module. Another thousand games mixed two emotional agents with two pure AI players, and the final batch included thousands of games of four AI players. To collect the data, a call-back function counted every time an emotion was changed from inactive to active. However, as the length of the game varied greatly, especially between the set using emotion and the set using AI, the results were divided by the number of turns. Multiple test runs were made and compared to make sure the results within the different groups were consistent and stable. While the different test groups showed significant differences between each other, the groups themselves did not.

The emotional agents always behaved in the same way, though in their case this happened naturally and was exactly the kind of emergent behaviour that the module was implemented for. Each player would end up with one liked ally and two disliked players, one of them usually disliked about twice as much as the other. These relationships were completely symmetrical. Since decisions were purely based on sympathy, it meant two players would always attack each other with one of the other two supporting him. As a result, games would last a very long time as squares would constantly go back and forth between these two players. Figure 3 demonstrates the longer duration of pure AE games in turns compared to mixed and pure AI groups. Once the first player was out, the remaining player would lose very quickly. Considering the very simple decision making rules of the application itself, the fact that agents automatically formed teams after a few moves is a good sign that complex behaviors could emerge in more interesting scenarios.

It turned out that games with only AI players showed the least cooperation, with only about 40% of the attacks being joint attacks and only 75% of the requests being answered positively. This is not surprising. The leading player would always be denied and would soon stop asking. This is also the reason why only 25% of requests were refused. Only the weakest players would regularly receive help and kept asking for it. Looking at the emotional players, over 90% of their attacks were joint attacks and almost 100% of them were granted. These 90% must be taken with caution, as an attack is counted as joint attack, if at least one other player is invited to join. As mentioned above, the emotional players would always have two enemies and one ally, so only one request was made each time. However, it is worth pointing out that the close to 100% success rate means that sympathy was always mutual. This is an interesting result, as no extra code was written to predict the other player's answer and guarantee a positive response.

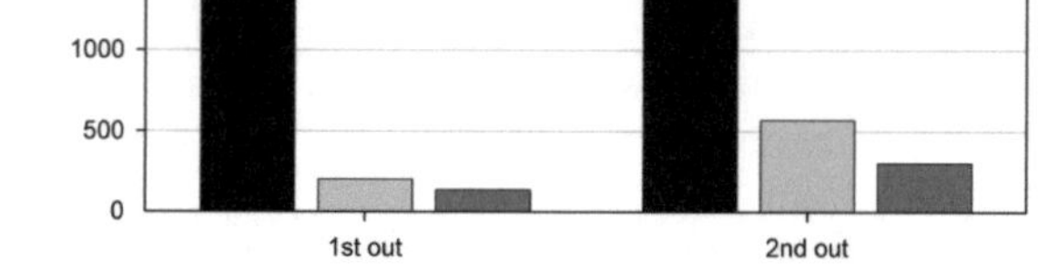

Fig. 3. Game duration comparing AE and AI players

Figure 4 (left side) shows examples of emotions "experienced" by agents in regard to their position in the game, i.e. whether they were winning or losing. Though almost all of the OCC emotions were triggered in the game we present only the most relevant ones for this analysis. Interestingly, the way the AI players immediately focused on the weakest player gave some insight into the different emotions of an agent that won without being attacked and one that was constantly attacked by everybody else. Surprisingly, the latter is not experiencing only negative emotions but shows a more interesting pattern.

With a few exceptions, *all* emotions are experienced a lot more often by the losing player, including positive ones. An explanation for this is the fact that there are more emotional triggers for this player in the game since he is attacked (and hence "interacts" with other players) more often than winning agents. The losing player (fourth place in the figure) "experiences" distress because of being attacked all the time and disappointment because of eventually losing; these emotions are logical and show the realism of the emotion engine. Resentment is also natural since the losing player obviously does not appreciate that the other players win square after square, ever worsening his position. The fact that pity is equally distributed among players also makes sense since there is no reason why an agent's rank in the game should influence his empathy and willingness to feel pity for other players. Why is the losing player experiencing more joy and relief, though? Although he is constantly under attack, a lot of those attacks fail because of mixed support the other players grant the winning player. Hence, there is high potential for joy (an attack successfully deflected, or the disliked other player not gaining support). Because the last player in rank is in constant fear of losing squares, relief will occur every time an attack fails.

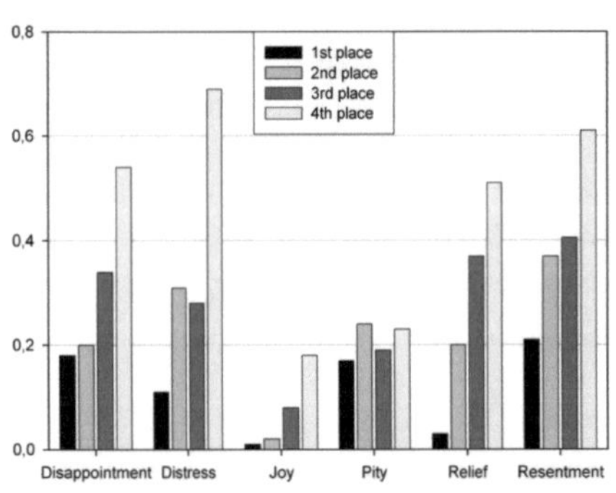

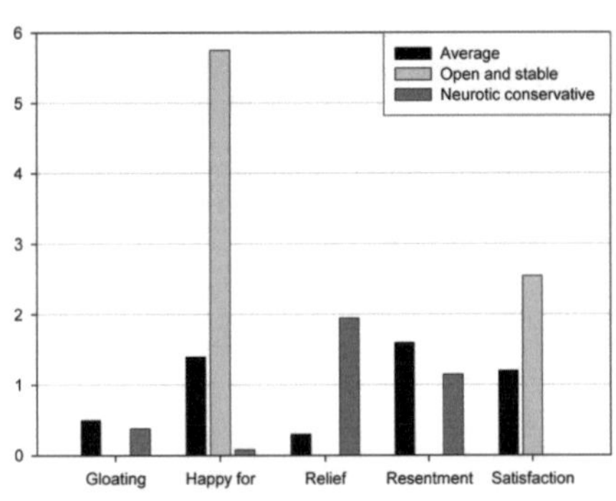

Fig. 4. Emotions by ranking (left side) and emotions by personality (right side)

Finally, figure 4 (right side) demonstrates the influence of extreme personalities on the emotions experienced. This was tested in a different run where predefined personality variables were modified systematically. The first personality was completely average as in previous games. The second one was an absolutely open, extroverted and non-neurotic person, while the third one was his exact opposite, a highly neurotic and introverted conservative. Though negative emotions were usually experienced more often in the other test runs with average personalities, the extroverted player forms an exception: his experience consisted almost only of positive emotions. "Happy-for" is triggered extremely often and is the result of this player "being the friend of everyone". Since there are multiple chances within a round to feel happy for other players' achievements, "happy-for" has a high value. "Satisfaction" is also occurring naturally as the open and stable player is optimistic and sees his hope often confirmed, partially due to good support from other players. In the opposite way, the neurotic person experienced nothing but negative emotions, again with the exception of relief, as his pessimism would not always turn out to be appropriate. This player seems to be always gloating and resentful. His lack in extroversion might also explain why only the most intense negative emotions came to the surface.

5. Conclusion

In this paper we presented SIMPLEX, a new model to simulate emotions. This model operates with three layers: personality, mood-states and emotions, which are interconnected in a believable way. Personality influences decisions on multiple levels. Mood-states are represented in a PAD space, they influence emotions and act as a means to form relationships to other agents. Emotions are generated according to OCC appraisal rules.

AI agents and AE agents whose emotions were generated by SIMPLEX were made to play a simple game. The data collected showed interesting emergent behavior. First, cooperation emerged between players. Second, the player losing the game is the one who experienced the most emotions, including positive ones.

It is questionable whether strictly separating AI from AE is realistic. Though it has been shown that in some cases, emotions may be triggered automatically, as when one freezes in front of a dangerous animal, in most cases emotions and cognition interact (Davidson, 2003; Ledoux, 1996). Cognitive evaluations of a situation, which are traditionally within the realm of AI, are also part of the appraisal processes necessary to trigger emotions. Frijda (1986) gives the example of how one can feel progressively overwhelmed by anger after having heard someone criticize a friend. On the contrary, Damasio (1996) has shown that emotions were necessary to cognitive processes.

Further research should thus investigate the behaviors of "Artifical-Emotionally-Intelligent" agents, which would be more realistic than AI or AE ones. This next generation of agents, which may be just as intelligent as AI ones, may then grow to be a little "emotionally creative" (Averill, 2004).

6. References

Averill, J. R. (2004). A tale of two snarks: Emotional intelligence and emotional creativity compared. *Psychological Inquiry*, 15, 228-233.

Bradley, M. M., & Lang, P. J. (1994). Measuring emotion: the Self-Assessment Manikin and the Semantic Differential. *J Behav Ther Exp Psychiatry*, 25(1), 49-59.

Damasio, A. R. (1996). The somatic marker hypothesis and the possible functions of the prefrontal cortex. *Philos Trans R Soc Lond B Biol Sci*, 351(1346), 1413-1420.

Davidson, R. J. (2003). Seven sins in the study of emotion: Correctives from affective neuroscience. *Brain and Cognition Affective Neuroscience*, 52(1), 129-132.

Frijda, N. (1986). The Emotions. New York: Cambridge University Press.

Gray, J. A., & McNaughton, N. (1996). The neuropsychology of anxiety: reprise. *Nebr Symp Motiv*, 43, 61-134.

LeDoux, J. E. (1996). The emotional brain: the mysterious underpinnings of emotional life. New York: Simon & Schuster.

McCrae, R. R., & Costa, P. T., Jr. (1987). Validation of the five-factor model of personality across instruments and observers. *J Pers Soc Psychol*, 52(1), 81-90.

Mehrabian, A. (1996). Analysis of the big-five personality factors in terms of the PAD temperament model. *Australian Journal of Psychology*, 48(2), 86-92.

Ortony, A., Clore, G. L., & Collins, A. (1988). The Cognitive Structure of Emotions. Cambridge: Cambridge University Press.

Reeves, B., & Nass, C. (1996). The Media Equation. How People Treat Computers, Television, and New Media like real People and Places. New York: Cambridge University Press.

Russell, J. A. (1978). Evidence of convergent validity on the dimensions of affect. *Journal of Personality and Social Psychology*, 36, 1152-1168.

Simon, H. A. (1967). Motivational and emotional controls of cognition. *Psychological Review*, 74, 29-39.

Staller, A., & Petta, P. (1999). Towards a Tractable Appraisal-Based Architecture for Situated Cognizers. In D. Canamero (Ed.), Grounding Emotions in Adaptive Systems. Zurich, Switzerland: Fifth International Conference of the Society for Adaptive Behaviour (SAB98).

Toda, M. (1982). Man, robot, and society. The Hague, Nijhoff.

Traue, H. C., & Kessler, H. (2003). Psychologische Emotionskonzepte. In A. Stephan & H. Walter (Eds.), Natur und Theorie der Emotion (pp. 20-33). Paderborn: Mentis.

Wilson, I. (2000). The Artificial Emotion Engine, Driving Emotional Behavior. Paper presented at the AAAI Spring Symposium.

14

From Signals to Emotions: Applying Emotion Models to HM Affective Interactions

Rita Ciceri and Stefania Balzarotti
Università Cattolica del Sacro Cuore, Milano
Italy

1. Introduction

In 1997 Rosalind Picard defined *Affective Computing* as the «computing that relates to, arises from, or deliberately influences emotions». Since then, research has developed to provide machines and computers with emotional skills similar to those of human users: among others, emotion recognition and expression. Within this approach, emotions are thought to constitute key components to achieve more effective Human Computer Interaction (HCI): «machines may never need all of the emotional skills that people need; however, there is evidence that machines will require at least some of these skills to appear intelligent when interacting with people» (Picard, Vyzas, & Healey, 2001). The core idea is that in the same way as emotion is crucial for human intelligent and rational functioning - as most recent psychology and neuroscience research has pointed out (Bechara & Damasio, 2005) - emotional abilities should be considered also in the development of intelligent computer systems.

Within the broad research area of *Affective Computing*, it is possible to distinguish two main work areas: on one side, *emotion simulation* is aimed at implementing artificial human-like autonomous agents able to interact with the user reproducing human facial and/or vocal emotional expressions, e.g. avatars, robots and ECAs (Breazeal, 2002; de Rosis et al., 2003; Lisetti et al., 2004); on the other side, *emotional decoding* is meant to design interfaces able to recognize the user's emotional responses from real-time capturing and processing of multiple signals (Lisetti et al., 2003). Whatever the research goal is - simulation or recognition - researchers have been confronted with the concept of emotion. Modelling emotions in HCI has revealed a complex challenge and different computational models have been developed to support its complexity and the multimodal richness of human *face-to-face* communication (Bianchi-Berthouze & Lisetti, 2002; Kort, Reilly, & Picard, 2001). Although the psychological study of emotion has brought to the development of different definitions of this construct, in the last years a widespread consensus has grown in psychological literature on the complexity of the emotional process and in particular on its *componential* nature (Scherer, 2005). All major theorists have stressed the need to analyze multiple response systems, such as physiology, behaviour and experience (Levenson, 2003).

In this chapter, we'll mainly focus on *emotional decoding*, i.e. the task to construct new generation interfaces able to sense and to respond to the user's affective feedback (Picard, Vyzas, & Healey, 2001). In particular, the major purpose of the chapter is to provide hints about the application of psychological emotion models to this research area. We'll first present a brief review of the two main theoretical approaches to the study of emotion: the *categorical* and the *dimensional* one, in the attempt to point out the main advantages and weak points when applied to the HCI. Secondly, we will focus on a dimensional semantic model (Multidimensional Emotional Appraisal Semantic Space, MEAS) which locates emotion in a four axis space, presenting its major features and application possibilities. Finally, we'll present some experimental data to support the use of our model.

2. Theoretical models of emotion: state or process?

As stated by Cowie et al. (2001) «constructing an automatic emotion recognizer depends on a sense of what emotion is. In the context of automatic emotion recognition, understanding the nature of emotion is not an end in itself. It matters mainly because ideas about the nature of emotion shape the way emotional states are described. They imply that certain features and relationships are relevant to describing an emotional state, distinguishing it from others, and determining whether it qualifies as an emotional state at all» (p.35). However, those ideas about what emotion is are not universally shared and different models of emotion are available within psychological literature. The selection and application of a certain model (the way emotion is conceived) to HCI and to the construction of artificial systems is not an irrelevant issue, since it will determine the way emotion is elicited, the way it is measured and the final performance of the system itself. Figure 1 displays three subtasks which can be differentiated within the broader scope of building an emotion detection system: signal capturing, feature extraction and semantic attribution. It should be noted that the selection of a specific model of what emotion is would influence each of these subtasks: which signals are needed, which features are the relevant ones and how they are labeled. In particular, a critical issue in the implementation of interfaces able to manage affective interactions with the user concerns the *semantic attribution*, i.e. the criteria or rules to attribute an emotional meaning to patterns of signals. In our chapter we will mainly focus on this subtask, considering patterns of signals - such as non verbal behavior and physiological responses - which are usually called *subsymbolic* and are thought to belong to the implicit channel of human communication (Cowie et al., 2001).

Figure 1. Three subtasks in the construction of emotion-sensitive interfaces.

A first theoretical approach to emotion is named *categorical* and has its roots in the evolutionary theories (Tomkins, 1962; Ekman, 1972), according to which emotions correspond to discrete and distinct units that are regulated by innate genetic-based mechanisms. Emotions are biologically determined and have evolved to address specific environmental concerns of our ancestors (for example, flight as a consequence of fear in situations that may be dangerous for the organism). Evolutionary theorists have pointed out the existence of a reduced number of *basic* or *primary* emotions (as for example anger, fear, disgust, happiness, sadness, surprise) each characterized by a specific response pattern, i.e. basic emotions may be clearly differentiated on the basis of their profile of physiological responses and facial expressions, which are universal. What happens when such an approach is applied to the HCI field? First of all, research will focus on primary emotions so that - for example - an automatic emotion recognizer will be taught to learn to detect if the user is happy, sad, angry, disgusted and so on. Second, research will consider stable and distinct response configurations each corresponding to a certain emotional label. To date, the main approach has been the attribution of a fixed emotional label to a specific configuration of signals. For example, the well-known Facial Action Coding System (FACS; Ekman & Friesen, 1978)- or better the EMFACS - involves a stable link between configurations of Action Units and six discrete basic emotions. This approach may be synthesized by the following formula:

$$\begin{aligned} &\text{if } s_{11} + s_{12} + \ldots + s_{1n}, \text{ then } e_1 \\ &\text{if } s_{21} + s_{22} + \ldots + s_{2n}, \text{ then } e_2 \\ &\quad \vdots \qquad\qquad\qquad\qquad \vdots \\ &\text{if } s_{k1} + s_{k2} + \ldots + s_{kn}, \text{ then } e_k \end{aligned}$$

where *s* are different signals and *e* the correspondent emotions: for example, if smile, then happiness; if lowered eyebrows, then anger, etc. Although they are useful to clarify the underlying core idea, these examples are obvious simplifications, since the detection and definition of pattern of signals is not so simple and immediate. Moreover, this subtask is complicated by a number of issues, such as the chance to regulate and hide non verbal signals or their intrinsic multiple communicative functions (Kaiser & Wehrle, 2001a), which however we will not consider here.

A second theoretical approach is named *dimensional.* It was started by Wundt (1905) and nowadays it is represented mainly by appraisal emotion theories and other theorists, such as Russell (1980;2003). Appraisal theories have suggested that the elicitation and differentiation of emotions are based on a process of *appraisal* of the situations that affect an individual's needs and goals (Arnold, 1960; Lazarus, 1991; Scherer, 1984). In this view emotions may be differentiated on the basis of *continuous* appraisal dimensions or criteria (and their patterns), according to which individuals evaluate situations and events. For instance, fear is generated by the evaluation of an event as new (novelty), unpleasant (valence) and exceeding the resources of the individual to cope with it (coping). This approach may be synthesized by the schema displayed in figure 2 where emotion (*e*) is the resultant of the intersection between different dimensions (d) whose values are determined by pattern of signals (s). In this view, the component-process model describes emotion as «the dynamic and constantly changing affective tuning of organisms as based on the continuous evaluative monitoring of their social and physical environment» (Scherer, 2005). Thus, emotion is considered as a *process* rather than a state: it is defined as an episode of temporary synchronization of all major subsystems of the organism functioning represented by five components - cognition; physiology; action tendencies; behavioural expression and subjective feeling. What happens when this second approach is applied to the HCI field?

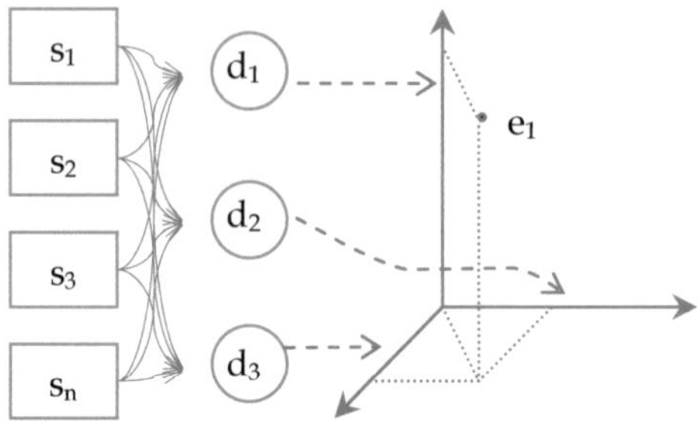

Figure 2. Dimensional models: emotions as resultant of underlying dimensions.

First of all, according to the researchers of this approach, the categorical view seems unable to account for the multiplicity of emotional signals that characterize human spontaneous interactions because it is limited to decode and interpret stereotyped sets of few basic emotions (Kaiser & Wehrle, 2001b). Since emotion is the *dynamic* product of the continuous process of appraisal, the interest is shifted from the detection and labeling of static response configurations to the modeling of the continuous modifications in multiple response systems - as for instance facial movements - with respect to specific dimensions such as novelty, pleasantness, activation and so on. These dimensions vary according to the model adopted: the definition of a reduced number of dimensions through which differentiate all emotional states and hence account for the *structure* of emotion is still a problematic issue. Ben-Ze'ev (2000) has used the expression «subtlety of emotions», to underlie how difficult the task is to account for the entire domain of human emotions through a few number of dimensions and their combinations.

3. Mutual tuning and joint action

Examining the categorical and dimensional approach, we suggested that the latter provides an alternative way to represent emotions rather than conceiving them as more or less discriminative lists of categories. Instead, the dimensional approach should enable researchers to go beyond the attribution of labels to static configurations of signals, since it is aimed at the analysis of patterns of signals in dynamically changing emotional episodes. Of course, this does not mean that prototypical (and universal) expressive configurations of basic emotions are denied; what is questioned is the usefulness of an approach which is limited to their analysis: regarding facial behaviour, Kaiser and Wehrle (2001b) have stated that «since such prototypical full-face expression patterns occur rather rarely in daily interactions, the question of whether and how single facial actions and partial combinations can be interpreted becomes crucial». In a similar way, in their contribute Cowie et al. (2001) have differentiated between full-blown and underlying emotional states, remarking the need for emotion technology to consider underlying emotion: «its priorities are pragmatic, in the sense that it has to deal with emotion as it occurs in real settings. In that context, it would be difficult to justify a policy of ignoring underlying emotion. For instance, it is a serious limitation if an alerting or tutoring system is blind to signs of emotions like boredom or anger until they become full blown» (p.35).
Thus, the risk seems twofold: on one side, it could be implemented an emotion-sensitive system able to recognize prototypical emotional reactions (fear, anger, happiness, etc.) which however occur so rarely within interactions that the system is almost useless; on the other side, the system could be sensitive to macroscopic (full blown) changes rather than to

more subtle response modifications which are crucial in the management of the interaction. Communication theorists have called *attunement* the set of behavioural units through which the agents manage, maintain and coordinate their communicative interactions (Giles et al., 2001; Siegman and Feldstein, 1979). Emotional non verbal signals play a central role within this process: in this sense, Cowie et al. (2001) have talked about *convergence*. Thus, applying the attunement perspective to HCI, the interchanges between user and machine cannot be reduced to or analyzed in terms of linear sequences of expressions and recognitions (Cappella & Pelachaud, 2001), but rather as a coordinated sequence of signals through which they attempt to mutual tuning. Emotional interfaces are thought to support HM interactions within different contexts, as for instance entertainment, tutoring or information retrieval. Therefore, it is reasonable to take into consideration that emotion recognition on the side of the machine is not an end in itself, but it should subserve the intent of improving the effectiveness of the dialog between the artificial system and the human user in the accomplishment of a certain goal. There is a joint (HM) action going on between user and artificial agent and whatever its nature is - having fun in a videogame, e-learning, retrieving information - the emotional reactions of the user arise within this context. In other words, we suggest that the machine should be able to *use* emotional signals to improve its attainment of the operational target (and eventually to adapt the task accordingly): the ability to *tune* emotionally to the user (through the processing of non verbal signals) can support and enhance the joint-action (Figure 3).

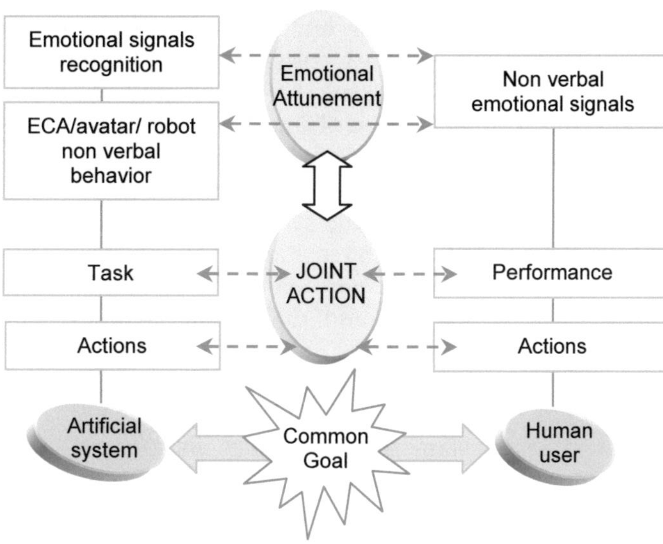

Figure 3. Emotional attunement and management of joint actions.

These two processes are conceived as simultaneous and interdependent: the artificial system and the human user are involved in a specific type of task (usually proposed by the machine) which implies certain types of action and a performance on the side of the user. The recognition of the user's emotional signals enables the machine to respond properly to his/her state through both pertinent non verbal behavior (performed for instance by an ECA) and the modification of the running task.

In this view, the correct recognition of the user's response cannot disregard contextual information such as the type of action or task and the related performance of the human:

«the concrete meaning of a facial expression can only be determined within the whole *temporal* and *situational* context» (Kaiser & Wehrle, 2001b). This also means that more *blended* emotional responses - for instance frustration, boredom, interest, satisfaction, amusement, etc. - are extremely relevant and that the attribution of an emotional meaning to a signal should always consider what's going on within the interaction (a smile could be a signal of embarrassment rather than of happiness).

4. Dimensional models: A proposal

Standing the importance of the attunement process in our modelling of HM interactions, we started working on a model of emotion which could be applied to any situation where an emotion-sensitive system would be likely to operate and could support the subtask of semantic attribution. In the following paragraphs, we'll outline its main features: since the work is still in progress, it is important to note that the model is by no means meant as exhaustive or definitive. We believe that it can provide useful hints for the research in this area, but we will also present the limits and weak points we are still trying to face. First of all, we had clear in mind that the model should entail three main properties: dimensionality, situatedness and multimodality.

Dimensionality. To model the structure of emotion, we chose a dimensional rather than a categorical approach. As reported above, the dimensional approach has accounted for the *temporal dimension* of emotion, i.e. it has underlined the importance of monitoring the constant modifications of the emotional response, which - in each moment - corresponds to the result of the continuous process of appraisal of the situation. It should be clear that if one considers (as we do) the task of recognition of emotional signals as functional to the constant process of emotional attunement in the HM interaction, the need to consider emotion as a process becomes crucial. Thus, we started to conceive the user's emotions as represented by a set of continuous axes, which are normally set to zero but that can move within a certain range of positive and negative values as a result of a change in the status of the user. Given these assumptions, a question remained: how many and which dimensions are necessary to account for the structure of emotion and differentiate between the huge number of emotional responses?

To address this question, we turned to the dimensional models of emotion proposed by psychological literature. A first dimensional model is the *circumplex model* of Russell (1980) which considered two relevant dimensions, *activation* and *valence* - the definition of these two dimensions was derived by the results of various analysis techniques (factor analysis, scaling, etc.) on emotion related words. According to this model, emotions are represented by different points which are distributed within a two-dimensional space forming approximately a circle. Emotions are then organized around two axes: the horizontal one corresponds to valence, i.e. pleasantness vs. unpleasantness of a certain emotional state; the vertical one is defined as activation, i.e. how dynamic the state is (activation vs. calm). In sum, every emotional state can be described as a specific point of intersection between these two axes. The valence and activation dimensions have been used by other psychological models of emotion (Plutchik, 1980) and have also been applied to HCI (Cowie et al., 1999). However, «representations of that kind depend on collapsing the structured, high-dimensional space of possible emotional states into a homogeneous space of two dimensions. There is inevitably loss of information» (Cowie et al., 2001). In other words,

these two dimensions alone do not allow to differentiate between all emotional states: for example, both fear and anger are characterized by high activation and negative valence.
Secondly, we directed our attention to appraisal dimensions and in particular to the Stimulus Evaluation Checks (SECs) proposed by Scherer (2001): novelty, intrinsic pleasantness, goal conduciveness, coping potential, norm/self compatibility. According to this author, all different emotions may be derived from a particular pattern of these appraisal dimensions. More recently, Scherer (2005) has proposed an instrument for the assessment of subjective experience (Geneva Emotional Wheel, GEW) «going beyond a simple valence-arousal space in order to be better able to differentiate qualitatively different states that share the same region in this space» (p.721). The structure given to the emotional categories included in the instrument is based on appraisal dimensions (or SECs) and in particular on goal conduciveness (vs. obstructiveness) and coping potential (low vs. high power), since - according to Scherer - research has demonstrated that these are the dimensions which have the strongest impact on emotion differentiation.
Starting from the theoretical issues (based on empirical findings) presented above, we chose to locate emotion in a four axis space defined by: novelty, valence, coping and arousal. Because of the reference to the appraisal framework, we named our model *Multidimensional Emotional Appraisal Semantic Space* (MEAS, Ciceri & Balzarotti, 2007). Thus, in our model, every emotion can be described by the formula: e_j (x,y,z,k), where x, y, z, and k define the coordinates in a four-dimensional space. Although they are theoretically conceived as continuous, due mainly to practical reasons, the MEAS axes can assume five different discrete intensity values, ranging from -2 to +2. A graphical representation of the model is displayed in Figure 4.

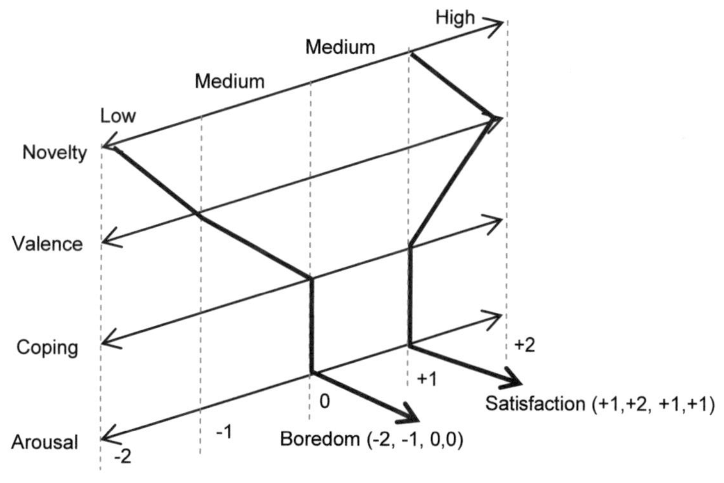

Figure 4. The MEAS model: emotions are conceived as the intersection of four emotional axes (novelty, valence, coping and arousal) which can assume different levels of intensity.

It should be remarked that unlike the other models outlined (mainly concerned with subjective experience), our model was meant as an instrument to attribute emotional meaning to patterns of signals (semantic attribution). In other words, what we tried (and are still trying) to develop is a system of rules able to link signals to underlying emotional dimensions so that 1) emotional episodes can be differentiated from non emotional behaviour; 2) an automatic emotion recognizer using these rules may be able to monitor the responses of the user continuously, detecting the relevant episodes of changes in the user's state. Thus, as it will be shown concerning *multimodality*, the MEAS system and its scoring are tightly linked to the multimodal analysis of both physiological and non verbal signals, whose modifications provide information for the scoring of the axes.

Besides theoretical assumptions on the structure of emotion, the selection of the four axes (novelty, valence, coping and arousal) was dependent on the possibility to score them on the basis of observable responses. In this sense, the most problematic dimension seems the coping one, since «coping» represents an internal state of the individual, i.e. the evaluation of his/her personal resources to cope with the situation. The issues regarding the scoring of the axes will be further considered in the following paragraphs.

The MEAS model presents a number of limitations: a) first of all, a four axis space is complicated to handle and it seems likely to be a long time before automatic emotion recognizers will incorporate all the subtleties considered in it: nonetheless, we believe that it could provide useful directions to work on, which may be absent in simpler models; b) although it is based on the analysis of previous studies on emotion structure, the selection of the dimensions is still arbitrary and others axes could be more effective at differentiating emotions; c) the definitions of rules linking signals to dimensions is still in progress, as we will show in the next paragraphs.

5. Embodiment: situatedness and action

The application of the concept of attunement to HCI represents an attempt to shift empirical attention from a perspective of uncontextual emotion recognition to its grounding in joint actions between human and artificial agents in which the two participants act in coordination with each other to accomplish goals that are part of their joint activities (Clark, 1996; Brock & Trafton, 1999). In this view, the emotion detection system to be implemented is not an automatic labeler, but rather an artificial agent able to exploit emotional signals to manage the interaction with the user properly tuning to his/her current state. To do this, the system has to be provided with contextual information in some way, since HM Emotional interactions are always *situated* within a certain context, as for instance, videogame-playing, information retrieval services, e-learning, etc. Within HCI, the context may be defined by the particular nature of the interaction itself, i.e. the type of task to accomplish which in turn determines two key elements: the common goal that user and artificial agent share (have fun, give/receive information, tutoring) and the actions performed. The core idea is that it is almost impossible to attribute the accurate emotional meaning to the user's behaviour unless this contextual information is available.

Besides the attunement perspective, the central role attributed to *action* is also justified by the reference to the recently formulated *enactive* view (Varela et al., 1991). Within this psychological approach to cognition, it has been theorized that the mind is embodied, i.e. the body - and the sensorimotor processes - constitutes the medium of the interaction with the world and for this reason it plays a central role in cognition and in adaptation. Since the organism inevitably interacts with the world through his own body, action directly influences perception, categorization and other cognitive processes: «cognition depends upon the kinds of experience that come from having a body with various sensorimotor capacities [...]. By using the term *action* we mean to emphasize once again that sensory and motor processes, perception and action, are fundamentally inseparable in live cognition» (Varela et al., 1991). The concept of embodied (body-mediated) interaction has become increasingly relevant within the domain of HCI. Concerning simulation, for instance, the Embodied Conversational Agents (ECAs) are defined as embodied because they have bodies (similar to the human ones) through which they can communicate multimodally with the user using voice, face, gaze, posture, etc. (Pelachaud & Poggi, 2002). Concerning recognition, interfaces and artificial agents are provided with sets of sensors able to detect a wide range of body signals and human motion. Moreover, besides multimodal interfaces, a new research area has started to work on *enactive interfaces* (ENACTIVE NoE), i.e. interfaces which are thought to interact through perception, action and motion rather than through icons and symbols (e.g. Reactive Robots).

In this perspective, to accomplish the definitions of possible rules of semantic attribution which are part of the MEAS model, two different factors were considered in addition to patterns of (physiological and non verbal) emotional signals. The first factor corresponded to the event, i.e. the type of stimulus/task (what the user is doing): for instance, signals of frustration may be expected within a difficult learning task that exceeds the user's abilities; signals of boredom such as yawning may be expected within repetitive tasks, or within unsuccessful entertainment contexts and so on. According to appraisal theories, emotion is generated by the cognitive evaluation of certain situations: through the systematic manipulation of types of events in a computer game (losing a ship, passing to the next game level), Van Reekum, et al. (2004) have demonstrated the influence of appraisal dimensions (intrinsic pleasantness and goal conduciveness) on physiological reactions and vocal behaviours.

The second factor corresponded to action and included 1) the performance to the task (e.g. doing right/wrong, win/lose, etc.); 2) body movements signaling approach or withdrawal. As to this last component, it has been showed that emotions are linked to different action tendencies, e.g. avoid, approach, interrupt, change strategy, attempt, reject, etc. and involve states of action readiness (Frijda, 2007). Both these elements are used in the scoring of the MEAS dimensions: 1) the performance in the task provides information about two axes, valence and coping; for instance, doing wrong may change from positive to negative the valence of a smile and usually involves low coping; 2) body movements signalling approach and withdrawal provide information about the three axes of novelty, valence and coping; for instance, approaching may signal interest and curiosity towards something new, whereas withdrawing may indicate unpleasantness and low coping (turning one's head), or even low novelty (boredom).

6. Multimodality

Multimodal interfaces are a new-generation class of interfaces designed to recognize two or more combined user input modalities - as for example speech and facial movements - relying on recognition-based technologies increasingly improved by the development of new sensors and input/output devices now becoming available (Oviatt, 2002) together with new algorithms for real-time pattern detection, as in facial tracking (McKenna & Gong, 1996; Cohn, Zlochower, Lier, & Kanade, 1999; Anisetti, Bellandi, Beverina, Damiani, 2005). In this way, they are thought to support more efficient and powerful HM interaction. Multimodality seems an essential property especially for interfaces aimed at automatic emotion detection, since (as stated at the beginning of the chapter) psychological literature has highlighted the *componential* nature of the emotional process (Scherer, 2005) stressing the need to analyze multiple response systems (Levenson, 2003).

Computation research has based empirical investigation including the combination of multiple modalities collecting various body measures that may capture aspects of an affective state in the attempt to reproduce the multimodal richness of the emotional process. Combining all the features extracted might also provide consistent information in order to increase the accuracy and reduce the error related to the use of single parameters (Picard, Vyzas, & Healey, 2001). In this sense, multimodality is tightly linked to the two subtasks of signal capturing and feature extraction (Picard, Vyzas, & Healey, 2001), i.e. how emotion is measured. In the last decades, these two subtasks have been faced by several studies and research teams (e.g. HUMAINE NoE), which however will not be considered here since they are beyond the purpose of this chapter.

What we are interested in is the translation of multimodal signals into an emotional semantic, i.e. a model to link patterns of signals belonging to different response system to emotional meanings. The MEAS model is designed to receive information from different types of signals (as the ones which multimodal interfaces should handle): a first distinction concerns two macro categories, *physiological* and *communicative* responses.

Many researchers have introduced the interesting and important use of *biosignals* as possible indicators of emotion and arousal (Prendinger et al., 2003; Picard, Vyzas, & Healey, 2001). The Autonomic Nervous System (ANS) is one of the most elicited apparatus from which understand and detect arousal, which is either consciously or mainly unconsciously modified. Since 1953, researchers have proposed some correlations between physiological signals and ANS responses and nowadays it is possible to infer from these signals useful information to understand that something is changing in the emotional condition (Kim et al, 2004; Picard et al, 2001): among the most exploited input signals, skin temperature, electrodermal activity, heart rate, the respiratory rate, etc. However, the chance of differentiating configurations of physiological signals specific for each emotion is still controversial (Cacioppo & Tassinary, 1990) and it may be questioned whether a system relying exclusively on biosignals could be able to discriminate the emotional reactions of the user - or at least reactions which do not fall under the basic emotion categories (Picard, Vyzas, & Healey, 2001). Besides the investigation of specific physiological correlates of emotional categories, other studies have showed that physiological changes are linked to emotional dimensions such as valence and arousal (Cacioppo et al., 2000; Picard, Vyzas, & Healey, 2001).

For these reasons, in our model, physiological signals act as a generic and transverse layer besides the specific channels used to realize the communicative interaction between Human and Machine. In other words, the principal use of the physiological signals we do in our framework is as detectors of the beginning of emotional arousal in the human agent: for this reason, biosignals provide information for the scoring of the *arousal* dimension. Since we are still working on the translation of two types of signals (HR and EDA) into one single arousal axis, we will mainly focus on communicative responses.

Communicative non verbal signals ranging from facial expression, vocal features, gestures, gaze direction, posture have been widely exploited in HCI (for a review about voice and face see Cowie et al., 2001). Psychological research on multimodal communication has suggested that human expressive systems are characterized not only by semantic redundancy - multiple signals belonging to different systems converge to transmit the same message - but also by semantic interdependence, in which each signal in relation to the others participates in the meaning construction (Ciceri, 2001). For example, one can shake his head to deny and smile at the same time to lower the negativity of the situation or to signal its only partial unpleasantness. We can observe action units like lip corner depressor and lowering eyebrows to signal disgust and at the same time an approaching movement towards the screen to signal simultaneously attention and willingness to better explore. The coordinated use of signals belonging to different response systems enables humans to soften, to stress, to modify the expression of their emotional states to accomplish different communicative intentions. For these reasons, it becomes relevant to focus on the role of different signal systems in emotional expression, as showed in figure 5.

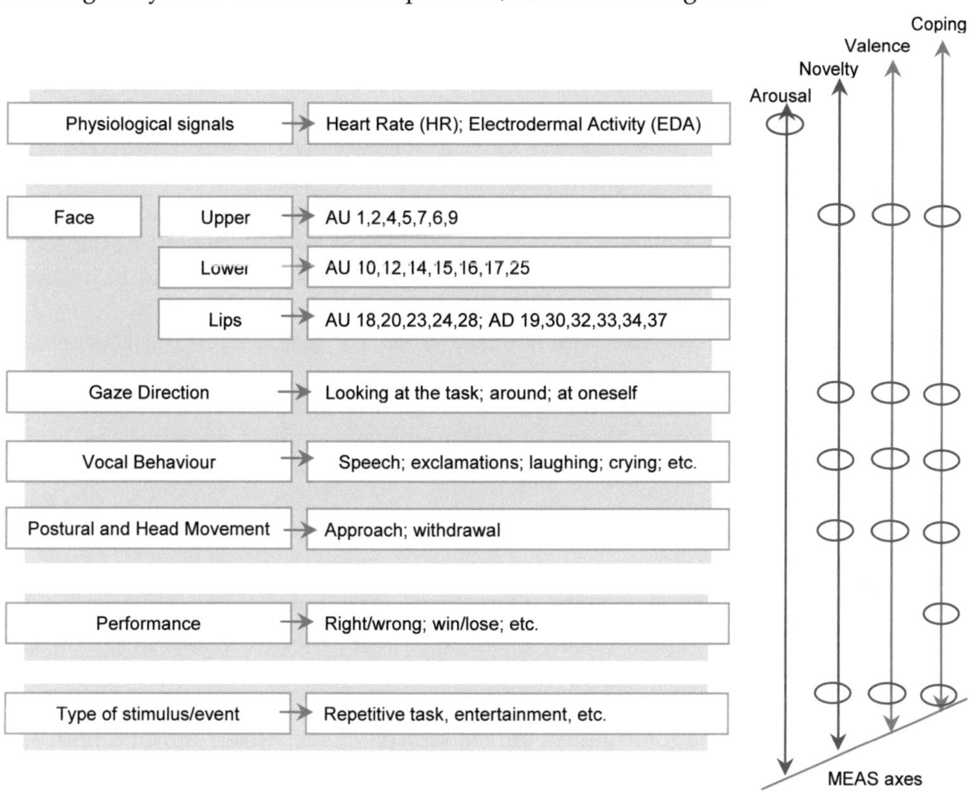

Figure 5. Response systems and emotional axes.

The figure displays the different types of signals considered in our model and the emotional axes which is possible to score on the base of each of them. Physiology provides information to the arousal dimension, whereas communicative signals to novelty, pleasantness and coping. The coping dimension is scored also on the base of the performance to the task. Finally, the type of eliciting event or stimulus may influence novelty, pleasantness and coping.

The procedure of scoring of the four MEAS dimensions is always based on a preceding analysis of the signals belonging to the different response systems taken into account (non verbal and physiological). Since all signals are characterized by large inter-individual variability, this level of analysis should always take into account a *baseline* level for each subject. Although the procedure to compare a certain response to the baseline is widespread in the analysis of physiological signals, it is less common in behavioural analyses. In this case, the risk is to overestimate (or underestimate) a certain behaviour - since it may be part of the individual's «personal style» of expression.

Regarding non verbal behaviour, the first level of application of the MEAS method consists in a behavioural *frame by frame* micro-analysis (25 fps) of the clip obtained from the video recording of the human subject. This analysis is based on the previous elaboration of a coding grid, i.e. the selection of behavioural units to be extracted. The left side of figure 4 displays the major categories of the Behaviour Coding system (BCS), through which we conduct our analyses (Ciceri, Balzarotti, & Colombo, 2005). The BCS considers four macro-categories:

1) *Facial movements*: the fundamental muscle movements that comprise the Facial Action Coding System (Ekman & Friesen, 1978) were selected. We considered action units relating to upper and lower face and to lip movements (20 AUs and 10 ADs). For each unit, intensity is rated on a 3 point scale (Low, Medium, High);
2) *Gaze direction:* this category considers where the gaze - and thus the attention - of the subject is directed: for instance, the subject may look at the task (mainly at the computer screen), at the keyboard, or he may be distracted and look around, or at oneself (this usually happens when the subject is wired);
3) *Posture and head movement*: behavioural units of approaching/withdrawing are considered (see 5);
4) *vocal behaviour:* since the coding system is applied to a video, we restrict here the analysis to the recording of the use of speech or other kinds of vocalizations. However, more subtle analyses on supra-segmental features may be conducted extracting the vocal stream.

Reliabilities between different coders need to be calculated. Moreover, statistical analysis performed through THEME Software (Magnusson, 2001) is used for the detection of multimodal recurrent pattern analysis (T-pattern). The number of different T-patterns detected in a behavioural stream, their average and/or maximum length (number of event types involved) and their average/maximum level (number of hierarchical levels in a pattern) may be used as measures of complexity or overall synchrony.

Non verbal signals provide information for the scoring of three axes: novelty, pleasantness and coping. At this second level of analysis, the three axes derived from SECs are scored on a 5 point rating scale by a group of three judges to describe the user emotional state. The judges do the scoring on the base of the MEAS rules, which link pattern of signals to positive or negative scores on a certain emotional dimension: examples are showed in Table 1. Novelty is scored in correspondence of behavioural units signalling the individual's evaluation that a change in the pattern of external or internal stimulation occurred (e.g. raising eyebrows, brow lowering, widening eyes, etc.) or that a stimulus is already known, well explored and too expected (moving gaze away, yawning, etc). Valence is scored in correspondence of behavioural units signalling the evaluation that a stimulus event as pleasant (e.g. smile, approach tendencies) or unpleasant (nose wrinkle, avoidance tendencies, etc.). Coping is scored in correspondence of behavioural units signalling the evaluation that the coping potential, i.e. the degree of control over the event is high (approach tendencies, nodding, right performance, etc.) or low (withdrawal, closing eyes or moving gaze away, wrong performance, etc.). The level of intensity attributed to the emotional axes depends on both the level of intensity (High, Medium, Low) and the number of the behavioural units activated. Inter-judge agreement is calculated.

At present, we have available a group of rules which we derived from indications found in literature (Kaiser & Wehrle, 2001a; Wehrle et al., 2000; Wallbott, 1998) and from the results of the previously mentioned analysis of patterns and configuration of multimodal signals applied to the MEED database (Ciceri, Balzarotti, Beverina, Manzoni, & Piccini, 2006) as we'll describe in the next paragraph. However, we are working at the development of this initial group to a more extended set of rules. Moreover, although at present the MEAS method requires manual annotations (with the aid of software for the analysis of observational data) and human expert judges who receive a training to perform the coding, in the future the rules may be tested and implemented through connectionist architectures to build up the semantic of an emotion detection interface[1]. Facing the problem of «the definition of appropriate models of the relation between realistic emotions and the coordination of behaviours in several modalities» - though applied to the construction of believable ECAs - Martin et al. (2006) have stated that «regarding the analysis of videos of real-life behaviours, before achieving the long-term goal of fully automatic processing of emotion from low levels (e.g. image processing, motion capture) to related behaviours in different modalities, a manual annotation phase might help to identify the representation levels that are relevant for the perception of complex emotions».

7. MEAS multimodal database

We conclude the chapter presenting the grounding of the MEAS system on the analysis of a multimodal database (Multidimensional Emotion Ecological Database, MEED; Ciceri, Balzarotti, Beverina, Manzoni, & Piccini, 2006): audiovisual corpora have been proposed as an important source of knowledge on multimodal behaviour occurring during real-life complex emotions (Douglas-Cowie et al., 2003).

The MEED database includes the collection of naturally occurring samples of emotions (audio, video and physiological data) elicited by two different kinds of stimuli in experimental situations: a) in a first condition, 36 subjects were video recorded while watching segments extracted from three famous movies; b) in a second experimental setup, 24 subjects were video recorded while playing with five different kinds of computer games especially developed to elicit emotional reactions. In this chapter we will focus on this second condition since it better represents a typical HM interaction and it offers an experimental situation where the subject is involved not just as a simple observer since he has to act and react. The videogames were developed through the manipulation of appraisal dimensions and types of game events in a similar way as in Van Reekum et al (2004).

---

[1] In partnership with the Laboratory of Neural Networks (Laren) directed by prof. Bruno Apolloni, State University, Milano.

Dimensions	Rules (+1, +2)	Rules (-1, -2)
Novelty: behavioural units signalling that a change in the pattern of external or internal stimulation occurred	AU 1, AU2, AU 1+2 AU 1+2+17 AU 1+2+25+26 AU 5, AU 1+5 AU 4, AU 4+7 AU 5+ head backward AU 7 + head forward AU 7+20+23 AU 25, 26,AU 16+25 Head/posture forward	AU 41 AU 43 Look away Head backward Head tilted Posture backward
Valence: behavioural units signalling pleasantness or unpleasantness	AU 12 AU 6+12 AU 6+12+25 AU 6+12+20 AU 6+14+20 Approaching	AU 15 AU 6+4 AU 6+17 AU 9 AU 9+16+25 AU 10 AU 6+7+9 AU 16+20+25 Withdrawal Head turned
Coping: behavioural units signalling that the degree of control over the stimulus is high or low	AU 6+20+24 AU 23+24 AU 6+12+right performance Nodding	AU 2 AU 1+4+10 AU 15 + 17 AU 4+17 AU 5+17 AU 17+22 AU 17+23 +head backward/turned Shaking head Wrong performance

Table 1. Examples of signals used to score the MEAS dimensions.

We started from the analysis of emotional responses to address three questions which lied at the base of the task to define rules linking signals to underlying emotional axes:

1) which behavioural systems are used most frequently during HM interactions and thus which signals are the most relevant to consider (multimodality);
2) which behavioural units are usually associated in the same behavioural patterns (multimodality);
3) how these patterns vary in correspondence to certain types of stimulus/event (embodiment);
4) how behavioural units dynamically change in time (attunement).

A preliminary *frame by frame* micro-analysis (25 fps) was performed as previously explained through the Behaviour Coding System (BCS) by two independent judges who had received a training in the analysis of multimodal behaviour. The analysis was conducted with the aid of The Observer 5.0® software for the analysis of observational data (NOLDUS, The Netherlands). The computerized procedure of analysis allowed the automatic extraction of behavioural indexes such as rate (number of occurrences/total time) and duration which were used as dependent variables to submit to statistical analysis. Moreover, inter-judge reliability was calculated (averaged Cohen's Kappa=.89). Figure 6 displays the mean rates calculated for each behavioural category in correspondence of the five different types of videogames.

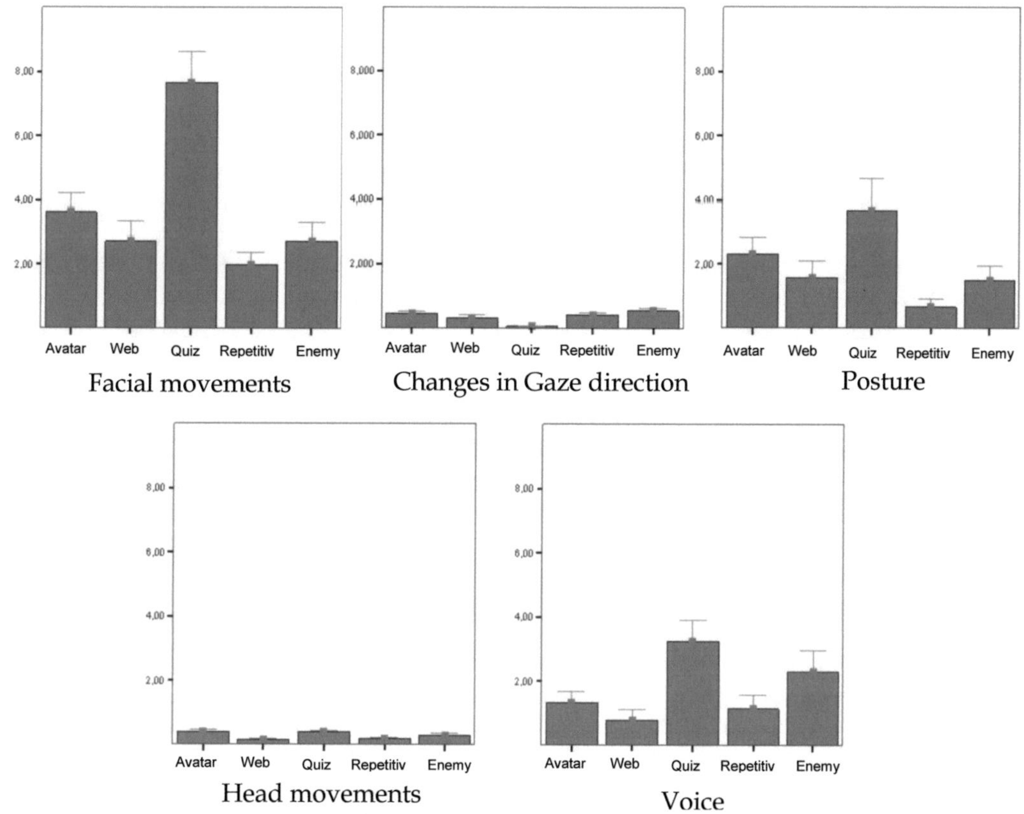

Figure 6: Mean rates calculated for Facial Movements, Gaze Direction, Posture, Head Movements and Vocal Behaviour in correspondence of five different types of video games.

Within the different multimodal signals considered in our analysis, mean rates clearly indicated that some behavioural categories - face, voice and posture - are more frequently exhibited than others. In particular facial movements seemed the most used expression system to signal emotion and thus the most informative. These results were confirmed by a repeated measure ANOVA which showed a significant main effect of the behavioural category ($F=24.807$; $df=4$ $p < .001$). Moreover, Bonferroni adjusted pairwise comparisons confirmed that face differed from all the other expressive systems.

A second significant effect concerned the type of stimulus ($F = 26.402$; df=4; $p < .001$) and its interaction with the type of behavioural category ($F = 16.873$; df=16; $p < .001$), i.e. the rate of exhibition of a certain behavioural category is influenced by the kind of running task. To better explain the role of the stimulus, we provide hereafter a brief description of the games used in our study. Five different activities were selected in order to simulate different interactive levels on one side and to elicit specific emotional reactions on the other. The first purpose required the manipulation of both the kind of procedural actions on the side of the player and the interactive structure of the game. The second goal involved the manipulation of game events through underlying appraisal dimensions (Van Reekum et al., 2004).

1) In the first activity (avatar), participants interacted with and listened to an avatar constituted by a computerized Italian speaking voice which guided participants across the different computer activities.
2) The second activity (web) consisted in the exploration of a university web site: in particular, some pages regarding university courses were selected as assumed to be emotionally neutral. As to the expected interaction structure, we supposed a low interaction level as participants were confronted with a non finalized task simply requiring to explore a controlled number of virtual pages.
3) The third activity (quiz) was constituted by a quiz game: fifteen questions of general culture were presented to subjects who had to select the right answer among four alternatives.
4) The fourth activity (repetitive) was a boring game: in this game, subjects moved a rabbit character on the screen and had to collect a large number of carrots (50). Carrots appeared one by one and always in the same positions, hence creating a repetitive task.
5) The last activity corresponded to a classical video game: subjects controlled a rabbit character that had to collect carrots while avoiding an enemy. The game presented four different levels of difficulty. The players won points for every carrot collected and every level successfully completed. From the possible events in the game that may elicit particular patterns of appraisal, three different types of events were selected: losing a life (being captured by the enemy or hitting an obstacle), bonus appearing and passing successfully to the next game level. The first type of event is obstructive to the goal of winning the game, while the latter conducive in the pursuit of gaining points.

The games were structured to provide participants with different kind of interactions: for instance, the quiz game had a very quick question/answer structure, hence very similar to a conversational exchange; in the second and third game participants moved and controlled a rabbit and had to act «as if» they were this character to reach specific goals (e.g. gain carrots, avoid the enemy). In the third game, five different interactive episodes (positive vs. negative bonus, invisibility bonus, poisoned carrot, new level) were added where the computer used verbal messages to interact with the participant and this active intervention was aimed at eliciting the subject's response. The whole session lasted about 30 minutes.

Our experimental results showed that the user's communicative responses changed with respect to the interactivity level of the tasks and the related emotional events. More in detail, it is possible to observe that high interactive tasks (e.g. the quiz game, the avatar interaction and the enemy game) elicited more communicative signals, not only when compared to the web control condition, but also with the repetitive-boring task. In particular, Bonferroni adjusted pairwise comparisons showed that the quiz game differed from all the other activities, eliciting the highest number of responses. Therefore, the evaluation of the emotional experience requires the elaboration of situated rules closely linked to the ongoing task and the subject's performance, which can influence the relevance of an event: think, for example, how different can be a wrong answer during a job interview and a wrong answer during a game.

Secondly, THEME Software 5.0® was used for the detection of multimodal recurrent pattern analysis (minimum number of occurrences=15; α=.0005). The principal aim of the Theme software is to provide aid in discovering and understanding the structure of behavioural streams (Magnusson, 2001).

Thus, whereas the previous statistical analysis considered the mean rate of behavioural categories, this analysis was aimed at examining the *temporal structure* and the associations between specific classes of behavioural units. For instance, figure 7 shows the temporal occurring of all the behavioural units scored for one subject: time is represented by the x-axis, whereas the number of scored events is displayed by the y-axis. Behavioural units are concentrated in the initial part of the HM interaction (avatar and quiz game), whereas few responses characterize the central section (web and repetitive task). At present, we are working on this kind of temporal analysis of behavioural responses, on the detection of the patterns of association between different units and on the possibility to differentiate a reduced number of emotional episodes though the application of the MEAS system (not all behaviour is necessary emotional).

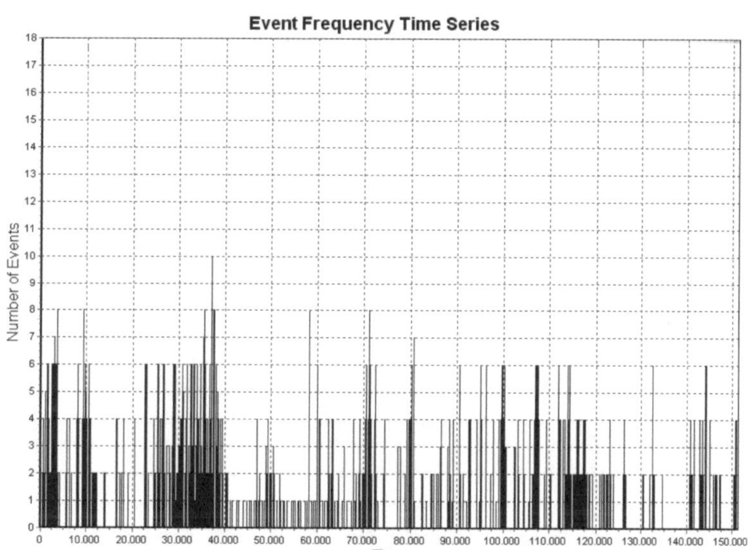

Figure 7. Number of behavioural units scored and temporal dimension

THEME results showed a high number of non random temporal patterns in the event time series of behavioural units. Thus, the detected patterns indicated that non verbal behaviour during computer interaction is highly temporally structured. A qualitative analysis distinguished two different kinds of patterns: patterns connecting behavioural units belonging to the same category (e.g. facial movements) and patterns connecting units belonging to different categories (e.g. facial and vocal behaviour), indicating a multimodal organization and structure. Figure 8 shows one of the most frequent modal patterns (occurrences=17; length=8; duration =5116 frames), combining AU 15 and AU 17 and a multimodal one (occurrences=15; length=6; duration =15287) where vocal behaviour (speech) and facial movements AU 15+17 (lip corner depressor and chin raise) are connected.

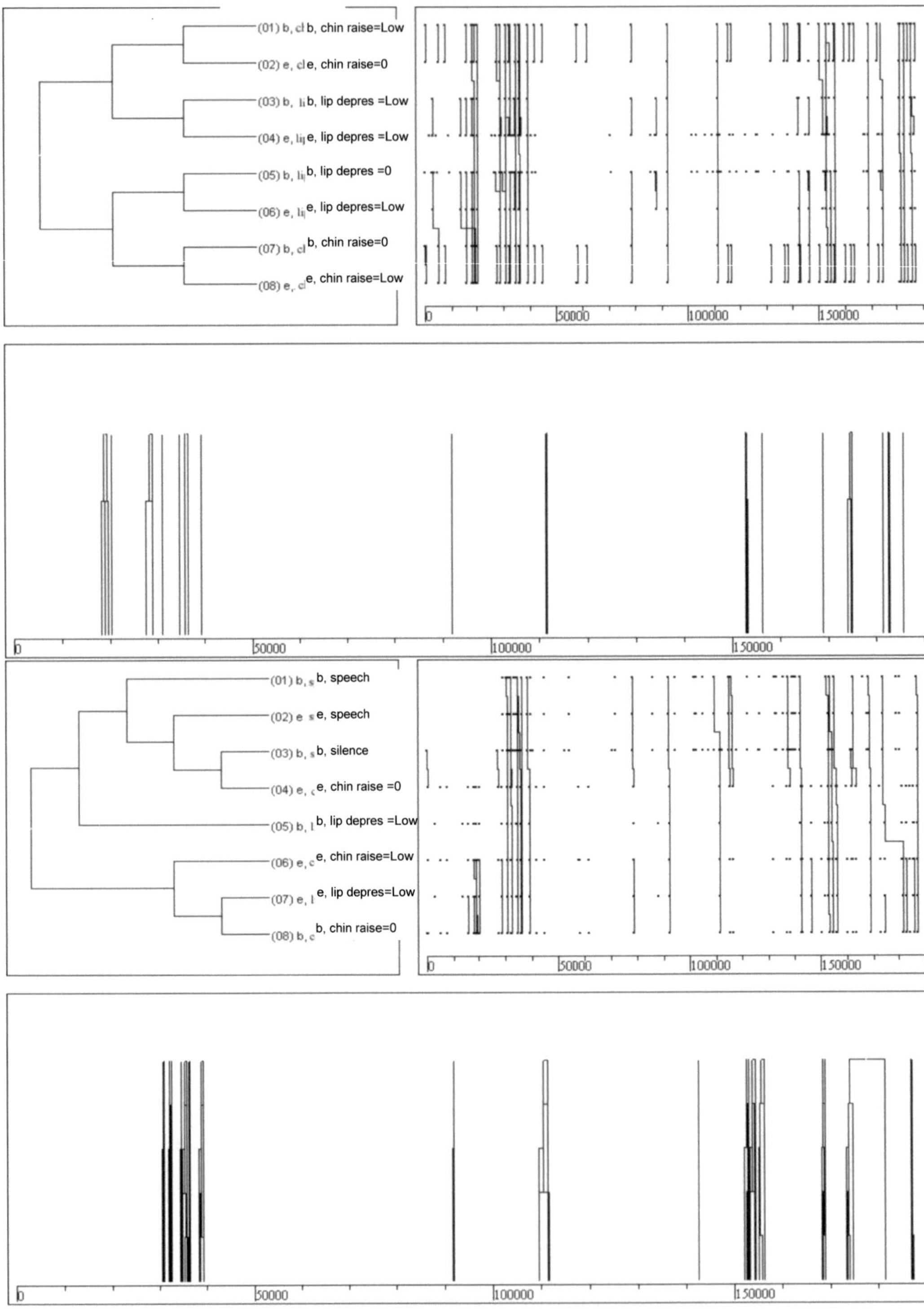

Figure 8. Statistical analysis of recurrent behavioural patterns.

Three diagrams are presented: 1) the pattern tree graph shows the event types composing the pattern (signalling begin or end) listed in the order in which they occur, while the pattern connections are on the left of the event list showing how many hierarchical levels are involved; 2) the connection graph deals with frequency and real-time distribution of events in the pattern: dots represent event occurrences and the lines connecting the dots represent pattern occurrences; 3) the instance graph provides information about the real-time structure of the pattern.
Finally, starting from the multimodal analysis explained above, the three axes of the MEAS systems (the fourth dimension, i.e. arousal, concerns physiological data which are not taken into account here) were scored by two judges who had received a previous training. Inter-judge reliability was calculated (Cohen's Kappa=.79). Figure 9 displays the durations (% interval) for each emotional dimension in correspondence of five different video activities (i.e. the percentage of time during which the dimensions were «active»).

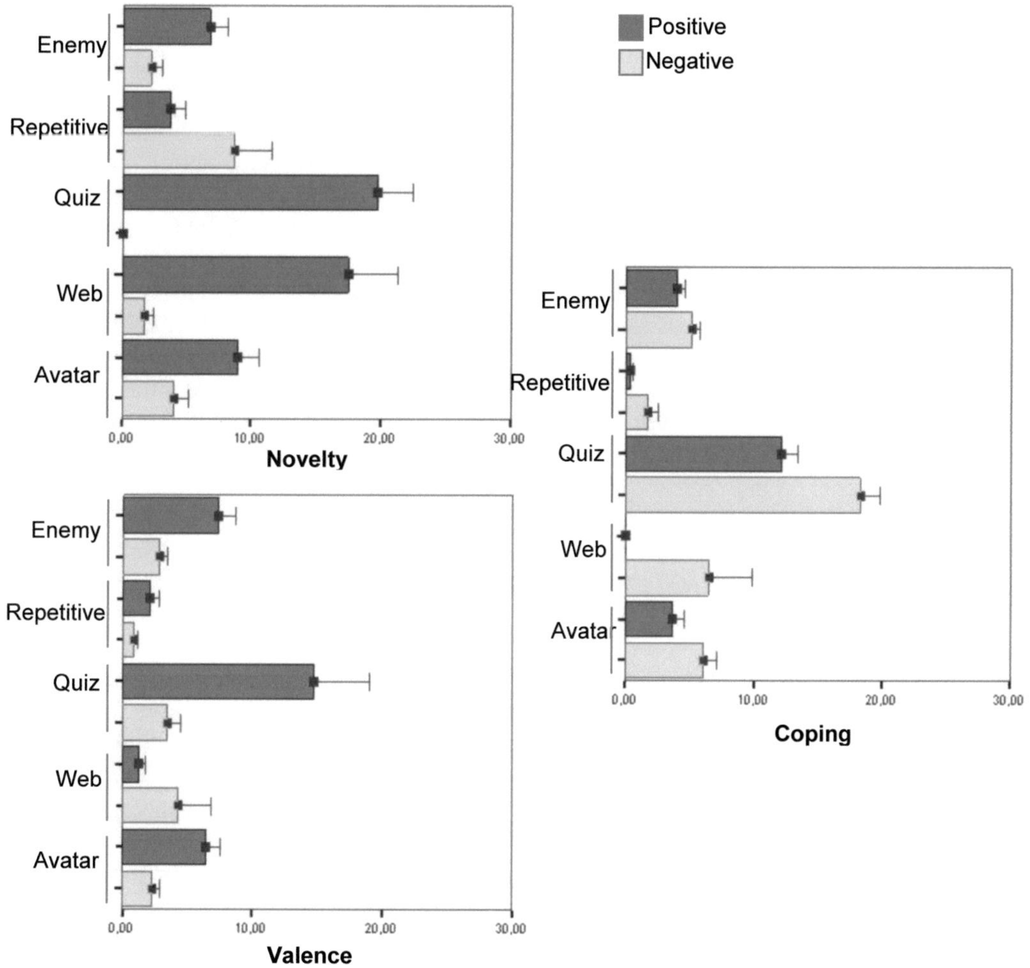

Figure 9. MEAS emotional axes: durations (% interval) for positive (+1, +2) and negative (-1, -2) scores.

First, our results showed that all three emotional axes were active for less than the 30% of the total duration of the activity, whereas they were set to zero for the remaining time: this means that through the application of the MEAS coding system a reduced number of emotional episodes was selected. Thus, emotion is a dynamic and continuous process which characterizes the whole HM interaction, yet not continually. In other words, emotional episodes arise all along the computer interaction without covering its entire duration but being restricted to limited intervals of time (Scherer, 2005). In particular, our results showed that emotional reactions occurred mostly within high interactive activities (for instance, the quiz game) and in response to manipulated eliciting events (Van Reekum et al., 2004).

Second, performing a repeated measure ANOVA, a main effect concerning the type of dimension was found ($F=8.685$; $df=2$; $p<.01$): in particular, the novelty dimension - which is linked to emotions such as interest, surprise, curiosity, boredom, etc. - was the most scored and differed from both coping and valence. Thus, although all dimensions were informative, novelty seemed to have the largest weight (this also because it was often simultaneously active when coping and valence were scored). These results seem consistent with Scherer's Stimulus Evaluation Checks (SECs, 1984), according to which novelty is the first appraisal dimension activated within the emotional process.

Third, positive scores recorded significantly longer durations than negative ones ($F=12.527$; $df=1$; $p<.01$). Both positive and negative scores provided information about the subject's emotional response: for instance, high levels of novelty characterized all the activities, but the quiz game, the web exploration, the interaction with the avatar and the final videogame were characterized by high durations of positive scores (i.e. surprise, interest, etc.), whereas the repetitive task totalized a high duration of the negative ones (i.e. boredom).

Finally, results showed a main effect of game ($F=38.461$; $df=4$; $p<.001$): in particular, the quiz game was the activity where the all the axes were most active and differed significantly from all the other activities. This result highlighted once again the role of the ongoing task in eliciting specific emotional reactions, as already explained concerning the analysis of multimodal behaviour. In sum, our results showed a global coherence between the manipulated events on one side and the emotional reactions (behavioural units and axes) on the other, thus supporting the use of the MEAS scoring procedure.

We conclude this section by presenting an example of synchronic analysis: figure 10 displays a video-segment (44 sec) corresponding to the first set of five questions of the quiz game. We decided to extract the example from the quiz game since previous analyses had demonstrated that this activity obtained the highest number of responses. The figure presents: a) the image sequence extracted from the video of one of our subjects and the related analysis of the main multimodal behavioural units exhibited; b) the scoring of the MEAS axes; c) the task events and the performance of the subject. The synchronic analysis shows that each task event, i.e. the appearance of a new question was followed by the activation of behavioural units concerning novelty, as for instance eyebrow raising and head moving towards the screen and successively by units signalling a low coping potential, as for instance lip corner depressor and chin raise. Despite the facial movements exhibited before answering, the subject gave the right answer to all five questions and showed positive signals such as a smile: on the base of both the performance (right) and the behavioural response, the coping and valence dimensions were then scored as positive (pleasantness and high coping). Thus, the emotional reactions of the subjects were *tuned* to the contextual elements, such as task events and action performance.

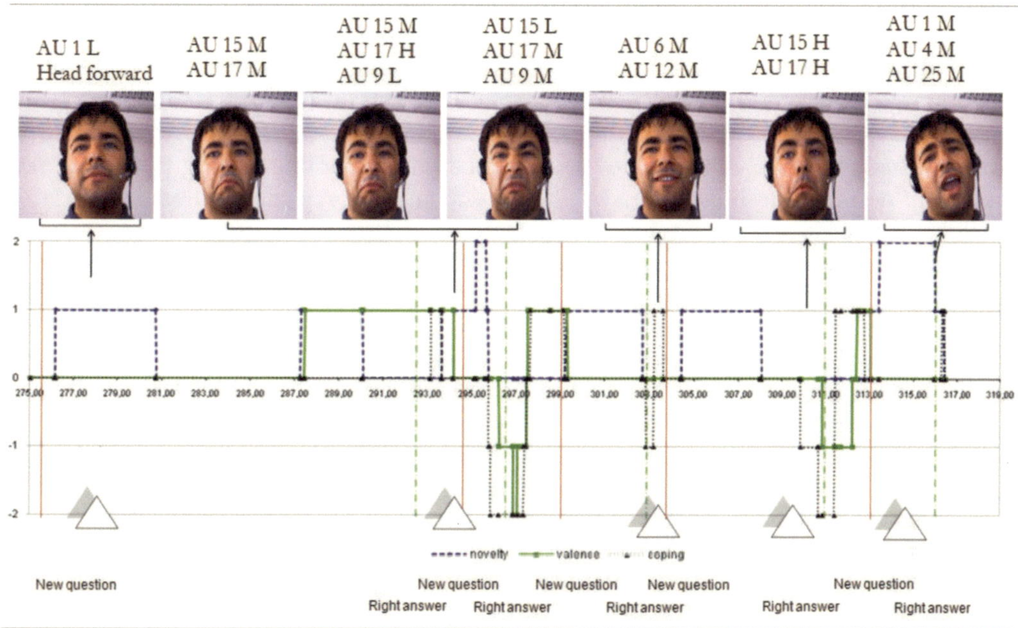

Figure 10. Synchronic analysis: an example of behavioural analysis and MEAS scoring.

8. Conclusions

In this chapter we presented a dimensional semantic model (Multidimensional Emotional Appraisal Semantic Space, MEAS) which locates emotion in a four axes space, in the attempt to detect rules linking pattern of signals to underlying emotional axes, such as novelty, valence, coping and arousal. Although the development of this set of rules is still in progress, this model is aimed at providing hints in the work area of *Affective Computing* concerning emotion decoding, i.e. the implementing and design of automatic emotion recognizers. In particular, within this field of studies, we addressed the subtask of semantic attribution: once the machine is able to capture and to process the multimodal signals (and pattern of signals) exhibited by the human user during the interaction, how is it possible to attribute to them an emotional meaning (or in other words, to label them)?

First of all, it is important to note that despite the use of the term «rule», the MEAS scoring system is not meant as a set of fixed and stable laws to be rigidly applied to every type of HM interaction and context. In fact, this would disclaim one of the principles on which the system is based (embodiment) and the more general conception of the HM interaction which is here proposed. Concerning the former - as previously explained - the MEAS system is thought as strictly linked to the context, that is to the type of running task and to the actions performed by the human user. Concerning the second, in our view, the machine should use the user's emotional signals to be able to *tune* to his/her emotional state (process of attunement). Moreover, as clearly showed by our data, the users themselves show emotional responses which are highly influenced and congruent with the type of eliciting stimuli and the way they are appraised. Therefore, the MEAS rules are flexible and may change according to these contextual elements adjusting to them.

Second, the MEAS system is designed to record the continuous modifications of emotional dimensions rather than the number of appearances of certain types of emotion categories, since it is based on a theoretical conception of emotion as a process rather than a state. As stated by Russell (2003): «The ecology of emotional life is not one of long periods of non-emotional "normal" life punctuated by the occasional prototypical emotional episode. [..] Emotional life consists of the continuous fluctuations in core affect, in pervasive perception of affective qualities, and in the frequent attribution of core affect to a single Object, all interacting with perceptual, cognitive, and behavior processes. Occasionally, these components form one of the prototypical patterns, just as stars form constellations». Thus, prototypical or basic emotions such as happiness, anger or fear occur occasionally, whereas emotion may be better conceived as a continuous modification of emotional dimensions (as, for instance, valence and arousal which form Russell's core affect).

The adoption of a dimensional model leaves open the issue concerning emotional labels. According to Cowie et al. (2001) «category labels are not a sufficient representation of emotional state, but they are probably necessary». Of course, emotional labels may be attributed to each intersection between the different axes considered (as for instance in figure 4). However, not all intersections correspond to different types of emotions, since they may simply represent a shift in the intensity of a certain emotional response. We won't consider here the translation of our dimensions into labels since we are still working on the preceding operation, i.e. the translation of signals into dimensions. Nonetheless, in our view, besides the usual contraposition between dimensions and categories, it should be pointed out the need to consider emotion as a continuous process, thus working on models actually able to account for its dynamical changing.

Another issue we leave open is the relation between non verbal communicative behavior and physiological signals. We are still working on the possibility to translate different physiological measures, such as heart rate and electrodermal activity[2], into a single dimension which should signal the beginning of the physiological arousal of the individual. Although in our model we do not consider biosignals as informative about the specific nature of the emotional response (which is signaled by the expressive-motor system), they are nonetheless an important source of information about the individual's state of body activation. Moreover, since emotion is thought to produce coordinated modifications in multiple response systems (Scherer, 2001), we are working on the hypothesis that a total absence of behavioural expressions together with a high level of activation may indicate that a process of regulation is going on - see for instance, the regulatory strategy of suppression studied by Gross and Levenson (1993).

Finally, the MEAS system includes the dimension of coping to differentiate emotion. As already stated about the main limits of the model, this dimension was the most problematic one, since it concerned an internal state of the individual, i.e. the evaluation of his/her own resources to cope with a certain event. For this reason, it seemed more difficult to link this dimensions to observable behaviour and the scoring of the coping axis was mainly linked to the action (approach vs. withdrawal) and the performance of the user. Nonetheless, we

[2] In partnership with Sensibilab, Politecnico di Lecco.

believe that this dimension may provide useful information to an emotional interface, since it signals the capability of the human user to accomplish a task or not. For instance, if we imagine an e-learning tutoring context, it would be crucial for the virtual tutor to detect when the task proposed to the user is too difficult and to change it accordingly.

9. Acknowledgments

This study was part of a wider research project (ALEA) and we would like to thank all the people who are involved and cooperated in its realization. We would like to thank prof. Bruno Apolloni, Computer Science Department, State University, Milan; Eng. Luca Piccini and Giuseppe Andreoni, Sensibilab, Politecnico di Lecco; to Eng. Fabrizio Beverina and Giorgio Palmas, STMicroelectronics (Italy).

10. References

Anisetti, M.; Bellandi, V.; Damiani, E. & Beverina, F. (2005). Facial identification problem: a tracking based approach, *Proceedings of the First International Conference on Signal-Image Technology and Internet-Based Systems*, IEEE SITIS, Yaoundé, Cameroon.

Arnold, M.B. (1960). *Emotion and Personality, Psychological Aspects.* Columbia University Press, New York.

Bechara, A. & Damasio, A. R. (2005). The somatic maker hypothesis: A neural theory of economic decision. *Games and Economic Behavior*, 52, 2, 336-372.

Ben-Ze'ev, A. (2000). *The Subtlety of Emotions,* Massachusetts Institute of Technology Press, Cambridge, MA.

Breazeal, C. (2002). *Designing Social Robots*, MIT Press, Cambridge, MA.

Bianchi-Berthouze, N. & Lisetti, C. (2002). Modelling multimodal expression of user's affective subjective experience. *User Modelling and User-Adapted Interaction,* 12, 1, 49-84.

Brock, D. & Trafton, J.G. (1999). Cognitive representation of common ground in user interfaces. In: *User modeling: Proceedings of the seventh international conference,* Kay, J. (Ed.), Springer-Wien, New York, NY.

Cacioppo, J.T. & Tassinary, L.G. (1990). Interring Psychological Significance from Physiological Signals. *American Psychologist*, 45, 16-28.

Cacioppo, J.T.; Tassinary, L.G., Berntson, G.G. (2000). *Handbook of Psychophysiology,* 2nd Edition, Cambridge University Press, New York.

Cappella, N.J. & Pelachaud, C. (2001). Rules for responsive robots: Using human interactions to build virtual interactions. In: *Stability and Change in Relationships*, Vangelisti, A.L.; Reis, H.T. & Fitzpatric M.A., (Eds.), Cambridge University Press, New York.

Ciceri, M.R. (Ed), (2001). *Comunicare il Pensiero,* Omega Edizioni, Torino.

Ciceri, R.; Balzarotti, S. & Colombo, P. (2005). Analysis of the human physiological responses and multimodal emotional signals to an interactive computer, *Proceedings of AISB 2005 Annual Conference, Agents that want and like: emotional and motivational roots of cognition and action*, 12-15 April 2005, Hatfield.

Ciceri R.; Balzarotti, S.; Beverina, F.; Manzoni, F. & Piccini, L. (2006). MEED: The challenge towards a Multimodal Emotional Ecological Database, *Proceedings of LREC 2006,*

Multimodal Corpora: From Multimodal Behavior Theories To Usable Models, May 2006, Genova, Italy.

Ciceri, R. & Balzarotti, S. (2007). MEAS: Multidimensional Emotional Appraisal Semantic space. In: *Knowledge-based Intelligent Information and Engineering Systems. Lecture Notes in Computer Science,* (Vol. 4693/2007, pp. 395-402), Springer Verlag, Berlin/Heidelberg.

Clark, H. H. (1996). Arranging to do things with others. In: *Conference Companion of the Conference on Human Factors in Computing Systems – CHI'96,* Association for Computing Machinery.

Cohn, J.F.; Zlochower, A.J.; Lien J. & Kanade, T. (1999). Automated face analysis by feature point tracking has high concurrent validity with manual FACS Coding. *Psychophysiology*, 36, 35-43.

Cowie, R.; Douglas-Cowie, E.; Apolloni, B.; Romano, A. & Fellenz, W. (1999). What a neural net needs to know about emotion words. In: *Computational Intelligence and Applications,* Mastorakis, N. (Ed.), (pp. 109-114), World Scientific & Engineering Society Press.

Cowie, R.; Douglas-Cowie, E.; Tsapatsoulis, N.; Votsis, G.; Kollias, S., Fellenz, W. & Taylor, J. G. (2001). Emotion recognition in human-computer interaction. *IEEE Signal Processing Magazine*, 18, 32–80.

De Rosis, F.; Pelachaud, C.; Poggi, I.; Carofiglio, V. & De Carolis, B. (2003). From Greta's mind to her face: modelling the dynamics of affective states in a conversational embodied agent. *International Journal of Human-Computer Studies*, 59, 1, 81-118

Douglas-Cowie, E.; Campbell, N.; Cowie, R. & Roach, P. (2003). Emotional speech: Towards a new generation of databases. *Speech Communication*, 40, 33-60.

Ekman, P. (1972). Universals and Cultural Differences in Facial Expression of Emotion. In: *Nebraska Symposium on Motivation*, Cole, J.R. (Ed.), (pp. 207–83), University of Nebraska Press, Lincoln, Vol. IXX.

Ekman, P. & Friesen, W. (1978). *Facial Action Coding System (FACS): A technique for the measurement of facial movement*, Consulting Psychology Press.

Frijda, N.H. (2007). *The laws of emotion*. Erlbaum, Mahwah.

Giles, H.; Shepard, C.A. & Le Poire, B.A. (2001). Communication Accommodation Theory. In: *The new handbook of language and social psychology,* Robinson, W.P. & Giles, H. (Eds.), (pp. 33-56), Wiley, Chichester, UK.

Gross, J. J. & Levenson, R. W. (1993). Emotional suppression: Physiology, self-report, and expressive behaviour. *Journal of Personality and Social Psychology, 64*, 970-986.

Kaiser, S. & Wehrle, T. (2001a) Facial expressions as indicators of appraisal processes. In: *Appraisal processes in emotions: Theory, methods, research,* Scherer, K. R.; Schorr, A. & Johnstone, T. (Eds.), (pp. 285-300), Oxford University Press, New York.

Kaiser, S. & Wehrle, T. (2001b). The role of facial expression in intra-individual and inter-individual emotion regulation. In: *Emotional and Intelligent II: The Tangled Knot of Cognition,* Cañamero, D. (Ed.), (pp. 61-66), Papers from the 2001 AAAI Fall Symposium, Technical Report FS-01-02, AAAI Press, Menlo Park, CA.

Kim K. H.; Bang S. W. & Kim S. R. (2004). Emotion recognition system using short-term monitoring of physiological signals. *Medical and Biological Engineering and Computing*, 42, 419-427.

Kort, B.; Reilly R. & Picard, R.W. (2001). An affective model of interplay between emotions and learning: reengineering educational pedagogy—building a learning companion, *International Conference on Advanced Learning Technologies,* ICALT 2001, Madison, WI.

Lazarus, R.S. (1991). *Emotion and Adaptation,* Oxford University Press, New York.

Levenson, R. W. (2003). Blood, sweat, and fears: The autonomic architecture of emotion. In: *Emotions inside out,* Ekman, P.; Campos, J. J.; Davidson, R. J. & de Waal, F. B. M. (Eds.), (pp. 348–366), The New York Academy of Sciences, New York.

Lisetti, C. L.; Nasoz, F.; LeRouge, C.; Ozyer, O. & Alverez, K. (2003). Intelligent affective interfaces: A patient-modelling assessment for tele-home health care. *International Journal of Human-Computer Studies,* 59, 245-255.

Lisetti, C. L.; Brown, S.M.; Alverez, K. & Marpaung, A. H. (2004). A social informatics approach to human robot interaction with a service social robot, *IEEE Transactions on Systems, Man and Cybernetics,* Special Issue on Human-Robot Interaction, 195-209.

Magnusson, M. S. (2001). Discovering hidden time patterns in behavior: T-Patterns and their detection, behavior research method. *Instruments and Computers,* 32, 1, 93-110.

Martin, J.C.; Buisine, S.; Pitel, G. & Bernsen, N.O. (2006). Fusion of Children's Speech and 2D Gestures when Conversing with 3D Characters. *Signal Processing Journal,* Special issue on multimodal interfaces, 86, 12, 3596-3624.

McKenna, S. J. & Gong, S. (1996). Tracking faces, *Proceedings of the 2nd International Conference on Automatic Face and Gesture Recognition,* pp. 271-276.

Oviatt, S.L. (2002). Multimodal interfaces. In: *Handbook of Human-Computer Interaction,* Jacko, J. & Sears, A. (Eds), Lawrence Erlbaum, New Jersey.

Pelachaud, C. & Poggi, I. (2002). Subtleties of facial expressions in embodied agents. *Journal of Visualization and Computer Animation,* 13, 301-312.

Picard, R.W. (1997). *Affective Computing,* The MIT Press, Cambridge, MA.

Picard, R.W. & Healey, J. (2001). Toward machine emotional intelligence: Analysis of affective physiological state. *IEEE transaction on Pattern Analysis and Machine Intelligence,* 23, 10, 1175-1193.

Picard, R. W.; Vyzas, E. & Healey, J. (2001). Toward machine emotional intelligence: Analysis of affective physiological state. *IEEE Transactions Pattern Analysis and Machine Intelligence,* 23, 10, 1185-1191.

Plutchik, R. (1980). A psychoevolutionary theory of emotions. *Social Science Information,* 21, 529–553.

Prendinger, H.; Mayer, S.; Mori, J. & Ishizuka, M. (2003). Using bio-signals to measure and reflect the impact of character-based interfaces, Workshop on Assessing and Adapting to User Attitudes and Affect: Why, When and How?, in conj. with User Modeling (UM-03), pp. 39-44, Johnstown, USA.

Russell, J. A. (1980). A circumplex model of affect. *Journal of Personality and Social Psychology,* 39, 1161-1178.

Russell, J.A. (2003). Core Affect and the Psychological Construction of Emotion. *Psychological Review,* 110, 1, 145-172.

Scherer, K.R. (1984) On the nature and function of emotion: A component process approach. In: *Approaches to Emotion,* Scherer, K.R. & P. Ekman (Eds.), (pp. 293–317), Erlbaum, Hillsdale, NJ.

Scherer, K.R. (2001). Appraisal Considered as a Process of Multi-Level Sequential Checking. In: *Appraisal Processes in Emotion: Theory, Methods, Research*, Scherer, K.R.; Schorr, A. & Johnstone, T. (Eds.), (pp. 92–120), Oxford University Press, New York.

Scherer, K.R. (2005). What are emotions? And how can they be measured? *Trends and developments: Research on emotions,*, 44, 4, 695-729.

Siegman, A.W. & Feldstein, S. (1979). *Of Speech and Time,* Erlbaum, Hillsdale.

Tomkins, S.S. (1962). *Affect, Imagery, Consciousness: Vol. I, The Positive Affects*, Springer, New York.

Van Reekum, C.M.; Johnstone, T.; Banse, R.; Etter, A.; Wehrle, T. & Scherer, K.R. (2004). Psycho physiological responses to appraisal dimensions in a computer game. *Cognition and Emotion*, 18, 5, 663-688.

Varela, F.; Thompson, E. & Rosch, E. (1991). *The Embodied Mind*. MIT Press, Cambridge, MA.

Wallbot, H.G. (1998). Bodily expression of emotion. *European Journal of Social Psychology*, 28, 879-896.

Wehrle, T.; Kaiser, S.; Schmidt, S. & Scherer, K. R. (2000). Studying the dynamics of emotional expression using synthesized facial muscle movements. *Journal of Personality and Social Psychology*, 78, 1, 105-119.

Wundt, W. (1905). Grundzüge der physiologischen Psychologie, Engelmann, Leipzig.

15

The Information Processing Role of the Amygdala in Emotion

Wataru Sato
Kyoto University
Japan

1. Introduction

The term "emotion" usually refers to brief and intense affective feelings. Numerous philosophers and writers have noted since ancient times that emotion greatly influences our lives. Thus, researchers and laypersons both are very interested in emotion. Recently, neuroscientific studies exploring the neural substrate for emotion have suggested the involvement of the amygdala in emotion, but its specific role remains unclear.

This article reviews previous research and attempts to summarize how the amygdala processes information on emotion. First, I discuss emotion as a series of information processes based on evidence from the psychological literature. Then, I present compiled anatomical information on the amygdala and give evidence for the involvement of the amygdala in emotion. Finally, I explain the general framework and details about how the amygdala processes information on emotion.

2. Psychological discussion on emotion

Emotion is a subject in psychology that also draws the attention of non-psychologists, but a large difference exists between the popular concept and psychological perspectives of emotion. Popularly, people tend to emphasize the subjective aspects of emotion (Cornelius, 1996) and sometimes wonder whether emotion is too personal to be a subject of scientific research. Psychological research provides a different perspective on emotion, and although summarizing the psychological research on emotion is difficult because it is extremely varied, I believe that three findings are important for the study of emotion when we discuss the relationship to its neural mechanisms.

First, emotion clearly includes widespread responses. For example, some research on expressions has indicated that emotions induce specific expressive behaviors. Ekman et al. (e.g., Ekman & Friesen, 1975) found that people commonly display specific facial expressions when they feel specific basic emotions (e.g., anger). In addition, emotion generates physiological responses. Some studies measuring autonomic nervous activity have shown that each type of emotion generates a specific physiological response pattern (Levenson, 1991). Moreover, emotion modulates cognitive activities, including perception (Öhman et al., 2001) and memory (Bradley et al., 1992). Studies that recorded multiple measures simultaneously indicated that the subjective, physiological, behavioral, and cognitive responses of emotion are intimately related (Lang et al., 1998).

Second, emotion is proposed to be an adaptive function of the mind acquired in the evolutionary process (e.g., Tooby & Cosmides, 1990). Darwin (1872/1998) first analyzed emotion from an evolutionary perspective and provided some evidence to support his idea. Subsequent Darwinist researchers systematically gathered evidence of inter- and intra-species universalities for emotional expressions, which strongly suggested that human emotion was acquired evolutionarily (Ekman, 1999). From the perspective of evolutionary functionalism, emotion can be viewed as a biological function designed for adaptation, promoting the survival and reproduction of individuals in response to the environment. Emotion still has an adaptive function that may partially reflect past environments (Keltner & Gross, 1999).

Third, researchers pointed out that before an emotional response is produced, one conducts a process of appraisal (e.g., Arnold, 1960). Indeed, for the identical stimulus, the emotional responses can differ from individual to individual. In addition, the emotional response of an individual can differ depending on the context. Before producing an emotional response, the appraisal mechanism must assess the relevance of the stimulus in terms of the current state of the individual. Many researchers (e.g., Arnold, 1960) have posited that the appraisal process in emotion is not necessarily intentional, but is automatic and sometimes cannot be accessed subjectively. Although the nature of appraisal in emotion remains inconclusive, most researchers appear to agree that emotion involves an appraisal process.

Taken together, emotion, as discussed in the psychological literature, is a series of information processes that appraise the adaptive significance of stimuli and generate various adaptive responses accordingly (Fig. 1).

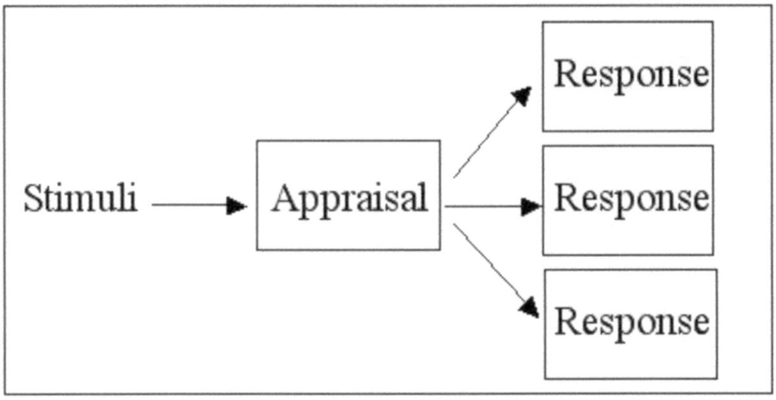

Fig.1. Emotion as a series of information processes.

Emotion is regarded as a series of information processes that evaluate the adaptive significance of stimuli and produce distributed adaptive responses accordingly.

3. Anatomy of the amygdala

The anatomy of the brain sets important constraints on and provides clues to cognitive functions. Hence, I will briefly summarize the anatomy of the amygdala. The amygdala is an almond-shaped mass of gray matter located bilaterally within the anteromedial part of the temporal cortex. The volume of the amygdala on one side is about 1700 mm^3 based on the overall mean across studies (Brierley et al., 2002).

Although it is a small organ, the amygdala has a complicated internal structure comprising a complex of nerve nuclei. Anatomical studies in monkeys suggest that it consists of 13 distinct nuclei (Amaral, 2002) that form an intricate neural network (Aggelton & Saunders, 2000), including multistage serial processing pathways that process sensory signals. For example, the visual signals are input from the temporal cortex to the lateral nucleus, which projects them onto the basal nucleus; the basal nucleus then projects them onto the central and medial nuclei. In addition, parallel processing pathways are involved, for example, the lateral nucleus projects on the accessory basal nucleus, as well as the basal nucleus.

Anatomical studies in monkeys have revealed intriguing relationships between the amygdala and other brain regions. As inputs, the amygdala receives projections from one or more sensory regions representing each sensory modality (Amaral et al., 1992), which suggests that the amygdala can process sensory stimuli of all modalities. Concerning the visual and auditory modalities, input projections travel via both subcortical and cortical structures. For example, while the optic pathway goes through the primary visual cortex in the occipital lobe, bypassing projection pathways to the amygdala are routed via the superior colliculus and pulvinar, enabling the rapid processing of sensory information. As outputs, the amygdala has dense projections to many brain regions that are important in implementing various types of bodily and cognitive responses, including the brain stem, hypothalamus, hippocampus, basal ganglion, and cortical regions (Amaral et al., 1992).

In summary, the amygdala is a neural region that has a complex inner structure, receiving input from all sensory modalities and sending output to various brain regions.

4. Evidence for involvement of the amygdala in emotion

Lesions studies in monkeys provide clear evidence that the amygdala is involved in emotion. A seminal study by Kluver and Bucy (1939) reported dramatic changes in the emotional behaviors of monkeys after lesioning the anterior temporal cortex, which included the amygdala. For example, the lesioned monkeys approached snakes, which normal monkeys fear. Subsequent studies showed that the impaired emotional behavior was caused by selective lesions of the amygdala. For example, Amaral et al. (2003) examined the effect of selective amygdala damage in monkeys. The monkeys with damaged amygdala did not show fear in response to threatening environmental stimuli, such as snakes. In addition, when the lesioned monkeys were put in a cage with unfamiliar individuals—a situation in which normal monkeys become nervous and aggressive - the subjects did not show any emotional arousal.

Human studies also provide evidence of the involvement of the amygdala in emotion. For example, a neuropsychological study reported that a patient with bilateral amygdala damage showed the loss of subjective and behavioral responses involving certain negative emotions (Tranel et al., 2006). Electric stimulation studies in epileptic patients have revealed that stimulation of the amygdala sometimes induced subjective experiences and the facial expressions of fear (Gloor, 1997). A functional neuroimaging study (Breiter et al., 1996) measured the brain activities in normal participants using functional magnetic resonance imaging (fMRI) while observing facial expressions showing fear, happy, and neutral emotions. Emotional facial expressions of others have been shown to induce contagious emotional responses in observers (e.g., Johnsen et al., 1995). The amygdala was more active in response to fearful and happy facial expressions than to neutral expressions.

In summary, these findings demonstrate that the amygdala is indeed involved in emotion.

5. Information processing related to emotion in the amygdala

What information does the amygdala process regarding emotion?

Electrophysiological studies in animals have shown that the amygdala neuron activity in response to external stimuli reflects the adaptive significance of stimuli and not their sensory characteristics. For example, Ono and Nishijo (1992) conducted single unit recordings in a monkey and investigated the amygdala activity in response to visual stimuli. First, they identified the amygdala neurons that responded to the sight of food, such as an orange. Then, they salted the food and made the monkey taste it. As a result, the amygdala activity in response to the sight of an orange disappeared immediately. When the researchers gave unsalted food to the monkey, the responses of the amygdala neurons to the sight of food recovered quickly. Note that the salted food looked the same as normal food, but differed in its adaptive significance. These results suggest that the amygdala is not engaged in the basic sensory analysis of environmental stimuli, but in appraising their significance.

Lesion studies in monkeys and rats have also indicated that selective damage to the amygdala impairs the triggering of emotional responses to emotionally significant stimuli (Aggleton & Young, 2000). For example, a series of experiments in rats by LeDoux and his colleagues (LeDoux, 1998) indicated that the freezing response to fearful stimuli disappears after destroying the central nucleus of the amygdala, which projects to the central gray matter in the brain stem. The amygdala, however, is not involved in the response itself. In this case, even when the amygdala was destroyed, the freezing response could be elicited by electric stimulation of the central gray matter. Therefore, the production of the emotional response "freezing" should be regarded as relating to the central gray matter directly. The amygdala likely generates commands for other brain regions regarding appropriate responses that are based on appraisals of their significance.

In line with these animal data, human neuroimaging studies have demonstrated that amygdala activity corresponds to the emotional significance of stimuli and emotional responses. For example, an fMRI study (Sato et al., 2004) examined this issue using the interaction between facial expressions and face directions (Fig. 2). Angry and neutral expressions looking toward and away from participants were presented in unilateral visual fields. The emotional significance of the angry expressions differed markedly between face directions, although the physical features of the stimuli were comparable. After acquiring the image, the participants' experience of negative emotion for the stimuli was also investigated. The study yielded two main results. First, the amygdala showed an interaction between emotional expression and face direction, with greater activity for angry expressions looking toward the subjects than angry expressions looking away from them. Second, the amygdala activity showed a positive relationship with the emotion experienced. The first result matches the idea that the amygdala is involved in appraising significance after the basic sensory processing of stimuli. The second result supports the idea that the amygdala is related to the emotional response.

Combined, the animal and human data suggest that the amygdala is involved in multiple processes that first evaluate the adaptive significance of stimuli and then generate commands for other brain regions regarding adaptive responses (Fig. 3). This concurs with the hardware characteristics of the amygdala. As the amygdala has a complex inner structure and receives all sensory inputs, it is well equipped to evaluate environmental stimuli. In addition, the amygdala sends output to several regions that are related to emotional responses.

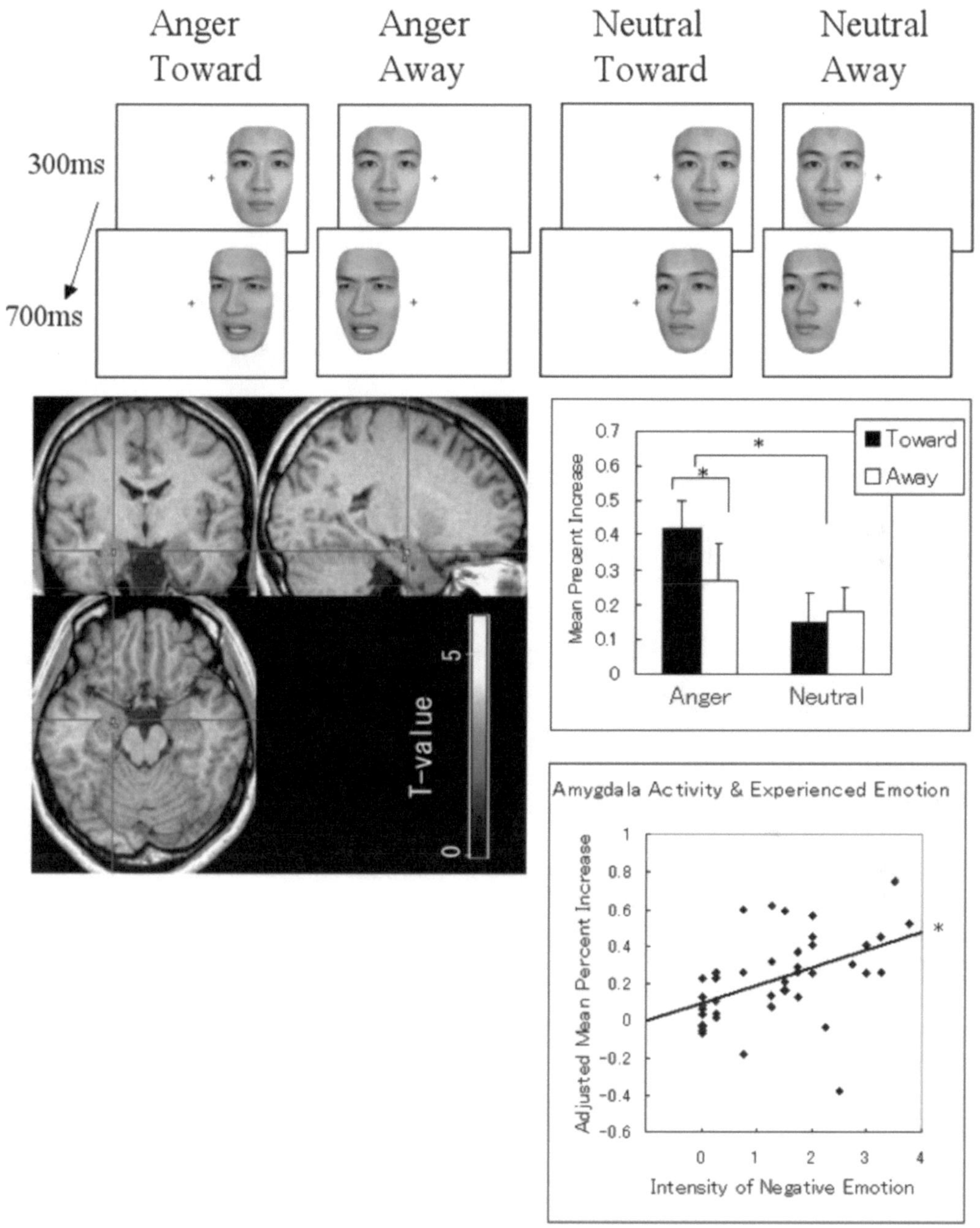

Fig.2. Experiment in the study of Sato et al. (2004).

Top: Examples of stimulus presentations. Four conditions are involved with two expressions (angry and neutral) in two directions (toward and away). Middle left: Areas in the left amygdala demonstrate the interactions of expressions and directions. Middle right: Patterns of activity in the left amygdala. Bottom: Positive relationship between the activity of the left amygdala and the subjective emotional response.

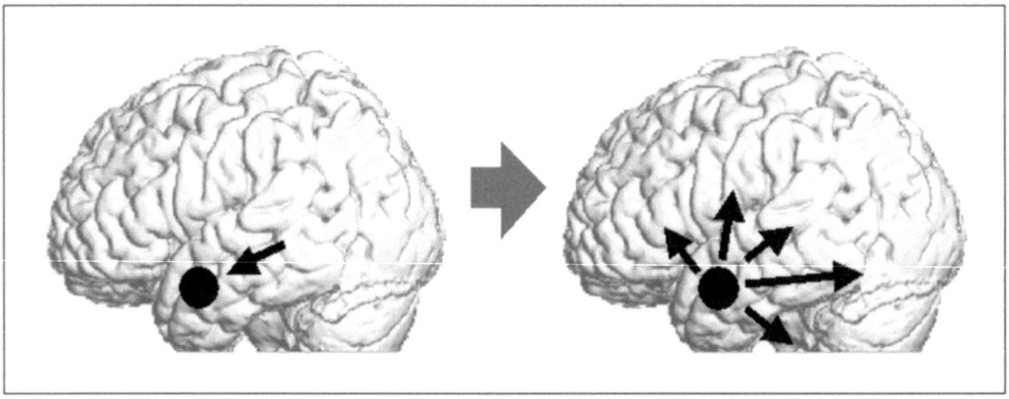

Fig.3. Information processing of the amygdala in emotion

In emotion, the amygdala is involved in the processes that evaluates the adaptive significance of stimuli, and accordingly generates the commands of adaptive responses, which are implemented in other brain regions.

6. Information processing by the amygdala at each emotion-processing stage

In this section, I discuss the details of the processing of emotion in the amygdala during the subprocesses of significance appraisal and response command generation. For the latter, I limit my discussion to three emotional responses as examples: bodily responses, perceptual enhancement, and memory facilitation.

6.1 Subconscious and conscious appraisals of emotion: amygdala activation by sensory inputs via subcortical and cortical routes

Psychological studies have shown that emotion can be elicited with or without the conscious awareness of stimuli (Robinson, 1998).

In addition to evidence of the involvement of the amygdala in processing emotion with conscious awareness (e.g., Sato et al., 2004), some studies have provided evidence that the amygdala is involved in processing emotion without awareness. For example, a neuropsychological study (Kubota et al., 2000) investigated patients with unilateral amygdala damage in which emotionally negative or neutral slides were presented to their unilateral visual fields subliminally. Higher electrodermal responses to negative versus neutral stimuli were observed when stimuli were presented to the intact, but not lesioned, hemispheres. A neuroimaging study (Morris et al., 1999) measured the brain activity when angry facial expressions were presented subliminally with and without fear conditioning. With conditioning, angry faces induced stronger activity of the right amygdala, compared to without conditioning. Regression analyses revealed that the amygdala activity was positively related to the activity of the superior colliculus and pulvinar. Together, these data suggest that the processing of emotions by the amygdala can occur subconsciously and that it may be implemented by sensory input via subcortical routes.

An intracranial field potential recording study in humans (Oya et al. 2002) demonstrated that the amygdala could be activated within as early as 50-150 ms from the stimulus onset in response to emotional stimuli. Since visual awareness has been proposed to be related to the activity of the visual cortices at about 200-300 ms (Treisman & Kanwisher, 1998), the rapid activity of the amygdala could correspond to subconscious emotional processing.

In summary, ample evidence indicates that the amygdala begins to process emotion quickly, before the conscious awareness of stimuli. Since the amygdala has multiple sensory input pathways, including cortical and subcortical projections, it may conduct multistage appraisals of stimulus significance according to the resolution of the sensory inputs.

6.2 Bodily responses of emotion: outputs from the amygdala to the brain stem and hypothalamus

Psychological studies have shown that emotion induces widespread body responses (Levenson, 1991).

The emotional bodily responses are related to the activity of the brain stem and hypothalamus (Buck, 1999). The brain stem consists of functionally different regions, each of which engages with a specific bodily response. For example, the solitary nucleus regulates the activity of the parasympathetic branch of the autonomic nervous system, and the central gray matter is related to freezing behavior. The hypothalamus also consists of different functional regions and is very involved in controlling the body responses by sending output to the brain stem or releasing hormones to the body directly.

Animal research has revealed that the outputs from the amygdala to the brain stem and hypothalamus are related to the emotional body responses. For example, lesion studies in rats demonstrated that the local destruction of the amygdala impaired a specific component of the body responses (LeDoux, 1998). Research in monkeys showed that cooling the amygdala, which produces reversible neuronal lesions, modulated the activity of the hypothalamus neurons for visually presented emotional stimuli (Ono & Nishijo, 1992).

Human neuroimaging studies have also demonstrated the involvement of the amygdala in emotional body responses. For example, an fMRI study (Williams et al., 2001) depicted the brain activity while participants were observing fearful and neutral facial expressions, and measured the electrodermal activity simultaneously. The amygdala was active for fearful expressions inducing clear electrodermal responses, but not for fearful faces failing to elicit electrodermal activity.

In summary, animal and human data indicate that the amygdala outputs to the brain stem and hypothalamus are related to the body responses of emotion.

6.3 Perceptual enhancement by emotion: output from the amygdala to the visual area

Psychological studies have indicated that emotional significance enhances the perception of stimuli (Öhman et al., 2001).

A neuropsychological study (Anderson & Phelps, 2001) confirmed that the amygdala is related to the perceptual enhancement of emotional stimuli. The researchers used the attentional blink phenomenon, in which the identification of the first targets impairs that of the second targets. In normal controls, the transient impairment of conscious awareness for the second targets was attenuated when the second targets were emotional words. In contrast, in patients with unilateral or bilateral amygdala damage, no difference was observed between emotional and neutral words.

As related evidence, some neuroimaging and electrophysiological studies have reported that emotional stimuli, compared to neutral ones, enhance the activity of the visual cortices, coinciding with the amygdala activity. For example, an fMRI study (Breiter et al., 1996) revealed that that the presentation of fearful and happy faces activated the ventral visual cortices and amygdala more strongly than neutral faces. Sato et al. (2001) recorded event-related potential (ERP) while viewing fearful, happy, and neutral facial expressions. The fearful and happy expressions induced higher activity over the posterior temporal areas during 200–300 ms after stimulus onset compared to neutral expressions. Independent component analyses indicated that the negative potential of the posterior cortices was coupled with positive potential of the anterior midline region functionally, implying limbic system activity. One can interpret these data as showing that the rapid enhancement of the visual area activity for emotional stimuli is realized by the direct output from the amygdala. The activity of the visual area within 200–300 ms has been suggested as being related to perceptual awareness (Treisman & Kanwisher, 1998); hence, this heightened activity of the visual area might cause the perceptual enhancement of emotional stimuli.

In summary, human data suggest that the amygdala is related to perceptual enhancement by emotion, possibly via the rapid output from the amygdala to the visual area.

6.4 Memory facilitation by emotion: outputs from the amygdala to the hippocampus, basal ganglion and neocortex

Psychological studies have suggested that emotional significance enhances the memory performance for stimuli (Bradley et al., 1992).

Research with rats has indicated that the influence of the amygdala on other brain regions is related to this memory facilitation. A series of studies by McGaugh and his colleagues (1999) revealed that the learning of avoidance behaviors to emotionally aversive stimuli was facilitated by the electric stimulation of the amygdala; in contrast, when the amygdala was damaged, the performance became poorer. The stimulation of the amygdala affected both spatial memory and procedural memory. Since these two memory functions are related to the hippocampus and basal ganglion, respectively, the data suggest that the amygdala influences these regions. Electrophysiological recordings further revealed that amygdala activity modulated the activity of the neocortex related to memory consolidation.

Human data have also indicated the involvement of the amygdala in memory enhancement by emotion. For example, a neuropsychological study (Adolphs et al., 1997) investigated the memory performance for a story including an emotional scene. While the normal controls performed better for the emotional scene than for other scenes, the patients with bilateral amygdala damage did not show an advantage regarding the emotional scene. A neuroimaging study (Cahill et al., 1996) measured the brain activity while presenting unpleasant and neutral films and subsequently tested memory performance. The memory performance was better for the unpleasant films than for the neutral ones, and the amygdala activity was positively related to the memory performance for the unpleasant films.

Together, the evidence indicates that the amygdala sends outputs to other brain regions, including the hippocampus, basal ganglion, and neocortex, facilitating the memory performance for emotional stimuli.

7. Conclusion

This article reviewed research on the amygdala and discussed its role in emotion. Psychological studies have revealed that emotion is a series of information processes that evaluates the adaptive significance of stimuli and generates adaptive responses accordingly. Neuroscientific evidence indicates that in terms of emotion, the amygdala is involved in appraising the significance of stimuli and generating response commands for other regions. Emotion is appraised rapidly in the amygdala through sensory inputs via subcortical routes, before the conscious awareness of stimuli. The outputs from the amygdala induce diverse emotional responses by activating other brain regions.

Although this article focused on the amygdala, other brain regions appear to process emotion similarly, including the orbitofrontal cortex and nucleus accumbens. Evidence suggests that these regions are related to different sorts of appraisals of emotion and different emotional responses. As the amygdala and these regions have close interconnections, these areas may form a neural network and thus be involved in more complex emotion processing.

Many issues remain to be clarified regarding the role of the amygdala in emotion. For example, no consensus exists as to what types of emotion involve the amygdala. However, neuroscientific studies on emotion are making dramatic progress. As our understanding of the brain mechanisms, especially of the amygdala, advances, we will gain more profound knowledge regarding the mechanisms of emotion.

8. References

Adolphs, R.; Cahill, L.; Schul, R. & Babinsky, R. (1997). Impaired declarative memory for emotional material following bilateral amygdala damage in humans. *Learning & Memory*, 4, 3, 291-300, 10720502.

Aggelton, J. P. & Saunders, R. C. (2000). The amygdala-what's happendned in the last decade? In: *The amygdala: A functional analysis*, J. P. Aggleton (Ed.), 1-30, Oxford University Press, 0198505019, New York.

Aggleton, J. P. & Young, A. W. (2000). The enigma of the amygdala: On its contribution to human emotion. In: *Cognitive neuroscience of emotion*, R. D. Lane & L. Nadel (Eds.), 106-128, Oxford University Press, 019511888X, New York.

Amaral, D. G. (2002). The primate amygdala and the neurobiology of social behavior: implications for understanding social anxiety. *Biological Psychiatry*, 51, 1, 11-17, 00063223.

Amaral, D. G.; Bauman, M. D.; Capitanio, J. P.; Lavenex, P.; Mason, W. A.; Mauldin-Jourdain, M. L. & Mendoza, S. P. (2003). The amygdala: Is it an essential component of the neural network for social cognition? *Neuropsychologia*, 41, 4, 517-522, 00283932.

Amaral, D. G.; Price, J. L.; Pitkanen, A. & Carmichael, S. T. (1992). Anatomical organization of the primate amygdaloid complex. In: *The amygdala: Neurobiological aspects of emotion, memory, and mental dysfunction,* J. P. Aggleton (Ed.), 1-66, Wiley-Liss, 0471561290, New York.

Anderson, A. K. & Phelps, E. A. (2001). Lesions of the human amygdala impair enhanced perception of emotionally salient events. *Nature,* 411, 6835, 305-309, 00280836.

Arnold, M. B. (1960). *Emotion and personality, vol. 1. Psychological aspects.* Columbia University Press, 0231089392, New York.

Bradley, M. M.; Greenwald, M. K.; Petry, M. C. & Lang, P. J. (1992). Remembering pictures: Pleasure and arousal in memory. *Journal of Experimental Psychology Learning, Memory, and Cognition,* 18, 2, 379-390, 02787393.

Breiter, H. C.; Etcoff, N. L.; Whalen, P. J.; Kennedy, W. A.; Rauch, S. L.; Buckner, R. L.; Strauss, M. M.; Hyman, S. E. & Rosen, B. R. (1996). Response and habituation of the human amygdala during visual processing of facial expression. *Neuron,* 17, 5, 875-887, 08966273.

Brierley, B.; Shaw, P. & David, A. S. (2002). The human amygdala: a systematic review and meta-analysis of volumetric magnetic resonance imaging. *Brain Research Brain Research Reviews,* 39, 1, 84-105, 01650173.

Buck, R. (1999). The biological affects: A typology. *Psychological Review,* 106, 2, 301-336, 0033295X.

Cahill, L.; Haier, R. J.; Fallon, J.; Alkire, M. T.; Tang, C.; Keator, D.; Wu, J. & McGaugh, J. L. (1996). Amygdala activity at encoding correlated with long-term, free recall of emotional information. *Proceedings of the National Academy of Sciences of the United States of America,* 93, 15, 8016-8021, 00278424.

Cornelius, R. R. (1996). *The science of emotion: Research and tradition in the psychology of emotions.* Prentice Hall, 0133001539, Upper Saddle River.

Darwin, C. (1872/1998). *The expression of the emotions in man and animals.* Oxford University Press, 0195112717, Oxford.

Ekman, P. (1999). Facial Expressions. In: *Handbook of cognition and emotion,* T. Dalgleish & T. Power (Eds.), 301-320, John Wiley & Sons, 0471978361, Sussex.

Ekman, P. & Friesen, W. V. (1975). *Unmasking the face: A guide to recognizing emotions from facial clues.* Prentice-Hall, 013938183X, Englewood Cliffs.

Gloor, P. (1997). *The temporal lobe and limbic system.* Oxford University Press, 0195092724, New York.

Johnsen, B. H.; Thayer, J. F. & Hugdahl, K. (1995). Affective judgment of the Ekman faces: A dimensional approach. *Journal of Psychophysiology,* 9, 3, 193-202, 02698803.

Keltner, D. & Gross, J. J. (1999). Functional accounts of emotions. *Cognition and Emotion,* 13, 5, 467-480, 02699931.

Kluver, H. & Bucy, P. C. (1939). Preliminary analysis of functions of the temporal lobes in monkeys. *Archives of Neurology and Psychiatry,* 42, 6, 979-1000, 00966754.

Kubota, Y.; Sato, W.; Murai, T.; Toichi, M.; Ikeda, A. & Sengoku, A. (2000). Emotional cognition without awareness after unilateral temporal lobectomy in humans. *Journal of Neuroscience,* 20, 19, RC97: 1-5, 02706474.

Lang, P. J.; Bradley, M. M. & Cuthbert, B. N. (1998). Emotion, motivation, and anxiety: Brain mechanisms and psychophysiology. *Biological Psychiatry,* 44, 12, 1248-1263, 00063223.

LeDoux, J. E. (1998). *The emotional brain: The mysterious underpinnings of emotional life.* Simon & Schuster, 0684836599, New York.

Levenson, R. W. (1991). Autonomic nervous system differences among emotions. *Psychological Science,* 3, 1, 23-27, 09567976.

McGaugh, J. L.; Rozendaal, B. & Cahill, L. (1999). Modulation of memory storage by stress hormones and the amygdaloid complex. In: *The New Cognitive Neurosciences, 2nd ed.,* S. M. Gazzaniga (Ed.), 1081-1098, MIT Press, 0262071959, Cambridge.

Morris, J. S.; Öhman, A. & Dolan, R. J. (1999). A subcortical pathway to the right amygdala mediating "unseen" fear. *Proceedings of the National Academy of Sciences of the United States of America,* 96, 4, 1680-1685, 00278424.

Öhman, A.; Flykt, A. & Esteves, F. (2001). Emotion drives attention: Detecting the snake in the grass. *Journal of Experimental Psychology: General,* 130, 3, 466-478, 00963445.

Ono, T. & Nishijo, H. (1992). Neurophysiological basis of the Kluver-Bucy syndrome: responses on monkey amygdaloid neurons to biologically significant objects. In: *The amygdala: Neurobiological aspects of emotion, memory, and mental dysfunction,* J. P. Aggleton (Ed.), 167-190, Wiley-Liss, 0471561290, New York.

Oya, H.; Kawasaki, H.; Howard, M. A. & Adolphs, R. (2002). Electrophysiological responses in the human amygdala discriminate emotion categories of complex visual stimuli. Journal of Neuroscience, 22, 21, 9502-9512, 02706474.

Robinson, M. D. (1998). Running from William James' bear: A review of preattentive mechanisms and their contributions to emotional experience. *Cognition and Emotion,* 12, 5, 667-696, 02699931.

Sato, W.; Kochiyama, T.; Yoshikawa, S. & Matsumura, M. (2001). Emotional expression boosts early visual processing of the face: ERP recording and its decomposition by independent component analysis. *Neuroreport,* 12, 4, 709-714, 09594965.

Sato, W.; Yoshikawa, S.; Kochiyama, T. & Matsumura, M. (2004). The amygdala processes the emotional significance of facial expressions: An fMRI investigation using the interaction between expression and face direction. *Neuroimage,* 22, 2, 1006-1013, 10538119.

Tooby, J. & Cosmides, L. (1990). The past explains the present: Emotional adaptations and the structure of ancestral environments. *Ethology & Sociobiology,* 11, 4-5, 375-424, 01623095.

Tranel, D.; Gullickson, G.; Koch, M. & Adolphs, R. (2006). Altered experience of emotion following bilateral amygdala damage. *Cognitive Neuropsychiatry,* 11, 3, 219-232, 13546805.

Treisman, A. M. & Kanwisher, N. G. (1998). Perceiving visually presented objects: recognition, awareness, and modularity. *Current Opinion in Neurobiology,* 8, 2, 218-222, 09594388.

Williams, L. M.; Phillips, M. L.; Brammer, M. J.; Skerrett, D.; Lagopoulos, J.; Rennie, C.; Bahramali, H.; Olivieri, G.; David, A. S.; Peduto, A. & Gordon, E. (2001). Arousal dissociates amygdala and hippocampal fear responses: evidence from simultaneous fMRI and skin conductance recording. *Neuroimage,* 14, 5, 1070-1079, 10538119.

16

A Physiological Approach to Affective Computing

Mincheol Whang and Joasang Lim
Division of Digital Media Technology, Sangmyung University Seoul, Korea

1. Introduction

Psychologists, cognitive scientists and neuroscientists have studied emotion for more than a century (Darwin, 1872). Only recently has computer science research shown an increasing interest in incorporating emotion into computers (Picard, 1997; Whang *et al.*, 2003). Given that the computers are built to operate logically and computing work is intended to be rational, however, this interest is rather challenging and controversial (Hollnagel, 2003). As technological developments progress at a rapid pace, computers are ubiquitous and disappearing. They become regarded even as 'social agents' rather than just a machine (Marakas *et al.*, 2000). As a result, it is deemed that communication with computers should be more natural and friendlier than the traditional one chiefly relying on hand driven movement using the mouse or the keyboard. Efforts are underway to improve the interface with more intrinsic medium through voice, face expression or gesture and computers are getting human-like (Marsic *et al.*, 2000). Even so it is still far short of what is needed.
What we feel conveys an essential context in the human-human communication and computers with the capability to recognize and express the emotion is definitely friendlier and more of human-like. There exist some theoretical foundations what brings up certain emotion and somatic changes. It is certain, however, that emotion naturally arises in our daily life when we encounter a certain situation or make a risky decision. Emotion affects many different aspects of human behavior, cognition and decision making (Cowie *et al.*, 2001), often leading to some heuristic shortcuts and cognitive biases (De Martino *et al.*, 2006). Surely it is a challenging task to build computers to serve the users mechanically, intelligently or even further emotionally. Recent research has reported some cases where emotion aware computing may be useful. For example, people like to signal their emotional state in email or SMS with so-called emoticons (Curran & Casey, 2006). Emotion recognition also has a part to play in tutoring, remote education (Nasoz & Lisetti, 2006) and computer entertainment such as game (Mandryk & Atkins, 2007).
Despite the role of emotion that has been shown in the literature, it is not clear the effect of emotion on the human computer interaction (HCI). Many studies have analyzed the artificial data that were taken from the subjects off-line and used them to recognize what emotional states they were in. On the other hand, our approach is made with on-line data that were read from the sensors attached on the mouse. This physiological data were

processed to build an algorithm to enable the computers to understand the emotion in real-time. What we aim is to build an emotional computer which is more sympathetic with the computing work and behave more intelligently in recognizing users' emotion and responding to it in an appropriate manner.

2. Related literature on emotion recognition

Emotion is not a simple phenomenon. The term emotion, despite being much used in our daily life, is still controversial in academia (Forgas, 1989). In the context of affective computing, however, the exact definition may not be consequential as the focus is pointed to the automatic recognition of the expressed emotion or feelings. We will use the term emotion to include both affect and mood. Emotion and mood are related but distinct phenomena in terms of cause, duration, control, experience, and consequences (Beedie *et al.*, 2005). The term emotion will be used to refer to a relatively intense state that has been induced for a short duration and involves a definite cause (Forgas, 1992). Given this definition, an emotion differs from a mood because the former is typically about something specific, its onset/offset time-course is more rapid and it is more intense at its peak.

Research has shown that emotion impacts upon human behavior and decision processes in a variety of ways and its effects can occur in the perception, storage and use of information. For instance, affect can influence the processes of search, acquisition and retrieval of information (Bower, 1981) and the selection of decision strategies for a task (Isen & Means, 1983). It may be contrary to the view that emotion can lead to irrational thinking of human and thus should be inhibited. Rather emotion can help people act more intelligently and choose more rational choice (Bechara & Damasio, 2005). This argues that people would behave differently what emotional state they are in. More relevant to affective computing, emotion, as an important medium of expression, plays a crucial role in human-human communication.

Among the theories for categorizing or structuring emotions, two main views include either discrete or dimensional. The former claims the existence of universal 'basic' emotions. One of the typical perspectives was from Ekman (1993), who empirically showed six basic emotions of anger, disgust, fear, joy, sadness and surprise. An alternative view on emotion is a dimensional approach, assuming the existence of two or more major dimensions which describe different emotions and distinguish between them (Russell, 1980). There is still debate on which view best captures the structure of emotion even though some attempts have been made to merge the two (Russell & Barrett, 1999). Both perspectives have received little unanimous support from physiological studies (Cacioppo *et al.*, 2000).

Here introduced is a brief overview of computing approaches to automatic human affect recognition. The references in Table 1 are representative of existing empirical studies and are by no means exhaustive. More details on the automatic recognition of human emotion as well as more complete lists of references can be found in Picard (2000). Table 1 shows primarily two approaches to automatically recognizing human emotion based on audio or visual cues that are expressed through linguistic or paralinguistic channels. Machines need to be trained to learn the patterns that signal emotion as contained in speech, face, bodily movements or in combination. Unfortunately, none of the studies perfectly estimate human emotion embedded in these channels. This may be attributed partly to the fact that pattern learning algorithms are imperfect to learn the properties of the human emotion. Data may get noised due to sensing capability or be subject to vulnerable to unwanted thoughts during data capturing. An alternative explanation could be related to the nature of emotion expression and regulation, often hidden and contextually dependant (Ekman & Friesen, 1975). Some studies (see for a review Murray & Arnott (1993) & Scherer (2003)) have empirically investigated acoustic and prosodic characteristics such as pitch variables and speaking rate, which are taken into emotion recognition models and this approach has shown varying detection rates (Devillers *et al.*, 2005). Table 1 shows some of the recognition accuracy of empirical evidence in the range of between 50% (Nakatsu *et al.*, 2000) and 83.5% (Grimm *et al.*, 2007). It should be noted that the accuracy may be dependent on the number of emotional states attempted in the studies. Facial expressions and movements such as a smile or a nod (Essa & Pentland, 1997; Fasel & Luettin, 2003) have been also extensively used to map into emotion (see Fasel & Luettin (2003) for a review). Due to delicate face muscle movements, however, some emotional states (e.g., happiness) seem to be easier to recognize than others (e.g., fear). Motion captured data with markers placed on human body are collected and analyzed to recognize emotion (Bianchi-Berthouze & Klemsmith, 2003; Castellano *et al.*, 2007). Or an attempt has made to analyze images of body gestures. The problem for this method is related to separating the movement from the background. People may have to wear a certain colored dress or need to be trained for some manual initial markings (see for a review Wang et al. (2003)). Thus some research tends to take a multimodal approach in consideration of the importance of non-verbal cues (Kapoor *et al.*, 2007; Zhihong *et al.*, 2007). Interestingly enough, in communicating feelings, non-verbal cues (e.g., 38% for voice tone & 55% for gestures) often carry more informative messages than do verbal ones (7%) (Mehrabian, 1971).

Approaches	Recognition Rates
Vocal	50% (Nakatsu et al., 2000),73% (Lee et al., 2006), 83.5% (Grimm et al., 2007)
Facial	98% (Essa & Pentland, 1997), 86% (Anderson & McOwan, 2006), 78% (Ioannou et al., 2005)
Body gestures	84-92% (Kapur et al., 2005),44-90% (Castellano et al., 2007), 60% (10% noise added) (Bianchi-Berthouze & Klemsmith, 2003)
Physiological	61.2% (Kim et al., 2004), 70-90% (Lisetti et al., 2003), 81% (Picard et al., 2001)
Multimodal	31-98% (voice, face & speech) (Fragopanagos & Taylor, 2005), 91.1% (face & gestures) (Gunes & Piccardi, 2007)72% (face & speech) (De Silva & Pei Chi, 2000)

Table 1: Some of the empirical approaches to emotion recognition

Of the above mentioned approaches, a physiological approach is promising in that inner bodily changes are reflected in autonomous nervous systems and thus, integrally related to human emotion (Picard et al., 2001; Lisetti et al., 2003; Zhihong et al., 2007). For example, there is empirical evidence that physiological activities in face, finger, and body (e.g., EMG, PPG, EEG) are related to emotions. Thus, measuring these somatic activities would make it possible to obtain information about the emotional states. Research has been recently growing in the discipline of human–computer interaction to study the emotion-related physiological signals. Kim et al. (2004) employed pattern learning algorithms to recognize four types of emotions (sadness, anger, stress & surprise) from four physiological signals (ECG, SKT, EDA & PPG). Considering the large number of subjects participated in their study, recognition rates were relatively high in the range of 78.4% for three and 61.8% for four emotions. Lissetti et al. (2003) have made an attempt to recognize some basic emotions such as anger, fear, sadness and frustration and the recognition accuracy was varied depending upon the emotional states from 70% to 90% (70% for frustration, 80% for anger & fear, 90% for sadness). Picard et al. (2001) used a single subject design methodology and instead more number of emotions were put into machine learning techniques. GSR, EMG (jaw), BVP and respiration signals were taken from a subject repeatedly over many days and the accuracy was comparatively high. Some of the issues worthy attention in physiological studies include obtrusiveness (e.g., sensors and gel), noise and environmental context that may pollute data. Given the alternative approaches discussed by thus, it is hard to compare results across studies or to draw any conclusion about the applicability of emotion recognition due to different techniques used in the studies. Techniques used in the studies are varied as to the way emotion is defined, elicited and controlled.

3. Automatic emotion recognition: an experiment

As discussed, the most pertinent agenda for affective computing would be understanding what emotional state one is in. The authors have been studying this issue in three aspects of emotion modeling, recognition and adaptive interaction. We report here mainly as to our physiological approach to affective computing with individualization capability.

3.1 Physiological measurement

Autonomic parameters were chosen for emotion recognition with discretion in full consideration of easiness and convenience of measurement. Electrodes were applied to the fingers and palm region of the hand. Photoplethysmogram (PPG), galvanic skin response (GSR) and skin temperature (SKT) were representative parameters of autonomic nervous responses. GSR was measured as an indicator for sympathetic activity (Boucsein, 1992), skin temperature (SKT) for parasympathetic activity and PPG for arousal and orienting. GSR, as one of electrodermal responses, is low in frequency. Its amplitude measures the degree of arousal as calculated by the difference in conductance level between the tonic and the peak of the response. SKT is slower in frequency and represents a state of relaxation. PPG as measured at the fingertips is relatively faster in frequency with a peak every 0.8 and is a useful index for orienting response. Therefore, the physiological parameters were analyzed from the amplitude of PPG and GSR, and the slope of SKT and mapped with subjective emotional states for emotion recognition.

3.2 Emotional computer

The specially designed mouse was constructed as shown in Figure 1 to record three measures that signal the most salient aspects of autonomic activities. It was optimally shaped for a firm contact between skin and sensors of PPG, GSR and SKT in order to avoid measurement noise. Ten curvatures were designed on the mouse in reference to the Korean anthropometric data collected from the 20- year-old subjects in 1992. The mouse was 9-10 cm in width and 18-19cm in length.

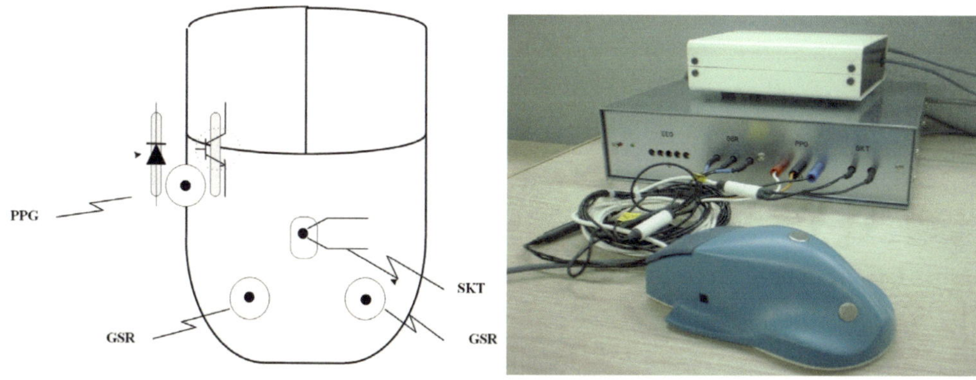

Figure 1: Emotional mouse with sensors for PPG, SKT & GSR.

As the mouse is capable of estimating human emotion, we named it as 'emotional mouse.' The emotional mouse was developed as shown in Figure 1. PPG signals were collected from the thumb, the GSR from the low part of the palm and the SKT from the center of the palm respectively. Three curvatures as depicted in Figure 1 according to the natural profiles of a right hand were designed to prevent noise signals, which may occur due to any unstable contacts between sensors and skin. Included were the thenar-hypothenar curvature for GSR (Boucsein, 1992) and the curvature of the inner palm for SKT. Both the curvature of the thumb and a special wing were modeled for PPG to minimize any movement effect.

The data acquisition board was specially configured to filter, amplify and digitally convert analog signals produced from three data channels simultaneously. The prototype for the board was produced separately from the mouse as seen in Figure 2. This was later reduced in size and stacked in a multi-layered structure to fit into the emotional mouse. It supports the RS 232 or the USB port.

Attention was paid to the chance of overloading due to incoming data from the emotional mouse, which may slow down the computer. This study has taken the client-server architecture to tackle any possible system delay. The client-side computer was given the role of data acquisition and display while the server was responsible for more demanding jobs such as data processing, emotion analysis and evaluation. The measurements along with user profiles were put into the data base for a more personalized service. The emotional mouse hooked up to the client side computer read the physiological data (PPG, GSR & SKT) and transmitted them to the server. The server then processed and analyzed the data to evaluate the emotion based on the inference algorithm (to be discussed in a following section). The results were transferred back to the client computer to be made available what emotional state was in.

3.3 Emotion inference

The term emotional computer is designed to operate emotionally as the term denotes, which may sound illogical. The inference algorithm was designed in this study to have emotion as background intelligence. The procedure required to assess the physiological data and map them to the emotional states is depicted in Figure 2. As discussed earlier, the dimensional emotion model as proposed by Larsen and Diener (1992) was adopted and PPG, GSR and SKT were analyzed into two dimensional measurements such as arousal and valence. In most of the time, however, users were in a neutral state of emotion, which was not defined in the theoretical dimensional model. The neutral emotion refers to a state that is free from any emotional influence and thus set as a reference state in the course of assessing the emotional state. Each physiological signal of PPG, GSR, and SKT needs setting a neutral band based on subjective evaluation of the emotional states. As a result, the four categories (i.e., (1) pleasantness-arousal, (2) pleasantness-relaxation, (3) unpleasantness-arousal, and (4) unpleasantness-relaxation) were added with neural states. This resulted in nine categories of emotional states with five more states added; that is, (5) pleasantness-neutral arousal, (6) unpleasantness-neutral, (7) neutral pleasantness-arousal, (8) neutral pleasantness-relaxation, and (9) neutral pleasantness-neutral arousal.

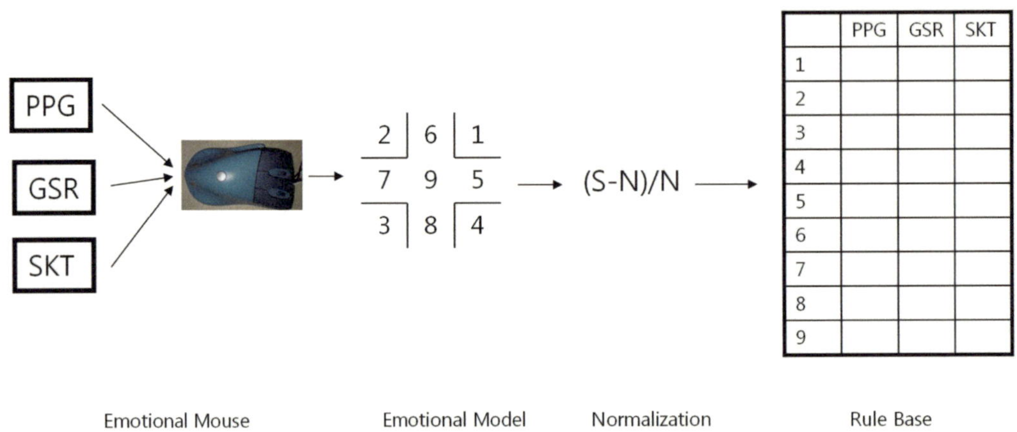

Figure 2: Process to assess the emotional states

The neutral state of emotion was not identical across individuals due to their physical and psychological characteristics. This certainly leads to variations in individual emotional experience, which was manifested for both within and between subjects. This problem has been also reported in literature and some (Picard et al., 2001) used one subject over long period of time. To overcome the hurdle of individualization, the neutral band was introduced and automatically decided in reference to the subjectively assessed values of self-emotion to accommodate some likely individual differences.

The neutral band was used to normalize physiological data. As shown in Equation 1, E refers to the percent changes of physiological signals and is computed as the difference between stimulated state (S) and neutral state (N) divided by neutral state (N). Thus, normalization values should lie in the range of between 0 and 1.

$$E = (S-N)/N \tag{1}$$

Each physiological signal was normalized and assigned into one of the three states, i.e., increase, decrease and no variation. The three possible states for three physiological signals yielded 27 cases. Individual difference was also taken into account in developing the rule base. The rule set was defined for each individual with individualistic neutral band and responses to emotional events. This algorithm was updated by mapping subjectively assessed scores of valence and arousal states to incoming physiological signals. The recognition accuracy of the emotional computer was empirically validated. Five university students participated in 100 repetitive experiments for three consecutive days. Their subjectively reported self-emotions were compared to the one estimated according to the inferential algorithm. The recognition rates were 70-90%. Higher accuracy was found for arousal than for valence of the emotion.

4. Conclusion

Emotion is one of the intellectual traits that may distinguish human beings from computers (Picard, 1997; Oatley, 1998). Despite considerable efforts over the past decades, computers are far from understanding the delicacy of human emotion and this would certainly lead users to perceive computers being challenging and inhumane. This study has shown that the computer may be capable of recognizing emotion in an automatic way with the physiological signals such as PPG, GSR, and SKT. The computers were designed to be equipped with some devices that evaluated the emotional state of computer users and could trigger appropriate actions adaptively depending upon the changes in emotion. In this context, the physiological data of users were read into the signal processor of emotional computers to assess the state of users' emotion. It should be, however, noted that there may be a number of factors that could contribute to the accuracy of emotion evaluation. Accuracy may be greatly related, among others, to data measurement and preprocessing of measured data and mathematical models to classify the state of human emotion. Also, there have been very few studies which evaluated 'live' emotion. Most studies captured the signals and analyzed them off-line. Physiological computing raises the issue of obtrusiveness. The size and number of sensors required for the collection of physiological data may be obtrusive. The time and chemicals to affix sensors onto human body may also be cumbersome. Individual differences should also be taken into account that emotion may not be necessarily consistent over individuals and over days. Our approach with on-line physiological data would be valuable to provide insights into the notion of emotional computers and further research is required in this respect.

5. References

Anderson, K. & McOwan, P. W. (2006). "A real-time automated system for the recognition of human facial expressions." IEEE Transactions on Systems Man and Cybernetics Part B-Cybernetics 36(1): 96-105.

Bechara, A. & Damasio, A. R. (2005). "The somatic marker hypothesis: A neural theory of economic decision." Games and Economic Behavior 52(2): 336-372.

Beedie, C. J., Terry, P. C. & Lane, A. M. (2005). "Distinctions between emotion and mood." Cognition & Emotion 19(6): 847-878.

Bianchi-Berthouze, N. & Klemsmith, A. (2003). "A categorical approach to affective gesture recognition." Connection Science 15(4): 259-269.

Boucsein, W. (1992). Electrodermal Activity. New York, Plenum Press.

Bower, G. H. (1981). "Mood and Memory." American Psychologist 36(2): 129-148.

Cacioppo, J. T., Berntson, G. G., Larsen, J. T., Poehlmann, K. M. & Ito, T. A., Eds. (2000). The psychophysiology of emotion. Handbook of Emotions. New York, The Guilford Press.

Castellano, G., Villalba, S. D. & Camurri, A. (2007). "Recognising human emotions from body movement and gesture dynamics." Affective Computing and Intelligent

Interaction. Proceedings Second International Conference, ACII 2007. (Lecture Notes in Computer Science vol. 4738): 71-82.

Cowie, R., Douglas-Cowie, E., Tsapatsoulis, N., Votsis, G., Kollias, S., Fellenz, W. & Taylor, J. G. (2001). "Emotion recognition in human-computer interaction." IEEE Signal Processing Magazine 18(1): 32-80.

Curran, K. & Casey, M. (2006). "Expressing emotion in electronic mail." Kybernetes 35(5-6): 616-631.

Darwin, C. (1872). Expression of the Emotions in Man and Animals. London, John Murray.

De Martino, B., Kumaran, D., Seymour, B. & Dolan, R. J. (2006). "Frames, biases, and rational decision-making in the human brain." Science 313(5787): 684-687.

De Silva, L. C. & Pei Chi, N. (2000). "Bimodal emotion recognition." Proceedings Fourth IEEE International Conference on Automatic Face and Gesture Recognition (Cat. No. PR00580): 332-5 | xiv+560.

Devillers, L., Vidrascu, L. & Lamel, L. (2005). "Challenges in real-life emotion annotation and machine learning based detection." Neural Networks 18(4): 407-422.

Ekman, P. (1993). "Facial Expression and Emotion." American Psychologist 48(4): 384-392.

Ekman, P. & Friesen, W. (1975). Unmasking the Face. Englewood Cliffs, NJ, Prentice-Hall.

Essa, I. A. & Pentland, A. P. (1997). "Coding, analysis, interpretation, and recognition of facial expressions." IEEE Transactions on Pattern Analysis and Machine Intelligence 19(7): 757-763.

Fasel, B. & Luettin, J. (2003). "Automatic facial expression analysis: a survey." Pattern Recognition 36(1): 259-275.

Forgas, J. P. (1989). "Mood Effects on Decision-Making Strategies." Australian Journal of Psychology 41(2): 197-214.

Forgas, J. P. (1992). "Affect in Social Judgments and Decisions - a Multiprocess Model." Advances in Experimental Social Psychology 25: 227-275.

Fragopanagos, N. & Taylor, J. G. (2005). "Emotion recognition in human-computer interaction." Neural Networks 18(4): 389-405.

Grimm, M., Kroschel, K., Mower, E. & Narayanan, S. (2007). "Primitives-based evaluation and estimation of emotions in speech." Speech Communication 49(10-11): 787-800.

Gunes, H. & Piccardi, M. (2007). "Bi-modal emotion recognition from expressive face and body gestures." Journal of Network and Computer Applications 30(4): 1334-1345.

Hollnagel, E. (2003). "Commentary - Is affective computing an oxymoron?" International Journal of Human-Computer Studies 59(1-2): 65-70.

Ioannou, S. V., Raouzaiou, A. T., Tzouvaras, V. A., Mailis, T. P., Karpouzis, K. C. & Kollias, S. D. (2005). "Emotion recognition through facial expression analysis based on a neurofuzzy network." Neural Networks 18(4): 423-435.

Isen, A. M. & Means, B. (1983). "The influence of positive affect on decision-making strategy." Social Cognition 2(1): 18-31.

Kapoor, A., Burleson, W. & Picard, R. W. (2007). "Automatic prediction of frustration." International Journal of Human-Computer Studies 65(8): 724-736.

Kapur, A., Kapur, A., Virji-Babul, N., Tzanetakis, G. & Driessen, P. F. (2005). Gesture-based affective computing on motion capture data. Affective Computing and Intelligent Interaction, Proceedings. Berlin, Springer-Verlag Berlin. 3784: 1-7.

Kim, K. H., Bang, S. W. & Kim, S. R. (2004). "Emotion recognition system using short-term monitoring of physiological signals." Medical & Biological Engineering & Computing 42(3): 419-427.

Larsen, R. J. & Diener, E. (1992). Promises and problems with the circumplex model of emotion. Newbury Park, CA., Sage.

Lee, K. K., Cho, Y. H. & Park, K. S. (2006). Robust feature extraction for mobile-based speech emotion recognition system. Intelligent Computing in Signal Processing and Pattern Recognition. Berlin, Springer-Verlag Berlin. 345: 470-477.

Lisetti, C., Nasoz, F., LeRouge, C., Ozyer, O. & Alvarez, K. (2003). "Developing multimodal intelligent affective interfaces for tele-home health care." International Journal of Human-Computer Studies 59(1-2): 245-255.

Mandryk, R. L. & Atkins, M. S. (2007). "A fuzzy physiological approach for continuously modeling emotion during interaction with play technologies." International Journal of Human-Computer Studies 65(4): 329-347.

Marakas, G. M., Johnson, R. D. & Palmer, J. W. (2000). "A theoretical model of differential social attributions toward computing technology: when the metaphor becomes the model." International Journal of Human-Computer Studies 52(4): 719-750.

Marsic, I., Medl, A. & Flanagan, J. (2000). "Natural communication with information systems." Proceedings of the IEEE 88(8): 1354-1366.

Mehrabian, A. (1971). Silent messages. Belmont, California, Wadsworth.

Murray, I. R. & Arnott, J. L. (1993). "Toward the Simulation of Emotion in Synthetic Speech - a Review of the Literature on Human Vocal Emotion." Journal of the Acoustical Society of America 93(2): 1097-1108.

Nakatsu, R., Nicholson, J. & Tosa, N. (2000). "Emotion recognition and its application to computer agents with spontaneous interactive capabilities." Knowledge-Based Systems 13(7-8): 497-504.

Nasoz, F. & Lisetti, C. L. (2006). "MAUI avatars: Mirroring the user's sensed emotions via expressive multi-ethnic facial avatars." Journal of Visual Languages and Computing 17(5): 430-444.

Oatley, K. (1998). "Emotion." The Psychologist: 285-288.

Picard, R. W. (1997). Affective Computing, MIT Press.

Picard, R. W. (2000). "Toward computers that recognize and respond to user emotion." IBM Systems Journal 39(3-4): 705-719.

Picard, R. W., Vyzas, E. & Healey, J. (2001). "Toward machine emotional intelligence: Analysis of affective physiological state." IEEE Transactions on Pattern Analysis and Machine Intelligence 23(10): 1175-1191.

Russell, J. A. (1980). "A Circumplex Model of Affect." Journal of Personality and Social Psychology 39(6): 1161-1178.

Russell, J. A. & Barrett, L. F. (1999). "Core affect, prototypical emotional episodes, and other things called Emotion: Dissecting the elephant." Journal of Personality and Social Psychology 76(5): 805-819.

Scherer, K. R. (2003). "Vocal communication of emotion: A review of research paradigms." Speech Communication 40(1-2): 227-256.

Wang, L. A., Hu, W. M. & Tan, T. N. (2003). "Recent developments in human motion analysis." Pattern Recognition 36(3): 585-601.

Whang, M. C., Lim, J. S. & Boucsein, W. (2003). "Preparing computers for affective communication: A psychophysiological concept and preliminary results." Human Factors 45(4): 623-634.

Zhihong, Z., Maja, P., Glenn, I. R. & Thomas, S. H. (2007). A survey of affect recognition methods: audio, visual and spontaneous expressions. Proceedings of the 9th international conference on Multimodal interfaces. Nagoya, Aichi, Japan, ACM.

17

iFace: Facial Expression Training System

Kyoko Ito* **, Hiroyuki Kurose **, Ai Takami ** and Shogo Nishida **
** Center for the Study of Communication-Design, Osaka University,*
***Graduate School of Engineering Science, Osaka University,*
Japan

1. Introduction

Nonverbal information, such as that contained in facial expressions, gestures, and tone of voice, plays an important role in human communications (Kurokawa, 1994). Facial expressions, especially, are a very important media for visually transmitting feelings and intentions (Yoshikawa, 2001; Uchida, 2006). At least one study has shown that more than half of all communication perceptions are transmitted through visual information (Mehrabian, 1981).

However, the person transmitting a facial expression cannot directly see his or her own expression. Therefore, it is important to understand the expression being transmitted and identifying the target facial expression in order to ideally express it. Facial muscles play a critical role in human facial expressions.

Facial expression training has recently garnered attention as a method of improving facial expressions (Inudou, 2007; Inudou, 1997; COBS ONLINE, 2007; Practice of Facial Expression, 2007). In facial expression training, exercises are performed that target a specific part of the face and those facial muscles. The muscles used in facial expressions are strengthened by training and when the facial expression is softened, the ideal facial expression can be expressed. Facial expression training has effective applications not only in daily communications, but also within the realm of business skills and rehabilitation. Facial expression training can take multiple forms, one of which is a seminar style experience with a trainer. Another method uses self training books or information on the Internet to serve as a guide. Some seminars are very expensive, and time and space are restricted. Alternatively, in a self training venue, it is difficult to clearly see your target facial expression when alone, and to compare your ideal facial expression with the present one.

The aim of this study is the proposal of an effective expression training system using the computer to achieve the target facial expression. As an initial step, an interface to select the target facial expression is proposed. Next, the expression training system, including the target expression selection interface, is developed.

A previous study (Miwa et al., 1999), one that used a virtual mirror, developed a facial expression training system that created a support system for facial expression training by utilizing a computer. The virtual mirror study was a facial expression training system displaying a facial expression by emphasizing the person's features with a virtual mirror. This study, however, is different from the virtual mirror study because this study instead selects the target facial expression of an actual face.

2. A facial expression training system that achieves the target facial expression

2.1 Support process

In this study, the following steps are taken within facial expression training to achieve the target facial expression.

1) The target facial expression is identified.
2) The current facial expression is expressed in an attempt to achieve the target facial expression.
3) The current facial expression is compared with the target facial expression.
4) The muscles used for facial expression are trained.

In this study, the above enumerated processes are supported by a computer. This study also aims to develop a facial expression training system that can achieve target facial expressions. A computer is utilized to support each process of this method as follows:

1) For support in making the target facial expression;
2) For support in recognizing the current expression;
3) For support in comparing the current facial expression with the target facial expression;
4) For support in understanding the facial expression muscles that require training to achieve the target facial expression.

A primary objective of this study is the first item, above, to support making the target facial expression, and a user interface is proposed to achieve this goal. A proposal for the user interface is described below.

2.2 Support method

In this study, the following parameters are observed in making the target facial expression:
(a) Your own face is used.
(b) Your target facial expression must correspond to the movement of a real human face, the expression which is achievable.

The first item above, (a), that the target facial expression be made by using a real face is important because each human face is different from the next one. Your facial expression corresponds to your facial features.

The second item above, (b), necessitates making the target expression one that can actually be anatomically expressed using your real face. It is also important to be able to naturally make a satisfactory target facial expression.

Using these parameters, a user interface to select the target facial expression is considered. In addition, the following two stage approach is considered so that the user may select a satisfactory target facial expression:

- First stage: Rough expression selection
- Second stage: Detailed expression selection

During the first stage, based on "Emotion Map" (as illustrated in Figure 1) (Kurose et al., 2006) in Figure 1 proposed in our previous study, an interface (as illustrated in Figure 2) is proposed. Such an interface protects the user from having to worry about details and allows the user to intuitively select the target expression.

As shown in Figure 2, the interface consists of six facial images, each displaying a different potential facial expression, all arranged around a big circle in the center (Schlosberg, 1952). These six images are designed to correspond with six basic facial expressions: pleasure, surprise, displeasure, anger, fear, and sadness. Additionally, it is possible to both mix expressions from two different images and choose an expression strength level by selecting a point on the circle at the center.

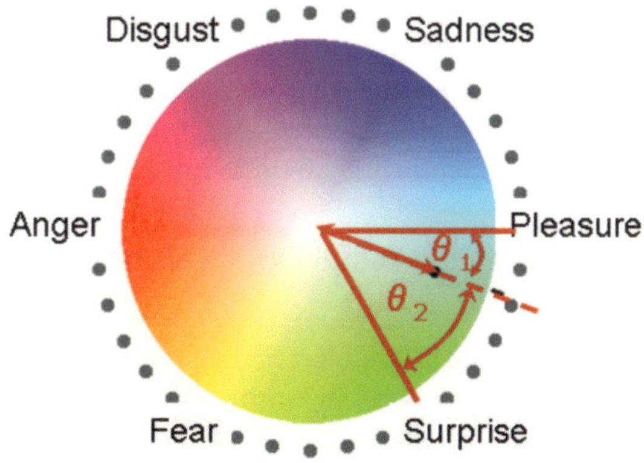

Fig. 1. Emotion Map

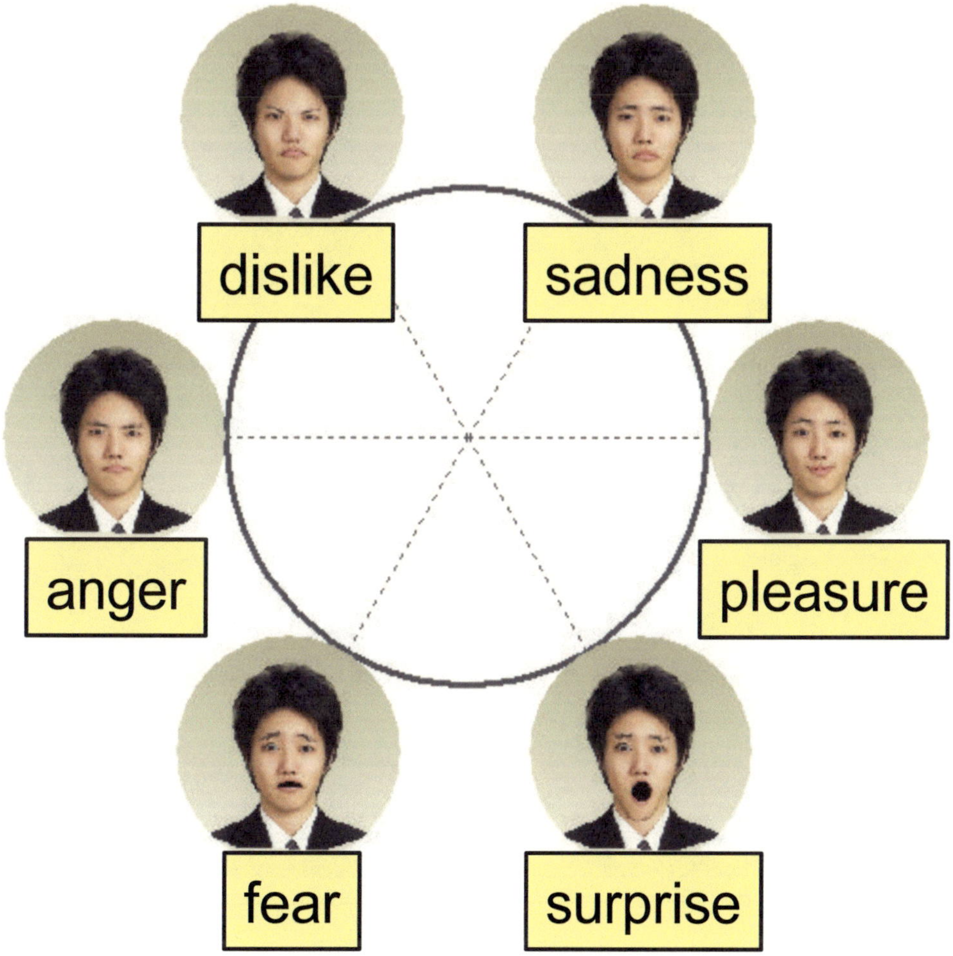

Fig. 2. Interface for selecting the target facial expression.

In the second stage, for the user's satisfaction, another user interface is employed that enables a user to be able to control further details. In this stage, an action unit (AU), derived from Ekman et al's (Ekman et al., 1978) previous research about facial expression features is used. The elements of each feature as measured in AU can be thus established in detail. These features are comprised of eyebrows, eyes, cheeks, mouth, and mandibles. Action units of 3, 5, 2, 10, and 5 are used in each feature. In total, 25 kinds of AU are used.

3. Design and development of the facial expression training system

A facial expression training system including the above mentioned processes and the interface for selecting the target facial expression has thus been developed.

First, a personal computer camera is used to capture the current facial expression of the user. Figure 3 shows the hardware setup. Visual C++6.0 is used as the software for the development of this system. In order to fit the user's face with a wire frame model, FaceFit (Galatea Project, 2007) is used. The facial expression training system developed (Parke, 1991; Waters, 1987) has been named "iFace." The following procedures are utilized in iFace:

1) User registration;
2) Selection of the target facial expression;
3) Expression of the current facial expression; and
4) Comparison of the current facial expression and the target facial expression.

Fig. 3. Hardware setup

Figure 4 shows a screen of the user registration for the fitting. The screens for selecting the target facial expression with a rough setting and a detailed setting are shown in Figures 5 and 6, respectively. Figure 7 shows the screen presenting the result of comparing the current facial expression with the target facial expression.

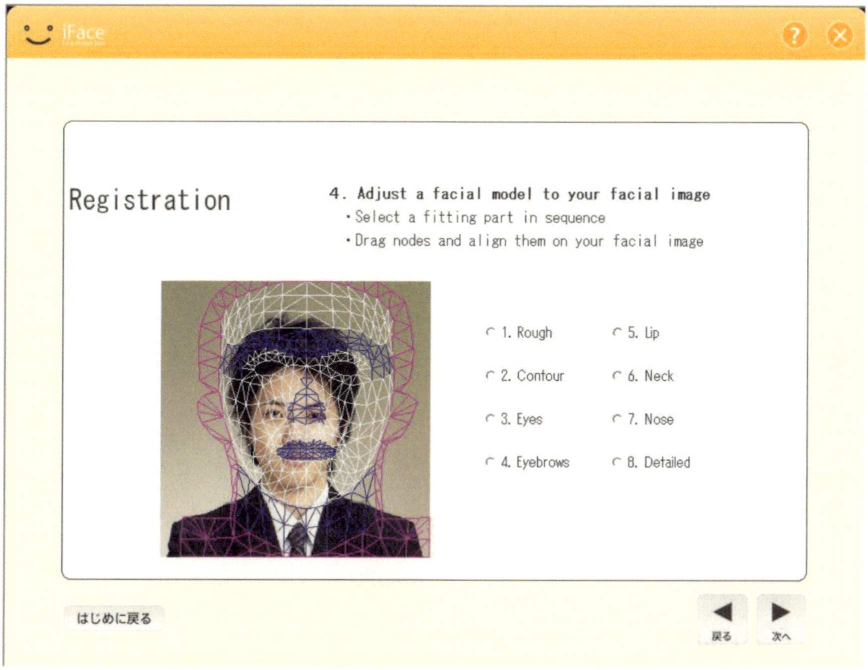

Fig. 4. A screen example of a user registration for fitting.

Fig. 5. Rough setting screen.

Fig. 6. Detailed setting screen.

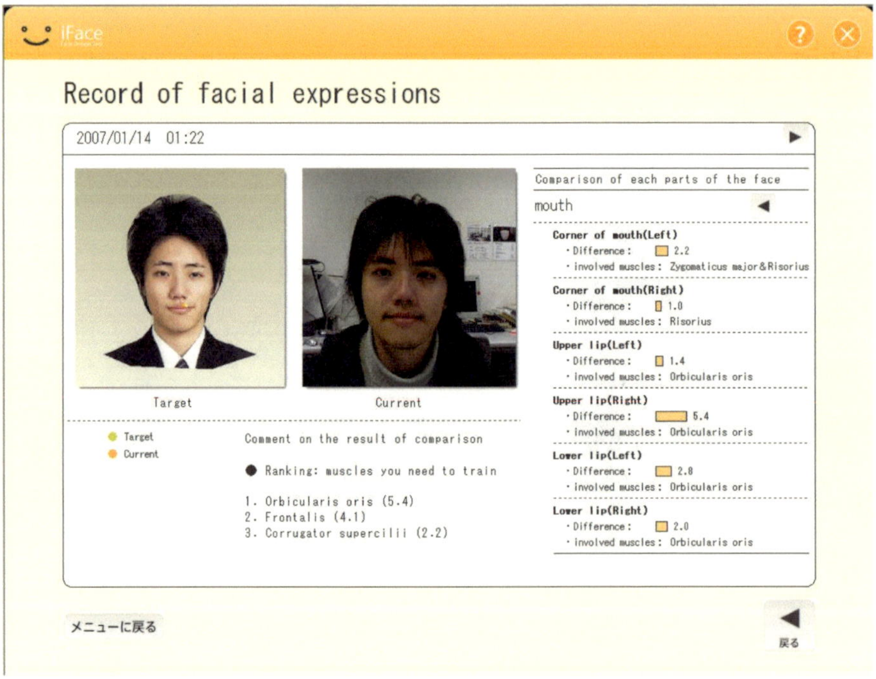

Fig. 7. An example of a screen showing a comparison between current and target

4. Evaluation of the facial expression training system

4.1 Purposes

In order to examine the effectiveness of the target facial expression selection interface and the facial expression training system, an evaluation experiment was conducted. This evaluation experiment specifically aimed to examine the following points:

- The effectiveness of the target facial expression selection interface for a facial expression training system; and
- The potential for a facial expression training system.

4.2 Methods

A. Experimental procedure

1) The target facial expression is selected by the user by employing the facial expression training system.
2) A user attempts to enact the self-selected target facial expression, while the user's current facial expression is digitally captured.
3) The user's current facial expression is then compared with the target facial expression, and the results are presented.

Each user can select two target facial expressions. One target is the user's ideal smile, and the other is an elective choice by the user. The user's current facial expression is expressed three times in attempting to achieve each target expression. Therefore, a total of six expressions of the current facial expression are attempted.

B. Experiment participants

- 12 females (dentists)

C. Methods of analysis

The results of a questionnaire administered both before and after the experiment are used. In addition, data obtained during use of the facial expression training system are used.

4.3 Results

- Effectiveness of the target facial expression selection interface

Table 1 shows the results of the questionnaire regarding the effectiveness of the target facial expression selection interface. Answers to the questionnaire are ranked on a seven point

#	Questionnaire item	Avg.
1	Did you satisfactorily achieve the target expression? (Asked regarding the first target expression)	-0.3
2	Did you satisfactorily achieve the target expression? (Asked regarding the second target expression)	1.7
3	Was the facial expression selection interface both intuitive and comprehensible?	2.2
4	Did you experience the synthesized facial expression in a way that felt natural?	-0.3

Table 1 Questionnaire results regarding the effectiveness of the target facial expression selection interface

scale of +3 to -3. Questionnaire results reflected an average satisfaction rating scores of -0.3 for the first target expression attempt (#1) and 1.7 for the second target expression attempt (#2). The questionnaire results also show that the satisfaction rating on the smile selection is lower than that of the elective choice expression.

In addition, the time required for selecting the target facial expression is shown in Figure 8 with separate amounts for a rough setting and a detailed setting at the smile selection. In a comparison between a rough setting and a detailed setting, it was demonstrated that there were many people who spent more time in a detailed setting.

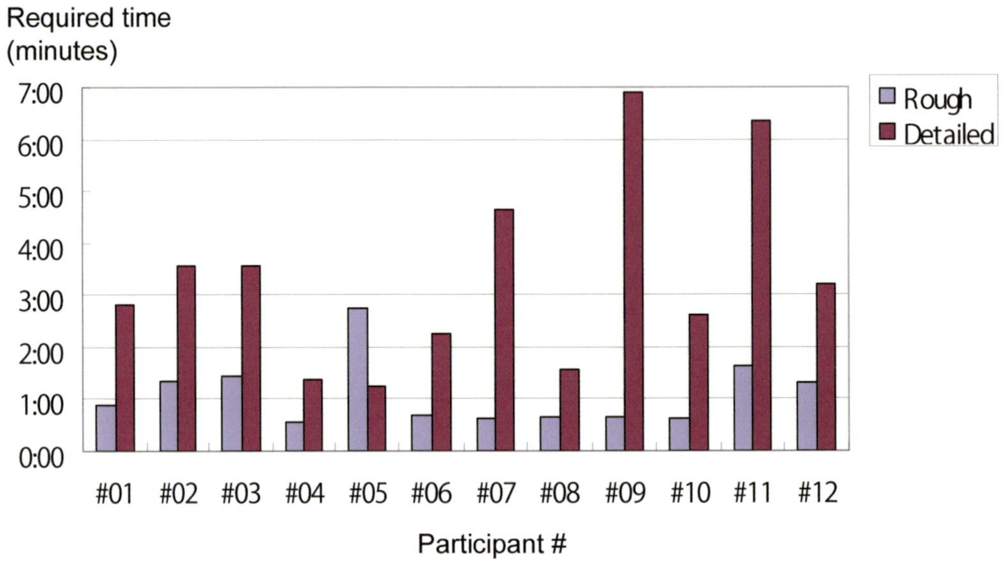

Fig. 8. The time required for rough and detailed selections of target facial expressions by each user.

#	Questionnaire item	Avg.
5	Was the training method for deciding the target facial expression both concrete and comprehensible?	2.6
6	Was it easy to express your actual expression by comparing the current facial expression with the target facial expression?	2.5
7	Would you want to use the facial expression training system daily?	1.8

Table 2 Questionnaire results regarding facial expression training system potential

- Facial expression training system potential

Table 2 shows the questionnaire results for facial expression training system potential. The questionnaire answers are ranked on a seven point scale of +3 to -3. The results demonstrate that the facial expression training system was positively evaluated.

The following comments were obtained from comments written on the questionnaire:

- I think that they can use it [a facial expression training system] to undergo rehabilitation for a paralytic face.
- My motivation for facial expression training increased when I made the target facial expression.

5. Conclusion

In this study, a target facial expression selection interface for a facial expression training system and a facial expression training system were both proposed and developed. Twelve female dentists used the facial expression training system, and evaluations and opinions about the facial expression training system were obtained from these participants.
In the future, we will attempt to improve both the target facial expression selection interface and the comparison of a current and a target facial expression. Successful development of an effective facial expression training system can then lead to actual and varied usage.

6. References

COBS ONLINE Business good face by facial muscles training (January, 2008). http://cobs.jp/skillup/face/index.html (In Japanese)

Ekman, P., and W. V. Friesen (1978). The Facial Action Coding System, Consulting Psychologists Press.

Galatea Project (January, 2008). http://hil.t.u-tokyo.ac.jp/~galatea/index-jp.html (In Japanese).

Kurokawa, T. (1994). Nonverbal interface, Ohmsha, Ltd., Tokyo (In Japanese)

Inudou, F. Facening Official Site (January, 2008). http://www.facening.com/ (In Japanese)

Inudou, F. (1997). Facening, Seishun Publishing Co., Ltd., Tokyo (In Japanese)

Kurose, H., Ito, K. and Nishida, S. (2006) A Method for Selecting Facial Expression based on Emotions and Its Application for Text Reading, Proc. of IEEE International Conference on Systems, Man, and Cybernetics(SMC2006), pp.4028-4033.

Mehrabian, A. (1981). Silent messages, Implicit Communication of Emotions and Attitudes, 2nd Ed., Wadsworth Pub. Co.

Miwa, S., H. Katayori and M. Inokuchi (1999). Virtual mirror: Proposal of Facial expression training system by face image data processing, Proc. 43th conference of the institute of system, control and information engineers, pp.343-344.

Parke, F. I. (1991). Techniques for facial animation, New Trends in Animation and Visualization, pp.229-241.

Practice of Facial Expression (January, 2008). http://www.nikkeibp.co.jp/style/biz /associe/expression/ (In Japanese)

Schlosberg, H. (1952). The description of facial expression in terms of two dimensions, Journal of Experimental Psychology, Vol.44.

Uchida, T. (2006). Function of facial expression, Bungeisha, Co., Ltd. (In Japanese)

Yoshikawa, S. (2001). Facial expression as a media in body and computer, pp.376-388, Kyoritsu Shuppan Co., Ltd. (In Japanese)

Waters K. (1987). A Muscle Model for Animating Three dimensional Facial Expression, Computer Graphics, SIGGRAPH'87, Vol.2, No.4, pp.17-24.

18

Affective Embodied Conversational Agents for Natural Interaction

Eva Cerezo, Sandra Baldassarri, Isabelle Hupont and Francisco J. Seron
Advanced Computer Graphics Group (GIGA)
Computer Science Department, Engineering Research Institute of Aragon(I3A),
University of Zaragoza,
Spain

1. Introduction

Human computer intelligent interaction is an emerging field aimed at providing natural ways for humans to use computers as aids. It is argued that for a computer to be able to interact with humans it needs to have the communication skills of humans. One of these skills is the affective aspect of communication, which is recognized to be a crucial part of human intelligence and has been argued to be more fundamental in human behaviour and success in social life than intellect (Vesterinen, 2001; Pantic, 2005).

Embodied conversational agents, ECAs (Casell et al., 2000), are graphical interfaces capable of using verbal and non-verbal modes of communication to interact with users in computer-based environments. These agents are sometimes just as an animated talking face, may be displaying simple facial expressions and, when using speech synthesis, with some kind of lip synchronization, and sometimes they have sophisticated 3D graphical representation, with complex body movements and facial expressions.

An important strand of emotion-related research in human-computer interaction is the simulation of emotional expressions made by embodied computer agents (Creed & Beale, 2005). The basic requirement for a computer to express emotions is to have channels of communication such as voice, image and an ability to communicate affection over those channels. Therefore, interface designers often emulate multimodal human-human communication by including emotional expressions and statements in their interfaces through the use of textual content, speech (synthetic and recorded) and synthetic facial expressions, making the agents truly "social actors" (Reeves & Nass, 1996). Several studies have illustrated that our ability to recognise the emotional facial expressions of embodied computer agents is very similar to that of identifying human facial expressions (Bartneck, 2001). Related to agent's voice, experiments have demonstrated that subjects can recognize the emotional expressions of an agent (Creed & Beale, 2006) whose voice varies widely in pitch, tempo and loudness and its facial expressions match the emotion it is expressing.

But, what about the impact of these social actors? Recent research focuses on the psychological impact of affective agents endowed with the ability to behave empathically with the user (Brave et al., 2005; Isbister, 2006; Yee et al., 2007; Prendinger & Ishizuka, 2004; Picard, 2003). The findings demonstrate that bringing about empathic agents is important in human-computer interaction. Moreover, addressing user's emotions in human-computer interaction significantly enhances the believability and lifelikeness of virtual humans (Boukricha et al., 2007). This is why the development of computer-based interfaces capable of understanding the emotional state of the user has been a subject of great interest in recent affective computing researches. Nevertheless, to date, there are no examples of agents that can sense in a completely automatic and natural (both verbal and non-verbal) way human emotion, and respond realistically. In fact, few works related to agent-based human-like affective interaction can be found in literature. In some of them, the user communicates with an affective agent through a dialogue based on multiple choice test, without any kind of non-inmersive automated emotional feedback from the user to computer (Prendinger & Ishizuka, 2005; Anolli et al., 2005). In other works, the interaction is enriched by a speech recognition and generation system that allows a minimum instructional conversation with the agent (Elliott et al., 1997) or by an automatic emotion recognizer that transmits the user's emotion to the agent which reacts accordingly (Burleson et al., 2004). In spite of the difficulties and limitations, this type of social interface has been demonstrated to enrich human–computer interaction in a wide variety of applications, including interactive presentations (Seron et al., 2006), tutoring (Elliott et al., 1997), e-learning (Anolli et al., 2005) and health-care (Prendinger & Ishizuka, 2004), and user support in frustrating situations (Prendinger & Ishizuka, 2004; Klein et al., 2002).

Our research focuses on developing interactive virtual agents that support multimodal and emotional interaction. Emotional interaction enables us to establish more effective communication with the user and multimodality broadens the number of potential users by making interaction with disabled users (for example hearing-impaired or paraplegics) and people of different ages and with different levels of education (people with or without a knowledge of computers) possible. The result of our efforts has been Maxine, a powerful engine to manage real-time interaction with virtual characters. The consideration of emotional aspects has been a key factor in the development of our system. Special emphasis has been done in capturing the user's emotion through images and in synthesizing the emotion of the virtual agent through its facial expressions and the modulation of the voice. These two aspects will , therefore constitute the core of the chapter.

The chapter is organized as follows. In Section 2, Maxine, the platform for managing virtual agents is briefly described. Section 3 details the system developed for capturing user's emotion whereas Section 4 is devoted to discuss the natural language communication between the user and the agent. In section 5 evaluations of Maxine agents are commented and, finally, in Section 6, the conclusions are presented and current and future work are outlined.

2. A platform for managing affective embodied conversational agents

2.1 Overall description

Maxine is a script-directed engine for the management and visualization of 3D virtual worlds. In Maxine it is possible to load real-time models, animations, textures and sounds. Even though it is a very generic engine, it has been oriented to the work with virtual characters in 3D scenarios. It has been written in C++ and employs a set of open source libraries.

The modules that conform Maxine are: the Sensory/Perception Modules, that process the inputs of the system, the Generative/Deliberative Modules, in charge of managing the appropriated reactions according to the inputs, and the Motor Module, that generates and coordinates the final outputs of the system.

While reasoning based on a user's directly input behaviours is important and useful, it is also limited. Therefore, an endeavour is also made to collect the largest possible amount of information on the user by means of body language or facial expression, without requiring him or her to enter data. The ultimate aim is to enhance interaction and establish emotional communication between the user and the virtual character as well as providing the user with different communication modalities. The available inputs are:

- Voice Interaction. The user can communicate with the character through voice, formulating an order, a question or any sentence in natural language. One of the requisites of our system was that it should be able to "understand" and speak Spanish. This constraint prevented us from using existing libraries, all of them in English. Details are given in section 4.
- Image Interaction: a webcam takes pictures of the user's face. The aim of these pictures is to obtain additional information on the user and, in particular, on his or her emotional state. This kind of input is detailed in section 3.
- Console (keyboard)/mouse commands: advanced users can fully control the scene and the agent thanks to the scripting language used, LUA (Lua, 2008). For non-programmer users, it is also possible to associate the execution of a command to the pressing of a certain key or clicking the mouse and, due to the power of the scripting language used, options are very varied.

Regarding the agents' reactions, two kinds of actions are distinguished:

- Purely reactive: for example, if the user keys in something, the virtual agent interrupts his/her speech, if a lot of background noise is detected, it requests silence, etc. These reactions are managed in the generative module.
- Deliberative: the choice of the reaction of the virtual character calls for more complex analysis. This analysis is done in the deliberative module, which, for example, is in charge of obtaining an answer from the user when interaction is made via voice, as it will be explained later on.

These reactions generally produce outputs, basically facial and body animations and speech with appropriated lip-synchronization.

Detailed description of Maxine is given elsewhere (Baldassarri et al., 2007b).

2.2 Maxine virtual agents

The basic aim of the system has been to make it easier to developers the inclusion of these agents in their applications. Therefore, default models, rigged and textured, with basic animations, visemes and expressions are prepared to be loaded in the system. Advanced users' can create their own chacters by using commercial software, as appropriated converters have been developed.

In Maxine, the virtual agent is endowed with the following differentiating features:

- it supports interaction with the user through different channels: text, voice (through natural language), peripherals (mouse, keyboard), which makes the use of the generated applications available to a wide range of users, in terms of communication ability, age, etc.
- it gathers additional information on the user and the environment: noise level in the room, image-based estimate of the user's emotional state, etc.
- it has its own emotional state, which may vary depending on the relationship with the user and which modulates the agent's facial expressions, answers and voice.

To study the potential and usefulness of Maxine agents different applications have been developed. In particular:

- Virtual presenters for PowerPoint like presentations: a like-life character presents PowerPoint information on a graphic display. This kind of presenter has demonstrated to be specially useful when the same presentation has to be repeated several times or given in a different language (for example in English by a non-fluent English speaker). The application, MaxinePPT (Seron et al., 2006), is capable of creating and performing a virtual presentation in a 3D virtual scenario enriched with virtual actors and additional information such as videos, images, etc. from a classical PowerPoint file. All the aspects of the virtual presentation are controlled by an XML-type language called PML (Presentation Markup Language). The PML instructions are added to the page notes of the PowerPoint slides in order to determine, for example, the text to be spoken by the virtual presenter. Once the presentation has been created, user intervention is not necessary. Figure 1 shows some screenshots of a virtual presentation.

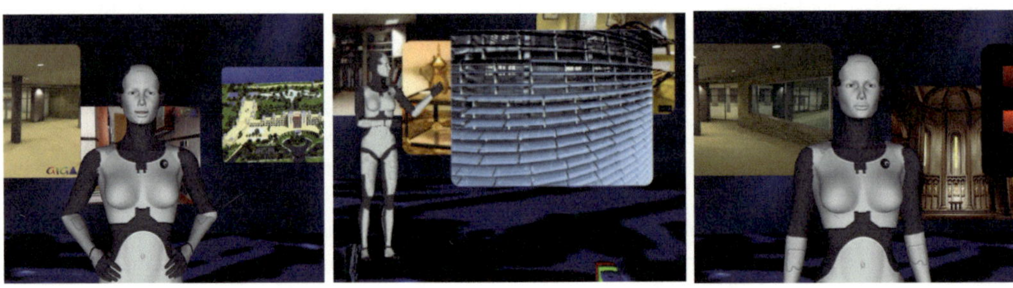

Fig. 1. Some screenshots from the presentation performed by a virtual agent

- Virtual assistants for controlling a domotics environment: a virtual agent, called Max, was created and used as an interactive interface (see Figure 2) for the access and remote control of an intelligent room (Cerezo et al., 2007). The user can ask Max to do different tasks within the domotics environment (to turn on/off the lamps, the tv, the electric kettle, etc.), and, also, may do queries about the different devices of the intelligent room (the state of the door, for example). Presently, adaptation of the agent interface to other devices such as mobile phones and PDAs is being performed.

Fig. 2. User interacting with the domotics environment through Max, the virtual agent

- Virtual Interactive pedagogical agents for teaching Computer Graphics: Maxine has also been used for the development of a learning platform to simplify and improve teaching and practice of Computer Graphics subjects (Seron et al., 2007) in the Computer Science degree. The interactive pedagogical agent helps students in two ways: acting as a virtual teacher to expose some specific topics, and allowing the interaction and handle of a 3D scene to make it easier to understand difficult topics of CG subjects (see Figure 3). Results are promising as it will be discussed in section 5.

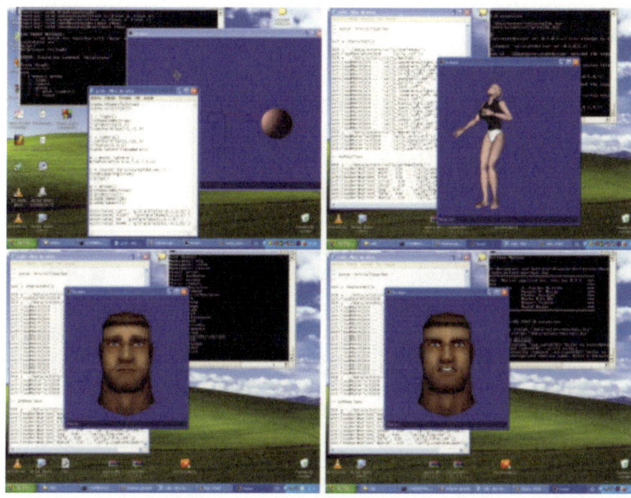

Fig. 3. "Playing" with the Maxine engine: managing a 3D scene (above left), loading and blending animations (above right) and changing characters' expressions (below)

3. Capturing user's emotions

As pointed out, the recognition of emotional information is a key step toward giving computers the ability to interact more naturally and intelligently with people. Nevertheless, to develop a system that interprets facial expressions is not easy. Two kinds of problems have to be solved: facial expression feature extraction and facial expression classification. Our work focuses on the second problem: classification. This implies the definition of the set of categories and the implementation of the categorization mechanisms.
Facial expression analyzers make use of three different methods of classification: patterns, neuronal networks or rules. If a pattern-based method is used (Edwards et al., 1998; Hong et al., 1998; Lyons et al., 1999), the face expression found is compared with the patterns defined for each expression category. The best matching decides the classification of the expression. Most of these methods first apply PCA and LDA algorithms to reduce dimensionality. In the systems based on neuronal networks (Zhang et al., 1998; Wallace et al., 2004), the face expression is classified according to a categorization process "learned" by the neuronal network during the training phase. In general, the input to this type of systems is a set of characteristics extracted from the face (points or distances between points). The rule-based methods (Pantic & Rothkrantz, 2000a) classify the face expression into basic categories of emotions, according to a set of face actions previously codified. In (Pantic & Rothkrantz, 2000b) an excellent state-of-the-art on the subject can be found.

In any case, the development of automatic facial classification systems presents several problems. Most of the studies on automated expression analysis perform an emotional classification based on the emotional classification of Ekman (Ekman, 1999). It describes six universal basic emotions: joy, sadness, surprise, fear, disgust and anger. Nevertheless, the use of Ekman's categories for developing automating facial expression emotional classification is difficult. First, his description of the six prototypic facial expressions of emotions is linguistic and, thus, ambiguous. There is no uniquely defined description either in terms of facial actions or in terms of some other universally defined facial codes. Second, classification of facial expressions into multiple emotion categories should be possible (e.g. raised eyebrows and smiling mouth is a blend of surprise and happiness). Another important issue to be considered is individualization. The system should be capable of analyzing any subject, male or female of any age and ethnicity and of any expressivity, which represents a really challenging task.

3.1 Image-based interaction process

The stages of the image-interaction process are shown in Figure 4. In the following paragraphs, each of the three stages is explained.

Stage 1: Feature extraction

A webcam takes pictures of the user and the tracking of some points enables to extract relevant facial features.

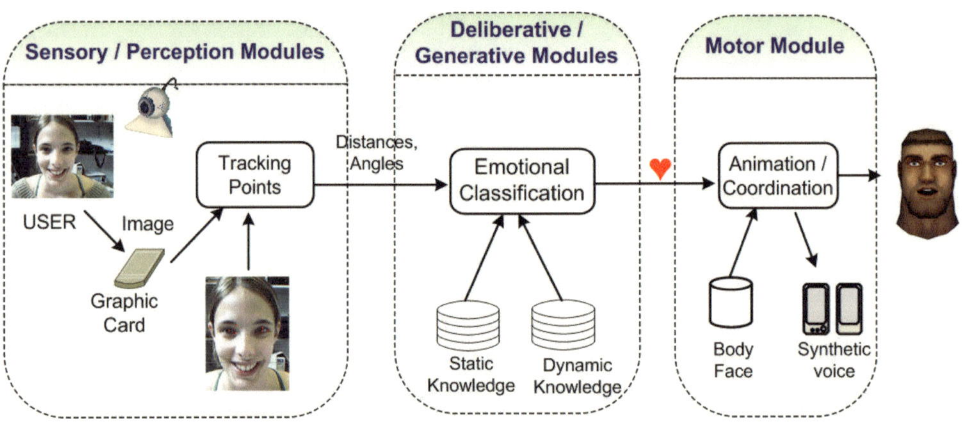

Fig. 4. Stages of the user-avatar image interaction process

Feature selection

The first step of the method consists of extracting the 20 feature points of the face that will later allow us to analyze the evolution of the face parameters (distances and angles) that we wish to study. Figure 5 shows the correspondence of these points with the ones defined by the MPEG-4 standard (MPEG-4, 2002). The characteristic points are used to calculate the five distances shown in Figure 6. These five distances can be translated in terms of MPEG-4 standard, putting them in relation to the feature points shown in Figure 5 and with some FAPs defined by the norm. All the distances are normalized with respect to the distance between the eyes (MPEG FAPU "ESo"), which is a distance independent of the expression. This way, the values will be consistent, independently of the scale of the image, the distance to the camera, etc.

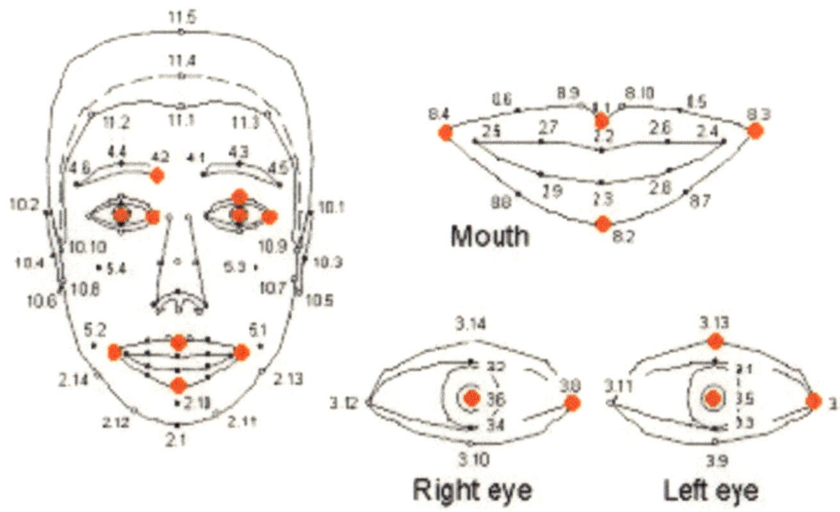

Fig. 5. Facial feature points used for the later definition of the parameters to analyze, according to MPEG-4 standard.

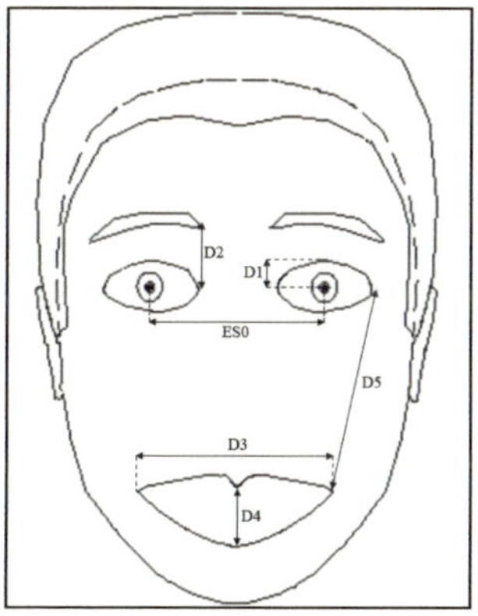

MPEG-4 FAPs NAME	FEATURE POINTS USED FOR DISTANCES
close_upper_l_eyelid close_lower_l_eyelid	D1=d(3.5, 3.1)
raise_r_i_eyebrow	D2=d(4.2, 3.8)
stretch_l_cornerlip stretch_r_cornerlip	D3=d(8.4, 8.3)
open_jaw	D4=d(8.1 , 8.2)
raise_r_cornerlip	D5=d(8.3, 3.7)

Fig. 6. Characteristic distances used in our method (left). On the right, relationship between the five characteristic distances and the MPEG-4 FAPs and feature points.

Tracking

The emotional classifier was first developed and tuned based on the tracking of features on static images. Thanks to a collaboration, the Computer Graphics, Vision and Artificial Intelligence Group of the University of the Balearic Islands provided us with a real-time facial tracking module to test our classifier. The features extraction system is non-invasive and is based on the use of a simple low cost webcam (Manresa et al., 2006). The parameters corresponding to the neutral face are obtained calculating the average of the first frames of the video sequence, in which the user is supposed to be in the neutral state. For the rest of the frames, a classification takes place following the method explained in the next sections.

The automatic features extraction program allows the introduction of dynamic information in the classification system, making it possible the study of the time evolution of the evaluated parameters, and the classification of user's emotions from live video.

Psychological investigations argue that the timing of the facial expressions is a critical factor in the interpretation of expressions. In order to give temporary consistency to the system, a temporary window that contains the emotion detected by the system in each one of the 9 previous frames is created. A variation in the emotional state of the user is detected if in this window the same emotion is repeated at least 6 times and is different from the detected in the last emotional change.

Stage 2: Emotional classification

From the extracted facial features, emotional classification is performed in stage 2.

The core of our work has been, in fact, the development of the emotional classifier. It is based on the work of Hammal et al. (Hammal et al., 2005). They have implemented a facial classification method for static images. The originality of their work consists, on the one hand, in the supposition that all the necessary information for the recognition of expressions is contained in the deformation of certain characteristics of the eyes, mouth and eyebrows and, on the other hand, in the use of the Belief Theory to make the classification. Nevertheless, their method has important restrictions. The most important restriction comes from the fact that it is only able to discern 3 of the 6 basic emotions (without including the neutral one). This is basically due to the little information they handle (only 5 distances). It would not be viable, from a probabilistic point of view, to work with many more data, because the explosion of possible combinations would remarkably increase the computational cost of the algorithm.

Our method studies the variation of a certain number of face parameters (distances and angles between some feature points of the face) with respect to the neutral expression. The objective of our method is to assign a score to each emotion, according to the state acquired by each one of the parameters in the image. The emotion (or emotions in case of draw) chosen will be the one that obtains a greater score. For example, let's imagine that we study two face parameters (P_1 and P_2) and that each one of them can take three different states (C^+, C^- and S, following the nomenclature of Hammal). State C^+ means that the value of the parameters has increased with respect to the neutral one; state C^- that its value has diminished with respect to the neutral one; and the state S that its value has not varied. First, we build a descriptive table of emotions, according to the state of the parameters, like the one of the Table 1. From this table, a set of logical tables can be built for each parameter (Table 2). That way, two vectors of emotions are defined, according to the state taken by each one of the parameters (C^+, C^- or S) in a specific frame. Once the tables are defined, the implementation of the identification algorithm is simple. When a parameter takes a specific state, it is enough to select the vector of emotions (formed by 1's and 0's) corresponding to this state. If we repeat the procedure for each parameter, we will obtain a matrix of as many rows as parameters we study and 7 columns, corresponding to the 7 emotions. The sum of 1's present in each column of the matrix gives the score obtained by each emotion.

	P1	P2
Joy	C-	S/C-
Surprise	C+	C+
Disgust	C-	C-
Anger	C+	C-
Sadness	C-	C+
Fear	S/C+	S/C+
Neutral	S	S

Table 1. Theoretical table of parameters' states for each emotion (example with only two parameters).

Compared to the method of Hammal, ours is computationally simple. The combinatory explosion and the number of calculations to be made have been considerably reduced, allowing us to work with more information (more parameters) of the face and to evaluate the seven universal emotions, and not only four of them, as Hammal does.

		E1 joy	**E2 surprise**	**E3 disgust**	**E4 anger**	**E5 sadness**	**E6 fear**	**E7 neutral**
P1	**C+**	**0**	**1**	**0**	**1**	**0**	**1**	**0**
	C-	1	0	1	0	1	0	0
	S	0	0	0	0	0	1	1
		E1 joy	**E2 surprise**	**E3 disgust**	**E4 anger**	**E5 sadness**	**E6 fear**	**E7 neutral**
P2	**C+**	0	1	0	0	1	1	0
	C-	**1**	**0**	**1**	**1**	**0**	**0**	**0**
	S	1	0	0	0	0	1	1

Table 2. Logical rules table for each parameter.

Stage 3: Animating facial expressions

The information about the emotional state of the user can be used to adapt the emotional state of the agent and consequently to modify its facial animations, which are generated and coordinated in this stage.

The technique used for facial animation is the skeletal one and the nomenclature followed is that of the VHML standard (VHML, 2001). Each agent has got the corresponding animation of the 6 Ekman emotions (see Figure 7).

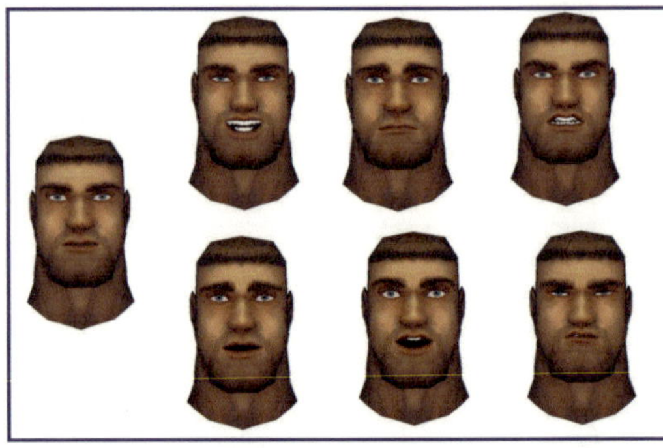

Fig. 7. Neutral face plus Ekman facial emotions: happiness, sadness, anger, fear, surprise and disgust.

3.2 Emotional classification: describing emotions

<u>Databases</u>

In order to define the emotions in terms of the parameters states, as well as to find the thresholds that determine if parameter is in a state or another (as explained in last section), it is necessary to work with a wide database. In this work we have used two diferent facial emotions databases: the FG-NET database (FG-NET, 2006) that provides video sequences of 19 different caucasian people; and the MMI Facial Expression Database (Pantic et al., 2005) that holds 1280 videos of 43 different subjects from different races (caucasian, asian and arabic). Both databases show the 7 universal emotions of Ekman (Figure 8).

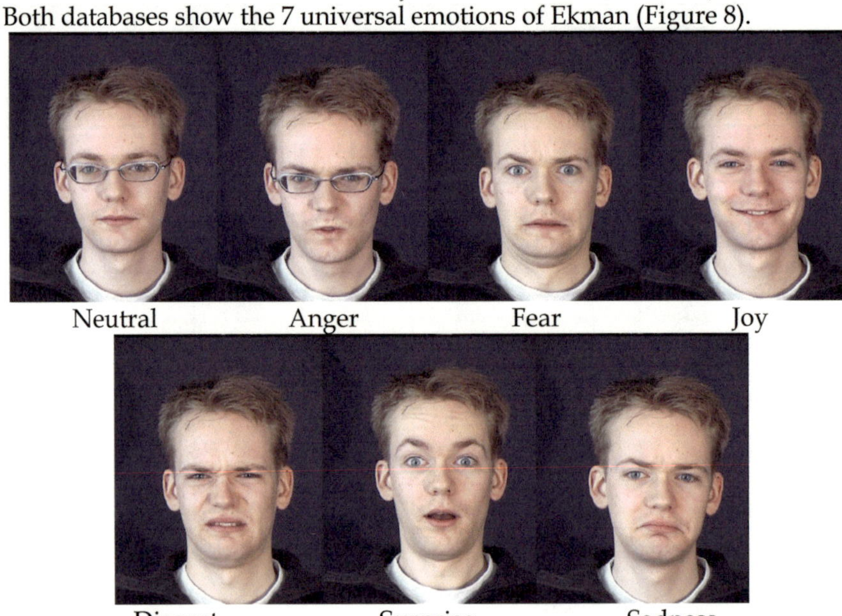

Fig. 8. Example of selected frames of the MMI Facial Expression

<u>Emotions' definitions and thresholds</u>

In order to build a descriptive table of each emotion in terms of states of distances, we must determine for each distance the value of the states that define each emotion (C+, C- or S), as well as evaluate the thresholds that separate a state from another. To do this, we studied the variation of each distance with respect to the neutral one, for each person of the database and for each emotion. An example of the results obtained for distance D4 is shown in Figure 9. From these data, we can make a descriptive table of the emotions according to the value of the states (Table 3).

	D_1	D_2	D_3	D_4	D_5	Wrinkles	Ang 1	Ang 2	W/H
Joy	C-	S/C-	C+	C+	C-	No	C+	S/C+/C-	S/C-
Surprise	S/C+	S/C+	S/C-	C+	S/C+	No	C-	C+	C-
Disgust	C-	C-	S/C+/C-	S/C+	S/C-	Yes	S/C+/C-	S/C+	S/C-
Anger	C-	C-	S/C-	S/C-	S/C+/C-	Yes	C+	C-	C+
Sadness	C-	S	S/C-	S	S/C+	No	S/C+/C-	S/C-	S/C+
Fear	S/C+	S/C+/C-	C-	C+	S/C+	No	C-	C+	C-
Neutral	S	S	S	S	S	No	S	S	S

Table 3. Theoretical table of the states taken by the different studied characteristics for each emotion. The distances (D1,..D5) are those shown in Figure 6. Some features do not provide any information of interest for certain emotions (squares in gray) and in these cases they are not considered. Note also that the distances D1, D2 and D5 have a symmetric facial distance (one in each eye). Facial symmetry has been assumed after having calculated the high correlation between each distance and its symmetric.

One step necessary for our method to work is to define the values of the thresholds that separate a state of another one, for each studied distance. Two types of thresholds exist: the upper threshold (marks the limit between neutral state S and state C+) and the lower threshold (the one that marks the limit between neutral state S and state C-). The thresholds' values are determined by means of several tests and statistics on all the subjects and all the expressions of the databases. Figure 9 shows an example of thresholds estimation for the distance D4.

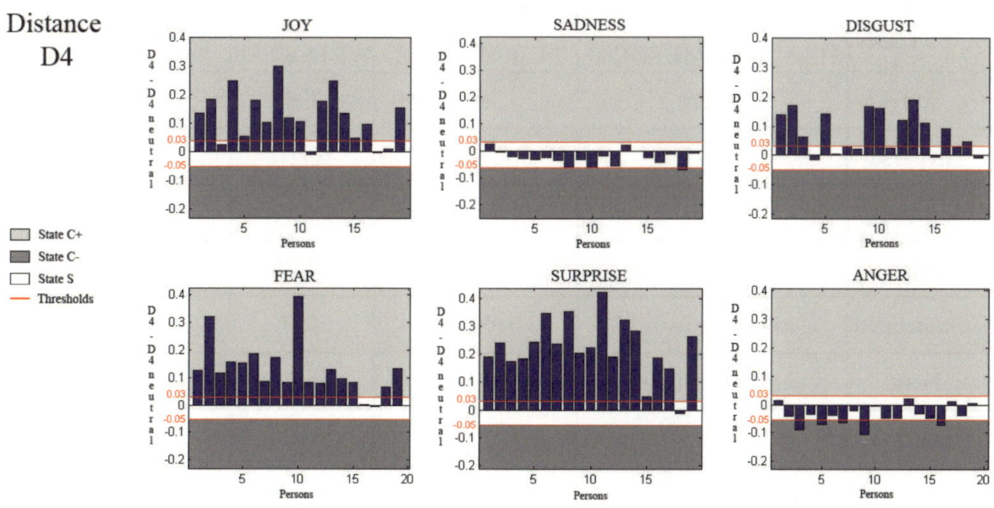

Fig. 9. Statistics results obtained for distance D4. Thresholds estimations are also shown.

3.3 Results

Classification rates

The algorithm has been proved on the images of the databases. In the evaluation of results, the recognition is marked as "good" if the decision is coherent with the one taken by a human being. To do this, we have made surveys to 30 different people to classify the expressions shown in the most ambiguous images. For example, in the image shown in Figure 10, the surveyed people recognized it as much "disgust" as "anger", although the FG-NET database classifies it like "disgust" exclusively. Our method obtains a draw.
First we considered to work with the same parameters as the Hammal method, ie, with the 5 characteristic distances shown in Figure 6. The obtained results are shown in the third column Table 4. As it can be observed, the percentage of success obtained for the emotions "disgust", "anger", "sadness", "fear" and "neutral" are acceptable and similar to the obtained by Hammal (second column). Nevertheless, for "joy" and "surprise" the results are not very favorable. In fact, the algorithm tends to confuse "joy" with "disgust" and "surprise" with "fear", which comes justified looking at Table 3, where it can be seen that a same combination of states of distances can be given for the mentioned pairs of emotions.

Fig. 10. Frame classified like "disgust" by the FG-NET database (FG-NET, 2001).

EMOTION	% SUCCESS HAMMAL METHOD	% SUCCESS OUR METHOD	% SUCCES WRINKLES	% SUCCESS MOUTH SHAPE
Joy	87,26	36,84	100	100
Surprise	84,44	57,89	63,16	63,16
Disgust	51,20	84,21	94,74	100
Anger	not recognized	73,68	94,74	89,47
Sadness	not recognized	68,42	57,89	94,74
Fear	not recognized	78,95	84,21	89,47
Neutral	88	100	100	100

Table 4. Classification rates of Hammal (Hammal et al., 2005) (second column), of our method with the 5 distances (third column), plus wrinkles in the nasal root (fourth column) plus mouth shape information (fifth column).

In order to improve the results obtained in "joy", we have introduced a new face parameter: the presence or absence of wrinkles in the nasal root, typical of the emotions "disgust" and "anger". This way, we are able to mark a difference between "joy" and "disgust". The obtained success rates are shown in the forth column in Table 4. We observe, as it was expected, a considerable increase in the rate of successes, especially for "joy" and "disgust". However, the rates still continue to be low for "sadness" and "surprise", which indicates about the necessity to add more characteristics to the method. A key factor to analyze in the recognition of emotions is the mouth shape. For each one of the 7 basic emotions, its contour changes in many different ways. In our method, we have added the extra information about the mouth behaviour that is shown in Figure 11. Results are shown in the fifth column in Table 4. As it can be seen, the new information has introduced a great improvement in our results. The importance of the mouth shape in the expression of emotions is thus confirmed.

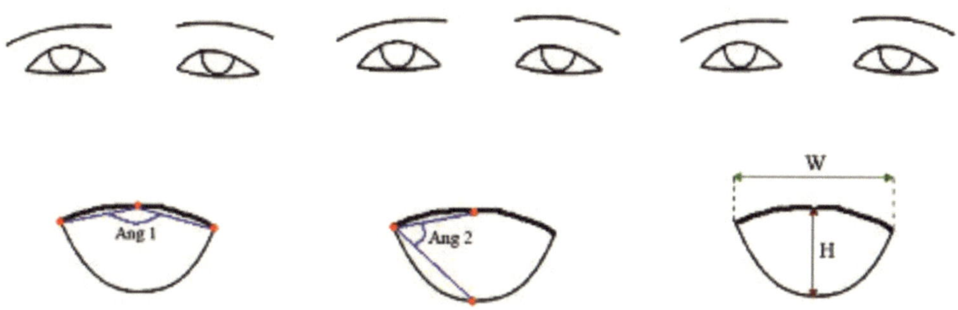

Fig. 11. Extra information added about the mouth shape

The method has also been tested with other databases different from the ones used for the threshold establishment, in order to confirm the good performance of the system. Related to classification success, it is interesting to realize that human mechanisms for face detection are very robust, but this is not the case of those for face expressions interpretation. According to Bassili (Bassili, 1997), a trained observer can correctly classify faces showing emotions with an average of 87%.

Once satisfactory classification rates were achieved, the system has been used to analyze the influence of gender and race in the studied face characteristics. Details of the results can be found in (Hupont & Cerezo, 2006).

Analysing video sequences: real-time interaction

The features extraction program captures each facial frame and extracts the feature points which are sent to the emotion classifier. When an emotional change is detected, the output of the 7-emotion classifier constitutes an emotion code which is sent to Maxine's character. For the moment, the virtual character's face just mimics the emotional state of the user (Fig. 12), accommodating his/her facial animation and speech. More sophisticated behaviour may be implemented.

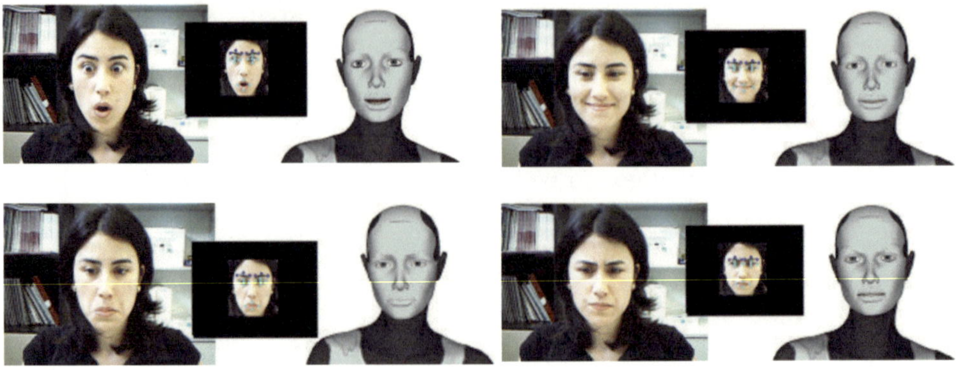

Fig. 12. Examples of the integrated real-time application: detection of surprise, joy, sadness, anger. For each example, images caught by the webcam, small images showing automatic features' tracking and synthesized facial expressions are shown. The animated character mimics the facial expression of the user.

4. Voice-based interaction

Natural language is one of the most used communication methods, and although it has been extensively studied, relevant aspects still remain opened. As stated before, in order to obtain a more natural and trustworthy interaction, HCI systems must be capable of responding appropriately to the users with affective feedback. Within verbal communication it implies the addition of variability in the answers and the synthesis of emotions in speech (Cowie et al., 2000).

The incorporation of emotion in voice is carried out by changes in the melodic and rhythmic structures (Bolinger, 1989). In the last years, several works focus on the synthesis of voice considering the components that produce emotional speech. However, most of the studies in this area refer to the English language (Murray & Arnott, 1993, Shroder, 2001). Related to the Spanish language, the work of Montero et al (Montero et al., 1999) focus on the prosody analysis and modelling of a Spanish emotional Speech Database with four emotions. They make an interesting experiment about the relevance of voice quality in emotional state recognition scores. Iriondo et al. (Iriondo et al., 2000) present a set of rules that describes the behaviour of the most significant speech parameters related with the expression of emotions and validate the model using speech synthesis techniques. They simulate the 7 basic emotions. A similar study was made in (Boula et al., 2002), but getting the expressions of emotions of videos performed by professional actors in English, French and Spanish.

Our system performs emotional voice synthesis in Spanish, but unlike the previous works, it allows interaction, supporting real time communication with the user in natural language. Moreover, in this conversational interface the emotional state (that may vary depending on the relationship with the user along the conversation) is considered and expressed by the modulation of the voice and by selecting the right answer. For this purpose, the system keeps information about the "history" of the conversation.

4.1 User-avatar communication process

The overall process of communication between user and avatar through voice is shown in Figure 13. In the following paragraphs, each of the three stages is explained.

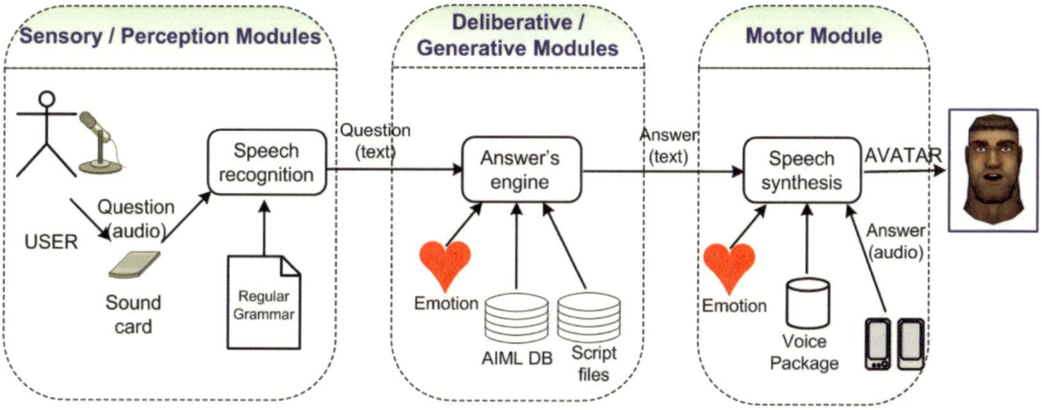

Fig. 13. Stages of the user-avatar voice communication process

Stage 1: Audio Speech Recognition (ASR)

The aim of this first stage is to obtain a text chain from the words said by the user in Spanish. To do this, a voice recognition engine has been constructed on the basis of the commercial Loquendo ASR (Audio Speech Recognition) software. The ASR is based on a dynamic library that enables a recognition device to be created and integrated ad hoc within a certain system; however, the disadvantage is that it has to be developed largely from scratch; in particular, it is necessary to pick up the audio and prepare it for processing by the recogniser and to develop a grammar with the words that are going to be recognised. Loquendo ASR only enables three possible context-free grammars, ABNF (Augmented BNF), XMLF (XML Form) and JSGF (Java Speech Grammar Format). We have chosen JSGF syntax as it avoids complex labelling of the XML and is used by a broader community than ABNF syntax.

One of the requisites of our system is that it must be able to "understand" and speak Spanish. This constraint prevented us from using existing open-source libraries, all of them in English. Moreover, during the development of the recogniser, some problems that are specific to Spanish had to be solved: specifically, Loquendo ASR is not capable of distinguishing between words with or without 'h' (this letter is not pronounced in Spanish), with 'b' or 'v', or with 'y' or 'll' (these letter pairs correspond to single phonemes).

Stage 2: Getting the right answers

This stage is basically in charge of generating the answer to the user's questions in text mode and it is based on the recognition of patterns, to which fixed answers are associated (static knowledge). These answers, however, vary depending on the virtual character's emotional state (explained later on), or may undergo random variations so that the user does not get the impression of repetition if the conversation goes on for a long time (dynamic knowledge). In our case, this type of answer's system has proved to be sufficient because, for the moment, we use it restricted to specific topics (education domains or specific orders for managing domotics systems).

The system we have developed is based on chatbot technology under GNU GPL licences: ALICE (ALICE 2007) and CyN (CyN 2004). However, CyN is only designed to hold conversations in English, so we had to modify the code to support dialogues in Spanish. The main differences lie in the work with accents, dieresis and the "ñ" character, and in the use of opening interrogation and exclamation marks.
The knowledge of the virtual character is specified in AIML -Artificial Intelligence Markup Language- (AIML, 2001). AIML is an XML derivative, and its power lies in three basic aspects:
- AIML syntax enables the semantic content of a question to be easily extracted so that the appropriate answer can be quickly given.
- The use of labels to combine answers lends greater variety to the answers and increases the number of questions to which an answer can be given.
- The use of recursivity enables answers to be provided to inputs for which, in theory, there is no direct answer.
The AIML interpreter has been modified to include commands or calls to script files within the AIML category. These commands are executed when the category in which they are declared is activated, and their result is returned as part of the answer to the user. This makes it possible, for example, to consult the system time, log on to a website to see what the weather is like, etc.
Stage 3: Text to Speech Conversion (TTS) and Lip-sync
The synthesis of the voice is made using Windows SAPI5, but the function uses packages of Spanish voice offered by Loquendo. SAPI gives information about the visemes (visual phonemes) that take place pronouncing the phrase wanted to be synthesized, what allows to solve the problem of the labial synchronization: a lip-sync module specially developed for Spanish language has been implemented. In order to avoid the voice sounding artificial, it has been equipped with an emotional component, as it will be described in next section.

4.2 Emotional voice generation

The voice generated by text-voice converters usually sounds artificial, which is one of the reasons why avatars tend to be rejected by the public. To succeed in making the synthesiser appear "alive", it is essential to generate voice "with emotion". In our system we work with the six universal emotion categories of Ekman. SAPI5 enables tone, frequency scale, volume and speed to be modified, which is why we have used it as a basis. To represent each emotion, fixed values are assigned to the parameters that enable the relevant emotion to be evoked. The configuration of these emotional parameters is based on several studies (Boula et al., 2002; Francisco et al., 2005; Iriondo et al., 2000). The process carried out to find the values at which these parameters must be fixed for each emotion was voice assessment by users. The three assessment paradigms used were: Forced Choice, providing the subjects with a finite set of possible answers that take in all emotions that have been modelled, Free Choice, where the answer is not restricted to a closed set of emotions and Modified Free Choice in which neutral texts were used together with emotion texts. The values of the emotional parameters validated by the tests are shown in Table 5. Details of the evaluation process are given in (Baldassarri et al., 2007a).

Emotion	Volume (0-100)	Speed (-10 -10)	Pitch (-10 -10)
Joy	80	3	4
Disgust	50	3	-6
Anger	70	3	0
Fear	56	1	2
Neutral	50	0	0
Surprise	56	0	3
Sadness	44	-2	2

Table 5. Setting volume, speed and tone parameters for emotional voice generation.

4.3 Emotional management

Emotion is taken into account not only in the voice synthesis (as it was previously explained) but also in the generation of the answers at two levels:

- The answer depends on the avatar's emotional state. For this reason, the AIML <random> command has been redesigned to add this feature, as it can be seen in the following example. There may be more than one answer with the same label, in this case, one of these answers would be given at random. There must always be an answer (applied to neutral emotional state) that does not have an associated label.

```
<category>
  <pattern> I BELIEVE THAT WE WOULD HAVE TO LEAVE THIS CONVERSATION
   </pattern>
   <template> <random>
                 <li> <sad/>Well, I suppose I am not what you expected
                 </li>

                 <li> <angry/>But what is the matter with you?
                               Don't you like me?
                 </li>

                 <li><surprised/> Why? We were having such a good time!
                 </li>

                 <li><happy/>Come on, let's talk a little more
                 </li>

                 <li>Ok, we will continue another time
                 </li>
   </random> </template>
```

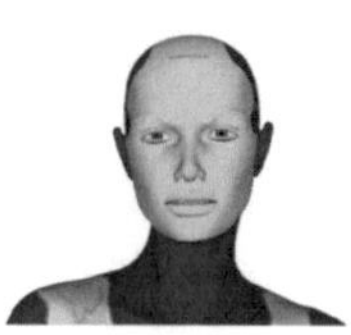

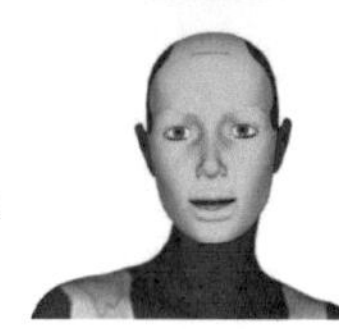
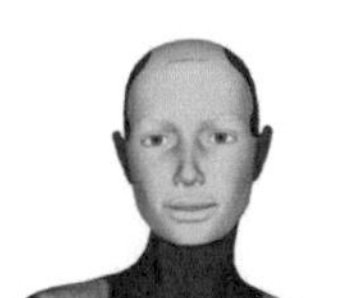
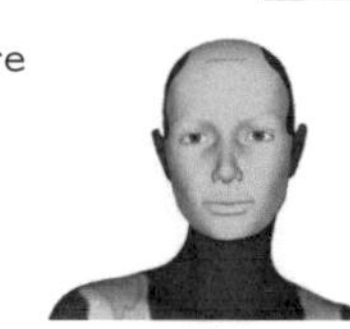

- Besides, the emotional state of the virtual character may change during a conversation, depending on how the conversation develops. That is, if it the conversation is on a topic that pleases the character, it gets happy; if it is given information it was not aware of, it is surprised; it is insulted, it gets angry; if it is threatened, it gets frightened, etc.

4.4 Results

The system developed makes it possible for the user to maintain a conversation in Spanish with the virtual character. For example, in the virtual presenters application (see Section 2) the user can ask questions about the presentation and get answers from the character. As far as the voice interface is concerned, we have endeavoured to reduce to a minimum the time that elapses between the point at which the user finishes speaking and the point at which the answer begins. Excessive lead time decreases the sensation of interactivity and would not be readily accepted by the user. The duration of each stage in the communication process has been measured with sentences that are liable to be used during a conversation, in which the longest sentence is no longer than 20 words. The voice recognition and synthesis tests were all carried out in Spanish. The time measurements in the search for results were carried out with Alice's brain, which has some 47,000 categories. Table 6 shows a time study carried out through several conversations. In the table, both for synthesis and voice recognition, the maximum time applies to the recognition or synthesis of the longest sentences.

Stages of a conversation	Min Time	Max Time	Average
Speech recognition	1.6s	2.01s	1.78s
Text to Speech	0.18s	0.2s	0.3s
Search of Answers	0.1s	0.17s	0.2s

Table 6. Time measurements of the different stages of a conversation (in seconds).

5. Evaluating Maxine agents

As we mentioned in section 2, Maxine system has been used to develop a learning platform to simplify and improve teaching and practice of Computer Graphics subjects. One of the ways the interactive pedagogical agent helps students is by exposing some specific topics, acting as a virtual presenter. Last term students have been asked to evaluate Maxine agents in these virtual presentations and their usefulness. Two questionnaires, one before and one after, have been done; their objectives are:

- To evaluate the previous knowledge of the subject that will be presented
- To assess the effectiveness of the "information provision" aspect of the message, ie, the Maxine's effect on the presentation subjects' comprehension
- To measure the perceptions about the Maxine agent.

Specifically, an introductory presentation about CG and its applications has been evaluated. The students are asked to evaluate their knowledge about different topics of CG before and after the presentation, evaluating it from 1 (very low) to 10 (very deep). In Figure 14 mean values are shown (classified by gender). It is interesting to realize that female students systematically rate their knowledge lower than male students; explanation of this behaviour cannot be based on objective facts, as they all are in the same university level, having coursed almost the same subjects and having female students usually higher marks.

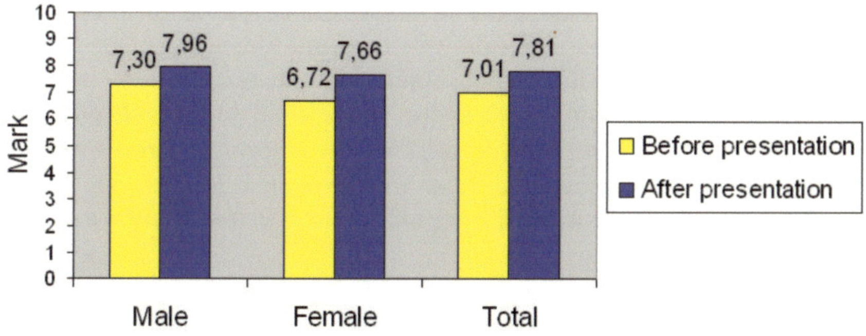

Fig. 14. Effectiveness on the subjects' comprehension after one of Maxine's presentations

Students are also asked about the aspects of the virtual agent that have attracted their attention (results in Figure 15) and which attributes would they use to describe the presenter (see Figure 16). Most of them think that this kind of "virtual teachers" only can be used as a tool and can not replace tutors (75%), but could be a good option for distance training (92%).

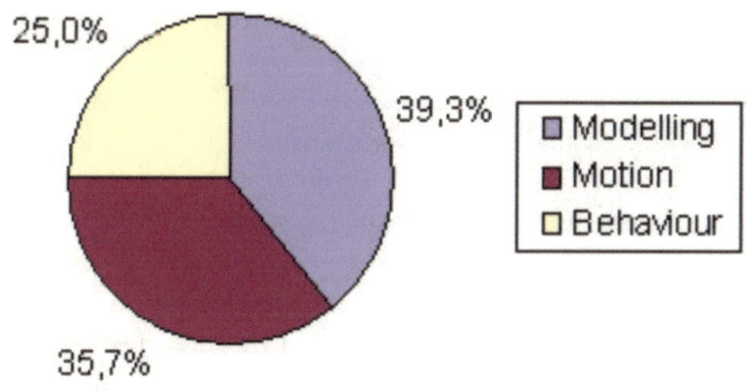

Fig. 15. Remarkable aspects of the virtual presenter

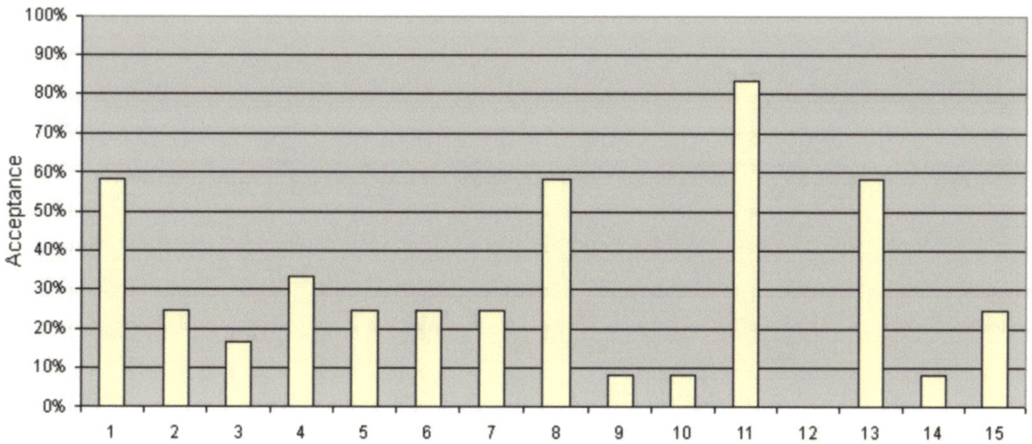

Fig. 16: Acceptance of the following virtual presenter's attributes (1-Helpful, 2-Intelligent, 3-Likable, 4-Reliable, 5-Believable, 6-Competent, 7-Friendly, 8-Clear, 9-Natural, 10- Not very convincing, 11-Stiff, 12-Happy, 13-Neutral, 14-Sad, 15-Coherence expression-message)

The students are also asked to describe the agent (see Table 7) and, by an open question, to compare it with other virtual characters they know (from videogames, programs,...). Their answers are all positive, considering it good, simple but effective. Students are also asked to point out which aspects contribute most to the realism and to the lack of realism of the virtual agent. The answers have been divided into two groups: those corresponding to students being used to videogames and those that are not. It is especially interesting the different consideration about the aspects contributing most to the lack of realism (see Figure 17).

Statement	Rank (1-10)
The virtual actor looks real	7.7
The movements of his/her head look natural	7.7
His/her gaze looks natural	7.0
His/her facial expressions look natural	8.0
Good lip-synchronization is achieved	7.5
Voice modulation is always coherent	6.6
Coherence between facial expression and voice	6.9

Table 7. Description of the virtual actor

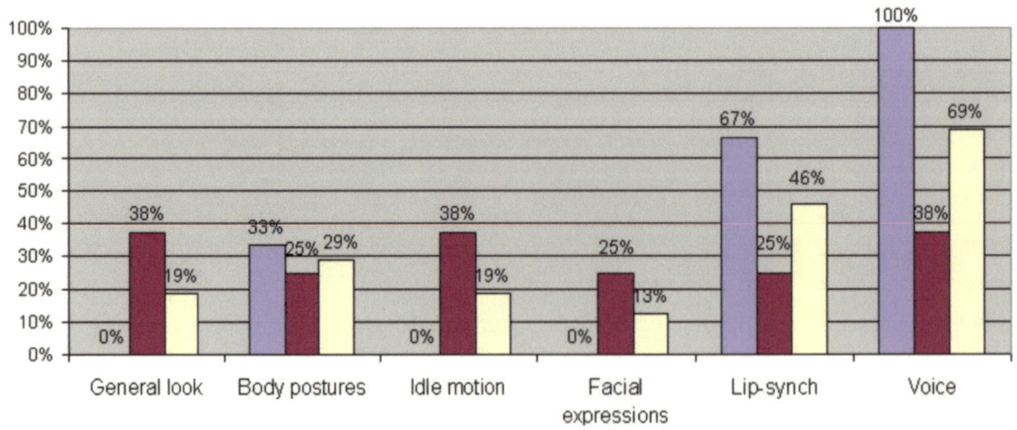

Fig. 17. Aspects contributing to the lack of realism. Opinion of students that: usually don't play videogames (blue), usually play videogames (red), total (yellow)

6. Conclusions and future work

This chapter presents a completely automated real-time character-based interface, where a scriptable affective humanoid 3D agent interacts with the user. Special care has been taken in making it possible multimodal natural user-agent interaction: communication is accomplished via text, image and voice (natural language). Our embodied agents are equipped with an emotional state which can be modified throughout the conversation with the user, and depends on the emotional state detected from the user's facial expressions. In fact, this nonverbal affective information is interpreted by the agent, which responds in an empathetic way by acompasing its voice intonation, facial expression and answers. These agents have been used as virtual presenters, domotic assistants and pedagogical agents in different applications and results are promising.

The chapter has focused on two main aspects: the capture of the user emotional state from web cam images and the development of a dialog system in natural language (Spanish) that takes also emotional aspects into account.

The facial expression recognizer is based on facial features' tracking and on an effective emotional classification method based on the theory of evidence and Ekman's emotional classification. From a set of distances and angles extracted from the user images and from a set of thresholds defined from the analysis of a sufficiently broad image database, the classification results are acceptable, and recent developments has enabled us to improve success rates. The utility of this kind of information is clear: the general vision in that is a user's emotion could be recognized by a computer, human computer-interaction would become more natural, enjoyable and productive.

The dialog system has been developed so that the user can ask questions, give commands or ask for help to the agent. It is based on the recognition of patterns, to which fixed answers are associated. These answers, however, vary depending on the virtual character's emotional state, or may undergo random variations so that the user does not get the impression of repetition if the conversation goes on for a long time. Special attention has also been paid in adding an emotional component to the synthesized voice in order to reduce its artificial nature. Voice emotions also follow Ekman's ones and are modeled by means of modifying volume, speed and pitch.

Several research lines remain open:

- Regarding Maxine, next steps are:
  - to allow not only facial expressions but body postures to be affected by the emotional state of the agent,
  - to use the user emotional information in a more sophisticated way: the computer could offer help and assistance to a confused user or try to cheer up a frustrated user and, hence, react in ways more appropriated than simply ignoring the user affective states, as is the case in most current interfaces,
  - to consider not only emotion but personality models for the virtual agents,
  - to give the system learning mechanisms, so that it can modify its display rules based on what appears to be working for a particular user, and improve its responses while interacting with that user, and
  - to carry out a proper validation of Maxine system and characters.

- In the case of the facial emotional classifier the next step is to introduce fuzzy models and fuzzy rules to the classification algorithm in order to obtain wider information from the emotional state of the user. The objective is to obtain the membership percentage of the displayed user emotion to each one of the 7 basic emotions (for example 70% happiness, 20% surprise, 10% neutral, 0% others).
- Regarding the interaction via voice, it will be important to improve the dynamic knowledge of the system because, till now, only the "history" of the conversation is stored. In this way, the system should be able to learn and should possess a certain capacity of reasoning or deduction to manage basic rules of knowledge. An other interesting field is the extraction of emotional information from the user's voice. As we are not specialist in the subject contacts have been established with a voice-specialised group.

7. Acknowledgements

The authors wish to thank the Computer Graphics, Vision and Artificial Intelligence Group of the University of the Balearic Islands for providing us the real-time facial tracking module to test our classifier and to David Anaya for his work in the natural language dialog system. This work has been partly financed by the Spanish "Dirección General de Investigación", contract number N° TIN2007-63025 and by the Aragon Government through the WALQA agreement (ref. 2004/04/86) and the CTPP02/2006 project.

8. References

AIML (2001). Artificial Intelligence Markup Language (AIML) Version 1.0.1, *http://www.alicebot.org/TR/2001/WD-aiml/*

ALICE (2007).Artificial Intelligence Foundation, *http://www.alicebot.org/*

Anolli, L.; Mantovani, F.; Balestra, M.; Agliati, A.; Realdon, O.; Zurloni, V.; Mortillaro, M.; Vescovo, A. & Confalonieri, L. (2005). The Potential of Affective Computing in E-Learning: MYSELF project experience. *International Conference on Human-Computer Interaction (Interact 2005), Workshop on eLearning and Human-Computer Interaction: Exploring Design Synergies for more Effective Learning Experiences*, Rome, Italy September 2005

Baldassarri, S.; Cerezo, E. & Anaya, D. (2007a). Interacción emocional con actores virtuales a través de lenguaje natural (in Spanish). *Proceedings VIII Congreso Internacional de Interacción Persona-Ordenador*, ISBN 978-84-9732-596-7, Zaragoza, Spain, September 2007, Thomson

Baldassarri, S.; Cerezo, E. & Seron, F. (2007b). An open source engine for embodied animated agents. *Proceedings CEIG'07: Congreso Español de Informática Gráfica*, pp. 35–42, ISBN 978-84-9732-595-0, Zaragoza, September 2007, Thomson

Bartneck, C. (2001). How convincing is Mr. data's smile: Affective expressions of machines. *User Modeling and User-Adapted Interaction,* Vol. 11, No.4, pp. 279-295, ISSN 0924-1868

Bassili, J.N. (1997). Emotion recognition: The role of facial movement and the relative importance of upper and lower areas of the face. *Journal of Personality and Social Psychology,* Nº 37, pp. 2049-2059, ISSN: 0022-3514

Bolinger, D. (1989) *Intonation and its uses: melody and grammar in discourse,* Stanford Universiy Press, ISBN-13: 978-08-0471-535-5

Boukricha, H.; Becker, C. & Wachsmuth, I. (2007). Simulating Empathy for the Virtual Human Max, *Proceedings 2nd International Workshop on Emotion and Computing in conj. with the German Conference on Artificial Intelligence (KI2007),* pp. 22-27, ISSN 1865-6374, Osnabrück, Germany.

Boula de Mareuil, P. ; Celerier, P. & Toen J. (2002). Generation of Emotions by a Morphing Technique in English, French and Spanish. *Proceedings of Speech Prosody 2002,* pp. 187-190, ISBN 9782951823303, Aix-en-Provence, France, April 2002

Brave, S.; Nass, C. & Hutchinson, K. (2005). Computers that care: investigating the effects of orientation of emotion exhibited by an embodied computer agent, *International journal of human-computer studies,* Vol. 62, Issue 2, pp. 161-178, ISSN 1071-5819

Burleson, W.; Picard, R.W.; Perlin, K. & Lippincott, J. (2004). A platform for affective agent research. *Workshop on Empathetic Agents, Third International Joint Conference on Autonomous Agents and Multi-Agent Systems,* ISBN 1-58113-864-4, New York, United States, August 2004

Casell, J.; Sullivan, J.; Prevost, S. & Churchill, E. -eds.- (2000). *Embodied Conversational Agents,* MIT Press, ISBN 0-262-03278-3, Cambridge Massachusetts

Cerezo, E.; Baldassarri, S.; Cuartero, E.; Seron, F.J., Montoro, G.; Haya, P.A. & Alamán X. (2007). Agentes virtuales 3D para el control de entornos inteligentes domóticos (in Spanish). *Proceedings VIII Congreso Internacional de Interacción Persona-Ordenador,* ISBN 978-84-9732-596-7, Zaragoza, España, Septiembre 2007

Cowie, R.; Douglas-Cowie, E. & Shroder, M. –eds- (2000). *Proceedings ICSA Workshop on Speech and Emotion: a Conceptual Framework for Research,* Belfast

Creed, C. & Beale, R. (2005). Using Emotion Simulation to Influence User Attitudes and Behavior, *Proceedings of the 2005 Workshop on the role of emotion in HCI,* September 2005, Edinburgh, UK

Creed, C. & Beale, R. (2006). Multiple and Extended Interactions with Affective Embodied Agents, *Proceedings of the 2006 Workshop on the role of emotion in HCI,* September 2006, London, UK

CyN (2004). Proyect CyN, http://www.daxtron.com/cyn.htm

Edwards, G.J.; Cootes, T.F. & Taylor, C.J. (1998). Face Recognition Using Active Appearance Models, *Proceedings of the European Conf. Computer Vision,* Vol. 2, pp. 581-695, ISBN 3540646132, Freiburg, Germany, June 1998, Springer

Ekman, P. (1999). Facial Expression. *In: The Handbook of Cognition and Emotion.* John Wiley et Sons, pp. 45-60, ISBN: 0471978361, Sussex, UK

Elliott, C.; Rickel, J. & Lester, J.C. (1997). Integrating affective computing into animated tutoring agents. Proceedings of the IJCAI Workshop on Animated Interface Agents: Making Them Intelligent, pp. 113-121, Nagoya, Japan, August 1997

FG-NET (2006). http://www.mmk.ei.tum.de/~waf/fgnet/feedtum.html

Francisco, V.; Gervás, P. & Hervás, R. (2005). Expression of emotions in the synthesis of voice in narrative contexts (in Spanish). Proceeding of the Symposium on Ubiquitous Computing & Ambient Intelligence (UCAmI'05), pp.353-360, Granada, Spain, September 2005

Hammal, Z.; Couvreur, L.; Caplier, A. & Rombaut, M. (2005). Facial Expressions Recognition Based on the Belief Theory: Comparison with Diferent Classifiers, *Proceedings of the 13th International Conference on Image Analysis and Processing*, ISBN: 3-540-28869-4, Cagliari, Italy, September 2005, Lecture Notes in Computer Science, Vol. 3617, Springer Verlag

Hong, H.; Neven, H. & von der Malsburg, C. (1998). Online Facial Expression Recognition Based on Personalized Galleries, *Proceedings of the. Int'l Conf. Automatic Face and Gesture Recognition*, pp. 354-359, ISBN: 0818683465, Nara Japan, April 1998, IEEE

Hupont, I. & Cerezo, E. (2006). Individualizing the new interfaces: extraction of user's emotions from facial data. *Proceedings of SIACG'06 (Iberoamerican Symposium on Computer Graphics)*, pp. 179-185, ISBN: 3-905673-60-6, Santiago de Compostela, July 2006, Spain

Iriondo, I.; Guaus, R.; Rodriguez, A.; Lázaro, P., Montoya, N., Blanco, J. M.; Bernadas, D.; Oliver, J.M.; Tena, D. & Longth, L. (2000). Validation of an acoustical modelling of emotional expression in Spanish using speech synthesis techniques. *Proceedings of ISCA Workshop on Speech & Emotion* , pp.161-166, Belfast, Northern Ireland, 2000

Isbister, K. (2006). *Better game characters by design: A psychological approach*, Elsevier/Morgan Kaufmann, ISBN-13: 978-1-55860-921-1, Boston

Klein, J.; Moon, Y. & Picard, R. (2002). This computer responds to user frustration: theory, design and results, *Interacting with Computers*, Vol. 14, pp. 119–140, ISSN 0953-5438, Elsevier

Lyons, M.J.; Budynek, J. Akamatsu, S. (1999). Automatic Classification of Single Facial Images. *IEEE Trans. Pattern Analysis and Machine Intelligence*, Vol. 21, nº12, pp. 1357-1362, ISSN: 0162-8828, IEEE

Lua (2008) *http://www.lua.org/*

Manresa-Yee, C.; Varona J. & Perales, F.J. (2006). Towards hands-free interfaces based on real-time robust facial gesture recognition. In: *Lecture Notes in Computer Science*, Nº4069, Perales, F.J. & Fisher B. (Eds.), pp. 504-513, ISBN 103-540-36031-X, Springer

Montero, J.M.; Gutierrez-Arriola, J.; Colas, J.; Enriquez, E. & Pardo, J.M. Analysis and modelling of emotional speech in Spanish. *Proceedings of the 14th International Conference on Phonetic*, pp. 957-960, San Francisco, United States

MPEG-4 (2002). MPEG-4 Overview - (V.21), ISO/IEC JTC1/SC29/WG11 N4668, March 2002 http://www.chiariglione.org/mpeg/standards/mpeg-4/mpeg-4.htm

Murray, I. & Arnott, J. (1993). Toward the Simulation of Emotion in Synthetic Speech: A Review of the Literature on Human Vocal Emotion. *Journal of the Acoustical Society of America*, Vol. 93, Nº2, pp. 1097-1108, ISSN: 0001-4966

Pantic, M. (2005). Affective Computing, *Encyclopedia of Multimedia Technology and Networking*, M. Pagani (ed.) , Vol. 1, pp. 8-14, Idea Group Reference, USA.

Pantic, M. & Rothkrantz, L.J.M. (2000a). Expert System for Automatic Analysis of Facial Expression. *Image and Vision Computing J.*, Vol. 18, N°. 11, pp. 881-905, ISSN: 0262-8856

Pantic, M.; Rothkrantz, L.J.M. (2000b). Automatic Analysis of Facial Expressions: The State of the Art. *IEEE Transactions on Pattern Analysis and Machine Intelligence,*, Vol. 22, Issue 12, pp. 1424–1445, **ISSN** 0018-9340

Pantic, M.; Valstar, M.F.; Rademaker, R. & Maat, L. (2005). Web-based Database for Facial Expression Analysis. *Proceedings of the.* IEEE *Int'l Conf. Multmedia and Expo* (ICME'05), July 2005, IEEE

Picard, R.W. (2003). Affective Computing: Challenges, *International Journal of Human-Computer Studies*, Vol. 59, No. 1, pp. 55-64, ISSN 1071-5819

Prendinger, H. & Ishizuka, M. (2004). What Affective Computing and Life-like Character Technology Can Do for Tele-Home Health Care, *Workshop on HCI and Homecare: Connecting Families and Clinicans (Online Proceedings) in conj. with CHI-04*, Vienna, Austria, April 2004

Prendinger H. & Ishizuka, M. (2005). The Empathic Companion: A Character-Based Interface That Addresses Users' Affective States. *Applied Artificial Intelligence*, Vol. 19, N°. 3-4, pp. 267-285, Taylor & Francis, ISSN 0883-9514

Reeves, B. & Nass, C. (1996). *The media equation: How people treat computers, televisions and new media like real people and places*, CLSI Publications, ISBN-10 1-57586-053-8, New York.

Seron, F.J.; Baldassarri, S. & Cerezo, E. (2006). MaxinePPT: Using 3D Virtual Characters for Natural Interaction. *Proceedings WUCAmI'06: 2nd International Workshop on Ubiquitous Computing and Ambient Intelligence*, pp. 241–250, ISBN 84-6901744-6, Puertollano, Spain, November 2006

Seron, F.J.; Baldassarri, S. & Cerezo, E. (2007). Computer Graphics: Problem-based Learning and Interactive Embodied Pedaggiacal Agents. *Proceedings Eurographics 2008, Education papers,* Crete, Greece, April 2007 (to appear)

Shroder, M. (2001). Emotional Speech Synthesis: A review. *Proceedings of the 7th European Conference on Speech Communication and Technology (EUROSPEECH'01)*, Vol. 1, pp.561-564, Aalborg, Denmark, September 2001

Vesterinen E. (2001). Affective computing. *Tik-111.590 Digital media research seminar*, Finland.

VHML, (2001).Virtual Human Markup Language, VHML Working Draft v0.3, http://www.vhml.org

Wallace, M.; Raouzaiou, A.; Tsapatsoulis, N. & Kollias, S. (2004). Facial Expression Classification Based on MPEG-4 FAPs: The Use of Evidence and Prior Knowledge for Uncetainty Removal, *Proceedings if the IEEE International Conference on Fuzzy Systems (FUZZ-IEEE)*, Vol. 1, pp. 51-54, Budapest, Hungary, July 2004

Yee, N.; Bailenson, J.N.; Urbanek, M.; Chang, F. & Merget, D. (2007). The Unbearable Likeness of Being Digital: The Persistence of Nonverbal Social Norms in Online

Virtual Environments. *The Journal of CyberPsychology and Behavior*, Vol. 10, No. 1, pp. 115-121, Mary Ann Liebert Inc Publ, ISSN 1094-9313.

Zhang, Z.; Lyons, M.; Schuster, M. & Akamatsu, S. (1998). Comparison between Geometry-Based and Gabor Wavelets-Based Facial Expression Recognition Using Multi-Layer Perceptron, *Proceedings. Int'l Conf. Automatic Face and Gesture Recognition*, pp. 454-459, Seoul, Korea, May 2004

19

Exploring Un-Intentional Body Gestures for Affective System Design

Abdul Rehman Abbasi[1], Nitin V. Afzulpurkar[1] and Takeaki Uno[2]
[1]*Asian Institute of Technology*
[2]*National Institute of Informatics*
[1]*Thailand,*
[2]*Japan*

1. Introduction

Imagine the following situation: a student is attempting a tutorial through an intelligent tutoring system (ITS). During the learning session, he starts scratching on his head. What might be the reason for this action? Is he anxious, or having a problem with his hair?

Now imagine how effective the intelligent tutoring system (ITS) could be if it could correctly realize students' mental state and consequently adopt a suitable instructive strategy to address the situation.

Human affect-sensitive system such as envisioned here, capable of interpreting its users' affect and promising applications proposed by Picard (2000) and others (Brave & Nass, 2002) are source of inspiration for growing interest in researching affective systems. However, reliable recognition of affect needs to address uncertainty and context dependency when mapping affect from human behavioral cues. Uncertainty comes from the fact that affective interpretations vary from person to person and likewise being context dependent these interpretations vary with situation quite often. Here, we discuss our approach to address both of these issues.

As such no precise and generally agreed definition of affect or emotion exists. Recently, (Minsky, 2006) describes emotional state as not different from the process such as thinking. Human affect may consist of emotional and/or mental state of a person. Beside verbal expression there are non-verbal means of expressing affect by humans. They include visual cues that may inform about the human affective state. Gestures from face, hand and body are part of human body language (Sebe & Lew, 2003), and may communicate affect in various situations. We consider human body gestures for affect interpretation, and use them for designing affective systems.

In this chapter, we report an extension of our earlier work (Abbasi et al., 2007) that explores the presence of body gestures that we found as common among a group of students attending a class lecture. Most of these gestures involve hand movements around the face and are unintentional in nature. We map these gestures to affective states reported by students. We propose using this information for designing an intelligent tutoring system or an affective class barometer.

To address the uncertainty in subjective interpretations, we propose using a probabilistic approach. These interpretations are dependent on situational context as they occur in a particular scenario such as in a class room situation. Preliminary analyses from our proposed model advocates suitability and applicability of our approach. At the end, we conclude with limitations and future directions for this work.

2. Related work

Affective computing is an emerging approach for intelligent and effective system design while vision-based human affect analysis proposes execution of this approach. Some researchers have considered extracting affect automatically from facial expressions (Pantic & Rothkrantz, 2000; Pantic et al., 2005; Tian et al., 2005) while others have analyzed hand gestures to extract affective information (Kim et al., 2006; Lee, 2006).

A recent survey by Mitra & Acharya (2007) provides current state of art in gesture recognition but this development still needs reliable means to map gestures to correct affective states that can be used for devising valuable affective systems. Although, previous works are much focused on improving detection methods, and mostly exclude contextual information, yet they do augment the overall research effort.

Earlier studies by Darwin (1872) on facial expression and those followed by Ekman & Friesen (1975, 1978) report the presence of universal emotional categories. Mehrabian (1968) reveals through his studies that 55 percent of emotional message in face-face communication results from body language. Ambady & Rosenthal (1992) suggest both facial expressions and body gestures as most significant human behavioural cues. Lately, Gunes & Piccardi (2007) show better recognition results using both modalities while augmenting their work (Gunes & Piccardi, 2006) on forming a database of both modalities.

Dadgostar et al. (2005) utilize non-verbal information to assist intelligent tutoring system. They relate gestures with students' skills. Pantic et al. (2005) and Kapoor et al. (2004) use audio-visual channels for affect recognition while Balomenos et al. (2004) consider visual channel alone with multiple modalities. They report recognition of six prototypic emotions, using facial expressions and hand gestures.

As such intended hand gestures, appearing in a human-to-human interaction are well established cues that communicate intentions or emotions while mostly these are used to convey sign language. On the other hand, un-intentional body movements which were not earlier perceived as showing affective state, seem to be providing informative clues about the mental or/and emotional state of a person in specific situational context.

A recent analysis of non-stylish body movements' by Bernhardt & Robinson (2007) shows promising results to detect implicitly present affect. They report that emotions such as happiness, sadness and anger could be inferred from motions such as knocking and walking. Similarly, Coulson (1992) and Burgoon et al. (2005), too correlate body actions to the emotions such as a shoulder shrug showing uncertainty or a contracted body showing fear.

Different to earlier approaches, we consider extracting affective information from people in a real world interaction such as a student-instructor interactive scenario, where we note down the observed gestures from the students and then obtain self-reports from these students in a post-experiment interview. These gestures involve unintentional hand movements relative to face such as a head scratch or an eye rub. Preliminary analysis of this work is reported in (Abbasi et al., 2007) while here we extend our work by proposing a method to exploit this information. We believe that subjective human studies such as this are crucial as models are formed on the basis of these studies. They certainly raise the confidence level for interpreting *true* affective state.

3. Experimental description

We carried out the experiment involving four students attending a preliminary Japanese language class lecture. These students were from different cultural and educational backgrounds. One European, second an American-resident and rest were Asians while two of these sutdents were females. These students were recurited as volunteers.
Goal of the experiment was to record unitnetional movements of these students during the lecture. Students were not told about the exact nature of the experiment however, they were briefed about participating in a HCI study.

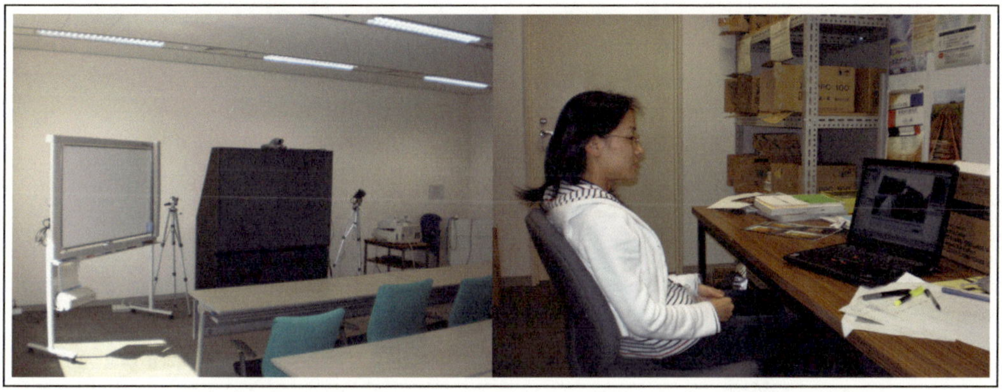

Fig. 1. Experimental set up (left), Post-Experiment interview with a student (right)

Two video sessions of about two hours were recorded for these students. Two passive cameras were used to record their activities as shown in Fig. 1 (left). During the first session, activities of two students were recorded, and in the second session, activities of the other pair of students were recorded. Once the recorded video was secured, the next phase was manual labeling of observable gestures by the experimenters (Refer Fig. 2).
The experimenters manually labeled the participants' hand gestures into discrete categories. These categories were determined through an initial preview of video recordings. Later, a post-experiment interview was conducted to determine the actual affective state, reported by the participants. We then compared the manual labels to the reported affect for analysis.

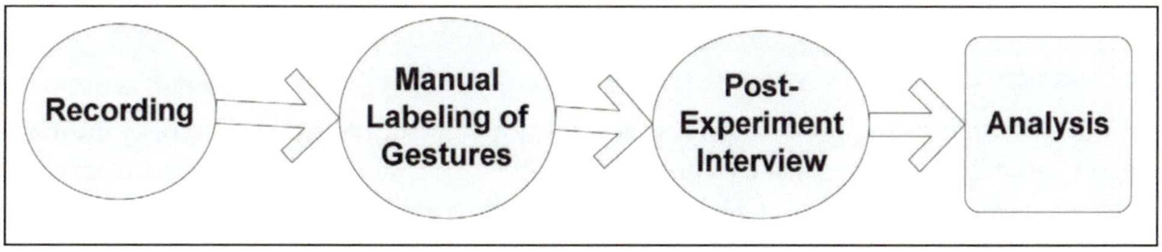

Fig. 2. Procedural steps for the Experiment

In fact, in the free format response which we retained from post-experiment interview, participants used a variety of words to describe their feelings. Therefore, we normalized them using Geneva Affect Label Code (GALC; Scherer, 2005).

Actually, GALC classifies such type of free form responses into well defined categories as it provides labels for 36 defined categories in differnt languages. Finally, we grouped participants' affective states with the corresponding images of gestures from the recorded video, some of these are shown in Fig. 3.

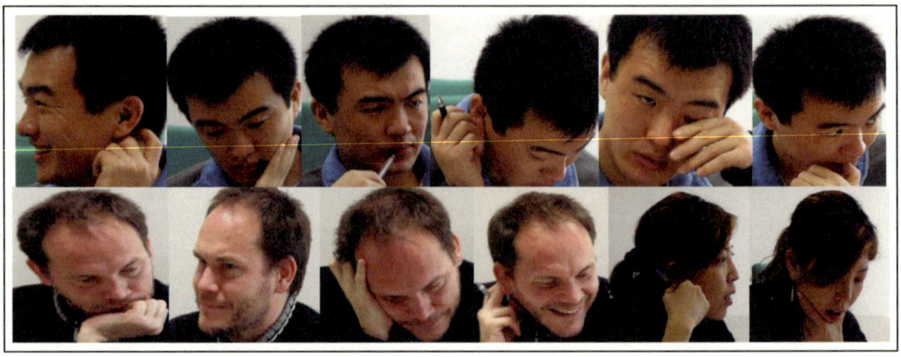

Fig. 3. Gestures observed during the Experiment

4. Data acquisition

In the data from video recordings, there were 28 gestures for student A, 37 for student B, 35 for student C and 27 for student D. Total time for each student recording was 25 minutes. Distribution of these gestures versus non-gestures for all students is shown in Fig. 4.

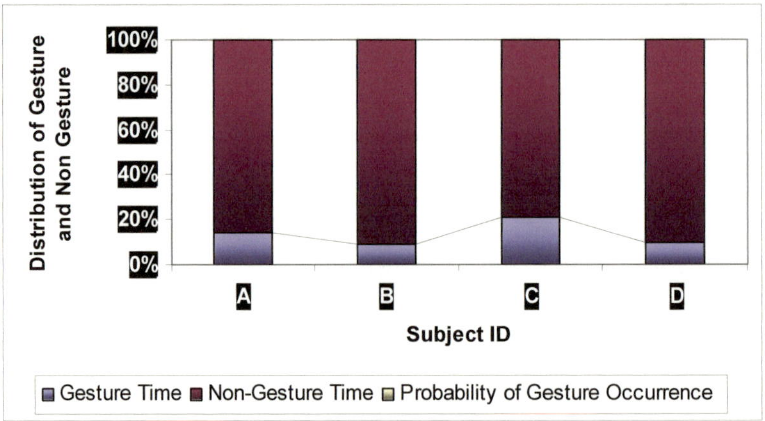

Fig. 4. Presence of gesture versus non-gestures over time for all four students

Distribution as shown in Fig. 4 refers the occurrence of gestures in a real world interaction. Average probability of occurrence of any kind of gesture calculated over all four students is 15.9 percent(with a maximum of 26.3 percent). There were about 14 gestures in all but for our analysis here; we only considered seven of these that were commonly found in the Experiment for all four students. The gestures categorized are *Head Scratch, Nose Itch, Lip Touch, Eye Rub, Chin Rest, Lip Zip and Ear Scratch.* The distribution of these gestures over all four students is shown in Fig. 5 and *Chin Rest* is the most frequent gesture among these.

From the post-experiment interview, we found that students were able to associate their gestures with some affective states. The relationship between the gestures and affective states that could be established is illustrated through Table 1.
In Table 1, the confidence level is calculated as number of times a student could correlate the gesture with the reported affective state with certainty and for remaining occasions students were reported saying *nothing* or they were not sure about the state. So, we categorized that state as having *No Emotion*. The presence of all affective states alongwith *No Emotion* state is shown in Fig. 6.

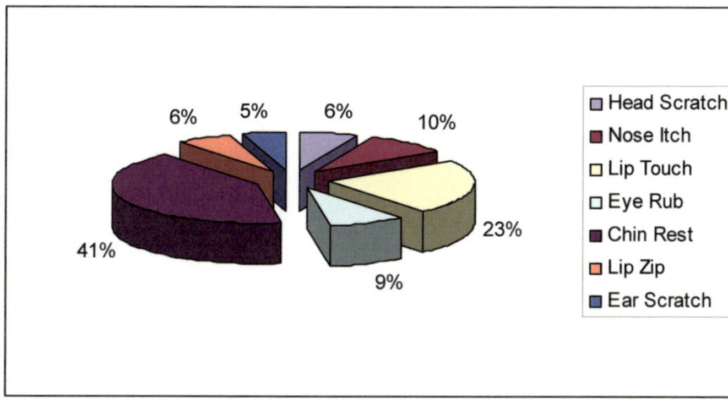

Fig. 5. Distribution of different gestures commonly found in the Experiment for all students

Gesture	Reported Affective State	Confidence Level in Reporting
Head Scratch	Recalling	100 %
Nose Itch	Satisified	77.5%
Lip Touch	Thinking	88.75 %
Eye Rub	Tired	81 %
Chin Rest	Thinking	90 %
Lip Zip	Bored	100 %
Ear Scratch	Concentrating	83.33%

Table 1. Self-reported affect and co-occurring gestures with confidence level

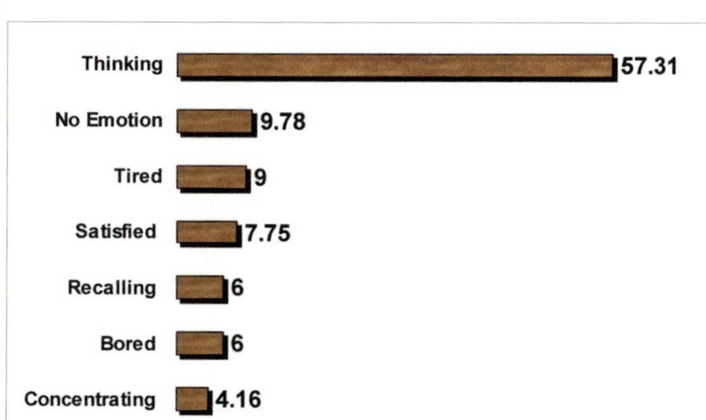

Fig. 6. Presence of affective states co-occurring with gestures, averaged over all students (in percentage of total instances)

5. Proposed model

From the experimental data, we formed a small domain knowledge that could be used to infer useful affective information. The novelty in our work is to propose a knowledge based affect interpretation system able to work in particular situational context, i.e. during a class lecture or student-instructor interaction. Our proposed system alongwith its component is illustrated through Fig. 7.

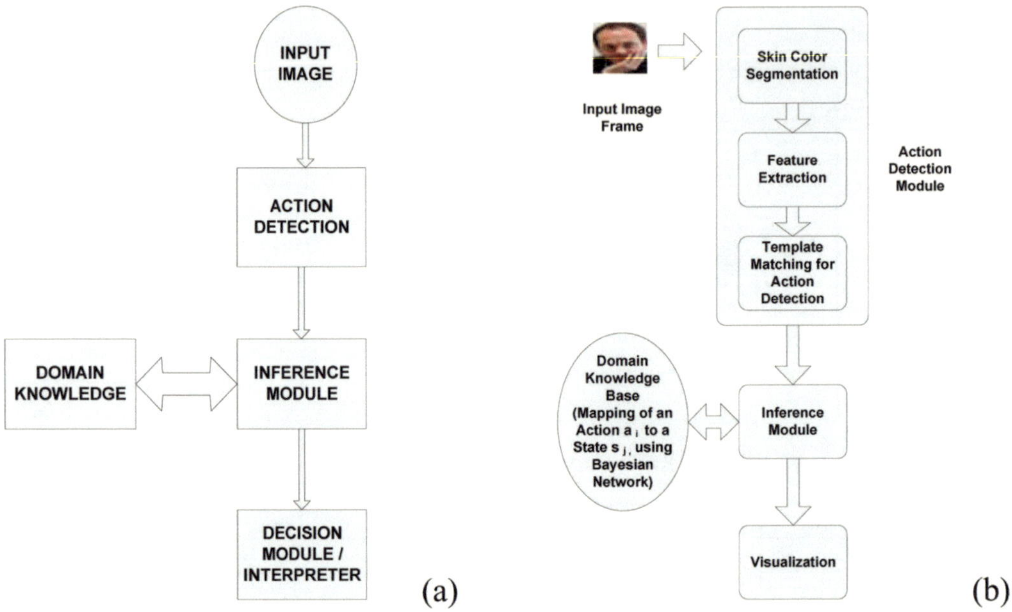

Fig. 7. (a) Conceptual model of proposed system, (b) Details of proposed system

The Action Detection module is basically the gesture detection system that may use some image processing technique to classify a particular gesture. But, for this work we consider manually labelled gestures, to provide a preliminary analysis of the proposed approach. Once a labelled gesture is given to the inference module, the next step is to infer the most probable affective state using the information from the Domain Knowledge stored in the form of prior and class conditional probabilities.

Considering the nature of data acquired from our Experiment, we use a probabilistic approach to infer useful meanings out of gesture information. In our case, number of participants and number of gestures are small. Furthermore, there is uncertainty in interpretations by the students therefore; we find probabilistic approach better than conventional statistical methods which may not be useful due of absence of complete data.

Bayesian inference uses a numerical estimate of degree of belief (prior) in a hypothesis before evidence is observed and then again computes it (posterior) after evidence is presented (Pearl, 1988). At present, Bayesian networks are widely used in artificial intelligence applications. These include medical diagnosis, image understanding, speech recognition, multi-sensor fusion and environmental modelling. Here, in our approach we use Bayesian network to model affective states as causes, and gestures as effects.

The stochastic relationship between the seven gestures and six affective states is modelled by a Bayesian network as shown in Fig. 8.

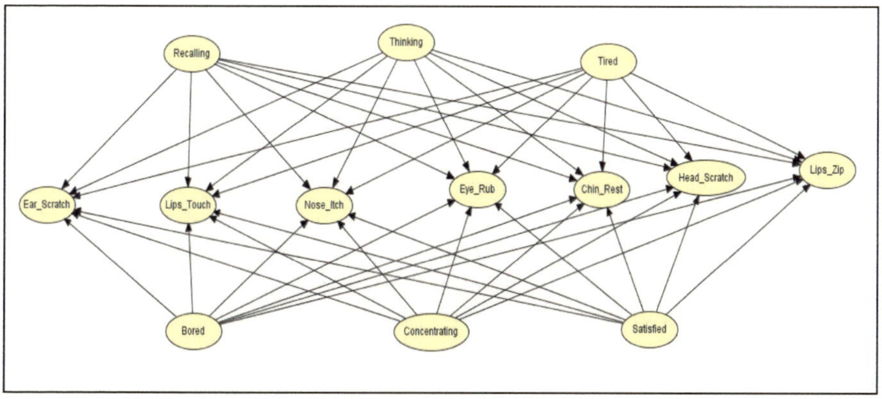

Fig. 8. Bayesian network showing cause-effect relationship of gestures and affect

6. Discussion on results and issues

A preliminary evaluation of the proposed Bayesian model for the four students is reported by Abbasi et al. (2008). They have reported 100 percent recognition rate over the cases where the student reported an affective state using a four fold cross validation. The classification was based on a maximum a posteriori Bayesian classifier. In contrary, recognition rate was found to be around 80 percent when they include cases where the students were uncertain.
These preliminary evaluations indicate that the proposed approach might to be suitable to model such kind of system where information involves uncertainty. However, it still needs to confirm system performance following the automation of gesture detection module. Inherently gesture detection module may involve inaccuracy that may lead to false classification of gestures thus resulting in declined model accuracy.
Furthermore, the data is secured from a limited study where the numbers of gestures is small and number of participants is few. However, these gestures are well known to occur during any interaction such as we studied but remained unnoticed as no study has found their relationship with subjects' emotional or mental state. These un-intentional clues may become part of gesture taxonomy that may be transformed to affective states as shown in Fig. 9.

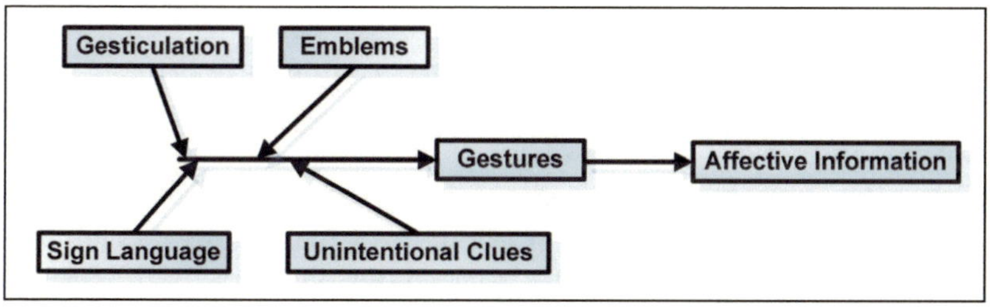

Fig. 9. Unintentional cues being part of gesture taxonomy turning to affective information

Gesticulation is referred as gestures co-occurring with speech (Kendon, 1986) which are different from autonomous gestures, conveyed independent of speech (Queck, 1994; Queck, 1995). Emblems are specific gestures used to convey an idea or concept and are more closed to sign language. There are also other gesture types more specific to situation. An earlier work by Pavlovic et al. (1997) mention that unintentional movements of arm/hand do not convey any meaningful information, however, from our Experiment we have found that unintentional movements may be useful to predict affective states of a person in a particular situational context.

Apparently, prior to this study, we could not find any work that considers unintentional movements in context. As such human body sends message unconsciously, to signal affect or feelings but these movements cannot be identified truly without considering the context. Other unintentional movements such as folded arms, tapping forehead, crossed legs and leaning down the head could be meaningful if studied in context.

Another aspect in processing gesture information is related to the detection of a particular gesture. A recent survey by Mitra & Acharya (2007), presents the current state of art in the gesture recognition techniques however, variation in pose or style of a person or different people for the same gesture (Refer Fig. 10) is a challenging problem which needs to be resolved for a reliable gesture detection system.

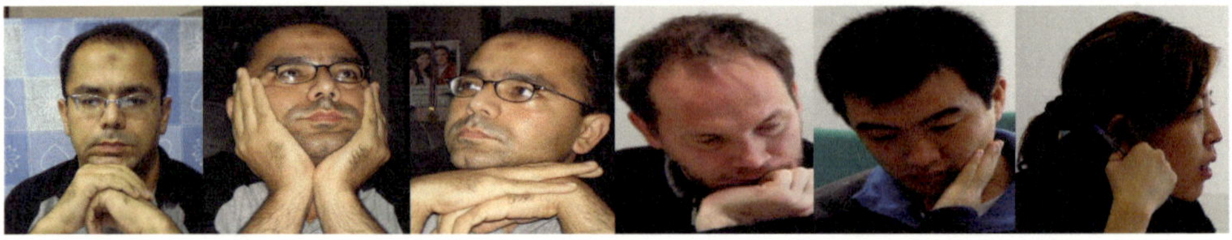

Fig. 10. Few variations in the pose for the same gesture of *Chin Rest*

7. Conclusion & future work

Human body language has recently been explored as part of human non-verbal behavior understanding for various applications involving human-computer interaction. Body from head to toe can express itself such as an eye rub showing weariness or a chin rest showing thinking state. However, the expression and its understanding is context dependent.

We observed some unintentional movements that usually remain unnoticed while we provide meaningful correlations between these movements and probable affective state. Although, these observations are subjective but using objective measures alone to the exclusion of subjective interpretations, might be misleading to understand affective states (Boehner, 2007). Therefore, we advocate subjective analysis considering situational context to correlate actions and affect.

Natural interface between human and computers such as gaze and wink is replacing traditional keyboards and mouse clicks but at present very few systems are in commercial use. Many useful applications can benefit from studies and approach such as presented here. This includes monitoring student affective state during class lecture, web-based learning systems, automated tutoring and also drivers' or pilots' fatigue or weariness monitoring during driving or flight respectively.

In our future work, we will focus on extending scope of our analysis by gathering further data. Furthermore, we will also focus on automating gesture detection system with reasonable accuracy which is itself a challenging problem.

8. Acknowledgments

We acknowledge the volunteer participation of students and researchers from National Institute of Informatics, Japan. We are also thankful to the kind permission granted by Springer Science and Business Media for using some of the material published by Abbasi et al. (2007). Thanks to Asian Institute of Technology, Thailand for its support to publish this report.

9. References

Abbasi, A.R. ; Uno, T. ; Dailey, M.N. & Afzulpurkar, N.V. (2007). Towards knowledge-based affective interaction : Situational interpretation of affect, *Proceedings of 2nd Int. Conf. Affective Computing & Intelligent Interaction*, Lecture Notes in Computer Science Vol. 4738, pp. 452-463, Lisbon, Portugal, Sep., 2007, Springer-Verlag, Heidelberg.

Abbasi, A.R. ; Dailey, M.N. ; Afzulpurkar, N.V. & Uno, T. (2008). Probabilistic prediction of student affect from hand gestures. *Proceedings of Int. Conf. Automation, Robotics and Control Systems*, 7-10 July, 2008, Orlando, Fl., USA. (Accepted manuscript)

Ambady, N. & Rosenthal, R. (1992). Thin slices of expressive behavior as predictors of interpersonal consequences: a metaanalysis. *Psychological Bulletin*, Vol. 111, No. 2, pp. 256–274.

Balomenos, T. ; Raouzaiou, A. ; Ioannou, S. ; Drosopoulos, A.; Karpouzis, K. & Kollias, S.D. (2004). Emotion analysis in man–machine interaction systems. *Lecture Notes in Computer Science*, Vol. 3361, Springer, pp. 318–328.

Bernhardt, D. & Robinson, P. (2007). Detecting affect from non-stylished body motions, *Poceedings of 2nd Int. Conf. Affective Computing & Intelligent Interaction*, Lecture Notes in Computer Science Vol. 4738, pp. 59-70, Lisbon, Portugal, Sep., 2007, Springer-Verlag, Heidelburg.

Boehner, K., DePaula, R., Dourish, P. & Sengers, P. (2007). How emotion is made and measured. Int. J. Human-Computer Studies, Vol. 65, pp. 275-291.

Brave, S. & Nass, C. (2002). Emotion in HCI. In: Jacko J, Sears A (Ed.). *The Human–Computer Interaction Handbook: Fundamentals, Evolving Technologies and Emerging Applications.* Hillsdale, NJ: Lawrence Erlbaum Associates.

Burgoon, J.K. ; Jensen, M.L. ; Meservy, T.O. ; Kruse, J. & Nunamaker, J.F. (2005). Augmenting human identification of emotional states in video, *Proceedings of Int. Conf. Intelligent Data Analysis.*

Coulson, M. (1992). Attributing emotion to static body postures: recognition accuracy, confusions, and viewpoint dependence. *J. Nonverbal Behavior*, Vol. 28, No. 2, pp.117–39.

Dadgostar, F. ; Ryu, H. ; Sarrafzadeh, A. & Overmyer, S.P. (2005). Making sense of student use of nonverbal cues for intelligent tutoring systems, *Proceedings of Int. Conf. ACM SIGCHI*, Vol. 122, pp. 1-4.

Darwin, C. (1872). *The Expression of Emotions in Man and Animals*, J. Murray, London.

Ekman. P. & Friesen,W.V. (1978), *Facial Action Coding System (FACS): Manual*, Palo Alto: Consulting Psychologists Press.

Ekman, P. & Friesen, W.V. (1975). *Unmasking the Face: a Guide to Recognizing Emotions from Facial Clues.* Englewood Cliffs, NJ, Prentice-Hall.

GALC, available at http://www.unige.ch/fapse/emotion/resmaterial/GALC.xls

Gunes, H. & Piccardi, M. (2007). Bi-modal emotion recognition from expressive face and body gestures. *J. Network and Computer Applications*, Vol. 30, pp. 1334–1345.

Gunes, H. & Piccardi, M. (2006). A bi-modal face and body gesture database for automatic analysis of human nonverbal affective behavior, *Proceedings of IEEE Int. Conf. Pattern Recognition*, pp. 1148–53.

Kapoor, A. ; Picard, R.W. & Ivanov, Y. (2004). Probabilistic combination of multiple modalities to detect interest, *Proceedings of IEEE Int. Conf. Pattern Recognition*, pp. 969–972.

Kim, K. ; Kwak, K. & Chi, S. (2006). Gesture analysis for human-robot interaction, *Proceedings of 8th Int. Conf. Advanced Communication Technology (ICACT)*, Korea, pp. 1824-1827.

Kendon, A. (1986). Current issues in the study of gesture. In : Nespoulous, J., Peron, P. & Lecours, A. (Ed.). *The Bilological Foundations of Gestures : Motor and Semiotic Aspects.* Lawrence Erlbaun Assoc., pp. 23-47.

Lee, S. (2006). Automatic gesture recogntion for intelligent human-robot interaction, *Proceedings of 7th Int. Conf. Automatic Face and Gesture Recognition (FGR06),* pp. 645-650.

Mehrabian, A. (1968). Communication without words. *Psychology Today*, Vol. 2, No. 4, pp. 53-56.

Minsky, M. (2006). *The Emotion Machine : Commonsense Thinking, Artificial Intelligence, and the Future of the Human Mind*, Simon and Schuster, New York.

Mitra, S. & Acharya, T. (2007). Gesture recognition : A survey, *IEEE Trans. SMC–Applications and Reviews*, Vol. 37, No.3, pp. 311-324.

Pantic, M. ; Sebe, N. ; Cohn. J. & Huang, T. (2005). Affective multimodal human–computer interaction, *Proceedings of ACM Int. Conf. Multimedia*, pp. 669–676.

Pantic, M. & Rothkrantz, L.J.M. (2000). Automatic analysis of facial expressions- the state of the art. *IEEE Trans. Pattern Analysis and Machine Intelligence*, Vol. 22, No.12, pp. 1424-1445, December.

Pavlovic, V., Sharma, R. & Huang, T. (1997). Visual interpretation of hand gestures for human-computer interaction: A review. *IEEE Trans. Pattern Analysis and Machine Intelligence*, Vol. 19, No. 7, pp.677-695, July.

Pearl, J. (1988). *Probabilistic Reasoning in Intelligent Systems : Networks of Plausible Inference,* Morgan Kaufmann Publishers, California.

Picard, R.W. (2000). *Affective Computing,* MIT Press, Cambridge, MA.

Sebe, N. & Lew, M.S. (2003). *Robust Computer Vision- Theory & Applications*, Kluwer Academy Publishers.

Shcerer, K. (2005). What are emotions ?And how can they be measured ? *Social Science Information*, Vol. 44, No. 4, pp. 695-729.

Tian, Y. ; Kanade, T. & Cohn, J. (2005). Facial expression analysis, In : *Handbook of Face Recognition*, Li, S & Jain, A. (Ed.) , Springer.

Queck, F. (1994). Towards a vision-based hand gesture interface, *Conf. On Virtual Reality Software and Technology*, pp. 17-31.

Queck, F. (1995). Eyes in the interface. Image & Vision Computing, Vol.13, No. 6, pp. 511-525.

20

Towards Affect-sensitive Assistive Intervention Technologies for Children with Autism

Karla Conn, Changchun Liu, Nilanjan Sarkar,
Wendy Stone and Zachary Warren
Vanderbilt University
USA

1. Introduction

Investigation into technology-assisted intervention for children with autism spectrum disorder (ASD) has gained momentum in recent years. Therapists involved in interventions must overcome the communication impairments generally exhibited by children with ASD by adeptly inferring the affective cues of the children to adjust the intervention accordingly. Similarly, an intelligent system, such as a computer or robot, must also be able to understand the affective needs of these children - an ability that the current technology-assisted ASD intervention systems lack - to achieve effective interaction that addresses the role of affective states in human-computer interaction (HCI), human-robot interaction (HRI), and intervention practice. In this chapter we present a physiology-based affect-inference mechanism for emotion modeling, emotion recognition, and emotion-sensitive adaptive response in technology-assisted intervention. This work is the first step towards developing "understanding" interactive technologies for use in future ASD intervention. We address the problem of how to make computer-based ASD intervention tools affect-sensitive by designing therapist-like affective models of the children with ASD based on their physiological responses. By employing these models, we explain how a robot can detect the affective states of a child with ASD and adapt its behaviors accordingly. Experimental results with 6 children with ASD from computer-based cognitive tasks and a proof-of-concept experiment (i.e., a robot-based basketball game) are presented. A Support Vector Machines (SVM) based affective model yielded approximately 82.9% success for predicting affect inferred from a therapist. The robot learned the individual liking level of each child with regard to the game configuration and selected appropriate behaviors to present the task at his/her preferred liking level. Results show the robot automatically predicted individual liking level in real time with 81.1% accuracy. This is the first time, to our knowledge, that the affective states of children with ASD have been detected via a physiology-based affect recognition technique in real time. This is also the first time that the impact of affect-sensitive closed-loop interaction between a robot and a child with ASD has been demonstrated experimentally.
While there is at present no single accepted intervention, treatment, or known cure for ASD, there is growing consensus that intensive behavioral and educational intervention programs can significantly improve long term outcomes for individuals and their families (Rogers,

1998). Despite the urgent need and societal import of intensive treatment (Rutter, 2006), appropriate intervention resources for children with ASD and their families are often extremely costly when accessible (Jacobson et al., 1998; Tarkan, 2002). Therefore, an important new direction for research on ASD is the identification and development of assistive intervention tools that can make application of intensive treatment more readily accessible.

In response to this need, a growing number of studies have been investigating the application of advanced interactive technologies to address core deficits related to autism, namely computer technology (Bernard-Opitz et al., 2001), virtual reality environments (Pares et al., 2005; Parsons & Mitchell, 2002), and robotic systems (Dautenhahn & Werry, 2004; Kozima et al, 2005; Michaud & Theberge-Turmel, 2002; Pioggia et al., 2005; Scassellati, 2005). Initial results indicate that such technologies may hold promise for rehabilitation of children with ASD. Computer and virtual reality (VR) based intervention may provide a simplified but exploratory interaction environment for children with ASD (Moore et al., 2000; Parsons & Mitchell, 2002). Various software packages and VR environments have been developed and applied to address specific deficits associated with autism, e.g., understanding of false belief (Swettenham, 1996), attention (Trepagnier et al., 2006), expression recognition (Silver & Oakes, 2001), and social communication (Bernard-Opitz et al., 2001; Parsons et al., 2005). Research suggested that robots can allow simplified but embodied social interaction that is less intimidating or confusing for children with ASD (Dautenhahn & Werry, 2004). Michaud & Theberge-Turmel (2002) investigated the impact of robot design on the interactions with children and emphasized that systems need to be versatile enough to adapt to the varying needs of different children. Pioggia et al. (2005) developed an interactive life-like facial display system for enhancing emotion recognition in individuals with ASD. Robots have also been used to teach basic social interaction skills using turn-taking and imitation games, and the use of robots as social mediators and as objects of shared attention can encourage interaction with peers and adults (Dautenhahn & Werry, 2004; Kozima et al, 2005). Interactive technologies pose the advantage of furnishing robust systems that can support multimodal interaction and provide a repeatable, standardized stimulus while quantitatively recording and monitoring the performance progress of the children with ASD to assess the intervention approaches (Scassellati, 2005). By employing human-computer interaction (HCI) and human-robot interaction (HRI) technologies, interactive therapeutic tools can partially automate the time-consuming, routine behavioral therapy sessions and may allow intensive intervention to be conducted at home (Dautenhahn & Werry, 2004). For the purpose of using our affective computing tools, computers or robots could be the mode of technology for assisted ASD interventions. We will use the term intelligent system primarily in this text to imply both computer and robot interactive technologies.

Even though there is increasing research in assistive technologies for autism intervention, the authors found no published studies that specifically addressed how to automatically detect and respond to affective cues of children with ASD. This could be important since research suggests that people tend to interact with computers as they might relate to other people, provided that the technology behaves in a socially competent manner (Reeves & Nass, 1996). We believe that such ability could be critical given the importance of human affective information in HRI (Fong et al., 2003; Picard, 1997) and the significant impacts of the affective factors of children with ASD on the intervention practice (Seip, 1996). Common in autism intervention, therapists who work with children with ASD continuously monitor affective cues of the children in order to make appropriate decisions about adaptations to their intervention strategies. For example, 'likes and dislikes chart' is recommended to record the children's preferred activities and/or sensory stimuli during interventions that could be used as reinforcers and/or 'alternative behaviors' (Seip, 1996). Children with autism are particularly vulnerable to anxiety and intolerant of feelings of frustration, which requires a therapist to plan tasks at an appropriate level of difficulty (Ernsperger, 2003). The engagement of children with ASD is the ground basis for the 'floor-time therapy' to help them develop relationships and improve their social skills (Wieder & Greenspan, 2005).

The potential impacts brought by an intelligent system that can detect the affective states of a child with ASD and interact with him/her based on such perception could be various. Complex social stimuli, sophisticated interactions, and unpredictable situations could be gradually but automatically introduced when the robot recognizes that the child is comfortable or not anxious at a certain level of interaction dynamics for a reasonably long period of time. A therapist could use the child's affective records to analyze the therapeutic approach. With the record of the activities and the consequent emotional changes in a child, an intelligent system could learn individual affective characteristics over time and thus could adapt the ways it responds to the needs of different children.

The primary objective of the current research is to investigate how to augment HCI and HRI to be used in autism intervention by endowing the intelligent system with the ability to recognize and respond to the affective states of a child with ASD. To achieve this objective, the research is divided into two phases. Phase I represents the development of affective models through psychophysiological analysis, which includes designing cognitive tasks for affect-elicitation, deriving physiological features via signal processing, and developing affective models using machine learning techniques. Phase II is characterized by the investigation of affect sensitivity during closed-loop interaction between a child with ASD and the intelligent system (i.e., computer, VR environment, or robot). A proof-of-concept experiment was designed wherein a robot learns individual preferences based on the predicted liking level of the children with ASD and in real time selects an appropriate behavior accordingly.

The chapter is organized as follows: The scope and rationale of this work is presented in Section 2. Section 3 describes our use of physiological indices for affect recognition and our proposed framework for automatically detecting and responding to affective cues of children with ASD in closed-loop interaction, as well as the experimental design. This description is followed by a detailed results and discussion section (Section 4). Finally, Section 5 summarizes the contributions of the paper and outlines possible future directions of this research. In addition, the machine learning algorithms employed in this study is presented in the Appendix.

2. Scope and rationale

The overview of the affect-sensitive closed-loop interaction between a child with ASD and an intelligent system is presented in Fig. 1. The physiological signals from the children with ASD are recorded when they are interacting with the system. These signals are processed in real time to extract features, which are fed as input into the models developed in Phase I. The models determine the perceived affective cues and return this information as an output.

The affective information, along with other environmental inputs, is used by a controller to decide the next course of action for the intelligent system. The child who engages with the system is then influenced by the system's behavior, and the closed-loop interaction cycle begins anew. The impact of such an interaction with a robot as the intelligent system is evaluated in Phase II.

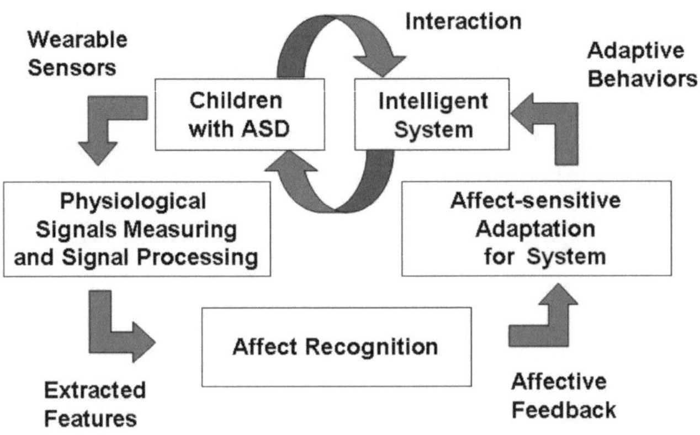

Fig. 1. Framework overview

Human interactions with technology are characterized by explicit as well as implicit channels of communication with presumed underlying affective states (Picard, 1997). While the explicit channel transmits overt messages, the implicit one transmits hidden messages about the communicator (e.g., his/her intention and attitude). There is a growing consensus that endowing an intelligent system with an ability to understand implicit affective cues should permit more meaningful and natural HCI and HRI (Picard, 1997). There are several modalities such as facial expression (Bartlett et al., 2003), vocal intonation (Lee & Narayanan, 2005), gestures and postures (Asha et al., 2005; Kleinsmith et al., 2005), and physiology (Kulic & Croft, 2007; Liu et al., 2006; Mandryk & Atkins, 2007; Picard et al., 2001; Rani et al., 2004) that can be utilized to evaluate the affective states. In this work we chose to create affective models based on physiological data for several reasons. Children with ASD often have communicative impairments (both nonverbal and verbal), particularly regarding expression of affective states (DSM-IV-TR, American Psychiatric Association, 2000; Green et al., 2002; Schultz, 2005). These vulnerabilities place limits on traditional conversational and observational methodologies; however, physiological signals are continuously available and are not necessarily directly impacted by these difficulties (Ben Shalom et al., 2006; Groden et al., 2005; Toichi & Kamio, 2003). As such, physiological modeling may represent a methodology for gathering rich data despite the potential communicative impairments of children with ASD. In addition, physiological data may offer an avenue for recognizing aspects of affect that may be less obvious for humans but more suitable for computers by using signal processing and pattern recognition tools. Furthermore, there is evidence that the transition from one affective state to another state is accompanied by dynamic shifts in indicators of Autonomic Nervous System (ANS) activity (Bradley, 2000). The physiological signals that have been used in this research consist of various cardiovascular, electrodermal, electromyographic, and body temperature signals, all of which have been extensively investigated in psychophysiology literature (Bradley, 2000).

An important question when estimating human affective response is how to operationalize the affective states. Although much existing research on affective modeling categorizes affective states into "basic emotions," there is no consensus on a set of basic emotions among the researchers (Cowie et al., 2001). This fact implies that pragmatic choices are required to select target affective states for a given application (Cowie et al., 2001). In this research we chose anxiety, engagement, and liking to be the target affective states. Anxiety was chosen for two primary reasons. First, anxiety plays an important role in various human-machine interaction tasks that can be related to task performance (Brown et al., 1997). Second, anxiety frequently co-occurs with ASD and plays an important role in the behavior difficulties of children with autism (Gillott et al., 2001). Engagement, defined as "sustained attention to an activity or person," has been regarded as one of the key factors for children with ASD to make substantial gains in academic, communication, and social domains (Ruble & Robson, 2006). With 'playful' activities during the intervention, the liking of the children (i.e., the enjoyment they experience when interacting with an intelligent system) may create the urge to explore and allow prolonged interaction for the children with ASD, who are susceptible to being withdrawn (Dautenhahn & Werry, 2004).

Notably, there is evidence that several affective states could co-occur at different arousal levels (Vansteelandt et al., 2005), and different individuals could express the same emotion with different characteristic response patterns under the same contexts (i.e., phenomenon of person stereotypy) (Lacey & Lacey, 1958). The novelty of the presented affective modeling is that it is individual-specific to accommodate the differences encountered in emotional expression, and it consists of an array of recognizers - each of which determines the intensity of one target affective state for each individual. In this work, a therapist observed the experiments (described in Section 3.2.2) and provided subjective reports based on expertise in inferring presumable underlying affective states from the observable behaviors of children with ASD. The therapist's reports on perceived intensity of the affective states of a child and the extracted physiological indices (described in Section 3.2.4) were employed to develop *therapist-like* affect recognizers that predict high/low levels of anxiety, engagement, and liking for each child with ASD.

Once affective modeling was completed in Phase I, the recognizers equipped the intelligent system with the capability to detect the affective states of the children with ASD in real time from on-line extracted physiological features, which could be utilized in future interventions even when a therapist is not available. As stated in (Dautenhahn et al., 2003), it is important to have robots maintain characteristics of adaptability when applied to autism intervention. In Phase II, we designed and implemented a proof-of-concept experiment (robot-based basketball) wherein a robot adapts its behaviors in real time according to the preference of a child with ASD, inferred from the interaction experience and the predicted consequent liking level. This work is the first time, to our knowledge, that the feasibility and the impact of affect-sensitive closed-loop interaction between a robot and a child with ASD have been demonstrated experimentally. While the results are achieved in a non-social interaction task, it is expected that the real-time affect recognition and response system described in this work will provide a basis for future research into developing technology-assisted intervention tools to help children with ASD explore social interaction dynamics in an affect-sensitive and adaptive manner.

3. Experimental investigation

3.1 Participants

Given the nature of autism (a spectrum disorder) which implies vast individual differences, the works on autism intervention assistive tools are generally guided by the individual characteristics, needs, and preferences of the children (i.e., individual-specific approach) and focus on one sect of the population to develop a method with the flexibility to make future modifications for a wider part of the population (Pioggia et al., 2005; Robins et al., 2005; Robins et al., 2004; Werry et al., 2001). The spectrum nature of autism and the phenomenon of person stereotypy (Lacey & Lacey, 1958) led us to choose an individual-specific approach to work on a long-term basis with a small group of children with ASD in order to evaluate our affect-sensitive intelligent system.

Six participants within the age range of 13 to 16 years old volunteered to partake in the experiments with the consent of their parents. Each of the participants had a diagnosis on the autism spectrum, either autistic disorder, Asperger's Syndrome, or pervasive developmental disorder not otherwise specified (PDD-NOS), according to their medical records. Due to the nature of the designed cognitive tasks (as described in Section 3.2.1), the following were considered when choosing the participants: (i) having a minimum competency level of age-appropriate language and cognitive skills and (ii) not having any history of mental retardation. Each child with ASD underwent the Peabody Picture Vocabulary Test III (PPVT-III) (Dunn & Dunn, 1997) to assess cognitive function. The PPVT-III is a measure of single-word receptive vocabulary that is often used as a proxy for intelligence quotient (IQ) testing (Dunn & Dunn, 1997). It provides standard scores with a mean of 100 and a standard deviation of 15. The PPVT-III measure has high correlations with standardized tests such as the Stanford-Binet Intelligence Scale and the Wechsler Intelligence Scale for Children (Bee & Boyd, 2004), and DSM-IV-TR (2000) classifies full scale IQ's above 70 as nonretarded. Inclusion in our study was characterized as obtaining a standard score of 80 or above on the PPVT-III measure. Table 1 shows the characteristics of the participants in the experiments. The group sizes and the cardinality of participant age range of many studies on technology-assisted autism intervention are commensurate with our work when an individual-specific approach was used (Pioggia et al., 2005; Robins et al., 2005; Robins et al., 2004; Werry et al., 2001). The affective modeling was performed based on a large sample size of observations (approximately 85 epochs over 6 hours) for each child with ASD, which is comparatively more extensive than many other works (Groden et al., 2005; Pioggia et al., 2005; Robins et al., 2004).

Child ID	Gender	Age	Diagnosis	PPVT-III Score
A	Male	15	Autistic Disorder	99
B	Male	15	Asperger's Syndrome	80
C	Male	13	Autistic Disorder	81
D	Male	14	PDD-NOS	92
E	Male	16	PDD-NOS	93
F	Female	14	PDD-NOS	83

Table 1. Characteristics of Participants.

3.2 Phase I – affective modeling

While the impact of Phase II is evaluated on affect-sensitive human-robot interaction, we built the affective models using physiological data gathered from two human-computer interaction tasks. Our previous work (Rani et al., 2006a) showed that affective models built through human-computer interaction tasks could be successfully employed to achieve affect recognition in human-robot interaction for typical individuals. This observation suggests that it is possible to broaden the domain of tasks for affective modeling, thus reducing the habituation effect of continuous exposure to the same robotic system.

3.2.1 Task design for affect elicitation during cognitive tasks

Two computer-based cognitive tasks - an anagram-solving task and a Pong-playing task - were designed to evoke varying intensities of the following three affective states: anxiety, engagement, and liking, from the participants. Affective responses were manipulated by presenting the participant with anagrams of varying difficulty levels. For example, a long series of trivially easy anagrams caused less engagement. The Pong task involved the participant playing a variant of the classic video game "Pong." Various parameters of the game were manipulated to elicit the required affective responses: ball speed and size, paddle speed and size, sluggish or over-responsive keyboard, and the level of the computer opponent player. For examples, very high speeds and sluggish or over-responsive keyboard caused anxiety at times and playing against a moderate-level computer player usually generated liking. The task configurations were established through pilot work.

Each task sequence was subdivided into a series of discrete trials/epochs that were bounded by the subjective affective state assessments. These assessments were collected using a battery of five questions regarding the three target affective states and the perceived difficulty and performance rated on an eight-point Likert scale where 1 indicated the lowest level and 8 indicated the maximum level. Each participant took part in six sessions - three one-hour sessions of anagrams and three one-hour sessions of Pong - on six different days.

3.2.2 Experimental setup

Fig. 2 shows the setup for the experiment. A child with ASD was involved in the cognitive tasks on computer C1 while his/her physiological data was acquired via wearable biofeedback sensors and the Biopac system (www.biopac.com). After being amplified and digitized, physiological signals were transferred from the Biopac transducers to C2 through an Ethernet link and stored. C1 was also connected to the Biopac system via a parallel port, through which the physiological data were recorded in a time-synchronized manner. To gain perspective from different sources and enhance the reliability of the subjective report, a therapist with experience in working with children with ASD and a parent of the participant were also involved in the study, who may best know the participant. We video recorded the sessions to cross-reference observations made during the experiment. The signal from the video camera was routed to a television, and the signal from the participant's computer screen where the task was presented was routed to a separate computer monitor M2. The therapist and a parent were seated at the back of the experiment room, watching the experiment from the view of the video camera and observing how the task progressed on the separate monitor.

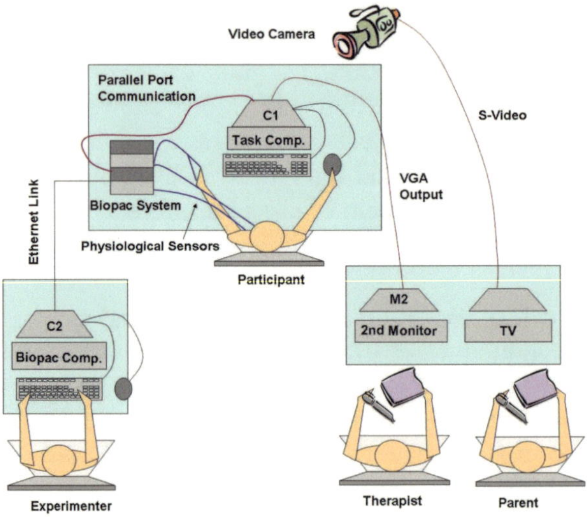

Fig. 2. Experimental setup for affective modeling tasks

3.2.3 Experimental procedure

On the first visit, participants completed the PPVT-III measurement to determine eligibility for the experiments. After initial briefing regarding the tasks, physiological sensors from a Biopac system were attached to the participant's body. Participants were asked to relax in a seated position and read age-appropriate leisure material while a three-minute baseline recording was performed, which was later used to offset day-variability. Each session lasted about an hour and consisted of a set (13-15) of either 3-minute epochs for anagram tasks or up to 4-minute epochs for Pong tasks. Each epoch was followed by subjective report questions rated on an eight-point Likert scale. The three sets of reports were used as the possible reference points to link the objective physiological measures to the participant's affective state.

3.2.4 Physiological indices for affective modeling

There is good evidence that the physiological activity associated with affective states can be differentiated and systematically organized (Bradley, 2000). Cardiovascular and electromyogram activities have been used to examine positive and negative affective states of people (Cacioppo et al., 2000; Papillo & Shapiro, 1990). Electrodermal activities have been shown to be associated with task engagement (Pecchinenda & Smith, 1996). The variation of peripheral temperature due to emotional stimuli was studied by Kataoka et al. (1998). In this work, we exploited the dependence of physiological responses on underlying affective states to develop affective models for children with ASD by using the machine learning method as described in Section 3.2.5 and Appendix 1. The physiological signals we examined were: various cardiovascular activities including electrocardiogram (ECG), impedance cardiogram (ICG), photoplethysmogram (PPG), and phonocardiogram (PCG)/heart sound; electrodermal activities (EDA) including tonic and phasic responses from skin conductance; electromyogram (EMG) activities from corrugator supercilii, zygomaticus major, and upper trapezius muscles; and peripheral temperature. These signals were selected because they are likely to demonstrate variability as a function of the targeted affective states, as well as they can be measured non-invasively, and are relatively resistant to movement artifacts (Lacey & Lacey, 1958; Dawson et al., 1990). Further details of the physiological signals examined in this work along with the features derived from each signal can be found in our supplementary publication Rani et al. (2006b).

The physiological signals were acquired using the Biopac MP150 data acquisition system (www.biopac.com). ECG was measured from the chest using the standard two-electrode configuration. ICG describes the changes of thorax impedance due to cardiac contractility and was measured by four pairs of surface electrodes that were longitudinally configured on both sides of the body. A microphone specially designed to detect heart sound waves was placed on the chest to measure PCG. PPG, peripheral temperature, and EDA were measured from the middle finger, the thumb, and the index and ring fingers of the non-dominant hand, respectively. EMG was measured by placing surface electrodes on two facial muscles (corrugator supercilii and zygomaticus major) and an upper back muscle (upper trapezius). Fig. 3 shows the sensor setup. The sampling rate was fixed at 1000 Hz for all the channels. Appropriate amplification and band-pass filtering were performed. Subsequently, emotional stimulus induced by cognitive tasks was applied in epochs of up to four minutes in length (as described in Section 3.2.1).

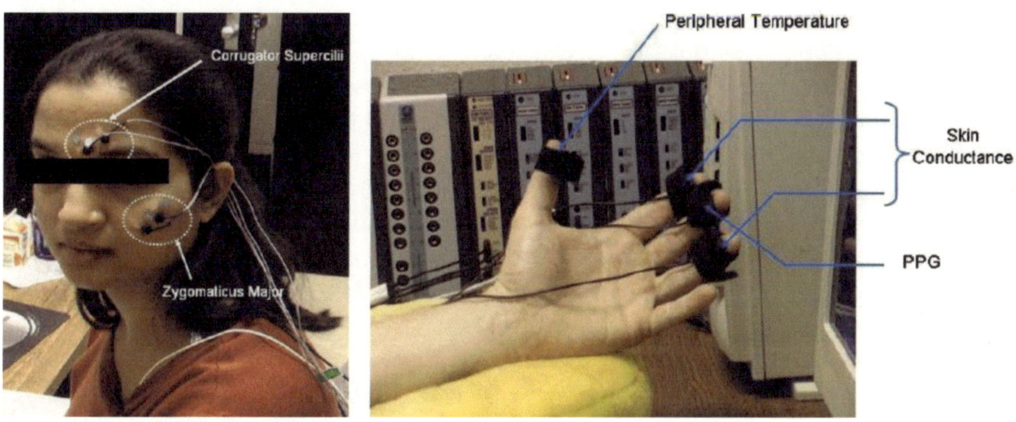

Fig. 3. Sensor Setup. (a) shows the position of facial EMG sensors and (b) shows the placement of sensors on non-dominant hand.

Signal processing techniques such as Fourier transform, wavelet transform, thresholding, and peak detection were used to derive the relevant features from the physiological signals. For example, inter beat interval (IBI) is the time interval between two "R" waves in the electrocardiogram (ECG) waveform. Power spectral analysis is performed on the IBI data to localize the sympathetic and parasympathetic nervous system activities associated with two frequency bands (i.e., high (0.15-0.4Hz) and low (0.04-0.15Hz) frequency components. Photoplethysmograph (PPG) signal measures changes in the volume of blood in the finger tip associated with the pulse cycle and provides an index of the relative constriction versus dilation of the blood vessels in the periphery. Pulse transit time (PTT) is estimated by computing the time between systole at the heart (as indicated by the R-wave of the ECG) and the peak of the pulse wave reaching the peripheral site where PPG is being measured. The features extracted from the heart sound signal consist of the mean and standard deviation of the 3rd, 4th, and 5th level coefficients of the Daubechies wavelet transform.

Bioelectrical impedance analysis (BIA) measures the impedance or opposition to the flow of an electric current through the body fluids contained mainly in the lean and fat tissue. A common variable in recent psychophysiology research, pre-ejection period (PEP) is derived from ICG and ECG and is most heavily influenced by sympathetic innervation of the heart. EDA consists of two main components - Tonic response and Phasic response. Tonic skin conductance refers to the ongoing or the baseline level of skin conductance in the absence of any particular discrete environmental events. Phasic skin conductance refers to the event related changes that occur, caused by a momentary increase in skin conductance (resembling a peak). The EMG signal from Corrugator Supercilii muscle (eyebrow) captures a person's frown and detects the tension in that region. This EMG signal is also a valuable source of blink information and helps determine the blink rate. The EMG signal from the Zygomaticus Major muscle captures the muscle movements while smiling. Upper Trapezius muscle activity measures the tension in the shoulders, one of the most common sites in the body for developing stress. Variations in the peripheral temperature mainly come from localized changes in blood flow caused by vascular resistance or arterial blood pressure and reflect the autonomic nervous system activity.

3.2.5 SVM-based affective modeling

Determining the intensity (e.g., high/low) of a particular affective state from the physiological response resembles a classification problem where the attributes are the physiological features and the target function is the degree of arousal. Our earlier work (Rani et al., 2006b) compared the efficacy of several machine learning algorithms (KNN, Bayesian Network Technique, Regression Tree, and SVM) to recognize the affective states from the physiological signals of typical individuals and found that SVM gave the highest classification accuracy. In this work, SVM was employed to determine the underlying affective state of a child with ASD given a set of physiological features. Details of the theory and learning methods of SVM can be found in (Vapnik, 1998) and are briefly described in Appendix 1.

As illustrated in Fig. 4, each participant had a data set comprised of both the objective physiological features and corresponding subjective reports on arousal level of target affective states from the therapist, the parent, and the participant. The physiological features were extracted by using the approaches described in Section 3.2.4). The individual range per affective state from each reporter on the subjective reports was normalized to [0, 1] and then discretized such that 0–0.50 was labeled as low level and 0.51–1 was labeled as high level. All three affective states were partitioned separately so that there were two levels for each affective state. Each data set contained approximately 85 epochs. The multiple subjective reports were analyzed, and one was chosen as the possible reference points to link the physiological measures to the participant's affective state. For example, a therapist-like affect recognizer can be developed when the therapist's reports are used. A SVM-based recognizer was trained on each individual's data set for each target affective state. In this work, in order to deal with the nonlinearly separable data, soft margin classifiers with slack variables were used to find a hyperplane with less restriction (Eqn. 1, Appendix 1) (Burges, 1998). RBF (Radial Basis Function) was selected as the kernel function because it often delivers better performance (Burges, 1998). A ten-fold cross-validation was used to determine the kernel parameter and regularization parameter (Eqn. 2, Appendix 1) of the recognizer.

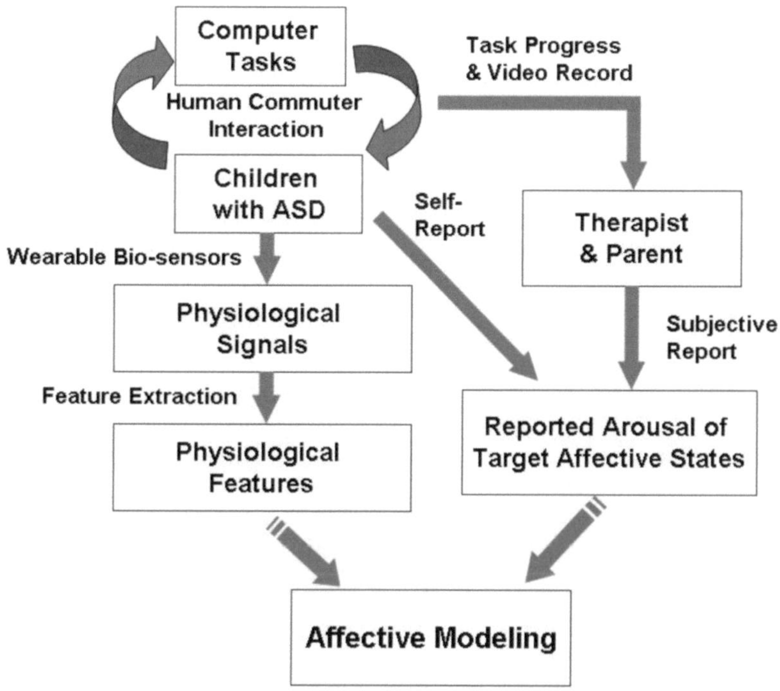

Fig. 4. Overview of affective modeling

Once affective modeling is accomplished, the affect recognizers can accept as input the physiological features extracted on-line and produce as output the probable level of the target affective state of a child with ASD while interacting with an intelligent system. In the design for the human-robot interaction task in Phase II, adequate measures were taken to avoid physical effort from overwhelming the physiological response.

3.3 Phase II - closed-loop human robot interaction

3.3.1 Task design for affect-sensitive behavior adaptation task

A closed-loop human robot interaction task, "robot-based basketball (RBB)," was designed. The main objective was two-fold: (i) to enable the robot to learn the preference of the children with ASD implicitly using physiology-based affective models as well as select appropriate behaviors accordingly; and (ii) to observe the effects of such affective-sensitivity in the closed-loop interaction between the children with ASD and the robot.

The affective model developed in Phase I is capable of predicting the intensity of liking, anxiety, and engagement simultaneously. However to designate a specific objective for the experiment in Phase II without compromising its proof-of-concept purpose, one of the three target affective states was chosen to be detected and responded to by the robot in real time. As has been emphasized in (Dautenhahn and Werry, 2004), the liking of the children (i.e., the enjoyment they experience when interacting with the robot) is a goal as desirable as skill learning for autism intervention. Therefore, liking was chosen as the affective state around which to modify the robot's behaviors in Phase II.

In the RBB task, an undersized basketball hoop was attached to the end-effector of a robotic manipulator, which could move the hoop in different directions (as shown in Fig. 5) with different speeds. The children were instructed to shoot a required number of baskets into the moving hoop within a given time. Three robot behaviors were designed as shown in Table 2. For example, in behavior 1 the robot moves towards and away from the participant (i.e., in the *X* direction) at a slow speed with soft background music, and the shooting requirement for successful baskets is relatively low. The parameter configurations were determined based on a pilot study to attain varied impacts on affective experience for different behaviors. From this pilot study, the averaged performance of participants for a given behavior was compiled and analyzed. Behavior transitions occurred between but not within epochs. As such, each robot behavior extended for the length of an epoch (1.5 minutes in duration) to have the participant fully exposed to the impact of that behavior.

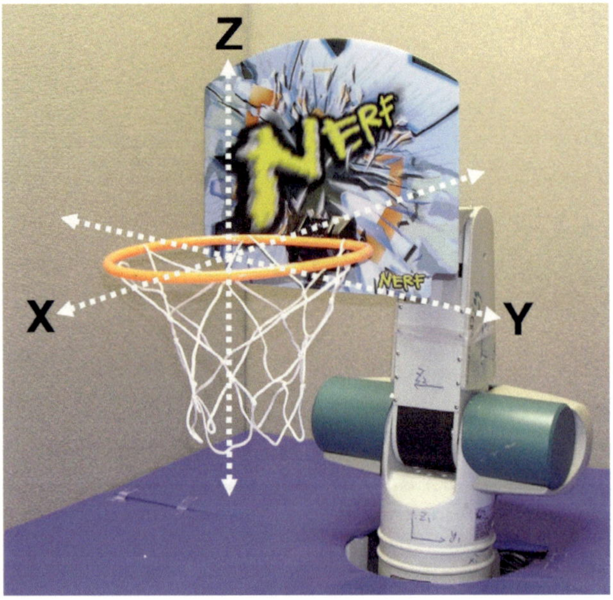

Fig. 5. X, Y, and Z directions for behaviors used in RBB

Behavior ID	Motion Direction	Speed (sec/period)	Threshold (shots/epoch)	Background Music
1	X	2	12	Serene
2	Y	4	20	Lively
3	Z	8	30	Irregular

Table 2. Robot behaviors

Each of the six participants took part in two robot basketball sessions (RBB1 and RBB2). In RBB1 (non-affect based) the robot selected its behavior randomly (i.e., without any regard to the liking information of the participant), and the presentation of each type of behavior was evenly distributed. This session was designed for two purposes: (i) to explore the state space and action space of the QV-learning algorithm used in RBB2 for behavior adaptation (described in Section 3.3.4); and (ii) to validate that the different robot behaviors have distinguishable impact on the child's level of liking. In RBB2 (liking-based), the robot continues to learn the child's individual preference and selects the desirable behavior based on interaction experiences (i.e., records of robot behavior and the consequent liking level of a participant predicted by the affective model). The idea is to investigate whether the robot can automatically choose the most-liked behavior of each participant as observed from RBB1 by means of physiology-based affective model and QV-learning.

3.3.2 Experimental setup

The real-time implementation of the RBB system is shown in Fig. 6. The set-up included a 5 degrees-of-freedom robot manipulator (CRS Catalyst-5 System) Two infrared (IR) transmitter and receiver pairs were attached to the basketball hoop to detect small, soft foam balls going through the hoop. Biological feedback equipment (Biopac system) was connected to a C1 that: (i) acquired physiological signals from the Biopac system and extracted physiological features on-line, (ii) predicted the probable liking level by using the affective model developed in Phase I, (iii) acquired IR data through the analog input channels of the Biopac system, (iv) ran a QV-learning algorithm that learns the participant's preference and chooses the robot's next behavior accordingly. Computer C1 was connected serially to the CRS computer (C2), which ran Simulink software. The behavior switch triggers were transmitted from C1 to C2 via a RS232 link. The commands to control the robot's various joints were transmitted from C2 to the robot. As in Phase I tasks, the therapist and a parent were also involved, watching the experiment from the TV that was connected to a video camera.

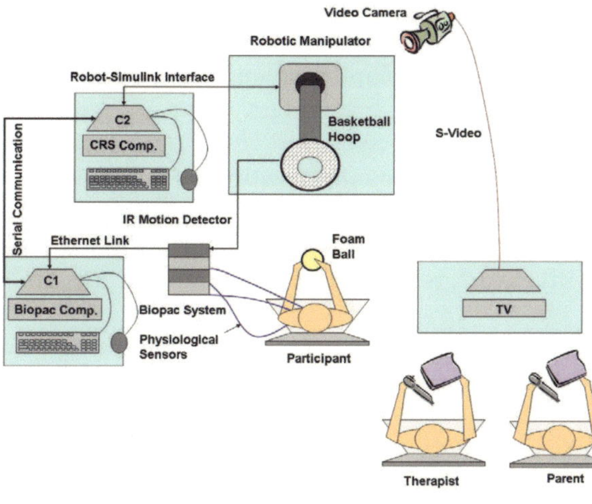

Fig. 6. Experimental set-up for robot basketball

3.3.3 Experimental procedure

Each basketball session (RBB1 or RBB2) was approximately 1 hour long and included 27 minutes of active human-robot interaction (i.e., 18 epochs of 1.5 minutes each). The remaining time was spent attaching sensors, guiding a short practice, taking a baseline recording, collecting subjective reports, and pausing for scheduled breaks. During the experiment, the participant was asked to take a break after every four epochs and the participant could request a break whenever he/she desired one. During each basketball epoch, the participant received commands and performance assessments from pre-recorded dialogue via a speech program running on C1 and the interaction proceeded as follows:

1. The participant was notified of the shooting requirement threshold.
2. A start command instructed the participant to start shooting baskets.
3. Once the epoch started, the participant was given voice feedback every 30 seconds regarding the number of baskets remaining and the time available.
4. A stop command instructed the participant to stop shooting baskets, which ended the epoch.
5. At the end of each epoch, the participant's performance was rated and relayed to him/her as excellent, above average, or below average.

Each epoch was followed by a subjective reporting procedure using the same protocol as Phase I that took 30-60 seconds to collect. After the subjective reports were complete, the next epoch would begin. To prevent habituation, a time interval of 7 days or more between RBB sessions was enforced.

3.3.4 Affect-sensitive behavior adaptation in closed-loop human robot interaction

We defined the state, action, state transition, and reward functions so that the affect-sensitive robot behavior adaptation problem could be solved using the QV-learning algorithm as described in (Wiering, 2005) and Appendix 2.

The set of states consisted of three robot behaviors as described in Table 2. In every state, the robot has three possible actions (1/2/3) that correspond to choosing behavior 1, 2, or 3, respectively, for the next time step (i.e., next epoch). Each robot behavior persists for one full epoch and the state/behavior transition occurs only at the end of an epoch. The detection of consequent affective cues (i.e., the real-time prediction of the liking level for the next epoch) was used to evaluate the desirability of a certain action. A reward function was defined based on the predicted liking level. If the consequent liking level was recognized as high, the contributing action was interpreted as positive and a reward was granted ($r = 1$); otherwise the robot received a punishment ($r = -1$). QV-learning uses this reward function to have the robot learn how to select the behavior that was expected to result in a high liking level and therefore positively influenced the actual affective (e.g., liking) experience of the child.

RBB1 enables state and action exploration through random, evenly distributed behavior-switching actions. The V-function and Q-function are updated using Eqn. (3) and Eqn. (4) from Appendix 2. After RBB1, the subjective reports are analyzed to examine the impacts of different behaviors on each participant's preference. In RBB2 the robot starts from a non-preferred behavior/state and continues the learning process by using Eqn. (3) and Eqn. (4). A greedy action selection mechanism is used to choose the behavior-switching action with the highest Q-value.

Because of the limited number of states and actions in this proof-of-concept experiment, tabular representation is used for the V-function and the Q-function. To prevent a certain action and/or state from being overly dominant and to counteract the habituation effect, the values of $Q(s, a)$ and $V(s)$ are bounded by using the reward or punishment encountered in the interaction. The parameters in Eqn. (3) and Eqn. (4) are chosen as $\alpha = 0.8$ and $\gamma = 0.9$. Before RBB1 begins, the initial values in the V-table and the Q-table are set to 0.

4. Results and discussion

In this section we present both the Phase I results of physiology-based affective modeling for children with ASD and Phase II results of the affect-sensitive closed-loop interaction between children with ASD and the robot.

4.1 Phase I – affect detection

One of the prime challenges of this work is attaining reliable subjective reports. Moreover, researchers are reluctant to trust the responses of adolescents on self-reports (Barkley, 1998). In order to overcome this difficulty, a therapist and a parent were involved by using the approaches described in the experimental setup. They observed the experiments and provided subjective reports based on their expertise/experience in inferring presumable underlying affective states from the observable behaviors of children with ASD.

To measure the amount of agreement among the different reporters, the kappa statistic was used (Siegel and Castellan, 1988). The kappa coefficient (K) measures pair-wise agreement among a set of reporters making category judgments, correcting for expected chance agreement. When agreement is complete, $K=1$; whereas, when there is only agreement as would be expected by chance, $K = 0$. Fig. 7 shows results for K averaged across the target affective states.

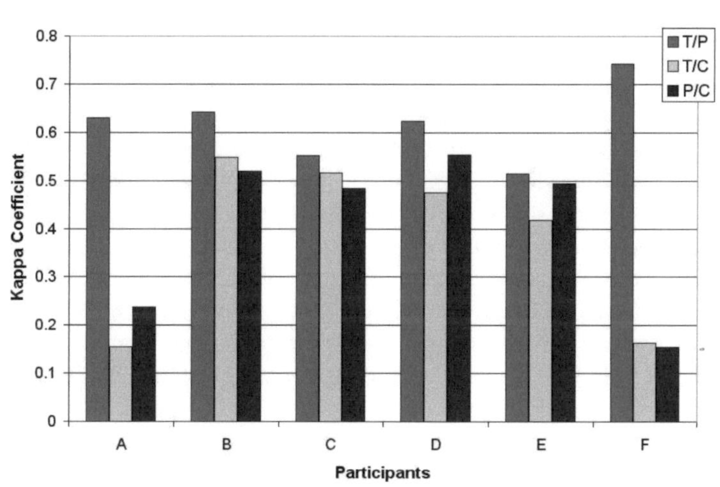

Fig. 7. Average Kappa Statistics between Reporters for Affective States

It was observed that the agreement between the therapist and parent (T/P) showed the largest K values (mean = 0.62) among the three possible pairs for each child ($p < 0.05$, paired t-test). When each child is examined individually, different trends arise, which revealed diverse affective characteristics of the children with ASD who partook in this study. The Kappa agreement between therapist and parent is substantial for Child A, Child B, Child D, and Child F and moderate for Child C and Child E. Such results might stem from the fact that it could be difficult for the therapist or parent to distinguish certain emotion for a particular child with ASD. For example, the agreement between therapist and parent for the anxiety level of Child C and Child E (K equals 0.352 and 0.372, respectively) are considerably less than the average level. In the experiment, Child A and Child F's ratings for liking, anxiety, and engagement were almost constant which resulted in lower K values for the therapist and child pair (T/C) and the parent and child pair (P/C) than those of the other participants. This may be due to the fact that the spectrum developmental disorder for children with autism manifests different abilities to recognize and report their emotions. The mean of the kappa statistic values between the children and either the therapist or the parent were relatively small (0.37 and 0.40, respectively). Although lack of agreement with adults does not necessarily mean that the self-reports of children with ASD are not dependable; however, given the fact that therapists' judgment based on their expertise is the state-of-the-art in most autism intervention approaches and the fact that there is a reasonably high agreement between the therapist and the parents for all of the six children, the subjective reports of the therapist were used as the reference points linking the objective physiological data to the children's affective state. To make the subjective reports more consistent, the same therapist was involved in all of the experiments. This choice allowed for building a *therapist-like* affective model. Once the affect modeling is completed, the recognizers will be capable of inferring the affective states of the child with ASD from the physiological signals in real-time even when the therapist is not available.

The performance of the developed affective model for each child (i.e., individual-specific approach) is shown in Fig. 8. The cross-validation method, 'leave-one-out', was used. The affective model produced high recognition accuracies for each target affective state of each participant. The average correct prediction accuracies across all participants were: 85.0% for liking, 79.5% for anxiety, and 84.3% for engagement, which are comparable to the best results achieved for typical individuals (Picard et al., 2001; Rani et al., 2006b). We also compared the performance of affective modeling to a control method that represents random chance. For example, in 48 out of 86 epochs the engagement of Child E was rated as low level, where a random classification could assign all test epochs to this category and make accurate classifications $(48/86)\times100 = 55.8\%$ of the time. We thus considered the level with a majority of epochs to represent the chance condition, which is denoted by dark grey bars in Fig. 8. While the physiology-based affective modeling alone did not provide perfect classification (i.e., 100%) of affective states of children with ASD, they did yield reliable matches with the subjective rating and significantly outperformed a random classifier (averaging 82.9% vs. 59.2%). This was promising considering that this task was challenging in two respects: (i) the reports were collected from the therapist who was observing the children as opposed to having typical adults capable of differentiating and reporting their own affective states and (ii) varying levels of arousal of any given affective state (e.g., low/high anxiety) were identified instead of determining discrete emotions (e.g., anger, joy, sadness, etc.).

To explore the effects of reducing the number of physiological signals and the possibility of achieving more economical modeling, we examined the performance of the affect recognizers when cardiovascular, electrodermal, and electromyographic activities and their combinations were used. As shown in Table 3, all the recognizers delivered better predication than random guess (mean prediction rate equals 52.9%), and with more information from physiological activities the performance of the affective models tends to improve (except the combination of electrodermal and electromyographic activities). While no combination of physiological activity surpassed the percent accuracy achieved when all signals were used, the results suggested it may be possible to selectively reduce the set of signals and obtain nearly-as-good performance (e.g., using a combination of cardiovascular and electrodermal signals).

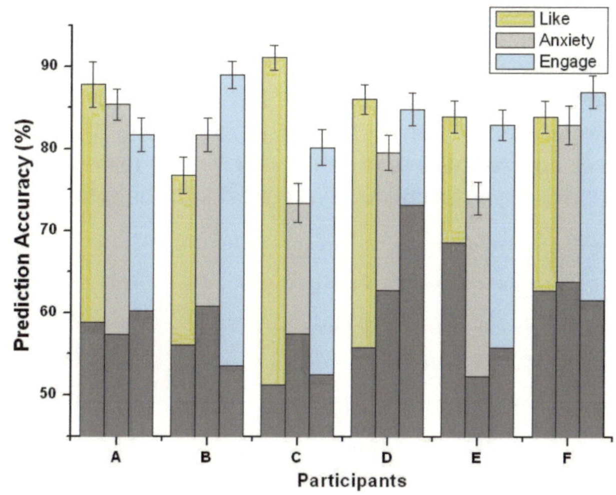

Fig. 8. Prediction Accuracy of the Affective Model

Physiological Signals	Liking	Anxiety	Engage	Mean
Cardiovascular	75.7	68.5	76.2	73.5
Electrodermal	73.4	72.3	73.3	73.0
Electromyographic	73.1	65.8	70.1	69.7
Electrodermal + Electromyographic	75.0	69.4	71.4	71.9
Cardiovascular + Electromyographic	79.6	70.2	79.9	76.6
Cardiovascular + Electrodermal	**79.9**	**74.3**	**81.9**	**78.7**
All	**85.0**	**79.5**	**84.3**	**82.9**

Table 3. Prediction Accuracy of the Affective Modeling based on Different Physiological Signals (%)*

4.2 Phase II – affect adaptation in robot-based basketball task

Six children with ASD who completed the Phase I experiments also took part in the robot basketball task. The results described here are based on the RBB1 (non-affect based) and RBB2 (liking-based) tasks.

First, we present results to validate that different behaviors of the robot had distinguishable impacts on the liking level of the children with ASD. To reduce the bias of validation, in RBB1 the robot selects behaviors randomly and the occurrence of each behavior is evenly

---

* Peripheral temperature has relatively few features derived and was not examined independently. Instead, it was studied conjunctively with the electrodermal activity, both of which were acquired from the non-dominant hand of a participant.

distributed. Fig. 9 shows the average labeled liking level for each behavior as reported by the therapist in RBB1. The difference of the impact is significant for five children (participants A, B, D, E, and F) and moderate for participant C. Across all participants, the differences of reported liking for the most-preferred, moderately-preferred, and least-preferred behavior are statistically significant ($p < 0.05$, ANOVA test). Furthermore, it was observed that different children with ASD may have different preferences for the robot's behaviors. These results demonstrated that it is important to have a robot learn the individual's preference and adapt to it automatically, which may allow a more tailored and affect-sensitive interaction between children with ASD and the robot.

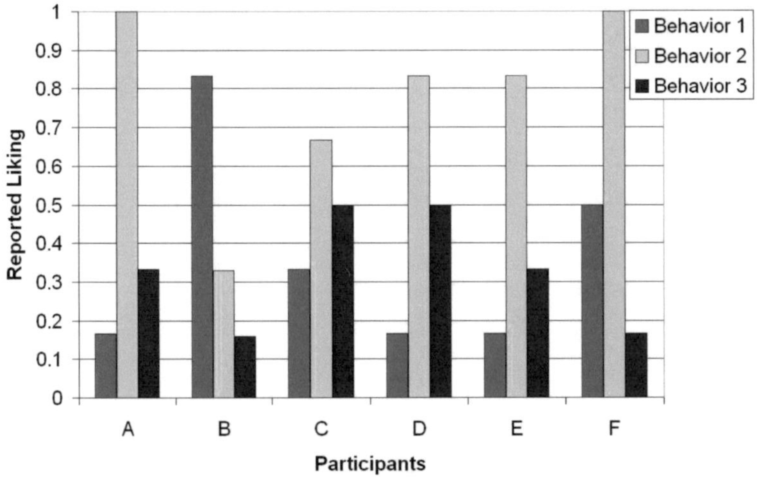

Fig. 9. Mean liking level for different behaviors in RBB1

Second, the predictive accuracy of how closely the real-time physiology-based quantitative measures of liking, as obtained from affective models developed in Phase I, matched with that of the subjective rating of liking made by the therapist during Phase II is discussed. The average predictive accuracy across all the participants was approximately 81.1%. The highest was 86.1% for Child D, and the lowest was 77.8% for Child B and Child E. Note that the affective model was evaluated based on physiological data obtained on-line from a real-time application for children with ASD. However, this prediction accuracy is comparable to the results achieved through off-line analysis for typical individuals (Rani et al., 2006b).

Third, we present results about robot behavior adaptation and investigate its impact on the interaction between the children and the robot. Table 4 shows the percentages of different behaviors that were chosen in RBB2 for each participant. The robot learned the individual's preference and selected the most-preferred behavior with high probability for all the participants. Averaged across participants, the most-preferred, moderately-preferred, and least-preferred behaviors were chosen 72.5%, 16.7%, and 10.8% of the time, respectively. The preference of a behavior was defined by the reported liking level in RBB1 as shown in Fig. 9. There could be several reasons why less-preferred behaviors were chosen in RBB2. The learned behavior selection policy might not have been optimal after the exploration in RBB1, and the QV-learning algorithm continued the learning process in RBB2. Another reason could be that the affective model is not 100% accurate and may return false reward/punishment, which may have given the robot imperfect instruction for behavior switches. Habituation to the most-preferred behavior during RBB2 could also be a factor that might have contributed to temporary changes in preference which led the robot to choose other behaviors.

Child ID	Most-Liked Behavior		Moderate-Liked Behavior		Least-Liked Behavior	
	ID	Proportion	ID	Proportion	ID	Proportion
A	2	82.4%	3	11.8%	1	5.8%
B	1	70.6%	2	17.7%	3	11.7%
C	2	58.8%	3	23.5%	1	17.7%
D	2	76.5%	3	11.8%	1	11.7%
E	2	76.5%	3	17.6%	1	5.9%
F	2	70.6%	1	17.7%	3	11.7%

Table 4. Proportion of Different Behaviors Performed in RBB2

In Fig. 10 we present results to demonstrate that active monitoring of participants' liking and automatically selecting the preferred behavior allowed children with ASD to maintain high liking levels. The average labeled liking levels of the participants as reported by the therapist during the two sessions were compared. The lighter bars indicate the liking level during the RBB1 session (i.e., when the robot selected behaviors randomly), and the darker bars show the liking level during the RBB2 session (i.e., when robot learned the individual preference and chose the appropriate behavior accordingly). For all participants liking level was maintained, and for five of the six children liking level increased.

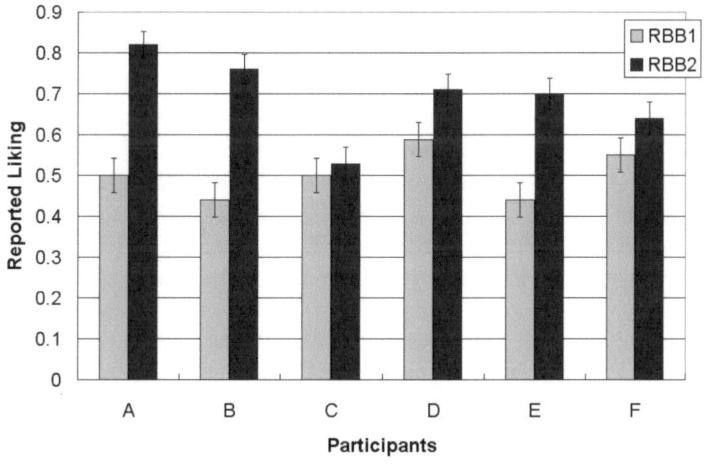

Fig. 10. Subjective liking as reported by therapist

There was no significant increase for Child C during the liking-based session as compared to the non-affect based session. The impact of the different robot behaviors on the liking level of Child C is not as significant as that of the others (refer to Fig. 9), which may impede the robot in finding the preferred behavior and hence impede the robot in effectively influencing the subjective liking level positively. Note that RBB1 presents a typically balanced interaction with equal numbers of most-preferred, moderately-preferred, and least-preferred epochs and the comparisons in Fig. 10 are not between liking-based sessions and sessions of least-preferred epochs. To determine whether this change in liking level was statistically significant across all the participants, a one-way ANOVA test was performed on the null hypothesis of no change in liking level between liking-based sessions and non-affect based sessions. The null hypothesis could be rejected at the 99.5% confidence level. This was a significant result as the robot continued learning and utilizing the information regarding the probable liking level of children with ASD to adjust its behaviors. This ability enables the robot to adapt its behavior selection in real time and hence keep the participant in a higher liking level.

5. Conclusions and future work

There is increasing consensus in the autism community that development of assistive tools that exploit advanced technology will likely make application of intensive intervention for children with ASD more readily accessible. In recent years, various applications of advanced interactive technologies have been investigated in order to facilitate and/or partially automate the existing behavioral intervention that addresses specific deficits associated with autism. However, the current technology-assisted intervention tools for children with ASD do not possess the ability of deciphering affective cues from the children, which could be critical given that the affective factors of children with ASD have significant impacts on the intervention practice. In this work, we have proposed a novel framework for affect-sensitive human-machine interaction where the intelligent system can detect the affective states of the children with ASD implicitly and respond to it accordingly.

The presented affective modeling methodology could allow the recognition of affective states of children with ASD from physiological signals in real time and provide the basis for future technology-assisted affect-sensitive interactive autism intervention. In Phase I, two cognitive tasks - solving anagrams and playing Pong - have been designed to elicit the affective states of liking, anxiety, and engagement for children with ASD that are considered important in autism intervention. To have reliable reference points to link the physiological data to the affective states, the reports from the child, the therapist, and the parent were collected and analyzed. A large set of physiological indices have been investigated to determine their correlation with the affective states of the children with ASD. We have experimentally demonstrated that it is viable to detect the affective states of children with ASD via a physiology-based affect recognition mechanism. A SVM-based affective model yielded reliable prediction with a success rate of 82.9% when using the therapist's reports.

In order to investigate the affect-sensitive closed-loop interaction between the children with ASD and an intelligent system, we designed a proof-of-concept task, robot-based basketball, and developed an experimental system for its real-time implementation and verification. The real-time prediction of liking level of the children with ASD was accomplished with an average accuracy of 81.1%. The robot learned individual preferences of the children with ASD over time based on the interaction experience and the predicted liking level and hence automatically selected the most-preferred behavior, on average, 72.5% of the time. We have observed that such affect-sensitive robot behavior adaptation has led to an increase in reported liking level of the children with ASD. This is the first time, to our knowledge, that the affective states of children with ASD have been detected via a physiology-based affect recognition technique in real time. This is also the first time that the impact of affect-sensitive closed-loop interaction between a robot and children with ASD has been demonstrated experimentally.

The presented work requires physiological sensing that has its own limitations. For example, one needs to wear physiological sensors, and use of such sensors could be restrictive under certain circumstances. Given the rapid progress in physiological sensing clothing and accessories (Picard, 1997), we believe that physiology-based affect recognition can be appropriate and useful for the application of interactive autism intervention and could be used conjunctively with other modalities (e.g., visual and audio) to allow flexible and robust affective modeling for children with ASD. Moreover, none of the participants in this study had any objection to wearing the physiological sensors.

Future work will involve designing socially-directed interaction experiments that address the social communication deficits of children with ASD. We will investigate how to augment the interactive autism intervention by having an intelligent system (e.g., computer, VR environment, or robot) respond appropriately to the inferred affects based on the affective model described here. Specifically, we plan to integrate the real-time affect recognition and response system described in this research with a life-like android face developed by Hanson Robotics (www.hansonrobotics.com) and separately with an interactive virtual reality environment developed with Vizard software (www.worldviz.com). These intelligent systems can produce accurate examples of common facial expressions that convey affective states. This affective information could be used as feedback for empathy exercises to help children recognize their own emotions. Enhancements on the intervention process could also be envisioned. For instance, the intelligent system could exhibit interesting behaviors to retain the child's attention when it detects his/her liking level is low. Additionally, we will investigate fast and robust learning mechanisms that would permit an intelligent system's adaptive response in the more complex interaction tasks.

6. Appendix

6.1 Pattern recognition using support vector machines

SVM, pioneered by Vapnik (1998), is an excellent tool for classification (Burges, 1998). Its appeal lies in its strong association with statistical learning theory as it approximates the structural risk minimization principle. Good generalization performance can be achieved by maximizing the margin, where margin is defined as the sum of the distances of the hyperplane from the nearest data points of each of the two classes. SVM is a linear machine working in a high k-dimensional feature space formed by an implicit embedding of n-dimensional input data X (e.g., a vector of derived physiology features as described in Section 3.2.4) into a k-dimensional feature space ($k > n$) through the use of a nonlinear mapping $\phi(X)$. This allows for the use of linear algebra and geometry to separate the data, which is normally only separable with nonlinear rules in the input space. The problem of finding a linear classifier for given data points with known class labels can be described as finding a separating hyperplane $W^T\varphi(X)$ that satisfies:

$$y_i\left(W^T\varphi(X_i)\right) = y_i\left(\sum_{j=1}^{k} w_j\phi_j(X_i) + w_0\right) \geq 1 - \xi_i \tag{1}$$

where N represents the number of training data pairs (X_i, y_i) indexed by $i = 1,2,\ldots, N$; $y_i \in \{+1, -1\}$ represents the class label (e.g., high/low intensity of a target affective state); $\varphi(X) =$

$[\phi_0(X), \phi_1(X),..., \phi_k(X)]^T$ is the mapped feature vector ($\phi_0(X) = 1$); and $W = [w_0, w_1,..., w_k]$ is the weight vector of the network. The nonnegative slack variable ξ_i generalizes the linear classifier with soft margin to deal with nonlinearly separable problems.
All operations in learning and testing modes are done in SVM using a so-called kernel function defined as $K(X_i, X) = \varphi^T(X_i)\varphi(X)$ (Vapnik, 1998). The kernel function allows for efficient computation of inner products directly in the feature space and circumvents the difficulty of specifying the non-linear mapping explicitly. The most distinctive fact about SVM is that the learning task is reduced to a dual quadratic programming problem by introducing the Lagrange multipliers α_i (Vapnik, 1998; Burges, 1998):

Maximize

$$Q(\alpha) = \sum_{i=1}^{N} \alpha_i - \frac{1}{2} \sum_{i=1}^{N} \sum_{j=1}^{N} \alpha_i \alpha_j y_i y_j K(X_i, X_j) \tag{2}$$

Subject to

$$\sum_{i=1}^{N} \alpha_i y_i = 0 \quad \text{and} \quad 0 \le \alpha_i \le C$$

where C is a user-defined regularization parameter that determines the balance between the complexity of the network characterized by the weight vector W and the error of classification of data. The corresponding α_i multipliers are only non-zero for the support vectors (i.e., the training points nearest to the hyperplane), which induces solution sparseness. The SVM approach is able to deal with noisy data and over-fitting by allowing for some misclassifications on the training set (Burges, 1998). This characteristic makes it particularly suitable for affect recognition because the physiology data is noisy and the training set size is often small. Another important feature of SVM is that the quadratic programming leads in all cases to the global minimum of the cost function. With the kernel representation and soft margin mechanism, SVM provides an efficient technique that can tackle the difficult, high dimensional affect recognition problem.

6.2 Behavior adaptation using QV-learning

QV-learning (Wiering, 2005), a variant of the standard reinforcement learning algorithm Q-learning (Watkins and Dayan, 1992), was applied to achieve the affect-sensitive behavior adaptation. QV-learning keeps track of both a Q-function and a V-function. The Q-function represents the utility value $Q(s, a)$ for every possible pair of state s and action a. The V-function indicates the utility value $V(s)$ for each state s. The state value $V(s_t)$ and Q-value $Q(s_t, a_t)$ at step t are updated after each experience (s_t, a_t, r_t, s_{t+1}) by:

$$V(s_t) := V(s_t) + \alpha\left(r_t + \gamma V(s_{t+1}) - V(s_t)\right) \tag{3}$$

$$Q(s_t, a_t) := Q(s_t, a_t) + \alpha\left(r_t + \gamma V(s_{t+1}) - Q(s_t, a_t)\right) \tag{4}$$

where r_t is the received reward that measures the desirability of the action a_t when it is applied on state s_t and causes the system to evolve to state s_{t+1}. The difference between (4) and the conventional Q-learning rule is that QV-learning uses V-values learned in (3) and is not defined solely in terms of Q-values. Since $V(s)$ is updated more often than $Q(s, a)$, QV-learning may permit a fast learning process (Wiering, 2005) and enable the intelligent system to efficiently find a behavior selection policy during interaction.

7. Acknowledgements

The authors gratefully acknowledge the MARI (Marino Autism Research Institute) grant, the staff support from the Vanderbilt Treatment and Research Institute for Autism Spectrum Disorders for guidance during the development of experiments involving children with ASD, and the parents and children who participated in the presented research.

8. References

American Psychiatric Association. (2000). *Diagnostic and statistical manual of mental disorders: DSM-IV-TR (4th ed.)*. American Psychiatric Association. Washington, DC

Asha, K., Ajay, K., Naznin, V., George, T., & Peter, F. D. (2005). Gesture-based affective computing on motion capture data, *Proceedings of the Int. Conf. on Affective Computing and Intelligent Interaction*, Beijing, China

Barkley, R. A. (1998). *Attention deficit hyperactivity disorder: A handbook for diagnosis and treatment (2 ed.)*. Guilford Press. New York, NY

Bartlett, M. S., Littlewort, G., Fasel, I., & Movellan, J. R. (2003). Real time face detection and facial expression recognition: development and applications to human computer interaction, *Proceedings of the Computer Vision and Pattern Recognition Workshop*, Madison, Wisconsin

Bee, H. & Boyd, D. (2004). *The Developing Child. (10th ed.)*. Pearson. Boston

Ben Shalom, D., Mostofsky, S. H., Hazlett, R. L., Goldberg, M. C., Landa, R. J., Faran, Y., McLeod, D. R., & Hoehn-Saric, R. (2006). Normal physiological emotions but differences in expression of conscious feelings in children with high-functioning autism. *J Autism Dev Disord*, 36(3):395-400

Bernard-Opitz, V., Sriram, N., & Nakhoda-Sapuan, S. (2001). Enhancing social problem solving in children with autism and normal children through computer-assisted instruction. *J Autism Dev Disord*, 31(4):377-384

Bradley, M. M. (2000). Emotion and motivation, In: *Handbook of Psychophysiology*, J. T. Cacioppo, L. G. Tassinary & G. Berntson, (Eds.), 602-642, Cambridge University Press. New York, NY

Brown, R. M., Hall, L. R., Holtzer, R., Brown, S. L., & Brown, N. L. (1997). Gender and video game performance. *Sex Roles*, 36(11-12):793 - 812

Burges, C. J. C. (1998). A tutorial on Support Vector Machines for pattern recognition. *Data Mining and Knowledge Discovery*, 2(2):121-167

Cacioppo, J.T., Berntson, G.G., Larsen, J.T., Poehlmann, K.M., & Ito, T.A. (2000). The psychophysiology of emotion, In: *Handbook of Emotions*, Lewis, M., & Haviland-Jones, J.M., (Eds.), The Guilford Press. New York, NY

Cowie, R., Douglas-Cowie, E., Tsapatsoulis, N., Votsis, G., Kollias, S., Fellenz, W., & Taylor, J. (2001). Emotion recognition in human-computer interaction. *IEEE Signal Processing Magazine*, 18(1):32-80

Dautenhahn, K., & Werry, I. (2004). Towards interactive robots in autism therapy: background, motivation and challenges. *Pragmatics & Cognition*, 12(1):1-35

Dautenhahn, K., Werry, I., Salter, T., Boekhorst, R. T. (2003). Towards Adaptive Autonomous Robots in

Autism Therapy: Varieties of Interactions, *IEEE International Symposium on Computational Intelligence in Robotics and Automation*, Kobe

Dawson, M. E., Schell, A. M., & Filion, D. L. (1990). The Electrodermal System. In: *Principles of Psychophysiology: Physical, Social, and Inferential Elements,* Cacioppo, J.T., & Tassinary, L.G., (Eds.), Cambridge University Press. Cambridge, MA

Dunn, L. M., & Dunn, L. M. (1997). *PPVT-III: Peabody Picture Vocabulary Test-Third Edition.*American Guidance Service. Circle Pines, Minnesota

Ernsperger, L. (2003). *Keys to Success for Teaching Students with Autism.* Future Horizons

Fong, T., Nourbakhsh, I., & Dautenhahn, K. (2003). A survey of socially interactive robots. *Robotics and Autonomous Systems,* 42(3-4):143-166

Gillott, A., Furniss, F., & Walter, A. (2001). Anxiety in high-functioning children with autism. *Autism,* 5(3):277-286

Green, D., Baird, G., Barnett, A. L., Henderson, L., Huber, J., & Henderson, S. E. (2002). The severity and nature of motor impairment in Asperger's syndrome: a comparison with Specific Developmental Disorder of Motor Function. *Journal of Child Psychology and Psychiatry and Allied Disciplines,* 43(5):655-668

Groden, J., Goodwin, M. S., Baron, M. G., Groden, G., Velicer, W. F., Lipsitt, L. P., Hofmann, S. G., & Plummer, B. (2005). Assessing Cardiovascular Responses to Stressors in Individuals with Autism Spectrum Disorders. *Focus on Autism and Other Developmental Disabilities,* 20(4):244-252

Jacobson, J.W., Mulick, J. A., & Green, G. (1998). Cost-benefit estimates for early intensive behavioral intervention for young children with autism - General model and single state case. *Behavioral Interventions,* 13:201-206

Kataoka, H., Kano, H., Yoshida, H., Saijo, A., Yasuda, M., & Osumi, M. (1998). Development of a skin temperature measuring system for non-contact stress evaluation. *IEEE Ann. Conf. Engineering Medicine Biology Society*

Kleinsmith, A., Fushimi, T., & Bianchi-Berthouze, N. (2005). An incremental and interactive affective posture recognition system, *Proceedings of the UM 2005 Workshop: Adapting the Interaction Style to Affective Factors,* Edinburgh, United Kingdom

Kozima, H., Nakagawa, C., & Yasuda, Y. (2005). Interactive robots for communication-care: A case-study in autism therapy, *Proceedings of the IEEE International Workshop on Robot and Human Interactive Communication,* Nashville, Tennessee, August

Kulic, D., & Croft, E. (2007). Physiological and subjective responses to articulated robot motion. *Robotica,* 25:13-27

Lacey, J. I., & Lacey, B. C. (1958). Verification and extension of the principle of autonomic response-stereotypy. *Am J Psychol,* 71(1):50-73

Lee, C. M., & Narayanan, S. S. (2005). Toward detecting emotions in spoken dialogs. *IEEE Transactions on Speech and Audio Processing,* 13(2):293-303

Liu, C., Rani, P., & Sarkar, N. (2006). Human-Robot interaction using affective cues. *Proceedings of the International Symposium on Robot and Human Interactive Communication,* Hatfield, United Kingdom

Mandryk, R. L., & Atkins, M. S. (2007). A fuzzy physiological approach for continuously modeling emotion during interaction with play technologies. *International Journal of Human-Computer Studies,* 65(4):329-347

Michaud, F. & Theberge-Turmel, C. (2002). Mobile robotic toys and autism. In: *Socially Intelligent Agents: Creating Relationships with Computers and Robots,* K. Dautenhahn, A. H. Bond, L. Canamero, and B. Edmonds, (Eds.), 125-132, Kluwer Academic Publishers

Moore, D. J., McGrath, P., & Thorpe, J. (2000). Computer aided learning for people with autism - A framework for research and development. *Innovations in Education and Training International*, 37(3):218-228

Papillo, J.F., & Shapiro, D., (1990). The cardiovascular system. In: *Principles of Psychophysiology: Physical, Social, and Inferential Elements,* Cacioppo, J.T., & Tassinary, L.G., (Eds.), Cambridge University Press. Cambridge, MA

Pares, N., Masri, P., van Wolferen, G., & Creed, C. (2005). Achieving dialogue with children with severe autism in an adaptive multisensory interaction: the "MEDIAte" project. *IEEE Trans Vis Comput Graph,* 11:734-743

Parsons, S., & Mitchell, P. (2002). The potential of virtual reality in social skills training for people with autistic spectrum disorders. *J Intellect Disabil Res,* 46(Pt 5):430-443

Parsons, S., Mitchell, P., & Leonard, A. (2005). Do adolescents with autistic spectrum disorders adhere to social conventions in virtual environments? *Autism,* 9(1):95-117

Pecchinenda, A., & Smith, C. A. (1996). The affective significance of skin conductance activity during a difficult problem-solving task. *Cogn. and Emotion,* 10(5):481-504

Picard, R. W. (1997). *Affective Computing*. The MIT Press. Cambridge, MA

Picard, R. W., Vyzas, E., & Healey, J. (2001). Toward machine emotional intelligence: Analysis of affective physiological state. *IEEE Transactions on Pattern Analysis and Machine Intelligence,* 23(10):1175-1191

Pioggia, G., Igliozzi, R., Ferro, M., Ahluwalia, A., Muratori, F., & De Rossi, D. (2005). An android for enhancing social skills and emotion recognition in people with autism. *IEEE Transactions on Neural Systems and Rehabilitation Engineering,* 13(4):507-515.

Rani, P., Liu, C., & Sarkar, N. (2006a). Affective feedback in closed loop human-robot interaction. *Proceeding of the 1st ACM SIGCHI/SIGART Conference on Human-Robot interaction,* Salt Lake City, Utah, USA, March

Rani, P., Liu, C. C., Sarkar, N., & Vanman, E. (2006b). An empirical study of machine learning techniques for affect recognition in human-robot interaction. *Pattern Analysis and Applications,* 9(1):58-69

Rani, P., Sarkar, N., Smith, C. A., & Kirby, L. D. (2004). Anxiety detecting robotic system - towards implicit human-robot collaboration. *Robotica,* 22:85-95

Reeves, B., & Nass, C. I. (1996). *The media equation: how people treat computers, televisions, and new media as real people and places.* Cambridge University Press. New York, NY

Robins, B., Dickerson, P., & Dautenhahn, K. (2005). Robots as embodied beings – Interactionally sensitive body movements in interactions among autistic children and a robot, *Proceedings of the 14th IEEE International Workshop on Robot and Human Interactive Communication,* Nashville, Tennessee, August

Robins, B., Dickerson, P., Stribling, P., & Dautenhahn, K. (2004). Robot-mediated joint attention in children with autism: A case study in robot-human interaction. *Interaction Studies,* 5(2):161–198

Rogers, S. J. (1998). Empirically supported comprehensive treatments for young children with autism. *J Clin Child Psychol,* 27(2):168-179

Ruble, L. A., & Robson, D. M. (2006). Individual and Environmental Determinants of Engagement in Autism. *J Autism Dev Disord.*

Rutter, M. (2006). Autism: its recognition, early diagnosis, and service implications. *J Dev Behav Pediatr,* 27(2 Suppl):S54-58

Scassellati, B. (2005). Quantitative metrics of social response for autism diagnosis, *Proc. IEEE International Workshop on Robot and Human Interactive Communication*, Nashville, Tennessee, August

Schultz, R.T. (2005). Developmental deficits in social perception in autism: the role of the amygdala and fusiform face area. *Int J Dev Neurosci*, 23:125-41

Seip, J. A. (1996). *Teaching the autistic and developmentally delayed: A guide for staff training and development*. Delta. British Columbia

Siegel, S., & Castellan, J. N. J. (1988). *Nonparametric Statistics for the Behavioral Sciences*. McGraw-Hill. New York, NY

Silver, M., & Oakes, P. (2001). Evaluation of a new computer intervention to teach people with autism or Asperger syndrome to recognize and predict emotions in others. *Autism*, 5(3):299-316

Swettenham, J. (1996). Can children with autism be taught to understand false belief using computers? *J Child Psychol Psychiatry*, 37(2):157-165

Tarkan, L. (October 21, 2002). Autism therapy is called effective, but rare. *New York Times*

Toichi, M., & Kamio, Y. (2003). Paradoxical autonomic response to mental tasks in autism. *J Autism Dev Disord*, 33(4):417-426

Trepagnier, C. Y., Sebrechts, M. M., Finkelmeyer, A., Stewart, W., Woodford, J., & Coleman, M. (2006). Simulating social interaction to address deficits of autistic spectrum disorder in children. *Cyberpsychol Behav*, 9(2):213-217

Vansteelandt, K., Van Mechelen, I., & Nezlek, J. B. (2005). The co-occurrence of emotions in daily life: A multilevel approach. *Journal of Research in Personality*, 39(3):325-335

Vapnik, V. N. (1998). *Statistical Learning Theory*. Wiley-Interscience. New York, NY

Watkins, C. J. C. H. & Dayan, P. (1992). Q-Learning. *Machine Learning*, 8, May

Werry I, Dautenhahn K, & Harwin W. (2001). Investigating a robot as a therapy partner for children with autism, *Proceedings of the 6th European conference for the advancement of assistive technology*, Ljubljana, Slovenia

Wieder, S., & Greenspan, S. (2005). Can Children with Autism Master the Core Deficits and Become Empathetic, Creative, and Reflective? *The Journal of Developmental and Learning Disorders*, 9

Wiering, M. A. (2005). QV (λ)-learning: A New On-policy Reinforcement Learning Algorithm, *European Workshop on Reinforcement Learning*, Napoli, Italy, October

21

Authoring Emotion

Nelson Zagalo, Rui Prada, Isabel Machado Alexandre and Ana Torres
Department of Communication Sciences, University of Minho
IST-Technical University of Lisbon and INESC-ID
Department of Science and Information Technologies, ISCTE and ADETTI
Department of Communication and Art, University of Aveiro

1. Chapter short description

It is wide accepted that emotion "guides perception, increases the selectivity of attention, helps determine the content of working memory, in sum, it motivate, organize and sustain particular sets of behaviours" (Izard e Ackerman, 2000:254). Therefore, emotion is a very powerful strategy to achieve the attention and the information retention of other people with whom we communicate. In fields as Entertainment, it is important for the creation of engagement with fiction because it strongly depends of the interest and attention of the viewers (Plantinga, 1999). Also in fields as Education, Health and Security, in which it is important to have people alertness and memorising new inputs, it is also highly relevant to catch attention of users. Examples as teaching how to follow health prescriptions; teaching difficult/boring matters; or teaching how we must react in emergencies demonstrates the need to have emotion authoring tools accessible and easy to use by people with little technology skills.

In this chapter, we will discuss the development of a plug-in for two authoring tools: Inscape[1] and Teatrix[2]. The plug-in aims at helping authors to easily create virtual interactive stories that explore the emotional dimension of characters and scenes in order to contribute to higher coherence of stories and simultaneously emphasize their communication purposes.

The focus discussed here is on the cognitive architecture for autonomous agents that play the characters. This architecture uses two main drives to decision making: (1) it makes use of emotions, based in Frijda's "emotion theory" (1986); (2) as well as a model of characters' roles proposed by Propp (1968). Characters' behaviour is, therefore, induced simultaneously by the intentions of the author, that specifies characters' roles and the emotions each scene should convey, and by the characters' own emotional experience while interacting with other characters in the story. The integration of both types of influence on characters' behaviour is crucial in systems, such as Teatrix, where users may play characters. The goal is to keep the author with some control over the story but at the same time not limit the user participation, since this would damage her/his interaction experience. This direct influence on the behaviour of the characters, and indirectly on the story, features the concept of

---

[1] Inscape is an authoring platform being developed in an EC-FP6 project.

[2] Teatrix is a tool that for helping children in the creation of stories.

agency defined by Murray (1997). This approach was already applied in Teatrix, since it merged the actor, author and spectator roles (Machado, 2004). Users were invited *to act* in an interactive story along with the other characters (autonomous characters controlled by the architecture or by other users), to create/author such a story by acting in it and to understand the others characters' actions - being a spectator - in order to respond to their behaviours. This new concept aims at overcoming one of the typical problems of interactive narratives/stories - *the higher degree of freedom that is given to the user to intervene in the narrative flow, the weaker is the power given to the author to decide on the progress of the story* (Clarke & Mitchell, 2001) - since the users and authors of the story are the same.

2. Authoring mode

We developed a plug-in to work with INSCAPE authoring platform and have been working on adapting it for the Teatrix platform, enhancing the characters affective autonomy. The plug-in is an authoring module that can orchestrate the main audiovisual aspects and then improve emotionality in virtual world scenes, characters and interactivity (Zagalo, 2007).
The communication model (see Fig. 1) behind the plug-in is defined as a group of templates that can be used to quickly generate atmospheres in story representations. The author is the person that starts the process and that uses the plug-in to build a more affective artefact and so reach more easily the *experiencer*. The author always has the final word in the entire process; deciding to use nothing, partially or fully what is proposed by the plug-in. On the other side, the *experiencer* approaches the final artefact in two different ways in affective terms, perceptually and emotionally. In the former, the *experiencer* can recognize the sequences as attached to specific affective states but not feel them. In the latter, the *experiencer* feels the emotions expressed by these affective states represented (consciously or unconsciously).

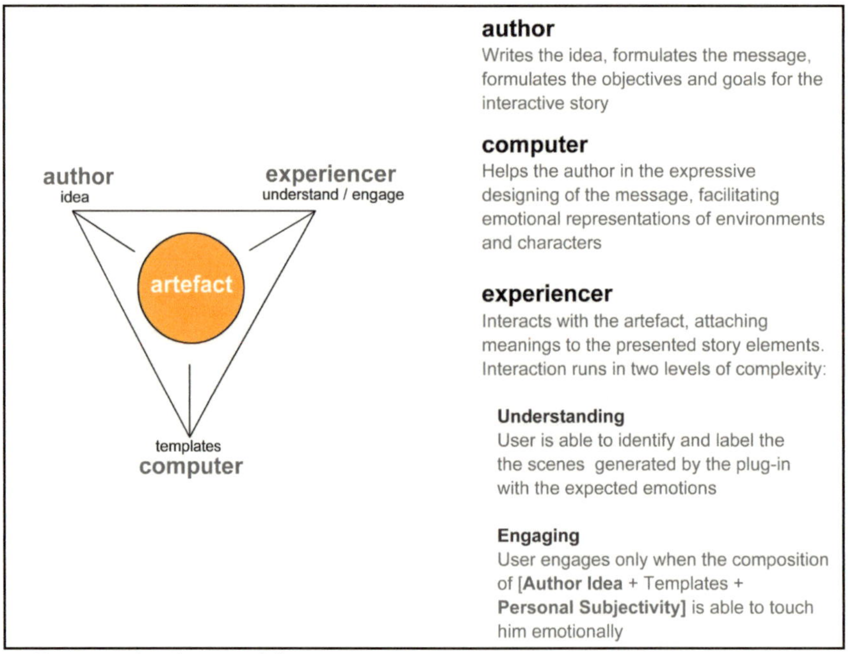

Figure 1. - Communication model

The plug-in is then targeted at producing a semantic intervention in the story that doesn't intend to transcend the storyteller work. The aim is to help authors to easily create interactive scenes that are identified by the authors and *experiencers* as attached to a specific type of atmosphere label and simultaneously to emphasize the communication process. The authoring intervention develops a pedagogical facet permitting the learning by the story authors about potential emotional uses of specific parameters.

The templates used by the plugin were made of audiovisual storytelling classes researched accordingly to their emotional impact in viewer. For the environment classes (see Table 1) they were firstly derived from Smith (2003) and were then verified through one or more authors (Block, 2001; Douglass & Harnden, 1996; Eisenstein, 1957; Mamet, 1992; Sonnenschein, 2001; Van Sijll, 2005). For the character's classes (see Table 1) we began within a theoretical approach from film studies (Smith, 1996) and videogames (Sheldon, 2004), then we have filtered this knowledge through communication theory (Knapp & Hall, 1997) and psychology (Argyle, 1975).

ENVIRONMENTS
Camera
Lenses, Motion, Position
Editing
Cuts and Pace
Time
Continuity and Variation
Frame
Composition and Shape
Screen Direction
3 axes (Up-Down; Left-Right; Back-
Music/Sound Qualities
Intensity, Pitch, Rhythm, Speed, Shape
Lighting
Motivation, Contrast, Tone
Color
Hue, Brightness, Saturation
Design Effects
Visual and Aural

CHARACTERS
Character's Space
Intimate, Personal, Social, Public
Physical Features
Clothes, Skin, Hair, Weight, Height
Body Movement
Posture, Gestures
Facial Expression
Face and Eyes
Touch
Types
Vocal Aspects
Tone, Types
Apparent Personality
Extraversion, Agreeableness, Consciousness, Neuroticism, Openness

Table 1. Environment and character's classes

All these classes were made part of a film content analysis study (Zagalo, 2007) performed with filmmakers and scriptwriters. The research conducted us to the creation of a storytelling affective parameters database. The plug-in then uses this database to act upon the environments and characters mixing different levels of expressivity. In terms of authoring the author can control an array of parameters through a simple set of sliders.

Thus, using a direct interface, the user is completely free to change the world and characters as he likes and in a much more straightforward way. Using one slider to add the percentage he wants, seeing 100% effect and deciding in real time to reduce it to only 25% of the effect if required. In addition, the user can consider mixing various emotional categories to attain the expressivity s/he prefers for the ideal scene s/he is building.

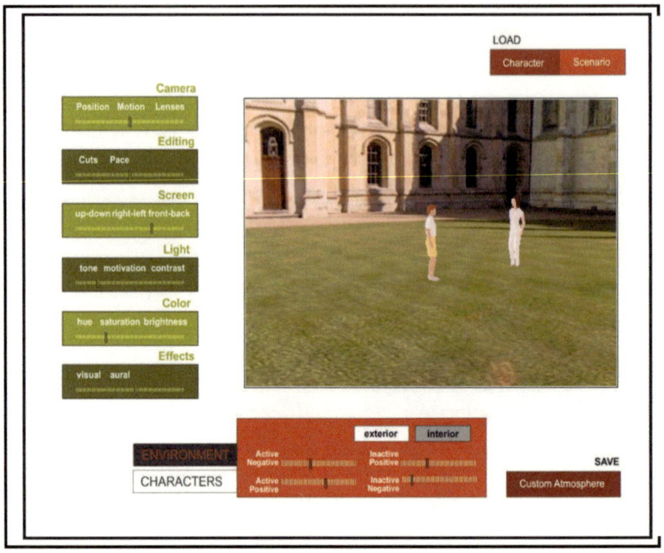

Figure 2. - The authoring plug-in interface

In terms of storytelling we can see in the fig. 3, this is a software module designed to act on form, and most specifically on story stylistics. This is a conscious choice in order to avoid the problem of entering the context and thematic domains, and also to avoid interfering too much with the Author core information message. With this storytelling approach, the author continues to be responsible for producing the idea, developing it and then, choosing the elements and interactions accordingly to needs.

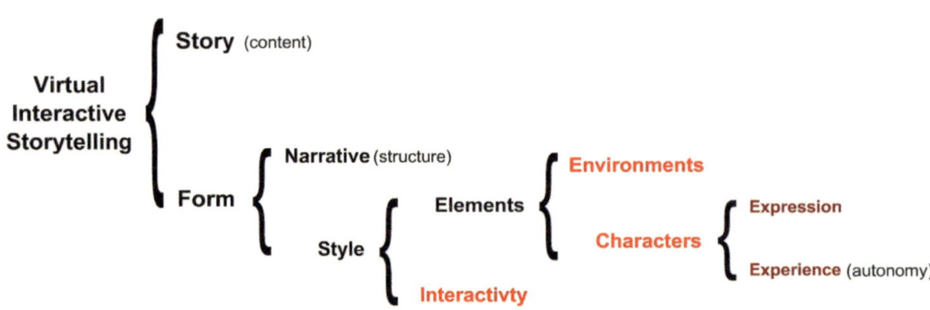

Figure 3 - The implementation process in the storytelling

Thus this leaves us with three variables to be effected by the authoring module - Environments, Characters and Interactivity - without causing direct interference in the author's work. For the authoring of characters, the author can start by assigning a predefined role accordingly to Propp (1968). This choice takes effect on the personality and so on cognitive model adopted by the agent, but then we have two emotion variables -

Expression and Experience. The Characters' expression refers to the visual expressions and movements performed by the characters in response to the emotional experience of the world. The experience encompasses the interpretation of the character/agent upon the stimulus received through own sensors of the world.
Next we'll explain the agent's architecture responsible for the character's interpretation and expression within the virtual world.

3. Agents' architecture

The architecture that drives characters' (*dramatis personae)* behaviour follows the approach of an agent being divided into well-defined parts: *mind* and *body* (see Fig. 4).
The *mind* component is responsible for cognitive activities of the agent, while the *body* component has as major function to receive and send directives to and from the story creation application. Usually, this component is also responsible for managing the physical appearance of the agent, but that representation is dependent on the specificity and requirements of story creation application, i.e., it is implemented within the application context. Nevertheless, within our architecture the bodies of the *dramatis personae* have a different interpretation and a different functioning because as *dramatis personae* they sense their world, process such information according to their reasoning processes and act in accordance with it. The body defines a set of sensors and actuators that are connected to the story world in order to enable the agent to receive the perceptions of what happened in the story and to send the action directives regarding the changes they want to produce in the story.

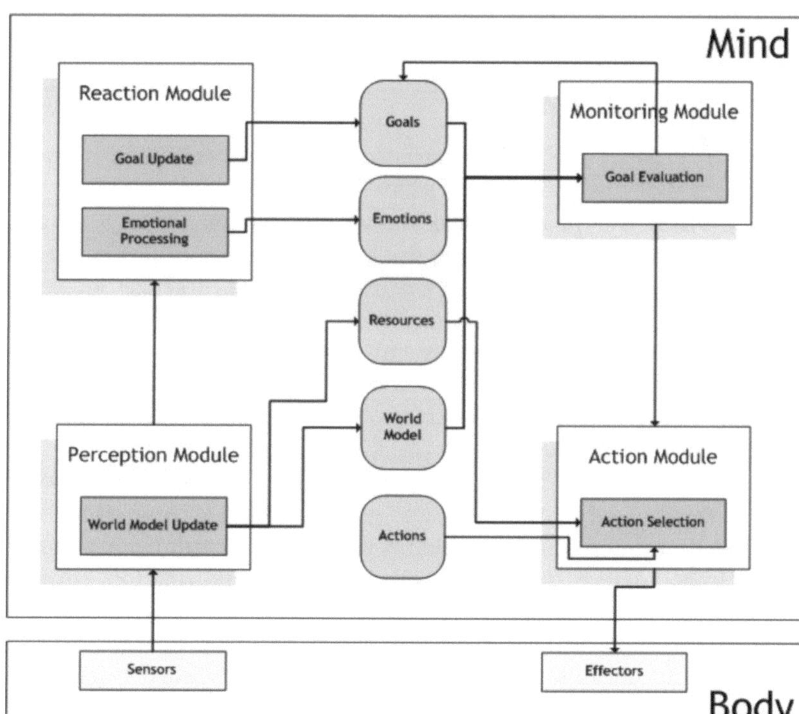

Figure 4. - Dramatis personae Architecture

This architecture is an extension of SAGA (Support And Guidance Architecture) and follows the work of C. Martinho (Martinho & Paiva, 1999), which had as its main goal the development of believable emotional agents – *pathematic* agents, and more specifically in Teatrix's story characters' architecture (Prada *et al.*, 2000). It is centred on the development of believable role-based characters, which play their specific roles in a particular story, adding an emotional perspective of their self experience in the story world.
The development of the *dramatis personae*'s behaviour is carried out according to a continuous cycle that goes from receiving a perception to the directive of performing an action by the agent's effectors. In the next sections, the different phases of the cycle are presented.

4. Perception phase (perception module)

In the Perception Phase, the dramatis personae's mind receives a perception from the story world. The perceptions received can contain several kinds of information: (1) an action performed in the story world by a particular dramatis personae; (2) an event describing the state of the story world, or an alteration of such state, e.g. a dramatis personae that entered a different scenario; (3) the introduction of a new prop in the story world.
By taking into account this perception, the dramatis personae decides if some change should be made to its internal world model. The world model contains the dramatis personae's point of view of the story world, i.e., the data contained in the world model corresponds to the perceptions received by the dramatis personae during the story evolution. Therefore, the dramatis personae constructs its world model from the events and actions already perceived.

5. Reaction phase (reaction module)

During the Reaction Phase, the character updates its internal structures, namely: the set of *goals*, the *physiological state*, and its *emotional state*.

- **Physiological state:** the physiological model comes from the need to incorporate internal states such as energy or "magical power" if , for example, the story allows characters to cast spells. These states can be used to control the level of activity of characters in the story, for example: (1) a character can be turned into *invisible*, it stays in the story but can only start to act if some magical prop is used and reverses this state; (2) it can be *immobilised*, being visible in the story world but without the possibility to perform any action, but could be saved by others; (3) or *neutralized*, being killed in the story, staying forever *immobilised*.
- **Goals:** in the reaction phase the character deliberates if it must alter its internal goals in accordance with the data received from its perception of the situation. Since this perception has been filtered in the previous phase, it is almost certain to have an effect on the character's active goals. Depending on the information contained in the perception, the character may have to deal with three different situations:
  1. *the information validates its current goal, and it continues to seek its attainment.* This validation only permits that the agent can proceed with the achievement of the current goal, i.e., meaning that the actions being performed are being successful and that the conditions for the further execution of the actions associated with such goal still verify;

2. *the information confirms the successful achievement of the current goal,* meaning that the current plot point was achieved by the character;
3. *the information confirms the failure of achievement of the current goal,* meaning that the story character may have to inspect its set of generic goals and choose another goal to be its current goal. This decision process is based on the assumption that its internal world model supports the necessary conditions for the goal activation.

- **Emotional state:** It is determined by the "emotion process" claimed by the cognitive appraisal theory of Frijda (Frijda, 1986). Frijda's emotion process consists into a decision system for action readiness and action determination. The core system is regulated by seven phases. Four of them are incorporated in the agent's Reaction Phase and three in the Action Phase:
  1. The first phase is an analyser that codifies events. This interpretation is based on the events acquired by the Perception Phase.
  2. In the second phase the event is evaluated according to its relevancy / irrelevancy to elicit pleasure, pain, surprise or desire. Emotions are held to arise when events are appraised as relevant to concerns[3].
  3. The third phase is a diagnostician that evaluates what can be made to cope with the event.
  4. The fourth is an evaluation system of the event strength, difficulty and seriousness. This phase is responsible to emit control sign of the results.

Frijda also argues that there are other factors responsible for the emotional responses determination (the humour, the activation state, the precedent experiences and the other people). It is also important to note that this model has a continuing feedback. Each emotion response is influenced by the precedent ones.

6. Monitoring phase (monitoring module)

All changes to the character's internal structures (e.g. goals, emotions, internal world model, physiological state) are evaluated to determine the most suitable behaviour to be carried out by the character. This behaviour may determine the need: (1) to activate a new goal, because the previous one failed to succeed or , on the contrary because it was successfully achieved; (2) to carry on with its completion of the current goal, or; (3) to trigger a reactive behaviour;
Reactive behaviours are needed to prevent the characters of performing their roles in an autistic way. The reason behind is the fact that in each story there can be autonomous and user-controlled characters. So, imagine that a user decides to direct her character in such a way that it would continuously use an attack/defence prop to harm an autonomous character. If that character did not have any particular interest in a direct interaction with the user-controlled character it would ignore the interaction and carry on with its actions. Thus, these reactive behaviours came from the need to accommodate user's needs and opinions during the story creation process. Furthermore, the introduction of reactive behaviours meets the requirements defined by Dautenhahn (1999) for a story-telling agent:

1. ability to recognise individuals;

[3] Concerns are defined "a disposition to desire occurrence or non-occurrence of a given kind of situation" (Frijda, 1986:335). It includes motives, major goals, personal sensitivities, attachments, and personal supra values.

2. ability to understand others;
3. ability to predict the behaviour of others and outcomes of interaction, and;
4. ability to remember and learn interactions with others and to build direct relationships.

The reactive behaviours are divided in two different categories:

1. **Friendly behaviours** - this apply to the behaviours taken by characters playing a compatible role to the one being played by the user-controlled character. Compatible roles are the ones shared by the characters playing roles that complement each other, in the sense that what a character contributes for the completion of another character's goals. The compatible roles are hero, donor, helper and others. This type of behaviour encompasses the friendly actions that are taken in response to a user-controlled character's interactions, such as: (1) respond in a friendly way to the questions posed by the user-controlled character; (2) share her/his goals with the user-controlled character; (3) give props that may be useful in the future actions.
2. **Unfriendly behaviours** - this category contains the behaviours taken in response of interactions elicited by incompatible roles. Incompatible roles are the ones played by the characters that have contradictory goals in the story. In saga, the incompatible roles refer to the opposition maintained by the villain character towards all the other roles. The unfriendly behaviour can be exemplified by the following actions: (1) respond in an aggressive way to the questions posed; (2) try to immobilise or neutralize the user-controlled character (e.g. by casting a spell); (3) never reveal their intentions and goals.

Additionally, there is also the need to include reactive behaviours in response to some of the plans elicited by some generic goals. For example, it is possible to detect some of these situations where the actions taken by the villain character directly affect the hero character or the beloved character, which presuppose that such characters must respond to them in some meaningful way. For example, if the villain character kidnaps the beloved character, she/he should respond in some way to this action - e.g. crying for help. To accommodate such direct interactions, it is decided that the set of active goals of such a character is added a new goal that is composed of a new plan to answer adequately to such direct interaction. It is important to say that the reactive behaviours can be primitive or non-primitive actions (see section Plans, Actions and Goals).

7. Action phase (action module)

In the Action Phase, the character has to decide which action should perform next. To support this decision the character considers the evaluation performed in the previous steps and chooses an action to execute. Before starting to execute a particular action the character must make sure that the pre-conditions for such particular action hold and that the necessary resources are available.

The choice of the action is performed in the following way. If there is not a reactive behaviour to be performed the character performs the action determined by the planning mechanism, otherwise the reactive behaviour always precede the execution of the other primitive actions. This process incorporates the last three phases of Frijda's emotion process (Frijda, 1986) already mentioned in the precedent Reaction Phase. The 3 phases corresponds to the following processes:

- The determination of the action plan, more precisely of the behaviours' sequences intended to put into action.
- The generation of the physiological change correspondent both to the emotional state originated and to the behaviours intended.
- The determination of the character action readiness to perform the action plan.

8. Roles

Each character has a role to play in the story, which was derived from the work of Propp which identified a set of functions that can be understood as both the actions of the characters and the consequences of these actions for the story. These functions are distributed among seven types of characters, such as villain, donor, helper, princess and father, dispatcher, hero and, false hero (see Table 2).

Character Type	Functions
Villain	villainy, struggle, pursuit, chase
Donor	1st donor function, receipt of agent
Helper	spatial change, liquidation, rescue, solution, transfiguration
Princess (and father)	difficult task, branding, exposure, punishment, wedding
Dispatcher	Absentation
Hero	counteraction, hero's reaction, wedding
False hero[4]	counteraction, hero's reaction, unfounded claims

Table 2 - Mapping of Propp's Character types into functions

Although, Propp's narrative morphology has been adopted as a starting point, it is clear that some of the functions must be adapted to today's reality and the context of usage. To accomplish this, the concept of function was extended to the concept of plot point - an important moment in the story (Mateas, 1999). At this stage, we go a step further in the specification of plot points and we establish that associated with each plot point is a set of generic goals. A generic goal is nothing more than a deeper elaboration of what the plot point stands for. For example, the plot point villainy has five associated different generic goals: theft, kidnapping someone, casting of a spell, imprisonment, and an order to kill/murder someone. Within each set, each generic goal is equally valid for reaching a particular plot point.

9. Plans, goals and actions

The goal structure is determined by the character's role in the story. The set of *goals* is determined by the set of *generic goals* associated with a specific *plot point*. Each of the generic goals is translated into a plan that guarantees the achievement of the correspondent plot point. At each moment, a *dramatis personae* has one active goal to pursuit. The methodology

[4] A false hero represents a character that pretends to be the hero and take his credits.

chosen for the definition of the plans associated with the generic goals was the Hierarchical Task Network (HTN) planning that creates plans by task decomposition.

Within our approach, the development of the story model was based on a hierarchical strategy - we started to define the major components of the model (the *functions* that were then *promoted* into *plot points*) and then to divide these *plot points* into smaller pieces that allowed their successful achievement.

Following the research of Kambhampati and his colleagues (Mali & Kambhampati, 1998), we assumed that there is no need to start from scratch to define a formalisation for HTN. The research followed by Kambhampati is based on the principle that most real-world domains tend to be *partially hierarchical*, which implies that a planner should apply an hybrid approach of using the reduction knowledge where possible and defaulting to primitive actions for other situations. The HTN approach here presented and applied is an extension of the action-based planning developed by (Kambhampati & Srivastava, 1995) to cover HTN planning (Kambhampati *et al.*, 1998). To these authors, HTN planning can be seen as a generalization of the classical planning problem where in addition to the primitive actions in the domain, the domain writer also specifies a set of non-primitive actions, and provides schemas for reducing the non-primitive actions into other primitive or non-primitive actions (Kambhampati *et al.*, 1998). It is a process where the tasks (non-primitive actions) are decomposed into smaller subtasks until primitive actions are found that can be performed directly (Tsuneto *et al.*, 1998; Kambhampati *et al.*, 1998).

To present this approach we start by introducing the notions of planning problem and partial plan. A planning problem is a 3-tuple $<\mathcal{I}, \mathcal{G}, \mathcal{A}>$ where:

- $\mathcal{I}$ is the complete description of an initial state;
- $\mathcal{G}$ is the partial description of the goal state, and;
- $\mathcal{A}$ is a set of actions (also called operators). An action sequence $\mathcal{S}$ is said to be a solution for the planning problem, if $\mathcal{S}$ can be executed from $\mathcal{I}$ and the resulting state of the world implies $\mathcal{G}$.

A partial plan $\boldsymbol{p}$ can be described in the form of a 5-tuple $<\mathcal{T}, \mathcal{O}, \mathcal{B}, \mathcal{ST}, \mathcal{L}>$ where:

- $\mathcal{T}$ represents a set of steps in the plan;
- $\mathcal{O}$ represents a set of ordering constraints;
- $\mathcal{B}$ represents a set of binding constraints on variables appearing in the pre and post conditions;
- $\mathcal{ST}$ maps a set of names to actions, and;
- $\mathcal{L}$ represents a set of auxiliary constraints that involve statements about truth of the specific conditions over particular time intervals.

The only extension required to the above definition of a partial plan representation to allow HTN planning is to include non-primitive actions into the plan. In particular, the steps $\mathcal{T}$ in the partial plan $<\mathcal{T}, \mathcal{O}, \mathcal{B}, \mathcal{ST}, \mathcal{L}>$ can map two types of actions: *primitive actions*, which correspond to the usual executable actions and *non-primitive actions*. These non-primitive actions have similar preconditions/effects structure as the primitive actions. The domain specification links each non-primitive action o to a set of reduction schemas. Each reduction schema S_i can be seen as a 2-tuple: $<\mathcal{P}_i, \mathcal{M}_i^{\mathcal{L}}>$ where $\mathcal{P}_i$ is the partial plan fragment which can replace o, and $\mathcal{M}_i^{\mathcal{L}}$ redirects the auxiliary constraints involving steps of $\mathcal{P}_i$.

Therefore, given a non-primitive action (also denoted as task) to accomplish, the planner chooses an applicable schema, instantiates it to decompose the non-primitive action into other non-primitive actions (also called as subtasks), and then chooses and instantiates other schemas to decompose the subtasks even further. If the constraints on the subtasks or the

interactions among them prevent the plan from being feasible, the planner will backtrack and try other schemas.
The first step of the application of HTN Planning in our architecture is the definition of the ***HTN domain description***. This definition aims at defining which are the primitive and non-primitive actions of the domain. The set of primitive actions considered are:

- ***Walk to*** *entity*, specifies that a character performs the action *walk* towards the *entity* (e.g. character **A walks to** character **B**);
- ***Talk with*** *character*, specifies that a character performs the action *talk* with the character (e.g. character **A talks with** character **B**);
- ***Give*** *prop* [***to*** *character*], specifies that a character performs the action *give* with the object being *prop* and the target of such action the *entity* (e.g. character **A gives** prop **x to** character **B**). If this action is performed without a target *character*, it means that the character drops *prop* and it is available in the story world - more specifically in a particular scene.
- ***Get*** *prop*, specifies that a character performs the action *get* with the target being *entity* (e.g. character **A gets** entity **x**). The props must have the property of being portable. When a character *gets* a particular *prop* it is assumed that it keeps it in its possession for later use.
- ***Use*** *prop* ***on*** *entity*, specifies that a character performs the action *use* of *prop* on *entity* (e.g. character **A uses** prop **x on** character **B**), and;
- ***Activate*** *prop*, specifies that a character performs the action *activate* of a specific *prop* (e.g. character **A activates** prop **x**). The props must have the property of being activated, for example: activate a door would mean to open if it is closed and to close if it is opened.

Table 3 presents the complete set of the primitive actions and their pre-conditions and effects.

PRIMITIVE ACTION	PRE-CONDITION	EFFECT
WALK_TO(X,Y)[5]		NEAR(X,Y)
TALK_WITH(X, TXT)[6]		
TALK_WITH(X, TXT, Y)	NEAR(X,Y)	
GIVE(X, A, Y)	HAS(X,A) AND NEAR(X, Y)	HAS(Y, A) AND NOT(HAS(X,A))
GIVE(X,A)	HAS(X,A)	NOT(HAS(X,A))[7]
GET(X,A)	IS_PORTABLE(A)	HAS(X,A)
USE(X,A, Y)	HAS(X,A) AND NEAR(X, Y)	DEPENDS ON THE TYPE OF PROP A
ACTIVATE(X,A)	NOT(ACTIVE (A)) AND NEAR(X,Y)	ACTIVE(A)

Table 3. - Primitive Actions

[5] Consider that X, Y denote a character and A a prop.
[6] Consider that TXT denotes the text being spoken.
[7] The object A is now available in the story world.

As one can realise from this set of primitive actions, the effect of some of the actions depend on the props used, mainly in actions *use* and *activate*. The specification of such details is performed by the *client* application when it defined the elements of its story world.
The set of primitive actions is very limited, but has the property of being easily extended because the majority of the actions depend on the props being used in such actions. In addition, the action ***talk*** can also be extended to something more complex like speech acts, and express things like *threathen, inform*, etc.
The set of non-primitive tasks is lengthy since it represents not only the whole set of generic goals associated with each plot point, but also the non-primitive actions that compose such generic goals. Table 4 presents a sample of the set of generic goals regarding the ***villain*** role. Note that, since the character performing each of the actions (primitive or non-primitive) in the reduction schemas is the character performing the ***villain*** role we decided to omit its explicit reference in the schemas.
Each reduction schema is a an expression of the form *Decompose*(***o***, ***p***), which means that a non-primitive action ***o*** can be decomposed into a partial plan ***p*** (Russel & Norvig, 1995). The representation of a partial plan ***p*** is represented as a 4-tuple $<\mathcal{T}, \mathcal{O}, \mathcal{B}, \mathcal{L}>$, which is a simplification of the 5-tuple $<\mathcal{T}, \mathcal{O}, \mathcal{B}, \mathcal{ST}, \mathcal{L}>$ presented above. We considered that each generic goal would only have one reduction schema for its achievement.

Generic Goal	Schema
Theft: It is considered that the object of theft is the desired entity established within the story goal.	Decompose(Theft(), Plan (Steps: {s_1: LookFor(desired prop[8]); s_2: Get(desired prop)}, Orderings: {$s_1 \rightarrow s_2$}[9], Bindings: { s_2: has(villain, desired prop)}, Links: {}))
Struggle with the hero: In this case, it is assumed that the villain wants to defeat the hero character by the use of a magical entity that would prevent her/him to go further in the story. This is performed by using a magical entity that turns the hero's energy level to immobilised. This energy state is different from neutralised one, since in this state it is still possible to use another magical prop that reverses it.	Decompose(Struggle(), Plan(Steps: {s_1: LookFor(magical prop); s_2: Get(magical prop); s_3: LookFor(hero); s_4: WalkTo(hero); s_5: Use(magical prop, hero)}, Orderings: {$s_1 \rightarrow s_2, s_2 \rightarrow s_3,$ $s_3 \rightarrow s_4, s_4 \rightarrow s_5$}, Bindings: { s_2: has(villain, magical prop); s_5: $(\text{hero})_{\text{ENERGY}}$ = immobilised}, Links: {$s_2 \xrightarrow{\text{MAGICAL PROP}} s_5$}))

Table 4. - Some generic goals for the **villain** role.

[8] DESIRED PROP denotes a prop with no specification of type.
[9] $s_i \rightarrow s_j$, which is read as s_i must occur sometime before s_j (but not necessarily immediately before).

10. Conclusion and perspectives

In this paper we've presented the architecture developed to sustain a storytelling authoring plug-in module based on Propp's functions and roles with support for emotional responses. Developed for the specificities of INSCAPE and Teatrix but having in mind adaptation to work within other virtual environments authoring tools.

The integration of Propp's guidelines to drive characters' behaviour gives some control of the story to the author, but adding an emotional dimension to the same characters withdraws part of this control from the author by allowing characters to have some personal experience in the story that affects their actions. This duality is essential in systems that promote user interaction (for example, where a user can play a character), since it brings some uncertainty and flexibility to the plot defined beforehand by the author. Thus, opens the opportunity for the user to play the role of author and have a feeling of ownership of the story.

Furthermore, apart the usability tests performed with the authoring module we intend to continue the testing making use of the integrated tests. These tests will put the user within an entire mode of story development and then give the opportunity to the author to use the authoring module during the story design. The main reason for this is to test the real value of having one module that works as an intermediary of the authoring process.

Also we intend to continue working and perfecting the character models and adapt the agent behaviours to the environments. Use the environment as a general entity controlled through an agent architecture in terms of emotional actions upon the characters.

On the other side we would like to expand the authoring module with another layer related with the control of events/information in the storytelling, making use of management models (Mateas and Stern, 2005) to control the flow of events presented to the agents and players.

11. References

Argyle, M. (1975), Bodily Communication (2nd ED), Madison: International Universities Press.

Block, B. A. (2001). The visual story: Seeing the structure of film, tv, and new media.Oxford: Focal

Clarke A. and Mitchell G. (2001). Film and Development of Interactive Narrative. In Proceedings of the International Conference in Virtual Storytelling - LNCS 2197. Springer, 2001.

Dautenhahn, H. (1999). The Lemur's Tale - Story-telling in Primates and Other Socially Intelligent Agents. In the Working Notes of the Fall Symposium Series of AAAI 1999 on Narrative Intelligence, AAAI Press, Menlo Park, CA, 1999.

Douglass, J. S., & Harnden, G. P. (1996). The art of technique: An aesthetic approach to film and video production.Boston, Mass.; London: Allyn and Bacon.

Eisenstein, S. (1957). Film form.New York: Harcourt.

Frijda, N. H. (1986). The emotions. Cambridge, Cambridge University Press.

Izard, C. E. and Ackerman, B. P. (2000). Motivational, organizational and regulatory functions of discrete emotions, In *Handbook of Emotion*, Lewis, M. & Haviland-Jones, M. (Eds.), (-),New York: Guilford Press.

Kambhampati, S. and Srivastava, B. (1995). Universal Classical Planner: An algorithm for unifying state space and plan space approaches. In New Trends in AI Planning: EWSP 95, IOS Press, 1995.

Kambhampati, S.; Mali, A. and Srivastava, B. (1998). Hybrid Planning for Partially Hierarchical Domains. Proceedings of the AAAI 1998, AAAI Press, 1998.

Knapp, M. L., & Hall, J. A. (1997). Nonverbal communication in human interaction (4. ed.). Fort Worth, Tex.: Harcourt Brace College Pub.

Machado, I. (2004). Children, Stories and Dramatic Games: A Support and Guidance Architecture for Story Creation, PhD Thesis, University of Leeds, 2004.

Mali, A. D. and Kambhampati, S. (1998). Encoding HTN Planing in Propositional Logic. In the Proceedings of International Conference on AI Planning Systems, 1998.

Mamet, D. (1992). On directing film.London: Faber.

Martinho, C. and Paiva, A (1999). Pathematic Agents: Rapid Development of Believable Emotional Agents in Intelligent Virtual Environments, in Proceedings of the Autonomous Agents'99, ACM Press, 1999.

Mateas, M. (1999). An oz-centric review of interactive drama and believable agents. In M. Wooldridge and M. Veloso, (Eds.), AI Today: Recent Trends and Developments. Lecture Notes in AI 1600. Berlin, NY: Springer. 1999.

Mateas, M., Stern, M., (2005), Structuring Content in the Façade Interactive Drama Architecture, AIIDE05, Conference on Artificial Intelligence and Interactive Digital Entertainment, Marina del Rey, USA

Murray J. H. (1997). Hamlet on the Holodeck - The future of the narrative cyberspace. The MIT Press, 1997.

Plantinga, C. (1999). Introduction. In C. R. Plantinga & G. M. Smith (Eds.), Passionate views: Film, cognition, and emotion. Baltimore, Md.: Johns Hopkins University Press.

Prada, R.; Machado, I. and Paiva, A. (2000). Teatrix: A Virtual Environment for Story Creation, Intelligent Tutoring Systems, Ed. G. Gauthier, C. Frasson & K. Van Lehn, Springer

Propp, V. (1968). Morphology of the folktale. Austin: University of Texas Press.

Pudovkin, V. I. (1961). Argumento e realização.Lisboa: Arcadia.

Russel, S. and Norvig, P. (1995) Artificial intelligence - a modern approach, Prentice Hall, 1995.

Sheldon, L. (2004). Character development and storytelling for games. Cambridge, Mass.; London: Course.

Smith, G. M. (1999). Local emotions, global moods, and film structure. In C. R. Plantinga & G. M. Smith (Eds.), Passionate views: Film, cognition, and emotion (pp. 301). Baltimore, Md.: Johns Hopkins University Press.

Smith, G. M. (2003), Film structure and the emotion system, Cambridge; New York, Cambridge University Press.

Sonnenschein, D. (2001). Sound design: The expressive power of music, voice and sound effects in cinema.Studio City, Calif.: Michael Wiese.

Tsuneto, R.; Hendler, J. and Nau, D. (1998). Analysing External Conditions to Improve the Effieciency of HTN Planning. Proceedings of the AAAI 1998, AAAI Press, 1998.

Van Sijll, J. (2005). Cinematic storytelling: The 100 most powerful film conventions every filmmaker must know.Studio City CA: Michael Wiese Productions.

Zagalo, N., (2007), Convergência entre o Cinema e a Realidade Virtual, PhD Thesis, Departamento de Comunicação e Arte, Universidade de Aveiro, Portugal

22

Computer-Assisted Regulation of Emotional and Social Processes

Toni Vanhala and Veikko Surakka
Research Group for Emotions, Sociality, and Computing, TAUCHI,
Department of Computer Sciences, University of Tampere
Finland

1. Introduction

Imagine a person who has a fear of other people. Let us call her Anna. She is afraid of people watching her every move as she stands in a line or walks down the street. Meeting new people is almost impossible as she always feels stared at and judged by everyone. This fear, or maybe even a phobia, can make Anna's life very complicated. It is difficult for her to travel through public spaces in order to get to work, to deal with a bus or taxi driver, shop for groceries, etc. Anna's leisure time activities are also very limited. The situation is indeed a vicious cycle, as it is even difficult for her to seek treatment and go to a therapist.

In USA alone, there are approximately 15 million people like Anna who suffer from social anxiety disorder (Anxiety Disorders Association of America, 2008). A total of 40 million people suffer from different anxiety disorders. The associated yearly costs of mental health care exceed 42 billion U.S. dollars. Thus, emotional disorders are a significant public health issue. There is a need for demonstrably effective and efficient new methods for therapy.

Computer systems have recently been applied to the treatment of many emotional disorders, including different phobias (Krijn et al., 2004; Wiederhold & Bullinger, 2005). These systems provide controlled virtual exposure to the object of the disorder, for example, a computer simulation of a spider or a room filled with other people. In this form of behavioural therapy, patients are systematically desensitized by gradual exposure to a computer generated representation of the object of their fear (Weiten, 2007; Krijn et al., 2004). At first, the level of exposure is kept mild and constant, for example, by keeping the object of the fear visually distant and far away. Then, the level of exposure is increased little by little, for example, by moving a virtual spider closer or increasing the number of virtual people. The underlying theory is that such exposure replaces anxiety provoking memories and thoughts with more neutral ones that are acquired in a safe, controlled environment.

It has been shown that people react to computer generated stimuli in the same manner as to authentic, real-life stimuli. For example, socially anxious people are cautious about disturbing embodied artificial characters in virtual reality (Garau et al., 2005). People have also reported higher anxiety and shown increased somatic responses when speaking to negative as compared to neutral and positive audiences consisting of virtual agent characters (Pertaub et al., 2002). As these studies have shown that virtual characters are able to evoke emotions or anxiety, computer generated stimuli show clear potential as a new method for treating different social and emotional disorders by enabling controlled exposure to anxiety provoking stimuli.

Advantages of computer generated stimuli include accurate control of the grade of exposure, the relative easiness of creating diverse stimuli and varying their characteristics, and the cost-efficiency of therapy. For example, a person who has a phobia of flying can experience a whole virtual air plane trip from take-off to landing at a relatively low cost. Further, the experience can be replicated again and again with small variations to factors that would be very difficult to control in real situations. Virtual environments even allow the re-enactment of traumatic episodes, such as bombings and car accidents. In fact, there are various conditions that have been successfully treated using virtual exposure to artificial stimuli, including fear of flying, fear of driving, fear of confined spaces, fear of public speaking, social phobia, post-traumatic disorders, and panic disorders (Krijn et al., 2004; Wiederhold & Bullinger, 2005). However, Krijn et al. (2004) concluded in their review of virtual exposure methods that there is little conclusive evidence about the relative effectiveness of virtual reality and real, *in vivo* exposure. One particular concern was the lack of evidence for the effectiveness of virtual exposure therapy as a stand-alone treatment.

There is evidence that the effectiveness of exposure therapy can be further improved by applying physiological measurements (Wiederhold & Wiederhold, 2003). For example, physiological signals can be registered and displayed to the patient during exposure therapy (Wiederhold & Bullinger, 2005; Wiederhold & Wiederhold, 2003). This way, the patient can gain awareness of physiological processes and learn to voluntarily control them. Voluntary control of emotion-related physiological functions has been shown to influence emotional reactions associated with, for example, fear and facial expressions (Vanhala & Surakka, 2007a; Wiederhold & Wiederhold, 2003). In other types of setups, the clinician can monitor these signals, estimate the progress of therapy, and adjust its intensity accordingly.

Previous research has established a number of physiology-based measures of emotional states that can be used as a basis for adapting the therapy (Vanhala & Surakka, 2007a; Vanhala & Surakka, 2007b; Partala et al., 2006; Anttonen & Surakka, 2005; Wilhelm et al., 2006; Surakka & Vanhala, accepted). These measures include electrical brain and facial muscle activity, heart rate, respiration, and skin conductivity. However, it is not possible to use a single measure as an index of emotional states, as each individual measure is affected by a number of psychological and physiological factors (Ward & Marsden, 2003). Emotions themselves are often categorized according to a number of dimensions, such as arousal and emotional valence (Bradley & Lang, 1994). Further, emotional processes are tightly interconnected with other psychophysiological processes, including cognition and attention (Surakka et al., 1998). Thus, it is necessary to take other psychophysiological processes (e.g., attention) into account when recognizing and analyzing emotions (Ward & Marsden, 2003).

As multi-signal, online monitoring of human psychophysiology involves signals with several varying characteristics (e.g. sample rate and frequency content) and as each measure reflects several inter-linked physiological systems, the amount of information can easily overwhelm a human operator. One way to deal with this challenge is to build perceptual intelligence into computers themselves (Pentland, 2000). Signal analysis of measured psychophysiological signals and states could be performed automatically. Further, the role of human actors in this kind of a virtual therapy system could be changed. Currently, humans need to process all information that is used to control the parameters of a virtual therapy system. Proactive computing could be used to remove this bottleneck (Tennenhouse, 2000). A system that responds to the emotional and physiological state of a person could automatically adapt the computer system according to the rules of desensitization. This way, both the person being treated and the therapist could focus on training to regulate emotions instead of actively interpreting and estimating them.

The main goal of the present work is to present a new model for computer systems that proactively support emotion regulation. First, in the next section we present examples of single and compound measures of psychophysiological states that could be used to build perceptual intelligence for this kind of a system. Then, in the following section we discuss studies demonstrating the effectiveness of computers in regulating emotions. In the process we identify several computer-generated stimuli that could be used to influence emotional and social processes. In the fourth section we combine these findings into a model that supports both computer-assisted regulation and voluntary control of emotion related psychological and physiological processes. Finally, we discuss the advantages and challenges of this model and suggest pertinent research areas for future work.

2. Measuring emotions

As our aim is to support the regulation of emotions, we need to be able to evaluate the results of this regulation, that is, changes in emotional responding. Researchers generally view emotions as a concurrent change in experiential, behavioural, and physiological systems that organize human motivational behaviour (e.g., Frijda, 1986; Mauss et al., 2005). Thus, our first task is to identify measures that capture a wide view of emotional processes. There have been two research traditions of emotions. The first tradition views emotions as discrete states, such as, disgust, fear, joy, sadness, and surprise (Ekman, 1993). The second tradition views emotions as a three-dimensional space varying in emotional valence, arousal, and dominance (Bradley & Lang, 1994; 2000). These traditions have direct consequences especially for measuring the experiential component of emotions. For example, one common method is to ask people to rate their experiences using bipolar scales of emotional valence (i.e., from negative to positive), arousal (i.e., from calm to aroused), and dominance (i.e., from feeling of being in control to being controlled).

The measurement of the experiential component of emotion often requires that the person is interrupted and asked to report her or his experiences. For example, during exposure therapy patients are periodically asked to rate the intensity of their anxiety using a scale of subjective units of discomfort (SUD) ranging from 0 to either 10 or 100 (see, e.g., review by Krijn et al., 2004). The rating is used to evaluate when the level of anxiety has changed and requires the therapist to adapt the exposure. When the anxiety is very high, the exposure may be decreased, for example, with instructed relaxation. Low anxiety suggests that the patient is ready to proceed to a higher level of exposure, for example, to take one step closer to a spider. This way, the person is gradually exposed to the object of their fear and habituated to ever increasing amounts of exposure in the process.

The drawback of reporting subjective experiences is that it distracts the person's attention from any ongoing tasks that she or he may be performing. This may hinder a person's experience of being present in the virtual therapy environment. There is some evidence pro the view that this feeling is critical for the success of exposure therapy, as it is required for the experience of relevant emotions and learning to regulate them (Krijn et al., 2004). In this sense, behavioural and physiological components of emotion are somewhat more convenient to measure. It is feasible to acquire these measures continuously and in real-time without distracting the person (Öhman et al., 2000; Teller, 2004; Wilhelm et al., 2006; Mandryk & Atkins, 2007). This also creates potential for more accurate timing of emotional responses. For example, the exact time of a reaction to some surprising event is more readily identified from changes in facial behaviour as compared to a post study questionnaire.

Measures of facial behaviour have been frequently used for detecting emotional responses. For example, Ioannou and others (2005) reported results from using an adaptive system to classify the facial behaviour of one person. The system classified emotional facial expressions into three classes based on features extracted from video images. The classes represented three out of four quadrants of a two-dimensional emotional space (i.e., high arousal - negative, high arousal - positive, low arousal - negative). The classification accuracy of a general (i.e., person-independent) model was about 58%. After adapting this model to the particular person, the performance increased to approximately 78%.

In contrast to Ioannou et al. (2005), typically the classes in video-based classification of facial behaviour have been based on a view of discrete emotions (see, e.g., reviews in Donato et al., 1999; Cowie et al., 2001). The accuracies for these kinds of classifiers are impressive at their best. For example, Sohail & Bhattacharya (2007) reported an average accuracy of over 90% in classifying six emotional facial expressions. However, discrete classifiers usually do not address the intensity of emotional states which is used in adapting the amount of virtual exposure. As an exception, Bailenson (in press) recently developed a classifier for both the discrete facial expression and the intensity of the expression. In any case, most previously investigated discrete classifiers are limited in their applicability to virtual therapy.

Video-based measures can be used to detect facial activity in a non-invasive manner, for example, without restricting the movements of the person by electrode wires. However, video-based methods can only be used to detect clearly visible facial behaviour, while electrophysiological measures have the potential to register very small changes in muscle activity (Ekman et al., 2002). There is also evidence that physiological measures can reflect emotional responses that do not evoke observable behaviour (e.g., Gross & Levenson, 1997). Furthermore, video-based measures are very sensitive to lighting and head orientation as well as to inaccuracies in detecting facial landmarks (e.g., Cowie et al., 2005). For these reasons, physiological measures may be seen to reflect a more objective (e.g., context-independent) view of the emotional response.

A common method for measuring the physiological activity that underlies visible facial behaviour is electromyography (EMG). Facial EMG is performed by attaching electrodes that register the electrical activity of facial muscles over specific muscle sites (Tassinary & Cacioppo, 2000). Especially the EMG activity of the *corrugator supercilii* (activated when frowning) and the *zygomaticus major* (activated when smiling) muscles has been frequently found to co-vary with subjective experiences of emotional valence (e.g., Lang et al., 1993; Larsen et al., 2003). The *corrugator supercilii* muscle which knits and lowers the brow is located in the forehead. Its activity has been found to increase when a person experiences negative emotions and to decrease during positive experiences. The *zygomaticus major* is a relatively large muscle located in the cheek. When activated it pulls up the corner of the mouth. The intensity of its activity varies with emotional valence in the opposite manner to the *corrugator supercilii* muscle.

Although some physiological reactions are quite straight-forward to interpret, humans do not normally evaluate emotional expressions of other people from electrophysiological data. Even one electrophysiological signal can contain lots of information, which may overwhelm a human observer. For example, facial EMG activity may reflect both the intensity of facial muscle activations and the fatigue in muscles (Tassinary & Cacioppo, 2000).

Automatic analysis and interpretation of physiological signals can help in perceiving which changes in signals are related to emotional processes. There is evidence that even the subjective component of an emotion (i.e., emotional experiences) can be automatically estimated from electrical facial muscle activity. For example, Partala and others (2005; 2006) were able to build systems that automatically estimated and classified emotional experiences evoked by picture and video stimuli. The first system (Partala et al., 2006) was adapted to the individual responses of each person as follows. First, participants were shown a calibration block of 24 pictures selected from the standardized set of International Affective Picture System (IAPS). After each stimulus, the participant rated the emotional valence that she or he experienced using a 9-point bipolar scale. Then, the statistical models that estimated the emotional valence were adapted to the person based on the ratings and the EMG data from the calibration block. Finally, the system was tested using 28 pictures and six videos that showed a female or a male actor crying, smiling, and portraying a neutral facial expression. Subjective ratings of emotional valence were collected after each stimulus. These ratings and the system's estimate of emotional valence were compared in order to determine the accuracy of the system. The results showed that the best models were able to separate negative and positive emotional responses with accuracies of over 70 percent for pictures and over 80 percent in the case of video stimuli. Further, the largest correlation between the subjective ratings and the system's estimate of emotional valence on a 9-point scale was over 0.9. Thus, the results of the first system showed that subjective emotional experiences can be estimated based on measures of electrical facial activity with relatively simple models in real-time. Although there is still room for improvement, the accuracy achieved in this study is already sufficient for many applications.

The second system was person-independent and therefore did not require a separate calibration period (Partala et al., 2005). The valence of emotional experiences was estimated based on the direction of change in EMG activity from a baseline period of 0.5 seconds before stimulus onset. This system was able to distinguish between reactions rated as positive or negative at an accuracy of nearly 70 percent for pictures and over 80 percent for videos. In summary, facial activity shows clear promise as a reliable measure for automatic, real-time classification of emotional valence, as both person-adapted and person-independent systems were demonstrated to perform at a reasonable accuracy.

In addition to measures of electrical facial muscle activity, there is a wide variety of other physiological measures that have been shown to vary between emotional reactions, such as the mean heart rate and its frequency components (Anttonen & Surakka, 2005; Levenson & Ekman, 2002; Bradley, 2000; Malliani et al., 1991). For example, Rainville and others (2006) investigated classification of emotional responses using a large set of heart activity and respiration related features. Participants recalled and experientially relived one or two autobiographical episodes associated with the experience of fear, anger, sadness, or happiness. The system was able to detect which of the four emotions the participant was experiencing (i.e., according to subjective ratings) at an accuracy of about 65%.

One challenge that has rarely been investigated in previous classification studies is the recognition and accurate timing of emotional responses. In other words, participants themselves have typically reported the onset and offset of emotional responses and data has been segmented by hand. It is clear that in order to react to the events in real-time, a system should be able to segment the collected data without human intervention. Vanhala & Surakka (2007b) recently reported a study of this kind of an online system. The system automatically detected the onset and offset of emotion related events (i.e., voluntary smiling and frowning) based on less than half a second of heart rate data. The onset of activity was detected with a statistically significant accuracy of 66.4% and the offsets were detected with an accuracy of 70.2%. However, the rate of false recognitions was 59.7% which is quite high. Thus, the results showed that the heart rate can be used to support recognition and classification of emotional responses, but it should be used as one of several corroborative measures in practical applications.

In fact, previous studies have usually employed more than one measure in classifying emotional states (e.g., Kim et al., 2004; D'Mello et al., 2007; Mandryk & Atkins, 2007). Otherwise, recognizing mental states and responses can be challenging, as physiological responses are person-dependent and they reflect several overlapping reactions and mental processes. For example, Bailenson and others (in press) compared classifiers that used facial activity as such or combined it with several physiological measures of heart activity, skin conductance, and finger temperature. The use of physiological measures significantly improved the precision of classification (i.e., the proportion of correctly classified samples in each classified group) as compared to classifiers that used only hand-coded facial features. The best improvements were over 15% for classifying sadness and about 9% for classifying amusement. Similarly, Zeng and others (2004) were able to improve the accuracy of their emotion classification system to 90 percent when both facial expressions and prosodic cues of speech were used. When only one of these modalities was used, the accuracies dropped to 56 and 45 percent, respectively. Busso and others (2004) achieved similar results with a system that recognized emotions from speech and facial expressions. In an earlier work, Picard and others (2001) identified specific physiological responses from four physiological signals (i.e., facial electromyogram, blood volume pressure, skin conductance, and respiration) and used these response patterns in classifying emotional experiences to eight classes. They achieved a classification accuracy of 81 percent.

The measurement of bioelectric signals can be criticized based on the complex arrangements (e.g., electrodes, amplifiers, and skin cleaning) that are required for measuring them. Recently, several wireless and non-invasive technologies have been developed for measuring physiological signals, including facial EMG (e.g., Anttonen & Surakka, 2005; Teller, 2004; Wilhelm et al., 2006). For example, the electrical activity of forehead muscles (e.g., *corrugator supercilii*) can be measured with an easy-to-wear wireless headband that contains embroidered silver thread electrodes (Vehkaoja & Lekkala, 2004; Nöjd et al., 2005). As another example of non-invasive and easily applied measurement technology, Anttonen and Surakka (2005; 2007) were able to reliably measure emotion related heart rate changes with a regular looking office chair. The chair contained embedded electromechanical sensors in the seat, arm rests, and back rest. The sensors can be used to detect pressure changes due to heart activity, body movement, or changes in posture. Based on these recent advances in non-invasive technologies, physiological measures are quickly catching up on the current benefits of video-based methods for tracking changes in emotion related behaviour.

In summary, there are several well-tried methods for measuring the different aspects of emotion. Our present review suggested that especially physiological measures show potential as objective and sensitive measures of emotion related processes. Thus, there is no need to rely on any single measure of emotional processes, such as SUD in adjusting the exposure in virtual therapy. In fact, typically several measures have been fused together in order to derive more accurate compound measures. This also helps in interpreting the data, as it can be pre-processed into a form that is more accessible to a human observer. Further, physiological measures are less prone to distract the person as they can be continuously acquired without intervention. However, monitoring emotion related processes can still require considerable human effort after integration and interpretation by the computer. The model that we present in the current paper is aimed to facilitate this work.

3. Regulating emotions with computers

Social and emotional cues from computers have been found to evoke significant responses in their human observers. For example, synthesized speech with emotional content has been found both to evoke positive emotions and to enhance problem solving activity (Partala & Surakka, 2004; Aula & Surakka, 2002). Aula & Surakka (2002) used synthesized speech to provide neutral, negatively, or positively worded auditory feedback that seemed to reflect participant's performance in solving arithmetic problems. In reality, the content of feedback was random and independent of the participant's performance. Nonetheless, positive feedback significantly facilitated the speed of solving problems. In a later study, Partala & Surakka (2004) investigated emotionally worded interventions after a pre-programmed mouse delay during computerized puzzle solving tasks. Similar to the previous study, problem solving performance was significantly better after positively worded interventions. In terms of facial EMG measurements, participants also smiled more and frowned less after positive interventions as compared to facial activity after neutral and negative interventions. These kinds of studies have shown that explicit feedback and interventions from computers can affect human cognitive and emotional processes. There is also evidence that even more subtle social and emotional cues are effective in human-computer interaction. For example, in one of the first studies of virtual proximity, Partala and others (2004) investigated reactions to the simulated distance of a virtual head. When the head appeared to be closer, participants rated that they felt dominated by it. Vice versa, when the head was further away, participants felt that they were controlling it. Vanhala and others (submitted) recently found similar subjective dominance reactions to the simulated proximity of an embodied computer agent. Some researchers have even described computers as social actors, meaning that people have a strong tendency to behave socially when interacting with computers (Nass et al., 1994; Reeves & Nass, 1996).

The effectiveness of virtual stimuli in evoking social and emotional reactions is the basis for virtual exposure therapy. The idea is that new neutral memory structures are formed during virtual exposure. These memory structures should replace the previous anxiety related structures when responding to real-life situations (Krijn et al., 2004). In other words, people should react to provoking virtual stimuli in the same manner as to authentic, real-life stimuli. There are some studies that support his view. For example, socially anxious people get highly distressed when they talk to or need to disturb embodied artificial characters in virtual reality (Pertaub et al., 2002; Garau et al., 2005). Further, the effects of virtual exposure to spiders have been found to generalize to real-life behaviour as measured by the Behavioural Avoidance Test (Garcia-Palacios et al., 2002). That is, people were able to approach a real spider more easily after exposure to a virtual one.

In addition to these computer generated stimuli that regulate emotional responses, emotions can also be actively self-regulated. Gross & Thompson (2007) have described the development of emotion self-regulation as a continuum. In the first stages emotions are consciously regulated. Later, emotion regulation becomes more automatic and effortless. Thus, the process of learning to regulate emotions resembles the process of skill acquisition in general (Anderson, 2000). In this view, less skilled emotion regulators use cognitive processes extensively to support the regulation. For example, they may deliberately rely on instructions and examples of successful regulation. After practise, the regulation of emotions becomes autonomous and efficient, demanding much less cognitive processing. For example, a skilled self-regulator does not need to explicitly apply instructions (e.g., from a therapist) in order to regulate emotions.

Instructions that support emotion regulation may be relatively simple. For example, Vanhala & Surakka (2007a) investigated whether computer-guided voluntary facial activations have an effect on autonomous nervous system activity. Participants were instructed to activate either the *corrugator supercilii* muscle or the *zygomaticus major* muscle at one of three intensity levels (i.e., low, medium, or high). Instructions for each task and real-time feedback about the intensity of facial muscle activations were provided to the participant on the computer screen. Subjective ratings of emotional valence were collected after the activation. It was found that different muscle activations produced both task-specific emotional experiences and significant changes in heart rate and heart rate variability. Thus, the results showed that relatively simple computer-instructions allow people to actively influence their involuntary physiological reactions and subjective experiences that are associated with emotions.

Physiological feedback as such can also help in learning to regulate emotions. Usually, either skin conductivity or breathing patterns are registered and displayed to the patient or the therapist during computer-assisted therapy sessions (Wiederhold & Bullinger, 2005). This way, a person can become aware of unconscious physiological responses and processes, which can enable voluntary control over them. As an impressive example in favour of the effectiveness of virtual exposure therapy, Wiederhold & Wiederhold (2003) followed the behaviour of a group of 10 patients inflicted with fear of flying who were treated using virtual exposure and physiological feedback. As the terrorist attacks on September 11th, 2001 were quite directly related to flying, they could have caused relapses in terms of intensifying the fear of flying in these patients. However, everyone of this group was able to fly without medication or further treatment just four months after the attacks.

Physiological data can also be collected for later reflection. For example, Lindström and others (2006) presented an "affective diary" that provided a multimodal (i.e., auditory and visual) representation of sensor data. A measure of arousal was extracted from the physiological measures and the estimated level of arousal affected the posture of a virtual character displayed on the screen. Users of the diary could later reflect their experiences and manipulate the character in order to match it to their recollection of those feelings. This application illustrates the interplay of involuntary emotion related physiological reactions (i.e., visually coded sensor data) and voluntary regulation of emotions (i.e., later reflection and adjustment in "affective diary"). However, a crucial component for supporting the training of emotion regulation is the online adjustment of emotional stimulation, for example, the amount of exposure to virtual stimuli. This requires a real-time system for the evaluation and reflection of psychological and physiological processes.

In summary, computer systems show potential for regulating human emotions. First, studies have shown that people react socially and emotionally to computers and virtual environments. Second, the effects of virtual stimuli (e.g., habituation of anxiety responses) have been further facilitated when feedback of emotion related physiological activity has been provided. Third, we found that voluntary regulation of emotion related processes seems to be a potential key factor both in learning the regulation as such but also in modulating the functioning of involuntary mechanisms activated during emotion related processes. Fourth, we reviewed a large number of physiological measures that show potential as sensitive and objective measures of emotional responses. The relevant information from these measures could be extracted using automatic classification of emotional responses. This way, it would be possible to avoid overwhelming a human observer, while still using all of the available information in order to maximally support emotion regulation. In the next section we present a model that supports this goal by integrating perceptual intelligence to the system.

4. Adaptive support for emotion regulation

Figure 1 shows a model of how virtual exposure therapy is currently performed. The model contains a set of different actors that take part in an interaction loop. First, the relevant emotional state is observed using different emotion related measures. Then, a human facilitator monitoring these measures decides how the virtual stimuli should be adapted. For example, if the patient reports a relatively low subjective experience of discomfort, the facilitator may proceed to increase the amount of exposure, for example, by moving a virtual spider closer. Note that the facilitator may in fact be the person who is being measured and treated, that is, the person may choose to control the amount of stimulation her or himself. Finally, the interaction loop in Figure 1 is closed after the adaptation by the newly modified stimulation. For example, if the virtual spider was moved closer, it may now provoke stronger anxiety reactions. These anxiety reactions are then reflected in the measures of emotion related processes, which leads to another cycle of interaction. The underlying idea of these continuous cycles is that the person learns to regulate emotional responses to increasing levels of stimulation.

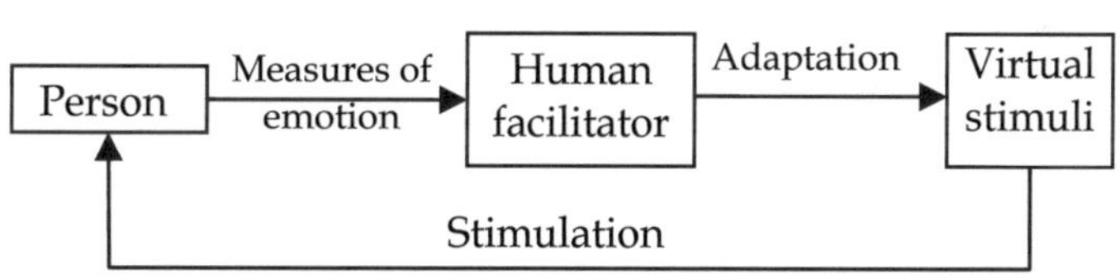

Fig. 1. A diagram of the current model used in virtual exposure therapy. Different actors are presented as boxes and labelled arrows represent the flow of information.

Although the model is quite compact and straight-forward, there are three major challenges involved when it is applied. First, although previous work has shown that virtual stimulation is effective in evoking similar emotional and social responses as real-life stimuli, the effects of virtual stimulation and its online adaptation have not been extensively investigated. It has also been found that computer-generated stimuli may significantly facilitate cognitive processing and effectively support regulation of anxiety responses. However, more information is still needed about how adapting the different parameters of stimulation in real-time affects emotion related processes. This challenge should be resolved by controlled experimental studies of each virtual stimulus in the future.

The second challenge is that there are several emotion related measures that provide complementary, non-overlapping information. There is a large amount of information contained in each of these measures. A human observer is often forced to choose between a broad view of the emotional state and an in depth analysis of it. Perceptual intelligence can be used to solve this challenge. Different methods for building computers that perceive emotion from physiological and behavioural measures were reviewed in the second section. These methods form the basis for the perceptual intelligence in our new model.

Figure 2 presents a model where perceptual intelligence has been included into the system. The model is similar to the previous one with the exception that the interpretation of emotion related measures is performed automatically. Thus, the facilitator has access to a higher level representation or a summary of information that is relevant to therapy. Simply stated, the computer acts as a kind of a translator that deciphers the information in the measured signals into a summary that is more accessible to the human observer. This way, the facilitator is less likely to be overwhelmed with the load of information available from different experiential, behavioural, and physiological measures. However, the actual adaptation is still controlled by a human facilitator acting on the basis of the summarized information.

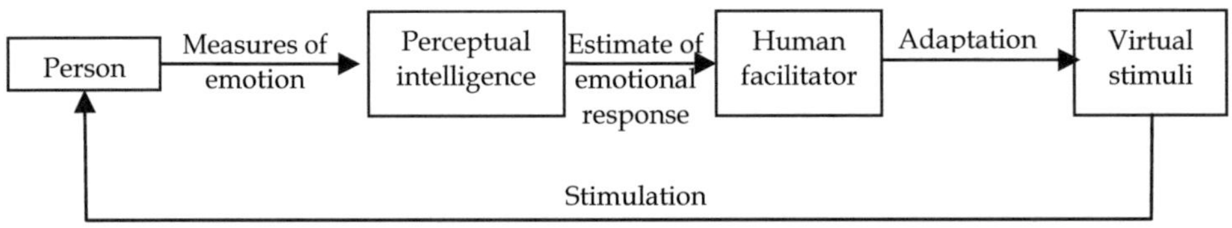

Fig. 2. A diagram of a perceptually intelligent model to be used in virtual exposure therapy. Different actors are presented as boxes and labelled arrows represent the flow of information.

The third and final challenge in using the conventional model is that it places the human facilitator as a part of the real-time system (see Figs. 1&2). This requires that a person must continuously attend to the measurements and decide when and how to react to any changes or even to a lack of changes. Figure 3 shows a final model designed to more efficiently support emotion regulation in virtual exposure therapy. The continuous monitoring of emotion related information is now built into the computer system itself. In contrast to conventional computer systems that place humans as a part of the processing loop, this model can support emotion regulation without distracting the person or requiring constant attention. The system provides this support by taking the initiative and adapting the stimulation when it is appropriate, that is, by being proactive (Tennenhouse, 2000).

In this kind of a system, the role of the human facilitator is to supervise the process of therapy. In order to perform this task, the supervisor needs information about the therapy process and the functioning of the system. Further, this information should be concise if we are to retain the main advantage of automatic signal analysis and reasoning which was to allow people to focus on the task at hand. One potentially efficient way to do this is to provide an explanation of the system's reasoning to the supervisor. This type of a model fits the definition of an expert system which solves problems in a narrow domain of expertise (i.e., virtual exposure therapy) and is able to explain its own reasoning (Bratko, 2001). For example, if the system moved the object of the phobia closer to the person, it could be asked why it did this. A brief explanation could be that, for instance, the physiological signals showed that the current level of anxiety was very low. Then, the person could further query the specifics of these signals, if she or he so desires. This way, the users confidence of the system's functioning could be increased by making it transparent to the user. Of course, this would also allow the system's reasoning to be monitored and tuned when appropriate.

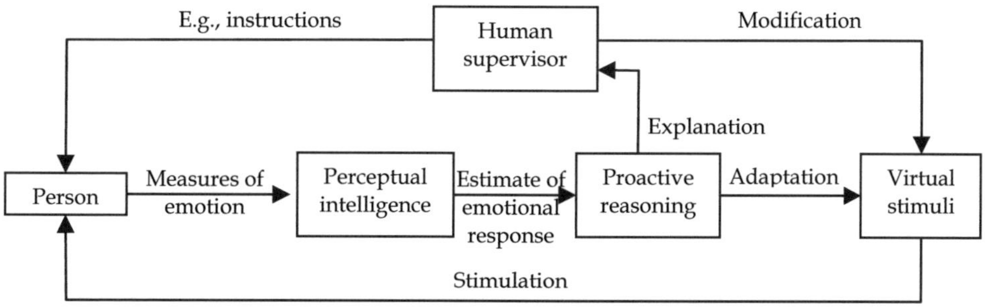

Fig. 3. A diagram of a proactive model for virtual exposure therapy. Different actors are presented as boxes and labelled arrows represent the flow of information.

During the operation of the system its supervisor may exert control over the system either by adapting the stimulation directly or through interaction with the person who is being trained. For example, a therapist may instruct the person to relax by performing controlled breathing exercises. This voluntary control affects the physiological state which is further reflected in the collected emotion related measures. As a result, the changes in these measures lead to corresponding adaptation of the stimulation. As another example, the person may directly influence those measures that affect the intensity of stimulation. This is feasible as the same expressive channels that reflect spontaneous emotional reactions can also be voluntarily controlled. For instance, the person may voluntarily frown in order to signal a high level of discomfort and move the spider further away. This also highlights another advantage of proactive adaptation. As responses to measured changes (i.e., voluntary activity) are explicit pre-programmed reactions, they can be guaranteed to be consistent. This might not be the case if the responses were selected by a human operator.

In summary, a perceptually intelligent and proactive system enables a wide variety of information to be used in regulating emotions. First, perceptual intelligence enables more efficient processing of measured emotion related signals. This enables the monitoring of a larger set of emotional measures, which then results in a more comprehensive and reliable view of the emotional state, for example, attending to multiple physiological and behavioural changes. Second, proactive reasoning may be used to adapt the stimulation in an appropriate and consistent manner. The adaptation can be based on findings that show how virtual stimulation affects human emotions and cognitive processing. As a whole, a system that uses this model can function independently without constant human supervision, helping people to regulate emotions without distracting them.

5. Discussion and future work

The current work presented a model for a computer system that supports the regulation of emotion related processes during exposure to provoking stimuli. We identified two main challenges for these kinds of systems. First, emotions as such are complex, multi-component processes that are measured with several complementary methods. The amount of information can overwhelm a human operator. Second, the adaptation of stimulation requires real-time reasoning about the current emotional state and the effects of adaptation. This reasoning may distract a human facilitator from tasks related to emotion regulation. Further, a human operator may respond inconsistently to changes in emotional processes, which effectively removes the control of the system from the person who is being trained.

In the present work we addressed the first challenge of identifying emotional reactions by including perceptual intelligence to our model. Several measures for automatic analysis of emotional state have been investigated in previous studies. Especially physiological measures were found to show potential as objective and reliable measures of emotional processes. For example, there are several new wireless and wearable measurement technologies that enable continuous and non-invasive measurement of emotion related physiology. Thus, automatic analysis of emotion related physiological activity can help to identify significant emotional responses during virtual exposure therapy. For a human observer, this pre-processed data is easier to interpret and apply to emotion regulation.

The second challenge of adapting virtual stimulation was addressed with proactive reasoning. First, we reviewed studies of human responses to virtual stimulation. These studies showed that human cognitive functioning and emotional responses may be significantly regulated using different computer-generated social and emotional cues, for example, virtual proximity. Second, we suggested a model where the computer automatically adapts the virtual stimulation according to the emotional state that it has perceived. This way, perceptual intelligence and artificial reasoning result in a proactive system that does not require humans to process data in real-time. In other words, when our model is applied to virtual exposure therapy, a person can focus on the training itself instead of monitoring and responding to measured physiological signals.

In spite of the promising findings from previous studies, there are still open questions in the computer perception of emotional responses to provoking stimuli. For example, some findings suggest that physiological reactions of phobics and healthy people may be significantly different (Wilhelm & Roth, 1998). Although the responses may be similar in terms of direction of change from a baseline (e.g., heart rate accelerated in both phobics and healthy subjects exposed to provoking stimulation), the differences in the magnitude of change may affect the results of automatic recognition. This raises the question whether automatic classification methods for emotional responses in healthy people provide information that is applicable to treating emotional disorders (i.e., abnormal emotional responses). Thus, there is a need to study systems where automatic perception has been included in a virtual therapy system.

The previous research on automatic classification of emotional states has used both person-independent methods and methods that are calibrated to each individual person. These two types of methods are suited for different kinds of applications (Bailenson et al., in press). Systems based on a universal model of emotional responses are suited when lots of people use the same interface, for example, a public computer at a library. An idiosyncratic model that adapts to each person is more suitable when the same person repeatedly uses the interface. The latter case is typical in virtual therapy applications, as the person is treated over multiple similar sessions (Krijn et al., 2004; Wiederhold & Wiederhold, 2005). However, a person-independent model could be used as a starting point for the adaptation, similar to the video-based system by Ioannou and others (2005). This would enable the system to provide estimates of emotional experiences even before a set of person-specific physiological data is collected and calibration is performed. Then, later adaptation of the model could be performed to improve its accuracy.

Another challenge in perceptual intelligence that has received little attention is the automatic segmentation of collected measures. Most previous studies of automatic classification of emotional responses have used hand-segmented data. Typically, a participant reports the onset and the offset of an emotional state and the data is segmented off-line. In contrast to these methods, virtual exposure therapy requires a system that analyses the data online and adapts to the emotional state of a person in real-time. If perceptual intelligence is to be included in this kind of a system, there is a need to investigate online, automatic segmentation of physiological data. Our preliminary results of heart rate responses have shown that such automatic segmentation is feasible (Vanhala & Surakka, 2007b). However, there is a need to investigate systems that use multiple complementary signals in order to improve the reliability and accuracy of methods.

On a general level, our review suggested that people appreciate computer systems that respond to their emotions, for example, display empathy (Klein et al., 2002; Brave et al., 2005). Although it seems a small step to assume that people would appreciate computers that administer virtual exposure therapy by responding to anxiety, there can be a fundamental difference. Emotion regulation aims not only to respond but also to change the emotional reactions to virtual and real-life emotional stimulation. There is a need to study how people experience this kind of a system and whether it helps in regulating emotions.

In summary, the present work showed how automatic perception of emotions and proactive adaptation of a computer system could help in facilitating virtual exposure therapy. The skill of regulating emotions is gradually acquired by adapting virtual stimuli according to the emotional state of the person. This principle is applicable to other emotionally intelligent applications as well. For example, we might be less likely to loose our temper if the desktop computer could display empathy when an important document gets accidentally deleted. Thus, research on perceptual intelligence and proactive reasoning in virtual exposure therapy systems has the potential to improve the quality of human-technology interaction in general. The current work identified the state-of-the-art and the future research that will help in reaching this goal.

6. Acknowledgements

This research was financially supported by the Graduate School in User-Centered Information Technology and the Academy of Finland (project number 1115997).

7. References

Anderson, J. R. (1999). *Learning and memory: An integrated approach*, Wiley, New York.

Anttonen, J. & Surakka, V. (2005). Emotions and heart rate while sitting on a chair, *Proceedings of CHI 2005*, 491-499, ACM.

Anttonen, J. & Surakka, V. (2007). Music, heart rate, and emotions in the context of stimulating technologies, *Affective Computing and Intelligent Interaction, LNCS*, 4738, 290-301.

Anxiety Disorders Association of America. (2008). *Statistics and facts about anxiety disorders*, http://www.adaa.org/AboutADAA/PressRoom/Stats&Facts.asp, Jan 30th, 2008.

Aula, A. & Surakka, V. (2002). Auditory Emotional Feedback Facilitates Human-Computer Interaction, *Proceedings of HCI 2002*, 337-349, Springer.

Bailenson, J. N.; Pontikakis, E. D.; Mauss, I. B.; Gross, J. J.; Jabon, M. E.; Hutcherson, C. A.; Nass, C. & John, O. (in press). Real-time classification of evoked emotions using facial feature tracking and physiological responses. *International Journal of Human-Computer Studies.*

Bradley, M. M. (2000). Emotion and Motivation, In: *Handbook of Psychophysiology*, Cacioppo, J. T.; Tassinary, L. G. & Berntson, G. G. (Ed.), 602-642, Cambridge University Press.

Bradley, M. M. & Lang, P. J. (2000). Affective reactions to acoustic stimuli. *Psychophysiology*, 37, 204-215.

Bradley, M. M. & Lang, P. J. (1994). Measuring emotions: the self-assessment manikin and the semantic differential. *Journal of Behavioral Therapy and Experimental Psychiatry*, 25, 1, 49-59.

Bratko, I. (2001). *Prolog Programming for Artificial Intelligence*, 3rd ed., Pearson.

Brave, S.; Nass, C. & Hutchinson, K. (2005). Computers that care: investigating the effects of orientation of emotion exhibited by an embodied computer agent. *International Journal of Human-Computer Studies*, 62, 161-178.

Busso, C.; Deng, Z.; Yildirim, S.; Bulut, M.; Lee, C. M.; Kazemzadeh, A.; Lee, S.; Neumann, U. & Narayanan, S. (2004). Analysis of emotion recognition using facial expressions, speech and multimodal information, *Proceedings of ICMI*, 205-211.

Cowie, R.; Douglas-Cowie, E.; Taylor, J.; Ioannou, S.; Wallace, M. & Kollias, S. (2005). An intelligent system for facial emotion recognition, *Proceedings of IEEE ICME*, 4 pp.

Cowie, R.; Douglas-Cowie, E.; Tsapatsoulis, N.; Votsis, G.; Kollias, S.; Fellenz, W. & Taylor, J. (2001). Emotion Recognition in Human-Computer Interaction. *IEEE Signal Processing Magazine*, 18, 1, 32-80.

D'Mello, S.; Graesser, A. & Picard, R. W. (2007). Toward an affect-sensitive AutoTutor. *IEEE Intelligent Systems*, 22, 4, 53-61.

Donato, G.; Bartlett, M. S.; Hager, J. C.; Ekman, P. & Sejnowski, T. J. (1999). Classifying facial actions. *IEEE Transactions on Pattern Analysis and Machine Intelligence*, 21, 974-989.

Ekman, P. (1993). An argument for basic emotions. *Cognition and Emotion*, 6, 3, 169-200.

Ekman, P.; Friesen, W. V. & Hager, J. C. (2002). *Facial Action Coding System: Investigator's Guide*, A Human Face, Salt Lake City, USA.

Frijda, N. H. (1986). *The Emotions*, Cambridge University Press.

Garau, M.; Slater, M.; Pertaub, D. & Razzaque, S. (2005). The Responses of People to Virtual Humans in an Immersive Virtual Environment. *Presence: Teleoperators & Virtual Environments*, 14, 1, 104-116.

Garcia-Palacios, A.; Hoffman, H.; Carlin, A.; Furness, T. A. & Botella, C. (2002). Virtual reality in the treatment of spider phobia: a controlled study. *Behaviour Research and Therapy*, 40, 9, 983-993.

Gross, J. J. & Levenson, R. W. (1997). Hiding feelings: The acute effects of inhibiting negative and positive emotion. *Journal of Abnormal Psychology*, 106, 1, 95-103.

Gross, J. J. & Thompson, R. A. (2007). Emotion regulation: Conceptual foundations, In: *Handbook of Emotion Regulation*, Gross, J. J. (Ed.), 3-24, Guilford Press.

Ioannou, S. V.; Raouzaiou, A. T.; Tzouvaras, V. A.; Mailis, T. P.; Karpouzis, K. C. & Kollias, S. D. (2005). Emotion recognition through facial expression analysis based on a neurofuzzy network. *Neural Networks*, 18, 4, 423-435.

Kim, K. H.; Bang, S. W. & Kim, S. R. (2004). Emotion recognition system using short-term monitoring of physiological signals. *Medical and Biomedical Engineering and Computing*, 42, 3, 419-427.
Klein, J.; Moon, Y. & Picard, R. W. (2002). This computer responds to user frustration: Theory, design, and results. *Interacting with Computers*, 14, 119-140.
Krijn, M.; Emmelkamp, P.; Olafsson, R. & Biemond, R. (2004). Virtual reality exposure therapy of anxiety disorders: A review. *Clinical Psychology Review*, 24, 259-281.
Lang, P. J.; Greenwald, M. K.; Bradley, M. M. & Hamm, A. O. (1993). Looking at pictures: Affective, facial, visceral, and behavioral reactions. *Psychophysiology*, 30, 261-273.
Larsen, J. T.; Norris, C. J. & Cacioppo, J. T. (2003). Effects of positive and negative affect on electromyographic activity over the zygomaticus major and corrugator supercilii. *Psychophysiology*, 40, 776-785.
Levenson, R. W. & Ekman, P. (2002). Difficulty does not account for emotion-specific heart rate changes in the directed facial action task. *Psychophysiology*, 39, 397-405.
Lindström, M.; St, A.; Höök, K.; Sundström, P.; Laaksolahti, J.; Combetto, M.; Taylor, A. & Bresin, R. (2006). Affective diary: designing for bodily expressiveness and self-reflection, *CHI '06 extended abstracts*, 1037-1042, ACM, New York.
Malliani, A.; Pagani, M.; Lombardi, F. & Cerutti, S. (1991). Cardiovascular neural regulation explored in the frequency domain. *Circulation*, 84, 482-492.
Mandryk, R. L. & Atkins, M. S. (2007). A fuzzy physiological approach for continuously modeling emotion during interaction with play technologies. *International Journal of Human-Computer Studies*, 66, 329-347.
Mauss, I. B.; Levenson, R. W.; McCarter, L.; Wilhelm, F. H. & Gross, J. J. (2005). The tie that binds? Coherence among emotion experience, behavior, and physiology. *Emotion*, 5, 2, 175-190.
Nass, S.; Steuer, J. & Tauber, E. R. (1994). Computers are Social Actors, *Proceedings of CHI'94*, 72-78.
Nöjd, N.; Puurtinen, M.; Niemenlehto, P.; Vehkaoja, A.; Verho, J.; Vanhala, T.; Hyttinen, J.; Juhola, M.; Lekkala, J. & Surakka, V. (2005). Wireless wearable EMG and EOG measurement system for psychophysiological applications, *Proceedings of the 13th Nordic Baltic Conference on Biomedical Engineering and Medical Physics*, 144-145
Öhman, A.; Hamm, A. & Hugdahl, K. (2000), Cognition and the Autonomic Nervous System: Orienting, Anticipation, and Conditioning, In: Handbook of Psychophysiology, Cacioppo, J. T.; Tassinary, L. G. & Berntson, G. G. (Ed.), 533-575.
Partala, T. & Surakka, V. (2004). The effects of affective interventions in human-computer interaction. *Interacting with Computers*, 16, 2, 295-309.
Partala, T.; Surakka, V. & Vanhala, T. (2006). Real-time estimation of emotional experiences from facial expressions. *Interacting with Computers*, 18, 208-226.
Partala, T.; Surakka, V. & Vanhala, T. (2005). Person-independent estimation of emotional experiences from facial expressions, *Proceedings of IUI 2005*, 246-248, ACM.
Pentland, A. (2000). Perceptual intelligence. *Communications of the ACM*, 43, 3, 35-44.
Pertaub, D.; Slater, M. & Barker, C. (2002). An Experiment on Public Speaking Anxiety in Response to Three Different Types of Virtual Audience. *Presence: Teleoperators & Virtual Environments*, 11, 1, 68-78.

Picard, R. W.; Vyzas, E. & Healey, J. (2001). Toward machine emotional intelligence: Analysis of affective physiological state. *IEEE Transactions on Pattern Analysis and Machine Intelligence,* 23, 1175-1191.

Rainville, P.; Bechara, A.; Naqvi, N. & Damasio, A. R. (2006). Basic emotions are associated with distinct patterns of cardiorespiratory activity. *International Journal of Psychophysiology*, 61, 5-18.

Reeves, B. & Nass, C. (1996). *The Media Equation: How People Treat Computers, Television, and New Media Like Real People and Places,* Cambridge University Press, New York.

Sohail, A. S. M. & Bhattacharya, P. (2007). Classification of Facial Expressions Using K-Nearest Neighbor Classifier, *Proceedings of MIRAGE 2007*, 555-566, Springer.

Surakka, V. & Vanhala, T. (accepted). Emotions in human-computer interaction, In: *Multi-channel communication on the Internet*, Kappas, A. (ed.), Cambridge University Press.

Surakka, V.; Tenhunen-Eskelinen, M.; Hietanen, J. K. & Sams, M. (1998). Modulation of human auditory information processing by visual emotional stimuli. *Cognitive Brain Research*, 7, 159-163.

Tassinary, L. G. & Cacioppo, J. T. (2000). The skeletomotor system: Surface electromyography, In: The Handbook of Psychophysiology, Cacioppo, J. T.; Tassinary, L. G. & Berntson, G. G. (Ed.), 163-199, Cambridge University Press.

Teller, A. (2004). A platform for wearable physiological computing. *Interacting with Computers*, 16, 917-937.

Tennenhouse, D. (2000). Proactive computing. *Communications of the ACM*, 43, 5, 43-50.

Vanhala, T. & Surakka, V. (submitted). Virtual proximity and facial expressions regulate human emotions and attention. *International Journal of Human-Computer Studies.*

Vanhala, T. & Surakka, V. (2007a). Facial activation control effect (FACE), *Affective Computing and Intelligent Interaction, Lecture Notes in Computer Science*, 4738, 278-289.

Vanhala, T. & Surakka, V. (2007b). Recognizing the Effects of Voluntary Facial Activations Using Heart Rate Patterns, *Proc. of the 11th WSEAS Int. Conf. on Computers*, 628-632.

Vehkaoja, A. & Lekkala, J. (2004). Wearable wireless biopotential measurement device, *Proceedings of the IEEE EMBS 2004*, 2177-2179.

Ward, R. D. & Marsden, P. H. (2003). Physiological responses to different WEB page designs. *International Journal of Human-Computer Studies*, 59, 199-212.

Weiten, W. (2007). *Psychology: Themes and variations*, Thomson.

Wiederhold, B. K. & Bullinger, A. H. (2005). Virtual reality exposure for phobias, panic disorder, and posttraumatic disorder: A brief sampling of the literature, *Proceedings of HCII 2005*, CD-ROM, Lawrence Erlbaum Associates.

Wiederhold, B. K. & Wiederhold, M. D. (2003). Three-Year Follow-Up for Virtual Reality Exposure for Fear of Flying. *CyberPsychology and Behavior*, 6, 441-445.

Wilhelm, F. H.; Pfaltzl, M. C. & Grossman, P. (2006). Continuous electronic data capture of physiology, behavior and experience in real life: towards ecological assessment of emotion. *Interacting with Computers*, 18, 171-186.

Wilhelm, F. H. & Roth, W. T. (1998). Taking the laboratory to the skies: Ambulatory assessment of self-report, autonomic, and respiratory responses in flying phobia. *Psychophysiology*, 35, 5, 596-606.

Zeng, Z.; Tu, J.; Zhang, T.; Rizzolo, N.; Zhang, Z.; Huang, T. S.; Roth, D. & Levinson, S. (2004). Bimodal HCI-related affect recognition, *Proceedings of ICMI*, 205-211.

23

Generating Facial Expressions with Deep Belief Nets

Joshua M. Susskind[1,2,3], Geoffrey E. Hinton[2],
Javier R. Movellan[3] and Adam K. Anderson[1]
[1]*Department of Psychology, Univ. of Toronto,*
[2]*Department of Computer Science, Univ. of Toronto,*
[3]*Institute of Neural Computation, Univ. of California at San Diego*
[1,2]*Canada*
[3]*USA*

1. Introduction

Realistic facial expression animation requires a powerful "animator" (or graphics program) that can represent the kinds of variations in facial appearance that are both possible and likely to occur in a given context. If the goal is fully determined as in character animation for film, knowledge can be provided in the form of human higher-level descriptions. However, for generating facial expressions for interactive interfaces, such as animated avatars, correct expressions for a given context must be generated on the fly. A simple solution is to rely on a set of prototypical expressions or *basis shapes* that are linearly combined to create every facial expression in an animated sequence (Kleiser, 1989; Parke, 1972). An innovative algorithm for fitting basis shapes to images was proposed by Blanz and Vetter (1999) . The main problem with the basis shape approach is that the full range of appearance variation required for convincing expressive behavior is far beyond the capacity of what a small set of basis shapes can accommodate. Moreover, even if many expression components are used to create a repertoire of basis shapes (Joshi, Tien, Desbrun, & Pighin, 2007; Lewis, Matt, & Nickson, 2000), the interface may need to render different identities or mixtures of facial expressions not captured by the learned basis shapes. A representation of facial appearance for animation must be powerful enough to capture the right constraints for realistic expression generation yet flexible enough to accommodate different identities and behaviors. Besides the obvious utility of such a representation to animated facial interfaces, a good model of facial expression generation would be useful for computer vision tasks because the model's representation would likely be much richer and more informative than the original pixel data. For example, inferring the model's representation corresponding to a given image might even allow transferring an expression extracted from an image of a face onto a different character as illustrated by the method of expression cloning (Noh & Neumann, 2001).

In this chapter we introduce a novel approach to learning to generate facial expressions that uses a deep belief net (Hinton, Osindero, & Teh, 2006). The model can easily accommodate different constraints on generation. We demonstrate this by restricting it to generate expressions with a given identity and with elementary facial expressions such as "raised eyebrows." The deep belief net is powerful enough to capture the large range of variations in expressive appearance in the real faces to which the net has been exposed. Furthermore, the net can be trained on large but sparsely labeled datasets using an unsupervised learning approach that employs an efficient contrastive form of Hebbian learning (Hinton, 2002). The unsupervised approach is advantageous because we have access to large corpuses of face images that are only sparsely labeled. Furthermore, since the human brain learns about faces through exposure in addition to explicit linguistic labeling, the unsupervised approach may lead to a better understanding of how the brain represents and processes faces for expression interpretation. It is unlikely that neural representations are learned by ignoring everything in the facial signal other than what correlates with occasional linguistic labels, because the labels do not provide enough information to organize a flexible and powerful representation of the face. The deep belief net approach to facial expression generation should be of interest to neuroscientists and psychologists concerned with facial expression representation in the brain because the multiple layers of representation that it uses are all learned from the data rather than being pre-specified.

2. Strategies for facial expression generation

A good criterion for determining the usefulness of a facial expression animation program is whether generation can be controlled easily. The challenge is finding a class of generative model that is powerful enough to generate realistic faces but simple enough to be learned from sparsely labeled data. Assume for a moment that we have access to a facial animation program with sensible controls, some face images, and a corresponding set of labeled data representing the controls the animation program would need to generate those images. For example, faces can be labeled using the Facial Action Coding System (FACS), which encodes expressions in terms of configurations of facial muscles and associated changes to the surface appearance (Ekman & Friesen, 1978). FACS is a kind of universal grammar for faces that describes the many different patterns of muscle actions that faces can express. FACS-based face models have been used to control facial animation (e.g. Wojdel & Rothkrantz, 2005). Currently, state of the art methods for realistic facial animation used in video games and feature films use FACS to drive models derived from motion capture data (Parag, 2006). However, this performance-driven approach to facial animation requires more information than images and labels, including motion capture technology, extensive calibration, and processes to clean data prior to modeling. This may be infeasible in most cases where we only have face images and associated high-level animation labels. With a sufficient number of FACS-labeled images, we could learn to control our animation program to do various tasks such as mimic face images by inferring the latent variables that control the generative model given an image and then generating a reconstruction from the model. However, learning the required nonlinear mapping from pixels to animation controls is likely to be a difficult problem requiring huge amounts of data and processing time. For instance, varying the intensity of a smile has highly nonlinear effects on pixel intensities. It is an even greater challenge to tailor the animation program to be flexible enough to accommodate arbitrary facial appearance. Rather than starting with an existing face model or using human animation knowledge to develop a complicated animation program, in this chapter we will learn to animate faces by training a type of general-purpose generative model on many examples of faces and associated high-level descriptors including FACS and identity labels.

A widely used technique for learning face structure from images is principal component analysis (PCA). PCA is a dimensionality reduction method that can be used to extract components from face images for use in face recognition (Turk & Pentland, 1991) and expression coding (Calder, Burton, Miller, Young, & Akamatsu, 2001). PCA is the optimal *linear* method for data compression when measured using squared error (provided we ignore the cost of coding the projections onto the components and we force the dimensions to be orthogonal). PCA, however, may ignore subtle, low-contrast cues in the interior of a face image, especially if the contrast between the face and the background is large, so that very accurate reconstruction of the boundary location is essential for minimizing squared error. A much more powerful method can be constructed using a twist on the standard PCA approach that factors faces into separate shape and texture sources. The active appearance model (AAM) is one such technique that uses information about the positions of facial feature landmarks (i.e. eyebrows, eyes, nose, mouth and facial contour) to warp face pixels to a standard reference frame (Cootes, Edwards, & Taylor, 1998). In this model, PCA is applied separately to the facial landmark coordinates and the shape-normalized pixels. The high-level controls are latent variables that linearly combine the feature coordinates and the texture map. To produce face images from a given vector of latent variables, texture and feature vectors are extracted and the shape-normalized textures are nonlinearly warped from the reference frame to the feature locations specified in the shape vector. This is a more sensible mapping from latent variables to pixels because faces can be modeled very accurately. The overall mapping is highly nonlinear even though variables controlling texture have linear effects on shape-normalized pixels, and variables controlling shape have linear effects on feature coordinates.

While appearance modeling approaches including AAMs have been used for facial expression recognition and generation (Abboud & Davoine, 2005) their applicability is limited in a number of ways because they are restricted to hard-coded transformations of images into sources such as shape, texture or lighting. Furthermore, as with standard PCA, the generative process in this type of model is deterministic and relies on heuristics such as selecting a number of model parameters using percentage of variance cutoffs. A more fundamental problem is the major cost of hand-annotating facial features to create a shape model. Due to the reliance on manual annotation, it is difficult to extend the representational capacity of trained AAMs to model additional sources of variance such as new identities or expression types. Likewise, it is difficult to make use of unlabeled data during training because feature points are not provided. Finally, while appearance models can generate realistic facial expressions spanning the kinds of variations common in the training set, fitting the model to test data is a separate problem. In an AAM, computing the underlying representation of test faces involves a search scheme (Cootes et al., 1998). The search scheme requires an initial "guess" for the location of the face in the image and it uses an iterative refinement procedure for uncovering the underlying model representation that can often fail if the guess is not already almost correct.

Another strategy is to treat facial expression generation as an unsupervised density estimation problem without the linear restrictions of standard PCA. If we have a large source of data, we can use it to learn a model of faces even if most of the images are not labeled; however, we need a good objective for adjusting model parameters. The key assumption is that there is rich structure in face images that can be uncovered without requiring labeled training data. One objective for unsupervised learning is optimal reconstruction from a reduced code space. PCA is a linear example of this type of unsupervised approach. It learns codes for face images by finding a subspace of a particular dimensionality that minimizes squared reconstruction error. However, beyond the problems with PCA and the associated appearance model techniques mentioned above, squared reconstruction error is not always a perceptually meaningful measure. For instance, two different views of the same person are perceptually more similar than two different people in the same view even though measuring squared error of the pixels would suggest the opposite (Prince & Elder, 2005). Thus, although minimal reconstruction error may be an obvious objective for unsupervised learning of facial structure, it may not always be the most useful. This is especially true if our goal is to generate plausible expressions for a given context rather than to "mimic" expressions. Moreover, if the purpose is not to compress data, but to develop a good animation model, our objective should be to learn good "causes" for faces that lead to sensible generation of face images. If we have a good model for how to generate face images, those causes can be used for other tasks such as mapping image causes to high-level labels or driving an animation program.

A recent breakthrough in machine learning makes it relatively easy to learn complex, probabilistic, nonlinear generative models of faces using *deep belief nets* (Bengio, Lamblin, Popovici, & Larochelle, 2007; Hinton et al., 2006). A deep belief net (DBN) is a generative model that uses multiple layers of feature-detecting neurons. The net learns to represent plausible configurations of features (Hinton, 2007b). For example, a DBN could model the useful property of faces that the eyes are always situated above the nose. Given reasonable training data, the net would be highly surprised by a new face in which all the features were face-like but the eyes were below the nose. DBNs have been used successfully to learn generative models of handwritten digits (Hinton & Salakhutdinov, 2006), of natural image patches (Osindero & Hinton, 2008), and of millions of small color images (Torralba, Fergus, & Weiss, 2008). A logical extension is to apply DBNs to modeling facial expressions, thereby demonstrating the wide applicability of the approach to learning useful structure from complicated, high-dimensional data.

3. Using labels to control the generative model

Within the context of affective computing, it is important to be able to control a face animation program to output particular expressions, identities, or other domain specific attributes. However, prototypical examples of specific categories like happy, sad, or angry do not capture the full repertoire of expressive behaviors important for realistic interaction. In fact, thousands of distinct facial expressions have been catalogued (J. F. Cohn & Ekman, 2005). In our generative approach to expression modeling, we will learn a joint model of images, FACS labels, and identities. Once it has been learned, this model can generate an image with a pre-specified blend of identities and any desired combination of FACS labels. A key facet of our approach is the use of high-level descriptions, including identity and expressive facial action labels that provide rich information to usefully constrain the underlying representations used for generating image data.

Labeling facial expressions using FACS consists of describing expressions as constellations of discrete muscle configurations known as action units (AUs) that cause the face to deform in specific ways. While FACS can code muscle configurations that people commonly recognize as emotions such as anger or fear (Ekman & Rosenberg, 1997), it describes underlying anatomy rather than expression categories per se. This extends its usefulness in tasks such as fine-grained detection of micromomentary expressions (subtle expressions appearing for mere microseconds) (Ekman & Rosenberg, 1997), detection of facial markers of deceit (Frank & Ekman, 1997), and characterization of spontaneous emotional behavior (Schmidt, Ambadar, Cohn, & Reed, 2006). Although FACS is a popular coding system, human-based coding of AUs is a labor intensive process requiring significant expertise, especially when applied to tasks such as labeling huge image datasets or sequences of video frames. Accordingly, developing an automated method for FACS labeling is an important challenge for computer vision and machine learning. Existing automated methods for FACS labeling rely on pre-processing expression data using expert knowledge of facial features (J. Cohn, Zlochower, Lien, & Kanade, 1999), or supervised feature selection methods (M.S. Bartlett et al., 2006). One obstacle to high quality automatic FACS labeling is that only a small number of datasets with coded AUs are available publicly; yet there exist many images of faces that could be used to develop an automated model if there was a sensible way to make use of this additional unlabeled data. By using a generative approach to expression modeling, we can learn useful image structure from huge numbers of faces without the need for many labeled examples. This approach enables us to learn associations between FACS labels and image structure, but is not limited only to these associations. This is important because FACS labels alone do not code additional attributes for realistic animation such as identity characteristics or fine surface texture changes.

Although faces are complex objects with often subtle differences in appearance, deep belief nets can be applied to learn a representation of face images that is flexible enough for animating as well as visually interpreting faces. State-of-the-art discriminative performance was recently achieved using DBNs as a pretraining method for handwritten digit recognition (Hinton et al., 2006) and for determining face orientation from images (Salakhutdinov & Hinton, 2008). In this chapter we apply an analogous method to learning a model for facial expressions. The DBN approach is capable of generating realistic expressions that capture the structure of expressions to which it is exposed during training, and can associate the high-level features it extracts from images with both identity and FACS labels.

4. Learning in deep belief nets

Images composed of binary pixels can be modeled by using a "Restricted Boltzmann Machine" (RBM) that uses a layer of binary feature detectors to model the higher-order correlations between pixels. If there are no direct interactions between the feature detectors and no direct interactions between the pixels, there is a simple and efficient way to learn a good set of feature detectors from a set of training images (Hinton, 2002). We start with zero weights on the symmetric connections between each pixel i and each feature detector j. Then we repeatedly update each weight, w_{ij}, using the difference between two measured, pairwise correlations

$$\Delta w_{ij} = \varepsilon\left(<s_i s_j>_{data} - <s_i s_j>_{recon}\right) \tag{1}$$

where ε is a learning rate, $<s_i s_j>_{data}$ is the frequency with which pixel i and feature detector j are on together when the feature detectors are being driven by images from the training set and $<s_i s_j>_{recon}$ is the corresponding frequency when the feature detectors are being driven by reconstructed images. A similar learning rule can be used for the biases.

Given a training image, we set the binary state, s_j, of each feature detector to be 1 with probability

$$p(s_j = 1) = \frac{1}{1 + \exp(-b_j - \sum_{i \in \text{pixels}} s_i w_{ij})} \tag{2}$$

where b_j is the bias of feature j and s_i is the binary state of pixel i. Once binary states have been chosen for the hidden units we produce a "reconstruction" of the training image by setting the state of each pixel to be 1 with probability

$$p(s_i = 1) = \frac{1}{1 + \exp(-b_i - \sum_{j \in \text{features}} s_j w_{ij})} \tag{3}$$

The learned weights and biases of the features implicitly define a probability distribution over all possible binary images. Sampling from this distribution is difficult, but it can be done by using "alternating Gibbs sampling". This starts with a random image and then alternates between updating all of the features in parallel using Eq. 2 and updating all of the pixels in parallel using Eq. 3. After Gibbs sampling for sufficiently long, the net reaches "thermal equilibrium". The states of pixels and features detectors still change, but the probability of finding the system in any particular binary configuration does not.

A single layer of binary features is not the best way to model the structure in a set of images. After learning the first layer of feature detectors, a second layer can be learned in just the same way by treating the existing feature detectors, when they are being driven by training images, as if they were data (Hinton, 2007a). To reduce noise in the learning signal, the binary states of feature detectors (or pixels) in the "data" layer are replaced by their real-valued probabilities of activation when learning the next layer of feature detectors, but the new feature detectors have binary states to limit the amount of information they can convey. This greedy, layer-by-layer learning can be repeated as many times as desired. Provided the number of feature detectors does not decrease and their weights are initialized correctly, adding an extra layer is guaranteed to raise a lower bound on the log probability of the training data (Hinton et al., 2006). So after learning several layers there is good reason to believe that the feature detectors will have captured many of the statistical regularities in the set of training images and will constitute a good generative model of the training data.

After learning a deep belief net, perception of a new image is very fast because it only involves a feedforward pass through the multiple layers. Generation from the multilayer model is slower. At the end of the layer-by-layer training, the weight between any two units in adjacent layers is the same in both directions and we can view the result of training three hidden layers as a set of three different RBM's whose only interaction is that the data for the higher RBM's is provided by the feature activations of the lower RBM's. It is possible, however, to take a very different view of exactly the same system (Hinton et al., 2006). We can view it as a single generative model that generates data by first letting the top-level RBM settle to thermal equilibrium using alternating Gibbs sampling (which may take a very long time), and then performing a single top-down pass to convert the binary feature activations in the penultimate layer into an image. In the top-down, generative direction, the weights between the lower layers form part of the overall generative model, but in the bottom-up, recognition direction they are not part of the model. They are merely an efficient way of inferring what hidden states probably caused the observed image.

5. A deep belief net for facial expressions

5.1 Facial expression dataset

In order to learn a generative model from a large and varied corpus of faces, we combined datasets that capture a significant degree of expression variation. Spontaneous expressions were collected during interviews in which participants were either deceptive or truthful (M. S. Bartlett et al., 2005). Additionally, a mixture of spontaneous and posed facial actions were collected from subjects in the MMI database (Pantic & Rothcrantz, 2000). Finally, posed facial actions were collected from the Cohn-Kanade FACS database (Kanade, Cohn, & Tian, 2000), the Ekman and Hager directed facial actions set (M.S. Bartlett, Hager, Ekman, & Sejnowski, 1999), and the Pictures of Facial Affect database (Ekman & Friesen, 1976). Identity labels accompany almost all faces. A subset of the data was coded by expert human raters, providing FACS labels for training the model to associate AUs with image features.

5.2 Preprocessing

We extracted over 100,000 face patches from the combined datasets using an automatic face detector (I. Fasel et al., 2004), which extends a previous approach (Viola & Jones, 2001). Modifications include employing a generative model framework to explain the image in terms of face and non-face regions, Gentleboost instead of Adaboost for feature selection, estimated eye and mouth corner feature detection, and a cascading decision procedure (I. R. Fasel, Fortenberry, & Movellan, 2005). Face patches were resized and cropped to 24x24 pixels. We then randomly selected 30,000 unlabeled faces and 3,473 labeled faces from the pool of detected face patches (see Table 1 below). The 8 AUs chosen for this experiment are common facial actions representing changes to the top and bottom half of the face (see Figure 4 below). The AUs representing the top half of the face are AU 1 and AU 2, which code inner, and outer eyebrow raises, respectively, AU 4, which codes brow lowering, and AU 5, which codes upper eyelid raise. The AUs representing the bottom half of the face are AU 10, which codes for upper lip raise, AU 12, which codes for lip corner raise, AU 14, which codes for cheek dimpling, and AU 20, which codes for horizontal mouth stretching.

		FACS Action Units (AUs)								
Faces	**ID**	**1**	**2**	**4**	**5**	**10**	**12**	**14**	**20**	**--**
3,473	151	0.28	0.22	0.15	0.08	0.08	0.18	0.07	0.05	0.35
27,863	205	--	--	--	--	--	--	--	--	--

Table 1. Faces, unique identities, and AU labels in the dataset. The first row describes faces with labeled action units, including the number of unique faces, and identities, and the proportion of labeled faces displaying a particular AU. The second row indicates the number of unique faces and identities in the larger set of faces with missing AU labels.

The extracted face images exhibited a large range of lighting conditions because of the differences in lighting control across datasets. To avoid learning lighting features at the expense of face details, pixel brightness was first normalized within and then across faces. First, all pixel values in a given face image were standardized across all pixels (i.e. separate linear transformations for each face). Then, each pixel value was normalized across faces to unit variance (i.e., each pixel intensity was divided by a separate constant). Finally, pixels that were beyond ±3 standard deviations from the average pixel brightness were truncated, and the images were rescaled to range between [0-255]. These preprocessing steps produced symmetric brightness histograms that were roughly normally distributed with minimal preprocessing artifacts.

To facilitate training the first-level RBM with binary visible units, which are easiest to train, a heuristic procedure was used to convert brightness normalized face images into "soft" binary images. The method involved: (1) stretching the brightness-normalized face images using a hand-tuned logistic function resulting in contrast-enhanced pixel values, maintaining a range between [0-255], and (2) multiplying the pixels by 2 and truncating values exceeding 255. The ensuing images had dark edge features and bright regions elsewhere and retained perceptually important identity and expression attributes (see Figure 1a).

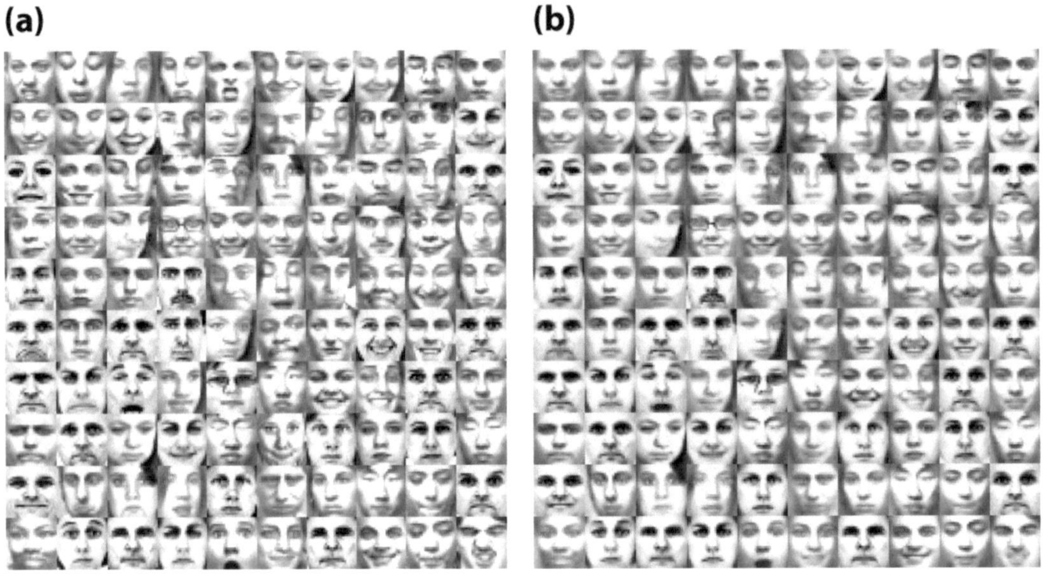

Figure 1. (a) Randomly selected soft binary training images. (b) RBM reconstructions (probabilities are shown instead of binary samples to produce smoother images).

To see how much critical information about expression is lost by the soft binarization procedure, two different neural nets were trained with backpropagation to discriminate FACS labels from real-valued versus soft binary images. The performance was slightly worse for the net trained using soft binary images (see Appendix).

5.3 Net architecture

Figure 2 depicts the deep belief net used to model the joint distribution of face images, identities, and FACS labels. In this model, 576 soft binarized pixel inputs are connected to a hidden layer of 500 logistic units, which is connected to a second layer of 500 hidden units. The penultimate hidden layer is then concatenated with identity and FACS label units, and the resulting vector serves as the visible layer of a top-level RBM with 1000 logistic hidden units. During training, each ascending pair of layers in the deep belief net is trained as an RBM, using the hidden activities computed from the previous RBM below as visible units for training the next RBM. After greedy layer-wise training, the complete net forms a hybrid model consisting of directed connections between lower layers and an undirected associative memory at the top (Hinton et al., 2006). This top-level associative memory binds features and labels, and can thus be sampled by letting the RBM settle on likely configurations of features and label units. To generate from the net, the FACS AU label units in the penultimate layer can be clamped to particular values, and the associative memory can be sampled to find features that satisfy the label constraints, or the features can be clamped to values computed from an up-pass starting from an image, and the associative memory will fill in FACS labels. Given a particular configuration of features in the penultimate layer, the generative directed connections (pointing from higher to lower layers) convert the deep layers of feature activities into observed pixel face images.

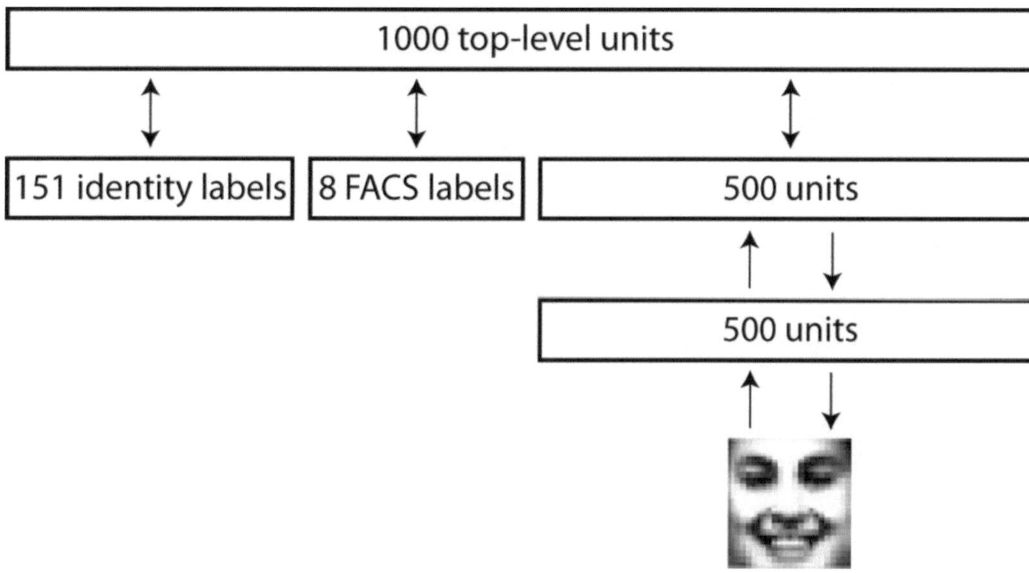

Figure 2. Architecture for deep belief net trained to generate facial expressions, identity labels, and FACS labels.

5.4 Greedy layer-wise training of the deep belief net

For training each RBM, the biases and weights connecting visible to hidden units were initialized to randomly sampled values from a normal distribution (μ=0, σ =.03). Training consisted of multiple passes through a full set of minibatches of 100 visible vectors with the weight being updated after each minibatch. To encourage the hidden layers to develop sparse representations, a penalty term was added to the weight updates for the first and second-level RBMs to pressure features to turn on 20% of the time. To reduce over-fitting, a weight decay of .00005 was used.

The first-level RBM connecting pixel visible units to 500 hidden units was trained for 200 epochs through the training data. A learning rate of .01 was used for the visible-to-hidden connections and .05 was used to update the weights on the visible and hidden biases. Figure 3 below shows receptive fields of some of the features learned by the first-level RBM. Since all the faces in the dataset were roughly aligned and scaled based on a consistent face and eye detection scheme, the positions of local features learned by the RBM tended to correspond to recognizable face parts, often characterizing local receptive fields comprising the eyebrows, eyes, cheeks, nose, or mouth.

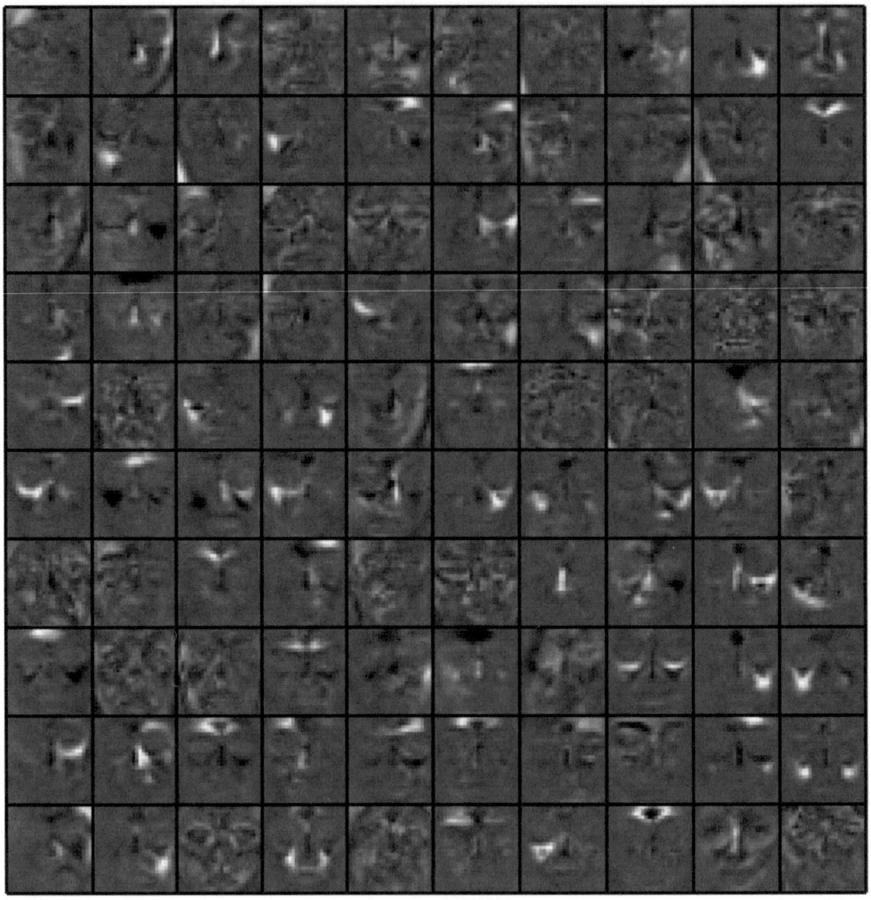

Figure 3. Receptive fields of some features learned by the first-level RBM. White indicates a positive weight to a pixel and black indicates a negative weight. Many features contain moderately to highly local receptive fields, indicating componential structure useful for representing distinct features and edges. Other features are more global.

Even though the first-level RBM was trained completely unsupervised, it learned useful structure in its features relating to different FACS AU label units.

Figure 4 shows a subset of features that correlate the most with different AUs. One interesting set of features includes salient positive weights to the whites of the eyes and negative weights to the pupils for detecting AU 5 (which codes for raised upper eyelids). These detailed features were likely learned because the automatic face detector aligns face patches to have roughly the same eye positions. Also evident from

Figure 4 is that some action units correlate with the same features because the changes in facial anatomy overlap. For instance, the same wide-eyed feature is highly correlated with AUs 1, 2, and 4, which code for raised inner brow, raised outer brow, and raised upper eyelid, respectively. Similarly, AUs 10 and 12, which code upper lip raise and upturned mouth corners, both correlate negatively with bright regions lateral to the mouth corners. A raised upper lip is a typical feature of disgust faces while upturned lip corners relate to smiling; both of these actions may occur along with activation of the Zygomaticus muscle, serving to raise the cheeks, which leaves darker creased regions below.

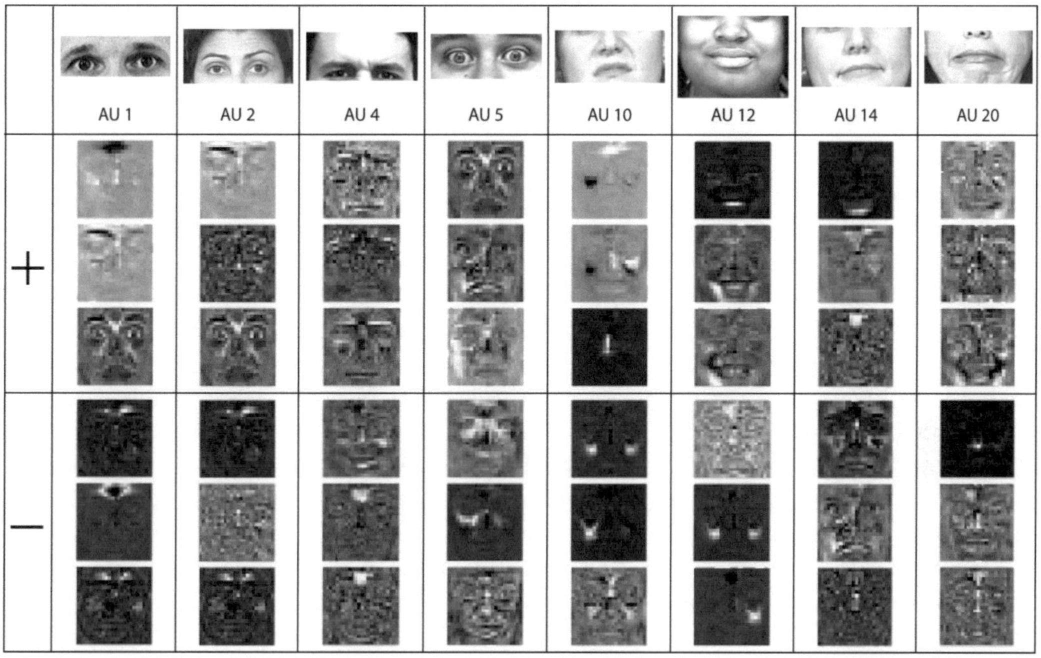

Figure 4. Unsupervised features (rows) that are highly correlated with particular action units (columns). The first 3 rows show positively correlated features with a particular AU, and the bottom 3 rows show negatively correlated features.

The visible units of the second-level RBM were initialized during training to the hidden probabilities computed by the first-level RBM after training. The second-level RBM was also trained for 200 epochs through the training data using the same learning rates and sparsity targets as were used to train the first-level RBM.

5.5 Learning the joint distribution of FACS labels and penultimate features

After training the second-level RBM, its feature activities were concatenated with discrete label units representing both identity and AU labels. The combined vector then became the visible units of the top-level RBM. Since a face image can only be associated with a single identity, a 1-of-K "softmax" coding scheme was used to represent the identities. Once binary states have been sampled for the hidden units, we generate identity labels by setting the state of each identity element to be 1 with probability

$$p(ID_i = 1) = \frac{\exp(b_i + \sum_{j \in \text{features}} s_j w_{ij})}{\sum_{k \in \text{identities}} \exp(b_k + \sum_{j \in \text{features}} s_j w_{kj})} \qquad (4)$$

On the other hand, more than one FACS unit can be active for a face. Thus, the AU label vector comprises independent binary units for each of the 8 AUs. AU labels and feature activities are both generated independently for each unit using Eq. 3.

The third-level RBM was trained using N-step contrastive divergence (Carreira-Perpignan & Hinton, 2005) in 100 epoch sets using CD-3, CD-5, CD-7, CD-9, and CD-10 with the learning rate annealed in step increments from .001 to .0005 across the 500 epochs, and a weight decay of .00005. Training continued at CD-10 for a total of 4000 epochs.

5.6 Expression generation

After training, the deep belief network was tested as a face animation program by generating faces given different configurations of identity and AU labels. To generate from the DBN, one or more identity and/or AU labels are first clamped to particular values (where 0 = "off" and 1 = "on"). Next, the remaining visible units of the top-level RBM are sampled randomly according to their bias terms. This initializes the visible data vector for the top-level RBM to a reasonable unbiased starting point. Next, alternating Gibbs sampling is run for 1,000 steps, after which it is assumed the network has settled close to its equilibrium distribution given the clamped labels. Then, a single top-down pass converts the binary feature activations in the penultimate layer into an image consistent with the sample from the top-level RBM.

An innovative facial animation program would allow a user to specify some diffuse attributes, such as facial actions and/or identities, without requiring very specific controls. In other words, one should be able to specify a high-level description to the animation program without specifying every detailed feature contributing to that composition. The trained DBN is capable of this type of high-level control over face generation. Figure 5 below shows examples of the DBN generating faces after specifying a particular facial action unit. Although the network is capable of highly specific combinations of facial actions, such as all AUs off except for raised eyebrows, here we allow the net to determine its own combinations of facial actions given a single clamped unit. Thus, for example, when AU 1 is on (inner brow raise), the network often fills in other facial actions in addition to AU 1 such as AU 2 (outer brow raise), AU 4 (lowered brow), and AU 5 (raised eye lids). Note that AUs 1 and 4 can co-exist because there are multiple muscles involved in brow movement. The network's ability to generate combinations of AUs is evident in many other instances in Figure 5, such as the combination of AU 20 (horizontal lip stretcher) with AU 12 (raised lip corners), which is consistent with grinning, and AU 20 with AU 1 (inner brow raise), AU 2 (outer brow raise), and AU 5 (raised upper eye lid) which is characteristic of fear.

In addition to generating faces by specifying particular facial actions, the DBN can generate faces conforming to particular identities. Figure 6 below shows examples of the DBN generating faces after specifying a particular identity label. Since identity labels are "softmax" units, the network has learned during training not to blend identities. This is evident in Figure 6, where most faces generated for a particular identity look like that identity. Since the DBN is capable of settling on different combinations of AUs given a particular identity label, the generated faces vary in expression, sometimes exhibiting multiple AUs. However, since not all identities in the training set exhibited all facial actions, some expressions occur more often for some identities than others.

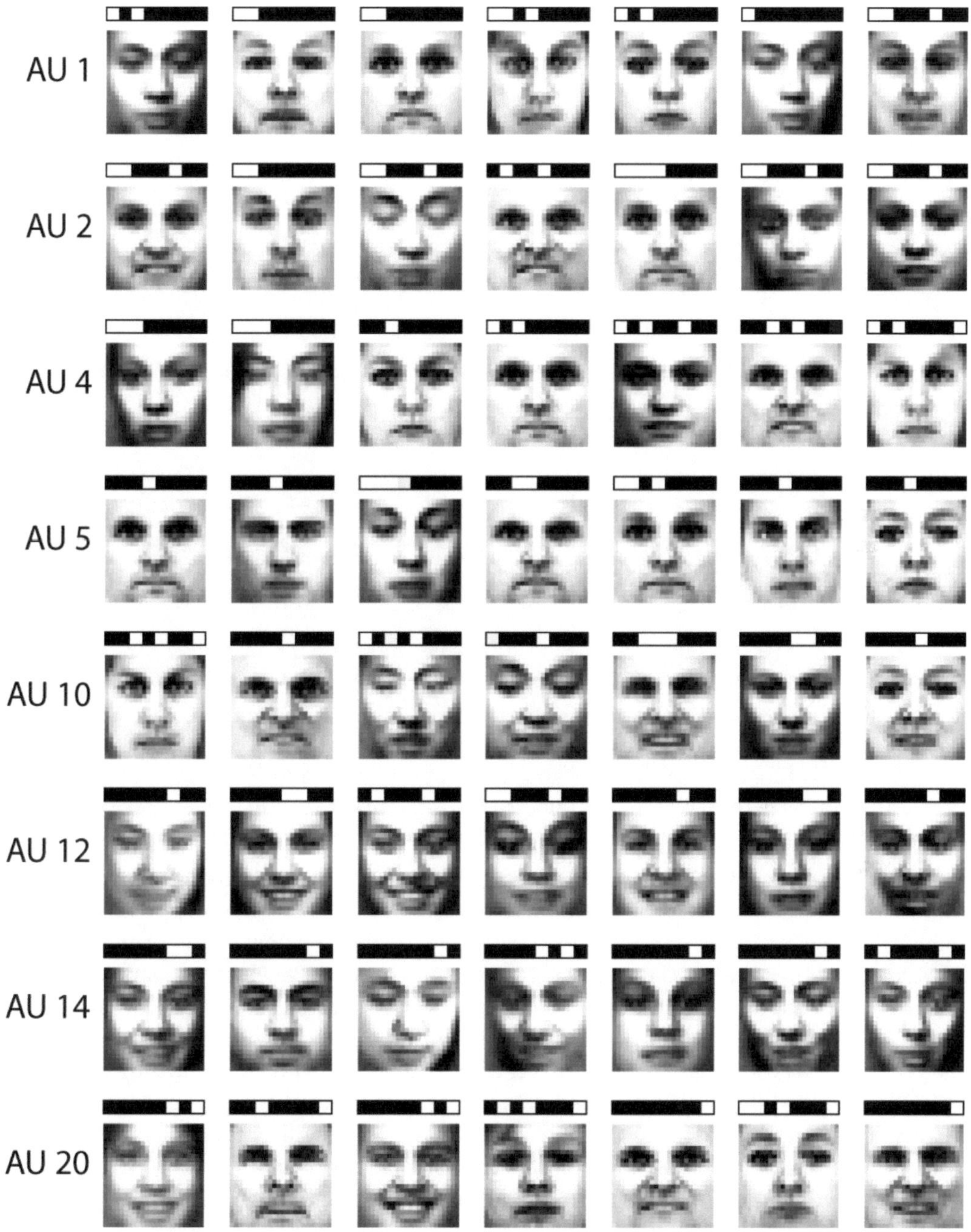

Figure 5. Face images sampled from the conditional distribution of features and AUs given an AU label. Each row shows 7 results after clamping a particular AU label to "on" and running alternating Gibbs sampling at the top-level RBM for 1000 iterations, and generating an image via a directed down-pass through the network, resulting in pixel probabilities observed at the visible image layer. Above each face image is the associated AU vector that the network settled on, indicating from left to right AUs 1, 2, 4, 5, 10, 12, 14, and 20.

Figure 6. Face images sampled from the conditional distribution of features and AUs given an identity label. Each row corresponds to faces generated with a particular identity label clamped on. The first column shows example faces from the training set representative of the clamped identity for the corresponding row. The samples vary in expression in ways representative of the expressions posed by that identity in the training set.

The DBN is also capable of generating a face given both a set of AUs and a specific identity. This is an important ability for an animation program to possess because often the intent is to animate the expressions of a particular individual. Figure 8 below shows examples of the DBN generating faces after clamping specific identity and AU labels. For example, the first row of Figure 8 shows 5 different examples of the same identity exhibiting AU 10 (upper lip raise), which is a facial action often associated with disgust. Sometimes the network also filled in other AUs such as AU 12, which can occur together with AU 10 during happiness. Note that the middle face in the first row appears to change identity even though the identity label is clamped. Since the DBN is stochastic, this will occasionally happen. The second row of Figure 8 demonstrates both a consistent identity and the likely co-occurrence of AU 1 (inner brow raise) with AU 2 (outer brow raise), and AU 5 (upper eye lid raise), which are combinations that often occur in conjunction with fear and surprise.

Finally, we demonstrate the DBN has the capacity to generate faces that are restricted to a subset of more than one identity. Occasionally in this case the network will generate blends of identities since the feature representation contains many local features consistent with both identities. Figure 7 below shows examples of the DBN generating faces after specifying two different identity labels with equal probability. These examples demonstrate that the

DBN is capable of generalizing beyond the training examples to create novel blends of identities that vary in expression.

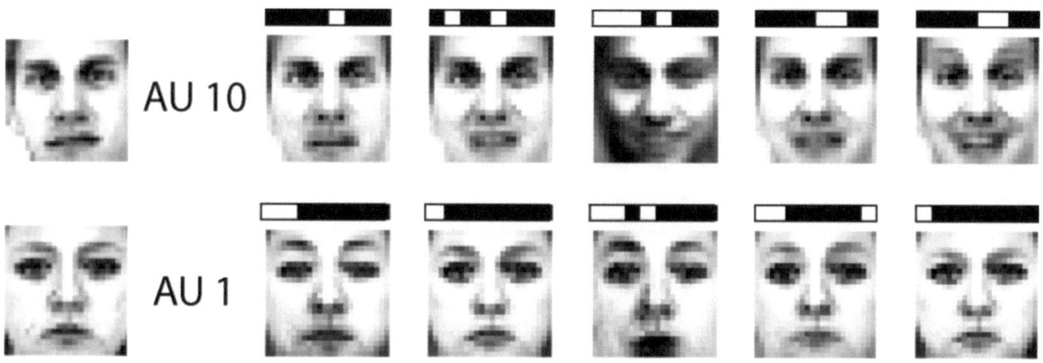

Figure 8. Face images sampled from the conditional distribution of features and AUs given both an identity label and an AU label. Each row corresponds to faces generated with both a particular identity label and an AU label clamped on. Row 1 shows that the network settles on faces congruent with a consistent identity label (corresponding to the face in column 1) that all exhibit variations on the upper lip raise (AU 10). Similarly, row 2 shows different variations on the inner brow raise (AU 1) consistent with the corresponding given identity.

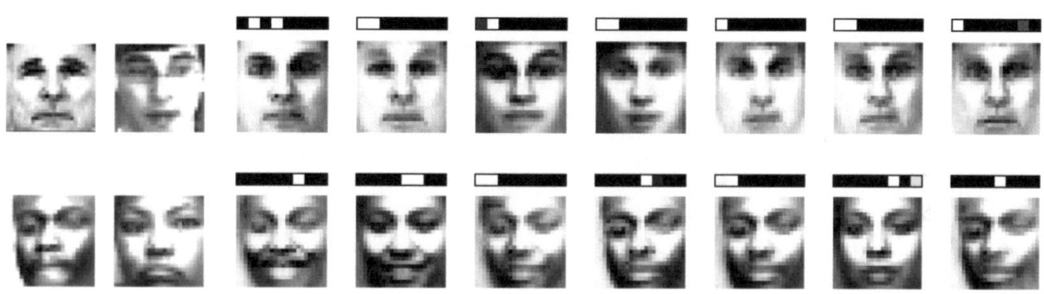

Figure 8. Face images sampled from the conditional distribution of features and AUs given a blend of two identity labels clamped on. Each row shows sample faces consistent with the identity labels for the two left-most faces in that row. Some faces are more consistent in visual appearance with one of the identities, while other faces seem to settle on blends of the two identities, indicating the identities contain compatible features.

6. Conclusion

In this chapter we showed that it is possible to train a deep belief net with multiple layers of features to function as an animation system capable of converting high-level descriptions of facial attributes into realistic face images. By specifying particular labels to the DBN, we were able to generate realistic faces displaying specific identities and facial actions. In addition, the DBN could generalize from the associations it learned during training to synthesize novel combinations of identities and facial actions. Thus, like the human brain, the DBN can remember faces it has seen during training, can associate faces with particular identities, and can even "imagine" faces it has never seen before by blending identities and/or facial actions. By sampling from the DBN, we demonstrated that it is possible to investigate how a neural net represents faces and associates them with high-level descriptions. Samples that the DBN generates represent beliefs it has about faces. In particular, the top-level RBM acts as a constraint satisfaction network, finding sets of image features that the network considers likely to be associated with a given set of identities and action units. A question for future research is the extent to which the representations that the DBN learns resemble the neural representations used by humans. For instance, humans often confuse certain facial expressions like fear and surprise, presumably because these expressions share underlying muscle configurations and are thus visually similar (Dailey, Cottrell, Padgett, & Adolphs, 2002; Susskind, Littlewort, Bartlett, Movellan, & Anderson, 2007). Likewise, humans may confuse some identities more than others due to ways in which the faces are perceptually similar. Does the DBN capture human-like perceptual similarity? In order to answer this question we would need to measure how similarly the network represents different faces. One way this could be done is by correlating average feature activities in the DBN to different faces and comparing the degree of similarity between faces to human judgments of similarity.

Our DBN results demonstrate that different types of facial attributes can be represented by the same distributed set of image features, suggesting in particular that identity and expression are not entirely independent facial attributes. The current study did not attempt to investigate the interdependence of identity and expression directly, but the ability of the network to associate identities and facial actions with facial appearance suggests these different attributes can make use of the same distributed neural representation. One way to examine the relative interdependence of expression and identity in the network is to examine whether some facial actions are more likely to be generated given one identity label rather than another, which would indicate that expression depends on identity. The DBN can model the notion that different people smile in different ways, expressing the same facial action with different constellations of visual features. Some evidence that the brain encodes facial expression in an identity-specific manner comes from behavioral studies examining high-level facial expression adaptation to different identities (Ellamil, Susskind, & Anderson, in press; Fox & Barton, 2007).

The deep belief network approach demonstrates that given a large enough set of training data, a neural network can learn sensible representations of face images directly from image pixels, without requiring expert feature selection methods to pre-process the image. Although in this approach the DBN was trained to generate facial expressions given high-level identity and FACS AU labels, the representation of faces that it learned may also be useful for recognizing these and other expressive attributes when presented with a face image. In fact, after learning multiple layers of image features using RBMs, the DBN can be further fine-tuned for discriminating high-level labels from images using the backpropagation algorithm (Hinton & Salakhutdinov, 2006). However, the discriminative network would lose its capacity to generate faces. More appropriately for the purposes of facial animation, the DBN can be fine-tuned to recognize high-level descriptions of faces while maintaining its generative capacity to animate facial expressions using generative fine-tuning methods such as a contrastive version of the wake-sleep algorithm (Hinton et al., 2006). The authors show that this approach works well for generating and recognizing hand-written digits. Although better generation and recognition performance might be achieved with fine-tuning, we have demonstrated that a relatively simple unsupervised learning algorithm can develop a powerful internal representation of faces.

7. References

Abboud, B., & Davoine, F. (2005). Bilinear factorisation for facial expression analysis and synthesis. *VISP, 152*(3), 327-333.

Bartlett, M. S., Hager, J., Ekman, P., & Sejnowski, T. (1999). Measuring facial expressions by computer image analysis. *Psychophysiology, 36*, 253-264.

Bartlett, M. S., Littlewort, G. C., Frank, M. G., Lainscsek, C., Fasel, I. R., & Movellan, J. R. (2006). Automatic Recognition of Facial Actions in Spontaneous Expressions. *Journal of Multimedia, 1*(6), 22-35.

Bartlett, M. S., Movellan, J. R., Littlewort, G., Braathen, B., Frank, M. G., & Sejnowski, T. J. (2005). Towards automatic recognition of spontaneous facial actions. In P. Ekman (Ed.), *What the Face Reveals*: Oxford University Press.

Bengio, Y., Lamblin, P., Popovici, D., & Larochelle, H. (2007). Greedy Layer-Wise Training of Deep Networks. In B. Scholkopf, J. Platt & T. Hoffman (Eds.), *Advances in Neural Information Processing Systems 19* (pp. 153-160). Cambridge, MA: MIT Press.

Blanz, V., & Vetter, T. (1999). *A morphable model for the synthesis of 3D faces.* Paper presented at the Proceedings of the 26th annual conference on Computer graphics and interactive techniques.

Calder, A. J., Burton, A. M., Miller, P., Young, A. W., & Akamatsu, S. (2001). A principal component analysis of facial expressions. *Vision research, 41*(9), 1179-1208.

Carreira-Perpignan, M. A., & Hinton, G. E. (2005). On Contrastive Divergence Learning. *Artificial Intelligence and Statistics.*

Cohn, J., Zlochower, A., Lien, J. J., & Kanade, T. (1999). Automated face analysis by feature point tracking has high concurrent validity with manual FACS coding. *Psychophysiology, 36.*

Cohn, J. F., & Ekman, P. (2005). Measuring facial actions. In J. A. Harrigan, R. Rosenthal & K. Scherer (Eds.), *The New Handbook of Methods in Nonverbal Behavior Research* (pp. 9-64). New York, USA: Oxford University Press.

Cootes, T. F., Edwards, G. J., & Taylor, C. J. (1998, 1998). *Active Appearance Models.* Paper presented at the European Conference on Computer Vision.

Dailey, M. N., Cottrell, G. W., Padgett, C., & Adolphs, R. (2002). EMPATH: A Neural Network that Categorizes Facial Expressions. *Journal of cognitive neuroscience, 14*(8), 1158-1173.

Ekman, P., & Friesen, W. (1976). Pictures of facial affect.

Ekman, P., & Friesen, W. V. (1978). *The facial action coding system.* Palo Alto, California: Consulting Psychologists Press.

Ekman, P., & Rosenberg, E. L. (1997). *What the face reveals: Basic and applied studies of spontaneous expression using the Facial Action Coding System (FACS).* New York: Oxford University Press.

Ellamil, M., Susskind, J. M., & Anderson, A. K. (in press). Examinations of identity invariance in facial expression adaptation. *Cognitive, Affective, & Behavioral Neuroscience.*

Fasel, I., Dahl, R., Hershey, J., Fortenberry, B., Susskind, J. M., & Movellan, J. R. (2004). Machine perception toolbox, http://mplab.ucsd.edu/software/mpt.html.

Fasel, I. R., Fortenberry, B., & Movellan, J. R. (2005). A generative framework for real-time object detection and classification. *Computer Vision and Image Understanding, 98.*

Fox, C. J., & Barton, J. S. (2007). What is adapted in face adaptation? The neural representations of expression in the human visual system. *Brain Research, 1127*, 80-89.

Frank, M. G., & Ekman, P. (1997). The ability to detect deceit generalizes across different types of high-stake lies. *Journal of Personality and Social Psychology, 72*, 1429-1439.

Hinton, G. E. (2002). Training products of experts by minimizing contrastive divergence. *Neural Computation, 14*(8), 1711-1800.

Hinton, G. E. (2007a). Learning Multiple Layers of Representation. *Trends in Cognitive Sciences, 11*, 428-434.

Hinton, G. E. (2007b). To recognize shapes, first learn to generate images In P. Cisek, T. Drew & J. Kalaska (Eds.), *Computational Neuroscience: Theoretical Insights into Brain Function.*

Hinton, G. E., Osindero, S., & Teh, Y. W. (2006). A fast learning algorithm for deep belief nets. *Neural Computation, 18*(1527-1554).

Hinton, G. E., & Salakhutdinov, R. R. (2006). Reducing the Dimensionality of Data with Neural Networks. *Science, 313*(5786), 504-507.

Joshi, P., Tien, W., Desbrun, M., & Pighin, F. (2007). Learning Controls for Blendshape-based Realistic Facial Animation. In *Data-Driven 3D Facial Animation* (pp. 162-174).

Kanade, T., Cohn, J. F., & Tian, Y. (2000). *Comprehensive database for facial expression analysis.* Paper presented at the Proceedings of the fourth IEEE International conference on, Grenoble, France.

Kleiser, J. (1989). *A fast, efficient, accurate way to represent the human face.* Paper presented at the SIGGRAPH '89 Course Notes 22: State of the Art in Facial Animation.

Lewis, J. P., Matt, C., & Nickson, F. (2000). *Pose space deformation: a unified approach to shape interpolation and skeleton-driven deformation.* Paper presented at the Proceedings of the 27th annual conference on Computer graphics and interactive techniques.

Noh, J.-y., & Neumann, U. (2001). *Expression cloning.* Paper presented at the Proceedings of the 28th annual conference on Computer graphics and interactive techniques.

Osindero, S., & Hinton, G. E. (2008). *Modeling image patches with a directed hierarchy of Markov random fields.* Paper presented at the Advances in Neural Information Processing Systems 20.

Pantic, M., & Rothcrantz, J. M. (2000). Automatic analysis of facial expressions: State of the art. *IEEE Trans on Pattern Analysis and Machine Intelligence, 22*(12), 1424-1445.

Parag, H. (2006). *Sony Pictures Imageworks.* Paper presented at the ACM SIGGRAPH 2006 Courses.

Parke, F. I. (1972). *Computer generated animation of faces*Paper presented at the Proceedings ACM annual conference.

Prince, S. J. D., & Elder, J. H. (2005). Creating invariance to "nuisance parameters" in face recognition. *Computer Vision and Pattern Recognition.*

Salakhutdinov, R., & Hinton, G. (2008). Using Deep Belief Nets to Learn Covariance Kernels for Gaussian Processes. In J. C. Platt, D. Koller, Y. Singer & S. Roweis (Eds.), *Advances in Neural Information Processing Systems 20*. Cambridge, MA: MIT Press.

Schmidt, K. L., Ambadar, Z., Cohn, J. F., & Reed, L. (2006). Movement differences between deliberate and spontaneous facial expressions: Zygomaticus major action in smiling. *Journal of Nonverbal Behavior, 30*, 37-52.

Susskind, J. M., Littlewort, G., Bartlett, M. S., Movellan, J., & Anderson, A. K. (2007). Human and computer recognition of facial expressions of emotion. *Neuropsychologia, 45*(1), 152-162.

Torralba, A., Fergus, R., & Weiss, Y. (2008). *Small codes and large image databases for recognition*. Paper presented at the Computer Vision and Pattern Recognition (CVPR-08).

Turk, M., & Pentland, A. (1991). Eigenfaces for Recognition. *Journal of Cognitive Neuroscience, 3*(1).

Viola, P., & Jones, M. (2001). *Robust real-time object detection.* Paper presented at the ICCV Second International Workshop on Statistical and Conceptual Theories of Vision.

Wojdel, A., & Rothkrantz, L. J. M. (2005). Parametric Generation of Facial Expressions Based on FACS. *Computer Graphics Forum, 24*(4), 743-757.

Appendix

In a control experiment to ensure no critical loss of information, we compared two different classifiers trained with backpropagation to predict FACS labels, using faces preprocessed with and without the soft binarization step. Results are shown below in
Table 2 for nets trained with 100 hidden units[1]. Area under the ROC curve was computed separately as an

Net	Area under ROC							
Architecture	AU1	AU2	AU3	AU4	AU5	AU6	AU7	AU8
MLP100	0.78	0.74	0.76	0.90	0.78	0.87	0.75	0.77
BINMLP100	0.77	0.74	0.76	0.88	0.76	0.87	0.75	0.75

Table 2. FACS classification results for feedforward nets trained with backpropagation, with and without the soft binarization preprocessing step (top and bottom row, respectively).

index of classification accuracy for each FACS label. The net trained with soft binarized inputs (BINMLP100) achieved comparable results to the net trained without this extra

[1] Separate nets were tested with 50-500 hidden units. The 100 hidden unit nets were optimal as assessed by error on the labeled validation cases.

preprocessing step (MLP100). In addition, Figure 1b shows reconstructions from a trained RBM showing that treating the set of soft binarized pixel intensities as Bernoulli probabilities is appropriate for capturing essential identity and expression features in the training images, even though the RBM does not optimize image reconstruction. These results indicate that the soft binarization step does not eliminate diagnostic expression features, which validates the use of binary visible units to train the first-level RBM.